P9-DHF-028

Rajasthan, Delhi & Agra

Lindsay Brown
Amelia Thomas

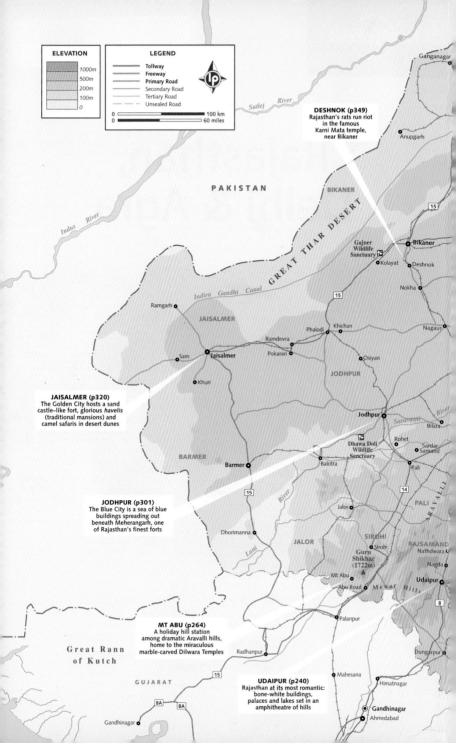

ELEVATION

1000m
500m
200m
100m
0

LEGEND

Tollway
Freeway
Primary Road
Secondary Road
Tertiary Road
Unsealed Road

0 ——— 100 km
0 ——— 60 miles

Sutlej River

Indus River

PAKISTAN

GREAT THAR DESERT

Indira Gandhi Canal

Ganganagar

Anupgarh

15

DESHNOK (p349)
Rajasthan's rats run riot
in the famous
Karni Mata temple,
near Bikaner

BIKANER

Gajner
Wildlife
Sanctuary
Kolayat

Bikaner
Deshnok

Nokha

Nagaur

Ramgarh

JAISALMER

Sam

Jaisalmer

Khuri

Ramdevra

Pokaran

Phalodi

Khichan

Osiyan

JODHPUR

JAISALMER (p320)
The Golden City hosts a sand
castle–like fort, glorious *havelis*
(traditional mansions) and
camel safaris in desert dunes

BARMER

Barmer

15

Luni River

Jodhpur

Rohet

Dhawa Doli
Wildlife
Sanctuary
Balotra

Saraswati River

Bilara

Sardar
Samand

Pali

14

PALI

ARAVALLI

JODHPUR (p301)
The Blue City is a sea of blue
buildings spreading out
beneath Meherangarh, one
of Rajasthan's finest forts

Dhorimanna

Jalor

JALOR

SIROHI

Guru
Shikhar
(1722m)

Mt Abu

Abu Road

Sirohi

Mewat Hills

RAJASAMAND

Nathdwara

Nagda

Udaipur

8

Great Rann
of Kutch

MT ABU (p264)
A holiday hill station
among dramatic Aravalli hills,
home to the miraculous
marble-carved Dilwara Temples

Radhanpur

Palanpur

Dungarpur

GUJARAT

15

8A   8A

Gandhinagar

Mahesana

UDAIPUR (p240)
Rajasthan at its most romantic:
bone-white buildings,
palaces and lakes set in an
amphitheatre of hills

Himatnagar

Gandhinagar

Ahmedabad

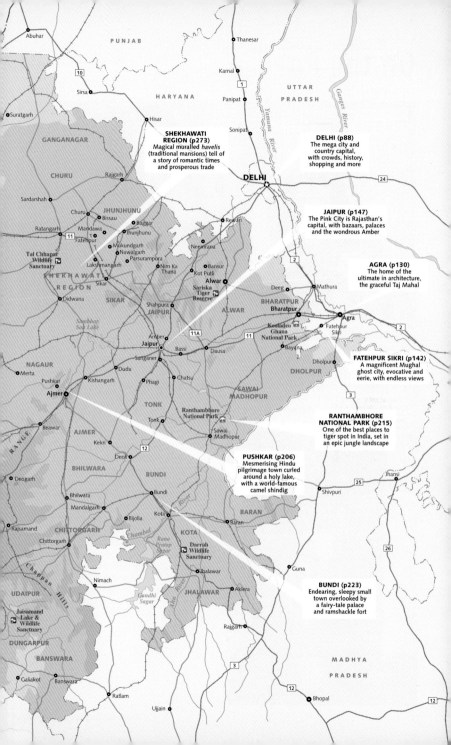

SHEKHAWATI REGION (p273)
Magical muralled *havelis* (traditional mansions) tell of a story of romantic times and prosperous trade

DELHI (p88)
The mega city and country capital, with crowds, history, shopping and more

JAIPUR (p147)
The Pink City is Rajasthan's capital, with bazaars, palaces and the wondrous Amber

AGRA (p130)
The home of the ultimate in architecture, the graceful Taj Mahal

FATEHPUR SIKRI (p142)
A magnificent Mughal ghost city, evocative and eerie, with endless views

RANTHAMBHORE NATIONAL PARK (p215)
One of the best places to tiger spot in India, set in an epic jungle landscape

PUSHKAR (p206)
Mesmerising Hindu pilgrimage town curled around a holy lake, with a world-famous camel shindig

BUNDI (p223)
Endearing, sleepy small town overlooked by a fairy-tale palace and ramshackle fort

On the Road

LINDSAY BROWN Coordinating Author

As a Lonely Planet author your path is not always your own. Publishers, editors, cartographers, previous authors, readers, even centuries-old trade routes have a habit of, if not mapping out your destiny, then dictating your itinerary. Still, chance and serendipity, the predictable unpredictability of India and perhaps even karma are daily companions providing distracting detours and temptations to lead you astray. Following the hastily emailed directions of a reader, I weave through the narrow lanes of sky-blue old Jodhpur and come face to face with Shiva.

AMELIA THOMAS It's 7am, New Year's Day, New Delhi, and new baby (on the way in two-months' time) is kicking hungrily for breakfast. Connaught Place is – possibly for the first time ever – silent and deserted. Except for a few post-party revellers and a doorman shivering in the chilly air, we're the only ones wandering its once grand colonnaded walkways. We savour the scent of wood fires and watch hawks soaring over the central park, then duck into a South Indian cubbyhole restaurant. Delhi, one of my favourite cities, has never seemed so serene – and *dosas* (lentil-flour pancakes) have rarely tasted so good.

For full author biographies see p402.

Highlights

Here we share some fleeting or quintessential travel moments that were captured by our readers – a bird skimming the pool of water at the Taj Mahal, a match-lit perspective on a palace interior, a brief but intense sunrise illuminating the sights of Jaipur…the highlights of the Golden Triangle are unique and personal. For some, it's contemplating the pink sandstone and blue rooftops of Rajasthan; for others, it's soaking in the timeless landscape from the back of a camel or elephant – or maybe the chance to enthusiastically participate in one of India's many spirited festivals.

Do you have your own mustn't-miss travel experiences that you want to share? Post your highlight at lonelyplanet.com/india.

ANDREW BAIN

① TAJ MAHAL, AGRA

We sat at the end of the long pool, its surface only disturbed by the swallows that skimmed across it; their wing tips brushing the water, sending undulating ripples scurrying across its surface as the first light hit the dome. This was the Taj Mahal (p133), the gem of Agra. The semiprecious stones gleamed and glinted in the golden beams.

Been_jamin, Traveller

BLUE CITY, JODHPUR

2

The view from Jodhpur's Mehrangarh Fort (p304), perched on a hill, is a breathtaking ocean of blue rooftops. Originally coloured to mark the higher-caste house (Brahmin) from the lower, today the blue walls keep the locals from the mosquito menace.

elizabethsoumya, Traveller

3

JAISALMER FORT

This 12th-century fort (p324) is a warren of narrow streets carved from sandstone, harbouring a palace, temples and hundreds of deceptively simple-looking *havelis* (traditional residences). A quarter of the city's population lives here, surrounded by its 99 bastions.

Alex Landragin, Lonely Planet Staff

FABULOUS FESTIVALS

Barely a week goes by when there isn't some form of festival being celebrated in Rajasthan. Hindu, Muslim, Jain and Christian – each has contributed to the festival and ceremonial calendar; and, as elsewhere in India, the celebrations are by and large not exclusive to caste, class and religion. When there's an opportunity to prepare rich culinary treats or sticky sweets, to throw on colourful clothes, to ignite fireworks or to paint an elephant (as pictured below, Jaipur's Elephant Festival, see p148), usually everyone likes to join in. Though many festivals are age-old and deeply spiritual, others have evolved to celebrate the rich traditions and unique characteristics of Rajasthan in a rapidly modernising world.

Lindsay Brown, Lonely Planet Author

RICHARD I'ANSON

RICHARD I'ANSON

BUNDI PALACE, SOUTHERN RAJASTHAN

Bundi boasts an extraordinary, decaying puzzle-palace (p225) with fading gold-and-turquoise murals. Previously shut up and left to the bats and monkeys, it's since been cleaned up and opened to the public, although you will get lost without a guide.

**Alex Landragin,
Lonely Planet Staff**

5

CAMEL SAFARI IN THE SAM SAND DUNES

Take an overnight trip by camel into Rajasthan's Thar Desert (p330) to see gazelles, sleep on a sand dune, make chapati (unleavened Indian bread) over an open fire, and meet desert-dwelling villagers who are capable of growing watermelons and wheat in sand. You can organise a camel safari in the cities of Jaisalmer and Bikaner.

cheryn, Traveller

6

JOHN SONE

7

JASON EDWARDS

RANTHAMBHORE NATIONAL PARK

There are few places left to see the world's largest cat in the wild. Ranthambhore National Park (p215) is one such place. Lush forests, remarkable landscape, ancient palaces – it's an unforgettable setting.

zac83, Traveller

KEREN SU

8

RAJASTHAN: COLOUR ME BRIGHT

Geography will tell you Rajasthan is a barren, desert land. Aesthetics will tell you it is anything but. Festive and colourful, the sight of its forts and palaces, local folk in colourful costumes (as pictured above at Gangaur Festival, Udaipur, see p224), unique handicrafts and roadside musicians is a delight.

pujamad, Traveller

RICHARD I'ANSC

9 FATEHPUR SIKRI

The mists that hung low over Fatehpur Sikri (p142) created an eerie ambience as we made our way through the old Mughal capital. After we emerged from Emperor Akbar's intricately carved debating chambers, the heavens opened and it bucketed down. We took shelter under the red-sandstone verandas of the courtyard and watched the central pools of this royal city (abandoned for its lack of water) overflow.

Robin Stewart-Crompton, Traveller

RICHARD I'ANSC

10 JANTAR MANTAR OBSERVATORY, JAIPUR

Can't find your watch? Need to calculate the altitude of the sun? Then you've come to the right place. When you enter Jantar Mantar observatory (p156) in Jaipur, you'll be forgiven for thinking you've stumbled onto the set of a science-fiction movie. This futuristic landscape constructed centuries ago is home to an impressive collection of huge astronomical instruments; some are still used to forecast weather and the intensity of monsoons. The centrepiece here is a 23m-high sundial with staircase leading to the top; it tells the time to within 20-seconds' accuracy. Look out for the Hawa Mahal (Palace of the Winds) peeping over the observatory walls in the distance; its ornate pink-sandstone façade resembling Krishna's crown.

Alison Ridgway, Lonely Planet Staff

SMELL A RAT, BIKANER

If rats send a shiver up your spine, take a trip to the Karni Mata temple (p348) in Deshnok, Rajasthan. After stepping through the marble entrance you will be greeted by the swarms of holy rodents that devotees believe to be reincarnated souls saved from Yana, the god of death. Don't panic if one runs over your foot – it's considered lucky.

susannacsmith, Traveller

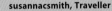

12

BRENT WINEBRENNER

PATRICK HORTON

11 RAJ GHAT, DELHI

Pay your respects to India's father of Independence at Raj Ghat (p98). The site of Mahatma Gandhi's cremation is now a sacred place. His black-granite cremation platform is covered in garlands of bright-orange marigolds, and an eternal flame burns at its side – a very simple memorial for a man who lived by the simple philosophies of truth and nonviolence. India's heart lies here.

Alison Ridgway, Lonely Planet Staff

LINDSAY BROWN

13 EXPERIENCE PUSHKAR

The colour, jewellery, desert, tribespeople and camels at the annual Pushkar Camel Fair (p209) are phenomenal! There's camel everything! Camel taxis, camel shoes, camel accessories including saddles and bells…but no camel on the menu!

travel_trail, Traveller

14 EXQUISITE INTERIORS

The phenomenal wealth of feudal princes and maharajas was as exclusive as it was vast. Only by luck of birth or special invitation could one have experienced the splendours of Rajasthan's palaces and grand *havelis* in their halcyon days. All that has changed and the always indulgent interiors are now open to the hoi polloi. Many of the region's most flamboyant and artistic rooms (such as Samode Palace, pictured left, see p181) can be enjoyed for the cost of admission to a museum.

Lindsay Brown,
Lonely Planet Author

15 AMBER FORT

Escape the frantic streets of Jaipur and slow things down by ascending the nearby hills on elephant-back to Amber Fort (p178). Our elephant was 27 years old and her name was Lakshmi (they all seemed to be called Lakshmi). As she gently carried us high above the valley, she took good care of us, even trumpeting away hawkers as they approached us. Once at the fort, we marvelled at the imposing three-storey gateway that shimmered in the sun. We lit a match inside the dark Sheesh Mahal chamber and gasped as our flame was reflected in thousands of tiny mirrors embedded in the walls and ceiling, like stars in the night sky.

Carol Andrades, Traveller

Contents

Regional Map Contents

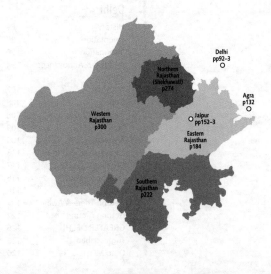

Destination Rajasthan, Delhi & Agra

Here is India at its high-definition, surround-sound best. Prowling tigers, swaying elephants, hot and spicy bazaars, fabulous festivals, stunning saris and twisted turbans; all a pageant of colour and curiosity set against a backdrop of desert sands, secluded jungles, marble palaces and impenetrable stone forts.

This book also celebrates the Golden Triangle – a traveller's trigonometric survey of emblematic India. Starting at the daunting megametropolis of Delhi with its majestic Mughal heritage, it then angles towards Agra, where the world's most famous tomb, the Taj Mahal, defines a city, before heading to Jaipur, the city painted pink with a palace of winds and bustling bazaars, and the gateway to Rajasthan.

Covering an area 342,236 sq km, about the size of Germany, Rajasthan represents 10.4% of the Indian landmass, with much of it embracing the Thar Desert, a vast area of heat, dunes and dust. The chronic drought of recent times has accelerated migration from the parched agricultural lands to the already overburdened cities.

In recent years, Rajasthan's life-giving monsoon has become less and less predictable, and the desperate scarcity of rain has affected people's livelihoods as well as the greater environment. For those who remain on the land, it has become a battle for survival. No wonder then, that there were tears of joy as the waters from the Sardar Sarovar dam, part of the controversial Narmada River Project in neighbouring Gujarat, finally trickled into the deserts around Barmer and Jalore in 2008. Bringing drinking and irrigation water to millions of people affected by drought was a political triumph, but the ultimate financial, social and environmental costs have yet to be counted.

Snapshots of the everyday in Rajasthan capture India at its most evocative: You can catch it in the twirl of a moustache, a veiled glance, or a puff of blue hashish smoke. Witnessing turbaned men bartering camels brings history to life. This is Rajasthan's famous heritage which has bestowed legacies of pride and tradition, magnificent palaces and forts, as well as stunning handicrafts and fine arts developed through patronage of the Maharajas. Rajasthan is India's major drawcard in the lucrative tourist trade – 40% of all visitors to India come to Rajasthan, bringing with them cash, providing jobs, affording its magnificent heritage to be maintained, encouraging the region's splendid arts and provoking cultural exchange.

However, there is another side to the heritage coin: the state's feudal burden slows development, and in many respects – women's rights, health and education – Rajasthan lags behind the other states in the country. The position of women – especially rural women – is a particular cause for concern. In rural areas female education is not valued, largely because of the expense of sending girls to school. But it is also because women have a low status (for more information, see p40). Access to education and health resources in Rajasthan is affected by gender, caste and class far more than elsewhere in the country. It's not all doom and gloom though. The figures for literacy, at around 61% (44.2% for women), have doubled since 1991. Statistics also indicate a decline in poverty and infant mortality.

FAST FACTS

Population Rajasthan: 56.5 million

Population Delhi: 12.8 million

Population Agra: 1.3 million

Population Growth Rate: 2.5%

GDP growth rate: 9%

Inflation: 5.2%

Unemployment: 5.5%

No of camels: 400,000

No of tigers: 16-20 (all in Ranthambhore National Park)

No of maharajas (and rajas): 19

The entire Indian economy, including Rajasthan's tourism, agriculture and business sectors, has undeniably made giant strides in recent years; however, the challenges for today's politicians – redistribution of wealth and environmental conservation – remain unresolved. Rajasthan continues to lose its wildlife and vegetation, and India is expected to become the world's third-largest emitter of carbon by 2015. In a land where juxtaposition of old and new has become a hackneyed slogan, the visitor must still marvel at the scene of elaborate cenotaphs of erstwhile rulers and rich silk-route traders now crowded by state-of-the-art wind turbines helping to address India's burgeoning energy and pollution crisis.

Getting Started

Rajasthan holds India's greatest wealth of places to visit, and is conveniently adjacent to the international gateway of Delhi and the internationally famous destination of Agra. This area of India is very accessible and easy to travel around, with air, bus and train connections that make all sorts of routes feasible. The only problem you may face is deciding how many of Rajasthan's extraordinary sights you can fit into your visit. While puzzling this out, make sure you allow some time to visit out-of-the-way places too, as your experience in a rural hamlet or little-visited village will be a world away from that in the major towns and cities.

Rajasthan suits all budgets – you can travel on a shoestring, emulate the maharajas or go for a middle-path sojourn, and in each case have an astonishing, romantic time, staying in wondrous places that evoke the region's past in varying degrees of luxury.

Travel in India can be exasperating, challenging and stressful, so choose your companions with care. Women travelling alone will encounter some hassle (see p372 for more information) but this is usually irritating rather than dangerous – it's generally a safe place to travel solo whatever your gender. Travel with children is rewarding here, too. In such a family-centred society, children are fêted everywhere and will be your ticket to feeling welcome wherever you go! That said, it's much harder in the hectic, traffic-congested cities, so you'll need to plan your route carefully to allow lots of respite on the way. For more information, see p354.

For disabled travellers, India is very challenging – crowds, uneven surfaces, lack of adequate facilities, and toilets (often of the squat variety) that test the most able-bodied are all hurdles for any traveller. However, the advantage with travelling here is that you can always find help at hand to assist with lifting, carrying or just about anything. With planning and research there's no reason to rule Rajasthan out because you have a disability. See p369 for more details.

You can choose to get around by train, plane, bus or taxi. Many travellers, particularly those short of time, choose to travel solely by taxi – this allows you complete flexibility, and means you can cover a lot of ground and visit out-of-the-way places with ease. Part of the joy of travel in India, however, can be to take trains – always an experience in itself and a good way of mingling with others. If it suits your needs, trip and budget, the most flexible and rewarding way to get around is a mishmash of methods – taking the occasional train, buses when it suits, and taxis for the more inaccessible places or when you need your own space or are just a bit tired. For more discussion of the pros and cons of different forms of transport, see p376.

WHEN TO GO

Rajasthan is at its best in the balmy winter months (November to March), when the days are warm and sunny (average temperatures across the state are around 25°C), and the nights are cool. However, as this is when most people go, hotel prices are at their highest and you'll also have to plan (and book) ahead if you want to stay in the better-known midrange and top-end hotels, particularly the palaces, *havelis* (traditional, ornately decorated residences) and hunting lodges for which Rajasthan is renowned. In March and in the postmonsoon season from mid-September to the end of November, it's a bit hotter, but still fine to visit, with average maximum temperatures in October of around 35°C and an average minimum of around 20°C. These periods are

See Climate Charts (p354) for more information.

also good as places won't be so busy and rooms at those charismatic hotels will be easier to find.

Another factor you should watch out for is travelling during Indian holiday times. If you want to catch a train during the Diwali holiday (p360), for example, you'll need to book your ticket weeks in advance. Otherwise you can usually book train and plane tickets just a few days in advance to be assured a place.

Rajasthan is a startlingly vibrant state, and some of its most colourful festivals, such as the Desert Festival in Jaisalmer (p301) and the famous Pushkar Camel Fair (p209), take place in winter. In October/November it's Diwali, the festival of lights, when people go crazy with noisy fireworks, and oil lamps line the streets. In late February/early March there's Holi (p360), India's most exuberant festival, when everyone throws coloured water and powder at each other. Rajasthan's own Gangaur Festival (see p148) is celebrated in March/April, as is Udaipur's Mewar Festival (p224). Jaipur's Elephant Festival (see p148) is held in March. For more on festivals, see the boxed text at the beginning of each regional chapter and p358.

Winter is also a good time to visit Rajasthan's best-known wildlife sanctuaries: Keoladeo Ghana National Park (p188), Ranthambhore National Park (p215) and Sariska Tiger Reserve (p198).

If a summer visit is your only option, be aware that it will be horrendously hot. Premonsoon, which extends from April to June, is the hottest season, with temperatures ranging from 32°C to 45°C. There is little relief from the scorching onslaught, particularly in the arid zone to the west and northwest of the Aravalli Hills, where temperatures often climb above 45°C. Mt Abu registers the lowest temperatures at this time (the daytime maximum reaches around 32°C). The monsoon is a welcome arrival in late June in the eastern and southeastern regions of the state, finally falling in mid-July in the desert zones. It is preceded by dust and thunderstorms. Unless the rains are insubstantial, the monsoon is accompanied by a decrease in temperatures, with average maximums dropping to 29°C to 32°C in the south and southeast of Rajasthan, and an average of above 38°C in the northern and northwestern regions. But take comfort in the fact that hotel prices will be at their lowest, you won't have to book ahead anywhere, and plan on taking it easy and doing your sightseeing early or late in the day.

DON'T LEAVE HOME WITHOUT...

- Your passport, visa (p369), tickets and travel insurance (p361)
- Sleeping-bag sheet – good if you're unsure about the hotel linen and essential if you're travelling overnight on a 2nd- or 3rd-class sleeper train
- Packets of wet wipes
- Tampons – available in main tourist centres, but it's worth bringing your own stock
- Sunscreen and sunglasses – the local versions aren't reliable
- A small torch (flashlight) – the sort you wear on your head to keep your hands free is ideal
- A universal sink plug – useful in cheap hotels
- Insect repellent – you can't buy the really good stuff
- A voltage stabiliser – a good idea if you're bringing sensitive electronic equipment
- A water bottle – if you use water-purification tablets or filters (see Drinking Water, p391) you'll avoid adding to Rajasthan's plastic waste problem

COSTS & MONEY

Prices vary depending on the season and how busy a place is. In the low season, or even on an off day during the high season, you can get big discounts just by asking. Costs will escalate during festivals or other special events. Costs in the larger cities (such as Jaipur, Delhi and Agra) and popular tourist destinations (such as Jaisalmer and Udaipur) are often higher, though accommodation can be cheap at these places because of all the competition.

Costs also vary depending on whether you are travelling solo or in a group. It's more economical travelling with one or more people, as you can save money by sharing hotel rooms, taxis, rickshaws and car hire.

Whatever budget you have, you'll get so much more for your money than in most other countries – Rajasthan is amazing value.

That said, during the high season, prices for top-end hotels can vie with similar places elsewhere in the world. If you stay in luxurious converted forts and palaces, fly between the main cities of Rajasthan, and buy exquisite arts and crafts, you can sail through enormous amounts of cash. It's easy to blow US$200 a night in a swanky palace hotel without even poking your nose out the door.

If you stay in dormitories or the cheapest hotels, travel on public buses, and subsist on dhal and rice, you could see Rajasthan on about US$20 a day.

If you're looking for something between these extremes, you could spend around US$40 to US$60 a day staying in good budget and midrange hotels, eating in good restaurants and taking trains and autorickshaws rather than uncomfortable buses.

HOW MUCH?
Internet access per hr Rs 20-60
Rajasthani puppet Rs 100-500
Kurta pyjamas Rs 300
Camel safari per day Rs 650
Henna painting per hand Rs 80

Admission Fees

Most tourist sites have an admission fee, and many levy a fee for the use of cameras and videos (they haven't yet adapted for digital cameras that can take videos). Many sites charge a substantially lower admission fee for Indian residents than they do for foreigners. In case you're wondering, if you're of Indian descent (but not an Indian resident), the foreigners' rate officially applies, although you may escape detection or even be knowingly offered the lower local rate.

Admission to the Taj Mahal now costs Rs 750 for foreigners, but most other places are nowhere near as expensive, averaging around Rs 250 for major sites.

TRAVELLING RESPONSIBLY

Since its inception in 1973, Lonely Planet has encouraged readers to tread lightly, travel responsibly and enjoy the magic that independent travel affords. International travel is growing at a jaw-dropping rate, and we still firmly believe in the benefits it can bring – but, as always, we encourage you to consider the impact your visit will have on both the global environment and the local economies, cultures and ecosystems. For a range of ways to travel responsibly see Responsible Travel (p82).

TRAVEL LITERATURE

Robyn Davidson's *Desert Places* is a remarkable account of the author's journey by camel with the Rabari (a nomadic tribal group) on their annual migration through the Thar Desert. It offers compelling insight into the plight of the nomads, as well as recounting the reflections of a solo female traveller in Rajasthan.

TOP PICKS

PUT YOURSELF IN THE PICTURE

Take the effort to seek out some of the region's most spectacular, picturesque and evocative experiences and take home a lifetime of memories.

- The monument to love – the Taj Mahal (p133)
- Sunrise overlooking Pushkar from Saraswati Temple (p209)
- The mighty Mehrangarh (p304), Rajasthan's most imposing fort
- Tiger spotting in Ranthambhore National Park (p215)
- The sand-castle fort of Jaisalmer (p320)
- Bird-watching in Keoladeo Ghana National Park (p188)

ROMANTIC ROOMS & PALATIAL DIGS

Whether it's an old fort with metre-wide walls, an opulent palace, or a luxury tent in the wide outdoors, you'll sleep like royalty in our top hotel picks.

- Lake Palace Hotel (p253) – opulence with movie-set credentials and a perfect location
- Khem Villas (p218) – luxurious tents and bungalows in jungle environs owned and run by dedicated conservationists
- Rambagh Palace (p169) – lavish lawns and serene surroundings seem to slow down time
- Umaid Bhawan Palace (p310) – sheer luxury in this swan song of maharaja indulgence
- Shiv Niwas Palace Hotel (p253) – sumptuous suites and a gorgeous marble pool

GOING GREEN

Though there are many claiming to be on the green wagon, Rajasthan is not an overly green destination. Nonetheless, there are some commendable efforts blending sustainable tourism with environmental awareness.

- Apani Dhani (p281) – an award-winning accommodation option that uses organic farm alternative energy, including solar cookers and water heaters, compost toilets and biogas
- Barefoot College (p207) – supports rural outreach programmes in Rajasthan with an emphasis on empowering women and
- conserving the natural environment and traditional knowledge
- Sanganer's paper manufacturers (p180) – use recycled fabric rather than wood pulp
- Anokhi (p174) – a modern textile outlet, with branches blossoming all over India, that has helped revive traditional dyeing and hand-block printing

FESTIVALS & EVENTS

Rajasthan is alive with festivals year-round and the following are our top 10 picks (for more on the wealth of festivals and events in Rajasthan, see p358).

- Jaisalmer Desert Festival (p301) in January and February in Jaisalmer
- Holi (p224) in February and March in Udaipur
- Gangaur (p148) in March and April in Jaipur
- Teej (p148) in July and August in Jaipur
- Dussehra (p224) in October and November in Kota
- Pushkar Camel Fair (p209) in October and November in Pushkar
- Kolayat Fair (p301) in November in Bikaner

Rajasthan Stories, Rudyard Kipling's tales about the state, make for an old-fashioned ripping yarn; the three slim volumes are available in bookshops in Jaipur (p150).

City of Djinns, by William Dalrymple, is a fascinating book about Delhi – its history intertwined with the author's personal struggles to get to grips with the city. It also records a visit to the Sufi shrine at Ajmer during pilgrimage time.

In Rajasthan, by Royina Grenal, is part of Lonely Planet's travel literature series and gives a different slant on solo female travel – from a local (if privileged middle-class) perspective.

Lost in Transmission, by Jonathan Harley, is an engaging and entertaining account of a foreign correspondent finding his way in the subcontinent. It is interestingly linked to another book, *Holy Cow,* by Sarah MacDonald. This is a lightweight, amusing book about the author's life in Delhi (thanks to new husband, Jonathan Harley), travels around India, and her cursory investigations of different religions – her conclusions feel a bit glib, but it's very entertaining on the way.

Scoop-wallah, by Justine Hardy, follows the author's work on the *Indian Express* in Delhi. It's a tantalising glimpse into the world of Indian journalism that journeys through the author's frustrations and her canny observations of contemporary Delhi.

No Full Stops in India, by BBC correspondent Mark Tully, is a fascinating read that details his travels around India and puts forward some interpretations of contemporary Indian society.

INTERNET RESOURCES

The website of the state tourism authority, **Rajasthan Tourism Development Corporation** (RTDC; www.rajasthantourism.gov.in), offers some useful information on what's happening in Rajasthan.

There are zillions of websites on India and Rajasthan, but you'll find that many are nothing more than glossy, inaccurate public-relations puff. For reliable information scan trusted newspapers and current-affairs sites:

Hindu (www.thehindu.com) The website of this quality broadsheet.

Hindustan Times (www.hindustantimes.com) Another reasonable broadsheet with a reasonable website.

India Today (www.india-today.com) A popular magazine on India's current affairs.

Indian Express (www.indianexpress.com) Useful coverage on this popular broadsheet's site.

Times of India (www.timesofindia.com) National coverage with a tabloid feel, and a curious selection of international news.

Itineraries
CLASSIC ROUTES

This traditional circuit linking the big-ticket attractions of Delhi, Agra and Jaipur is ideal for travellers short on time. You will cover just over 700km and though the road and rail connections are excellent, book your bus or train seats early on this popular trail.

THE GOLDEN TRIANGLE

One route is so well loved it even has a name: the Golden Triangle – the classic Delhi–Agra–Jaipur trip, which can be squeezed into a week.

Spend a day or two in **Delhi** (p88) finding your feet and seeing the big-draw sights, such as the magnificent Mughal **Red Fort** (p96) and **Jama Masjid** (p98), India's largest mosque. Then catch a convenient train to **Agra** (p130) to spend a day being awed by the world's most extravagant monument to love, the **Taj Mahal** (p133) and exploring the mighty **Agra Fort** (p135). Only an hour away is **Fatehpur Sikri** (p142), a beautiful Mughal city dating from the apogee of Mughal power, which is amazingly well preserved and deserves another day.

If you have time, take a rural respite at **Keoladeo Ghana National Park** (p188), one of the world's foremost bird reserves. Though suffering from lack of water, it is a relaxing, beautiful and intriguing place to visit. Having chilled, you can train it to **Jaipur** (p147) for a couple of days in and around Rajasthan's hectic, dusky-pink capital, seeing the **City Palace** (p154) and **Amber Fort** (p178), and stocking up on blue pottery, Rajasthani puppets and other shopping delights before heading back to Delhi.

MAHARAJA CIRCUIT

With a fortnight to spare, you can forget triangles and go all out for a multifaceted loop taking in Rajasthan's most spectacular cities, all erstwhile capitals of former princely states.

Again, start from **Delhi** (p88) and make your way to **Jaipur** (p147), possibly via **Agra** (p130) and the **Taj Mahal** (p133).

From Jaipur, take a long trip to the sacred lake of **Pushkar** (p206) and then on to the romantic lake-town of **Udaipur** (p240), visiting the fine **City Palace** (p244) and the impressive **Jagdish Temple** (p247) as well as doing some shopping and relaxing on rooftops while peering at the lake. From Udaipur head to the extraordinary, bustling, blue city of **Jodhpur** (p301), but not before taking time to stop at the milk-white Jain temple complex of **Ranakpur** (p261) and the isolated, dramatic fortifications of **Kumbalgarh** (p259), one of Rajasthan's most remote and impressive forts. As they are fairly close together you can visit them comfortably en route to Jodhpur in a day. In Jodhpur itself, visit the spectacular **Mehrangarh** (p304), a fort that glowers over the city like a storybook fortress.

Next take an overnight train to the Golden City, **Jaisalmer** (p320), a giant sand castle in the desert, with its beautiful Jain temples and exquisite merchants' *havelis* (traditional, ornately decorated mansions). Take a short camel safari through bewitching desertscapes if you get a chance, and break your journey back to Delhi with a stop in the desert city of **Bikaner** (p338), home to the impregnable **Junagarh Fort** (p339).

Taking in the famous palaces and forts of royal Rajasthan, this 2000km loop explores the length and breadth of the romantic desert state. Though certainly feasible in a couple of weeks, you'll be tempted to linger and lap up the luxury.

A MONTH-LONG SOJOURN

With **Agra** (p130) and the **Taj Mahal** (p133) as your first stop after **Delhi** (p88), head to **Fatehpur Sikri** (p142) and the World Heritage–listed bird-watching paradise of **Keoladeo Ghana National Park** (p188), followed by **Ranthambhore National Park** (p215) if tigers are your bag.

Take the train southwest to Kota for a stop at the charming small town of **Bundi** (p223), before taking the train on to **Chittorgarh** (p236) and then **Udaipur** (p240), where you can relax from your travels with a few easy days of sightseeing, grazing and shopping.

From Udaipur it's worth side-tripping to **Mt Abu** (p264) to see the magnificent **Dilwara Temples** (p265) before going north to **Jodhpur** (p301), or travel directly to Jodhpur, stopping at **Ranakpur** (p261) and **Kumbalgarh** (p259) on the way. From Jodhpur it's an easy train ride to **Jaisalmer** (p320), the golden desert town, from where you can take a camel trek into the desert. After Jaisalmer, head to **Bikaner** (p338) via **Phalodi** (p318) and **Khichan** (p318), where you can observe the village's renowned demoiselle cranes.

From Bikaner head south, stopping at the challenging and fascinating rat temple of **Deshnok** (p349) and the sleepy cattle-fair town of **Nagaur** (p316) before coming to rest at the sacred pilgrimage town of **Pushkar** (p206) to relax for a few days…or more.

From Pushkar it is a short hop to **Jaipur** (p147) with its fabulous citadel at Amber and great shopping. From Jaipur head north to **Shekhawati** (p273) for a few days, inspecting *havelis* at **Mandawa** (p294), **Nawalgarh** (p277) and **Fatehpur** (p291), before returning to Delhi.

This 2500km plus circuitous expedition delves into the spiritual heart of Rajasthan, combining lesser-known palaces, secretive tigers, and astonishing temples with the more famous attractions of the region. Factor in several rest days in a quiet corner or a plush palace hotel.

TAILORED TRIPS

UNDISCOVERED GEMS

Many out-of-the-way places in Rajasthan don't see that many tourists – amazing when you consider how many visitors the state receives, and wonderful when you want to escape from the major tourist haunts and see an entirely different side of the state.

Our top picks include the Shekhawati region with its colourful *havelis* and rural pace. The town of Mandawa aside, the area has escaped much tourism, and seeking out the amazing murals in its small towns is like a treasure hunt. Some towns worth discovering are **Nawalgarh** (p277), **Fatehpur** (p291), **Dundlod** (p282) and **Mahansar** (p289). Other lesser-known places include **Kolayat** (p348), a remote town around a holy lake near Bikaner; **Osiyan** (p317), an ancient desert town filled with Jain temples; some of the sights around Sariska, such as the ghost town of **Bhangarh** (p199); **Dungarpur** (p263), a royal town with an eccentric empty palace and serene lake; **Jhalawar** (p233), near a magnificent fortress and the ancient City of Temple Bells; and **Karauli** (p219), which has a beautiful, worn palace.

Other wonderful escapes are the countryside around **Udaipur** (p240), with its undulating hills and tiny villages, trekking in the hills around **Mt Abu** (p264) or **Kumbalgarh** (p259), and the barren landscape surrounding **Pushkar** (p206).

ARTS & CRAFTS

Rajasthan's desolate, muted landscape seemingly galvanises its inhabitants to produce some of India's most vivid paintings, textiles and jewellery.

Shekhawati's small towns are packed with brilliantly painted *havelis*; in **Nawalgarh** (p280) you can attend craft workshops, and you can take painting lessons at **Jhunjhunu** (p287).

Jaipur (p147) is the artistic nerve centre, with some wonderful shops and opportunities to see artisans, particularly jewellers, at work. Nearby is **Sanganer** (p180), where you can visit workshops specialising in paper making and block printing, and take block-printing or pottery **lessons** (p163). Also nearby is the woodcarving centre of **Bassi** (p235). **Kishangarh** (p205) is renowned for its production of miniature paintings.

Around **Jodhpur** (p301), villagers produce woollen *dhurries* (rugs).

Udaipur (p240) is another major centre for the arts – a splendid place to buy miniatures, textiles, woodcarving and jewellery, take lessons in painting and see traditional dance. Outside the city is **Shilpgram** (p247), which displays, demonstrates and sells traditional handiwork.

In the west, **Barmer** (p337) is another place to see block printers at work, and in **Bikaner** (p338) you can see artisans producing *usta* (gold-painted camel leather) work.

RAJASTHAN'S WILD SIDE

You can wildlife-spot till you drop in Rajasthan's beautiful sanctuaries, commune with tamer creatures at regional festivals or ride them out on safari.

World Heritage site **Keoladeo Ghana National Park** (p188) is one of the world's foremost bird sanctuaries. Rambling **Ranthambhore National Park** (p215) is one of the best places in India to spot tigers. Though there are no tigers at **Sariska Tiger Reserve** (p198), it is another scenic sanctuary protecting leopards, hyenas, blue bulls and lots of birdlife.

Catch up with all the latest trends in camel fashion at the epic **Pushkar Camel Fair** (p209) or the more business-oriented version at **Nagaur** (see Festivals in Western Rajasthan, p301) in January/February. To get an

even closer look at Rajasthan's ships of the desert, take a camel safari from **Jaisalmer** (p330), **Khuri** (p336), **Osiyan** (p317), **Pushkar** (p210) or **Bikaner** (p343).

Going horse riding around **Udaipur** (p248) is a wonderful way to take in the countryside as well as some rural life. Between Udaipur and Jodhpur, **Kumbalgarh Wildlife Sanctuary** (p259) offers some fantastic scenery and is famous for its wolves.

Finally, do not miss **Khichan**, located between Jaisalmer and Nagaur, where you can see the spectacular sight of over 7000 demoiselle cranes descending to feed on grain spread around for them by villagers (see The Demoiselle Cranes of Khichan p318).

FORT COLLECTING

Water may be a problem, but one thing Rajasthan's not short of is forts. You'll definitely want to bag as many of these architectural wonders on your trip as you can.

Delhi (p88) is a good place to start on your fort-finding mission, with the city-centre Mughal **Red Fort** (p96). To the east, in Agra, is its red-sandstone cousin, **Agra Fort** (p135), which contains exquisite Mughal buildings. For something straight out of the *Jungle Book*, visit **Ranthambhore Fort** (p216), perched on a craggy mountain in Ranthambhore National Park, surrounded by jungle. At Sariska Tiger Reserve is **Kankwari Fort** (p198) – a fortified pipsqueak compared to many others, but one that offers superb views. **Taragarh**

(p225) at Bundi is overgrown, crumbling and a fantastic place for a ramble. Plateau-top **Chittorgarh** (p236) is Rajasthan's most legendary fort, containing palaces, temples and a mass of myths. Even more spectacular is **Kumbalgarh** (p259), a noble, remote edifice between Udaipur and Jodhpur. Near Jhalawar is little-visited **Gagron Fort** (p235), which towers over the confluence of two rivers.

Most dramatic of all is **Mehrangarh** (p304) in Jodhpur, rising from a rock face like an epic movie set. Also striking is **Jaisalmer** (p324), the golden sandstone fort that resembles a sand castle and is alive with inhabitants, while Bikaner's **Junagarh** (p339) claims the region's most spectacular interiors.

History Anirban Mahapatra

A popular Indian saying goes that the state of Rajasthan alone has more history than the rest of the country put together. Given that its name literally translates as 'the land of kings', perhaps the theory is true. Strewn with fascinating palaces, forts and ruins, with a colourful and diverse culture to boot, Rajasthan is an exotic land that intrigues as much as it enthrals. Throw in the neighbouring medieval capitals of Delhi and Agra, and you've got a heady cocktail laced with a thousand royal legends, potent enough to work its charm on even the most prosaic of imaginations.

But all good things come at a price. And Rajasthan, along with its neighbouring areas, has had to pay heavily in the past in order to inherit the rich heritage it calls its own today. Over the centuries, the province has had to cope with waves of ruthless invasions lashing in from the geographically vulnerable northwest, and later the south. These raids, undertaken by everyone from treasure hunters to religious crusaders, have brought along their own share of carnage, vandalism and desecration. Uncertainty and political turmoil have been a way of life here. Delhi, for instance, has been razed and rebuilt by different dynasties at least nine times throughout the ages. And the crisis has often been compounded by severe infighting among princely states in the area. Ironically, it is this very streak of collective unrest that has contributed immensely towards shaping the character of the terrain and its people, leaving behind a legacy unparalleled by any other part of the nation.

Anirban Mahapatra is a journalist, writer and photographer based in Delhi, and has travelled extensively through Rajasthan and northern India during his three-year stay in the Indian capital. His primary interests include exploring the multifaceted culture and living tradition of India and its people.

BACK WHERE IT ALL BEGAN

Archaeologists have inferred that the desert and scrub areas of Rajasthan have been home to humans for several thousand years. Excavations in Kalibangan, near Ganganagar in northern Rajasthan, have unearthed terracotta pottery and jewellery that date back to around 3000 BC, conclusively dating the earliest spread of settlements in the state to that time. Some of these urban centres were presumably absorbed into the Harappan segment of the Indus Valley civilisation, where they flourished until the settlement was mysteriously abandoned 3700 years ago. The mass exodus, possibly triggered by flooding or a severe climatic change, rendered Rajasthan devoid of human settlement for some time, until indigenous tribes such as the Bhils and the Minas moved in to set up their own squabbling small kingdoms, thereby commencing the long history of argumentative neighbours in the region.

But even as the tribes tore away at each other, another civilisation was sprouting in the fertile plains to the east of Rajasthan, between the rivers Yamuna and Ganga (Ganges). Though their exact origins are difficult to determine, the settlers in this fledgling colony are widely assumed to

The oldest natural relics in Rajasthan are fossilised remains of a 180-million-year-old forest, located at the Akal Wood Fossil Park (p337) in the Thar Desert near Jaisalmer.

TIMELINE

c 2600–1700 BC	c 1500 BC	c 1000 BC
The heyday of the Indus Valley civilisation. Spanning parts of Rajasthan, Gujarat and the Sindh province in Pakistan, the settlement takes shape around metropolises such as Harappa and Mohenjo-Daro.	The Indo-Aryan civilisation takes root in the fertile plains of the Indo-Gangetic basin. The settlers here speak an early form of Sanskrit, from which several Indian languages, including Hindi, later evolve.	Indraprastha, Delhi's first incarnation, comes into being. Archaeological excavations at the site where the Purana Qila now stands continue even today, as more facts regarding this ancient capital keep coming to light.

belong to a seminomadic race of Indo-European origin, who were known as Aryans or 'noblemen'. It was in this civilisation that Hinduism first evolved as a religious tradition and a way of life, along with a complex patriarchal social structure and the tiered caste system that the greater Indian society adheres to even today. By 1000 BC, the province had seen the establishment of at least two prominent kingdoms: the Matsya territory of Viratnagar encompassing Alwar, Bharatpur, Dholpur and Karauli; and Indraprastha, the earliest-known incarnation of Delhi, which was successively built on by several dynasties to come.

The website www.har appa.com provides an illustrated yet scholarly coverage of everything you need to know about the ancient Indus Valley civilisation, including the significance of recent archaeological finds.

Little is known of Rajasthan's development at this time. However, it was an era that saw few incursions, as the mighty empires which were then strengthening their hold on the subcontinent, surprisingly, chose to pass on the state for one reason or another. Alexander the Great, who came to Asia on his epic conquest, was forced to return when his troops, homesick and weary after the campaign, convinced him to retreat. The Mauryan empire (323–185 BC) had minimal impact too, largely due to its most renowned emperor, Ashoka, taking to nonviolent ways after he converted to Buddhism. In stark contrast to the atrocities he had inflicted on the eastern Indian kingdom of Kalinga, the only evidence Ashoka left of his reign in Rajasthan were Buddhist caves and stupas (Buddhist shrines; p235) near Jhalawar, rock-cut edicts at Bairat, an ancient Buddhist site near Sariska (p198), and a 13m-high pillar he inscribed in Delhi (p99).

The concepts of zero and infinity are widely believed to have been devised by eminent Indian mathematicians such as Aryabhatta and Varahamihira during the reign of the Guptas.

MARAUDING HUNS & THE ADVENT OF KINGS

The insulation that Rajasthan enjoyed through its early years came to an abrupt end during the 5th century AD, when armies of fierce Hun warriors rode in from Central Asia to carry out a series of pillaging raids across north India. These raids were to alter the course of the region's history in two major ways. To begin with, they resulted in the disintegration of the Gupta dynasty, which had taken over from the Mauryas as a central power and had reigned over the country 320–550. But more importantly, they triggered a parallel invasion, as the Rajputs finally came to make Rajasthan their home and, in the absence of an overarching monarchy, grew from strength to strength to usher in the golden age of Rajasthan.

Rajput armies primarily consisted of cavalries. They were known to breed pedigree horses such as the Marwari and Kathiawari, which were inducted into their forces.

Historical evidence suggests that the Rajputs (their name meaning 'children of kings') fled their homelands in Punjab, Haryana, Gujarat and Uttar Pradesh to settle in Rajasthan, primarily to escape the wrath of the White Huns (and later the Arabs) who had begun to storm in from Pakistan and Afghanistan. Once they had arrived in Rajasthan, the Rajputs trampled over the Bhils and Minas, and set up their own small fiefdoms in the face of mounting local chaos. Though they largely belonged to the lower rungs of Hindu society, volatile circumstances demanded that the Rajputs don the role of warriors, if only to fend off further advances by foreign invaders. So in

c 540 BC	326 BC	323–185 BC
The writing of the *Mahabharata* begins. The longest epic in the world, it takes nearly 250 years to complete, and mentions settlements such as Indraprastha, Pushkar and Chittorgarh.	Alexander the Great invades India. He defeats Porus in Punjab to enter the subcontinent, but a rebellion within his army keeps him from advancing beyond the Beas River in Himachal Pradesh.	India comes under the rule of the Maurya kings. Founded by Chandragupta Maurya, this Pan-Indian empire is ruled from Pataliputra (Patna), and briefly adopts Buddhism during the reign of Ashoka.

spite of rigid social norms, which didn't allow for any kind of self-promotion, early Rajput clans such as the Gurjara Pratiharas crossed the caste barriers to proclaim themselves Kshatriyas, members of the warrior class, who came second only to the Brahmins (priests) in the caste hierarchy.

To facilitate their smooth transition through social ranks, and to avoid stinging criticism from the Brahmins, these early Rajput clans chose to jettison their worldly ancestry and took to trumpeting a mythological genealogy that supposedly evolved from celestial origins. From the 6th century onward, some of the clans began calling themselves Suryavanshis (Descendants of the Sun), while others chose to be known as Chandravanshis (Descendants of the Moon). A third dynasty, on the other hand, traced their roots to the sacrificial fire that was lit on Mt Abu during the Mauryan era, thereby naming themselves Agnivanshis (Fire-Born).

As the Rajputs slowly consolidated their grip over Rajasthan, they earned a reputation for their chivalry, noble traditions and strict code of conduct. Their sense of honour matched perhaps only by Arthurian knights or the Japanese samurai, the Rajputs gave rise to several well-known dynasties, who in turn established some of the most renowned princely states of Rajasthan. The largest of these kingdoms, and the third largest in India after Kashmir and Hyderabad, was Marwar. Founded by the Suryavanshi Rathores who rode in from Uttar Pradesh, it was initially ruled from Mandore, before the seat of power was relocated to the Mehrangarh Fort (p304) in nearby Jodhpur. The Sisodias migrated from Gujarat to assemble in the folds of the Aravalli Hills to the south, where they formed the state of Mewar (see boxed text, p32) encompassing Chittorgarh and Udaipur. The Kachhwahas, from Gwalior in Madhya Pradesh, settled in Jaipur in eastern Rajasthan, their capital nestled in the twin fort complex of Amber (p178) and Jaigarh (p179). Meanwhile, a fourth kingdom, called Jaisalmer, was established in the Thar Desert by the Bhattis, who belonged to the lunar dynasty. Obscured by the dunes, the Bhattis remained more or less entrenched in their kingdom until Jaisalmer was integrated into the state of Rajasthan after Independence.

Over the years, Rajasthan saw the mushrooming of many other smaller dynasties, each of which staked claim to its own patch of territory in the region and ruled with complete autonomy, often refusing to submit to the whims of the bigger kingdoms. A few temporary alliances forged through cosmetic treaties or marriages didn't help much, as their fierce sense of pride and independence kept these states from growing and functioning as a unified force. Besides, the clans were so content with their tiny fiefdoms that they rarely thought of looking beyond their borders to explore and conquer newer territories.

One dynasty, however, proved to be an exception. The Chauhans, who belonged to the Agnivanshi race, moved in from Gujarat around the 8th century to settle in the city of Ajmer, from where they gradually extended their

Upon losing Delhi to the Afghans, Prithviraj Chauhan was captured and taken back to Mohammed of Ghori's court in Ghazni, where he was later blinded and killed.

AD 320–550	AD 500–600	1024
The period of the Gupta dynasty, the second of India's great monarchies after the Mauryas. This era is marked by a creative surge in literature and the arts.	The emergence of the Rajputs in Rajasthan. Stemming from three principal races supposedly of celestial origin, they form 36 separate clans who spread out to claim their own kingdoms across the region.	Mahmud of Ghazni raids India for the last time, ransacking on this occasion the Somnath Temple in Gujarat, where he purportedly smashes the idol with his own hands.

empire across the neighbouring states of Haryana and Uttar Pradesh. Within Rajasthan, the Hada offshoot of the Chauhans crossed over to the Hadoti region and captured the cities of Bundi and Kota, while the Deora branch took over the nearby Sirohi area, making way for successive generations to zero in on the provinces of Ranthambore, Kishangarh and Shekhawati. The most illustrious of the Chauhan kings, Prithviraj III, went a notch further by leading his troops to invade Delhi, which had been reduced to insignificance after the fall of Indraprastha and was being governed by local chieftains. Keen to set up a new capital here, Prithviraj Chauhan commissioned the building of a settlement called Qila Rai Pithora, the ramparts of which can still be seen near the Qutb Minar (p126) in Mehrauli. One of the few Hindu kings to hold fort in Delhi, Prithviraj Chauhan administered his empire from the twin capitals of Qila Rai Pithora and Ajmer, before his reign was put to an end by Islamic warriors, who galloped in by the thousands to change the face of the region forever.

THE SWORD OF ISLAM

Some 400 years after Prophet Mohammed had introduced Islam into Arabia, northern India saw the arrival of Muslim crusaders. It was to be expected. With the banner of Islam fluttering high, the crusaders had taken over the province of Sindh (in Pakistan) long ago, and, once they had managed to occupy Ghazni in neighbouring Afghanistan, it was obvious that India would figure next on their agenda. So at the beginning of the 11th century, zealous Turk warriors led by the fearsome Sultan Mahmud of Ghazni descended upon India, razing hundreds of Hindu temples and plundering the region to take away vast amounts of wealth to fill their coffers back home. The Turks made their raids into India almost an annual affair, ransacking the northern part of the country 17 times in as many years. Jolted out of their internal bickering, the Rajput princes organised some hasty defence, but their army was torn to shreds even before they could retaliate. Rajasthan had been lost to Islam.

Razia Sultana, who headed the Mamluks from 1236 to 1240, was the only woman ever to reign in Delhi. She was dislodged from the throne by her brother, Bahram Shah.

Delhi, located further east, was initially spared the wrath of the crusaders, as the Sultan largely confined his raids to Rajasthan and parts of Gujarat. Trouble, however, came by the name of Mohammed of Ghori, governor of Ghazni, who invaded India in the late 12th century, taking up where his predecessor had left off. He was thwarted on his first campaign by Prithviraj Chauhan, but the resolute Ghori returned a year later to defeat the Rajput king in the Second Battle of Tarain. Having convincingly stamped his victory over the region, Ghori trotted back to Ghazni, leaving Delhi under the governorship of Qutb-ud-din Aibak, a former Turk slave who had risen to command forces in India. When news of Ghori's death arrived in Delhi a decade and a half later, Qutb-ud-din shrugged off competition from rivals to stake claim to the Indian part of Ghori's empire. He declared himself Sultan

1192	1206	1303
Prithviraj Chauhan loses Delhi to Mohammed of Ghori. The defeat effectively ends Hindu supremacy in the region, exposing Rajasthan and the subcontinent to subsequent Muslim invaders trooping in from the northwest.	Ghori is murdered during a prayer session while returning to Ghazni from a campaign in Lahore. In the absence of an heir, his kingdom is usurped by his generals. The Delhi Sultanate is born.	Ala-ud-din Khilji sacks Chittorgarh with the intention of carrying away the beautiful Sisodia queen Padmini. The queen immolates herself to escape humiliation – the first recorded instance of *sati* in Rajasthan.

of the region, and founded the Mamluk or Slave dynasty, giving Delhi the first of its many Islamic monarchies.

AN AGE OF TREACHERY & EXPLOITS

The enthronement of Qutb-ud-din Aibak flagged off the Sultanate era of Delhi, which lasted for about 350 years. Throughout this period, Delhi was ruled by six different Islamic dynasties, with a break between 1526 and 1540, when Delhi was captured by the Mughals. The six dynasties produced a line of 38 rulers, who gradually pushed the boundaries of their kingdoms to conquer new land. The whole of the Gangetic basin soon came under the Sultanates' control, as did Rajasthan and Gujarat – the princely states there had little option but to bow down to their might.

Apart from expanding their empire, the Sultanate kings also significantly urbanised Delhi. The Mamluks created the city of Mehrauli, whose most famous monument is the Qutb Minar. The Khiljis, on their part, seated their capital at Siri (p89). The Tughlaqs constructed the forts of Tughlaqabad (p126) and Firoz Shah Kotla (p99), while Sher Shah Suri, the most renowned of the Sur kings, chose to rule from Shergarh, built on the site of the Purana Qila (p104) which he had won from the Mughal emperor Humayun.

Despite the glorious developments, however, the Sultanate era was marked by prolonged phases of political turmoil and administrative tension. Having become the jewel of foreign eyes, Delhi was persistently being attacked from the northwest by Mongol, Persian, Turk and Afghan raiders, who all wanted to set up their own outposts in the city. Within the empire, stability had given way to turncoat politics, conspiracy and internal strife, as deceitful kings contrived bloody assassinations and coups to either remove or upstage their predecessors. Things got murkier with time, until two noblemen who were disgraced by Emperor Ibrahim Lodi decided to get even with the Sultan by inviting Babur, prince of Kabul, to invade Delhi. Ironically, in plotting their revenge, the two men unknowingly paved the way for the most celebrated Islamic dynasty to roll into India.

ENTER THE MUGHALS

Babur, whose Turkic-Mongol lineage included great warriors such as Genghis Khan and Timur the Lame, marched into India through Punjab, defeating Ibrahim Lodi in the First Battle of Panipat (1526) to establish the Mughal dynasty in the country. Once he had seized Delhi, Babur focused his attention on Rajasthan, where many princely states, anticipating his moves, had already banded together to form a united front under the Sisodia king Rana Sanga. Taking advantage of the chaos in Delhi, the Rajputs had meanwhile clawed back in the power race, and states such as Mewar had become formidable enough to pose a considerable threat to the rulers of Delhi. Babur, however, squared everything by defeating the Rajput alliance in a blood-spattered battle

---

While the construction of the Qutb Minar in Delhi was started by Qutb-ud-din Aibak in 1193, it was completed during the reign of Firoz Shah, more than 150 years later.

The eccentric Tughlaq emperor Mohammed Tughlaq reduced Delhi to a ghost town for two years by moving the entire population to a new capital called Daulatabad, more than 1100km away in the Deccan.

To improve connectivity within his kingdom, Sher Shah Suri built the Grand Trunk Road, the oldest and longest road in the subcontinent, which runs from Bengal to Peshawar in Pakistan.

1398	1498	1504
Timur the Lame invades Delhi, on the pretext that the Sultans of Delhi are too tolerant with their Hindu subjects. He executes more than 100,000 Hindu captives before the battle for Delhi.	Vasco da Gama, a Portuguese voyager, discovers the sea route from Europe to India. He arrives in Kerala and engages in trade with the local kings.	Agra is founded on the banks of the Yamuna by Sikandar Lodi. Its glory days begin when Akbar makes it his capital, and the city is briefly called Akbarabad during his reign.

THE INDOMITABLE SISODIAS

In a region where invasions and political upheavals were historical norms, the Sisodias of Mewar stood out as an exception, using everything from diplomacy to sheer valour to retain an iron grip over their land. Pillage and blood baths notwithstanding, the dynasty administered its kingdom in southern Rajasthan without a hiatus for some 1400 years. Lorded over by 76 monarchs throughout the ages, the Sisodias also enjoy the rare distinction of having had one of the longest-serving dynasties in the world.

While they claim to be Suryavanshis, the lineage of the Sisodia kings can be traced back to a prince named Guhil, born to a Rajput queen sometime in the 6th century AD. Orphaned soon after birth and his kingdom ransacked by Huns, Guhil grew up among native Bhils in the forests of the Aravalli Hills. When he was 11, he forged an alliance with a Bhil chieftain to establish a dynasty called the Guhilots. The chieftain also granted Guhil a tract of forested land in the mountains, which was to later expand and flourish as the state of Mewar.

The Guhilots shifted base from the hills in the 12th century to a place called Ahar. It was here that the family split, resulting in a breakaway faction that relocated to the town of Sissoda and rechristened themselves Sisodias. The separatists soon took over Chittorgarh, an ancient garrison which remained under their control (despite being attacked by Ala-ud-din Khilji) until it was sacked by Mughal emperor Akbar in 1568. Though it came as a major military setback, the Sisodias lost no time in retreating into the Aravalli Hills, where they put together a new capital called Udaipur (p240). A serenely beautiful city, Udaipur was never lost to the enemy, and remained the capital of Mewar until the kingdom was absorbed into the state of Rajasthan following India's Independence.

Known for their resilience and courage, the Sisodias have been credited with producing some of the most flamboyant kings ever to have reigned in Rajasthan. The family boasts names such as Rana Sanga, who died a valiant death in 1527 while fending off Mughal troops under Babur, and Maharana Pratap (1540–97), who made several daring though unsuccessful attempts to win Chittorgarh back from Akbar during his time in power. Being prolific builders, the Sisodias also gave Mewar some of its finest structures, including the Victory Tower (p238) at Chittorgarh, the grand City Palace (p244) in Udaipur, the elegant Monsoon Palace (p248) atop Sajjangarh Hill and the spectacular Lake Palace (p243), which stands on an island amid the placid waters of Lake Pichola, also in Udaipur. A part of the City Palace now houses a museum, open to the public, which contains countless artefacts showcasing and documenting the glorious heritage of Mewar.

where several Rajput chiefs, including Rana Sanga, fell to the enemy's wrath. The defeat, which shook the foundations of the Rajput states, also left the Mughals as the undisputed rulers of northern India.

When Timur sacked Delhi, he spared all the builders so that they could build him a city, much like the one he had plundered, back in Samarkand.

Mughal supremacy was briefly cut back in the mid-16th century by Sher Shah Suri, who defeated Babur's successor Humayun to give Delhi its sixth and final Sultanate. Humayun reclaimed Delhi 14 years later, and was succeeded upon his accidental death by his 13-year-old son Akbar. Known as the greatest of the Mughal emperors, Akbar ruled for a period of 49 years,

1526	1540	1568
Babur conquers Delhi and stuns Rajasthan by routing its confederate force, gaining a technological edge on the battlefield due to the early introduction of matchlock muskets in his army.	The Sur dynasty briefly captures Delhi from the Mughals, after Sher Shah Suri's victory over Humayun in the Battle of Kanauj. The loss forces the Mughals to temporarily seek help from the Rajputs.	Akbar leads his army to Chittorgarh and wrests it from the Sisodias. Udai Singh, then king of Mewar, survives the onslaught and transfers his capital to the new city of Udaipur.

and, being a master diplomat, used both tact and military force to expand and consolidate the Mughal empire in India. Realising that the Rajputs could not be conquered on the battlefield alone, Akbar arranged a marriage alliance with a princess of the important Kachhwaha clan which held Amber (and later Jaipur), and even chose Rajput warriors to head his armies. Honoured by these gestures, the Kachhwahas, unlike other Rajputs, aligned themselves with the powerful Mughals, as Akbar indirectly succeeded in winning over one of the biggest Rajput states.

Of course, when diplomacy didn't work, Akbar resorted to war; he conquered Ajmer, and later proceeded to take the mighty forts of Chittorgarh and Ranthambhore. Gradually, all the important Rajput states except Mewar had acknowledged Mughal sovereignty to become vassal states. But even as he was well on his way to becoming the supreme ruler of India, Akbar became more tolerant in many ways. He married a Hindu Rajput princess and encouraged good relations between Hindus and Muslims, giving Rajputs special privileges so that they were embraced within his empire. A monarch with great social insight, he discouraged child marriage, banned *sati* (ritual suicide of a widow on her husband's funeral pyre) and arranged special market days for women. Akbar's reign also saw an unprecedented economic boom in the country, apart from great development in art and architecture.

THE LAST OF THE MUGHAL GREATS

Jehangir, Akbar's son, was the next Mughal emperor (1605–27), and he ruled alongside his adored Persian wife, Nur Jahan, who wielded considerable power and brought Persian influences to the court. Nur Jahan also commissioned the beautiful Itimad-ud-Daulah (p136), the first Mughal structure to be built in marble, in Agra for her parents. The Rajputs maintained cordial relationships with the Mughals through Jehangir's rule, a notable development being that Udai Singh, king of Udaipur, ended Mewar's reservations about the Muslims by befriending Jehangir.

Good times, however, came to an end soon after Jehangir's period in office, as his descendants' greater emphasis on Islam began to rock the relative peace in the region. Upon Jehangir's death, the prince Khurram took over, assuming the title Shah Jahan, which meant 'monarch of the world'. His reign was the pinnacle of Mughal power. Like his predecessors, Shah Jahan was a patron of the arts, and some of the finest examples of Mughal art and architecture produced during his reign, including the Taj Mahal (p133), an extravagant work of extreme refinement and beauty. Shah Jahan also commenced work on Delhi's seventh incarnation, Shahjahanabad, constructing the Red Fort (p96) and the Jama Masjid (p98).

Unfortunately, the emperor harboured high military ambitions, and often bled the country's financial resources to meet his whims. His exhaustion of the state treasury didn't go down well with the Rajputs, and towards the end

Driven by nostalgia, Babur ordered his architects to design a series of gardens across Delhi in a way that they would remind him of his former capital Kabul.

Though Fatehpur Sikri had every making of a great capital, it had an acute shortage of water which became so severe with time that Akbar was forced to move his seat of power to Agra.

Known for his religious tolerance, Akbar propounded a cult called Din-I-Ilahi, which incorporated the best elements of the two principal religions of his empire, Hinduism and Islam.

1608	1631	1674
Granted trading rights by way of a royal charter, the first ships of the British East India Company sail up the Arabian Sea to drop anchor at Surat in Gujarat.	Construction of the Taj Mahal begins after Shah Jahan, overcome with grief following the death of his wife Mumtaz Mahal, vows to build the most beautiful mausoleum in the world in her memory.	Shivaji establishes the Maratha kingdom, spanning western India and parts of the Deccan and north India. He assumes the supercilious title of Chhatrapati, which means 'Lord of the Universe'.

of Shah Jahan's rule, the Rajputs and the Mughals had resigned to accept each other as unsatisfactory bedfellows. Things worsened when Aurangzeb became the last great Mughal emperor in 1658, deposing his father who died in imprisonment at the Musamman Burj (p136) in Agra eight years later. An Islamic hardliner, Aurangzeb quickly made enemies in the region. His zeal saw him devoting all his resources to extending the Mughal empire's boundaries. His government's emphasis on Islam alienated his Hindu subjects. Aurangzeb imposed punitive taxes, banned the building of new temples, even destroying some, and forbade music and ceremonies at court. Challenges to his power mounted steadily as people reacted against his dour reign. And when he claimed his rights over Jodhpur in 1678, his relations with the Rajputs turned into full-scale war. Before long, there was insurgency on all sides, which only increased as Aurangzeb died in 1707 to leave the empire in the hands of a line of inefficient successors given to Bohemian excesses, who had little or no interest in running the state. The Mughal empire was on a one-way journey towards doom.

The booty carried back by Nadir Shah from India was so rich that, upon reaching Iran, he relieved his subjects from paying taxes for a period of three years.

MARATHAS & PERSIANS RUN RIOT

The death of Aurangzeb marked the beginning of Delhi's Twilight Years, a period through which the degenerating Mughal empire was laid to waste by the Marathas and the Persians. The Marathas had risen to prominence between 1646 and 1680 led by the heroic Shivaji, under whom their empire was administered by the *peshwas*, or chief ministers, who later went on to become hereditary rulers. At a time when the Mughals were struggling to hold their empire together, the Marathas trooped in from the south and gained a stranglehold on Delhi, primarily by supplying regiments to the Mughal army who soon went out of control and began to take possession of the land. Contemporary Mughal kings, who were both ineffective and cowardly, failed to curb their unruly behaviour. The resulting confusion was capitalised on by the Persian invader Nadir Shah, who sacked Delhi in 1739 and robbed the city of much of its wealth. When the Marathas were unable to put up any resistance on behalf of the Mughals, they joined the Persians in pillaging the capital. They soon sucked Delhi dry of all its treasures, and when there was nothing left to rob, the Marathas turned their eyes on Rajasthan. Raids and skirmishes with the Rajputs followed; cities were sacked, lives were lost, and the Marathas began to win large tracts of Rajput land in the state. The absence of a central Indian authority only contributed to the mayhem, so much so that India had to wait till the early 19th century for another invasion to bring the country under a single umbrella once again.

Captain James Tod's *Annals and Antiquities of Rajasthan* (published 1829-32) is a historical masterpiece, with the captain's fascinating observations on a region previously undocumented by Europeans.

THE BRITISH DROP ANCHOR

The British invaders came by the sea, following the Portuguese explorer Vasco da Gama, who had first discovered the sea route from Europe to

1707	1739	1756
Death of Aurangzeb, the last of the Mughal greats. His demise triggers the gradual collapse of the Mughal empire, as anarchy and rebellion break out across the country.	Nadir Shah plunders Delhi, and carries away with him the Peacock Throne as well as the Kohinoor, a magnificent diamond which changes many hands to eventually become property of the British royalty.	The rise of the notorious Jat dynasty of Bharatpur in Rajasthan. Under the leadership of Suraj Mahl and his son Jawahar Singh, the Jats soon join the Marathas and Persians in looting Delhi and Agra.

India around Africa in 1498. The British East India Company, a London trading firm that wanted a slice of the Indian spice trade (having seen how well the Portuguese were doing), landed in India in the early 1600s. Granted trading rights by Jehangir, the company set up its first trading outpost in Surat in Gujarat, and gradually went about extending its influence across the country, harbouring interests that went beyond mere trade. Extraordinarily enough, this commercial firm ended up nominally ruling India for 250 years.

Sooner or later, all leading European maritime nations came and pitched tent in India. Yet none managed to spread out across the country as efficiently as the British. The early English agents became well assimilated in India, learning Persian and intermarrying with local people, which gave them an edge over other European hopefuls. When the Mughal empire collapsed, they made a calculated political move, filling the power vacuum and taking over the reins of administration through a series of battles and alliances with local rulers. By the early 19th century, India was effectively under British control, and the British government in London had begun to take a more direct role in supervising affairs in India, while leaving the East India Company to deal with day-to-day administrative duties.

Outside British territory, the country was in a shambles. Bandits were on the prowl in the rural areas, and towns and cities had fallen into decay. The Marathas' 32 raids in Rajasthan continued, and though the British at first ignored the feuding parties, they soon spotted an opportunity for expansion and stepped into the fray. They negotiated treaties with the leaders of the main Rajput states, offering them protection from the Marathas in return for political and military support. The trick worked. Weakened by habitual wrangling and ongoing conflicts, the kings forfeited their independence in exchange for protection, and British residents were installed in the princely states. The British ultimately eliminated the Maratha threat, but, in the process, the Rajputs were effectively reduced to puppets. Delhi's prominence as a national capital dwindled too, as the British chose to rule the country from Calcutta (now Kolkata).

The later British authorities had an elitist notion of their own superiority that was to have a lasting impact on India. The colonisers felt that it was their duty to civilise the nation, unlike the first agents of the East India Company who had seen and recognised the value in India's native culture. During the first half of the 19th century, the British brought about radical social reforms. They introduced education in the English language, which replaced Persian as the language of politics and governance. New roads and canal systems were installed, followed by the foundation of schools and universities modelled on the British system of education. In the later stages, they brought in the postal system, the telegraph and the railways, introductions that remain vital to the Indian administrative system today.

William Dalrymple's *City of Djinns* is a wonderful book that draws upon his personal experiences in Delhi, and chronicles the fascinating history of the city in its many incarnations.

The Doctrine of Lapse, a policy formulated by Lord Dalhousie, enabled the East India Company to annex any princely state if its ruler was either found incompetent or died without a direct heir.

1757	1857	1885
Breaking out of its business mould, the East India Company registers its first military victory on Indian soil. Siraj-ud-Daulah, nawab of Bengal, is defeated by Robert Clive in the Battle of Plassey.	The short-lived First War of Independence breaks out across India. In the absence of a national leader, the rebels coerce the last Mughal king Bahadur Shah Zafar to proclaim himself emperor of India.	The Indian National Congress, India's first home-grown political organisation, is set up. It brings educated Indians together and plays a key role in India's freedom struggle.

The 2005 film *The Rising* retells the story of the 1857 rebellion through the life and death of its most celebrated hero, the soldier Mangal Pandey, played by Aamir Khan.

But at the same time, British bureaucracy came with controversial policies. Severe taxes were imposed on landowners and, as raw materials from India were used in British industry, cheap British-produced goods began to flood Indian markets and destroy local livelihoods. Mass anger in the country began to rise, and found expression in the First War of Independence in 1857. Soldiers and peasants took over Delhi for four months and besieged the British Residency in Lucknow for five months before they were finally suppressed by the East India Company's forces. Rajasthan also saw uprisings among the poor and middle classes, but there was little effect in the royal circles as Rajput kings continued to support the British, and were rewarded for their loyalty after the British government assumed direct control of the country the following year.

INDEPENDENCE, PARTITION & AFTER

Following a lengthy freedom movement, India finally freed itself of British domination in 1947. The road to Independence was an extraordinary one, influenced by Mohandas Karamchand Gandhi, later known as the Mahatma (Great Soul), who galvanised the peasants and villagers into a nonviolent resistance that was to spearhead the nationalist movement. A lawyer by qualification, he caused chaos by urging people to refuse to pay taxes and boycott British institutions and products. He campaigned for the Dalits (the lower classes of Hindu society, who he called Harijans or the 'Children of God'), and the rural poor, capturing public imagination through his approach, example and rhetoric. The freedom struggle gained such momentum under him that the British Labour Party, which came to power in 1945, saw Indian independence as inevitable. The process of the handover of power was initiated, but Hindu-Muslim differences took their toll at this crucial moment, and saw the country being divided on religious lines, with Pakistan being formed to appease the Muslim League which sought to distance itself from a Hindu-dominated country.

Mahatma Gandhi argued that the leader of the Muslim League, Mohammed Ali Jinnah, should lead a united India if that would prevent the partition of the country.

Prior to the change of guard, the British had shifted their capital out of Calcutta (now Kolkata) and built the imperial city of New Delhi through the early 1900s, work on which was overseen by architect Edwin Lutyens. Meant to be an expression of British permanence, the city was speckled with grand structures such as the Rashtrapati Bhavan (p104), the Central Vista and hundreds of residential buildings that came to be known as Lutyens Bungalows. After Independence, many of these Colonial buildings were used to house the brand-new Indian government, as Delhi was reinstated to its former status as the administrative and political capital of the country.

The 24-spoke wheel, an emblem designed by Ashoka, has been adopted as the central motif on the national flag of India, where it is rendered in blue against a white background.

Agra, sadly, did not get as much recognition as its counterpart. Being predominantly a satellite capital, where power occasionally spilt over from Delhi, the city had lost most of its political importance after the Mughals had departed. In the modern context, it made little sense to invest it with any kind of government machinery, so much so that it lost out to Lucknow when it came to selecting a state capital for Uttar Pradesh. Nonetheless, Agra

1911	1947	1948
Architect Edwin Lutyens begins work on New Delhi, the newest manifestation of Delhi, subsequently considered in architectural circles as one of the finest garden cities ever to have been built.	India gains independence on 15 August. Pakistan is formed a day earlier. Partition is followed by cross-border exodus, as thousands of Hindus and Muslims brave communal riots to migrate to their respective nations.	Mahatma Gandhi is assassinated during a public walk in New Delhi by Nathuram Godse on 30 January. Godse and his co-conspirator Narayan Apte are later tried, convicted and executed.

continues to be high up on the tourism map of India, as travellers throng the city to visit its many historic sites and monuments.

The long history of insurgency and unrest in India did not end with Independence. In 1962, India had a brief war with China over disputed border territories, and went on to engage in three battles with Pakistan over similar issues. Political assassinations didn't recede into history either. Mahatma Gandhi was slain soon after Independence by a Hindu extremist who hated his inclusive philosophy. Indira Gandhi, India's first woman prime minister, was gunned down by her Sikh bodyguards in retaliation to her ordering the storming of the Golden Temple, the holiest of Sikh shrines, in 1984. Her son, Rajiv, who succeeded her to the post of prime minister was also assassinated by Tamil terrorists protesting India's stance on Sri Lankan policies. Rajiv's Italian-born widow, Sonia, was the next of the Gandhis to take up the dynastic mantle of power. In 2004, she was chosen as president of the Congress Party, which has fed on the reputation and charisma of the Gandhis since its formative years and is currently a principal political alliance in one of the world's largest democracies.

RAJASTHAN IS BORN

Ever since they swore allegiance to the British, the Rajput kingdoms subjugated themselves to absolute British rule. Being reduced to redundancy, they also chose to trade in their real power for pomp and extravagance. Consumption took over from chivalry and, by the early 20th century, many of the kings were spending their time travelling the world with scores of retainers, playing polo and occupying entire floors of expensive Western hotels. Many maintained huge fleets of expensive cars, a fine collection of which can be seen in the automobile museum in Udaipur (p240). While it suited the British to indulge them, the maharajas' profligacy was economically and socially detrimental to their subjects, with the exception of a few capable rulers such as Ganga Singh of Bikaner. Remnants of the Raj (the British government in India before 1947) can be spotted all over the region today, from the Mayo College in Ajmer to the colonial villas in Mt Abu, and black-and-white photographs, documenting chummy Anglo-Rajput hunting expeditions, which deck the walls of any self-respecting heritage hotel in the state.

After Independence, from a security point of view, it became crucial for the new Indian union to ensure that the princely states of Rajasthan were integrated into the new nation. Most of these states were located near the vulnerable India–Pakistan border, and it made sense for the government to push for a merger that would minimise possibilities of rebellion in the region. Thus, when the boundaries of the new nation were being chalked out, the ruling Congress Party made a deal with the nominally independent Rajput states to cede power to the republic. To sweeten the deal, the rulers were offered lucrative monetary returns and government stipends, apart from being allowed to retain their titles and property holdings. Having fallen on hard times, the kings couldn't but agree

India got its first president from the Dalit community when KR Narayanan was sworn in to office in 1997. The current president, Pratibha Patil, is the first woman to hold the top post.

The Sariska and Ranthambhore tiger reserves, Rajasthan's best-known national parks, were originally used as private hunting grounds by the maharajas of Alwar and Ranthambore respectively.

1948–56	1952	1992
Rajasthan takes shape, as the princely states form a beeline to sign the Instrument of Accession, giving up their territories which are incorporated into the newly formed Republic of India.	The first elections are held in Rajasthan, and the state gets its first taste of democracy after centuries of monarchical rule. The Congress is the first party to be elected into office.	Hindu-Muslim rivalry rears its ugly head once again as the Babri Masjid, presumably built by Babur on a Hindu shrine in Ayodhya, is demolished by Hindu activists.

with the government, and their inclination to yield to the Indian dominion gradually brought about the formation of the state of Rajasthan.

To begin with, the state comprised only the southern and southeastern states of Rajasthan. Mewar was one of the first kingdoms to join the union. Udaipur was initially the state capital, with the maharaja of Udaipur becoming *rajpramukh* (head of state). The Instrument of Accession was signed in 1949, and Jaipur, Bikaner, Jodhpur and Jaisalmer were then merged, with Jaipur as the state's new capital. Later that year, the United State of Matsya was incorporated into Rajasthan. The state finally burgeoned to its current dimensions in November 1956, with the additions of Ajmer-Merwara, Abu Rd and a tract of Dilwara, originally part of the princely state of Sirohi that had been divided between Gujarat and Rajasthan. Rajasthan is now India's largest state.

The fate of the royal families of Rajasthan since Independence has been mixed. A handful of the region's maharajas have continued their wasteful ways, squandering away their fortunes and reducing themselves to abject poverty. A few zealous ones, who hated to see their positions of power go, have switched to politics and become members of leading political parties in India. Some have skipped politics to climb the rungs of power in other well-known national institutions, such as sports administration bodies or charitable and nonprofit organisations in the country. Only a few have chosen to lead civilian lives, earning a name for themselves as fashion designers, cricketers or entertainers.

The majority of kings, however, have refused to let bygones be bygones, and have cashed in on their heritage by opening ticketed museums for tourists and converting their palaces to lavish hotels. With passing time, the luxury hospitality business has begun to find more and more takers from around the world. The boom in this industry can be traced back to 1971, when Indira Gandhi, then India's Prime Minister, abolished the privileges granted to the Rajasthan princes at the time of accession. Coming as a massive shock to those at the top of the pile, the snipping of the cash cord forced many kings to inadvertently join the long list of heritage hotel owners.

In spite of the abolition, many kings choose to continue using their royal titles for social purposes till this day. While these titles mean little more than status symbols in the modern context, they still help in garnering enormous respect from the common public. On the other hand, nothing these days quite evokes the essence of Rajput grandeur as much as a stay in palatial splendour surrounded by vestiges of the regal age, in places such as the Rambagh Palace (p158) in Jaipur and the Umaid Bhawan Palace (p306) in Jodhpur. Not all the royal palaces of Rajasthan are on the tourist circuit, though. Many of them continue to serve as residences for erstwhile royal families, and some of the mansions that were left out of the tourism pie are crumbling away, ignored and neglected, their decaying interiors empty and full of bats.

Discover the bygone days of Rajasthan's royalty in *A Princess Remembers*, the memoirs of Gayatri Devi, maharani of Jaipur. Cowritten by Santha Rama Rau, it's an enthralling read.

1998	2004	2007
India declares itself a nuclear power after conducting underground tests near the town of Pokaran in Rajasthan. Pakistan follows suit, and the twin tests subject the subcontinental neighbours to global condemnation.	A deadly tsunami strikes the eastern shores of India on 26 December, killing more than 15,000 people.	India and the US release the draft of the 123 Agreemeent for mutual exchange of nuclear power and logistics. The draft is widely criticised by Indian opposition parties.

The Culture Anirban Mahapatra

RAJASTHANI IDENTITY

It's not the turbaned maharajas, or the self-obsessed white-collars, or even the stereotypical beggars, for that matter. The first people you run into upon your arrival in Rajasthan or Delhi are a jostling bunch of overly attentive locals, who ambush you the moment you step out of the airport or the railway station to drown you in a sea of unsolicited offers. Great hotels, taxi rides at half price, above-the-rate currency exchange…the list drags on, interspersed with beaming smiles you would only expect from long-lost friends. Famed Indian hospitality at work? This is no reception party; the men are touts out on their daily rounds, trying to wheedle a few bucks off unsuspecting travellers, and most of them can lie through their teeth. There's no way you can escape them, though a polite but firm 'no thank you' often stands you in good stead under such circumstances. It's a welcome each and every newcomer is accorded in India.

It's hard not to get put off by the surprise mobbing. But brush it off anyway, and don't let the incident make you jump to the hasty conclusion that every local, given half a chance, is out to hound the daylights out of you. Walk out of the terminal and into the real India, and things suddenly come across as strikingly different. With little stake in your activities, the people you now meet are genuinely warm (even if overtly curious), hospitable and sometimes helpful beyond what you'd call mere courtesy. For example, someone might volunteer to show you around a monument expecting absolutely nothing in return. And while it's advisable to always keep your wits about you (see the boxed text, p44), going with the flow often helps you understand the north-Indian psyche better, apart from making your trip to the region all the more memorable.

Broadly speaking, people in North India are easy to get along with. Punjabi-dominated Delhi has an inherent back-slapping culture where friendship is quickly forged over a stiff whisky. Rajasthan, on the other hand, is surprisingly cosmopolitan. Most rickshaw pullers in Jaipur or Udaipur have picked up a European language or three to attract more tourist dollars. And in spite of adhering to a rigid social code among themselves, Rajasthanis are willing to make concessions for tourists in more ways than one. Remember, it's the dollars brought in by travellers that makes much of the region's economy tick, and there's no way the locals are going to upset the apple cart.

The spin-off, however, is that Rajasthanis often tend to overdo things to play up their fabled identity built on chivalry and fortitude, if only to preserve an image that the world is willing to pay to see. From growing ornamental moustaches to weaving tall tales about their glorious ancestry, the people here leave no stone unturned in showcasing their regal past. But then, maybe it's just as well, for what would Rajasthan be without its history anyway?

DAILY LIFE
Contemporary Culture

Urbanity and exposure to the outside world notwithstanding, North Indian society remains conservative at heart. Cities such as Delhi and Jaipur may have acquired a liberal sheen on the outside, thanks to globalisation, but within the walls of a typical home, little has changed through time. The man of the house still calls the shots; conversations relating to sex don't make it to the dinner table; and moving in with a partner is considered immoral, if not a sign of blatant promiscuity. Western influences are apparent in the

The common gesture used to greet strangers in India is that of joining palms at chest-level in a *namaste*. Women generally don't shake hands, unlike some men.

Moustachioed personnel in some troops of the Indian Army, such as the Rajput regiment, are paid a monthly allowance of Rs 100 to maintain their whiskers.

The number of mobile phone connections in India is currently upward of 75 million, and is expected to grow to about 600 million by 2012.

public domain. Satellite TV rules the airwaves, mobile phones are nothing short of a necessity, and coffee shops are jam-packed on the weekends. But ask a young man in front of his parents what his girlfriend does, and you needn't look beyond several pairs of flushed cheeks to realise you've made a faux pas. Urban India prefers to wallow in a state of conscious denial. Some things are best left unsaid.

In the region's backyard, the scene is rather stark. Rural Rajasthan remains one of the poorest areas in the country. Being in close proximity to the Thar Desert, the climate here is harsh, and people dwelling in the region's villages are locked in a day-to-day battle for survival, as they have been for ages. Unemployment is rife, and has resulted in mass frustration, which in turn has led to problems such as debt, drug abuse (with synthetic drugs rapidly replacing age-old indulgences like opium and marijuana), alcoholism and prostitution. Indigenous tribes have been the worst affected, and it isn't uncommon to see members from their communities begging or performing tricks at Delhi's traffic signals in return for loose change.

Rajasthan also lags behind on the education front, its literacy rate being about 4% behind the national average of 65.4%. In 2001, the government implemented a nationwide 'education-for-all' programme, which aims to impart elementary education to all Indian children by 2010. The project focuses on the education of girls, who have historically been deprived of quality schooling. Rajasthan is expected to benefit immensely from the programme, and the authorities are optimistic that the forthcoming 2011 census will throw up positive results and set the record straight.

Status of Women

Traditionally objectified to the extent of being seen as child-bearing machines, women in rural Rajasthan are yet to rub shoulders with their menfolk in many ways. Being socially disadvantaged, their freedom has been seriously clipped, and, as keepers of a family's honour, they have been forbidden from mingling freely with strangers. Try approaching a village belle on the street, and you'll see her beat a quick retreat into the privacy of her home, her face hidden behind her sari. A Rajasthani woman's beauty, after all, is only for her family to appreciate.

Screened from the outside world, most women in rural Rajasthan are sentenced to a lifetime of strenuous household chores. If they are allowed to work at all, they are paid less than their male counterparts. Besides all this, the radically patriarchal society still doesn't recognise them as inheritors of family property, which almost always goes to male heirs. The birth of a girl child is often seen as unlucky, since it not only means an extra mouth to feed but a generous dowry that needs to be given away at the time of her marriage. Embryonic sex determination, despite being illegal, is practised on the sly, and local newspapers occasionally blow the lid off surgical rackets where conniving surgeons charge huge amounts of money to carry out female-foeticide operations.

Progress has been made, however, in the form of development programmes run by the central and state governments, as well as nongovernmental organisations (NGOs) and voluntary outfits that have swung into action. Organisations such as the Barefoot College, Urmul Trust and Seva Mandir all run grass-roots programmes in Rajasthan, devoted to awareness, education, health issues and female empowerment, and volunteering opportunities are never lacking (see p369).

In the cities, the scene is much better. Urban women in Delhi and Jaipur have worked their way to social and professional recognition, and feminists are no longer dismissed as fringe lunatics. Even so, some of India's first-

Opium was traditionally served to guests at social functions by several indigenous communities of Rajasthan. Though the sale of opium is now illegal, it continues behind law-enforcers' backs.

Mala Sen's *Death by Fire: Sati, Dowry Death & Female Infanticide in Modern India* is a disturbing and impassioned account, written from the perspective of three different women.

DOS & DON'TS

India has retained many time-honoured traditions and reservations regarding public behaviour. While you won't be expected to get everything right, common sense and courtesy will take you a long way. If in doubt about how you should behave, watch what the locals do, or simply ask.

Dressing conservatively (for both women and men) wins a warmer response from locals. Short skirts and spaghetti straps invite unwanted attention, especially in crowded places. Kissing and cuddling in public aren't condoned by society, so open displays of affection are best avoided.

Religious Etiquette

Visits to sacred sites require you to dress and behave respectfully – no shorts or sleeveless tops (this rule applies to both men and women). Head cover (not baseball caps!) is necessary at some places of worship. Jain temples request the removal of leather items and may ask women not to enter if menstruating. In some places, men may have to sit apart from women. Loud and intrusive behaviour isn't appreciated, nor is smoking. There are some sites that don't admit women and some that deny entry to nonadherents of their faith.

Before entering a holy place, remove your shoes and check if photography is allowed. Religious etiquette advises against touching locals on the head, or directing the soles of your feet at a person, religious shrine or deity. It's also offensive to touch someone with your feet or to touch a carving of a deity.

Eating & Visiting Etiquette

If you're invited to someone's home, it's considered good manners to remove your shoes before entering the house and wash your hands before a meal. Wait to be served or until you are invited to help yourself; if you're unsure about protocol, wait for your host to direct you. Indians eat with their hands, and cutlery is found only in urban households. You can always ask for a fork, but if the family can't provide you with one, simply proceed with your right hand. The left hand is only used for unsavoury actions, such as toilet duties. While drinking water from a shared container, hold it slightly above your mouth, so as to avoid contact with your lips – no swigging.

Photography Etiquette

Always ask before taking photographs. Incidents of people posing for photos only to ask for money afterward are common, and some women find it offensive to be photographed. Taking photos of shrines, funeral proceedings, religious ceremonies or of people bathing publicly can be considered impolite, and requesting permission in advance helps clear up any confusion. Flash photography may be prohibited in certain shrines or heritage monuments.

---

generation female executives recall a time not very long ago when employers would go into a tizz every time a woman put in a request for maternity leave, as motherhood had been precluded as an occasion that merited time off from work.

Treatment of Gays & Lesbians

Homosexuality is not endorsed by Indian culture per se. The Indian Penal Code still defines sodomy as a punishable offence for being 'against the order of nature'. Lesbianism, in contrast, has been left unaddressed by the law of the land. But if that leads you to believe that homosexual relations are unheard of in Indian society, the fact remains that India has more than 70 million gay, lesbian, bisexual and transgender (GLBT) people. Unfortunately, the absence of legal cover, along with fears of being rejected by society, keeps most people confined to the closet.

On a brighter note, the intelligentsia in cities such as Delhi have of late begun to mobilise public opinion against obsolete legal sanctions, besides actively rallying for gay rights. In recent years, several books have been

The government-run website www .exploreruralindia. org has a great deal of information about travel options in the backyards of several states across the country, including Rajasthan.

written and films made on same-sex relations, with the objective of dispelling social reservations regarding alternative sexuality.

Apart from the GLBT community, India has a sizable but marginalised population of transvestites and eunuchs, who dress in women's clothing and are collectively called *hijras*. A handful of them are born hermaphrodite; the others are either gay or are kidnapped and castrated at a young age by other *hijras* so as to add to their dwindling community. Disliked for their queer ways and brash behaviour, *hijras* earn a living by working as uninvited entertainers at weddings and celebrations of the birth of children. When their luck runs out, they have no option but to resort to prostitution.

Manvendra Singh Gohil, a Gujarati prince, is the only person among Indian royalty to have come out as gay. Now an activist, he plans to open a hospice for HIV-positive people.

Attitude towards HIV/AIDS

After South Africa, India has the world's highest number of HIV-positive people, with 5.2 million reported cases as of 2006. But even as the virus spreads rampantly through unprotected sex, prostitution and intravenous drug use, a large number of Indians continue to shy away from tackling the problem head on. Despite a flurry of awareness programmes, myths regarding the ailment abound, and HIV-positive people are often made to bear the brunt of social ostracism. Condom usage hasn't picked up either; many in suburban and rural India are still iffy about purchasing prophylactics across the counter in full public view.

Marriage & Divorce

Indian marriages were always meant to unite families, not individuals. In rural Rajasthan, the case remains much the same today. Unlike in cities, where people now find love through online dating sites, weddings in villages and small towns are still arranged by parents. Those actually getting married (read perfect strangers) have little say in the proceedings, and cross-caste marriages are still a no-no. Few move out of their parents' homes after tying the knot; setting up an independent establishment post marriage is often considered an insult to the elderly.

According to Hindu astrologers, people born under the influence of the planet Mars supposedly make bad wedding matches. Called *mangliks*, they are believed to bring bad luck to their in-laws' families.

By and large, marriages in rural areas are initiated by professional matchmakers who strike a suitable match based on family status, caste and compatible horoscopes. Once a marriage is finalised, the bride's family arranges for a dowry to be paid to the groom's parents, as an appreciation of their graciously accepting the bride as a member of their family. Sometimes running into hundreds of thousands of rupees, dowries can range from hard cash to items such as TVs, motorcycles, household furniture, utensils and even toiletries. Despite the exact amount of dowry being finalised at the time of betrothal, there have been sporadic cases reported where the groom's family later insists that the girl's parents cough up more, failing which the bride might be subjected to abuse and domestic violence. Stories of newly married girls dying in kitchen 'accidents' are not uncommon either. In most cases, they leave the grooms free to remarry and claim another dowry.

Not giving two hoots about Indian law, which sets the marriageable age of men and women at 21 and 18 respectively, child marriages continue to be practised in rural Rajasthan. It is estimated that one in every two girls in the state's villages are married off before they turn 15. Divorce, on the other hand, remains forbidden, thereby complicating things in case marriages don't work out. Even if a divorce is obtained, it is difficult for a woman to find another husband; as a divorcée, she is considered less chaste than a spinster. Given the stigma associated with divorce, few people have the courage to walk out on each other, instead preferring to silently live through botched marriage.

Death

Hindus cremate their dead. Deaths are mourned by Rajasthanis for a period of 12 or 13 days, after which a feast known as *mosar, barwa, kariyawar* or *terwa* is held, which formally ends the mourning. As a symbolic gesture, the aggrieved family has to entertain a group of community leaders and Brahmins by treating them to an elaborate meal, regardless of their financial standing. If the deceased happens to be a family patriarch, the 12th day also features a turban-tying ceremony where a successor to the male head is recognised by the family and society.

In the past, male deaths in Rajasthan warranted that widows end their lives by immolating themselves on their husband's funeral pyres. Known as *sati*, the act was traditionally seen as an event that relieved women of the ignominies of widowhood, and was widely practised in Rajasthan until the princely state of Jaipur outlawed it in 1846. Mewar initially resisted the ban, compelling Queen Victoria to issue a proclamation forbidding *sati* in 1861. After Independence, Indian legislation stuck with the proclamation, though intermittent cases of *sati* were still reported in the state, the last case coming to light as late as 1987.

Moral policing is a favourite pastime for some Indians, especially those associated with hardline politico-religious outfits. Violent demonstrations over trivial or absurd issues aren't uncommon either.

ECONOMY

Rajasthan trails the nation's per capita income figures by many notches. Agriculture has traditionally been the region's mainstay, and almost 70% of rural households are engaged in working the fields. Yet, the occupation is far from profitable, and has lately become even less viable, as periodic droughts followed by freak flash floods have repeatedly wreaked havoc on the regional harvest. Big-city dreams have started taking their toll too. Thousands of Rajasthani youths now leave home and hearth behind to migrate to urban centres, only to land menial jobs ranging from daily wage labourers to waiters at roadside eateries, with monthly salaries ranging from a meagre Rs 2000 to Rs 5000 (US$50 to US$120).

The recent surge in the tourism industry, however, has provided many locals with alternative career options. A large number of young Rajasthanis now earn a living from the circuit by working in guest houses, manning counters at souvenir shops or sprucing up their knowledge of history to become tourist guides.

On the other end of the economic rainbow are the well-heeled tech geeks and corporate honchos of Delhi, who bring money into the capital by tapping out strings of high-end computer codes or riding the real-estate boom. The business process outsourcing (BPO) industry has emerged as a lucrative industry in the past five years or so. Scores of outsourcing firms (commonly referred to as call centres) now dot the skylines of Delhi's suburbs, providing employment to hordes of urban graduates, who take home anything from Rs 15,000 to Rs 75,000 (US$350 to US$1765) per month for their services. Easy money has predictably bumped up living standards, bringing previously unaffordable luxuries within arm's reach of urban India's generation next.

POPULATION

Rajasthan's population has nearly doubled since 1951. There are several issues that have contributed to the phenomenon, such as improved infrastructure and better medical facilities, which have led to a considerable drop in the mortality rate. Ironically, the local mindset has still not registered these new-age boons, which is why procreation still follows the norm of having 'an heir and a spare', just in case one offspring falls

---

TRAVELLING TIPS

Navigation

Asking for directions in India can be a harrowing affair. Few locals are good at giving directions, and some would rather lead you the wrong way than admit their ignorance. It's worth noting that the commonly used sideways wobble of the head doesn't necessarily mean 'no'. It can translate to: 'yes', 'maybe' or 'I have no idea'. So never pose questions in a leading manner, like pointing and saying 'Is this the way to the museum?' since you're almost certain to get 'yes' for an answer. 'Which way to the museum?' is better. Even if you're given directions, crosscheck with other people along the way.

Tipping

If done with discretion, tipping can work wonders in India. There's no rule of thumb regarding how much you should tip, but, if you want an idea, here goes. Roadside eateries expect no more than Rs 20; errand boys are happy with Rs 10. In budget or midrange hotels, tip the room service guys about Rs 20 to Rs 50 when you check in; this ensures they don't ignore you through your stay. Then pass off another Rs 50 while checking out. Indians don't tip for public services such as rickshaw rides, haircuts or porterage. Delhi's cabbies would expect you to round off the fare, though.

Diplomacy

Indians are naturally curious, especially about foreigners. People are likely to strike up a conversation on a train journey, and some questions can be rather nosy – marital status, income, food habits – so expect anything. While it's advisable not to snub them, you can always laugh off awkward questions. In cases where they persist, be a sport – answer politely, then ask them back. It's an effective way to check the volley of queries.

Following the Crowd

If the bus you're on breaks down in the middle of nowhere, don't fret. Keep your wits about you, and go with the public. The locals know best how to tackle an emergency. And being in the company of people means you're never left to handle a crisis all by yourself.

Bombay Calling, a 2006 documentary produced by National Geographic, provided an in-depth look into India's BPO industry by profiling the work environment and employees of a call centre in Mumbai.

prey to untimely death. The reluctance to practise contraception is yet another reason behind the sharp rise in the head count; government-sponsored family-planning programmes are valiantly fighting a losing battle on this front.

Demographically speaking, most of the region's population still lives in its villages. The desert areas are scantly inhabited; western Rajasthan has the lowest population density in the region. The metropolises, alternatively, have attracted people from all walks of life to come and reside within their city limits, and thus boast a high-density, multiethnic population. Religious ghettos can be found in places such as Ajmer and Jaipur, where a fair number of Christian families currently live; the Ganganagar district, which is home to a large number of Sikhs; and parts of Alwar and Bharatpur, where the populace is chiefly Muslim. Though most Muslims in Rajasthan belong to the Sunni sect, the state also has a small but affluent community of Shi'ias, called the Bohras, living to the southeast.

Tribes & Indigenous Communities

Rajasthan has a large indigenous population, comprising communities that are native to the region and have lived there for centuries. Called Adivasis (ancient dwellers), most of these ethnic groups have been listed as Scheduled Tribes by the government. The majority of the Adivasis are pagan, though some have either taken to Hindu ways or converted to Christianity over time.

BHILS

The largest of Rajasthan's tribes, the Bhils live to the southeast, spilling over into Madhya Pradesh. They speak their own distinct native language and have a natural talent for archery and warfare. Witchcraft, magic and superstition are deeply rooted in their culture. Polygamy is still practised by those who can afford it, and love marriages are the norm.

Originally a hunter-gatherer community, the Bhils have survived years of exploitation by higher castes to finally take up small-scale agriculture. Some have left their villages to head for the cities. Literacy is still below average and not too many Bhil families have many assets to speak of, but these trends are slowly being reversed. The Baneshwar Fair (see boxed text, p224) is a huge Bhil festival, where you can sample the essence of their culture first hand.

For comprehensive information on India's native and tribal communities, check out the website www.tribal.nic.in, maintained by the Ministry of Tribal Affairs under the Government of India.

MINAS

The Minas are the second-largest tribal group in Rajasthan and live around Shekhawati and eastern Rajasthan. The name Mina comes from *meen* (fish), and the tribe claims it evolved from the fish incarnation of Vishnu. Minas once ruled supreme in the Amber region, but their miseries began once they were routed by the Rajputs. To make matters worse, they were outlawed during the British Raj, after their guerrilla tactics earned them the 'criminal-tribe' label. Following Independence, the criminal status was lifted, and the Minas subsequently took to agriculture.

Festivities, music and dance form a vital part of Mina culture, and they excel in performances such as swordplay and acrobatics. Minas view marriage as a noble institution, and their weddings are accompanied by enthusiastic celebrations. They are also known to be friendly with other tribes, and don't mind sharing space with other communities.

BISHNOIS

The Bishnois are the most progressive of Rajasthan's indigenous communities, and even have their presence on the internet (www.bishnoi .org). However, they can't be strictly classified as a tribe. The Bishnois owe their origin to a visionary named Jambho Ji, who in 1485 shunned the Hindu social order to form a casteless faith that took inspiration from nature. Credited as the oldest environmentalist community in India, the Bishnois are animal-lovers and take an active interest in preserving forests and wildlife. Felling of trees and hunting within Bishnoi territory is strictly prohibited.

RELIGION

Hindus comprise nearly 90% of Rajasthan's population. Much of the remaining 10% are Muslims, followed by decreasing numbers of Sikhs, Jains, Christians and Buddhists respectively. In spite of this religious diversity, tolerance levels are high, and incidents of communal violence are rare, at least in comparison to the volatile nature of things in the neighbouring state of Gujarat. Most people here mind their own business, without nosing around in others' affairs.

Look up the BBC website www.bbc.co.uk/religion /religions for a concise rundown of the world's major religions. The site also lists some interesting links you can access for further details.

Hinduism & the Caste System

Hinduism is among the world's oldest religious traditions, with its roots going back at least 3000 years. Theoretically, Hinduism is not a religion; it is a way of life, an elaborate convention that has evolved through the centuries, in contrast to many other religions which can trace their origins to a single founder. Despite being founded on a solid religious base, Hinduism doesn't

HINDU GODS & GODDESSES

According to Hindu scriptures, there are around 330 million deities in the Hindu pantheon. All of them are regarded as a manifestation of Brahman (the supreme spirit), which otherwise has three main representations, known as the Trimurti – the trio of Brahma, Vishnu and Shiva.

Brahma

The only active role that Brahma ever played was during the creation of the universe. Since then, he has been immersed in eternal meditation and is therefore regarded as aloof. His vehicle is a swan and he is sometimes shown sitting on a lotus (see also boxed text, p210).

Vishnu & Krishna

Being the preserver and sustainer of the universe, Vishnu is associated with 'right action'. He is usually depicted with four arms, each holding a lotus, a conch shell, a discus and a mace respectively. His consort is Lakshmi, the goddess of wealth, and his vehicle is Garuda, a creature that's half bird, half beast. Vishnu has 10 incarnations, including Rama, Krishna and Buddha. He is also referred to as Narayan.

Krishna, the hugely popular incarnation of Vishnu, was sent to earth to fight for good and combat evil, and his exploits are documented in the Mahabharata. A shrewd politician, his flirtatious alliances with *gopis* (milkmaids) and his love for Radha, his paramour, have inspired countless paintings and songs.

Shiva & Parvati

Although he plays the role of the destroyer, Shiva's creative role is symbolised by his representation as the frequently worshipped lingam (phallus). A hippie of sorts, he lives in the Himalayas, smokes marijuana, smears his body with ash, and has a third eye on his forehead that symbolises wisdom. With snakes draped around his neck, he is sometimes shown holding a trident while riding Nandi the bull. With 1008 names, Shiva takes many forms, including Pashupati, champion of the animals, and Nataraja, performer of the *tandava* (cosmic dance of fury). He is also the lord of yoga.

Shiva's consort is the beautiful goddess Parvati, who in her dark side appears as Kali, the fiercest of the gods who demands sacrifices and wears a garland of skulls. Alternatively, she appears as the fair Durga, the demon slayer, who wields supreme power, holds weapons in her 10 hands and rides a tiger or a lion.

Ganesh

The jolly, pot-bellied, elephant-headed Ganesh is held in great affection by Indians. He is the god of good fortune, prosperity and the patron of scribes, being credited with writing sections of the Mahabharata. Ganesh is good at removing obstacles, and he's frequently spotted above doorways and entrances of Indian homes.

Hanuman

Hanuman is the hero of the Ramayana and is Rajasthan's most popular god. He is the loyal ally of lord Rama, and the images of Rama and his wife Sita are emblazoned upon his heart. He is king of the monkeys, and thus assures them refuge in temple complexes across the country.

have a specific theology, or even a central religious institution. It also has no provision for conversion; one is always born a Hindu.

Being an extremely diverse religion, Hinduism can't be summed up by a universal definition. Yet, there are a few principal tenets that most Hindu sects tend to go by. Hindus believe that all life originates from a supreme spirit called Brahman, a formless, timeless phenomenon manifested by Brahma, the Hindu lord of creation. Upon being born, all living beings are required to engage in dharma (worldly duties) and samsara

RAJASTHAN'S FOLK GODS & GODDESSES

Folk deities and deified local heroes abound in Rajasthan. Apart from public gods, families are often known to pay homage to a *kuladevi* (family idol).

Pabuji is one of many local heroes to have attained divine status. His is a particularly violent and chivalrous tale: Pabuji entered a transaction with a woman called Devalde, in which, in return for a mare, he vowed to protect her cows from all harm. The time to fulfil this obligation came, inconveniently, during Pabuji's own marriage. However, Pabuji immediately went to the aid of the threatened livestock. During the ensuing battle, he, along with all the male members of his family, perished at the hands of a villain called Jind Raj Khinchi. To preserve the family line, Pabuji's sister-in-law cut open her own belly and produced Pabuji's nephew, Nandio, before committing *sati* (a widow's act of self-immolation on her husband's funeral pyre).

A community of professional storytellers called Bhopas have traditionally paid homage to the hero by performing *Pabuji-ka-phad*, in which they recite poetry in praise of Pabuji while unfurling *phad* (cloth-scroll) paintings that chronicle the life of the hero. You can attend these performances at places such as Chokhi Dhani (see p172) or Jaisalmer, if they happen at a time when you're around.

Gogaji was a warrior who lived in the 11th century and could cure snakebite; today, victims are brought to his shrines by both Hindu and Muslim devotees. Also believed to cure snakebite is Tejaji who, according to tradition, was blessed by a snake which decreed that anyone honouring Tejaji by wearing a thread in his name would be cured of snakebite.

Goddesses revered by Rajasthanis include incarnations of Devi (the Mother Goddess), such as the fierce Chamunda Mata, an incarnation of Durga; Sheetala Mata, the goddess of smallpox who is invoked by parents who want their children to be spared from the affliction; and Karni Mata, worshipped at Deshnok (see the Temple of Rats, p348) near Bikaner. Women who have committed *sati* on their husband's funeral pyres are also frequently worshipped as goddesses, such as Rani Sati, who has an elaborate temple in her honour in Jhunjhunu (p286), in Shekhawati. Barren women pay homage to the god Bhairon, an incarnation of Shiva, at his shrines, which are usually found under khejri trees. In order to be blessed with a child, the woman is required to leave a garment hanging from the branches of the tree. The deified folk hero Ramdev also has an important temple at Ramdevra (p319), near Pokaran in western Rajasthan.

(the endless cycle of birth, death and rebirth). It is said that the road to salvation lies through righteous karma (actions which evoke subsequent reactions), which leads to moksha (emancipation), when the soul eventually returns to unite with the supreme spirit.

If that's not complex enough, things are convoluted further by the caste system, which broadly divides Hindus into four distinct classes based on their mythical origins and their occupations. On top of the caste hierarchy are the Brahmins, priests who supposedly originated from Brahma's mouth. Next come the Kshatriyas, the warriors who evolved from the deity's arms – this is the caste that the Rajputs fit into. Vaishyas, tradespeople born from the thighs, are third in the pecking order, below which stand the Shudras. Alternatively called Dalits or Scheduled Castes, the Shudras comprise menial workers such as peasants, janitors or cobblers and are known to stem from Brahma's feet. Caste, by the way, is not changeable.

Islam

Islam was founded in Arabia by the Prophet Mohammed in the 7th century AD. The Arabic term 'Islam' means 'surrender', and believers undertake to surrender to the will of Allah (God), which is revealed in the Quran, the holy book of Islam. A devout Muslim is required to pray five times a day, keep daylong fasts through the month of Ramadan, and make a pilgrimage to the holy city of Mecca in Saudi Arabia, if possible.

In Hinduism, the syllable 'Om' is believed to be a primordial sound from which the entire universe takes shape. It is also a sacred symbol, represented by an icon shaped like the number three.

Darshan and *puja* are fundamental concepts of Hindu worship, which require people to visit a temple and make a ritual offering of flowers and fruits in return for divine blessings.

HINDU SACRED TEXTS & EPICS

Hindu sacred texts fall under two categories: those believed to be the word of God (*shruti*, meaning 'hearing') and those produced by people (*smriti*, meaning 'memory').

The Vedas

Introduced in the subcontinent by the Aryans, the *Vedas* are regarded as *shruti* knowledge and are considered to be the authoritative basis for Hinduism. The oldest works of Sanskrit literature, the Vedas contain mantras that are recited at prayers and religious ceremonies. The Vedas are divided into four Samhitas (compilations); the Rig-Veda, the oldest of the Samhitas, is believed to be written more than 3000 years ago. Other Vedic works include the *Brahmanas*, touching on rituals; the Aranyakas whose name means the 'wilderness texts', meant for ascetics who have renounced the material world; and the Upanishads, which discuss meditation, philosophy, mysticism and the fate of the soul.

Puranas, Sutras & Shastras

The Puranas comprise a post-Vedic genre that chronicles the history of the universe, royal lineages, philosophy and cosmology. The Sutras, on the other hand, are essentially manuals, and contain useful information on different human activities. Some well known Sutras are Griha Sutra, dealing with the nuances of domestic life; Nyaya Sutra, detailing the faculty of justice and debate; and Kamasutra, a compendium of love and sexual behaviour. The Shastras are also instructive in nature, but are more technical as they provide information pertaining to specific areas of practice. Vaastu Shastra, for example, is an architect's handbook that elaborates on the art of civic planning, while Artha Shastra focuses heavily on governance, economics and military policies of the state.

The Mahabharata

This 2500-year-old rip-roaring epic centres on the conflict between two fraternal dynasties, the Pandavas and the Kauravas, overseen by Krishna. Locked in a struggle to inherit the throne of Hastinapura, the Kauravas win the first round of the feud, beating the Pandavas in a game of dice and banishing them from the kingdom. The Pandavas, however, return after 13 years and challenge the Kauravas to an epic battle, from which they emerge victorious.

Being the longest epic in the world, unabridged versions of the Mahabharata incorporate the Bhagavad Gita, the holy book of the Hindus, which contains the worldly advice given by Krishna to Pandava prince Arjuna before the start of the battle.

The Ramayana

Composed around the 2nd or 3rd century BC, the Ramayana tells of Rama, an incarnation of Vishnu, who assumed human form to facilitate the triumph of good over evil. Much like the Mahabharata, the Ramayana revolves around a great war, waged by Rama, his brother Lakshmana and an army of apes led by Hanuman against Ravana, the demon king who had kidnapped Rama's wife Sita and had held her hostage in his kingdom of Lanka (Sri Lanka). After slaying Ravana, Rama returned to his kingdom of Ayodhya, his homecoming forming the basis for the important Hindu festival of Dussehra (see boxed text, p224).

Islam is monotheistic. God is held as unique, unlimited, self-sufficient and the supreme creator of all things. God never speaks to humans directly; his word is instead conveyed through messengers called prophets, who are never themselves divine. The religion has two prominent sects, the minority Shi'ias (originating from Mohammed's descendants) and the majority Sunnis, who split soon after the death of Mohammed owing to political differences, and have since gone on to establish their own interpretations and rituals. The most important pilgrimage site for Muslims in Rajasthan is the extraordinary dargah (burial place) of the saint Khwaja Muin-ud-din Chishti (p201) at Ajmer.

Sikhism

Now among the world's largest religions, Sikhism was founded on the sermons of 10 Sikh gurus, beginning with Guru Nanak Dev (1469–1539). The core values and ideology of Sikhism are embodied in the Guru Granth Sahib, the holy book of the Sikhs which is also considered the eternal guru of Sikhism. The Sikhs evolved as an organised community over time, and devoted themselves to the creation of a standing militia called the *khalsa*, which carried out religious, political and martial duties and protected the Sikhs from foreign threats. The religion, on its part, grew around the central concept of Vaheguru, the universal lord, an eventual union with whom is believed to result in salvation. The Sikhs believe that salvation is achieved through rigorous discipline and meditation, which help them overcome the five evils – ego, greed, attachment, anger and lust.

> Among all the deities in the Hindu pantheon, the gods Vishnu and Shiva have the largest number of devotees. Their followers are called Vashnavites and Shaivites respectively.

Jainism

The Jain religion was founded around 500 BC by Mahavira, the 24th and last of the Jain *tirthankars* (path finders). Jainism originally evolved as a reformist movement against the dominance of priests in Hindu society. It steered clear of complicated rituals, rejected the caste system, and believed in reincarnation and eventual moksha by following the example of the *tirthankars.*

Jains are strict vegetarians and revere all forms of life. The religion has two main sects. The Svetambaras (White Clad) wear unstitched white garments; the monks cover their mouths so as not to inhale insects and brush their path before they walk to avoid crushing small creatures. The monks belonging to the Digambaras (Sky Clad), in comparison, go naked. Jainism preaches nonviolence, and its followers are markedly successful in banking and business, which they consider nonviolent professions.

> Sufism is a mystic tradition derived from Islam, which originated in medieval times. Being largely secular, it has attracted followers from other religions and is widely practised in North India.

SPORT

Cricket is a national obsession in India. Nearly everybody claims to understand the game down to its finer points, and can comment on it with endless vigour. Shops down shutters and streets take on a deserted look every time India happens to be playing a test match or a crucial one-day game. The arrival of the Twenty20 format and new domestic leagues such as the Indian Premier League (IPL) has only taken the game's popularity a notch further.

While other mainstream sports pale in comparison to cricket, a few traditional pastimes continue to be patronised by niche spectators in Delhi and Rajasthan. In Old Delhi, people still take active interest in *kabutarbaazi* (pigeon flying). Despite lobbying by animal-rights activists, cock-fighting events are held now and then, and garner plenty of attention. The Nats, a roaming Rajasthani community, have long excelled in acrobatics, which they now perform as a means of revenue generation. The acts (tightrope walking, bamboo-pole balancing) can be seen at Chokhi Dhani (see p172) near Jaipur.

Interestingly, many people belonging to Rajasthan's elite classes retain a soft spot for polo, a game which was popularised in the state by the Rajput kings. Cities such as Jodhpur and Udaipur still foster a culture for the sport, and the royal houses maintain stables of thoroughbreds for use in the game.

ARTS

If the Rajputs knew how to fight, they also knew how to create art. Rajasthan's culture is a celebration of beauty, manifested through its architecture, music, dance, painting and poetry. The state also has a rich legacy of handicrafts

---

MUMAL & MAHENDRA

It was love at first sight for Mahendra of Umarkot. Every night he raced to the beautiful princess Mumal's chamber, borne by a swift camel named Chekal. As Mahendra had to travel at night to visit Mumal in the distant village of Lodhruva, near Jaisalmer, he had little energy left to perform his husbandly duties to the satisfaction of his eight wives. One day, the aggrieved wives – suspecting his nocturnal visits to the princess – beat up Chekal, leaving Mahendra at the mercy of a less-competent camel, which subsequently lost its way.

Meanwhile, Mumal's sister Sumal decided to pay her a visit. Sumal was in the habit of wearing men's clothes, and fell asleep next to Mumal. When Mahendra finally reached Mumal's apartment, he was confronted by the sight of her lying next to another man. He fled from the chamber, vowing never to lay eyes on her again, and bitterly cursing the inconstancy of women. Mumal waited every night for him, finally pining away with grief. When Mahendra heard of her death, and realised his misunderstanding, he was driven insane with grief.

---

which are prized the world over, both for their intricate craftsmanship and ornamental appeal (see Rajasthani Arts & Crafts, p53).

Literature

For a long time, Rajasthan's storytelling tradition was solely oral. Among the earliest known Rajasthani written works available today are paeans such as *Khuman Raso* (Songs of Khuman), the tale of a Sisodia king written by Dalapat Vijaya in the 9th century, and the epic *Prithviraj Raso* (Songs of Prithviraj), written by Prithviraj Chauhan's court poet Chand Bardai in the late 12th century.

The state-sponsored Sahitya Akademi in Delhi is devoted to the promotion of vernacular Indian literature. It grants annual awards of Rs 50,000 each in 22 language categories.

In subsequent years, Rajasthan produced several talented writers who wrote either in the Marwari dialect or Dingal – a literary form of Rajasthani which evolved in the 15th century. Common literary genres included folk tales, songs and ballads based on heroic accounts, religious legends and tragic love stories such as those of Dhola Maru (see boxed text, p292) and the princess Mumal (see boxed text, above). Apart from chronicling society, these works also helped purvey the image of the brave Rajput warrior, by glorifying traits such as heroism, chivalry, virtue and sacrifice.

Contemporary literature, in contrast, is heavily English-oriented, though many people still continue to write in vernacular languages. A few great titles which look into the social, psychological and historical aspects of the region include *Raj*, by Gita Mehta, a moving story of a young Rajput princess contracted in marriage to an arrogant prince; *Delhi: a Novel* by Khushwant Singh, a funny and irreverent take on Delhi's history through the experiences of several generations of inhabitants; and the novels *City of Djinns*, *The White Mughals* and *The Last Mughal* by William Dalrymple, the British author who calls Delhi his second home.

With Delhi-based writers Arundhati Roy, Rajkamal Jha and Pankaj Mishra bagging six-digit dollar advances for their novels in recent times, the city has lately become a literary capital, with scores of authors routinely churning out quality fiction and nonfiction. The trend has rubbed off on Jaipur, which is now home to an annual international literary festival, held there every year since 2006.

Cinema & Television

Television provides stock recreation for most Indian families. The opening up of the airwaves in the early 1990s brought satellite TV into the country, and the industry hasn't looked back since. Today, Indian viewers can choose from sports channels (ESPN, Star Sports), entertainment channels (MTV,

VH1, HBO), nature and travel networks (National Geographic, Discovery) and a host of newscasters, many of which compete with each other 24/7 by slapping the 'breaking-news' tag on trivial stories.

Out of home, it's cinema that rules. India has the world's biggest film industry. Films come in all languages, the majority pumped out by the Hindi tinsel town of Bollywood in Mumbai, and Mollywood, its Tamil counterpart, in Chennai. Most productions, however, are formulaic flicks that seize mass attention with hackneyed motifs – unrequited love, action that verges on caricature, slapstick humour, wet saris and plenty of sexual innuendo. Nonetheless, the past 10 years have seen upscale productions aimed at a burgeoning multiplex audience. Check out the cricket extravaganza *Lagaan*, the patriotic *Rang De Basanti*, or Shakespearean adaptations such as *Maqbool* (Macbeth) and *Omkara* (Othello). Some of these films have done the rounds at the Oscars, and shouldn't leave you disappointed.

Despite being far from popular, India also has a critically acclaimed, rock-steady art-house movement. Pioneered by the likes of Satyajit Ray, Adoor Gopalakrishnan, Ritwik Ghatak and Shyam Benegal, the tradition now boasts directors such as Mira Nair (*Salaam Bombay, Monsoon Wedding, The Namesake*) and Deepa Mehta (*Earth, Water, Fire*).

> Watching a Bollywood blockbuster in a neighbourhood cinema with the local audience is a terrific experience. Try Jaipur's Raj Mandir Cinema and Delite or Golcha in Old Delhi.

Music

Like elsewhere in India, Hindi pop songs and film soundtracks crackle joyfully out of speakers all over Rajasthan. But at the same time, folk music remains a vital, living part of traditional Rajasthani culture. Commonly, folk music comprises ballads that, like the region's literature, relate heroic deeds or love stories, and religious or devotional songs known as *bhajans* and *banis*. Various communities in the state, such as the Dhadhis and the Dholis, specialise in professional singing, and good places to hear some of it are the Jaisalmer Fort (p324), Shilpgram (p247) in Udaipur, and Chokhi Dhani (p172) outside Jaipur. Sufi hymns are a widely popular form as well, and there's always some of it happening either at the dargah in Ajmer (p201), or the shrine of Nizam-ud-din in Delhi (p106).

> The sitar, a musical instrument with sympathetic strings, seven of which are playable, is used widely by Indian classical musicians. It was popularised in the West by Beatle George Harrison.

In an attempt to popularise traditional music among the urban populace, a few contemporary musicians such as Ila Arun and Delhi fusion band Indian Ocean have dabbled in experimentation, thereby either reinventing folk music or fusing it with modern arrangements to create a unique sound which has clicked instantly with the city-bred (see boxed text, p52). Genres such as Indian and Western classical, rock 'n' roll and jazz have always had their own niche audiences, mostly in the cities. Blues is currently on an upswing; the Haze Bar (p117) in Delhi has live gigs on a regular basis, where bands from Kolkata, Mumbai and northeast India play out spirited 12-bar jams to a packed house.

Architecture

The magnificence of Delhi, Agra and Rajasthan's architectural heritage is astounding, and the province is home to some of India's best-known buildings. From temples and mosques to mansions and mausoleums, the region has it all. Most spectacular, however, are the fairy-tale forts and palaces, built by Rajputs and Mughals, which bear testimony to the celebrated history of North India.

TEMPLES

Rajasthan's earliest surviving temples date from the Gupta period. Built between the 4th and 6th century, these temples are small and their architecture restrained – the Sheetaleshvara Temple (p234) at Jhalrapatan is a notable

---

RECOMMENDED LISTENING

■ The albums *Banjaran, Vote for Ghaghra* and *Khichri* by folk singer Ila Arun. Noted for her husky voice, Arun's music oozes the essence of the desert and the spirit of wandering gypsies. Some of her songs are rather tongue-in-cheek with catchy tunes; others have a dash of blues or traditional courtly music thrown in.

■ *Kandisa* and *Jhini* by Indian Ocean, a fusion band from Delhi known for its signature sound and its inspiring compositions which are founded on Indian folk and classical music. *Desert Rain,* its live album recorded in 1997, hit number two on the iTunes world music charts in 2006.

■ The concert performances of Nusrat Fateh Ali Khan, a Pakistani musician who redefined Qawwali, the devotional music of the Sufis. As a musician ahead of his time, Khan, who died in 1997, was so devoted to spreading the message of Sufism that he collaborated heavily with Western artists such as Eddie Vedder and Peter Gabriel, and often sang into personal tape recorders of fans, without caring about piracy.

■ *Kailasa,* by Kailash Kher, a Delhi singer trained in classical music who happens to be one of India's most celebrated New Age singers. Kher's music also takes root in Sufism, but is open to experimentation and fusion.

■ The classical performances of Shubha Mudgal, the lady with a mesmerising voice who has often brought about a union of classical music with contemporary Indian pop. Look out for her cult mainstream release, *Ab Ke Sawan*.

---

example. Temple architecture (both Hindu and Jain) developed through the 8th and 9th centuries, and began to incorporate stunning sculptural work, which can be seen on temples at Osiyan (p317) and Chittorgarh (p238). Structurally, the temples usually tapered into a single *sikhara* (spire) and had a *mandapa* (pillared pavilion before the inner sanctum). The Dilwara complex (p265) at Mt Abu epitomises the architecture of this era. Built in the 11th century, it has marble carvings that reach unsurpassed heights of virtuosity.

The Archaeological Survey of India, a government body, currently protects and maintains heritage monuments of national importance, and conducts excavations at ancient sites.

Delhi, traditionally an Islamic stronghold, has few ancient temples to boast of. Nevertheless, the city is known for two spectacular modern structures. The Lotus Temple (p107), built in 1986 as a place of worship for the Bahai community, is a magnificent modern building shaped like a nine-sided lotus with marble-clad petals. It has won several architectural awards for its design. In 2005, Delhi got its second grand temple, Swaminarayan Akshardham, which holds a Guinness record for being the world's largest comprehensive Hindu temple. Made entirely out of stone, it features permanent exhibitions, boat rides, an IMAX theatre and musical fountains within its complex.

FORTS & PALACES

The courtyard of Delhi's Jama Masjid can hold up to 25,000 devotees during *namaz*. The mosque houses several relics, including a copy of the *Quran* written on deer skin.

The fabulous citadels of Rajasthan owe their origins to reasons ranging from mandatory fortification to the realisation of royal whims. Rajput kings often spent lavishly on these structures, to flaunt their status to the world, if nothing else. Sometimes, the beauty was heightened by having the palace reflected in an artificial pool or reservoir, such as in Deeg (p193) and Alwar (p194).

Most of Rajasthan's forts and palaces were built between the 15th and 18th centuries, which coincided with the Mughal reign in Delhi and saw the Rajputs borrowing a few architectural motifs from the Mughals. The concept of the *sheesh mahal* (hall of mirrors) was adopted from Muslim architecture, as was the use of pillared arches. Another ornamentation that was widely used across Rajasthan was the spired Bengal roof, shaped like an inverted

(Continued on page 61)

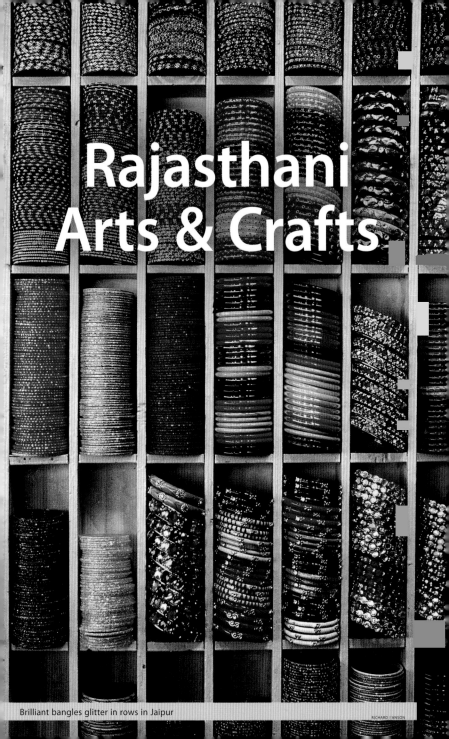

Rajasthani
Arts & Crafts

Brilliant bangles glitter in rows in Jaipur

Rajasthani dancers from a Bhil tribe create swirls of colour at Jaipur's Elephant Festival (p148)

PAUL BEINSS

The most vivid impression that visitors to Rajasthan take away with them is that of colour: searingly bright tribal dress, luminescent lorries and camels dressed to impress in a rainbow hotchpotch of bobbing baubles.

The local people have a passion for decoration, having historically taken advantage of their position on trade routes to learn new artistic skills. Their adoration of adornment is evident in the gorgeous painted houses of Shekhawati in northern Rajasthan, in the manifold variations of Rajasthani turbans (which are said to change in style every 10km) and in the state's women, from their block-printed *odhnis* (headscarves) right down to their brilliantly embroidered *jootis* (traditional Rajasthani leather shoes).

In a state whose natural environment is characterised by the stark, two-tone combination of sand and sky, the people of Rajasthan have created enduring, enchanting beauty to adorn a bleak and arid land.

RESPONSIBLE SHOPPING

Aside from not maxing out your credit card or buying too much to fit in your backpack, there are several ways to ensure that you're shopping responsibly in Rajasthan.

- Consider shopping at cooperatives, which have been set up to protect the income of day labourers and promote handicraft producers at a grass-roots level.
- Don't buy the assorted pieces of antique house fixtures you'll see up for sale, which may be slowly stripping the land of its traditional architecture.
- Ask to visit the place where a shop's items are manufactured. It's at least one way of seeing for yourself the conditions under which workers are producing goods.
- Check out the listings in Smart Shopping (p57), which includes shops and organisations dedicated to promoting Rajasthan's artisans.

PAINTING

Rajasthan's miniature painting flourished under princely patronage from the 11th century AD and beyond, with seven different 'schools', corresponding to seven Rajput principalities, each displaying its own individual conventions. Tackling religious and mythological subjects as well as plenty of courtly love, these tiny, delicate paintings were picked out in clear, bright colours and painted onto cotton, paper or silk; modern copies are widely available today.

The ancient art of *phad* (scroll) painting also survives in Rajasthan, whereby a long rectangular cloth is meticulously painted to depict the exploits of folk legend. Modern art, too, has its place in larger cities: try the splendid Juneja Art Gallery (p173) for a glimpse of contemporary Rajasthani art.

Finally, mural painting, especially in the Shekhawati region, has always played an important part in Rajasthan's artistic life. The region's painted *havelis* (traditional ornately decorated residences) form a sort of open-air art gallery, with work in a kaleidoscope of colour and styles (see p283). If the *havelis* inspire you, you can try mural painting yourself in Jhunjhunu (p287).

PAPER MAKING

Paper making is centred in Sanganer, near Jaipur, whose paper has traditionally been the most celebrated in India. The process makes environmentally friendly use of discarded fabric rags, which are soaked, pulped, strained, beaten and then spread out to dry on frames. Though some of the town's factories nowadays use machines, there are plenty of places that still perform the entire process by hand – view the racks of paper spread out to dry along Sanganer's river, or pop in for a visit at one of the town's 10 or so paper-making factories (p180).

Ornate frescoes cover the façade of the Haveli Nadine Le Prince (p292) in Fatehpur

JOHN SONES

Sparkling bangles adorn the arms of Rajasthani women dressed in vibrant saris

IAN CUMMING/ AXIOM

JEWELLERY, GEMS & ENAMELWORK

The patronage of Rajput princes historically helped Rajasthan's jewellery industry thrive. But jewellery in Rajasthan has never been entirely the domain of the rich. Even in the state's poorest villages, women can be seen bedecked in large and elaborate silver folk jewellery, along with armfuls of colourful bangles made of lac (resin), gold leaf and mirrorwork. The quality of the jewellery indicates the relative economic status of the wearer, along with their caste, ethnic group and social position, and consequently you may see women lugging around ornaments weighing as much as 5kg.

Two jewellery-making styles particularly prevalent in Rajasthan are *kundan* and *meenakari* work. *Kundan* involves setting gemstones into silver or gold pieces; one symbolic variation is known as *navratan,* in which

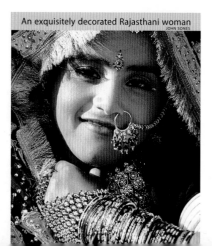

An exquisitely decorated Rajasthani woman

JOHN SONES

nine different gems are set into an item of jewellery, corresponding to the nine planets of Indian astrology. This way, it's an eternally lucky item to have about your person, since you will always be wearing, at any given time, the symbol of the ruling planetary body. *Meenakari*, meanwhile, is a gorgeous type of enamelwork, that is usually applied to a base of silver or gold. Jaipur's pieces of *meenakari* are valued for their vibrant tones – especially the highly prized rich ruby-red. A fantastic selection can be found on sale at the city's Johari Bazaar (p173).

SMART SHOPPING

■ Asha Handicrafts Association (www.ashahandicrafts.org) supports Rajasthani artisans, including producers of blue pottery, leather goods and block-printed textiles.

■ Barefoot College (www.barefootcollege.org; p207), based in Tilonia, runs artisan-development initiatives. Its craft output can be bought online at www.store.tilonia.com.

■ Seva Mandir (www.sevamandir.org; see also p370) is an Udaipur-based initiative that is dedicated to improving the lives of rural Rajasthani people. In Udaipur, you can buy their products at Sadhna (p256).

■ The Urmul Trust (see also p371) is a local NGO that sells artisans' diverse products at the Abhivyakti shop in Bikaner (p346).

■ Anokhi (p174) is a Jaipur clothing and textile manufacturer that produces high-quality items and provides good working conditions.

■ At Ranthambhore National Park, the Dastkar Craft Centre (p219) promotes handicrafts produced by low-caste women in local villages.

■ Sanganer's paper products (p180) are almost all made from recycled fabric, with not a felled tree in sight.

LEATHERWORK

Leatherworking has a long history in Rajasthan. Leather shoes known as *jootis* are produced in Jodhpur and Jaipur, often featuring ornate embroidery *(kashida)*. Strange to Western eyes and feet, there is no 'right' or 'left': both shoes are identical but after a few wears they begin to conform to the wearer's feet. Jaipur is the best place to buy *jootis*, with prices ranging from Rs 50 to Rs 700 per pair – don't miss the marvellous UN-supported Mojari (p174) shoe shop.

The town of Alwar is known for its beautiful leather book-bindings, a craft that flourished under Maharaja Banni Singh in the early 19th century. Bikaner, meanwhile, is famous for its *usta* (gold-painted camel leather) products. Some fine examples can be seen in Bikaner's Ganga Government Museum (p342); leather goods are sold, appropriately enough, on Usta St (p346).

Jootis (traditional Rajasthani leather shoes) embellished with rich embroidery and dazzling sequins
GUYLAIN DOYLE

TEXTILES

Rajasthan is renowned for its blazing textiles. Riotously woven, dyed, block or resist printed and embroidered, they are on sale almost everywhere you look throughout the state. You can also seek out specialist favourites, such as the *kota doria* (gold-woven) fabric from the village of Kaithoon near Kota (p228), woven in silk, cotton and pure-gold thread for exquisite, delicate saris. Intricate *bandhani* (tie-dye), whereby sections of fabric are tied and knotted before dyeing, often carries symbolic meanings when used to make *odhnis* (headscarves). A yellow background indicates that the wearer has recently given birth, while red circles on that background means she's had a son. You can buy tie-dyed cloth all over Rajasthan, and in Nawalgarh in Shekhawati you can even learn to do it yourself (see p280).

Block-printing fabric, Sanganer (p180)
LINDSAY BROWN

Traditionally, all Rajasthan's textile colours were derived from natural sources such as vegetables, minerals and even insects. Yellow, for instance, came from turmeric and buttermilk; green from banana leaves; orange from saffron and jasmine; black from iron rust; blue from the indigo plant; red from sugar cane and sunflowers; and purple from the kermes insect. Today, however, the vast majority are synthetically dyed; while they may not possess the subtlety of the traditional tones, they will, at least, stand a better chance in a 40°C machine wash.

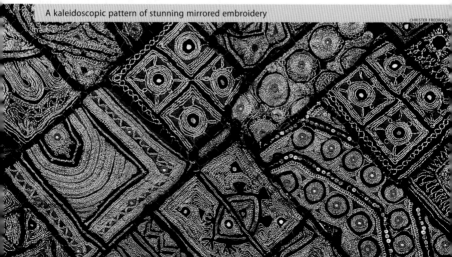

A kaleidoscopic pattern of stunning mirrored embroidery

CHRISTER FREDRIKSSON

A fine collection of *dhurries* (flat-woven rugs) carries striking designs

LINDSAY BROWN

EMBROIDERY

During the Mughal period, embroidery workshops known as *kaarkhanas* were established to train artisans so that the royal families were ensured an abundant supply of richly embroidered cloth. Finely stitched tapestries, inspired by miniature paintings, were also executed for the royal courts.

Today, Bikaner specialises in embroidery with double stitching, which results in the pattern appearing on both sides of the cloth. In Shekhawati, the Jat people embroider motifs of animals and birds on their *odhnis* and *ghaghara* (long cotton skirts), while tiny mirrors are stitched into garments in Jaisalmer. Beautifully embroidered cloth is also produced for domestic livestock, and ornately bedecked camels are a wonderfully common sight, especially at the Pushkar camel fair (p209).

CARPETS & WEAVING

Carpet weaving took off in the 16th century under the patronage of the great Mughal emperor Akbar, who commissioned the establishment of various carpet-weaving factories, including one in Jaipur. In the 19th century Maharaja Ram Singh II of Jaipur established a carpet factory at the Jaipur jail, and soon other jails introduced carpet-making units. Some of the most beautiful *dhurries* (flat-woven rugs) were produced by prisoners, and Bikaner jail is still well known for the excellence of its *dhurries*. Recent government training initiatives have seen the revival of this craft, and fine-quality carpets are once again being produced across Rajasthan.

A Rajasthani artisan skilfully applies cobalt oxide glaze to a piece of Jaipur's blue pottery

LINDSAY BROW

POTTERY

Of all the arts of Rajasthan, pottery has the longest lineage, with fragments recovered in Kalibangan dating from the Harappan era (around 3000 BC). Before the beginning of the 1st millennium, potters in the environs of present-day Bikaner were already decorating red pottery with black designs.

Today, different regions of Rajasthan produce different types of pottery, and most villages in Rajasthan have their own resident potter. He not only produces domestic vessels, but also clay images of the deities for ceremonial purposes. The most famous of Rajasthan's pottery is the blue pottery of Jaipur. The blue-glazed work was first evident on Mughal palace and cenotaph tiling, and later applied to pottery. Though, over the centuries, the tradition declined, it was revived in Jaipur in the mid-19th century, and an especially wide range of blue pottery is still available here (p173).

WOODWORK

Despite the paucity of wood in most parts of Rajasthan, the tradition of woodcarving dates back many centuries. Unfortunately, few medieval pieces have survived – if Rajasthan's arid climate didn't get them, the termites or the antique touts generally did.

Shekhawati was an important centre for woodcarving, and here you can still see the woodcarvers' talents in fantastically wrought doors, door and window frames, and in *pidas* – low folding chairs featuring decorative carving. On a smaller scale, Bassi (p235) is known for the production of wooden puppets and toys, and bright *kavads* – wonderful little portable shrines used by storytellers to relate tales of the gods. You can buy these from around Rs 100, as well as brilliantly painted tiny Hindu gods, for about Rs 20 apiece, which make great pocket-sized presents.

(Continued from page 52)

boat. Magnificent examples of Rajput architecture across the state include the Amber Fort (p178) and the Hawa Mahal (p157) in Jaipur, and the City Palace (p244) in Udaipur.

The forts and palaces of Delhi and Agra, conversely, adhere to the Islamic style, with intricate marblework, ornate *pietre dura* (stone inlay) panels, arched entrances and symmetrical, four-square gardens. Mausoleums and mosques, such as the Taj Mahal (p1330) and the Jama Masjid (p98), are capped by onion-shaped domes and flanked by minarets. Almost every dynasty that ruled in Delhi built its own fort and monuments in the city. Though they all follow Islamic architectural style, subtle differences exist among these structures due to their having come up centuries apart from each other.

Towards the end of the British era, a novel architectural style called the Indo-Saracenic school emerged in India, which blended Victorian and Islamic elements into a highly wrought, frilly whole. Some striking buildings were produced in this style, including Albert Hall (p158) and Jai Mahal (now a hotel, p169) in Jaipur, Lallgarh Palace (p342) in Bikaner and Mayo College (p201) in Ajmer.

> The Kumbalgarh Fort, a former Mewar stronghold in the Rajsamand district of Rajasthan, has the second-longest fortification in the world after the Great Wall of China.

HAVELIS

Rajasthani merchants built ornately decorated residences called *havelis*, and commissioned masons and artists to ensure they were constructed and decorated in a manner befitting the owners' importance and prosperity. The Shekhawati district of northern Rajasthan is riddled with such mansions that are covered with extraordinarily vibrant murals (see boxed text, p283). There are other beautiful *havelis* in Jaisalmer, constructed of sandstone, featuring the fine work of renowned local *silavats* (stone carvers).

WELLS, TANKS & CHHATRIS

Given the importance of water in Rajasthan, it's unsurprising that the architecture of wells and reservoirs rival other structures in the region. The most impressive regional *baoris* (step-wells) are Raniji-ki-Baori (p225) in Bundi and the extraordinary Chand Baori (p181) near Jaipur (see boxed text, p260).

Chhatris (cenotaphs) are a statewide architectural curiosity, built to commemorate maharajas and, as is the case in the Shekhawati district, wealthy merchants. In rare instances, *chhatris* also commemorate women, such as the Chhatri of Moosi Rani (p195) at Alwar. Literally translating to 'umbrella', a *chhatri* comprises a central dome, supported by a series of pillars on a raised platform, with a sequence of small pavilions on the corners and sides.

> Fascinating and detailed, *The Royal Palaces of India* by writer George Michell and photographer Antonio Martinelli is a comprehensive guide including maps to the grand residences of the Indian royalty.

Painting & Sculpture

MINIATURES

Rajasthan is famed for its miniatures – small-scale paintings that are executed on small surfaces, but cram in a surprising amount of detail by way of delicate brushwork. Originating in the 16th and 17th centuries, they led to the emergence of eminent schools such as Marwar, Mewar, Bundi-Kota, Amber and Kishangarh, among others. Each school had its own stylistic identity; while paintings from the Mewar school depicted court life, festivals, ceremonies, elephant fights and hunts, those from the Marwar school featured vivid colours and heroic, whiskered men accompanied by dainty maidens. Miniatures gained immense value as souvenirs with the coming of the tourism boom.

Rajasthani painters derived their colours mostly from natural sources; vegetables dyes were commonly used, as were pigments from minerals and crushed semiprecious stones. In ancient times, the vibrant gold and silver colouring used in many palaces was obtained from finely pounded pure gold and silver leaf. Miniatures can be spotted all over Rajasthan, on surfaces ranging from handmade paper to ivory, marble, wood, cloth and leather.

PHAD & FRESCO

Apart from miniatures, Rajasthan is also renowned for a kind of scroll painting called *phad*, which is done on cloth and portrays deities, mythology and legends of Rajput kings. Bhilwara, near Udaipur, is one of the better-known centres for *phad* scrolls. See also the Arts & Crafts colour section p61.

Fresco painting, originally developed in Italy, arrived in Rajasthan with the Mughals, and its finest examples can be seen in the exquisitely muralled *havelis* of Shekhawati. Other kinds of painted houses can be seen in certain tribal areas, where earthen walls are decorated with *pithoras* – naïve, appealing designs rendered in white – which were believed to bring luck and keep away evil spirits.

Nathdwara, 48km from Udaipur, is the centre for *pichwai* (religious paintings on home-spun cloth) which are hung behind images of Krishna (locally worshipped as Sri Nathji).

PORTRAITURE

Borrowed from the Mughals, the concept of royal portraiture was encouraged in Rajput courts from the 17th century onward. They took off on a stylised note, and depicted maharajas engaged in typical activities including hunting, fighting, wooing women and attending the durbar (royal court). Unlike the Mughals, who used muted colours to give their portraits a sense of shadow and depth, the Rajputs went overboard with bold primaries. The 19th century heralded a decline in portraiture in Rajasthan, perhaps reflecting the fading power of the maharajas, and the practice was diluted further with the arrival of photography soon after.

SCULPTURE & STONEWORK

The abundance of natural marble and sandstone deposits has helped breed generations of stonemasons and sculptors in Rajasthan. The most famous marble quarries were located in Makrana, from where the marble used in the Taj Mahal and the Dilwara Temples was sourced. The quarries of Dungarpur yielded a soft stone that was used for carving images of deities, which turned a rich, lustrous black when oiled. Most of Rajasthan, Delhi and Agra's forts were built out of red sandstone, which was mined from deposits in the Aravalli Hills. The exceptional Jaisalmer Fort (p324) and the Agra Fort (p135) were among the other group of sandstone structures, sculpted out of yellow sandstone.

Dance

Folk dance forms in Rajasthan are generally associated with indigenous tribes and communities of nomadic gypsies. Each region has its own dance specialities. The *ghoomer* (pirouette) is performed by Bhil women at festivals or weddings, and its form varies from one village to another. The Bhils are also known for *gair*, a men-only dance, that's performed at springtime festivities. Combine the two, and you get *gair-ghoomer*, where women, in a small inner circle, are encompassed by men in a larger circle, who determine the rhythm by beating sticks and striking drums.

Ghungroos are anklets made of metallic bells strung together, worn by Indian classical dancers to accentuate their complex footwork during performances.

Among other popular forms, the *kachhi ghori* dance of eastern Rajasthan resembles a battle performance, where dancers ride cloth or paper horses and spar away with swords and shields. To the south, the *neja* is danced by the Minas of Kherwara and Dungarpur just after Holi. A coconut is placed on a large pole, which the men try to dislodge, while the women strike the men with sticks and whips to foil their attempts. A nomadic community called the Kalbelias, traditionally associated with snake charming, performs swirling dances such as the *shankaria,* while the Siddha Jats of Bikaner are renowned for their spectacular fire dance, performed on a bed of hot coals, which supposedly leaves no burns. You could catch up on some of the action at tourist hubs such as Udaipur (see p256) and Chokhi Dhani (see p172).

Puppetry

Puppetry is one of Rajasthan's most acclaimed, yet endangered, performing arts. Puppeteers first emerged in the 19th century, and would travel from village to village like wandering minstrels, relaying stories through narration, music and an animated performance that featured wooden puppets on strings called *kathputlis.* Puppetry is now a dying art; waning patronage and lack of paying audiences has forced many puppeteers to give up the art form and switch to agriculture or menial labour. The puppets, however, have retained their value as souvenirs. Organisations such as the Barefoot College (see p207) now make use of puppetry as a medium to spread useful information on health, education and human rights.

Theatre

Modern theatre is firmly rooted in Delhi's thriving culture circuit. The city has a host of quality theatre institutions, including the prestigious National School of Drama, the Shri Ram Centre and Janam, founded in 1973 by late thespian-activist Safdar Hashmi. In recent years, the construction of state-of-the-art auditoriums and availability of corporate sponsorship has helped Delhi's theatre flourish in a significant way.

The website www .artindia.net keeps enthusiasts in tune with the best of classical music and dance happening around India, and has an excellent repository of articles on performing arts.

Food & Drink

Wherever you go in this region of India, you'll never be more than a step or two away from something tempting and delicious. From the sweet, decadent deep-fry of a Jaipur street-food stall, to the bliss of a hot cardamom-scented chai (tea) on a freezing Delhi January morning, to the opulence of a centuries-old Mughal or Rajput regal recipe, food is all around you, making it almost impossible to ever go hungry. Moreover, food is never just food here. It's intrinsically caught up in identity, ritual and tradition. Food marks celebrations and festivals, honours guests, and accompanies births, marriages and deaths.

Rajasthan's cuisine has developed in response to its harsh climate. Fresh fruit and vegetables are rare commodities in desert zones, but these parts of the state overcome the land's shortcomings by serving up an amazing and creative variety of regional dishes, utilising cereals, pulses, spices, milk products and unusual desert fruits in myriad ways. In these arid regions, water was traditionally so scarce and precious that milk was used as an alternative in cooking. In more fertile eastern areas, by contrast, food has always been prepared in a more conventional manner. Local cuisines have also been influenced by the area's martial history, with dishes having been developed that could last several days, be eaten on the move, and didn't require heating up before serving them.

Rajasthan, Delhi and Agra's regal feasts, meanwhile, are the stuff of legend. Delhi's princely Mughlai cuisine is traditionally rich and heavy, with plenty of butter, almonds, raisins and other expensive treats, often still cooked up the traditional way on brass pots over smoky wood fires. Rajasthan's ruling warrior class cooked up similar dishes, also heavy on the meat and cream. Modern Delhi, while not quite living up to these regal standards, ranks as one of the best restaurant destinations in the country. It has scores of establishments serving up everything from buttery kebabs to opulent international fusion cuisine, with enough choice to keep you eating at a different hotspot – cheap and cheerful or chic and complex – every day for several years.

> There's really no such thing, in India, as a 'curry'. The term is thought to be an anglicisation of the Tamil word *kari* (black pepper), coined by bewildered Brits for any dish that included spices.

STAPLES & SPECIALITIES
Bread

A meal is not complete in India unless it comes with a bountiful supply of roti, little round circles of unleavened bread (also known as chapati), made with fine wholemeal flour and cooked on a *tawa* (hotplate). In Rajasthan you'll also find *sogra*, a thick, heavy chapati made from millet; *makki ki* roti, a fat cornmeal chapati; and *dhokla,* yummy balls of steamed maize flour cooked with coriander, spinach and mint, and eaten with chutney. Yet another kind of roti is a pastry-like *purat* roti, made by repeatedly coating the dough in oil, then folding it to produce a light and fluffy result, from which you pull delicious bready strips to dip in sauce. *Cheelre,* meanwhile, is a chapati made with gram (legume) powder paste, while *bhakri* is a thick roti made from barley, millet or corn, eaten with pounded garlic, red chilli and raw onions by working-class Rajasthanis, and said to prevent sunstroke. It's probably best not to put too much trust in this theory, or to munch on a pungent stack of *bhakri* without your loved-one joining in.

Alongside the world of roti come *puris, parathas* and naans. A *puri* is a delicious North Indian snack of deep-fried wholemeal dough that puffs up like a soft, crispy balloon, and should be eaten finger-scaldingly fresh from the fryer. *Kachori* is a similar thing, but here the dough is pepped up with corn or dhal. Flaky *paratha* is a soft, circular bread, deliciously substantial and mildly elastic, which makes for a scrumptious early morning snack, and is often jazzed up with a small bowl of pickle and a stuffing of *paneer* (unfermented cheese), *aloo* (potato), or grated vegetables. Naan bread, made with white flour, is distinguished from roti by being much larger, thicker and doughier, cooked along the walls of a tandoor (oven) rather than on a *tawa*. Laced with garlic and lashings of butter, and filled with *paneer, aloo,* or coconut and raisins, naan is difficult to resist.

Rice

Rice is just as important in this region of India as in any other, and makes a nice change when you've had your fill of a dozen different kinds of roti. Aside from the plain long-grain white variety, you'll find *pilau* (also known as *pilaf*), a tasty, buttery rice dish, whose Rajasthani incarnations frequently include cinnamon, cardamom, cloves, and a handful or two of almonds and pistachios. Of all the varieties of rice you'll encounter, though, simple steamed basmati rice – slender and delicate – is generally considered the cream of India's crop, its name stemming from the Hindi phrase for 'queen of fragrance'.

Dhal & Cereals

India unites in its love for dhal (lentils or pulses), with around 60 different pulses slipping daily onto plates across the nation. In Rajasthan, the dhal of choice is *urad,* lentils boiled in water then cooked with *garam* (hot) *masala* (mixed spices), red chillies, cumin seeds, salt, oil and fresh coriander to make a spicy, fragrant broth.

The state's most popular and remarkable dhal-based dish is *dhal-bati-choorma,* which mixes dhal with *bati,* buttery hard-baked balls of whole-meal flour, and *choorma,* sweet fried wholemeal-flour balls mixed with sugar and nuts.

Frequently, instead of wheat flour, *besan,* or gram flour (made from ground chickpeas), and sometimes lentil flour, is used as a Rajasthani staple. Gram-flour dumplings known as *gatta* are a delicious dish usually cooked in a yogurt or masala sauce, while you might come across *mangodi,* lentil-flour dumplings, served in an onion or potato gravy. A speciality of Jodhpur is *kabuli Jodhpuri,* a dish made with meat, vegetables such as cauliflower, cabbage and peas, and yet more fried gram-flour balls. *Govind gatta* offers a sweet alternative: lentil paste with dried fruit and nuts all rolled into a sausage shape, then sliced and deep-fried. Pakora (fritters), *sev* (savoury nibbles) and other salted snacks generally known as *farsan* are all equally derived from chickpea gram, as is *gate ki sabzi* (or *besan gate*), spiced *besan* dough rolled into snakes, steamed and cooked in spicy gravy to create a delicious, if rather weighty, result.

For easy Rajasthani recipes - along with Mughlai, Gujarati and gorgeous breakfast recipes - search the extensive archive at www.indianfoodforever .com

Meat

While Rajasthan's Brahmins and traders traditionally stuck firmly to a vegetarian diet, the Rajputs have a far more carnivorous history. Goat (known as 'mutton' since the days of the British Raj), lamb and chicken are the mainstays; religious taboos make beef forbidden to Hindus, and pork to Muslims.

In the deserts of Jaisalmer, Jodhpur and Bikaner, meats are cooked without the addition of precious water, instead using milk, curd, buttermilk and plenty of ghee. Cooked this way, dishes keep for days without refrigeration, a practical advantage considering the searing heat of the desert. *Murg ko khaato* (chicken cooked in a curd gravy), *achar murg* (pickled chicken), *kacher maas* (dry lamb cooked in spices), *lal maas* (a rich red dish, usually made from mutton) and *soor santh ro sohito* (pork with millet dumplings) are all classic Rajasthani-desert dishes.

Maas ka sule, a Rajput favourite, is a dry dish that can be made from partridge, wild boar, chicken, mutton or fish. Chunks of meat are marinated in a paste of turmeric powder, coriander powder, ginger and garlic paste, salt, red-chilli powder, mustard oil and yogurt. The chunks are cooked on skewers in a *tandoor,* then glazed with melted butter and a tangy masala spice mix. Mughlai meat dishes, meanwhile, include rich korma and *rogan josh,* the former mild, the latter cooked with tomatoes and saffron, and both generously spiked with thick, creamy curd, equally popular today in their vegetarian incarnations.

Fruit & Vegetables

Rajasthan's delicious vegetable (*sabji*) dishes have to be admired for their inventiveness under frequently hostile growing conditions. Dishes you might come across include *papad ki sabzi,* a simple pappadam made with vegetables and *masala* (a mixture of spices), and *aloo mangori,* ground lentil paste dried in the sun then added with potato to a curry. Once rolled by hand, the paste is now often forced through a machine in a similar way to making macaroni. A common vegetarian snack whilst on the move is *aloo samosa,* triangular pastry cones stuffed with spicy potato, while another scrumptious local snack is *mirch bada,* a large chilli coated in a thick layer of deep-fried potato and wheatgerm, a Jodhpur speciality.

There are a few vegetables specific to the deserts of Rajasthan. These include *mogri,* a type of desert bean, which is made into *mogri mangori,* (similar to the *aloo mangori* described above) or into a sweeter version called *methi mangori* - *methi* being the leaf of a green desert vegetable. Another use for these *methi* leaves is in *dana methi,* where they are boiled with *dana* (small pea-shaped vegetables) and mixed with sugar, *masala* and dried fruit.

With developments in infrastructure, more vegetable dishes are now available in Rajasthan than during its barren, warrior-filled past. Heads of cauliflower are usually cooked dry on their own, with potatoes to make *aloo gobi,* or with other vegetables such as carrots and beans. Fresh green peas turn up stir-fried with other vegetables in *pilaus* and biryanis, in samosas along with potato, and in one of North India's signature dishes, *mattar paneer* (peas and fresh, firm white cheese). Brinjal (eggplant or aubergine), *bhindi* (okra or ladies' finger) and *saag* (a generic term for leafy greens) are all popular choices.

The desert bears a handful of fruits, too. *Kair* is a small, round variety, which grows on a prickly shrub and is a favourite of camels as well as local people, to whom it is usually served with mango pickle; *kachri* is a type of desert fruit frequently made into chutney. If you order something that arrives looking like a plate of dry sticks, these are *sangri* (dried wild desert beans). The seeds and beans are soaked overnight in water, boiled, and then fried in oil with *masala,* dried dates, red chillies, turmeric powder, shredded dried mango, salt, coriander and cumin seeds – and despite their dry-stick appearance are amazingly tender.

Fresh fruit is sold in mountains on street stalls at every turn: you'll find oranges (which are yellow-green), tangerines, custard apples, grapes, pink and white grapefruits, kumquats and sweet limes. Bananas are piled high, too, with many distinct varieties, rich in individual flavour and usually far tastier and juicier than the kind you'll get back home. You'll also find fruit –

Gorge yourself by reading about the extravagant royal recipes of Rajasthan in *Royal Indian Cookery* by Manju Shivraj Singh, the niece of the late Maharaja Bhawani Singh of Jaipur.

For a taste of the desert, try out a few dishes from the recipe collection, *Classic Cooking of Rajasthan* by Kaira Jiggs and Raminder Malhotra.

EATING INDIAN-STYLE

Most Indians eat with their right hand, using the tips of the fingers. *Never* eat with your left hand, which is reserved for unsavoury actions, such as toilet duties. The three-point plan to eating like a local goes as follows:

■ First, before a meal in any home, wash your hands thoroughly.

■ Next, mix your food with your fingers until it's thick and sticky. If you're having dhal and *sabzi*, mix only the dhal into your rice and take the *sabzi* in small scoops with each mouthful. If you're eating fish or meat curry, mix only the gravy into your rice and take the flesh off the bones from the side of your plate.

■ Finally, scoop up lumps of the mix and, with your knuckles facing the dish, use your thumb to shovel the food into your mouth. If you get messy in the process, discreetly wipe your hand on your bread, then consume the evidence.

---

especially lemons, limes and mangos – fashioned into a chutney or pickle, flavouring kulfi (ice cream) or other sweet treats.

Pickles, Chutneys & Relishes

You're in a pickle without a pickle, or *achar*: no Indian meal is complete without one, and, if possible, a couple of *chatnis* (chutneys) and relishes on the side. A relish can be anything from a roughly chopped onion to a delicately crafted fusion of fruit, nuts and spices. The best known is raita (mildly spiced yogurt or curd often containing cucumber, tomato or pineapple – served chilled as a side dish), which makes a delicious and refreshing counter to spicy meals. In Rajasthan it may be *bathua raita,* made with a handful of *bathua* (a spinach-like winter vegetable, also known as Pigweed) leaves, which are boiled, rinsed and then mixed with the yogurt.

Other regional variations include *goonde achar, goonde* being a green fruit that is then boiled and mixed with mustard oil and *masala. Kair achar* is a pickle with desert fruit as its base, while *lahsun achar* is an onion pickle. *Lal mirch* is a garlic-stuffed red chilli and *kamrak ka achar* a pickle made from *kamrak,* a type of desert vegetable with a pungent, sour taste. The best known, and most widely served, however, are made of raw mango, mixed with spices and mustard oil, with lime, shredded ginger, or with tiny whole shallots, jazzing up even the dullest dhal or rice dish.

'unmeltable paneer is a godsend for the vegetarian majority'

Dairy

Milk and milk products make a staggering contribution to Indian cuisine (hence the sanctity of the cow), and in Rajasthan they're even more important: *dahi* (curd) is served with most meals and is handy for countering heat in terms of both temperature and spiciness of dishes; firm, unmeltable *paneer* cheese is a godsend for the vegetarian majority and is used in apparently endless permutations; popular lassi (yogurt and iced-water drink) is just one in a host of nourishing sweet or savoury drinks, often with fruit such as banana or mango added for an extra zing; ghee (clarified butter) is the traditional and pure cooking medium (although not used nearly as much in India as in Indian restaurants abroad); and the best sweets are all made with plenty of condensed, sweetened milk or cream.

Sweets & Desserts

Indians have a heady range of tooth-jarringly sweet *mithai* (sweets), made from manifold concoctions of sugar, milk, ghee, nuts, and yet more sugar. Rajasthani varieties include *badam ki barfi,* a type of fudge made from sugar, powdered milk, almonds and ghee, and *chakki*, a *barfi* (milk-based fudge) made from gram flour, sugar and milk. Gram flour, sugar, cardamom, ghee and dried fruits combined make *churma*, while *ladoo* comes in ball-form, made from gram or wheat flour with dried fruit and sugar added.

Ghewar, another Rajasthani favourite for which Jaipur is famous, is a paste based on *urad* (a mung-bean type pulse) that's crushed, deep-fried, and dipped in sugar syrup flavoured with cardamom, cinnamon and cloves. It's served hot, topped with a thick layer of unsweetened cream and garnished with rose petals.

Kheer is perhaps India's favourite dessert. It's a delectable, fragrant rice pudding with a light, delicate flavour of cardamom, saffron, pistachios, flaked almonds, cashews or dried fruit. *Gulab jamun* comes next: spongy deep-fried balls of milk dough soaked in rose-flavoured syrup, satisfyingly treacle pudding–like and wonderful when served with chopped nuts or a rich kulfi ice cream. Kulfi is addictive once experienced; delicious, substantially firm-textured, made with reduced milk and flavoured with nuts, fruits and berries, and especially tasty in its pale-green pistachio incarnation.

Alongside these more sophisticated offerings are the sweets of the region's food stalls, which are weighed down with delights such as *jalebis* (orange-coloured whirls of fried batter dipped in syrup) which, served hot, melt in the mouth and hang heavy on the conscience. Taste these at your peril, since anyone with the slightest sweet tooth will inevitably find themselves drawn back for more.

'A glass of steaming sweet, milky, frothy chai is the perfect antidote to the heat'

Thalis

Thalis are the traditional cheap and filling meals made up of a combination of vegetable (or sometimes nonveg) curried dishes, served with relishes, pappadams, yogurt, *puris* and rice. The term 'thali' also covers the characteristic school-dinner type metal tray-plate on which the meal is frequently served. If you're strapped for cash, thalis are a saviour, especially at small, local hole-in-the-wall restaurants and at railway-station dining halls, since they're far heavier on the stomach than the wallet. In southern Rajasthan, many restaurants serve more sophisticated, sweet and lightly spiced Gujarati thalis, brought over from the adjoining state of Gujarat – one of the most famous and most delicious ways to sample a taste of Gujarati cuisine.

DRINKS
Nonalcoholic Drinks
TEA & COFFEE

India runs on chai (tea). It's a unique and addictive brew, more milk than water, stewed for a long time and frequently sugary enough to give you a much-needed energy boost. It's usually *masala* chai (mixed tea), with a few spices added, such as ginger and cardamom pods, to give it a delicious, exotic twist. A glass of steaming sweet, milky, frothy chai is the perfect antidote to the heat and stress of Indian travel; the disembodied voice droning 'chai, chai *garam*' (hot tea) at any dusty, sticky station will fast become one of the most familiar and welcome sounds of your trip.

If you never quite get the hang of chai but still crave a simple cuppa, many cafés and restaurants will serve you up 'tray tea' or 'English tea', where the teabag, milk, hot water and sugar are each served separately.

Whilst coffee used to be fairly unusual in the region, nowadays Delhi, along with parts of Rajasthan, has caught up with the double-mocha-latte ways of the West, and good – or complicated – coffee can generally be had at hotels, bars, traveller-orientated cafés, and at international coffee chains such as Costa and Barista. Coffee shops have increasingly become a popular hang-out for travellers and wealthier locals alike, though part of their appeal (beyond the paninis and carrot cake) might be the soothing jazz, chilly air-conditioning and clean toilets, as much as the quality of the ground beans.

At bus and train stations, though, coffee is still pretty much indistinguishable from chai: it's the same combination of water, boiled milk and sugar, but with just a dash of instant-coffee powder to allow connoisseurs to note the difference. That said, it offers the same restorative powers as chai, for just a fraction of the price tag of a frothy bucket-sized coffee-chain creation.

OTHER DRINKS

Aside from the usual gamut of Pepsis and 7Ups, India has a few of its own sugary bottled concoctions: the vaguely lemonish Limca and vivid-orange Mirinda. *Masala soda* is the quintessential Indian soft drink, though may be an acquired taste to the newcomer. Available at many drinks stalls, it's a freshly opened bottle of soda pepped-up with lime, spices, salt and sugar. Simple, freshly squeezed orange juice is also widely available – as are numerous sugar-enhanced carton versions – though the most popular street juices are made from sweet lemon and sugar cane, pressed in front of you by a mechanised wheel complete with jingling bells.

Less widespread but also popular, *Jal jeera* is one of the most therapeutic and refreshing indigenous drinks. It's made with lime juice, cumin, mint and rock salt and is sold in large earthenware pots by street vendors as well as in restaurants. *Falooda* is another nice option, a sweet rose-flavoured Muslim speciality made with milk, cream, nuts and strands of vermicelli.

By far the most popular of all Indian cold drinks, however, is a refreshing sweet or salty lassi (yogurt drink). Jodhpur is famous for its sweet *makhania* lassis, delicious thick, creamy lassis flavoured with saffron that are hearty enough to stand in for a meal. *Chach* and *kairi chach* are other Rajasthani specialities – the former is a thin, salted lassi and the latter is unripe mango juice with water and salt added, widely available in summer and allegedly a good remedy for sunstroke. There are also the infamous bhang lassis, to be attempted with caution: a mixture of yogurt and bhang, a heady marijuana derivative.

For information on water, see Drinking Water, p391.

> 'Masala soda is the quintessential Indian soft drink'

Alcoholic Drinks

There's a plethora of local and national brands of beer, but little to tell them apart as most are straightforward pilsners containing around 5% alcohol. Most travellers champion Kingfisher; Royal Challenge, Dansberg, Golden Eagle, London Pilsner and Sandpiper, imbibed ice-cold, are all equally refreshing. Local whiskies Peter Scott, Antiquity and Solan No 1 are all palatable if drunk with sufficient mixers.

Though the Indian wine industry is still in its infancy, there are signs that Indian wines are slowly being accepted into local and international markets. Currently, one of the best-known Indian wine producers is Sula Wines, which creates a whole slew of different tastes – from Zinfandel and Sauvignon Blanc, to a Chenin-Blanc dessert wine – with grapes grown in northern Maharashtra state. Meanwhile, Grover Vineyards, established in 1988 near Bangalore, also has a solid international reputation, with a smaller range of wines than Sula, including a nice Sauvignon Blanc and a tasty pink Shiraz. Both are worth seeking out whilst in India, rather than opting for a glass of something imported and inevitably overpriced.

At the other end of the scale, arak is what the poor drink to get blotto, poignantly called *asha* (hope) in the north of India. It's clear, distilled rice liquor, the effects of which creep up on you quickly and without warning.

Only ever drink this from a bottle produced in a government-controlled distillery. *Never, ever* drink it otherwise – hundreds of people die or are blinded every year in India as a result of drinking arak produced in illicit stills. Mahansar in Shekhawati (p289) produces a kind of 'wine' known as *daru* that tastes rather like Greek ouzo – it's homemade so, as with arak, proceed with caution.

CELEBRATIONS

Although statewide and national festivals are religiously resonant, they are also occasions for a huge nosh-up, each festival proffering its own special dishes. Sweets are considered the most luxurious of foods: *karanjis,* crescent-shaped flour parcels stuffed with sweet *khoya* (milk solids) and nuts, are synonymous with Holi, the most boisterous Hindu festival, which wouldn't be the same without its fair share of *malpuas* (wheat pancakes dipped in syrup), *barfi* fudges and *pedas* (multicoloured pieces of *khoya* and sugar). Diwali, the festival of lights, is the most widely celebrated national festival, each area producing specific Diwali sweets which are offered not only to revellers, but also to the gods themselves.

Ramadan is the Muslim month of fasting, when Muslims abstain from eating, smoking or drinking even water during daylight, replenishing themselves only before daybreak and at night. Each day's fast is broken by a huge *iftar* (sunset fast-breaking) meal and, during the Eid al-Fitr festival, a feast of heavy curries, nonvegetarian biryanis and squidgy, sumptuous sweets.

WHERE TO EAT & DRINK
Eating

Throughout Rajasthan, Delhi and Agra are multitudes of small, cheap and locally aimed restaurants, frequently known as 'hotels'. Most midrange restaurants serve one of two basic genres; South Indian (which means the sweeter, lighter vegetarian cuisine of Tamil Nadu and Karnataka) and North Indian (which comprises heavier, more meat-orientated Punjabi/Mughlai food). Rajasthan is a favourite holiday destination for affluent Gujaratis – from the famously foodie neighbouring state – which means places often specialise in Gujarati thalis. These include a selection of purely vegetarian, subtly flavoured dishes to delight the palate.

Dhabas (snack bars) are oases to the millions of truck drivers, bus passengers and anyone else who frequents India's crowded roadways. The rough-and-ready but extremely tasty food served in these hospitable shacks has become a genre on its own, known as '*dhaba* food'. In Rajasthan *dhabas* are known as *bhojanalyas,* from *bhojan* (food or meal) and *alya* (place). These simple eateries are great for travellers on a tight budget, but make sure your food comes freshly cooked, and not just reheated: you'll usually be able to judge quality in a *dhaba* by how busy its scattering of tables are or, in tableless versions, the length of the queue outside.

Delhi, these days, is a different culinary case from much of the rest of the country. Packed with expensive restaurants and cafés, it's a perfect place to splurge, if you're so-inclined, on stellar Mughlai food, or indeed on pretty much any world cuisine. But wherever you are in the region, don't be afraid to experiment in the 'I'll have what she's having' vein. Eating in Rajasthan is as much an adventure as the journey itself, and if you play it safe you may miss out on rich and memorable culinary experiences.

Drinking

You'll find no end of places to swig on a Kingfisher or sip on an expertly poured Manhattan in Delhi, particularly around Connaught Place and in the

Learn more about Sula Wines and their environmentally-friendly sustainable agriculture programmes at their website, www.sulawines .com.

Even deities have their favourite dishes. Krishna likes milk products, and Ganesh is rarely seen without a bowl of *modak* (sweet rice-flour dumplings).

wealthy suburbs, where some very stylish bars cater to the city's well-heeled after-work crowds. In Rajasthan, too, you won't find it too difficult to locate a cool glass of beer, except in Pushkar, which is officially a 'dry' town. 'Dry' days, too, may prevent you from quenching that thirst: Rajasthan has three per year (Republic Day, January 26; Independence Day, August 15; Gandhi Jayanti, October 2), while Delhi officially has 21.

Due to the expense of obtaining a liquor licence, many restaurants in Rajasthan don't list alcohol on the menu. Some won't mind if you bring your own; others may pop out to buy one for you (at an inflated price) whilst there are also those who will serve it to you despite their lack of licence – but surreptitiously, and in a teapot.

Quick Eats
STREET & PLATFORM FOOD

Whatever the time of day, people on the street are boiling, frying, roasting, peeling, juicing, simmering, mixing or baking some sort of food or beverage to tempt passers-by. Small operations usually have one special dish which they serve up all day, while other, slightly more sophisticated vendors offer different dishes for breakfast, lunch and dinner. The fare varies as you venture between neighbourhoods, towns and regions; it can be as simple as puffed rice or peanuts roasted in hot sand, as incongruous as a fried-egg sandwich with ketchup, or as complex as the riot of different flavours known as *chaat* (any snack foods seasoned with *chaat masala*).

Deep-fried treats are really where it's at on stations and streets, and you'll find samosas (deep-fried pyramid-shaped pastries filled with spiced vegetables and sometimes meat), *aloo tikka* (mashed potato patties) and *bhaji* (vegetable fritter fried in besan batter) in varying degrees of spiciness, along with *puris, kachoris,* and a whole host of other hot and battered delights. In most Muslim areas, you'll also find kebabs, doused in smooth curds and wrapped in warm bread, both filling and warming in equal measure.

For the full foodie experience whilst in Delhi, pick up the Times of India's *Times Food Guide* (Rs 100) which lists 2500 of Delhi's top eating destinations.

VEGETARIANS & VEGANS

India produces some of the best vegetarian food you'll find anywhere on the planet, and vegetarians will have absolutely no problem maintaining a varied and exciting diet no matter how long their stay.

Vegetarian food is sometimes divided up in India into 'veg' and 'pure veg', a frequently blurred and confusing distinction. As a general rule of thumb, 'veg' usually means the same as it does in the West: without meat, fowl or seafood, but possibly containing butter (in India's case, ghee), dairy products, eggs or honey. 'Pure veg' often refers to what the West knows as vegan food: dishes containing no dairy products, eggs or honey. Sometimes, as in the case of Jain or Hare Krishna–run eating establishments, 'pure veg' might also mean no onions, garlic or mushrooms (which some Hare Krishna believe can have a negative effect on one's state of consciousness) or even no root vegetables or tubers (since many Jains, according to the principles of ahimsa, are loathe to damage plants).

Though it's extremely easy to be vegetarian in India, finding vegan food – outside 'pure veg' restaurants – can be a bit trickier. Many basic dishes, including dhal, include a small amount of ghee, so ask whether a dish is 'pure veg', even in a vegetarian restaurant, before ordering.

EATING WITH KIDS

In such a family-centred society, children are welcomed everywhere and foreign children especially fêted. You'll never feel out of place, even in the swankiest of New Delhi restaurants, even if basics such as highchairs and

---

STREET FOOD DOS & DON'TS

There are obvious risks involved in eating on India's streets, but with a little common sense you're bound to discover culinary treasures: remember that fortune favours the brave.

■ Stick to street stalls that seem well-frequented, particularly by local families with children.

■ Check how and where utensils are cleaned, and whether food is covered when not on the flame. If the stall is very grimy or there are too many buzzing flies, beat a hasty retreat.

■ Avoid, in general, eating meat from street stalls, since food-poisoning risks are increased.

■ Choose sweet lemon, orange and sugar-cane drinks that are pressed in front of you, rather than dispensed from a jug.

■ Don't be tempted by pre-sliced fruit, which keeps its luscious veneer with a regular dousing of local tap water.

---

child-sized portions are a little lacking. For little ones with tamer palates, the cook at a simple eatery will usually be pleased to whip up a simple, spice-free dhal, roti and rice combination. At more sophisticated dining joints, there will generally be a choice of child-friendly dishes, both Indian and Western in orientation.

For vegetarian children, lassis and *paneer* in all its forms, are a great way to make sure they are getting an adequate dose of calcium. Fruit, bought from street stalls and peeled and washed in bottled water, is great for keeping everyone's vitamin C levels high, and bananas are particularly good for troubled tummies. Every small kiosk sells snacks (try Parle G biscuits for their chai-dunkable, malted-milk consistency) for on-the-go treats, while adventurous children will enjoy sampling the sweets and deep-fried delicacies of street stalls.

Breakfasts are a good time to stock up for the day ahead, where pancakes filled with sliced banana and honey or Nutella will soon become a firm favourite on every travelling-child's breakfast agenda. More adventurous children, meanwhile, will love the messy, hands-on experience of dipping *idlis* and *parathas* in *sambar* (dhal with vegetables) and curd, along with the vast, floppy *dosas* of the Indian breakfast table.

For more on travelling with children, see p354.

> To find out more about veganism in India, take a look at www.indian vegan.com. For recipe ideas, pick up a copy of *Spicy Vegan* by Sudha Raina.

HABITS & CUSTOMS

Three main meals daily is the norm in India, with as many tiffin (snacks) as can be consumed without sabotaging the appetite. Breakfast is a light meal, usually of *paratha* and chai – though for the modern Delhi commuter masses, it might just as likely be a croissant and cappuccino-to-go. Lunch is substantial, often a local version of a thali, or a slew of rice and curry dishes shared with friends or family, from the local eating joint.

Few are able to wait until dinner before eating again, so a substantial tiffin is tucked into at around 5pm. Indians eat their evening meal relatively late, so restaurants are often deserted before 9pm. Dinner will usually have fewer dishes than a thali lunch, but bigger portions. Whatever the meal time, dishes are rarely served in courses; rather they're served hot and all-together. In Delhi you'll see the masses tucking into cakes, ice creams or street-stall sweets until late in the evening, long after dinner is done and digested.

Food & Religion

Regardless of caste or creed, Indians share the belief that food is just as important for fine-tuning the spirit as it is for sustaining the body, though the country's Hindus, Muslims and Buddhists adhere to more culinary rules than its Sikhs, Christians and Parsis.

Most Hindus avoid foods that are thought to inhibit physical and spiritual development. The taboo on eating beef is the most rigid restriction, yet some – especially middle-class Hindus – eat it in restaurants and in non-Hindu homes. Some foods, such as dairy products, are considered innately pure and are eaten to cleanse the body, mind and spirit. Ayurveda, the ancient science of life, health and longevity, also heavily influences food customs.

Muslims have had a great influence on Indian food, and are responsible for most Indian meat dishes. Pork and alcohol are forbidden, and stimulants such as coffee and tea are avoided by the most devout. Halal is the term for all permitted foods, and haram for those prohibited.

Buddhists subscribe to the concept of ahimsa (the philosophy of non-violence), and most Indian Buddhists are largely vegetarian, though some eat fish and others abstain only from beef. Jainism's central tenet is ultra-vegetarianism, and rigid restrictions are in place to avoid even potential injury to any living creature – many Jains abstain from eating vegetables that grow underground; some, because of the potential to harm insects during cultivation, whilst others prefer to avoid harm to the plant itself.

COOKING COURSES

In Udaipur several places run cookery lessons (see p249), and you can also learn in Mt Abu at the Shri Ganesh Hotel (see p268). In Jhunjhunu in Shekhawati, Hotel Jamuna Resort (see p287) runs various courses, where lessons are coupled with field visits to different foodie families and establishments.

EAT YOUR WORDS
Useful Phrases
Do you accept credit cards?
  kyaa aap kredit kaard lete/letee haing? (m/f)
What would you recommend?
  aap ke kyaal meng kyaa achchaa hogaa?
I'm (a) vegetarian.
  maing hoong shaakaahaaree

I'd like the ... , please.
  muje ... chaahiye
Please bring a/the ....
  ... laaiye

bill	*bil*
fork	*kaangtaa*
glass	*glaas*
glass of wine	*sharaab kee kaa glaas*
knife	*chaakoo*
menu	*menyoo*
mineral water	*minral vaatar*
plate	*plet*
spoon	*chammach*

I don't eat ...
  maing ... naheeng kaataa/kaatee (m/f)
Could you prepare a meal without...?
  kyaa aap ... ke binaa kaanaa taiyaar kar sakte/saktee haing? (m/f)

beef	*gaay ke gosht*
fish	*machlee*

meat stock	gosht ke staak
pork	suar ke gosht
poultry	murgee
red meat (goat)	bakree

I'm allergic to ...
muje ... kee elarjee hai

nuts	meve
seafood	machlee
shellfish	shelfish

Food Glossary

achar – pickles and chutneys
aloo – potatoes
aloo tikka – mashed-potato patty, often filled with vegetables or meat
appam – South Indian rice pancake
arak – liquor distilled from coconut milk, potatoes or rice
baigan – eggplant; also known as *brinjal*
barfi – milk-based fudgelike sweet
besan – ground chickpea flour
betel – nut of the betel tree; chewed as a stimulant and digestive in *paan*; also called areca nut
bhajia – vegetable fritter fried in besan batter, often eaten as street food
bhang lassi – potent blend of lassi and bhang (a derivative of marijuana)
bhelpuri – thin fried rounds of dough with rice, lentils, lemon juice, onions, herbs and chutney
bhindi – okra (ladies' fingers)
biryani – rich, fragrant rice dish with meat or vegetables
bonda – mashed-potato patty
brinjal – eggplant/aubergine
butter chicken – a Delhi favourite: tandoori chicken in a rich butter and tomato sauce
chaat – any small, savoury snack
chai – sweet, spiced tea
chana – chickpeas
chapati – unleavened Indian bread, also known as roti
chatni – chutney
cheiku – small brown fruit that looks like a potato, but is sweet
dahi – curd or yogurt
dhal – curried lentil dish; a staple food throughout India
dhal makhani – black lentils and red kidney beans with cream and butter
dhansak – Parsi dish; meat, usually chicken, with curried lentils and rice
dosa – South Indian breakfast dish: a paper-thin lentil-flour pancake
falooda – rose-flavoured drink made with milk, cream, nuts and vermicelli
faluda – long chickpea-flour noodles
farsan – savoury nibbles
ghee – clarified butter
gram – legumes
gulab jamun – deep-fried balls of dough soaked in rose-flavoured syrup
halwa – soft sweetmeat made with vegetables, cereals, lentils, nuts and fruit
idli – South Indian spongy, round savoury rice cake, served for breakfast
jaggery – hard, brown unrefined sugarlike sweetener made from palm sap
jalebi – deep-fried coils of sweet batter dipped in sugar syrup
keema – minced meat
kheer – rice pudding
khichdi – heavy rice dish sometimes made with lentils, potatoes and peanuts
kofta – minced balls of meat or vegetables in a curry sauce
korma – rich, mild meat or vegetable dish, cooked with curd
kulcha – charcoal-baked bread

kulfi – flavoured (often with pistachio) ice-cream confection
ladoo – sweet ball made with gram flour and semolina; also spelt as *ladu*
lassi – refreshing yogurt and iced-water drink, served either sweet or salted
masala – a wide-ranging term referring either to a mixture of spices or a spicy dish
masala dosa – South Indian dish; large lentil-flour crepe *(dosa)* often stuffed with potatoes and vegetables, and served with *sambar* and coconut chutney
mattar paneer – peas and unfermented cheese in gravy
milk badam – invigorating morning drink made with saffron and almonds
mithai – Indian sweets
momo – Tibetan fried or steamed dumpling stuffed with vegetables or meat
murg – chicken
naan – flat bread cooked in a tandoor oven
paan – digestif made of betel nut (also called areca nut), lime paste and spices, with or without tobacco
pakora – bite-sized piece of vegetable dipped in gram-flour batter and deep-fried
palak paneer – unfermented cheese in spinach gravy
paneer – unfermented cheese
pani – water
paratha – bread made with ghee and cooked on a hotplate
pilau – rice cooked in stock and flavoured with spices; also spelt as 'pilaf' or 'pulao'
puri – flat dough that puffs up when deep-fried; also spelt as 'poori'
raita – mildly spiced yogurt or curd, often containing shredded or diced cucumber, carrot, tomato or pineapple; served chilled as a side dish
rasam – South Indian dish; thin tamarind-flavoured vegetable broth
rasgulla – sweet little balls of cream cheese flavoured with rose-water
rogan josh – spicy red curry, traditionally made with meat, cooked with saffron
roti – wheat-flour bread cooked on the *tawa (*hotplate)
sabji – any vegetable curry, also known as *sabzi*
saag – leafy greens, usually spinach or fenugreek
sambar – South Indian dish; thin, soupy dhal with cubed vegetables often served with *dosas* or *idlis*
samosa – deep-fried pastry triangles filled with spiced vegetables and/or meat
sonf – aniseed seeds; used as a digestive – usually comes with the bill after a meal and also known as *paan*
thali – 'all-in-one' meal served on a stainless-steel or silver plate
thukpa – thick Tibetan noodle soup
tiffin – snack; also refers to the stacked meal container, often made of stainless steel
tikka – spiced, marinated, chargrilled chunks of chicken, *paneer,* lamb or fish

Environment

THE LAND

The rugged Aravalli Range splits Rajasthan like a bony spine, running from the northeast to the southwest. These irregular mountains – at times lush and forested, at others bare and muscular – form a boundary between the Thar Desert to the west and the relatively lusher vegetation to the east. With an average height of 600m, in places the range soars to over 1050m; the highest point, Guru Shikhar (1722m), is near Mt Abu. It's thought to be the oldest mountain range in the world. A second hilly spur, the Vindhya Range, splays around the southernmost regions of Rajasthan.

The state's sole perennial river is the wide, life-giving swell of the Chambal. Rising in Madhya Pradesh from the northern slopes of the Vindhyas, the river enters Rajasthan at Chaurasigarh and forms part of Rajasthan's eastern border with Madhya Pradesh.

The south is drained by the Mahi and Sabarmati Rivers; the Luni, which rises about 7km north of Ajmer in the Aravalli, is the only river in western Rajasthan. Seasonal and comparatively shallow, the Luni sometimes billows out to over 2km wide.

The arid region in the west of the state is known as Marusthali or Marwar (the Land of Death), which gives some idea of the terrain. Sprawling from the Aravallis in the east to the Sulaiman Kirthar Range in the west is the Thar Desert, which covers almost three-quarters of the state. It's a barren, dry, inhospitable expanse – the eastern extension of the great Saharo-Tharian Desert – forming 61% of the area covered by desert in India.

Low, rugged, barren slopes occasionally punctuate the parched plains. About 60% of the region is also made up of sand dunes, which are formed by the erosion of these low hills and from sand blown from Gujarat's vast desert, the Great Rann of Kutch.

It's hard to believe, but this desolate region was once covered by massive forests and populated by huge animals. In 1996 two amateur palaeontologists working in the Thar Desert discovered animal fossils, some 300 million years old, that included dinosaur fossils. At the Akal Wood Fossil Park (p337), near Jaisalmer, you can visit the incredible remains of fossilised trees that are around 180 million years old. Plant fossils from 45 million years ago show that Rajasthan's metamorphosis into desert is relatively recent – and ongoing.

It's hard to make out where the desert ends and becomes semiarid. The semiarid zone nestles between the Aravallis and the Thar Desert, extending west from the Aravallis and encompassing the Ghaggar River Plain, parts of Shekhawati and the Luni River Basin.

Delhi lies on the vast flatlands of the Indo-Gangetic Plain, though the northernmost pimples of the Aravallis amount to the Ridge, which lies west of the city centre. The Yamuna River flows southwards along the eastern edge of the city. To the south, Agra lies on the banks of the Yamuna, in the neighbouring state of Uttar Pradesh.

Did you know? Around 180 million years ago the deserts of Rajasthan were lush forests home to dinosaurs.

WILDLIFE

For a place apparently so inhospitable, Rajasthan hosts an incredible array of animals and birds; the stars are the elusive tigers of Ranthambhore National Park (p215) and the birds of Keoladeo Ghana National Park (p188), although the status of the latter has dramatically declined owing to lack of water.

Animals

Arid-zone mammals have adapted to the lack of water in various resourceful ways. For example, some top up their fluids with insects that are composed of between 65% and 80% water, and water-bearing plants, while others retain water for longer periods. Faced with the incredible heat, many creatures burrow in the sand or venture out only at night – tricks that travellers in the hot season may feel like emulating.

ANTELOPES & GAZELLES

Blackbuck antelopes, with their long spiralling horns, are most common around Jodhpur, where they are protected by local Bishnoi tribes (see p315). Bishnoi conservation has also helped the chinkaras (Indian gazelles). These delicate little creatures (around 1m tall) are very fast and agile and found in small herds.

Also notable and relatively common in the national parks is the extraordinary nilgai, which is the largest of the antelope family – only the males attain the blue colour. It's a large, muscular animal whose front legs are longer than its rear legs, giving it an ungainly stance.

Elephas maximus – A Portrait of the Indian Elephant by Stephen Alter, reveals the princely pachyderm in all its wild grandeur as well as describing its influence in art, warfare and ceremony.

BIG CATS

Tigers were once found along the length of the Aravallis. However, royal hunting parties, poachers and habitat destruction have decimated the population, and tigers are now only found in Ranthambhore National Park. In 2008 there were plans to relocate the last four villages remaining in Sariska Tiger Reserve, and to then reintroduce tigers from Ranthambhore. The last of Sariska's original tigers were killed by poachers in 2004–05; (see p199).

The mainly nocturnal and rarely seen leopard, or panther, inhabits rocky declivities in the Aravallis, and parts of the Jaipur and Jodhpur districts. Anecdotal reports suggest an increase in numbers of leopards at Sariska Tiger Reserve following the demise of the tiger.

DOGS

Jackals are renowned for their unearthly howling, which enables them to find each other and form packs. Once common throughout Rajasthan, they would lurk around villages, where they scavenged and preyed on livestock. Habitat encroachment and hunting (for their skins) have reduced their numbers, though they are still a very common sight in Keoladeo Ghana, Ranthambhore and Sariska parks.

The wolf once roamed in large numbers in the desert, but farmers hunted it almost to the point of extinction. Wolves have begun to reappear over recent decades, due to concerted conservation efforts. The sanctuary at Kumbalgarh (p259) is known for its wolves.

The sandy-coloured desert fox is a subspecies of the red fox and was once prolific in the Thar Desert. As with wolves, the fox population has shrunk due to human endeavours, but it's still quite common to spot a single animal flitting across a desert road. Keep your eyes open for them scavenging roadkill on the highway near Jaisalmer.

The US-based Fund for the Tiger, www.fundfor thetiger.com, and Save the Tiger Fund, www .savethetigerfund.org are non-profit fundraisers who finance initiatives to assist tiger conservation in India and elsewhere.

RODENTS

Desert gerbils are small, but they're big trouble: they descend on crops in vast numbers, causing untold damage. In the arid zone an incredible 12,000 to 15,000 burrows per hectare have been identified. Each burrow opening shifts 1kg of soil, which is carried by the high-velocity winds, contributing to soil erosion and dust storms.

MONKEYS

Monkeys seem to be everywhere in Rajasthan. There are two common types: the red-faced and red-rumped rhesus macaque and the shaggy grey, black-faced langur, with prominent eyebrows. Both types are keen on hanging around human settlements, where they can get easy pickings. Both will steal food from your grasp at temples, but the macaque is probably the more aggressive and the one to be particularly wary of.

BEARS

In forested regions you might be greeted by a sloth bear – a large creature covered in long black hair with a prominent white V on its chest and peculiar muzzle with an overhanging upper lip. That lip helps it feed on ants and termites. Sloth bears feed mostly on vegetation and insects but aren't averse to a bit of carrion. The bears are reasonably common around Mt Abu and elsewhere on the western slopes of the Aravalli Range.

BIRDS

The Aravalli forests harbour orioles, hornbills, kingfishers, swallows, parakeets, warblers, mynahs, robins, flycatchers, quails, doves, peacocks, barbets, bee-eaters, woodpeckers and drongos, among others. Birds of prey include numerous species of owls (great horned, dusky, brown fishing and collared scops, and spotted owlets), eagles (spotted and tawny), white-eyed buzzards, black-winged kites and shikras.

The wetlands of eastern Rajasthan include the internationally renowned Keoladeo Ghana National Park. Although in recent years the lack of water has prevented the famous migratory flocks from returning, it is hoped that a new water supply will soon reinvigorate this wetland (p188). Migratory species include spoonbills, herons, cormorants, storks, open bills, ibis and egrets. Wintering waterfowl include the common, marbled, falcated and Baikal teal; pintail, gadwall, shoveler, coot, wigeon, bar-headed and greylag geese; and common and brahminy pochards. Waders include snipe, sandpipers and plovers. Terrestrial species include the monogamous sarus, which inhabits the park year-round, and the beautiful demoiselle crane. Other species resident throughout the year include moorhens, egrets, herons, storks and cormorants. Birds of prey include many types of eagles (greater spotted, steppe, imperial, Spanish imperial and fishing), vultures (white-backed and scavenger), owls (spotted, dusky horned and mottled wood), marsh harriers, sparrowhawks, kestrels and goshawks.

Common birds of the grasslands include various species of lark, including the short-toed, crested, sky and crowned finch-lark. Quails, including grey, rain, common and bush, can also be seen, as can several types of shrike (grey, rufous-backed and bay-backed), mynahs, drongos and partridges. Migratory birds include the lesser florican, seen during the monsoon, and the Houbara bustard, which winters at the grasslands. Birds of prey include falcons, eagles, hawks, kites, kestrels and harriers.

The Thar Desert also has a prolific variety of birdlife. At the small village of Khichan, about 135km from Jodhpur, you can see vast flocks of demoiselle cranes descending on fields in the morning and evening from the end of August to the end of March. Other winter visitors to the desert include Houbara bustards and common cranes. As water is scarce, water holes attract large flocks of imperial, spotted, pintail and Indian sandgrouse in the early mornings. Other desert dwellers include drongos, common and bush quail, blue-tailed and little green bee-eaters, and grey partridges. Desert birds of prey include eagles (steppe and tawny), buzzards (honey and long-legged), goshawks, peregrine falcons and kestrels. The most notable of the desert and

Did you know? When the desert gerbil senses danger, it thumps the earth with its hind feet; the entire colony then flees to the burrows.

dry grassland dwellers is the impressive great Indian bustard, which stands some 40cm high and can weigh up to 14kg.

ENDANGERED SPECIES

Some of Rajasthan's wildlife is disappearing due to encroachment on its habitat, but poaching is also a serious problem.

It's estimated that during the 1990s more than 20 tigers were slaughtered at Ranthambhore National Park and the last of the tigers of Sariska Tiger Reserve were killed in 2005. After the skin is removed, the bones inevitably find their way to China, where they form the basis of 'tiger wine', believed to have healing properties. The penis is coveted for its alleged aphrodisiac powers. For details on the recent tragedy see The Case of the Missing Tigers, p199.

National parks and sanctuaries are proving to be lucrative hunting grounds for poachers. Frequently, only main roads in parks are patrolled by (often poorly paid) guards, so poachers can trespass without fear of detection. From numbers in excess of 40,000 in the early 20th century, wild tigers in India have crashed to fewer than 1500 estimated in 2008. And many of these are in small, isolated and unsustainable populations.

Numbers of the great Indian bustard have also dwindled alarmingly due to hunting and because the bird's eggs are trampled by livestock. However, in Rajasthan, where the bird is the emblem of the state, there is no programme for conservation and this has led to calls for a national programme similar to Project Tiger to protect this majestic bird.

Three types of vulture have become endangered over the past few years. Once common, they joined the endangered ranks after the population in south Asia fell by 95%. The cause was exposure to a veterinary drug, which

The Tiger's Destiny, by Valmik Thapar, with photographs by Fateh Singh Rathore, is all about the besieged tigers of Ranthambhore National Park.

The most prominent organisation battling tiger poaching in India is the Wildlife Protection Society of India, www .wpsi-india.org.

ANIMAL AID SOCIETY

Praveen and Poonam met Americans Erika and Jim in 2000. Talking about their distress at seeing so many street animals in pain, together they began to realise a dream – to take action and address the problems of destitute animals. In March 2003 they completed a small hospital in Chota Hawala village, 3km northwest of Udaipur, which now treats around 200 animals per month.

The society's work includes emergency treatment of stray animals and projects such as spaying street dogs (20 to 40 per week). There are an estimated 10,000 ownerless dogs in the Udaipur district, so this helps keep numbers under control. They also travel to village communities to provide animals with treatments such as deworming.

If you've noticed donkeys weighed down with mammoth loads, you'll understand the Animal Aid Society's particular concern for these diminutive, overworked, long-suffering creatures. The hospital cares for retired donkeys and runs education programmes to prevent ill-treatment.

Another project is the Plastic Bag Education Campaign. Cows let loose on the street to graze often end up chowing down on indigestible plastic. The plastic sits in the cow's stomach, causing the animal to feel full. This means it will end up starving to death. Street cows who've been operated on have been found to have as much as 36kg of plastic in their gut. The society aims to educate people about the dangers of this kind of waste and so prevent cows from dying a slow and agonising death.

Visitors are welcome at the **hospital** (10am-5pm), in Chota Hawala village, near Udaipur. The Animal Aid Society relies on donations and volunteer help, so if you can give either money or time you'll be supporting excellent work. You could give a straightforward gift or sponsor a donkey. The society's website gives details of the projects your money could help with. Ideally, a volunteer should commit at least two weeks, working four or more hours a day, but if you have less time the society is happy to make other arrangements. Volunteers don't have to be skilled – you can help by just giving animals the care and attention that can speed recovery. For more details, call 0294-2513359 or check the website at www.animalaidunlimited.com.

the vultures absorbed while feeding from livestock carcasses. The reduction in vulture numbers has had knock-on ecological and health effects, as the birds once disposed of many carcasses, thus reducing risks of disease.

Plants

Vegetation in the desert zone is, not surprisingly, sparse and hardy. Only a limited range of grasses and slow-growing thorny trees and shrubs can grow here. The most common tree species are the ubiquitous khejri (*Prosopis cineraria*) and varieties of acacia. Rajasthan also has some dry teak forest, dry mixed deciduous forest, bamboo brakes and subtropical hill forests. Forest stocks are dwindling, however, as inhabitants scour the landscape for fuel and fodder.

A Guide to the Wildlife Parks of Rajasthan, by Dr Suraj Ziddi, with photographs by Subhash Bhargava, is a comprehensive guide to Rajasthan's reserves.

The hardy khejri, which is held sacred by the Bishnoi tribes of Jodhpur district (see p315), is drought resistant on account of its very deep roots (up to 30m below the surface). No part of the plant goes to waste: the thorny twigs are used to build barriers to keep sheep and goats away from crops, the leaves are dried and used for fodder, and the bean-shaped fruit can be eaten ripe or unripe. The latter, when cooked, is known as *sangri*. The wood is used to make furniture and the branches are burnt for fuel. The khejri twigs are used in the sacred fire that's lit during marriage ceremonies.

Another arid-zone tree is rohira (*Tecoma undulata*). Its pods form medicines that relieve abscesses, and its wood is used to make furniture. The Central Arid Zone Research Institute (p85) has had some success with the introduction of faster-growing exotic species to the desert, including various acacias.

NATIONAL PARKS & WILDLIFE SANCTUARIES

Among its numerous reserves, Rajasthan has some world-renowned wildlife sanctuaries and national parks (see the table opposite). Some of these, such as Ranthambhore, Keoladeo and Sariska, were originally the hunting reserves of the maharajas. Others, such as the Desert National Park in western Rajasthan, have been established to protect and preserve the unique plants and animals found in the arid zone.

ENVIRONMENTAL ISSUES

> *Oont chhode Akaro, Bakri chhode Kangro*
> The camel consumes everything other than *ak* (a thorny shrub) but the goat devours even that, leaving only the pebbles
> *Marwari proverb*

Rajasthan's challenging climate and human needs are responsible for its major environmental problems of drought, desertification and overgrazing, while Delhi and Agra's big burdens are air and water pollution.

Drought

Droughts are a recurrent spectre in Rajasthan, due to the unreliability of the monsoon. The propensity of drought conditions highlights the need for water-conservation strategies in the state, and many villages have been making impressive gains by reviving traditional water-harvesting techniques. However, the state still faces a huge water crisis. In western Rajasthan, even in good years, lack of water means cultivation barely meets subsistence requirements. Groundwater levels in cities such as Jaipur are lowering alarmingly.

Water scarcity has led to clashes between local people and conservationists. When it was suggested that water be re-diverted from Panchana Dam to

MAJOR NATIONAL PARKS & WILDLIFE SANCTUARIES

National park/ wildlife sanctuary	Location	Features	Best time to visit
Darrah WS	southern Rajasthan, p232	leopards, chinkaras, spotted deer, wild boar, wolves, sloth bears	Feb-May
Desert NP	western Rajasthan, p336	great Indian bustards, blackbuck, nilgai, wolves, desert foxes, crested porcupines	Sep-Mar
Dhawa Doli WS	western Rajasthan, p316	blackbuck, nilgai, partridges, desert foxes	Oct-Feb
Gajner WS	western Rajasthan, p347	desert cats, desert foxes, chinkaras	Oct-Mar
Jaisamand WS	southern Rajasthan, p262	crocodiles, leopards, chinkaras, beautiful *chhatris* (cenotaphs)	Nov-Jun
Keoladeo Ghana NP	eastern Rajasthan, p188	400 bird species, including migratory birds & waterbirds (wetlands)	Oct-Mar, Jul-Aug
Kumbalgarh WS	southern Rajasthan, p259	wolves in packs of up to 40, chow-singhas, four-horned antelopes, leopards, horse riding	Oct-Jun
Mt Abu WS	southern Rajasthan, p271	deciduous & subtropical forest, sloth bears, wild boar, sambars, leopards	Mar-Jun
National Chambal WS	southern Rajasthan,	gharial crocodiles, wolves, chinkaras, blackbuck, wild boar, caracals	Oct-Mar
Ranthambhore NP	eastern Rajasthan, p215	tigers, chitals, leopards, nilgai, chinkaras, bird life, ancient fort	Oct-Apr
Sariska Tiger Reserve	eastern Rajasthan, p198	leopards, chitals, chinkaras, birdlife, fort, deserted city & temples	Nov-Jun
Sitamata WS	southern Rajasthan, p263	ancient teak trees, deer, sambars, leopards, flying squirrels, wild boar	Mar-Jul
Tal Chhapar WS	northern Rajasthan, p298	blackbuck, chinkaras, desert foxes, antelopes, harriers, eagles, sparrowhawks	Sep-Mar

revive Keoladeo Ghana National Park, local farmers threatened to commit suicide. In Alwar district, villages have adopted traditional techniques to combat water shortages. The construction of *johars* (semi-circular earthen dams) slows the flow of monsoon run-off and thereby increases soil infiltration and the level of groundwater.

India's premier wildlife magazine, *Sanctuary*, has a website, www.sanctuaryasia.com, highlighting the latest conservation issues and with numerous related links.

Desertification

Desertification is partly a natural progression, as geological factors have given rise to warmer, drier climates, but it has been exacerbated by more and more humans and their domestic animals exploiting fewer and fewer resources. The Thar Desert is the most densely populated desert in the world, with an average of over 60 people per square kilometre.

An acute shortage of water, plus the problems of salinity, erosion, periodic droughts, overgrazing, overcultivation and overconsumption of scanty vegetation for fuel and timber, all either contribute to or are a consequence

RESPONSIBLE TRAVEL

You may feel that as an individual you are helpless to prevent environmental destruction, but there's a lot you can do, with little effort.

Rubbish Retaliation

Tourism contributes to the massive rubbish problem in Indian cities. In Udaipur the large number of hotels around Lake Pichola has contributed to widespread pollution within and around the lake. Travellers can help by encouraging hotel management to dispose of rubbish in an environmentally friendly manner. You can put similar pressure on the camel-safari operators who dump rubbish in the desert during their tours.

Plastic Peril

Many once-pristine regions are now vanishing under a sea of abandoned plastic mineral-water bottles. Travellers can make a significant difference by only buying products that use environmentally friendly packaging.

Discarded plastic bags are a very serious problem (see Animal Aid Society, p84). Avoid buying anything in plastic bags and bottles, and, if you must buy plastic, reuse it. Other ways of reducing Rajasthan's plastic peril include buying tea in terracotta cups at train stations (or in your own cup) rather than plastic, bringing your own canteen and purifying water rather than buying it in plastic bottles (see p391), and buying soft drinks in (recyclable) glass bottles.

Waste Not, Want Not

Traditionally, Rajasthanis have used ingenious methods of conserving every drop of water. In Jaisalmer the same water was used to bathe, wash clothes, wash the floor and water the garden. Today, however, Rajasthan has a water crisis. Across the state many people face a lack of drinking water, while in Jaisalmer increased water usage is causing the fort to crumble. There are various reasons for this, but the growing number of tourist facilities, particularly bathrooms, designed in line with Western standards, is definitely one of them.

of the continuing desertification of Rajasthan. As inhabitants scour the landscape for wood fuel, some species of vegetation face a severe threat. The roots of the phog plant (Calligonum polygonoides), which is one of the few species found on sand dunes, are removed and used for fuel. Once common in Jodhpur district, phog has now completely disappeared. The rohira tree has all but disappeared from the arid zone. Rohira wood, known locally as Marwar teak, is highly prized for furniture construction, and was traditionally used in the carved architraves and window frames of *havelis* (traditional, ornately decorated residences).

'concerns that air pollution was affecting the Taj Mahal led to the designation of a 4km traffic-free zone around the building'

Pollution

Deforestation and pollution are damaging many parts of Rajasthan, especially the southern region. Industrial waste has caused air, water and noise pollution; this is particularly noticeable around the industrial town of Kota. Marble mining has been especially harmful. Some areas of southern Rajasthan, including the region from Kota to Jhalawar, seem to be covered in a thin layer of marble dust, and around Rambagh, near Jaipur, the landscape is scarred by the (now closed) mines.

To address water pollution, the government has introduced policies that restrict building and development around lakes and rivers.

In Delhi, a shocking number of people die of air-pollution-related diseases every year. Road traffic is the chief cause of the problem, though recent measures, including the development of the metro and the conversion of all rickshaw engines to use compressed natural gas (CNG), have had an

You can make a difference by cutting down on the amount of waste water that you produce. Washing with a bucket uses around one-third of the water that's required for a shower. Similarly, using Indian rather than Western toilets reduces the amount of water that is flushed down the drain.

Animal Welfare
India's ancient reverence for the natural world manifests itself in myths, beliefs and cults that are an intrinsic part of the cultural fabric. But in a country where millions live below the poverty line, survival often comes before sentiment.

The World Society for the Protection of Animals (WSPA) works to raise awareness of cases of cruelty and exploitation. One campaign focuses on dancing bears. Cubs of endangered sloth bears are captured in the wild, and then their muzzles are pierced so rope can be threaded through the hole, and their teeth are pulled out. The bears' nomadic handlers ply tourist traps in Agra and Jaipur. According to the World Wide Fund for Nature (WWF), around 70,000 snakes (including the endangered king cobra) perish annually due to the dreadful living conditions they experience in captivity, particularly with snake charmers.

If you are concerned about the welfare of animals, don't take an interest in snake charming, bear dancing, photographic monkeys and other sideshow acts that exploit animals – don't take their photographs or give money. For information on elephant welfare, see The Amber Elephants, p179.

Monumental Mission
A number of monuments in Rajasthan are suffering irreparable damage from tourism and government indifference. One of the most threatened is Jaisalmer Fort, which has been listed in the New York–based World Monuments Watch list of 100 endangered sites worldwide. See Golden City Blues, p324, for information on how you can help save the fort. Other monuments in dire need of protection include the painted *havelis* (traditional, ornately decorated residences) of Shekhawati. You can help to reverse the damage by volunteering in conservation and restoration efforts – see p369.

impact. The Yamuna River is also horrendously polluted. In Agra, concerns that air pollution was affecting the Taj Mahal led to the designation of a 4km traffic-free zone around the building in 1994. In 1999 polluting factories in the area were closed, and illegal buildings within 500m were torn down (unfortunately, no provision was made for those affected by these rulings).

Plastic Waste
Almost everywhere in Rajasthan, Delhi and Agra, plastic bags and bottles clog drains, litter the city streets and deserts, and even stunt the growth of grass in parks. Of growing concern are the number of cows, elephants and other creatures that consume this plastic waste (see Animal Aid Society, p84). The antiplastic lobby estimates that about 70% of the plastics used in India is discarded within a week and only about 15% is recycled.

Deforestation
There are regular problems between villagers and the authorities running Rajasthan's sanctuaries as they battle over resources. The dense forests that covered the Aravalli Range prior to Independence are thinning rapidly. Before Independence, villagers were forbidden to encroach on these forests, which were the hunting preserves of the nobility. However, following Independence, huge numbers of trees were felled to meet increasing timber, fuel and fodder requirements, and in line with population growth this trend is continuing.

The alarming disappearance of the Aravalli forests has provoked government intervention, and some areas are now closed periodically to enable

'The alarming disappearance of the Aravalli forests has provoked government intervention'

JUST ADD WATER

Irrigating India's vast arid lands has long been the dream of rulers and politicians. The Indira Gandhi Canal was initiated in 1957 and, though it is still incomplete, it includes an amazing 9709km of canals, with the main canal stretching 649km. Critics suggest that the massive project, connected with Bhakra Dam in Punjab, was concerned with short-term economics and politics to the detriment of the long-term ecology of the region.

The canal has opened up large tracts of the arid western region for cash crops, but these tracts are managed by wealthy landowners rather than the rural poor. Environmentalists say that soil has been destroyed through over-irrigation, and indigenous plants have suffered, adding to the degeneration of the arid zone. Furthermore, sections of the Indira Gandhi Canal are built on traditional grazing grounds, to which graziers are now denied access. The canal has also been blamed for breeding malaria-carrying mosquitoes.

In 2008, the waters from India's largest westward flowing river, the Narmada, which were dammed in highly controversial circumstances, trickled into Rajasthan's drought-ravaged regions of Jalore and Barmer. The miraculous appearance of the water brought untold joy to the long-suffering villagers. However, the entire Narmada River project has been heavily criticised both on environmental grounds and for displacing a large number of tribal people in the Narmada Valley.

the forest to regenerate. However, the closed regions are poorly policed, and locals are also entitled to take dry wood from the areas. There is simply not enough wood for everyone, so villagers ringbark healthy trees, returning later to remove the dead timber. Residents of the villages that surround Ranthambhore and Sariska regularly clash with the authorities, as these villagers illegally remove wood from the protected areas.

Conservation

The best way to combat desertification is afforestation. Trees provide food, fodder, fuel and timber, and they also stabilise the earth and act as windbreaks, lessening the damage caused by sandstorms.

The first official recognition of the advancement of the Thar Desert and the alarming ramifications of this for the inhabitants of the arid zone occurred in 1951. As a result, in 1952 the Desert Afforestation Research Station was established in Jodhpur to conduct research into the problems of desertification (the research station became the Central Arid Zone Research Institute in 1959). This is the most important institute of its type in south Asia.

The institute's endeavours include stabilising the shifting sand dunes, establishing silvipastoral (where trees are grown alongside shrubs that can be used for livestock feed) and fuel-wood plantations, planting windbreaks to reduce wind speed and subsequent erosion, rehabilitating degraded forests, and starting afforestation of barren hill slopes.

Some of the institute's work has been criticised by conservationists, who claim that massive attempts to irrigate and afforest the arid zone alter its fragile composition. An afforestation project along the Indira Gandhi Canal has come under attack, as the indigenous phog plant is being uprooted and replaced with fast-growing non-native species such as a hybrid *Eucalyptus* and *Acacia tortilis*. Such species upset the desert ecosystem, are of little nutritional or practical use to villagers, and reduce traditional grazing grounds (animal husbandry is the economic staple and traditional livelihood for most of the inhabitants of Rajasthan's 11 desert districts). Environmentalists argue that development should promote the generation and conservation of desert species that are attuned and adapted to the local environment, and provide food, fodder and fuel.

Several organisations work to regenerate the ecosystem and promote environmentally sustainable development. **Tarun Bharat Sangh** (Young India Organisation; ☎ 01465-225043; www.tarunbharatsangh.org; Tarun Ashram, Bhikampura, Via Thangazi, District Alwar 301022) is an acclaimed nongovernmental organisation (NGO) involved in water-harvesting projects. It constructs small dams to collect rainwater using traditional technology and local labour. Since 1974 it has set up more than 4000 structures.

The **Central Arid Zone Research Institute** (CAZRI; ☎ 029-2740584, www.cazri.res.in; Light Industrial Area, Jodhpur 342003) focuses on the problems of desertification. It has a small pictorial museum with a photographic exhibition illustrating the institute's work.

Ubeshwar Vikas Mandal (chand67@bppl.net.in; 125 Priyadarshini Nagar Bedla Rd, Udaipur) is a small NGO studying and promoting sustainable agriculture, and focusing on methods such as rainwater harvesting.

In Shekhawati, Ramesh Jangid has pioneered inspirational ecological measures at his resort, Apani Dhani, a unique project in Rajasthan. See p277 for more information.

Delhi

JOHN HAY

DELHI

Delhi

Delhi, India's fascinating and frenzied capital, rewards those who refuse to allow its less-lovable elements to overshadow their stay. With patience, perseverance and a sense of humour, the creaky old city becomes increasingly more loveable the more time you spend here.

Some Delhi attributes work surprisingly well: the plentiful ATM machines, the train ticket booking system, the luxurious top-end hotels and the impressive metro system, whilst others – the greedy rickshaw drivers and crooked con-artists – stubbornly refuse to toe the line.

Broadly speaking, Delhi comprises two distinct halves. Spacious and planned, southern New Delhi was built in the early 20th century as the British imperial capital, with Lutyens' neoclassical architecture, wide boulevards and open spaces. This area remains a political and business hub, its southern and western suburbs home to semipermanent foreigners – many embassy workers.

Meanwhile, to the north, Old Delhi was once the capital of Islamic India, built by the Mughals in the 17th century. Today it's an eclectic blend of ancient history and modern chaos, housing many of Delhi's greatest sites, including Jama Masjid and the sprawling Red Fort.

As one of India's busiest international gateways, Delhi is a natural starting and ending point for travel into Rajasthan. With just a day or two to spare, you can easily dip beneath Delhi's surface, soaking up the medieval bazaars of Old Delhi, visiting top-notch museums, reviving over a frothy cappuccino, then taking your dining pick from anything from a local street-food extravaganza to a perfect wood-fired pizza.

HIGHLIGHTS

- Wander the **Red Fort** (p96), an evocative testament to the Mughal emperors
- Stroll through Lutyens' **New Delhi** (p101), experiencing Victorian imperial designs on a grand scale
- Gape at the **Jama Masjid** (p98), India's largest mosque, built by Shah Jahan
- Head out to the soaring **Qutb Minar** (p126) tower, built to proclaim the arrival of Islam
- Sip a mojito in a slick **Connaught Place bar** (p117), then chow down on **Old Delhi street food** (p113) near Chandni Chowk for a tenth of the price

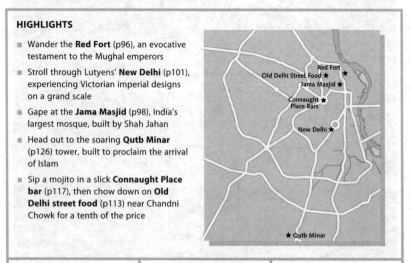

Red Fort
Old Delhi Street Food ★ ★
Jama Masjid ★
Connaught ★
Place Bars
New Delhi ★
★ Qutb Minar

| AREA: 1483 SQ KM | POPULATION: 12.8 MILLION | TELEPHONE CODE: 011 |

THE EIGHT INCARNATIONS OF DELHI

Remains of many of Delhi's eight cities are still visible today; here's a quick list of what was where, and when.

Qutb Minar area:

First City (1060) Lal Kot was founded by the Tomar Rajput clan, as the first 'official' Delhi incarnation.

Second City (1303) Siri, a citadel located near modern Hauz Khas village, was built by Central Asian king Ala-ud-din.

Third City (1321) Tughlaqabad (p126), a fortified city, was built by Ala-ud-din's successor; though short-lived, its ruins remain.

Fourth City (1326) Jahanpanah, a second Tughlaq creation, was proclaimed.

New Delhi Area:

Fifth City (1354) Firozabad (p99), a fortified palace, was founded by Firoz Shah Kotla.

Sixth City (1533) Purana Qila (p104), was founded by Afghan king Sher Shah Suri, located near the present day India Gate.

Old Delhi Area:

Seventh City (1638) Shahjahanabad (Old Delhi) was built by Mughal Emperor Shah Jahan.

New Delhi Area:

Eighth City (1931) New Delhi was inaugurated by the British, as the jewel in their colonial crown.

HISTORY

Delhi's history is as colourful and tumultuous as it is ancient. Many have desired and invaded the city, but the old saying that 'whoever establishes a new city at Delhi will doubtless lose it' has so far always come true – it remains to be seen whether its modern-day takeover by the moneyed middle classes will suffer the same fate.

Officially, Delhi has comprised eight distinct cities (only the last one of which was actually named Delhi), though in practice there have been many periods between the foundation of each separate 'city' during which control over Delhi changed hands multiple times. For a brief run-down of its various major incarnations, see the box above.

The first four cities of Delhi were all to the south, around the area where the Qutb Minar still stands. The far older settlement of Indraprastha, though, which featured in the epic Mahabharata over 3000 years ago, is the earliest known incarnation of Delhi (not officially counted as one of its eight incarnations) and was centred just east of India Gate in New Delhi.

In 1060, a Rajput clan named the Tomars founded Lal Kot, the first 'official' Delhi. This was followed by Siri (p107), a citadel built in 1303 by the unpopular king Ala-ud-din,

member of the Central Asian Turk clan, the Khiljis, who took Delhi in 1290. His lieutenant, Ghiyus-ud-din Tughlaq, followed in Ala-ud-din's footsteps, inaugurating Delhi's third incarnation, Tughlaqabad, in 1321, whose evocative ruins still stand (p126). The fourth Delhi, Jahanpanah, dates from 1326, a Tughlaq creation of Ghiyus-ud-din's successor.

The fifth Delhi, Firozabad (p99), consisting largely of a big fortified palace, was built in 1354 by next-in-line Sultan Firoz Shah Kotla in present-day New Delhi. Then, in 1398, Delhi fell prey to the whims of Central Asian warlord Tamerlane, and was completely sacked. Following a period of wrangling for power by the remaining locals, the area was re-established by the Punjabi Lodi sultans, whose mark can still be seen today in the tombs at the Lodi Gardens (p107).

The sixth city of Delhi, however, was not to appear until 1533, when the Afghan king Sher Shah Suri, also known as Emperor Sher Shah, took the city and built a citadel at Purana Qila (p104), near the spot where the ancient Indraprastha is thought to have stood. Emperor Shah Jahan, grandson of the famous Akbar who moved his court to the doomed Fatehpur Sikri (p142), constructed Shahjahanabad, Old Delhi, in 1638, thus shifting the Mughal capital back from Agra.

Finally, the eighth Delhi, New Delhi, was built almost 300 years later by the British, following the eventual fall of the Mughal empire and the rise of the British Raj. The moving of the capital of British India from Kolkata (Calcutta) to Delhi was announced in 1911 but construction was not finished, and the city officially inaugurated, until 1931. In 1947 it became the capital of modern India.

ORIENTATION

Although Delhi sprawls for miles (its official city limits encompass 1483 sq km), it's relatively easy to navigate. Probably the best way to get oriented is to begin by taking a stroll around central Connaught Place, upon which the characters of southern New Delhi and northern Old Delhi seem to converge.

Just north of Connaught Place, you'll find New Delhi railway station, the starting point for your journeys to Rajasthan and beyond. On the opposite side of the chaotic Chelmsford Rd is Paharganj, a labyrinthine conglomeration of bargain-basement hotels, souvenir shops and 'tourist restaurants', which services the needs of most of Delhi's budget travellers.

Further north, you'll reach Old Delhi, home to the Red Fort, Jama Masjid, and Chandni Chowk, Old Delhi's congested principal thoroughfare. In Old Delhi, you'll also find the main Inter State Bus Terminal (ISBT). Further north again, you'll find Majnu-ka Tilla, also known as the Tibetan Colony, a peaceful budget accommodation alternative to Paharganj.

Directly south from Connaught Place is India Gate and the impressive buildings of Lutyens' New Delhi. Broad, commanding Rajpath runs from India Gate to the Presidential Palace. Beyond this, to the south and west are affluent South Delhi suburbs and numerous pleasant shopping areas. Many top-end hotels are here, in the 'diplomatic enclave' of Chanakyapuri, tucked between central Delhi and the airport to the south-west.

Further south still, you'll find the Qutb Minar (p126), and the crumbling ruins of Tughlaqabad (p126).

To get around, either take an auto-rickshaw or taxi trip, for an 'on the ground' orientation, or the spanking new metro system (p125) which will whisk you – in underground serenity – to your chosen destination.

Maps

The free *AA City Maps Delhi Map*, which can be picked up in cafés and tourist spots, is a good basic map, with information on Delhi monuments, embassy phone numbers, train times and even a diagram of the airport. For exceedingly more detail, Eicher produces the 245-page *Eicher City Map* (Rs 290) and *Delhi Road Map* (Rs 75), available at most bookshops and newsstands.

INFORMATION
Bookshops

Delhi has dozens of wonderful bookshops, many conveniently located around Connaught Place. Other good areas to browse for books are the Khan Market (p120) and the Daryaganj Sunday Book Market (p119). For cut-price titles, you'll find plenty of roadside book stalls to peruse; beware that pages might be badly set, eclectically ordered, or missing that crucial last page telling you whodunnit.

CONNAUGHT PLACE AREA
Bookworm (Map p100; ☎ 23322260; 29 B-Block; ✆ 10.15am-7.30pm)
English Book Store (Map p100; ☎ 23415031; 17 L-Block; ✆ 10am-7pm Mon-Sat)
New Book Depot (Map p100; ☎ 23320020; 18 B-Block; ✆ 11am-8pm Mon-Sat)

KHAN MARKET
Bahri & Sons (Map pp102-3; ☎ 24694610; ✆ 11am-7.30pm Mon-Sat)
Full Circle Bookstore (Map pp102-3; ☎ 24655641; ✆ 10am-7.30pm Mon-Sat)

SOUTH EXTENSION
Timeless (Map pp92-3; ☎ 24693257; 46 Housing Society, South Extension Part 1; ✆ 10am-7pm) Tucked away in a back lane, Timeless specialises in quality coffee-table books and offers complimentary tea.

Cultural Centres & Libraries

Many of Delhi's libraries and cultural centres host exhibitions and seminars, dance, music and theatrical performances. Check listings (opposite) for details.
Alliance Française (Map pp102-3; ☎ 43500200; 72 Lodi Estate)
British Council (Map p100; ☎ 23710111; 17 Kasturba Gandhi Marg)
Delhi Public Library (Map p97; ☎ 23979297; SP Mukherjee Marg)

India Habitat Centre (Map pp102-3; ☎ 43662026; Lodi Rd)

Italian Embassy Institute of Culture (Map pp102-3; ☎ 26871901; 50E Chandragupta Marg, Chanakyapuri)

Max Mueller Bhavan (Map pp102-3; ☎ 23329506; 3 Kasturba Gandhi Marg)

Tibet House Library (Map pp102-3; ☎ 24611515; 1 Institutional Area, Lodi Rd)

Internet Access

There aren't too many internet cafés around Connaught Place, but Paharganj makes up for this with a whole slew of places to check your email. Most charge from Rs 5 to print a black-and-white A4 page and Rs 30 to scan or write a CD.

Cyber Graphics (Map pp102-3; Khan Market; per 30min Rs 50; ☽ 10.30am-7pm)

Cyber Station (Map p110; Main Bazaar, Paharganj; per 30min Rs 10; ☽ 7.30am-10pm)

DSIDC Cyber Café (Map p100; N-Block, Connaught Pl; per hr Rs 50; ☽ 9am-8pm Mon-Sat)

Laundry

Most budget and midrange hotels offer a laundry service for a decent rate (top-end places may charge an arm and a leg for a shirt and trousers). If you're feeling earth-conscious, lug your laundry to the 'eco friendly garment care' **Guardini Drycleaners** (Map pp102-3; Khan Market; ☎ 24622000; dry cleaning coat/suit/skirt Rs 185/280/175; ☽ 11am-7.30pm Mon-Sun).

Media

The charmingly old-fashioned, but very accurate, *Delhi City Guide* (Rs 20) and *Delhi Diary* (Rs 10) both include a Delhi map, as does *Explore Delhi* (Rs 20). *First City* (Rs 30) is a slick monthly magazine with comprehensive listings/reviews, while the fortnightly *Time Out Delhi* magazine (Rs 30) makes a great, hip introduction to the city. All are available at most newsstands and bookshops.

Medical Services

There are plenty of pharmacies around Connaught Place, and in all Delhi's markets.

All India Institute of Medical Sciences (AIIMS; Map pp92-3; ☎ 26588500, ambulance 1099; Ansari Nagar) Has a 24-hour ambulance emergency service.

Apollo Hospital (Off Map pp92-3; ☎ 26925858; www .apollohospdelhi.com; Mathura Rd, Sarita Vihar)

Dr Ram Manohar Lohia Hospital (Map pp102-3; ☎ 23365525; Baba Kharak Singh Marg) Another hospital with 24-hour emergency facilities.

East West Medical Centre (Map pp92-3; ☎ 24623738; www.eastwestrescue.com; B-28 Greater Kailash Part 1) A private clinic housed in an unassuming white building opposite N-Block Market.

Money
ATMS

ATMs (24 hours) linked to international networks are plentiful throughout Delhi. Most accept Visa, MasterCard, Cirrus, Maestro and American Express.

Bank of Punjab (Map p110; Hotel Ajanta, 36 Arakashan Rd, Paharganj)

Citibank Basant Lok (Map pp92-3; Vasant Vihar); cnr C-Block & K-Block (Map p100; Connaught Pl); Jeevan Bharati Bldg (Map p100; 3rd fl, Connaught Pl)

HDFC (Map p110; Main Bazaar, Paharganj)

ICICI Connaught Pl (Map p100; 9A Phelps Bldg); Paharganj (Map p110; Rajguru Rd).

UTI (Map p110; Rajguru Rd, Paharganj)

FOREIGN CURRENCY & TRAVELLERS CHEQUES

The following change major currencies and travellers cheques.

American Express (Map p100; ☎ 23719506; A-Block, Connaught Pl; ☽ 9.30am-6.30pm Mon-Fri, to 2.30pm Sat) Also has an Amex-only ATM.

Central Bank of India (Map pp102-3; ☎ 26110101, ext 3584; Ashok Hotel, Chanakyapuri; ☽ 24hr)

Chequepoint Foreign Exchange (Baluja Forex; Map p110; ☎ 51541523; 4596 Main Bazaar, Paharganj; ☽ 9am-8.30pm) Cash advances on MasterCard and Visa.

Thomas Cook (Map p100; ☎ 23416585; C-33, Connaught Pl; ☽ 10am-4pm Mon-Fri; 10am-1pm Sat) Exchanges travellers cheques, foreign currency, and provides cash advances on credit cards. Also arranges international money transfers. There's another branch at the Imperial Hotel (p113).

INTERNATIONAL MONEY TRANSFERS

Thomas Cook (see above) arranges money transfers from its Connaught Place branch.

Western Union (Map p100; ☎ 23311133; Sita World Travels, F-Block, Connaught Pl; ☽ 9.30am-9pm Mon-Sat, to 6pm Sun) There are numerous citywide branches, including a counter at the Connaught Place post office branch (see Post & Telephone).

Opticians

Delhi is a good place to pick up new frames, glasses or contact lenses. A good, swift central choice is listed here.

Optical Corner of India (Map p100; D-block, Connaught Pl; ☽ 10am-1.30pm, 2.30-7pm daily) Prescription and

DELHI

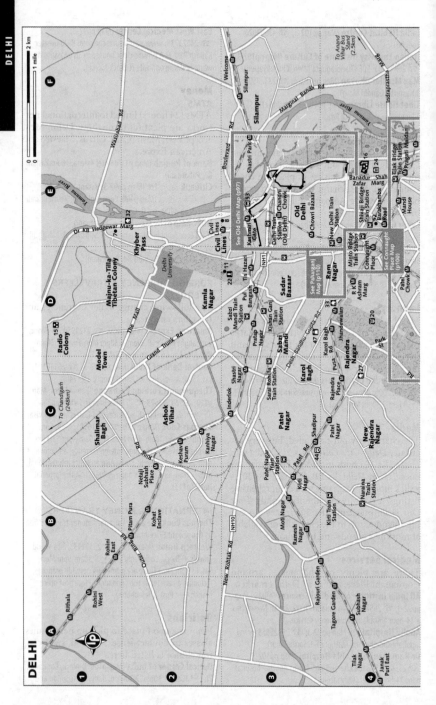

DELHI

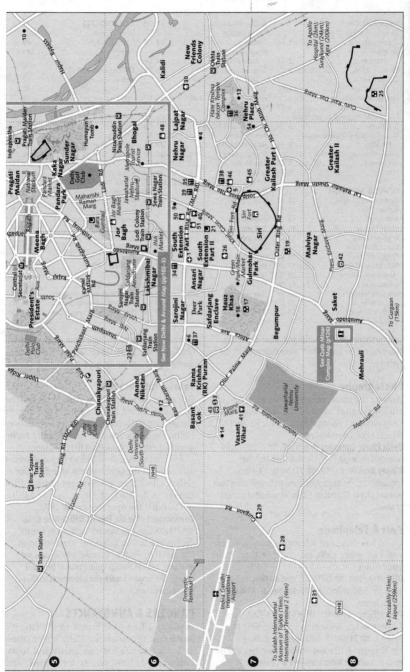

nonprescription glasses available with a one-day service. Also check out the lenses which 'allow more room for the eyelashes'.

Photography

Among the usual photographic services (including digital needs), the following both snap passport photos (four/10 for Rs 70/120), which take 10 minutes.

Delhi Photo Company (Map p100; ☎ 23320577; 78 Janpath, Connaught Pl; ☯ 9.30am-7pm Mon-Sat)

Kinsey Bros (Map p100; ☎ 23324446; 2 A-Block, Connaught Pl; ☯ 10am-7pm Mon-Sat) Downloading from memory card to CD costs Rs 170 for an unlimited amount of photos.

Post & Telephone

Delhi has scores of telephone kiosks, where you can make calls for cheaper than from your hotel.

DHL (Map p100; ☎ 23737587; Vandana Bldg, 11 Tolstoy Marg; ☯ 9.30am-8pm Mon-Fri, to 9pm Sat) A reliable courier option.

Post offices Connaught Pl (Map p100; 6 A-Block; 10am-7.30pm Mon-Sat); New Delhi main post office (GPO; Map pp102-3; ☎ 23364111; Baba Kharak Singh Marg; ☯ 10am-1pm & 1.30-5pm Mon-Sat, 10am-1pm Sun) The main post office is 500m southwest of Connaught Pl, and

has a poste-restante facility; ensure mail is addressed to GPO, New Delhi, 110001. The Connaught Pl branch is most conveniently located but has no poste restante.

Tourist Information

Beware of the many profit-driven, overpriced and substandard travel agencies and others posing as 'tourist information centres' all over Delhi. Do not be fooled – head straight to the government tourist office listed below.

For contact details of Indian regional tourist offices ask at the Government of India Tourist Office, check state government tourist office listings in the back of *First City* (see Media, p91) or dial the operator on ☎ 197.

Government of India Tourist Office (Map p100; ☎ 23320005/8; www.incredibleindia.org; 88 Janpath; ☯ 9am-6pm Mon-Fri, to 2pm Sat); international airport (☎ 25691171; ☯ 24hr) Dispenses advice, maps and brochures, and can arrange guided tours of Delhi and beyond. The Janpath branch also investigates tourism-related complaints.

DANGERS & ANNOYANCES

If you're a first-time visitor to the city, it's important to remember Delhi's reputation as India's centre for con artists and touts. Forewarned, however, is forearmed, and you'll generally find scammers fairly innocuous if you simply ignore them or call their bluff. Failing that, there's a special 'tourist police' squad, in clearly marked jeeps (each with English-speaking police, usually including one woman) stationed at tourist centres, including the international airport, New Delhi train station and Janpath. Female travellers should also take a look at p372.

Scams

There are a number of scams operating in Delhi – be extra cautious around tourist hubs. See Dodging Delhi's Dodgy Dealers (below) for a summary of practical tips.

HOTEL TOUTS

Touts often materialise in the form of taxi-wallahs, most frequently at the international airport. These sneaky drivers will try to persuade you that your hotel is full, poor value, or is no longer there at all, and will try to take you elsewhere. Some will go one step further, 'kindly' taking you to a 'tourist office' where a colleague in cahoots will phone your hotel on your behalf, and corroborate the driver's story. In reality, of course, he's talking to someone in the next room. The taxi-wallah will then drop you at the hotel of *his* choice, where he gets a plump commission and you get a high room rate.

TOURS & TOURIST INFORMATION SCAMS

No matter what the touts might tell you, there are only a couple of official, government-run tourist offices in the city. The others are privately owned, often offering inflated prices. For tourist information, only go to the tourist offices listed on opposite.

You should be even more careful when booking multiday tours out of Delhi. Lonely Planet receives frequent reports from travellers who booked and paid upfront, only to find that their 'all inclusive tour' failed to include entrance fees to major sites, provided terrible accommodation, or simply didn't travel to the places they were promised. Several travellers, too, have been sold 'lake' or 'river cruises', only to be ferried up to Kashmir, where violence and instability remain a security worry.

TRAIN TICKET SCAMS

At the New Delhi train station, touts may try to stop you from booking tickets at the upstairs (1st-floor) International Tourist

---

DODGING DELHI'S DODGY DEALERS

- Ignore taxi touts who tell you that your hotel is closed/full/burning down and try to take you to their 'booking office'. Tell persistent taxi drivers that you've paid for your hotel in advance, so there's no point taking you elsewhere and, if they continue, ask that they stop the car so that you can write down the registration plate number. Just to be sure, call or email to confirm your hotel booking, if possible, 24 hours before check-in.

- Walk on by the touts who congregate at the New Delhi Railway Station, and who'll do their best to convince you that the International Tourist Bureau is closed/being renovated/just across the road. They're lying, to which warning signs all over the station attest.

- Ignore touts who surreptitiously dirty one of your shoes or offer you a free, trial ear-cleaning in one ear.

- Agree in advance a fee for any journey by taxi or rickshaw, or insist the meter is put on (checking that it's been reset since the last passenger). If you run into any problems, threaten to telephone the tourist or transport police or, if you're near a prepaid booth, suggest you accompany the driver there to sort out the dispute.

- Beware of unscrupulous travel agents who'll try to sell you expensive, low standard tours, or trips to trouble spots (including Srinagar). If you're planning on booking a tour, only use agents accredited with organisations such as the Travel Agents Association of India, the Indian Association of Tour Operators and the Adventure Tour Operators Association of India – ask to see their accreditation.

- Never accompany any friendly individual who stops to offer help or directions, then suggests you should go to visit their shop: it'll likely be hard-sell all the way.

Bureau and attempt to divert you to one of the (overpriced and often unreliable) travel agencies over the road. Other tricksters may insist your ticket needs to be stamped (for a hefty fee payable to them) before it's valid – another scam. Still more may try to convince wait-listed passengers that there's a charge to check their reservation status – don't fall for it, no matter how hard the patter.

SIGHTS
Old Delhi & Around

The atmospheric, unruly remains of the 17th-century walled city of Shahjahanabad (Old Delhi) sprawl west from the Red Fort, though they were at one time surrounded by a sturdy defensive wall, only fragments of which now exist. The **Kashmiri Gate**, at the northern end of the walled city, was the scene of desperate fighting when the British retook Delhi during the 1857 Indian Uprising. West of here is the British-erected **Mutiny Memorial** (Map pp92–3), dedicated to soldiers who died during the Uprising. Near the monument is an **Ashoka Pillar** (Map pp92–3); like the one in Firoz Shah Kotla (p99), brought here by Firoz Shah.

RED FORT (LAL QILA)

The sandstone **Red Fort** (Map p97; Indian/foreigner Rs 10/250, children under 15 free, video Rs 25; ☽ sunrise-sunset Tue-Sun) once represented everything glorious about the peak of the Mughal empire; today, it seems a rather forlorn shadow of its former grand self.

Shah Jahan began construction of the fort in 1638 and it was completed a decade later. It was actually Shah Jahn's son, sly and conniving Aurangzeb, who moved his capital here from Agra, after deposing and imprisoning his father in Agra Fort. Aurangzeb himself became the first and last great Mughal emperor to rule from here.

Tickets to the fort are available from the dedicated tourist counter at the kiosk (Map p97) on the plaza to the left of the main Lahore Gate.

Lahore Gate

The fort's **main gate** (Map p97), named for the fact that it faces toward Lahore, now in Pakistan, became a symbol for the nationalist movement's fight against the British. The nationalists wished to see India's flag flown atop it; this was finally achieved in 1947. Entering the fort here, you immediately find yourself in the vaulted arcade

known as the **Chatta Chowk** (Covered Bazaar; Map p97). The shops in the arcade here once sold items that the royal household might have fancied – silks, jewellery and gold – though they now hawk tourist wares.

The arcade leads to **Naubat Khana** (Drum House; Map p97), where musicians used to play for the emperor. There's an **Indian War Memorial Museum** (Map p97; admission Rs 2; ☽ 10am-5pm Tue-Sun) upstairs. The open courtyard beyond the Naubat Khana once had galleries along either side, but these were removed by the British army when the fort was used as its headquarters. Other reminders of the British presence are the three-storey barrack blocks situated to the courtyard's north.

Diwan-i-Am

This elegant chamber (Hall of Public Audience; Map p97) was where the emperor would sit to hear complaints or disputes from his subjects, and was once set with precious stones, many of which were looted following the 1857 Uprising; it was restored following a directive from Lord Curzon, viceroy of India, between 1898 and 1905.

Diwan-i-Khas

Constructed of white marble, this room (Hall of Private Audience; Map p97) was the emperor's luxurious private meeting chamber. In 1760 the Marathas removed its silver ceiling, and today it's a shadow of its former glory.

Royal Baths

Next to the Diwan-i-Khas are the **hammams** (baths; Map p97), three large rooms surmounted by domes, with a fountain in the centre (one was set up as a sauna). The floors once had *pietra dura* (marble inlay), and the rooms were illuminated through panels of coloured glass in the roof.

Shahi Burj

This modest, three-storey, octagonal **tower** (Map p97) at the north-eastern edge of the fort was once Shah Jahan's private working area. From here, water used to flow south through the Royal Baths, the Diwan-i-Khas, the Khas Mahal and the Rang Mahal.

Moti Masjid

Built in 1659 by Aurangzeb for his own personal use, this small marble mosque (Pearl Mosque; Map p97) is next to the baths. Its

OLD DELHI

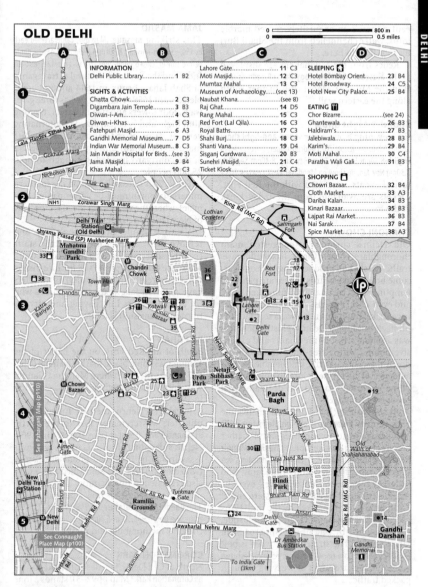

0 — 800 m
0 — 0.5 miles

INFORMATION
Delhi Public Library...............1 B2

SIGHTS & ACTIVITIES
Chatta Chowk.........................2 C3
Digambara Jain Temple..........3 B3
Diwan-i-Am...........................4 C3
Diwan-i-Khas.........................5 C3
Fatehpuri Masjid.....................6 A3
Gandhi Memorial Museum.....7 D5
Indian War Memorial Museum.8 C3
Jain Mandir Hospital for Birds...(see 3)
Jama Masjid...........................9 B4
Khas Mahal...........................10 C3

Lahore Gate..........................11 C3
Moti Masjid..........................12 C3
Mumtaz Mahal......................13 C3
Museum of Archaeology......(see 13)
Naubat Khana.......................(see 8)
Raj Ghat...............................14 D5
Rang Mahal..........................15 C3
Red Fort (Lal Qila)................16 C3
Royal Baths..........................17 C3
Shahi Burj.............................18 C3
Shanti Vana..........................19 D4
Sisganj Gurdwara..................20 B3
Sunehri Masjid......................21 C4
Ticket Kiosk.........................22 C3

SLEEPING
Hotel Bombay Orient............23 B4
Hotel Broadway....................24 C5
Hotel New City Palace..........25 B4

EATING
Chor Bizarre.......................(see 24)
Ghantewala..........................26 B3
Haldiram's............................27 B3
Jalebiwala............................28 B3
Karim's.................................29 B4
Moti Mahal...........................30 C4
Paratha Wali Gali..................31 B3

SHOPPING
Chowri Bazaar......................32 B4
Cloth Market.........................33 A3
Dariba Kalan.........................34 B3
Kinari Bazaar........................35 B3
Lajpat Rai Market..................36 B3
Nai Sarak.............................37 B4
Spice Market........................38 A3

outer walls are oriented exactly in symmetry with the rest of the fort, while the inner walls are slightly askew, so that it has the correct orientation toward Mecca.

Other Features

The **Khas Mahal** (Map p97), south of the Diwan-i-Khas, was the emperor's private palace, divided into rooms for worship, sleeping and living.

The **Rang Mahal** (Palace of Colour; Map p97), which is located further south again, took its name from its painted interior, which is now gone. This was once the residence of the emperor's chief wife, and is where the emperor ate. On the floor in the centre there's an exquisitely carved marble lotus; water channelled from the Shahi Burj used to flow to here.

Relics from the Mughal era are displayed at the **Museum of Archaeology** (Map p97; admission Rs 2) in the Mumtaz Mahal, still further south along the eastern wall.

Sound-&-Light Show

Each evening a one-hour **sound-and-light show** (adults/children Rs 50/20, children under 3 free; ☾ in English 8.30pm Feb-Apr, 9pm May-Aug, 8.30pm Sep-Oct, 7.30pm Nov-Jan, no show on Mondays) re-creates historical events associated with the Red Fort. Tickets are available from the ticket kiosk at the fort.

CHANDNI CHOWK

Old Delhi's chronically congested main thoroughfare, **Chandni Chowk**, has it all: noise, traffic, hassle, and produce ranging from fearsome bras to fake beards. There are plenty of tempting street treats at little, unnamed stalls, and even a McDonalds, should the particular urge strike. But it was not always so. Once the pinnacle of Mughal Delhi sophistication, this was a serene street of merchants and expensive homes, with a tree-lined canal flowing down the centre. You'll still be able to spot evidence of its former glory in some crumbling, intricately carved *haveli* (traditional residence) frontages.

At the eastern (Red Fort) end, there's the 16th-century **Digambara Jain Temple** (Map p97) You need to remove your shoes and all leather before entering this temple. The **Jain Mandir Hospital for Birds** (Map p97; ☎ 23090921; donations welcomed; ☾ 9am-6pm) here is run by the Jains, who believe in the preservation of all life – even the scruffiest of street pigeons. The western end of Chandni Chowk is marked by the mid-17th-century **Fatehpuri Masjid** (Map p97) mosque, commissioned by one of the emperor Shah Jahan's wives. The stretch in-between is best tackled either on foot, or by cycle-rickshaw, whose drivers are adept at weaving through packed traffic.

SUNEHRI MASJID

Just south of the Red Fort is the **Sunehri Masjid** (Map p97). In 1739 Nadir Shah, the Persian invader, stood on the roof of this mosque and watched calmly while his soldiers conducted a bloody massacre of Delhi's inhabitants.

JAMA MASJID

This striking **mosque** (Map p97; camera/video each Rs 150; ☾ non-Muslims 8.30am-12.30pm & 1.45pm-30min before sunset, closed noon-2pm Fri) is the largest in India and the final architectural extravagance of Shah Jahan, begun in 1644 and not completed until 1658. The mosque has three gateways, four towers and two minarets standing 40m high, and is constructed of alternating vertical strips of red sandstone and white marble. The main entry point is gate No 3, the courtyard inside big enough to hold 25,000 people.

For Rs 20 it's possible to climb the southern minaret (women must be accompanied by a male), where the views from the top, especially of New Delhi, are superb.

Visitors should dress respectfully and remove their shoes at the top of the stairs (pay the shoe-minder Rs 5 upon collection). There are **guides** (per person Rs 50) for hire inside; request accredited identification as travellers have reported fake (expensive) guides who try to fool visitors into paying an entry fee (mosque admission is free).

RAJ GHAT

South of the Red Fort, on the banks of the Yamuna, a simple black-marble **platform** (Map p97) marks the spot where Mahatma Gandhi was cremated following his assassination in 1948.

Jawaharlal Nehru, the first Indian prime minister, was cremated just to the north, at **Shanti Vana** (Forest of Peace; Map p97) in 1964. Nehru's daughter, Indira Gandhi, who was assassinated in 1984, and grandsons Sanjay (who died in 1980) and Rajiv (died 1991) were also cremated in this vicinity.

The Raj Ghat area is now a beautiful park. The **Gandhi Memorial Museum** (Map p97; ☎ 23311793; admission free; ☾ 9.30am-5.30pm Tue-Sun) inside it contains memorabilia and photos.

CORONATION PARK

North of Old Delhi, in a desolate field known as **Coronation Park** (Map pp92–3), stands a lone granite obelisk commemorating the crowning here of King George V as Emperor of India. It's hard to imagine that this forgotten and windswept site was the place where, in 1877 and 1903, grandiose theatrical durbars (ceremonial gatherings), featuring the full set of Indian rulers, paid homage to Queen Victoria and her successor, Edward VII.

FESTIVALS IN DELHI

Some of Delhi's festival dates and venues are variable – for this year's details and tickets to events listed below, contact the Government of India Tourist Office (p94). Delhi celebrates Diwali (p360) and Dussehra (p359) with particular verve. During Dussehra, theatrical renditions of the Ramayana are held.

Republic Day (26 Jan) At Rajpath, incorporating an impressive military parade, complete with floats, elephants and fly-past. Tickets for 'grandstand' viewing positions can be had for Rs 150 to Rs 300 and standing-room for Rs 20 to Rs 50.

Beating of the Retreat (29 Jan) The closing of the Republic Day celebrations is marked by the Beating of the Retreat outside the presidential palace, also entailing military pageantry. Tickets (from Rs 20 to Rs 50) are available for the dress rehearsal the day before, and, more scarcely, for the event itself (from Rs 100).

Delhi Flower Show (Jan/Feb) This event spans three to four days.

Mango Festival (Jun) Running for several days at the Talkatora Gardens, this festival includes awesome mango exhibitions and mango-eating competitions.

Independence Day (15 Aug) India celebrates Independence from Britain in 1947 and the prime minister addresses the nation from the Red Fort ramparts.

Qutb Festival (Oct/Nov) This festival runs for about a week at Qutb Minar, and features classical Indian music and dance performances.

Connaught Place & Around
CONNAUGHT PLACE (CP)

The geographical heart of New Delhi is **Connaught Place**, designed by Robert Tor Russel in 1932 in architectural imitation of the famous Royal Crescent in Bath, England. Because of its composition – three concentric, colonnaded circles with seven radial roads running out from them (for some reason known as Radial Rd 2 to 8, rather than 1 to 7) – it can be a bit confusing at first to navigate, though there is some method to the madness.

The inner circle (officially known as Rajiv Chowk, though this name is seldom used) is packed with expensive shops, Western chain restaurants, bookshops and street vendors. It's divided into blocks, from A to F. You'll see which block you're on from the letter painted onto the sides of buildings at each radial road junction, and often on individual establishments' signs.

In the centre of the circle is the calm **central park**, (☼ sunrise to sunset Tue-Sun) which makes a welcome place to sip a takeaway coffee in relative peace.

The middle circle, known, unsurprisingly, as 'Middle Circle', is the smallest and least significant of the three circles, with a backstreet feel and just a scattering of hotels and small eating establishments.

The outer circle (also known as 'Connaught Circus' or 'Indira Chowk' but commonly referred to simply as part of Connaught Place), is a road teeming with breakneck traffic, and plenty of cafés, bars and hotel accommodation. Like the inner circle, it's divided into blocks: this time, lettered from G through to N.

To keep things simple, we've used only 'Connaught Pl' in addresses throughout this chapter. Connaught Place addresses have a block letter and a number, but these are not always presented in a uniform way: some establishments use '50N Block', while others adopt 'N-50' or other variations. For shopping on and around Connaught Place, see p119.

JANTAR MANTAR

Just a short stroll south from Connaught Place, this impressive collection of salmon-coloured **structures** (Map p100; Sansad Marg; Indian/foreigner Rs 5/100, camera/video Rs 4/25; ☼ 9am-sunset) was one of Jaipuri Maharaja Jai Singh II's amazing observatories. Constructed in 1725 it's dominated by a huge sundial, which looks a lot like a staircase leading to nowhere, known as **Samrat Yantra**, or Prince of Dials. Other instruments were built to plot the course of heavenly bodies and predict eclipses and, though much of the original marble coating has long since been reappropriated, it's well worth a visit, not only for the learned astronomer.

FIROZ SHAH KOTLA

The ruins of Firozabad (the fifth city of Delhi; p89), erected by Firoz Shah in 1354, can be found at **Firoz Shah Kotla** (Map pp92-3; Indian/

CONNAUGHT PLACE

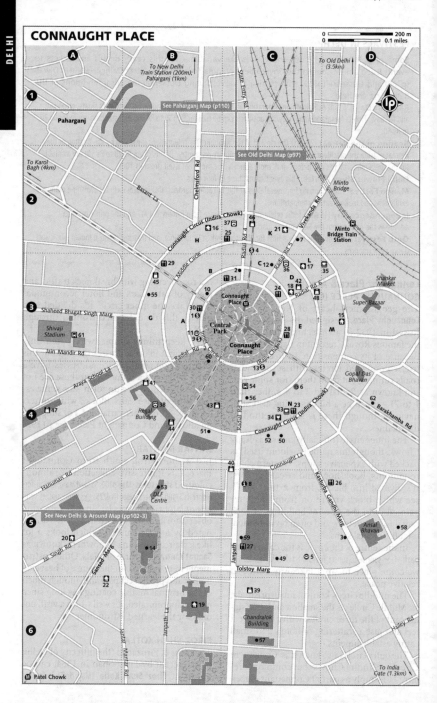

foreigner Rs 5/100, video Rs 25; ☼ sunrise-sunset), just off Bahadur Shah Zafar Marg. In the fortress-palace is a 3rd-century-BC, 13m-high sandstone Ashoka pillar where locals burn incense on Thursday nights to appease the spirits thought to live inside. The remains of an old mosque and a well can also be seen in the area, but most of Firozabad's ruins were used for the construction of later cities.

LAKSHMI NARAYAN TEMPLE (BIRLA MANDIR)

Directly west of Connaught Place is the large and welcoming Hindu **Lakshmi Narayan Temple** (Map pp92-3; Mandir Marg; ☼ 4am-1.30pm & 2.30-9pm), erected in 1938 by the rich industrialist BD Birla and opened in 1939 by Mahatma Gandhi. The main temple is dedicated to Lakshmi, goddess of wealth, while its soothing gardens make for serene respite from a Delhi day.

New Delhi & Around

New Delhi, designed by British architect Edwin Lutyens, was inaugurated on 9 February 1931 as the new administrative centre of the British empire. Though Lutyens himself hated Indian architecture, he eventually sought a compromise, creating buildings with neoclassical solidity but the occasional local flourish. Though some might argue that the two styles never really synthesised successfully, there's no doubting that New Delhi's commanding edifices remain as impressive today as when they formed the focal point of the British Raj.

RAJPATH

Immensely broad **Rajpath** (Kingsway) is a focal point of Lutyens' New Delhi where, on 26 January each year, thousands gather to witness the spectacle of the Republic Day parade (see p99).

At the eastern end of Rajpath is **India Gate** (Map pp102–3), around which families and couples like to mill aimlessly, particularly on weekends and warm evenings. Designed by Lutyens in 1921, it comprises a 42m-high memorial arch and bears the names of around 90,000 Indian army soldiers who died in WWI, the North-West Frontier operations and the 1919 Afghan fiasco. You'll also see an empty stone platform, which once held a statue of King George V, now banished to a remote spot in Coronation Park (p98).

DELHI

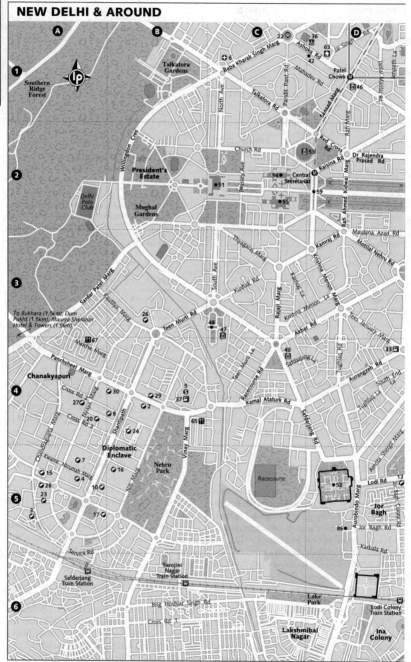

NEW DELHI & AROUND

Southern Ridge Forest

Talkatora Gardens

Baba Kharak Singh Marg

Ashoka Rd

North Ave

Talkatora Rd

Pandit Pant Marg

Mahadev Rd

Jai Singh Rd

Patel Chowk

Church Rd

Brassey Ave

President's Estate

Delhi Polo Club

Mughal Gardens

Red Cross Rd

Raisina Rd

Dr Rajendra Prasad Rd

Central Secretariat

Rafi Ahmed Kidwai Marg

Maulana Azad Rd

Thyagaraj Marg

Motilal Nehru Rd

Kamraj Rd

Sardar Patel Marg

Kautilya Marg

South Ave

Kushak Rd

Rajaji Marg

Krishna Menon Marg

Teen Murti Rd

Akbar Rd

Tees January Marg

To Bukhara (1.5km); Dum Pukht (1.5km); Maurya Sheraton Hotel & Towers (1.5km)

Melcha Marg

Teen Murti La

Racecourse Rd

Safdarjang Rd

Tughlaq Rd

Aurangzeb Rd

South End La

Panchsheel Marg

Chanakyapuri

Cross Rd 3

Nyaya Marg

Shantipath

Kamal Ataturk Rd

Vinay Marg

Tughlaq La

Chandragupta Marg

Kwame Nkrumah Marg

Diplomatic Enclave

Nehru Park

Racecourse

Lodi Rd

Jor Bagh

Nitti Marg

Amrita Shergil Marg

Aurobindo Marg

Jor Bagh Rd

Karbala Rd

Service Rd

Safdarjang Train Station

Sarojini Nagar Train Station

Lake Park

Lodi Colony Train Station

Brig Hoshiar Singh Rd

Cross Rd 1

Lakshmibai Nagar

Ina Colony

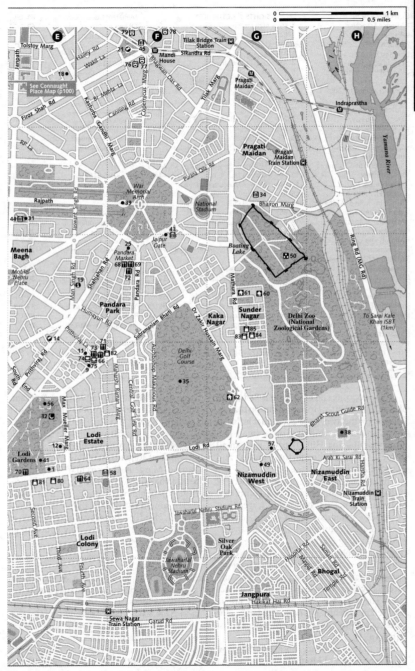

At the opposite end of Rajpath is **Rashtrapati Bhavan** (President's House; Map pp102–3), flanked by the two large **Secretariat buildings** (Map pp102–3) which sit on a small rise known as Raisina Hill. Topped with small domes, they now house the Finance and External Affairs ministries.

The official residence of the president of India, Rashtrapati Bhavan was completed in 1929. The palatial building – larger than Versailles – exhibits a blend of Mughal and Western architectural styles, includes the famous 23m-long Durbar Hall decorated with coloured marble, which took 20 years to complete. To its west is a **Mughal garden** (admission free, photography prohibited), styled on Mughal pleasure gardens by Lutyens, which occupies 130 hectares. The garden is only open to the public between mid-February and early March – for dates contact the Government of India Tourist Office (p94).

Prior to Independence, Rashtrapati Bhavan was the residence of Mountbatten, India's last viceroy, and required a vast retinue of servants to maintain the 340 rooms and extensive gardens: legend has it that there were 418 gardeners alone – 50 of them boys whose sole job was to chase away the birds.

North of Rajpath, standing at the end of Sansad Marg, is the circular, colonnaded **Sansad Bhavan** (Map pp102–3) which houses India's parliament. If you're keen to watch a parliamentary debate in progress (usually in Hindi), contact your embassy in Delhi, who will need to supply you with an introductory letter.

PURANA QILA

Back down Rajpath and east of India Gate, the crumbling citadel of **Purana Qila** (Map pp102-3; ☎ 24353178; Mathura Rd; Indian/foreigner Rs 5/110, children under 15 free, video Rs 25; ☉ sunrise-sunset) is known as the sixth city of Delhi (p89), built in 1533 by Afghan ruler Sher Shah. It's said to stand on the site of Indraprastha (p89) and marks a brief interruption in Dehli's Mughal history, the Afghan king defeating Mughal ruler Humayun, before Humayun regained control of India in 1545.

Entry is through the west gate, from which there are good views of Delhi, and beside which is a small **archaeological museum** (admission free; 10am-5pm Mon-Thu). Inside you'll find calming gardens, Sher Shah's beautifully patterned **Qila-i-Kuhran Mosque** (Mosque of Sher Shah) and, near the south gate, the small, octagonal redsandstone tower, the **Sher Mandal**, built as an observatory and later used by emperor Humayun as a library. It was while descending the stairs of this tower in 1556 that the emperor slipped and sustained injuries from which he later died. This, sadly, isn't Purana Qila's only grizzly tale: during Partition in 1947, Muslim refugees flocked here to await transport onward to Pakistan; many thousands of them didn't make it, being slaughtered on the way.

MUSEUMS & GALLERIES
National Philatelic Museum
Close to the parliament at Sansad Bhavan, this **museum** (Map pp102-3; ☎ 23036727; Sadar Patel Chowk, Sansad Marg; admission free, photography prohibited; 10am-5pm Mon-Fri) is tucked away in the Dak Bhavan post office. There are over 1600 exhibits, covering every single stamp issued since Independence, some extremely beautiful – though you really need to be a dedicated philatelist to fully appreciate the experience.

Crafts Museum
Near Pragati Maidan, due north of Purana Qila, is this tranquil **museum** (Map pp102-3; ☎ 23371817; Bhairon Marg; admission free; 10am-5pm Tue-Sun), containing a collection of traditional stalls displaying rural India's various crafts. There are craft demonstrations along with artisans selling direct to the buyer, all part of a contrived, yet still very impressive, 'village life' complex.

In addition to the reconstructed village homes is a fantastic indoor museum with several well-kept galleries; you'll also find a library and a nice fixed-price craft shop.

National Museum
On Janpath, not far from its junction with Rajpath, is the **National Museum** (Map pp102-3; ☎ 23019272; www.nationalmuseumindia.gov.in; Janpath; Indian/foreigner Rs 10/300, camera Indian/foreigner Rs 20/300, video prohibited; 10am-5pm Tue-Sun), with exhibits including Indian bronze, terracotta and wood

sculptures dating back to the Mauryan period, miniature and mural paintings, musical instruments, manuscripts, tapestries, tribal masks, swords, spears and plenty more. The most important exhibits are all grouped on the ground floor and, handily, an audio tour is included in the price of the ticket (though you'll need to leave a credit card, passport, or cash deposit). It's well worth a half-day of wandering, and perfect for a rainy monsoon morning.

Next door is the **Archaeological Survey of India** (Map pp102-3; ☎ 23010822; Janpath; 9.30am-1.30pm & 2-6pm Mon-Fri). Publications available at this office cover all the main sites in India.

National Gallery of Modern Art
This **gallery** (Map pp102-3; ☎ 23382835; Jaipur Gate; Indian/foreigner Rs 10/150, photography prohibited; 10am-5pm Tue-Sun), formerly the maharaja of Jaipur's grandiose Delhi residence, displays more than 300 contemporary paintings by Indian artists. Upstairs houses the impressive permanent collection, consisting of largely post-1930s works and representing all of India's great modern painters, while the ground floor is home to changing exhibits. Check *Time Out* or *First City* (p91) for current exhibition listings.

Nehru Memorial Museum & Planetarium
Teen Murti Bhavan, the former residence of Jawaharlal Nehru (India's first prime minister), just off Teen Murti Rd, was built as Flagstaff House for the British commander-in-chief, and now houses a **museum** (Map pp102-3; ☎ 23016734; admission free; 9.30am-5.30pm Tue-Sun) on Nehru's life and the Independence movement.

In the grounds there's also a **planetarium** (Map pp102-3; ☎ 23014504; 45min show Rs 15; in English 11.30am & 3pm Tue-Sun), one of Nehru's personal passions, which holds various wonders including equipment used by India's first cosmonaut in the 1980s.

Indira Gandhi Memorial Museum
The former residence of Prime Minister Indira Gandhi has been converted into a **museum** (Map pp102-3; ☎ 23010094; 1 Safdarjang Rd; admission free; 9.30am-4.45pm Tue-Sun). On show are some of her personal belongings, including the sari (with blood stains) she was wearing at the time of her assassination, as well as newspaper clippings, letters and photos, and the clothing

her son, Rajiv, was wearing when he too was assassinated, in 1991. On the way out, you'll pass an enclosed garden in which she walked moments before she was shot by two of her Sikh bodyguards. The path has been covered in crystal; the clear glass portion marks the spot where she collapsed.

National Museum of Natural History

Although nothing to rave about, this **museum** (Map pp102-3; ☎ 23314849; 2nd fl, FICCI Auditorium, Tansen Marg; admission free; ☻ 10am-5pm Tue-Sun) houses some noteworthy fossils such as the 160-million-year-old femur of a sauropod, the largest land animal ever to have roamed the earth. Other exhibits include stuffed armadillos and a Tibetan yak, making it a curiously diverting place to spend an hour or so.

Rail Transport Museum

Housing almost 30 locomotives and some interesting old carriages, this **museum** (Map pp92-3; ☎ 26880939; Chanakyapuri; admission Rs 10, children Rs 3, video Rs 100; ☻ 9.30am-5pm Tue-Sun) will be a hit with railway buffs. Exhibits include the maharaja of Mysore's personal train, an unusual 100-year-old monorail steam train that runs on Sundays, and various oddities such as the skull of an elephant that charged a mail train in 1894, and lost. It's an especially fun place for kids, who can travel round and round on the miniature steam train ride (an extra Rs 10/5 for adults/children), or paddle out onto the kayaking pond.

Sulabh International Museum of Toilets

Southwest of the city centre, this quirky **museum** (Off Map pp92-3; ☎ 25053646; Sulabh Complex, Mahavir Enclave, Palam Dabri Rd; admission free; ☻ 10am-5pm Mon-Sat) houses a small, intriguing collection of toilet-related paraphernalia (from 2500 BC to modern times). A free guided tour brings the loos to life.

TOMBS & SHRINES
Humayun's Tomb

Emperor Humayun had this impressive early-Mughal **tomb** (Map pp102-3; Indian/foreigner Rs 10/250, video Rs 25; ☻ sunrise-sunset), built for him in the mid-16th century by Haji Begum, his Persian-born senior wife. Elements in its design – a squat building with high arched entrances that let in light, topped by a bulbous dome and surrounded by formal gardens – were to be refined over the years to

eventually create the magnificence of Agra's Taj Mahal. Haji Begum is buried beside her husband, a fitting reward for a woman who camped outside, overseeing its construction, until it was complete.

Nizam-ud-din's Shrine

Across from Humayun's tomb, off Mathura Rd, is the popular **shrine** (Map pp102-3; ☻ 24hr) and tank of the great Muslim Sufi saint Nizam-ud-din Chishti, who died in 1325, aged 92. Its present incarnation dates from 1562, and comprises a marble building, with the inner tomb surrounded by lattice screens.

Other tombs in the area include the later grave of Princess Jahanara, favourite daughter of Shah Jahan, who stayed with her father in Agra's Red Fort during his imprisonment by Aurangzeb. Amir Khusru, disciple of Nizam-ud-din and considered by many to be the first Urdu poet, also has his tomb here, just in front of Nizam-ud-din's own mausoleum.

On most Thursdays and Fridays (from around 2pm to 8pm), the shrine plays host to hypnotic Qawwali (devotional singing), accompanied by a harmonium and tabla drums, providing a heady soundtrack with which to imbibe the land-that-time-forgot atmosphere of the tightly packed district of Nizamuddin surrounding the shrine itself.

Safdarjang's Tomb

The mid-18th-century **Safdarjang's tomb** (Map pp102-3; Aurobindo Marg; Indian/foreigner Rs 5/100, video Rs 25; ☻ sunrise-sunset) at the western end of Lodi Rd was built by the nawab of Avadh for his father, Safdarjang, and is one of the last examples of Mughal architecture created before the final remnants of the great empire collapsed. As such, it's an ornate and frothy reminder of all that was glorious and grand about the Mughals.

TEMPLES
Gurdwara Bangla Sahib

Delhi's largest **Sikh temple** (Map pp102-3; Ashoka Rd; ☻ sunrise-sunset), with its striking golden domes, is constructed at the site where the eighth Sikh guru, Harkrishan Dev, stayed when he visited Delhi in 1664. The temple tank contains water believed to have healing properties; locals still drink from it, though you might want to give that a miss. Dress conservatively, covering your head, and stop in at the information centre near the entrance to pick up a free registered guide.

Bahai House of Worship (Lotus Temple)

This 1986 **Bahai Temple** (Map pp92–3; ☎ 26444029; Kalkaji; ⏱ 9am-7pm summer, 9.30am-5.30pm winter, closed Mon), stunningly shaped like a white lotus, is especially spectacular at dusk when it's floodlit. It's set among pools and well-tended gardens, and welcomes adherents of all faiths to pray or meditate silently according to their own religion.

Remove your shoes before entering, turn off mobile phones and refrain from speaking. Photography is prohibited inside.

Akshardham Temple

On Delhi's outskirts is this huge, extravagant **temple** (Map pp92–3; www.akshardham.com; Noida Turning, National Hwy 24; admission free; ⏱ 9am-6pm Tue-Sun), a pink-sandstone and white-marble edifice inaugurated in 2005 and containing around 20,000 carved deities. Try to visit during weekdays, since the manifold attractions (including a musical fountain, a large-screen cinema and an animatronics 'Hall of Values') are best attempted when it's not too busy.

OTHER SIGHTS
Lodi Gardens

In these well-tended **gardens** (Map pp102-3; Lodi Rd; ⏱ 6am-8pm; admission free), popular with joggers and young lovers alike, are the crumbling 15th- and 16th-century tombs of a string of Sayyid and Lodi rulers, including Mubarak Shah (d 1433), Ibrahim Lodi (d 1526) and Sikander Lodi (d 1517). The **Bara Gumbad** (Map pp102–3) at the centre of the gardens is a 15th-century tomb that sports some interesting interior plasterwork, while if minitrees are your thing, head to the gardens, home to the **National Bonsai Park**, in which you can stroll Gulliver-like. It's especially nice here around 6pm, when the sun begins to set, the bats to swoop, and the tombs are illuminated, hiding – from a distance at least – centuries of graffiti.

Tibet House

Tibet House contains a small **museum** (Map pp102-3; ☎ 24611515; 1 Lodi Rd; admission Rs 10, photography prohibited; ⏱ 10am-1pm & 2-5.30pm Mon-Fri), exhibiting ceremonial items brought out of Tibet when His Holiness the Dalai Lama fled following Chinese occupation. Pieces include sacred manuscripts and *thangkas* (Tibetan cloth paintings).

There's also a library (p90), and the **Tibet House Book Corner**, which also sells Tibetan CDs (Rs 250), postcards (Rs 10), incense (from Rs 25) and prayer flags (Rs 70).

Hauz Khas Village

This urban **village** (Map pp92–3) surrounded by parkland and centred around a pleasant deer park, once held the reservoir for the second city of Delhi – Siri (p89) – the remains of which are visible on the western edge of the village. Today, Hauz Khas is a tiny, chic south-Delhi hideaway, filled with fashionable art galleries and boutiques.

A number of crumbling tombs are scattered about the reservoir area, including **Firoz Shah's tomb** (Map pp92–3), commemorating the founder of the fifth city of Delhi, while the woodlands surrounding it are a popular destination for early-morning joggers and late-evening canoodlers. Also part of the former old city of Siri, just east of Hauz Khas Village, is the **Moth-ki Masjid** (Map pp92–3), said to be one of the finest mosques in the Lodi style.

ACTIVITIES
Golf

Delhi Golf Club (Map pp92-3; ☎ 24362235; Dr Zakir Hussain Marg; foreigners weekdays/weekends Rs 1980/2640 ⏱ sunrise-sunset) is an old-fashioned institution with well-tended grounds; on weekends its fairways are pleasingly filled to capacity with Delhi notables, worthies and old-timers.

Massage & Ayurvedic Treatments

Ashtaang (Map pp92-3; ☎ 24101802; E-2 Anand Niketan; ⏱ 9am-6pm), opposite Delhi University (South Campus), offers authentic Keralan Ayurvedic treatments, such as *sirodhara* (warm oil drizzled on the forehead; 45 minutes costs Rs 1000) and *pzhichal* (oil-intensive body massage; 1¼ hours costs Rs 1200).

Beyond Looks (Map pp92-3; ☎ 26141517; lower ground fl, 15 Poorvi Marg, Vasant Vihar; ⏱ 8.30am-8.30pm) offers an olive/coconut oil massage (one hour costs Rs 400), shiatsu (one hour costs Rs 600) and *sirodhara* (1½ hours costs Rs 500).

LSA Homecare (☎ 9910397429; www.lsahomecare .com) is a (legitimate) massage service that will arrive to pamper you in your hotel room. Massages are Rs 600 to Rs 2000, facials Rs

DELHI

FAR FROM THE MADDING CROWD

If you find yourself frazzled by Delhi's oppressive summer heat, traffic snarls and pesky touts, there are some scenic spots to steal solace. In the cooler months, chill out in the pleasant grounds of **Humayun's tomb** (p106), **Qutb Minar** (p126), **Safdarjang's tomb** (p106), **Lodi Gardens** (p107), **Hauz Khas** (p107) and **Raj Ghat** (p98).

During hotter months, the bars at **top-end hotels** (p112) – with their powerful AC and comfy interiors – offer revitalising havens, worth the inflated prices for a reviving tipple. Likewise, many of Delhi's **bars** (p117) open around noon and provide cool respite, in both senses of the word. If a frothy iced-coffee would do the trick, Connaught Place is well equipped (p117), while if you just can't face the heat and hassle of yet another autorickshaw negotiation, plump for the AC comfort of the underground **metro system** (p125).

Delhi's modern AC **cineplexes** (p118) are also terrific spots to beat the summer heat without spending a fortune. Movie tickets range from Rs 50 to Rs 150, and that all-important popcorn will set you back around Rs 50.

1800 to Rs 2700, and nails and waxing Rs 650 to Rs 2700.

Swimming

Deluxe hotels have the best pools but they're restricted to guests. Some of the more modest upmarket hotels permit outsiders (for a stout amount). **Claridges Hotel** (Map pp102-3; ☎ 23010211; 12 Aurangzeb Rd; per person Rs 900), the **Radisson Hotel** (p113; per person Rs 500) and **Hotel Samrat** (Map pp102-3; ☎ 26110606; Chanakyapuri; per person Rs 300) are three to try.

COURSES

See p91 for publications containing up-to-the-minute details of various courses.

Meditation & Yoga

Telephone for session timings and, if not stated below, venues. Where there are no fees, donations are appreciated.

Ashtaang (Map pp92-3; ☎ 24101802; E-2 Anand Niketan; 1hr Rs 500) Beginner and advanced hatha yoga, including meditation.

Dhyan Foundation (www.dhyanfoundation.com) Meditation classes plus one-day workshops introducing participants to *sanatan kriya* (rotation exercises, yoga and meditation). Check the website for details and various Delhi branch phone numbers.

Laughter Yoga (☎ 27217164) Giggle yourself to well-being with an early-morning laughter yoga session in one of Delhi's parks.

Morarji Desai National Institute of Yoga (Map pp102-3; ☎ 23730417; www.yogamdniy.com; 68 Ashoka Rd) Includes pranayama and hatha yoga, meditation, stress-management and various diploma courses.

Studio Abhyas (☎ 26962757) Yoga classes (1¼ hours) combine asanas (fixed body positions), pranayama and

meditation. There's Vedic chanting on some evenings and Pilates classes too.

Sushumna Studio (☎ 9871930150) Ashtanga, yoga-lates (a yoga-Pilates combo) and other classes, taught by a London-trained expert.

Tushita Meditation Centre (☎ 26513400) Twice-weekly Tibetan/Buddhist meditation sessions.

DELHI FOR CHILDREN

Though Delhi might not seem the obvious destination for tiny people, there's a wealth of activities to entertain both big and small. Cultural centres often have activities on offer: check *Time Out* listings (p91).

For a day outdoors, head first to **Delhi Zoo** (Map pp102-3; Indians/foreigners Rs 10/50; ☼ 8am-6pm Sat-Thu in summer, 9am-5pm Sat-Thu in winter), the biggest zoo in India (though in quite a sorry state), with rare white Bengal tigers. Much more fun than the zoo, though, is the 1950s-throwback **Rail Transport Museum** (p106), the deer park at **Hauz Khas Village** (p107), and the **boating lake** (p104; Rs 40 per boat for 30 mins; ☼ noon-7pm summer, 11am-6pm winter) in front of Purana Qila. **Discover Delhi** (opposite) runs fortnightly tours of the city for children between the ages of four and 14.

For indoor activities, the **National Museum of Natural History** (p106) might amuse some children, while **Shankar's International Dolls Museum** (Map pp92-3; ☎ 23316970; Nehru House, 4 Bahadur Shah Zafar Marg; admission Rs 10; ☼ 10am-6pm Tue-Sun), with 6500 dolls from more than 80 countries, will appeal to others. Connaught Place has a number of bookshops, toy shops and stalls selling things both edifying and of the flashing, squealing variety, along with a legion of child-friendly Western-style eating options.

TOURS

Government of India Tourist Office (p94) Can arrange multilingual, government-approved guides for Rs 350/500 for a half-/full-day (maximum five people).

Salaam Balak Trust (contact Shekhar ☎ 9873130383; Rs 200; ⏰ 2½hr walks 10am daily) Former street children take you out into the Paharganj streets they know intimately, introducing you both to the neighbourhood and to the street children who fight there for survival.

Discover Delhi (Contact Kanchan ☎ 26891223; Rs 300 incl snack; ⏰ 9am fortnightly on Sat) Runs tours through various parts of historic Delhi, for children aged four to 14, guided by an educational and social activist.

Hotel Broadway (Map p97; ☎ 23273821; 4/15 Asaf Ali Rd; Rs 495) Operating from the hotel (p111), two-hour 'gastronomic walking tours' of Old Delhi include lunch at Chor Bizarre (see p113).

Master Guest House (Map pp92-3; ☎ 28741089; R-500 New Rajendra Nagar) This guesthouse (p112) offers personalised tours – such as 'Hidden Delhi' (includes Old Delhi) – with a knowledgeable guide. Tours cost the rupee equivalent of US$15, which includes breakfast and snacks.

SLEEPING

It's wise to book a room in advance as Delhi's most salubrious places can fill up in a flash, leaving new arrivals easy prey for commission sharks (see p95). During the low season (around mid-April to mid-August) room discounts of at least 20% are often negotiable.

Hotels with a minimum tariff of Rs 500 charge a 12.5% luxury tax. Some places, especially at the top end of the range, also whack on an additional service charge (of 6% to 10%); beware, too, that those charging in dollars may have a 'fixed' dollar rate that differs from the actual exchange rate of the day. Taxes aren't included in the reviews in this chapter unless indicated, and all rooms have private bathrooms unless otherwise stated.

Many hoteliers urge travellers to call or email to confirm their reservation 24 hours before arrival (hotel owners complain that travellers don't bother calling to cancel, just as frequently as travellers complain that their hotel bookings aren't always honoured).

Budget

Delhi's budget bunch of places to stay is decidedly lacklustre, with rooms typically small, cell-like and dreary. The truly diabolical, meanwhile, may be damp, mouldy, home to suspicious stains on the bed-linen, walls, or even the ceiling. On the plus side, however, there's plenty of choice, with new ventures opening up all the time, so with a bit of careful prodding and poking, you should be able to find something to suit your taste as well as your budget.

Most backpackers base themselves in Paharganj, a bustling, tourist-oriented enclave near New Delhi train station. For something much more mellow, but not nearly as central, try Majnu-ka Tilla, the Tibetan Colony. Here, the prices are low but the hotels generally cosier than in Paharganj. If it's your first time in Delhi, however, you may feel a bit disconnected from the action, and the enclave is quite hard to find, especially if you're arriving at night.

In the following budget listings, only the cheapest, non-AC room rates have been given; the AC rooms, where available, cost around several hundred rupees more.

NORTH DELHI
Old Delhi

Few travellers stay in Old Delhi since it's generally easier to be based near the amenities of Paharganj or Connaught Place, but for those who wish to, there are a couple of reasonable hotels near the Jama Masjid.

Hotel New City Palace (Map p97; ☎ 23289923; 725 Jama Masjid Motor Mkt; s/d Rs 250/350; 🕸) Clean though claustrophobic rooms but still better than most other Old Delhi cheapies; the pricier rooms have windows and AC, and there's plenty of hot water on tap.

Hotel Bombay Orient (Map p97; ☎ 23242691; s/d Rs 350/450) One of the most appealing choices in the area; ensure, though, that you look at a few rooms, as some are much newer and nicer than others.

Paharganj Area

Paharganj isn't everyone's cup of tea, with its reputation for drugs and shady characters. Nevertheless, it's walking distance from New Delhi train station and is *the* place to tap into the busy backpacker network. Most budget hotels offer nondescript, poorly ventilated and sun-starved rooms on the Main Bazaar main drag, or in the numerous (nameless) alleys snaking off it.

Hotel Navrang (Map p110; ☎ 23581965; Tooti Chowk, Main Bazaar; s/d Rs 100/120) Very rudimentary,

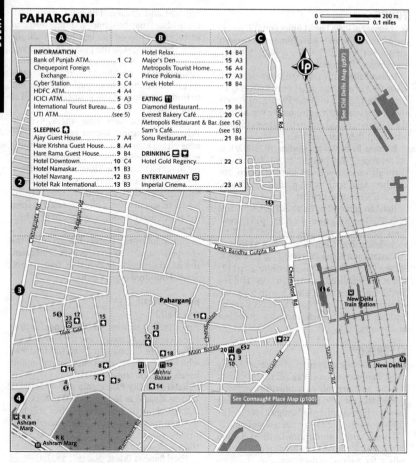

PAHARGANJ

INFORMATION		Hotel Relax...................14 B4
Bank of Punjab ATM.............1 C2		Major's Den....................15 A3
Chequepoint Foreign		Metropolis Tourist Home......16 A4
Exchange.....................2 C4		Prince Polonia.................17 A3
Cyber Station..................3 C4		Vivek Hotel....................18 B4
HDFC ATM......................4 A4		
ICICI ATM......................5 A3		EATING 🍴
International Tourist Bureau...6 D3		Diamond Restaurant.............19 B4
UTI ATM......................(see 5)		Everest Bakery Café............20 C4
		Metropolis Restaurant & Bar..(see 16)
SLEEPING 🏠		Sam's Café.....................(see 18)
Ajay Guest House...............7 A4		Sonu Restaurant................21 B4
Hare Krishna Guest House......8 A4		
Hare Rama Guest House.........9 B4		DRINKING 🍸🍷
Hotel Downtown...............10 C4		Hotel Gold Regency............22 C3
Hotel Namaskar...............11 B3		
Hotel Navrang................12 B3		ENTERTAINMENT 🎭
Hotel Rak International........13 B3		Imperial Cinema...............23 A3

cell-like rooms (especially the singles), but it's friendly, there's hot water by the bucketful for Rs 10, and the prices are among Delhi's lowest.

Hare Krishna Guest House (Map p110; ☎ 41541341; harekrishnagh@hotmail.com; 1572 Main Bazaar; s/d Rs 200/250) Apart from being smallish, the well-worn rooms are in pretty good shape (for Paharganj), it's fairly cosy, and there's a rooftop restaurant.

Hare Rama Guest House (Map p110; ☎ 35361301; harerama_2000@hotmail.com; T-298 Main Bazaar; s/d Rs 200/250; 🌐 🖳) Rooms are clean, good value and have cool tiled walls and floors, but some are notably sunlight deprived.

Hotel Downtown (Map p110; ☎ 51541529; 4583 Main Bazaar; s/d from Rs 200/300) The rooms are smallish

and some are much better than others, so check a selection before you move in. There's also a very basic dorm-bed option (Rs 80), with 16 beds, equipped with threadbare sheets, to one room.

Ajay Guest House (Map p110; ☎ 23583125; ajay5084@ hotmail.com; 5084 Main Bazaar; s/d Rs 250/350; 🌐 🖳) Luring travellers more for its chilled-out vibe than its insipid, ragged rooms, Ajay's has a rooftop café and pool table.

Hotel Namaskar (Map p110; ☎ 23583456; www .namaskarhotel.com; 917 Chandiwalan, Main Bazaar; d from Rs 300; 🌐) The star attractions of this hotel are its two helpful brothers, who, apart from dispensing useful advice, can arrange car hire and tours in and beyond Delhi and in Rajasthan. Most of the 32 simple rooms are painted in a cheerful shade of pink, and the place generally gets very good traveller feedback.

Hotel Rak International (Map p110; ☎ 23562478; Tooti Chowk, Main Bazaar; s/d Rs 300/400; ✗) All the rooms at this popular option have windows, making them a cut above much of the competition. Though modest, they're generally clean and the management is efficient.

Major's Den (Map p110; ☎ 23589010; d Rs 500-550; ✗) Away from the flurry of Main Bazaar, the rooms are extremely sparse and basic, but this is made up for, to some extent, by the charismatic presence of the spritely retired Major who lives on site, and who is exceedingly proud of his solar hot-water system.

Majnu-ka Tilla

Alongside the Yamuna, north of Civil Lines, is this peaceful enclave also known as the Tibetan Colony. Not nearly as centrally located as Paharganj, but with better-value rooms and less hype, it's perfect if you're all Delhi-ed out. There's a sprinkling of cheap Tibetan eateries, shops and internet centres.

Wongdhen House (Map pp92-3; ☎ 23816689; wongdhenhouse@hotmail.com; s/d from Rs 200/275; ✗) Hidden towards the bottom of an alleyway, this is the pick of the area's bunch, welcoming weary travellers with its sizable rooms, courteous staff and a breezy rooftop terrace sporting Yamuna River views. The restaurant cooks everything from banana pancakes (Rs 40) to *phing sha* (Tibetan noodles with mincemeat, Rs 50).

Peace House (Map pp92-3; ☎ 23939415; d AC/4th/3rd/2nd/1st fl Rs 725/175/275/325/325) Down a little side street and quite hard to spot, the hotel's sign mysteriously reads 'Peace STD' rather than 'hotel'. It offers plain but neat rooms and whenever hunger strikes, a nice plate of steamed *momos* (Tibetan dumplings, Rs 20) in its ground-floor restaurant.

Also recommended are:

IDA House (Map pp92-3; ☎ 23813960; d Rs 250)

Lhasa House (Map pp92-3; ☎ 23939777; d Rs 350; ✗)

White House (Map pp92-3; ☎ 23813944; d Rs 250; ✗)

CENTRAL DELHI
Connaught Place Area

Hotel Blue (Map p100; ☎ 23416666; hotelblue@indiatimes.com; 2nd fl, M-126; s/d Rs 800/1200, without bathroom Rs 600/800; ✗ 🖳) Up a dingy stairwell to the top floor, its 13 rooms are an acceptable choice if

all else fails, with a roof ter... reliable hot water. Avoid the ina... Hotel Bright downstairs.

Midrange
NORTH DELHI
Old Delhi

Hotel Broadway (Map p97; ☎ 23273821; broadway@oldworldhospitality.com; 4/15 Asaf Ali Rd; s/d Rs 1500/2595; ✗) Broadway's great Chor Bizarre restaurant (p113) and 'gastronomic walking tours' (p109) are more thrilling than the rooms which, though slightly gloomy, are certainly clean and well kept.

Paharganj Area

Prince Polonia (Map p110; ☎ 23581930; polinter@del3.vsnl.net.in; 2325 Tilak Gali; s/d Rs 900/1000; ✗ 🖳) Unusually for the area, most of Prince Polonia's rooms are equipped with windows, and some even go so far as to have balconies. The staff are friendly and keen to please, most rooms have TVs and attempts at decoration, and there's a nice rooftop restaurant, beside which is an empty swimming pool, sadly closed by order of the authorities.

Vivek Hotel (Map p110; ☎ 51541435; 1534-1550 Main Bazaar; d Rs 1000-1850; ✗ 🖳) Recently renovated, Vivek tries hard to provide its guests with a comfortable stay. Many double rooms come with bathtub and the owner's own line in headboards, and the suite is especially decent. Sam's Café (p114), up on the roof, serves a hearty line-up of dishes.

Hotel Relax (Map p110; ☎ 23562811; vidur109@hotmail.com; Nehru Bazaar; d Rs 1200; ✗) Its business cards, curiously, proclaim that this hotel offers 'day and night service'. The knick-knack filled hallways belie standard, spartan rooms, but the balconies make a good place to sit and watch bazaar life go by.

Metropolis Tourist Home (Map p110; ☎ 23561794; metravel@bom9.vsnl.net.in; 1634 Main Bazaar; d Rs 1200-1500; ✗) Good rooms (some with balcony) with TV, fridge and clean bathrooms that receive more natural light than most other Paharganj hotels. There's also a pleasant rooftop restaurant (p114).

West of Paharganj

Yatri House (Map pp92-3; ☎ 23625563; www.yatrihouse.com; 3/4 Panchkuian Marg; s/d Rs 3000/3500; ✗) Serenity just steps from the madness of Main Bazaar, on a lane off Panchkuian Marg, this guesthouse boasts a green lawn, open-air courtyard

...l rooms. For ...g area, it's by ...s price range; it's ...ons – well ahead ...sed.

M... ...p pp92-3; ☎ 28741089; www .master-g... ...500 New Rajendra Nagar; d from Rs 1850; ⚡) ...m residential guesthouse, located near the Shankar and Ganga Ram Hospital Rds crossing is run by a friendly couple. There are just four homely rooms (pick from 'Moghul', 'Ganesh', 'Krishna' and 'Lucky'), all clean and comfortable. Avnish runs tours of 'Hidden Delhi' (see p109).

CENTRAL DELHI
Ashoka Road
YWCA Blue Triangle Family Hostel (Map p102-3; ☎ 23360133; ywcadel@yahoo.co.in; Ashoka Rd; s/d Rs 1136/1975; ⚡ 💻) Open to both sexes, you must become a temporary member (Rs 20, valid for one month) to stay. The dormitory is commendable, if a tad tightly packed, and the private rooms are also nice, despite a lingering hint of fragrance à la mothball. All rates include tax and breakfast.

Sunder Nagar
The leafy, upmarket suburb of Sunder Nagar is about 3km southeast of Connaught Place.

Maharani Guest House (Map pp102-3; ☎ 24359521; mgh@vsnl.com; 3 Sunder Nagar; s/d Rs 2700/3300; ⚡ 💻) With clean, comfortable rooms lacking in atmosphere, this hotel is a veritable rabbit warren. Check out a few rooms before you decide (avoid the damp underground ones); the higher floors are generally airier and less claustrophobic.

La Sagrita Tourist Home (Map pp102-3; ☎ 2435 8572; www.lasagrita.com; 14 Sunder Nagar; s/d Rs 3690/4090; ⚡ 💻) A warm and friendly option, its rooms boast wooden floors, comfortable furniture and nice, clean bathrooms. There's 24-hour room service to make up for the lack of a restaurant.

Connaught Place Area
YMCA Tourist Hostel (Map p100; ☎ 23361915; ymcath@ ndf.vsnl.net.in; Jai Singh Rd; s/d Rs 1150/2000, without bathroom Rs 750/1400; ⚡ 💻 ⚡) This prim hostel takes both genders (Rs 30 membership; valid for one month); see several rooms, as some are dingy. All rates include tax, breakfast

and dinner; there's a pool and a gym for an extra fee.

YWCA International Guest House (Map p100; ☎ 23361561; www.ywcaindia.org; 10 Sansad Marg; s/d Rs 1556/1980; ⚡ 💻) With the same institutional feel as the YMCA, the rooms are certainly nothing exciting but they're secure and relatively clean.

York Hotel (Map p100; ☎ 23415769; K-Block; s/d Rs 1800/2950; ⚡) A '70s survivor with brown and beige everywhere you look. The rooms are plain and sparse, but functional and clean, some with new laminate flooring. Try to get a 'backside' room to cut down on traffic noise.

Hotel Fifty Five (Map p100; ☎ 23321244; bookings@hotel55.com; H-55; s/d Rs 2300/2800; ⚡) Small, warm and friendly, the 15 rooms are simple and clean, there's a nice rooftop terrace, reliable airport pickup service and free luggage storage.

Hotel Jukaso Inn (Map p100; ☎ 23415450; jukaso@ vsnl.com; L-Block; s/d Rs 3000/3850; ⚡ 💻) Though this place has decent, recently renovated rooms, even equipped with small flat-screen TVs, free wireless internet and a breakfast buffet, it gets bad reviews from travellers for its unfriendly staff.

SOUTH DELHI
Home Away from Home (Map pp92-3; ☎ 26560289; 1st fl, D-8 Gulmohar Park; s/d from Rs 1375/1575; ⚡) Owned by Mrs Kamte – who lives on site and keeps the place in tiptop condition – there are just two warm, clean rooms here, each tastefully furnished. Hush and Puppy, the pet basset hounds, appreciate a tummy tickle.

Top End
Devna (Map pp102-3; ☎ 24355047; 10 Sunder Nagar; d from Rs 5000; ⚡ 💻) Formerly known as Ten, this diminutive guesthouse has five lovely, antique-filled rooms and extremely friendly owners. Without doubt the best choice in Sunder Nagar for its personal touches, homely atmosphere and free wi-fi; be sure to enter through the right-hand gate, so as not to end up in the neighbours' house.

our pick **Hotel Palace Heights** (Map p100; ☎ 4352610; www.hotelpalaceheights.com; D26-28 Connaught Pl; s/d Rs 5000/5500; ⚡ 💻) At last – a comfortable, central and welcoming hotel, with top-end service without the exorbitant prices. The rooms might be smallish and scraping the upper edge of the mid-price category, but they're very well decorated, with powerful hot-water showers and a terrific tandoori restaurant attached. Eat a complimentary breakfast whilst gazing down at the early morning Connaught Place action. Highly recommended, as well, for people travelling with children.

The Manor (Map pp2-3; www.themanordelhi.com; d US$220; ✷ ☐) Tucked away in upscale New Friends Colony, this place might not have the hype or the extensive facilities of the usual top-end joints (there is, for instance, no pool) but it more than makes up for this in intimacy, great food and tip-top service. The suite, in particular, makes for a great stay, equipped with sculptures, comfy beds, and one of the biggest TVs you may have ever seen.

Oberoi (Map pp102-3; ☎ 24363030; www.oberoidelhi.com; Dr Zakir Hussain Marg; s/d from US$346/383; ✷ ☐ ✷) On the edge of the Delhi Golf Club, the Oberoi scores high marks. Discerning service and elegant rooms make it especially popular with business people.

Maurya Sheraton Hotel & Towers (Off Map pp102-3; ☎ 26112233; reservations.maurya@welcomgroup.com; Sardar Patel Marg; d from US$420; ✷ ☐ ✷) This world-class hotel has carved a name for itself as one of Delhi's finest, with a range of top-notch facilities, including a health club, business centre, and two excellent restaurants, Bukhara (p115) and Dum Pukht (see p115).

Imperial Hotel (Map p100; ☎ 23341234; www.theimperialindia.com; Janpath; d from US$495; ✷ ☐ ✷) the rates at this exceptionally fine old Delhi Art-Deco jewel continue to climb steeply, making it ever more expensive to sample its sumptuous interiors and top-class service. It's worth dropping in for a drink or dinner, though, if the tarrifs seem more ridiculous than sublime.

Airport Area

Shanti Palace (Map pp92-3; www.shantipalace.com; National Highway 8; ☎ 5732675; s/d Rs 5450/6600; ✷ ☐) This place receives good reports from travellers as a comfy, convenient option before an early departure or following a red-eye arrival.

Uppal's Orchid (Map pp92-3; ☎ 25061515; www.uphalsorchidhotel.com; National Highway 8; d from $US200; ✷ ☐ ✷) Billing itself as an 'environmentally conscious ecotel' this is another comfortable top-end choice near the airport.

Radisson Hotel (Map pp92-3; ☎ 26779191; www.radisson.com/newdelhiin; National Hwy 8; d US$225; ✷ ☐ ✷) Apart from its 256 stylish rooms, there's a

fitness centre and a few smart restaurants (see p117).

EATING
Catering to every palate and pocket, eating out in Delhi is a highlight. The following recommendations barely scratch the culinary surface of what the city has on offer: don't forget to just follow your nose – and the local in-the-know crowds – to discover your own slice of heaven.

Old Delhi & Around
RESTAURANTS
Karim's (Map p97; 16 Gali Kebabian, Jama Masjid; ☎ 23269880; mains Rs 75-180; ⏰ 7am-midnight; ✷) Iconic Karim's has been delighting Delhiites since 1913 with its flavoursome, predominantly nonvegetarian, heavy Mughlai cuisine. It is really a city institution and worth every second of the hunt to find the place; during Ramadan, it opens after sunset.

Moti Mahal (Map p97; ☎ 23273661; 3704 Netaji Subhash Marg, Daryaganj; mains Rs 100-225; ⏰ 11am-midnight; ✷) Though a bit shabby around the edges, this is another great Delhi institution. It's particularly noted for its succulent butter chicken (half/full chicken Rs 150/285), which tastes especially good when eaten outside, in summer, in the large courtyard.

Chor Bizarre (Map p97; ☎ 23273821; Hotel Broadway, 4/15 Asaf Ali Rd; mains Rs 115-250, veg/nonveg thalis Rs 260/325; ⏰ noon-3.30pm & 7.30-11.30pm; ✷) Wonderful Kashmiri and Mughlai fare in quirky surrounds – there's a vintage car that serves as a salad bar, and even a four-poster bed as a table. The *sharabi kababi tikka* – chicken in a rich cream-and-tomato sauce – is divine.

QUICK EATS
All along Chandni Chowk, you'll find stalls churning out both sweet and savoury treats. Make sure you pick a popular one, checking that the food's being cooked in front of you, and you shouldn't have any problems.

Paratha Wali Gali (Map p97; parathas Rs 30-40) In a lane just behind Ghantewala, off Chandni Chowk, opposite the Central Bank. Come here to feast on *parathas* (Indian flat bread) stuffed with fillings such as spiced *aloo* (potato), *gobi* (cauliflower) and *paneer* (unfermented cheese), all served with simple curries.

Jalebiwala (Map p97; Chandni Chowk; jalebis per 500g from around Rs 50; 9am-9pm) Near the Sisganj Gurdwara, Jalebiwala is *the* place to sink your teeth into fat, syrupy fried *jalebis* (deep-fried coils of sweet batter dipped in sugar-syrup).

Ghantewala (Map p97; 1862 Chandni Chowk; Indian sweets per kg around Rs 80; 8am-9pm) Also near the Sisganj Gurdwara, this simple sweets shop has been in business since 1790 and still has a loyal following. Try the divine *pista samosa*, of which you'll dream long after returning home.

Haldiram's (Map p97; Chandni Chowk; samosas/pakoras Rs 5/6, barfi per kg from Rs 100; 9am-10pm;) A Delhi legend since 1947, you can rest aching legs upstairs in the icily air-conditioned cafeteria, which serves terrific thalis (try the calorific Maharaja Thali for Rs 105), and even decent small pizzas. Alternatively, eat straight from the counter, filling up on *ladoos* (sweet gram-flour balls), *pistas* (pistachio sweets), *barfis* (fudgelike condensed-milk sweets) and *kajus* (cashew sweets) galore.

Paharganj Area

Sonu Restaurant (Map p110; mains Rs 25-100; 12-9pm) Cooks up plenty of South Indian *dosa* (lentil-flour pancake) fare, including bizarre egg and cheese versions – there's even a chocolate banana *dosa* (Rs 40) – as well as passable Chinese, Indian and Continental dishes.

Everest Bakery Café (Map p110; mains Rs 30-90; 7am-11pm) Opposite the Hotel Star Paradise, this teeny café boasts particularly enticing teas, nice with a big wedge of chocolate cake.

Diamond Restaurant (Map p110; mains Rs 40-100; 7.30am-11.30pm) The diminutive Diamond shines when it comes to pasta, but its Chinese, Continental and Israeli dishes can yield wobbly results. Breakfasts (Rs 50 to Rs 70) are reliable, as is the good music and the friendly vibe.

Sam's Café (Map p110; Vivek Hotel, 1534-1550 Main Bazaar; mains Rs 60-110; 8am-11pm) A dependable place to sip a *masala chai* (mixed tea) or strawberry lassi before diving into the filling plates of schnitzels, *momos*, falafel, thalis or roast chicken.

Metropolis Restaurant & Bar (Map p110; Metropolis Tourist Home, 1628 Main Bazaar; mains Rs 85-250; 8am-11pm) A relaxing rooftop restaurant with decent lasagne, sweet-and-spicy salmon fillets, spaghetti Bolognese, chicken wrapped in bacon, and plenty more.

Connaught Place & Around
RESTAURANTS

Sagar (Map p100; 15 K-Block; dosas Rs 32-50, thalis Rs 60; 8am-11pm;) A vegetarian *dosa* dreamland, Sagar is incredibly popular with Delhiites and its *uttappams* (crisp-collared rice-flour and coconut-milk pancakes from Rs 40) deserve special merit. Other favourites include the onion *rava masala dosa*, the *dahi vadas* (gram-flour balls smothered in spiced yogurt), and the cooling *dahi idli* (rice cake dunked in yogurt).

Saravana Bhavan (Map p100; 46 Janpath; dosas Rs 34-70, thalis Rs 65; 8am-11pm;) Heavenly Tamil food at this unmissable all-vegetarian joint. Great-value *dosas*, *idlis* and other southern specialities; don't miss the Tamil Nadu thali served at the sit-down restaurant on the first floor. Saravana also has a branch at 15 P-Block, Connaught Pl.

Banana Leaf (Map p100; 12 N-Block; dosas Rs 50-80, thalis Rs 70-95; 10am-11pm;) Apart from some top-notch South Indian vegetarian standards, including a delicious *Rawa Idli* made with cashews, tomato and carrot (Rs 50), there are some more-obscure options such as the Mysore dry fruit *masala dosa*. For a filling lunch, go for the Special Limited Thali (Rs 95).

Kwality Restaurant (Map p100; 7 Regal Bldg, Sansad Marg; mains Rs 85-180; noon-11pm;) Feeding Delhi for 65 years, Kwality may have rather tightly packed tables, but this venerable restaurant's food (especially the Indian dishes) lives up to its name. Try the *shahi paneer* (unfermented cheese in a creamy tomato sauce, Rs 110).

Embassy (Map p100; 11 D-Block; mains Rs 90-200; 10am-11.30pm;) Dimly lit and one of the oldest establishments in the area, Embassy attracts a clientele of notable oldies, including Delhi-based journalists and retired politicians. It serves up a scrummy *palak paneer* (unfermented cheese in spinach sauce) but is best known for its chicken supreme, apparently a favourite with its older clients.

Zen (Map p100; 25 B-Block; mains Rs 100-450; 10.30am-midnight;) Reasonable renditions of Chinese food. For lunch there's a decent, though not overly generous, set meal (veg /nonveg Rs 299/339). Dim sums go for Rs 109 to Rs 139 per portion.

Parikrama (Map p100; 66303394; 22 Kasturba Gandhi Marg; mains Rs 140-400; 12.30-11pm;) A revolving restaurant on the 24th floor where you can enjoy Indian or Chinese food while oh-so-slowly spinning (one revolution takes 1½ hours). The views are superlative, especially during the day and the food is decent, if not exceptional.

United Coffee House (Map p100; E-Block; mains Rs 165-345; ✆ 11am-11pm; ✖) With old-world charm and pleasing meals, this is a splendid spot to slow the pace beneath dusty chandeliers. The menu encompasses a bit of everything, from grilled-cheese sandwiches to rich, filling curries.

our pick **Veda** (Map p100; H26-27 Connaught Pl; ✆ 41513535; mains Rs 450-800; ✆ noon-3.30pm & 8-11.30pm) A Moulin Rouge fantasy of crushed velvet and chandeliers, serving an Indian-fusion menu, with highlights including tandoori grilled lamb chops. The food is great, but the atmosphere is really what you're coming for – sip a martini in plush, glamorous comfort, forgetting for a second that the clamour of Connaught Place is just outside the tinted windows.

The Spice Route (Map p100; The Imperial Hotel, Janpath; ✆ 23341234; mains Rs 500-1200; ✆ 12.30-3pm, 7-11.45pm; ✖) For a ritzy night out, this beautifully decorated restaurant in the glorious Imperial Hotel is hard to beat. The food roams through South India, Thailand, Burma and beyond, and dishes range from delicious to perfection itself. Reservations are recommended.

QUICK EATS

Wenger's (Map p100; A-Block; ✆ 10.30am-8pm) The legendary Wenger's bakes cakes (from Rs 27 per slice), savouries (coleslaw/chicken-tikka sandwiches Rs 28/40) and bread (cheese and jalapeno loaf Rs 25). Old-fashioned foil-wrapped chocolates – perfect for your great-great-aunt's birthday – are Rs 600 per kilo. It's almost always packed, largely because of its convoluted system of buying produce through a series of tickets, cashiers and counters.

Nizam's Kathi Kabab (Map p100; H5/6 Plaza Bldg-Block; ✆ 11am-11pm) Legendary takeaway kebabs: try the mutton kebab in *paratha* (Indian flat bread) with egg (Rs 65 to Rs 85); vegetarians will melt at the *paneer tikka* (spiced, marinated, chargrilled unfermented cheese) roll (Rs 80).

New Delhi & Around

DIPLOMATIC ENCLAVE & CHANAKYAPURI AREA

Fujiya (Map pp102-3; 12/48 Malcha Marg Market; mains Rs 85-210; ✆ noon-midnight; ✖) Small and friendly Fujiya serves Chinese and some Japanese dishes in a serene district of the diplomatic enclave. Whether it's Peking lamb, Szechwan chicken, or roast tofu with vegetables, diners are rarely disappointed. No reservations are taken so arrive early.

Basil & Thyme (Map pp102-3; Santushti Shopping Complex, Chanakyapuri; mains Rs 235-265; ✆ 10.30am-6pm Mon-Sat; ✖) A great bet if you're missing Western deli dishes; the menu is packed with home comforts such as asparagus tart and pasta with smoked salmon and dill, though, like the society ladies who lunch here, you'll be paying fairly substantially for the privilege.

Bukhara (Off Map pp102-3; ✆ 26112233; Maurya Sheraton Hotel & Towers, Sadar Patel Marg; mains Rs 495-695; ✆ 12.30-2.45pm & 7-11.45pm; ✖) Award-winning Bukhara serves North-West Frontier–style cuisine with aplomb, and is generally considered Delhi's very best restaurant. Almost anyone who's anyone has eaten here – including Bill Gates and Mick Jagger – making reservations pretty much essential; they are taken between 7pm and 8pm daily.

Dum Pukht (Off Map pp102-3; ✆ 26112233; Maurya Sheraton Hotel & Towers, Sadar Patel Marg; mains Rs 680-1000; ✆ 7.30-11.45pm daily, 12.30-2.45pm Sat & Sun; ✖) Another highly acclaimed Sheraton offering. The delectable dishes here are cooked in a *dum* style, a sort of slow-cooked stew with a pastry lid. Reservations (taken any time) are advised.

LODI COLONY

All American Diner (Map pp102-3; India Habitat Centre, Lodi Rd; mains Rs 150-250; ✆ 7am-11pm; ✖) Decked out in true diner style right down to the tunes, this place serves US classics from buttermilk pancakes and peanut-butter malts to hot dogs and onion rings.

Lodi, The Garden Restaurant (Map pp102-3; Lodi Rd; mains Rs 200-400; ✆ 11am-11.30pm; ✖) Its cuisine gets varied reports, but this pleasant eatery, with a garden setting, is a handy sustenance stop after a power-walking session at nearby Lodi Garden. One hit is the mezze platter, piled high with tabbouleh, hummus and aubergine salad.

PANDARA MARKET

Gulati (Map pp102-3; mains Rs 100-300; ✆ noon-12am; ✖) Incredibly popular with locals, this place does great Punjabi dishes, its two top hits being butter and *khadhai* (a tomato-and-chilli-infused masala) chicken. Rumour has it, too, that you might bump into a couple of

Bollywood legends, who arrive here regularly for a quick food fix.

Ichiban (Map pp102-3; mains Rs 100-300; 12.30-3.30pm & 7.30pm-1.30am;) If you're all curried-out, Ichiban specialises in Chinese and Japanese food, with perfectly reasonable versions of all your eastern favourites. Try the yummy stir-fried vegetables in almond sauce, salt-and-pepper chicken, and for dessert, crispy noodles in honey sauce (Rs 80).

Pindi Restaurant (Map pp102-3; mains Rs 100-300; noon-1am;) In an area with many *dhaba* (snack bar) Punjabi restaurants, this is probably the most famous, starting life as a simple, neon-lit affair and nowadays rather more sophisticated, with prices to match. Still, it's a good stop-off point for a large and delicious lunch, with particularly gratifying butter chicken (Rs 200) and *mattar paneer* (peas and cheese in gravy, Rs 160).

KHAN MARKET

Mrs Kaur's Premium Cookies (Map pp102-3; Khan Market; 9.30am-10pm) These scrummy, squidgy takeaway cookies range from Rs 30 for a super-choc chunk to Rs 600 for a giant birthday cookie. They also deliver, if you get caught with a craving.

Chona's (Map pp102-3; Khan Market; mains Rs 90-320; 11.30am-11.30pm Mon-Sat;) Linger with the locals at this simple institution over Indian, Chinese and Continental dishes, including their speciality veg or nonveg 'sizzlers' (Rs 190 to Rs 210). Some dishes work better than others but it's a good place to hang out with a 'chilli potato' or chicken-wing starter, watching the Khan Market world go by.

The Kitchen (Map pp102-3; Khan Market; mains Rs 150-350; 11am-11pm;) Friendly, cute and with an extensive menu, this is a great lunch spot, with a daily happy hour between 4pm and 7pm. Tuck into Irish stew (Rs 275), mixed-bean chilli (Rs 225) or attempt the 'complicated noodle salad' (Rs 180). Top this all off with a blueberry cheesecake or mocha fudge ice cream, and don't miss the framed poster of George Bushisms in the toilet.

HAUZ KHAS AREA

Naivedyam (Map pp92-3; 26960426; Hauz Khas Village; dosas Rs 50-75, thalis Rs 90; 11am-11pm;) A delightful, snug, South Indian restaurant decorated temple-style, with a small but great-value menu and happy atmosphere. The thalis come especially recommended.

Park Baluchi (Map pp92-3; 26859369; Hauz Khas Village; mains Rs 220-530; noon-11pm;) Set within the restful grounds of the deer park itself, this is a smart place drawing in a largely local crowd for its upmarket Indian cuisine. A favourite with wedding parties, it makes a nice place for a drink or a tandoori-chicken meal on a summer evening, after a calming stroll through the park.

La Piazza (Map pp92-3; 26791234, ext 1310; Hyatt Regency, Bhikaiji Cama Pl, Ring Rd; mains Rs 310-780; noon-3pm & 7-11.30pm;) Long acclaimed for its Italian food, this is an upmarket choice if you're simply craving a perfect wood-fired pizza, ravioli with ricotta and *pomodoro* (tomato), or have the taste for truffles.

DEFENCE COLONY & SOUTH EXTENSION AREA

Dilli Haat (Map pp92-3; Aurobindo Marg; www.dillihaat .org; admission Rs 15; 10.30am-10pm Oct-Mar, to 9.30pm Apr-Sep) Although this open-air market is rather contrived and more than a little touristy, it does offer the opportunity to sample regional Indian cuisine, even Manipuri veg thalis (Rs 60) and treats from the northeastern state of Assam.

Flavours (Map pp92-3; 24645644; 51-54C Moolchand Flyover Market, Ring Rd; mains Rs 150-310; noon-11pm;) Known by many – including its Italian owner – as 'the most authentic Italian eatery in Delhi'. Chef/owner Tarsillo Nataloni ensures you eat the *real* thing, whether it's bruschetta, risotto or, of course, pasta. Eat in the attractive restaurant or out in the garden, but beware that the service can sometimes be a little patchy.

Swagath (Map pp92-3; 14 Defence Colony Market; 24330930; mains Rs 180-600; 11am-11.30pm) Swagath serves up popular Indian and Chinese choices, the winner being seafood. Its most popular dishes include green masala pomfret and ladyfish fry.

GREATER KAILASH & EAST OF KAILASH

Govinda's Sweets (Map pp92-3; ladoo per kg Rs 140; 9am-1pm & 2-9pm) Next door to Govinda's. Sells delicious takeaway *mithai* (Indian sweets).

Govinda's (Map pp92-3; Hare Krishna Iskcon temple complex, East of Kailash; buffet Rs 225; breakfast 8-11am, lunch 12.30-3.30pm, afternoon snack 4-6.30pm, dinner 7-10pm;) Promising a 'transcendental dining experience', Govinda's pure-veg (no onion or garlic) Indian buffet is a good way to fill up in serene surroundings. Though the food itself is not necessarily spectacular, it's worth sampling if you're in the area, especially if you're keen to discuss George Harrison with an orange-robed devotee after dinner.

Shalom (Map pp92-3; ☎ 41632280; N Block Market, Greater Kailash Part I; mains Rs 400-700; ☉ 12.30-3.30pm & 7.30-12pm) Essentially a lounge bar with food, this is a grand place to dine if you need a complete break – both culinary and visual – from the chaos of Delhi. Step inside and you'll enter the Mediterranean, with a mostly Lebanese menu inspired by hints of Morocco and Spain. Vegetarians won't be disappointed with the extensive menu, one of the highlights being the Spanish corn crepes.

AIRPORT AREA

NYC (Map pp92-3; ☎ 26779191; Radisson Hotel, National Hwy 8; mains Rs 265-425; ☉ 24hr; ✸) A glam but pricey coffee shop with an overwhelmingly stars-'n'-stripes theme. It's worth stopping in if you're killing time in the airport area, and the food, though unspectacular, is a reasonable mix of sandwiches, soups and kebabs.

DRINKING

Delhi's bar scene, these days, is amazingly extensive, with new, hot places opening all the time. There are three main coffee chains – Barista, Coffee Day and Costa Coffee – which have taken Delhi with a vigour of which Starbucks would be proud. All offer cool respite from a hot Delhi day – or a welcome warm-up on a freezing Delhi winter morning.

Cafés

Barista (Map p100; 16 N-Block, Connaught Pl; snacks Rs 32-60; ☉ 9am-1am; ✸) Hip and happening, Barista serves comfort food, from smoked-chicken sandwiches to chocolate-chip muffins and a monstrous iced café mocha latte (Rs 72).

Costa Coffee (Map p100; L-8 Connaught Pl; ☉ 9am-1am; ✸) Though this central Connaught Place branch is one of the most popular and cosseting, no doubt you'll spot other branches popping up all over town. Great for a cup of something hot and steamy (try a large tiramisu latte for Rs 79), a piece of blueberry mousse cake (Rs 49) or a cheese-and-mushroom panini (Rs 69).

Big Chill (Map pp102-3; 68A Khan Market; mains Rs 90-190; ☉ noon-11pm Mon-Sat; ✸) Serves outrageously divine smoothies (Rs 70) and homemade ice cream, including a chocolate superfudge flavour (Rs 50 per scoop) in a cute, vintage movie-poster filled interior, along with a broad selection of veggie pasta and grill dishes.

Café Turtle (Map pp102-3; 2nd fl, Full Circle Bookstore, Khan Market; mains Rs 75-250; ☉ 10am-7.30pm Mon-Sat; ✸) Perfect for a languid cinnamon tea and a wedge of orange poppy-seed cake. Savoury eats include quiche, salads and sandwiches.

Bars & Nightclubs

In recent years, Delhi's bars have graduated from places for travellers to drown the sorrows of a miserable hotel room to places to see and be seen by hip urban Delhiites. Many of the best bars morph into nightclubs later in the evening, with top international DJs and prices to match those of more conventional clubbing capitals. The **Haze Bar** (☎ 41669008; 8 Basant Lok; 3pm-midnight) is a good place for a spot of live rock or blues; there's a Rs 500 bar minimum per person on days when a live band is performing.

PAHARGANJ

These licensed establishments serve drinks until around 11pm. Unlicensed eateries may also serve beer in a teacup if you're discreet about it.

Metropolis Restaurant & Bar (Map p110; Metropolis Tourist Home, 1634 Main Bazaar) This hotel's rooftop restaurant is a little pricey, but a good place for a cocktail sundowner (from Rs 90).

Hotel Gold Regency (Map p110; 4350 Main Bazaar) Sells cheap beer (a bottle of Kingfisher is Rs 80, including tax) at its bar and has live Indian music nightly except Tuesday.

CONNAUGHT PLACE AREA

Agni (Map p100; ☎ 2374 3000; Park Hotel, Parliament St; cover charge per couple Rs 2000 on Fri & Sat; ☉ 5pm-2am; ✸) A stylish lounge pad with a mixture of locals and travellers packing it out every night of the week, this hotel bar hosts dancing late into the night, with a 35ft-long bar holding every conceivable liquor your heart might desire. The Park also hosts exclusive poolside club **Aqua**, which bangs out techno music, then takes it down a notch with R&B, until around 1am. Bouncers here are selective, so dress for the occasion and be prepared for steep prices: Rs 225 for a pint of local beer; Rs 415 and above for cocktails.

DV8 (Map p100; ☎ 41500694; 13 Regal Bldg; ☉ noon-midnight; ✸) A place that is embraced by young professionals after a hard day at the office, this is a great destination if you've got a cocktail craving, with unusual beer-based cocktails on offer: try the 'American Rumble' (Rs 200) for a pick-me-up, whilst listening to the largely rock line-up. Check whether there's a live band playing while you're in town.

1911 (Map p100; Imperial hotel, Janpath; ☾ noon–1am; ⊠) For a true feel of colonial grandeur, imbibe in the company of oil-painted Maharajas, or lie back on bamboo deckchairs on the perfect-green lawn. Named after the year in which Delhi was proclaimed British India's capital, this grand bar claims to have over 500 beverages, as well as a simple bar-snacks menu if you're feeling peckish.

Blues (Map p100; 18 N-Block; ☾ noon–midnight; ⊠) Dimly lit with a cool vibe and a nice rock-and-pop change from the proliferation of lounge and techno Delhi's bar scene has on offer, Blues makes a relaxed place for a mug of draught beer (Rs 180) and a big plate of baked nachos (Rs 130). There's live music on Thursday and Saturday nights, and a generous happy hour between 4pm and 8pm.

Spirit (Map p100; 34 E-Block; ☾ noon–midnight; ⊠) A cosmopolitan lounge-bar-restaurant with a particularly pleasing wine list (Californian and Australian bottles for around Rs 1700); by the glass it's Rs 300/200 for foreign/domestic wine. There's a good menu specialising in Lebanese and Italian cuisine, and the barman knocks up a mean Long Island Iced Tea.

NEW DELHI & AROUND

Lizard Lounge (Map pp92-3; ☎ 32948208; 1st fl, E5 South Extension Part II; ☾ noon- midnight; ⊠) A world away from the rat race, this funky yet suave lounge is a desirable place to unwind over a cocktail or, if the mood is right, bubbly (Dom Perignon is a cool Rs 12,000). The volume is turned up after 11pm and there are a dozen flavours of hookah to choose from, including a curious cappuccino variety.

Delhi's Devils (Map pp92-3; 3rd fl, E3 South Extension Part II; cover charge weekdays Rs 300, weekends Rs 500; ☾ noon–midnight; ⊠) This cavernous bar is a good place to wind down, with lounge music on Mondays and Tuesdays, salsa nights on Thursdays, and hip-hop on Fridays.

Geoffrey's (Map pp92-3; Ansal Plaza, Khel Gaon Marg; ☾ 12.30-11pm; ⊠) If you're in the area, English-themed Geoffrey's pub is recommended for a mojito or two, accompanied by asparagus spears wrapped in smoked salmon (Rs 290).

Oxygen (Map pp92-3; D-Block Market, Poorvi Marg, Vasant Vihar; ☾ 11am-11.30pm; ⊠) Though really more restaurant than bar (and serving up a tasty vegetarian kebab), you can roll into Oxygen for a late-night cognac (Hennessy Rs 200) or choose from its massive selection of imported wines and spirits, to a mostly Bollywood soundtrack.

ENTERTAINMENT
Cultural Programmes

See Media (p91) for publications to pick up for to-the-minute listings of Delhi's dynamic cultural scene. The venues listed below reliably have something of some description going on.

Kamani Auditorium (Map pp102-3; ☎ 23388084; Mandi House, Copernicus Marg)

Sangeet Natak Akademi (Map pp102-3; ☎ 23387246; Rabindra Bhavan, Copernicus Marg)

Shri Ram Centre (Map pp102-3; ☎ 23714307; 4 Safdar Hashmi Rd)

Triveni Kala Sangam (Map pp102-3; ☎ 23718833; 205 Tansen Marg)

Cinemas

Most Delhi cinemas screen a fully Bollywood fare, rarely with English subtitles. There are several cinemas around Connaught Place including the **Odeon** (Map p100; ☎ 41517899) and the 1932-built **Regal** (Map p100; ☎ 23362245). There's also the enticingly ramshackle **Imperial Cinema** (Map p110; ☎ 55396702; Rajguru Rd, Paharganj) in Paharganj. Drop into the box office to check out screening times; tickets run to between Rs 30 and Rs 80.

You might be able to catch an international flick at one of the comfy, suburban cineplexes listed below: screening times are in newspapers and PVR cinema details are online at www.pvrcinemas.com.

PVR Anupam 4 (Map pp92-3; ☎ 51000458; Saket Community Centre, Saket)

PVR Plaza Cinema (Map p100; ☎ 27944194; H-Block Connaught Pl)

PVR Priya Cinema (Map pp92-3; ☎ 9810708625; 61 Basant Lok, Vasant Vihar)

Satyam Cineplex (Map pp92-3; ☎ 25893322; Patel Rd, Patel Nagar)

SHOPPING

Delhi has a magnificent mix of markets, from seething local bazaars to designer shopping enclaves, as well as fixed-price emporiums where you can finally take a break from

---

OLD DELHI'S BUZZING BAZAARS

Getting lost in the old city's colourful, convoluted bazaars (Map p97) is half the fun of shopping here; try, though, to arrive at around 11.30am, when most shops have opened but the jostling is at its most bearable.

For silver jewellery (and some gold) head for Dariba Kalan (Map p97), near the Sisganj Gurdwara. Nearby Kinari Bazaar has a focus on bridal gear, from fancy sari borders to iridescent tinsel decorations. The Cloth Market (Map p97) sells uncut material, as well as bed linen and towels, while electrical gadgets are the speciality of Lajpat Rai Market (Map p97). Chowri Bazaar (Map p97) is the wholesale paper and greeting-card market. Nearby, Nai Sarak (Map p97) deals in wholesale stationery and books and also has a portion devoted to saris.

Near the Fatehpuri Masjid, on Khari Baoli, is the aromatic Spice Market (Map p97), ablaze with fiery-red chilli powders and burnt-orange turmeric, as well as pickles, tea and nuts.

---

haggling. Outside these, bargain hard and remember that some taxi and autorickshaw drivers earn juicy profits (from you) via the commission racket – politely decline their shopping suggestions.

Top-end hotels have glitzy shopping arcades whose prices run to the stellar: for fun, check out the Valentino store at the **Shangri-la Hotel** (☎ 4119191919; www.shangri-la.com; Ashoka Rd), or the Louis Vuitton at the Oberoi (p113), from which you can order a cigar humidor that will set you back a smart Rs 3,600,000. At the other end of the spectrum you'll find indefatigable street hawkers on Chandni Chowk flogging everything from squeaky toys to fake beards for less than the price of a cup of chai.

Government & State Emporiums

Although the prices at these fixed-price emporiums can be marginally higher than elsewhere, you're assured of quality and don't have to haggle. If time permits, scout emporiums to get an idea of prices before exploring the markets – you can always return later if you didn't find comparable products at better prices in the bazaars.

Central Cottage Industries Emporium (Map p100; ☎ 23326790; Janpath; ⓥ 10am-7pm) A multilevel treasure-trove filled with India-wide handicrafts, including woodcarvings, silverware, jewellery, pottery, papier-mâché, brassware, beauty products, textiles and plenty more.

State Emporiums (Map p100; Baba Kharak Singh Marg; ⓥ 10am-6pm Mon-Sat) This string of side-by-side state government emporiums showcases authentic products from around the nation. Set aside several hours to do these fantastic shops justice, and bear in mind that some close for lunch between 1.30pm and 2.30pm.

Markets & Complexes

Many markets are closed once a week (indicated below), with most operating from roughly 10am to 7pm.

OLD DELHI & AROUND

Chandni Chowk (Map p97) is Old Delhi's famous shopping street, and wending your way through its offshoot jumble of chaotic bazaars is a head-spinning assault on the senses – see above for more information.

Daryaganj Sunday Book Market (Map p97; ⓥ 10am-5pm Sun) A bookworm's delight, this market north of Delhi Gate is a great place to spend a Sunday afternoon browsing and picking up out-of-print or hard-to-find titles for peanuts.

Karol Bagh Market (Map pp92-3; ⓥ Tue-Sun) Popular for its competitively priced clothing, shoes, homeware and general consumer goods. Spice things up here at **Roopak's** (Map pp92-3; 6/9 Ajmal Khan Rd; ⓥ 10am-8pm), two shops side by side that sell a similarly priced range of excellent, well-packed spices, most around Rs 100 per 100g.

CONNAUGHT PLACE & AROUND

Janpath (Tibetan) Market (Map p100; ⓥ 10am-7.30pm) This isn't really a market at all, but a series of permanent stalls running along Janpath to catch the moneyed tourists coming out from the Imperial Hotel towards Connaught Place. Because of this, prices are inflated and you'll have to haggle hard, but for those on a short trip, it's still a good place to pick up trinkets. For quality handmade paperware here, visit **Handpaper World** (Map p100; 12B Janpath Market).

Khadi Gramodyog Bhawan (Map p100; Regal Bldg, Sansad Marg; ⓥ 10am-7.45pm) Best known for its *khadi* (homespun cloth), but also ventures beyond textiles, with items such as handmade paper and delicately scented glycerine soaps. Watch out for the strange multicounter purchasing system.

Main Bazaar (Map p110; ☉ 10am-8pm) abounds with cheap T-shirts, shawls, costume jewellery, essential oil, incense and bindis. Although officially closed on Monday, many shops remain open, especially during the tourist season.

Palika Bazaar (Map p100; ☉ 11am-7.30pm Tue-Sun) This is a claustrophobic and frequently seedy bustling underground bazaar with competitively priced consumer goods (especially clothing) and Indian music CDs aimed at local clientele. Tourists are invariably quoted higher prices, so don't be shy to bargain.

People Tree (Map p100; Regal Bldg, Sansad Marg; ☉ 10.30am-7pm) The small and well-concealed People Tree sells avant-garde T-shirts, many with socio-political messages, as well as books, bags, clothes and costume jewellery.

Rangarsons Music Depot (Map p100; ☎ 23413831; 12 K-Block, Connaught Pl; ☉ 10am-5.30pm Mon-Sat) prides itself as being 'leading suppliers to the armed forces'. Items include brass-band instruments (trumpets Rs 2500), tablas (from Rs 1600) and sitars (from Rs 2500).

Rikhi Ram (Map p100; ☎ 23327685; Marina Arcade, 8 G-Block, Connaught Pl; ☉ 11.30am-8pm Mon-Sat) is patronised by some of India's most esteemed musicians. Sitars start at Rs 22,000 and tablas are upwards of Rs 4500.

Soma (Map p100; 1st fl, 44 K-Block; ☉ 10am-7pm) Soma has beautiful block-printed textiles from oven mitts and aprons, to children's clothing, cosmetic bags and scarves.

NEW DELHI & AROUND

Dilli Haat (Map pp92-3; Aurobindo Marg; admission Rs 10; ☉ 10.30am-10pm) sell reasonable regional handicrafts, such as shawls and woven baskets, but nothing you couldn't get in a government emporium. The food on offer is good, though, and the admission fee means a welcome break from hawkers.

Greater Kailash M-Block & N-Block Market (Map pp92-3; Greater Kailash 1; ☉ Wed-Mon) An upmarket shopping enclave best known for its garment, fabric and furnishings store **Fabindia** (Map pp92-3; N-Block Market; ☉ 10am-7.30pm) whose *dhurries* (cotton rugs) range from Rs 150 to Rs 15,000.

Hauz Khas Village (Map pp92-3; ☉ Mon-Sat) Another high-end shopping district, this one abounding with art galleries, boutiques

and furniture shops geared to society's upper crust.

C Lal & Sons (Map pp102-3; 9/172 Jor Bagh Market; ☉ 9.30am-7.30pm) Run by the lovely Mr Lal, this humble little 'curiosity shop' at Jor Bagh Market (Map pp102–3) is especially popular with expats for its charming handmade Christmas-tree decorations. The handicrafts (cheaper than those at tourist markets) include papier-mâché, blue pottery, candles, silk scarves and pretty glass beads.

Khan Market (Map pp102-3; ☉ 10am-7.30pm Mon-Sat) Rather a collection of shops and cafés than an actual market, this place is popular with expat diplomats and well-heeled locals for its boutiques and rash of skincare clinics. After splurging on books, CDs, clothes and organic toiletries, drop your remaining change into the permanent tin collection-box for stray cats, courtesy of the Windsor Pet Shop.

Lajpat Nagar Central Market (Map pp92-3; ☉ around 11am-9pm Tue-Sun) This market attracts bargain hunters on the prowl for household goods, clothing and jewellery. If you've fallen in love with the colourful jangly bangles widely worn by Indian women, you can find them here for around Rs 50 per two dozen.

South Extension Market Parts I & II (Map pp92-3; ☉ 11am-8pm Tue-Sun) sells high-class good in two enclaves, one on either side of the road. Music store **Planet M** (Map pp92-3; ☎ 26251620; ☉ 11am-8.30pm Tue-Sun) here has two well-arranged floors of English and Indian music.

Sunder Nagar Market (Map pp102-3; ☉ 10.30am-7.30pm Mon-Sat) Just south of Purana Qila, this genteel collection of shops specialises in Indian and Nepali handicrafts and 'antiques' (most are replicas). There are also two outstanding teashops: **Regalia Tea House** (Map pp102-3; ☉ 10am-7.30pm) and **Mittal Tea House** (Map pp102-3; ☉ 10am-7.30pm), both offering similar products (including wonderful loose teas and prepacked spices) and complimentary tea tastings.

Tailors

Tailors adeptly replicate ready-made garments so bring your favourite party frock. Ultracheap tailors can be shoddy – seek recommendations or try the following (reputable) outlets. Always confirm whether quotes include fabric; the following prices exclude material.

New Prominent Tailors (Map p100; ☎ 23418007; 25 K-Block, Connaught Pl; ☉ 11am-7.30pm Mon-Sat) A skirt (without lining) is Rs 150, men's trousers are Rs 300.

Vedi Tailors (Map p100; ☎ 23416901; 60 M-Block, Connaught Pl; ⏱ 11.30am-8pm Mon-Sat) Men's-only tailor. Charges Rs 300/2400 for trousers/suits.

GETTING THERE & AWAY

Delhi is a major international gateway to India. It's also a centre for domestic travel, with extensive bus, rail and air connections. Note that Delhi is prone to fog during the chilly winter months of December and January, which frequently disrupts airline schedules. For more details of arriving from overseas see p373.

Air

The domestic terminals (Terminal 1) of the Indira Gandhi International Airport (Map pp92–3) are around 15km south-west of Connaught Place, and the international terminal (Terminal 2) is a further 6km away. There's a free shuttle bus between the two terminals, or you can use the Ex-Servicemen's Air Link Transport Service (see p123). Allow 30 to 45 minutes to get to the domestic airport during the middle of the day, and 45 minutes to an hour to reach the international airport. If you're heading there at rush-hour, it's wise to double this, just to be sure.

At both domestic and international terminals, you *must* have your check-in baggage X-rayed and sealed before you check in – don't forget to do this or you'll be sent back. At the check-in counter, ensure you collect tags to attach to your hand luggage (mandatory to clear security later). For flight enquiries, call the **international airport** (☎ 25652011) or the **domestic airport** (☎ 25675126).

DOMESTIC
Arrivals & Departures

Check-in for domestic flights is one hour before departure. Note that if you've just arrived and have an onward connection within India, it may be with Air India, the country's international carrier, rather than its domestic carrier, Indian Airlines. If this is the case, you must check in at the international terminal (Terminal 2), not the domestic terminal.

Airlines

The most convenient **Indian Airlines office** (Map p100; ☎ 23313317; F-Block, Malhotra Bldg, Connaught Pl; ⏱ 10am-1pm & 2-5pm Mon-Sat) is at Connaught Place. There's also a ticket office at **Safdarjang**

airfield (Map pp102-3; ☎ 24631337; Aurobindo Marg; ⏱ 7am-11pm). For Indian Airlines' flight arrival and departure times, dial ☎ 1407.

Other major domestic airlines (it's usually quickest and cheapest to book tickets online):

Air Deccan (☎ 9818177008; www.air deccan.net)
Jet Airways (☎ 39893333; www.jetairways.com)
Kingfisher (☎ toll-free 18001800101; www.flyking fisher.com)
Spicejet (☎ toll-free 18001803333; www.spicejet.com)

INTERNATIONAL

The international airport's arrivals hall has 24-hour money-exchange facilities, a prepaid taxi counter and a tourist information counter. The railway booking counter is open from 8am to 8pm.

Airline Offices

Most airline offices listed below operate between around 10am and 5pm, Tuesday to Sunday.

Aeroflot (Map p100; ☎ 55302334; Tolstoy House, 15-17 Tolstoy Marg)
Air Canada (Map pp92-3; ☎ 41528181; 5th fl, World Trade Tower, Barakhamba Rd)
Air France (Map p100; ☎ 23466262; 7 Atma Ram Mansion, Connaught Pl)
Air India (Map p100; ☎ 23731225; 2nd fl, Jeevan Bharati Bldg, Connaught Pl)
British Airways (☎ 951244120747; DLF Plaza Tower, DLF Phase 1, Gurgaon)
El Al Israel Airlines (Map p100; ☎ 23357965; rm 303, Prakash Deep Bldg, 7 Tolstoy Marg)
Emirates (Map p100; ☎ 66314444; 7th fl, DLF Centre, Sansad Marg, Connaught Pl)
Gulf Air (Map p100; ☎ 23324293; 12 G-Block, Connaught Pl)
Japan Airlines (Map p100; ☎ 23324922; Chandralok Bldg, 36 Janpath)
KLM-Royal Dutch Airlines (Map p100; ☎ 23357747; Prakash Deep Bldg, 7 Tolstoy Marg)
Lufthansa Airlines (Map p100; ☎ 23724200; 56 Janpath)
Malaysian Airlines (Map p100; ☎ 41512121; Gopal Das Bhavan, 28 Bharakamba Rd)
Pakistan International Airlines (PIA; Map p100; ☎ 23737791; 23 Barakhamba Rd)
Qantas Airways (Map p100; ☎ 23321345; Prakash Deep Bldg, 7 Tolstoy Marg)
Royal Nepal Airlines Corporation (RNAC; Map p100; ☎ 23321164; 44 Janpath)
Scandinavian Airlines (SAS; Map p100; ☎ 43513202; Thapar House, 124 Janpath)

Singapore Airlines (Map p100; ☎ 23356283; 9th fl, Ashoka Estate Bldg, Barakhamba Rd)

Thai Airways International (THAI; Map pp92-3; ☎ 41497777; Park Royal Intercontinental Hotel, America Plaza, Nehru Pl)

Bus

Delhi's main bus station is the **Inter State Bus Terminal** (ISBT; Map pp92-3; ☎ 23868836; Kashmiri Gate; ✆ 24hr), north of the (Old) Delhi train station, about 20 minutes autorickshaw ride north of Connaught Place. It has a 24-hour left-luggage facility (Rs 10 per bag). 'Chaotic' can be an understatement here, so try to arrive at least 30 minutes ahead of your departure time.

Rajasthan Roadways (☎ 24864470; counter 36) and **Uttar Pradesh Roadways** (☎ 23868709; counter 38) sells onward tickets to Rajasthan and Agra at the bus station itself. You can also purchase tickets to Rajasthan at **Bikaner House** (Map pp102-3; ☎ 23383469), located near India Gate, where RTDC buses to and from Jaipur, Jodhpur, Ajmer and Udaipur arrive and depart. Services are seasonal, and vary wildly in price, time and comfort, so it's best to enquire here or at the bus station for up-to-the-minute options.

Train

STATIONS

There are two principal stations in Delhi – (Old) Delhi train station (Map pp92-3) 2km north of Connaught Place in Old Delhi, and New Delhi train station (Map p110) at Paharganj, a 15-minute walk from Connaught Place. It's another of Delhi's eccentricities that though the Old Delhi station is also known as the 'main station', most trains actually depart from the New Delhi train station. Do make sure you double-check which station serves your destination. If you're departing from the (Old) Delhi train station you should allow adequate time to tackle the slow-moving traffic of Old Delhi.

There's also the Nizamuddin train station (Map pp102-3), 5km southeast of Connaught Place, where some southbound and Agra connections departe or terminate. Some trains between Delhi and Jaipur, Jodhpur and Udaipur also operate out of the Sarai Rohilla train station (Map pp92-3), which is about 4km northwest of Connaught Place.

An essential (and oddly addictive) piece of reading matter for deciphering Delhi's rail services is the invaluable *Trains at a Glance* (Rs 50), available at newsstands, bookshops or at the International Tourist Bureau (see Ticket Bookings below). It offers complete listings updated every month, including prices per class and km, of all India's trains.

TICKET BOOKINGS

Foreign travellers should head directly to the **International Tourist Bureau** (Map p110; ☎ 23405156; 1st fl, New Delhi train station; ✆ 8am-8pm Mon-Sat, to 2pm Sun). Do *not* believe anyone who tells you it has shifted, closed or burnt down – this is a scam to divert you elsewhere (see p95).

In this large, air-conditioned upstairs office you'll find generally helpful staff, whose motto, advertised on the wall, is 'Service with a Smile', though this may be stretching it. You'll need to fill out a reservation card before heading to a counter, where tickets can be paid for in rupees, pounds sterling, US dollars, euros, or travellers cheques, but not by credit card. Take your passport along, and try to book onward tickets as early as possible before you intend to travel, since berths – especially first class and sleeper varieties – fill up fast. There are also counters here for buying, and making reservations with, Indrail passes.

GETTING AROUND

City buses can be hopelessly crowded, and unless you're travelling with a local, it's almost impossible to find the right one to serve your destination. Autorickshaws and taxis are in plentiful supply, but rates vary wildly, since it's frequently impossible to find one willing to turn on its official meter.

In certain parts of the city, cycle-rickshaws provide a swift way of cutting through Delhi traffic: this is most applicable on the short run from New Delhi train station to Connaught Place, and along the congested Chandni Chowk in Old Delhi.

Aside from walking, however, the very best way of getting around Delhi is by making use of its excellent metro system. Enter this serene, surreal underground world (keep an eye out for amazed locals struggling, Borat-like, with the escalators) and you'll be whisked about town quickly and sanely. New lines are still in the making, but for now the existing lines serve a good few of the main sights. Commuter hours may get sweaty and busy, but never worse than what's going on aboveground, or, for that matter, on London's Underground in August.

MAJOR TRAINS FROM DELHI

Destination	Train No & name	Fare (Rs)	Duration (hr)	Departures & station
Agra	2280 *Taj Exp*	91/199 (A)	2¾	7.15am HN
	2002 *Shatabdi Exp*	292/584 (B)	2	6.15am ND
Ajmer	2916 *Ashram Exp*	545/675/1194 (C)	8	3.05pm OD
Jaipur	2916 *Ashram Exp*	416/515/910 (C)	5½	3.05pm OD
	2958 *Rajdhani Exp*	473/656/1145 (C)	4½	8pm ND
Jaisalmer	4059 *Barmer Exp*	284/798/1153 (D) (1AC not available)	20	5.45pm OD
Jodhpur	2461 *Mandore Exp*	605/874/1546(C)	11	8.50pm OD
Udaipur	2963 *Mewar Exp*	555/801/1417 (C)	12	7pm HN

Train stations: ND – New Delhi, OD – Old Delhi, HN – Hazrat Nizamuddin
Fares: A 2nd class/chair car, B chair car/executive class, C 3AC/2AC/1AC, D sleeper/3AC/2AC/1AC

To/From the Airport

Airport-to-city transport is not as straightforward as it should be, due to predatory taxi and autorickshaw drivers who often target first-time visitors – see p95.

Many international flights arrive in the wee hours, making it wise to book your hotel in advance, notify it of your arrival time and, if possible, save yourself a lot of hassle by prearranging a pick-up.

PREARRANGED PICK-UPS

Arranging an airport pick-up through a hotel will inevitably be more expensive than taking a 'prepaid taxi' from one of the prepaid booths at the airport. It's worth the peace of mind though, especially if you're a first-time visitor to the city or your flight arrives in the middle of the night, since you know you'll end up at the right hotel and for a prearranged price. There's nothing more comforting after a long-haul flight than seeing someone holding a placard with your name on it.

BUS

The **Ex-Servicemen's Air Link Transport Service** (EATS; Map p100; ☎ 23316530; F-Block, Connaught Pl; ☷ 10am-10.30pm) has a bus service between the airport (both terminals) and its office in Connaught Place. The fare is Rs 50, plus Rs 10 per large piece of luggage, and tickets can be purchased from its counter in the arrivals hall. The bus will also drop you off at most major hotels en route, and at the Ajmeri Gate entrance to New Delhi train station (for Paharganj). There is no set timetable as the bus operates according to flight arrivals.

There is also a Delhi Transport Corporation (DTC) service (its counter is also in the arrivals hall), which operates frequent buses (Rs 50) into town, terminating at the ISBT (opposite) in Old Delhi. Since most travellers plump to stay in Paharganj or near Connaught Place, this service is generally much less useful than the EATS option.

TAXI

In the international terminal, there are several prepaid taxi booths in the arrivals hall area directly after customs; there's also a prepaid stand in the domestic terminal arrivals hall. It costs about Rs 250 to the city centre and there's a 25% surcharge between 11pm and 5am. If you're arriving at night or on your own, however, you may prefer to prearrange a pick-up from your hotel, since it's been known even for prepaid taxi drivers to attempt to take you to a different hotel in order to get a commission.

If you order a prepaid service, you'll be given a voucher at the booth with your destination on it. Never surrender your voucher until you actually get to your destination; it's a nice insurance that you'll actually get to where you've paid to go, since without that docket your driver won't get paid. To lodge complaints contact the **traffic police** (☎ 23378888; ☷ 24hr).

Bus

The Delhi Transport Corporation (DTC; Map p100) runs some buses, and others are privately owned, but they all operate along the same set routes. Tickets cost a maximum of Rs 15 for travel within the city precincts.

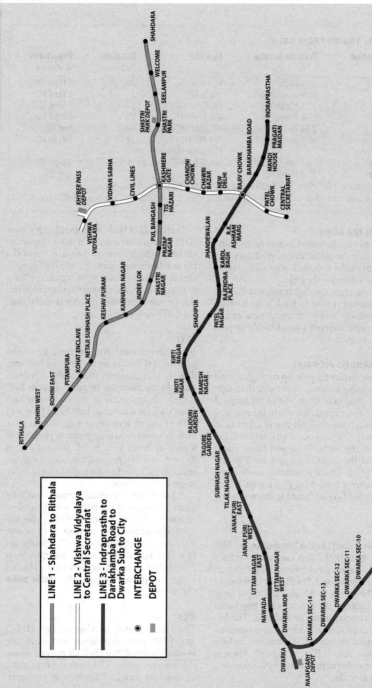

SHAHDARA
WELCOME
SEELAMPUR
SHASTRI PARK DEPOT
SHASTRI PARK
KHYBER PASS DEPOT
VIDHAN SABHA
CIVIL LINES
KASHMERE GATE
CHANDNI CHOWK
CHAWRI BAZAR
NEW DELHI
RAJIV CHOWK
BARAKHAMBA ROAD
PRAGATI MAIDAN
MANDI HOUSE
INDRAPRASTHA
PATEL CHOWK
CENTRAL SECRETARIAT
VISHWA VIDYALAYA
PUL BANGASH
TIS HAZARI
PRATAP NAGAR
SHASTRI NAGAR
INDER LOK
KANHAIYA NAGAR
KESHAV PURAM
NETAJI SUBHASH PLACE
KOHAT ENCLAVE
PITAMPURA
ROHINI EAST
ROHINI WEST
RITHALA
JHANDEWALAN
R.K. ASHRAM MARG
KAROL BAGH
RAJENDRA PLACE
PATEL NAGAR
SHADIPUR
KIRTI NAGAR
MOTI NAGAR
RAMESH NAGAR
RAJOURI GARDEN
TAGORE GARDEN
SUBHASH NAGAR
TILAK NAGAR
JANAK PURI EAST
JANAK PURI WEST
UTTAM NAGAR EAST
UTTAM NAGAR WEST
NAWADA
DWARKA MOR
NAJAFGARH DEPOT
DWARKA
DWARKA SEC-14
DWARKA SEC-13
DWARKA SEC-12
DWARKA SEC-11
DWARKA SEC-10
DWARKA SEC-9

LINE 1 - Shahdara to Rithala

LINE 2 - Vishwa Vidyalaya to Central Secretariat

LINE 3 - Indraprastha to Darakhamba Road to Dwarka Sub to City

INTERCHANGE

DEPOT

Whenever possible, try to board at a starting or finishing point, such as the **Shivaji Stadium terminal** (Map p100; Connaught Pl), as there's more chance of a seat.

Useful buses:

Buses 101, 104 & 139 Shivaji Stadium terminal to the Red Fort.

Bus 505 Janpath (from opposite the Imperial hotel) to Qutb Minar.

Buses 604, 620, 632 & 641 Connaught Pl (on Sansad Marg) to Chanakyapuri.

Car
HIRING A CAR & DRIVER
Numerous operators offer chauffeur-driven cars – for important tips see p379. Hotels can also often arrange cars but make absolutely sure there won't be hidden 'extra' charges before you depart. Three traveller-recommended options are cars arranged by the Vivek Hotel (p111), Hotel Namaskar (p110) and Yatri House (p111).

Kumar Tourist Taxi Service (Map p100; ☎ 2341 5930; kumar.tt.free.fr; 14/1 K-Block, Connaught Pl; ☺ 8am-9pm) is a tiny family-run outfit near the York Hotel and offers chauffeur-driven tours in Delhi and beyond. A day-long Delhi tour will cost between US$13 and $24 per car; a return daytrip from Delhi to Agra will be US$80–150 per car, prices varying depending on the size and air-conditioning situation of the car.

Cycle-rickshaw & Bicycle
Cycle-rickshaws are banned from Connaught Place and New Delhi, but are extremely handy for commuting between Connaught Place and Paharganj (about Rs 20). They're also recommended in Chandni Chowk (Old Delhi), as the drivers are veritable wizards at weaving through the crowds and gridlocks. You might decide to save your haggling skills for another occasion, since cycle-rickshaw drivers are usually some of Delhi's poorest (employed) residents, won't try to dupe you as frequently as autorickshaw drivers, face stiff competition among legions of others, and are restricted in their access to popular parts of the city.

If you want to purchase a bike, the largest range of new and secondhand bicycles can be found at Jhandewalan Cycle Market (Map pp92–3).

Metro
Delhi's **metro system** (www.delhimetrorail.com) opened to great acclaim in 2002 and is still in development, with work not expected to be finished until 2021. There are currently three lines in operation:

Red Line (Line 1) Runs northeast to northwest, from Shahdara to Rithala.

Yellow Line (Line 2) Runs south to north, from just south of the Central Secretariat to Vishwa Vidyalaya.

Blue Line (Line 3) Runs southeast to southwest, from Indraprastha to Dwarka.

Metros run daily every few minutes from 6am to 10pm and are an excellent, cost-effective way to get around the city. Purchase your token from the booth (fares start at Rs 6) or avoid queuing each time by purchasing an unlimited travel card (one-day/three-day card Rs 70/200). Children under 90cm tall travel for free.

Unlike on the London Underground, there is little indication, at each stop, what points of interest you might be near, so consult a map to find your nearest station. In general, the blue line is of most use to travellers, for shuttling between the sights of New and Old Delhi.

Motorcycle
To purchase or hire motorcycles (including legendary Enfields), head for Karol Bagh (p119) – do shop around and seek advice from fellow travellers in order to ensure you get the best deal. **Inder Motors** (Map pp92-3; ☎ 25728579; lallisingh@vsnl.com; 1740-A/55 Basement, Hari Singh Nalwa St, Karol Bagh Market) receives consistently positive reports; for more information see p382.

Taxi & Autorickshaw
All taxis and autorickshaws are metered but you'll usually find the meters are 'not working' or that drivers will simply refuse to turn them on. Unless you've got an iron will, you'll usually end up haggling over a price rather than standing for hours trying to find a meter-willing driver (taxis cost roughly double autorickshaws; as a guide, an autorickshaw from Connaught Place to Old Delhi should be Rs 40 to Rs 50). Prices will depend on how seasoned a traveller you appear to be, and the time of year. When there's less tourist trade in the winter months, you'll find that fares drop considerably. If you do get lucky with a working meter, remember that from 11pm to 5am, there's a 25% surcharge for autorickshaws and taxis.

To avoid shenanigans, you can try to catch an autorickshaw from a prepaid booth; locations are listed over page. In practice, though, unless you happen to be near a prepaid booth at a time of day when it's not only officially open, but also has someone sitting behind the counter, you'll have to resort to haggling hard.

Government of India Tourist Office (Map p100; 88 Janpath; 11am-7pm) The booth is just outside the tourism office.

New Delhi train station car park (Map p110; 24hr)

Palika Bazaar's Gate No 2 (Map p100; Connaught Pl; 11am-9pm)

GREATER DELHI

Two atmospheric sites well worth the trek out of the city are Tughlaqabad and the Qutb Minar complex, both evocative vestiges of the city's ancient past. You can visit both in a day trip from Delhi: Tughlaqabad lies around 15km southeast of Connaught Place, while the Qutb Minar is 13km to the south.

TUGHLAQABAD

The crumbling battlements of **Tughlaqabad** (Map pp92-3; Indian/foreigner Rs 5/100, video Rs 25; sunrise-sunset) once enclosed the third city of Delhi (p89). The walled city and fort with 13 gateways was built by Ghiyus-ud-din Tughlaq and was deserted soon after his death, possibly due to a dearth of fresh water nearby; not much remains, though 6.5km of walls, some halls, towers, and the outline of city streets can still be made out.

The city's construction involved a legendary quarrel between Ghiyus-ud-din and the saint Nizam-ud-din: when the Tughlaq ruler forbade workers moonlighting on the construction of Nizam-ud-din's shrine, the saint cursed the king, warning that his city would be inhabited only by shepherds. Today, along with legions of rhesus macaques, this is indeed the case.

An autorickshaw from Connaught Place should cost around Rs 200 for the return trip to Tughlaqabad, including half an hour waiting time.

QUTB MINAR

The imposing buildings of the **Qutb Minar complex** (26643856; Indian/foreigner Rs 10/250, video Rs 25; sunrise-sunset Tue-Sun) are the first monuments of Islamic rule in India and are fine examples of early Afghan architecture.

The Qutb Minar itself is a soaring tower of victory whose construction begun in 1193, immediately after the defeat of the last Hindu kingdom in Delhi. It's nearly 73m high and tapers from a 15m-diameter base to just 2.5m at the top.

The tower has five distinct storeys, each marked by a projecting balcony. The first three are of red sandstone, while the upper floors are of marble and sandstone. Although Qutb-ud-din began construction of the tower, he only finished the 1st storey; his successors completed it and, in 1368, Firoz Shah rebuilt the top storeys and added a cupola. An earthquake brought the cupola crashing down in 1803 and an Englishman replaced it with another in 1829. His dome, however, was deemed inappropriate and removed some years later.

Today, this impressively ornate tower has a slight tilt (making it no longer possible to climb), but otherwise has worn the centuries remarkably well. Scattered around it are a number of other remains; the **tomb of Imam Zamin** is beside the entrance gateway, while the **tomb of Altamish**, who died in 1235, is by the northwestern corner of the mosque. The largely ruined **madrasa of Ala-ud-din** stands at the rear of the complex.

There are also some **summer palaces** in the area, along with the **tombs** of the last kings of Delhi, who succeeded the Mughals. An empty space between two of the tombs was intended for the last king of Delhi, who died in exile in Yangon, Burma (Myanmar), in

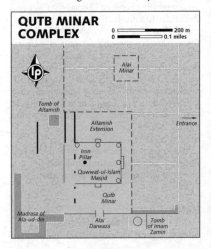

QUTB MINAR COMPLEX

0 — 200 m
0 — 0.1 miles

Alai Minar

Tomb of Altamish

Altamish Extension

Entrance

Iron Pillar

Quwwat-ul-Islam Masjid

Qutb Minar

Madrasa of Ala-ud-din

Alai Darwaza

Tomb of Imam Zamin

1862, following his implication in the 1857 Indian Uprising.

The Qutb Minar Festival is held here every October or November (p99).

Quwwat-ul-Islam Masjid

At the foot of the Qutb Minar stands the first mosque to be built in India, the Might of Islam Mosque. Qutb-ud-din began construction of the mosque in 1193, but various additions and extensions have been added over the centuries. Altamish, Qutb-ud-din's son-in-law, surrounded the original mosque with a cloistered court, built between 1210 and 1220. Ala-ud-din then added a court to the east along with the magnificent **Alai Darwaza gateway** in 1300. This gateway, the main entrance to the complex, was built of red sandstone in 1310 and stands just southwest of the Qutb Minar.

The mosque was built on the foundations of a Hindu temple, and an inscription over the east gate states that it was built with materials obtained from demolishing '27 idolatrous temples'. Many elements in the mosque's construction, however, still hark back to their Hindu or Jain origins.

Iron Pillar

This 7m-high pillar stands in the courtyard of the mosque, where it has stood since long before the mosque's construction. A six-line Sanskrit inscription indicates that it was initially erected outside a Vishnu temple, possibly in Bihar, and was raised in memory of Chandragupta II, who ruled from AD 375 to 413.

What the inscription does not mention is how the pillar was made, for the iron in the pillar is of quite exceptional purity. Scientists have never discovered how the iron, which has not rusted after almost 2000 years, could be cast using the technology of that time.

Alai Minar

When Ala-ud-din made his own additions to the mosque, he also conceived an ambitious second tower of victory, exactly like the Qutb Minar, but twice as high. By the time of his death the tower had reached 27m and was never completed; it now stands to the north of the Qutb Minar and the mosque.

Getting There & Away

Catch bus 505 (Rs 15) from the Ajmeri Gate side of New Delhi train station or from Janpath (opposite the Imperial hotel). Alternatively, Janpath's prepaid autorickshaw booth charges Rs 140 for the return trip to the Qutb Minar, including 30 minutes' waiting time (Rs 20 per extra hour).

Agra

PATRICK HORTON

Agra

Agra is home to one of the most famous monuments not only in India, but in the world: the semitranslucent, dreamlike Taj Mahal, a building that seems to glow with an ethereal light. The city was the Mughal capital from 1526, established by Emperor Babur on the banks of the Yamuna River, and for the next century Agra witnessed a remarkable spate of architectural activity as each emperor tried to outdo the grandiose monuments built by his predecessors – leaving behind a remarkable collection of Mughal masterpieces.

Today the city is sprawling, industrial and, for many travellers, just a bit too much hard work; the clamour and hustle a strident contrast to the otherworldly grace of the Taj Mahal. The hordes of rickshaw-wallahs, touts and souvenir-vendors are as persistent as monsoon rain and would test even the patience of Akbar, the most tolerant of Mughal emperors.

If you're on limited time, it's easy to visit the Taj on a whistle-stop day trip from Delhi, though Agra contains many other worthwhile Mughal wonders. Just an hour away by bus is the deserted city of Fatehpur Sikri, a destination highly recommended for its evocative sense of the Mughal empire at its peak.

HIGHLIGHTS

- Gaze in wonder at the **Taj Mahal** (p133), a quintessentially Indian jewel
- Explore the nooks and crannies of the awesome riverside **Agra Fort** (p135)
- Wander the eerie red-sandstone palaces of the lost city of **Fatehpur Sikri** (p142)
- Stroll the deer park at **Akbar's Mausoleum** (p136), final resting place of the greatest Mughal emperor, at Sikandra
- Admire the **Itimad-ud-Daulah** (p136), or Baby Taj, constructed of white marble and semiprecious stones

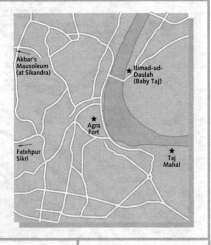

| ■ AREA: 82 SQ KM | ■ POPULATION:1,321,410 | ■ TELEPHONE CODE: 0562 |

AGRA

FESTIVALS IN AGRA & FATEHPUR SIKRI

Taj Mahotsav (18-27 Feb; Agra) Held in Shilpgram, a crafts village and open-air emporium, this festival features live music and dance, food-tasting and a Mughal procession with elephants and camels.

Kailash Fair (Aug-Sep; Kailash) Convened at Kailash, a 14km drive from Agra, the fair commemorates the appearance of Lord Shiva, in the form of a stone lingam, at its temple.

The Taj Mahal Marathon (Sep; Agra; www.thetajmahalmarathon.com) The new Taj Mahal marathon, running from the village of Niyamat Pur to the Taj Mahal, is set to become an annual event.

Eid al-Fitr (Dec/Jan; Fatehpur Sikri) Join the happy crowds in the bazaar and mosque at Fatehpur Sikri, near Agra, for end-of-Ramadan celebrations.

HISTORY

In 1504 Sultan Sikander Lodi established his capital here, but the city fell into Mughal hands in 1526, reaching its pinnacle of architectural innovation between the mid-16th and 17th centuries during the successive reigns of Akbar, Jehangir and Shah Jahan. In 1638 Shah Jahan built a new city in Delhi (now known as Old Delhi; see p96); his son Aurangzeb moved the capital there 10 years later, marking the end of Agra's munificence as imperial seat.

In 1761 Agra fell to the Jats, who looted its monuments, including the Taj Mahal. The Marathas took over in 1770, but were replaced by the British in 1803. Following the Indian Uprising of 1857, the British shifted administration of the province to Allahabad. Deprived of its administrative role, Agra developed as a centre for the chemicals industry and, consequently, atmospheric pollution – an environmental problem it still struggles to shake off – before tourism became a major source of income.

ORIENTATION

Agra sits on the Ganges plain on the western bank of the Yamuna River and has no real centre, its attractions being spread out in between a number of bazaar districts over an area more than 20 sq km.

Most of the city's Mughal masterpieces hug the banks of the Yamuna: Agra's massive fort and the city's main marketplace, Kinari Bazaar, are both in the northern half of the city, close to the riverbank. The Taj Mahal, meanwhile, is about 1.5km southeast of the fort, also beside the river.

The congested, confusing network of alleys immediately to the south of the Taj Mahal is known as Taj Ganj. Here you'll find the bulk of Agra's budget hotels, while most midrange and top-end hotels are located further south on Fatehabad Rd. West from Taj Ganj, on the opposite side of the leafy, British-built Cantonment district, is Sadar Bazaar, a smarter, more relaxed and serene alternative to Taj Ganj.

Most trains arrive and depart from the Agra Cantonment station in the southwest of the city, while long-haul buses arrive and depart the Idgah bus stand directly to the station's north. A few other trains also leave from the Agra Fort train station in the north of the city, just east of the Kinari Bazaar.

INFORMATION

A decent online guide to the city can be found at www.agra-india.net; there's also the state tourism website at www.up-tourism.com.

Bookshops

Aanee Bookshop (Map p137; Taj South Gate) Sells secondhand books at reasonable prices.

Emergency

Tourist police (Map p132; ☎ 2421204; UP Tourism office, Agra Cantonment train station; ⊗ 24hr) The guys in sky-blue uniforms are based at the tourism office.

Internet Access

There's internet access available all over Taj Ganj, usually costing around Rs 30 to Rs 40 per hour. One reliable option in Taj Ganj is **iWay Internet** (Map p137; per hr Rs 30; ⊗ 8am-11pm).

Left Luggage

Agra Cantonment train station (Map p132; ⊗ 24hr)
Yash Café (Map p137; Taj South Gate) A stone's throw from the Taj Mahal; this place charges Rs 50 for a whole day's luggage storage, with access to its showers thrown in.

Medical Services

District Hospital (Map p132; ☎ 2361099; Mahatma Ghandi (MG) Rd; ⊗ 24hr)
SN Hospital (Map p132; ☎ 2361314; Hospital Rd; ⊗ 24hr)

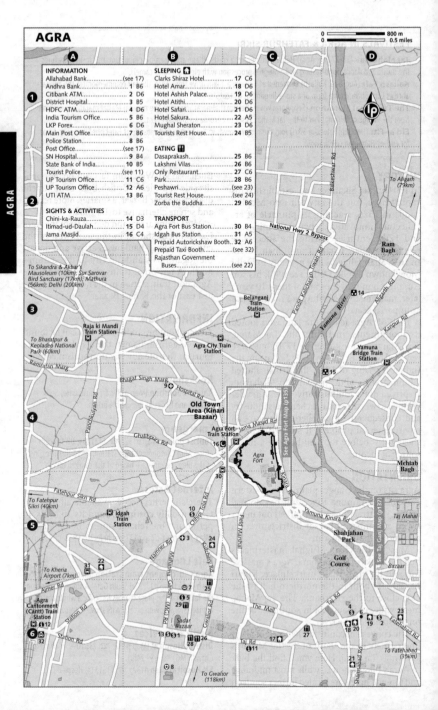

AGRA

| 0 | 800 m |
| 0 | 0.5 miles |

INFORMATION
Allahabad Bank....................(see 17)
Andhra Bank.................................1 B6
Citibank ATM.................................2 D6
District Hospital............................3 B5
HDFC ATM....................................4 D6
India Tourism Office.......................5 B6
LKP Forex.....................................6 D6
Main Post Office............................7 B6
Police Station................................8 B6
Post Office...............................(see 17)
SN Hospital...................................9 B4
State Bank of India.......................10 B5
Tourist Police...........................(see 11)
UP Tourism Office.......................11 C6
UP Tourism Office.......................12 A6
UTI ATM.....................................13 B6

SIGHTS & ACTIVITIES
Chini-ka-Rauza...........................14 D3
Itimad-ud-Daulah.......................15 D4
Jama Masjid...............................16 C4

SLEEPING 🏠
Clarks Shiraz Hotel......................17 C6
Hotel Amar.................................18 D6
Hotel Ashish Palace.....................19 D6
Hotel Atithi................................20 D6
Hotel Safari................................21 D6
Hotel Sakura...............................22 A5
Mughal Sheraton........................23 D6
Tourists Rest House......................24 B5

EATING 🍴
Dasaprakash...............................25 B6
Lakshmi Vilas..............................26 B6
Only Restaurant..........................27 C6
Park..28 B6
Peshawri................................(see 23)
Tourist Rest House...................(see 24)
Zorba the Buddha........................29 B6

TRANSPORT
Agra Fort Bus Station...................30 B4
Idgah Bus Station........................31 A5
Prepaid Autorickshaw Booth..32 A6
Prepaid Taxi Booth..................(see 32)
Rajasthan Government
    Buses..................................(see 22)

To Sikandra & Akbar's
Mausoleum (10km); Sur Sarovar
Bird Sanctuary (17km); Mathura
(56km); Delhi (200km)

To Bharatpur &
Keoladeo National
Park (60km)

To Fatehpur
Sikri (40km)

To Kheria
Airport (7km)

Agra
Cantonment
(Cantt) Train
Station

National Hwy 2 Bypass

To Aligarh
(79km)

Ram
Bagh

Balkeshwar Rd

Pandit Kalicharan Tiwari Rd

Yamuna River

Aligarh Rd

Kanpur Rd

Yamuna
Bridge Train
Station

Belanganj
Train
Station

Raja ki Mandi
Train Station

Agra City Train
Station

Ranitalan Marg

Panchkuiyan Rd

Bhagat Singh Marg

Hospital Rd

Old Town
Area (Kinari
Bazaar)

Jama Masjid Rd

Agra Fort
Train Station

Ghalibpura Rd

Agra
Fort

Mehtab
Bagh

Fatehpur Sikri Rd

Chippi Tola Rd

Field Marshal

Yamuna Kinara Rd

Shahjahan
Park

Golf
Course

Idgah
Train
Station

Mariner Rd

Mahatma Gandhi (MG) Rd

Kutchery Rd

Gwalior Rd

The Mall

Taj Rd

Taj Mahal

Bazaar

Sadar
Bazaar

Station Rd

Taj Rd

To Fatehabad
(35km)

Shahjahad Rd

To Gwalior
(118km)

To Fatehabad
Fatehabad Rd

See Agra Fort Map (p135)

See Taj Ganj Map (p137)

Money

Allahabad Bank (Map p132; Clarks Shiraz Hotel; ☽ noon-4pm Mon-Fri, noon-2pm Sat)

Andhra Bank (Map p132; Sadar Bazaar; ☽ 10am-4pm Mon-Fri, 10am-1pm Sat)

Citibank ATM (Map p132; Fatehabad Rd)

HDFC ATM (Map p132; Fatehabad Rd)

LKP Forex (Map p132; Fatehabad Rd; ☽ 9.30am-6pm Mon-Sat) Part of a reliable India-wide chain; exchanges currency and travellers cheques.

State Bank of India (Map p132; ☽ 10am-4pm Mon-Fri, 10am-1pm Sat) Just off Chhipi Tola Rd.

UTI ATM Sadar Bazaar (Map p132); Taj East Gate (Map p137)

Photography

Radhey Lal Colour Lab (Map p137; Taj South Gate) Can handle all your print and digital requirements.

Post

Main post office (Map p132; ☎ 2363886; the Mall; ☽ 10am-6pm Mon-Sat)

Post office (Map p132; Clarks Shiraz Hotel; ☽ 10am-5pm Mon-Sat)

Tourist Information

India Tourism office (Map p132; ☎ 2226378; www .incredibleindia.org; 191 the Mall; ☽ 9am-5.30pm Mon-Fri, 9am-2pm Sat & government holidays) Offers brochures, advice on hotels, and will fix you up with an official guide (up to 4 people half/full day Rs 350/650).

UP Tourism office (www.up-tourism.com) Agra Cantonment train station (Map p132; ☎ 2421204; ☽ 24hr); Taj Rd (Map p132; ☎ 2226431; 64 Taj Rd; ☽ 10am-5pm Mon-Sat)

DANGERS & ANNOYANCES

Many hotels, tourist shops and moneychangers pay hefty commissions to taxi drivers and rickshaw-wallahs who bring in customers; suspiciously cheap – or even free – rickshaw rides will often lead to a gem or souvenir shop.

Scams

Don't fall for the 'gem import scam', which has been conning tourists for decades. Travellers are invited to earn a quick buck by helping a shop avoid import duty. All they have to do is carry gems back to their home country, where a company representative will hand them a tidy profit. The travellers are asked to make a small credit-card payment 'as a sign of good faith'. Without exception, the gems are worthless, the representative never materialises and travellers are lumped with a huge credit-card bill.

Credit-card fraud is another scam operating widely in Agra. If at all possible, pay cash for everything and if you do decide to use your card, don't let it out of your sight. It's worthwhile checking your account regularly for errant transactions.

Several years ago, a few Taj Ganj restaurants allegedly went to the extent of deliberately poisoning travellers and rushing them off to crooked doctors who then billed insurance companies thousands of dollars. Lonely Planet has received several word-of-mouth traveller reports suggesting this has resurfaced: it's worth keeping an ear out for further news on this nasty practice.

Finally, in September 2007, two female Japanese tourists were allegedly raped in their hotel in Agra. Though this appears to have been a highly disturbing isolated incident, female travellers should remember the Staying Safe tips included on p372.

SIGHTS & ACTIVITIES

The vast majority of Agra's sights are based around the heady, extravagant and highly cultured world of the Mughals, who left their legacy dotted about the city.

Taj Mahal

ENTRY & INFORMATION

Described as the most extravagant monument ever built for love, this sublime Mughal **mausoleum** (Map p137; ☎ 2330498; Indian/foreigner Rs 20/750, children under 15 free, video Rs 25; ☽ 6am-7pm, south gate from 8am, closed Fri) is India's greatest tourist emblem. Many have tried to sum up its beauty – 'a teardrop on the face of eternity' according to Indian poet Rabindranath Tagore, 'the embodiment of all things pure' according to Indian-born British writer Rudyard Kipling.

Usually quiet and exceptionally magical at sunrise, it doesn't get invaded by tour groups until mid-morning. It's also great to visit around sunset, though you might find its iridescent sparkle subdued by lengthening shadows. Bear in mind that though the entrance price is pretty steep, it does entitle you to a modest saving at Agra's other points of interest. You'll get Rs 50 off entry to Agra Fort, and Rs 10 off entry to Akbar's tomb, Fatehpur Sikri and Itimad-ud-Daulah, provided you visit on the same day.

If you're in town on the night of the full moon plus two nights on either side, there are moonlight viewings of the Taj for the same price as a regular entry ticket. Batches of 50 visitors are allowed in at a time, with strict security measures, between 8pm and midnight. Tickets should be purchased a day in advance from one of the Taj's three ticket offices.

In attempts to preserve the monument for as long as possible, there's a long list of prohibited items (including food, drinks, drawing materials, tobacco, matches, mobile phones and camera tripods) all of which can be left without charge at the east and west gates. Cameras and camcorders are permitted, but you can't take photographs inside the mausoleum (there are instant fines in place). The top shot is of the gem-encrusted building reflected in the watercourse that runs through the gardens. Another popular choice is the 'Princess Diana' photo, with visitors seated on the famous bench where she was pictured alone in 1992. Note that the chances of obtaining a similarly solitary shot are pretty much impossible these days, though you can queue for a try.

TOURING THE TAJ

The Taj was built by Emperor Shah Jahan as a memorial for his second wife, Mumtaz Mahal, who died giving birth to their fourteenth child in 1631, aged 39. The death left the besotted emperor so heartbroken that his hair is said to have turned grey overnight. Construction began the same year and was not completed until 1653, with specialists brought in from as far afield as Europe to produce the exquisite marble screens and *pietra dura* (marble inlay work). The construction bill is believed to have run to Rs 3 million, equivalent to about US$70 million today.

Legends abound about its construction. Some say that Shah Jahan rather uncharitably cut off the chief mason's hand once the Taj

was finished, to prevent him from making another one; others, that the emperor wanted his own black-marble mausoleum on the opposite bank of the river. As he was imprisoned by his own son for his final years, however, this was never to be.

The Taj can be accessed through the west, south and east gates which all lead to an outer courtyard known as the **Chowk-i Jilo Khana**. From here, entry to the inner compound is through a 30m red-sandstone **gateway** on the south side of the forecourt, inscribed with verses from the Quran. The **ornamental gardens** are set out along classical Mughal *charbagh* (formal Persian garden) lines – a square quartered by watercourses, with an ornamental marble tank, representing the Quran's celestial pool of abundance, at the centre. To the west is a small **museum** (admission Rs 5; ☾ 9am-5pm Sat-Thu) housing original architectural drawings of the Taj, miniature paintings, and, most compellingly, some celadon-glazed plates, said to split into pieces or change colour if the food served on them contains poison.

The Taj Mahal **mausoleum** itself stands on a raised marble platform at the northern end of the ornamental gardens. Decorative slender white **minarets** grace each corner of the platform, which may have been designed to lean slightly outwards so that in the event of an earthquake, they would fall away from the Taj. The domed red-sandstone **mosque** to the west of the main structure is an important gathering place for Agra's Muslims. The identical building to the east, the **jawab**, was built for symmetry and probably used as travellers' accommodation.

The mausoleum is made of semitranslucent white marble, carved with flowers and inlaid with thousands of semiprecious stones. The whole structure is capped by four small domes

---

SERENITY NOW

Alongside security fears at the Taj, which suspended moonlight visits for two decades, there's another, more pressing danger to Agra's monuments. Air pollution, caused by a combination of heavy industry and traffic fumes is as sure a corroder over time as a vat of acid, and fears for the Taj's delicate marble work have been mounting.

To try to combat this, there is nowadays a 500m 'exclusion zone' around parts of the Taj Mahal, which prevents motorised vehicles from getting any closer. Though, in practice, there's still plenty of traffic around its south and west gates, the east gate is extremely peaceful. This may not really help save the Taj, but it does mean that if you're staying on its eastern side, roughly between the Amarvilas and Hotel Sheela, you'll likely be spared the traffic noise and fumes right outside your window.

surrounding the bulbous central dome, topped by a 17m brass spire. Entrance is through the south side, inside which is the **Cenotaph of Mumtaz Mahal**, an elaborate false tomb surrounded by an exquisite perforated marble screen. Beside it is the **Cenotaph of Shah Jahan**, who was interred here with little ceremony by his usurping son Aurangzeb in 1666. The real **tombs** of Mumtaz Mahal and Shah Jahan are directly below, in a locked basement room which cannot be viewed.

Agra Fort

Construction of this massive, majestic red-sandstone **fort and palace** (Map p135; ☎ 2364512; admission Indian/foreigner Rs 20/300, video Rs 25; ☼ sunrise-sunset) was begun by Emperor Akbar in 1565, with later additions made by Akbar's grandson Shah Jahan, who quite predictably (considering his efforts on the Taj Mahal) incorporated buildings using white marble. The fort, which stands on earlier Rajput fortifications, was built primarily as a military structure, but Shah Jahan upgraded it to a palace, and it became his gilded prison for his final eight years after his son Aurangzeb seized power in 1658. It was Aurangzeb, the last of the great Mughal emperors, who added the fort's ramparts.

The half-moon-shaped fort's colossal sandstone double outer walls rise over 20m in height and measure 2.5km in circumference, broken by a series of huge gates. Inside is a maze of buildings, forming a city within a city, of which only select parts are open to the public. Many of the fort's structures were, over the years, destroyed by Nadir Shah, the Marathas, the Jats and finally the British who used the fort as a garrison.

Nowadays, the **Amar Singh Gate** to the south is the sole entry point to the fort, its confusing design, comprising three separate gates, intended to flummox attackers. From here, a ramp leads to a second gate and a courtyard surrounding the beautiful **Diwan-i-Am** (Hall of Public Audience). This pillared hall was used by Shah Jahan for domestic government business, and features an ornate throne alcove where the emperor listened to petitioners, seated on the famous jewel-encrusted Peacock Throne. The throne itself was looted in 1739 and taken to Persia, where it was later destroyed.

In front of the Diwan-i-Am is the small and rather incongruous Gothic-style **tomb of John**

Colvin, a lieutenant-governor of the northwest provinces who died of an illness in the fort during the 1857 Uprising. To the north of the Diwan-i-Am courtyard, the **Moti Masjid** (Pearl Mosque) is usually closed to visitors, but don't miss the tiny but exquisite **Nagina Masjid** (Gem Mosque) on the upper level of the fort, built in 1635 by Shah Jahan for the ladies of his harem and made entirely of marble. Down below was the **Ladies' bazaar** where the court ladies were brought fine goods, which they could inspect in modesty from up above, standing on the small latticed balcony at the rear of the mosque.

Further up on the terrace, overlooking the river and the distant Taj Mahal, is **Takhti-i-Jehangir**, a huge slab of black rock with an inscription around its edge. This throne was made for the Emperor Jehangir when he was still just plain Prince Salim, apparently in defiance of his father Akbar. It was from here that he sat and watched elephant fights in the enclosure below, and dreamed of future glory. Facing the river, you'll see the **Diwan-i-Khas** (Hall of Private Audience) to your right, an incredibly ornately decorated reception area reserved by the emperor for important dignitaries or foreign representatives. Further on through the fort, the **Shish Mahal** (Mirror Palace) was another structure built for the ladies of the court, its walls inlaid with tiny mosaic-work mirrors. This is sadly not currently open to the public, so you'll have to crane your neck to catch a glimpse through the window.

Up ahead, you'll reach **Musamman Burj** and **Khas Mahal**, the wonderful white-marble octagonal tower and palace where Shah Jahan was imprisoned by his own son and from which he could gaze wistfully out at the Taj Mahal, the tomb of his beloved wife. The **Mina Masjid** was his own private mosque.

To the east of Shar Jahan's mosque, in the courtyard of the large harem quarters is **Anguri Bagh** (Grape Garden), a *charbagh* garden that has been brought back to life and now looks somewhat as it might have done in Shah Jahan's time.

South from here, the huge red-sandstone **Jehangir's palace** was possibly built by Akbar for his son Jehangir or otherwise for Akbar's own harem; the palace blends Hindu and Central Asian architectural styles, a reminder of the Mughals' Afghani cultural roots. In front of the palace is **Hauz-i-Jehangir**, a huge bowl carved out of a single block of stone, probably used for the emperor's bathing, when it would have been filled to the brim with rose-water. It's said, though hard to believe, that the emperor liked to lug this thing around with him on his travels, beating a bar of soap and a travel towel hands-down.

Akbar's Mausoleum

This outstanding sandstone and marble **tomb** (Off Map p132; ☎ 2641230; Indian/foreigner Rs 10/110, video Rs 25; ☼ sunrise-sunset) commemorates Akbar, the greatest of the Mughal emperors, who had it built himself, and was responsible for its curious mixture of styles. The huge courtyard is entered through its stunning **Buland Darwaza** (Great Gate). It has three-storey minarets

at each corner and is built of red sandstone strikingly inlaid with white-marble geometric patterns. The tomb itself lies in the centre of a peaceful garden, where deer still graze much as they did in Mughal times.

The mausoleum is located at Sikandra, 10km northwest of Agra Fort. Getting there is tricky but buses (Rs 10, 30 minutes) heading to Mathura from Agra Fort bus station go past the mausoleum. Alternatively, an autorickshaw should cost Rs 120 for a return journey including waiting time, (bear in mind it can be a long journey) while a taxi will charge double.

Itimad-ud-Daulah

Nicknamed the **Baby Taj** (Map p132; ☎ 2080030; Indian/foreigner Rs 15/110, video Rs 25; ☼ sunrise-sunset), this is the exquisite tomb of Mizra Ghiyas Beg, a Persian nobleman and Jehangir's *wazir* (chief minister). His daughter Nur Jahan, who married Jehangir, built the tomb between 1622 and 1628, in a style similar to the tomb she built for Jehangir himself, now near Lahore in Pakistan. Asmat Begum, Mizra Ghiyas Beg's wife, is buried next to him. Many of its design elements – including its marble construction and *pietra dura* work – foreshadow the stupendous Taj itself.

Chini-ka-Rauza

This is the riverside **tomb** (Map p132; ☼ 6am-6pm) of Afzal Khan, a Persian poet from Shiraz and high official in the court of Shah Jahan. It was built between 1628 and 1639, and is Agra's only purely Persian-style building. Rather neglected these days, it's hidden away down a shady avenue of trees. Bright-blue tiles still cover part of the exterior, giving an indication of how it once must have looked, and the interior is painted in floral designs. The upper storey offers fine views.

Mehtab Bagh

This **park** (Map p132; Indian/foreigner Rs 5/100; ☼ sunrise-sunset), which attempts to recreate a Mughal-style garden, is situated opposite the Taj Mahal, on the northern bank of the Yamuna River. Though pretty, it's really only worth visiting for its wonderful views of the back of the Taj. Alternatively, walk down to the Yamuna River on the path that runs alongside the park and view the Taj without any tourist crowds in a peaceful ambience of buffaloes and wading birds – though your peace may still be shattered by offers of autorickshaw rides, guided tours or boat rides across the river.

Taj Nature Walk

Follow the stone pathways through this **mini-wilderness** (Off Map p137; Taj East Gate Rd; admission Rs 50; ☺ 9am-6.30pm) exchanging Agra's rumble for a pleasant ramble among birds and butterflies, with the Taj hovering bewitchingly in the background.

Jama Masjid (Friday Mosque)

This fine red-sandstone **mosque** (Map p132; ☺ sunrise-sunset except prayer times) was built in 1648 by Shah Jahan and dedicated to his favourite daughter, Jahanara. It was originally connected, by way of a large courtyard, to the fort's main entrance, until the British ran a railway line between the two in the mid-1800s.

Beneath the Jama Masjid are the busy local streets of the colourful **Kinari Bazaar**, where you can haggle for everyday goods.

Swimming

Most swimming pools in Agra are reserved exclusively for guests of the hotels to which they belong. Some will make an exception, for a generally hefty fee: the best currently on offer are the Clarks Shiraz (p139; Rs 500) and Mughal Sheraton (p139; Rs 400) pools.

TOURS

UP Tourism runs lightning-fast **daily tours** (Indian/foreigner incl entry fees Rs 400/1700; ☺ daily except Friday) that leave the India Tourism office at 9.45am and Agra Cantonment train station between 10.20am and 10.30am. The tour includes the Taj Mahal, Agra Fort and Fatehpur Sikri with an hour-and-a-quarter stop in each place; for Rs 550 you can also join just for the afternoon portion to Fatehpur Sikri. Tours return to the station so that day-trippers can catch the *Taj Express* back to Delhi at 6.55pm. Contact either of the UP Tourism offices or the India Tourism office (p133) to book a seat.

SLEEPING

Agra, as you might expect, has plenty of hotels, but there's a lack of decent midrange accommodation and prices rise steeply towards the top end. If you're on a midrange budget, you might decide to save a few rupees by going for one of the better budget choices.

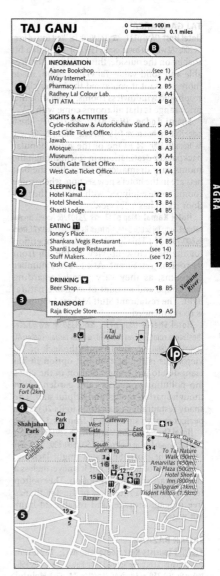

TAJ GANJ

INFORMATION	
Aanee Bookshop	(see 1)
iWay Internet	**1** A5
Pharmacy	**2** B5
Radhey Lal Colour Lab	**3** A4
UTI ATM	**4** B4

SIGHTS & ACTIVITIES	
Cycle-rickshaw & Autorickshaw Stand	**5** A5
East Gate Ticket Office	**6** B4
Jawab	**7** B3
Mosque	**8** A3
Museum	**9** A4
South Gate Ticket Office	**10** B4
West Gate Ticket Office	**11** A4

SLEEPING 🏠	
Hotel Kamal	**12** B5
Hotel Sheela	**13** B4
Shanti Lodge	**14** B5

EATING 🍴	
Joney's Place	**15** A5
Shankara Vegis Restaurant	**16** B5
Shanti Lodge Restaurant	(see 14)
Stuff Makers	(see 12)
Yash Café	**17** B5

DRINKING 🍷	
Beer Shop	**18** B5

TRANSPORT	
Raja Bicycle Store	**19** A5

Budget

The main centre for budget accommodation is Taj Ganj. Prices listed here are for rooms with private bathrooms, Western-style toilets and hot water, except where indicated. In summer, budget hotels tend to provide hot water in a bucket, whereas in winter it arrives more conveniently by pipe.

AGRA

TAJ GANJ AREA

Hotel Host (Map p137; ☎ 2331010; Taj West Gate; d from Rs 200, s/d without bathroom Rs 150/175) Though a bit shabby on the outside, this is a cheap, serviceable and solid-value Taj Ganj option, made more pleasant if you avoid the rather claustrophobic windowless rooms. A perk for this price range is that all rooms come with TV.

Shanti Lodge (Map p137; ☎ 2231973; shanti lodge2000@yahoo.co.in; Taj South Gate; d from Rs 200, with AC from Rs 500; 🕱) One of the most popular backpacker destinations in town, though the rooms vary dramatically in quality; the best bets are in the hotel's new section, where some rooms come equipped with TV and the top-floor room has a Taj view.

Hotel Kamal (Map p137; ☎ 2330126; hotelkamal@ hotmail.com; Taj South Gate; s/d from Rs 300/400, with AC from Rs 600/700; 🕱) This hotel wins the competition for the best close-up view of the Taj from its rooftop restaurant. Ask to see a number of rooms, as they vary greatly regarding size, shape and amount of available natural light. The restaurant Stuff Makers (opposite) is recommended.

Hotel Sheela (Map p137; ☎ 2333074; www.hotel sheelaagra.com; Taj East Gate Rd; d with fan/air cooler/AC Rs 400/600/800; 🕱 🖳) Despite the lack of Taj views this is the best budget option in Taj Ganj due to its serene situation in the city's 'no-pollution zone', its calm garden, clean though spartan rooms, and helpful staff. The shady restaurant (meals Rs 25 to Rs 70) is the perfect spot to sip a mixed-fruit lassi.

Hotel Sheela Inn (Off Map p137; ☎ 3293437; Taj East Gate Rd; d with fan/air cooler/AC Rs 500/600/800; 🕱) An offshoot of Hotel Sheela, it might lack the atmosphere of its sister, but it's nevertheless a clean, smart and friendly option. The rooftop restaurant has a nice view of the Taj, there's free luggage storage, and reliable 24-hour hot water.

SADAR BAZAAR

our pick Tourists Rest House (Map p132; ☎ 2463961; dontworrychickencurry@hotmail.com; Kutchery Rd; s Rs 150-300, d Rs 250-350, s/d with AC 350/450; 🕱 🖳) Helpful owners, a secure atmosphere, and spotless rooms grouped around a shady garden make this place widely regarded as Agra's best budget option. Though nowhere near as well-placed for the Taj Mahal as places in Taj Ganj, it's still such a perennial favourite that you need to book well ahead. There's internet, TV in most rooms and free pickup from the sta-

tion or bus station with 24 hours' notice. Also recommended are the trips around Rajasthan; ask for details and current prices.

OTHER AREAS

Hotel Sakura (Map p132; ☎ 2420169; ashu_sakura@ yahoo.com; Ajmer Rd; d Rs 200-500; 🖳) Another long-running favourite with clean rooms and a very friendly owner. It's close to Idgah bus stand, useful if you're planning an early start. The restaurant is recommended – try the butter chicken followed by a tasty *kheer* (rice pudding).

Hotel Safari (Map p132; ☎ 2480106; hotelsafari@hot mail.com; Shamsabad Rd; s/d Rs 300/350, with AC Rs 400/450; 🕱) Owned by the same people as the Tourists Rest House, this might lack the ambience of the former, but it's clean, comfortable and all rooms have TV. There's a rooftop terrace with a distant view of the Taj and the atmosphere is relaxed.

Midrange

Agra has very few midrange hotels worth their tarrif card; most of them are clustered together in Fatehabad Rd. It's well worth poking around a few, to make sure you get the best possible deal.

Taj Plaza (Off Map p137; ☎ 2232515; www.hoteltajplaza .com; Taj East Gate Rd; s/d Rs 600/900, with AC Rs 1000/1200; 🕱) A budget hotel gone upmarket, this place is small, clean and modern. Four of its pricier AC rooms are recommended for their Taj views, as is the rooftop restaurant.

Hotel Ashish Palace (Map p132; ☎ 2230032; Fatehabad Rd; s/d Rs 1200/1500; 🕱) Though it's one of the newer places on the Fatehabad Rd, its rooms equipped with fridge, TV and even shower caps, travellers have recently reported that it's starting to show telltale signs of wear and tear.

Hotel Atithi (Map p132; ☎ 2230040; www.hotel atithi.com; Fatehabad Rd; s Rs 1600-1900, d Rs 1900-2500; 🕱 🖳) Indoors, it's not an exciting choice, but the pool and lawn are the main draw here. There's also a restaurant serving good Indian food, where an evening meal will set you back Rs 400.

Hotel Amar (Map p132; ☎ 2331884; www.hotel amar.com; Fatehabad Rd; s Rs 2500-4000, d from Rs 3000; 🕱 🖳 🖳) The hotel, so the website boasts, 'beholds you with ultimate comfort'. This might be a bit much, but the rooms are certainly comfortable as well as colourful, ranging from an almost blindingly orange 'Mughal

Room' to a selection of lurid but airy suites. There's a good Indian restaurant, bar, pool, Ayurvedic health club and gym.

Top End

Clarks Shiraz Hotel (Map p132; ☎ 2226121; www.hotel clarksshiraz.com; Taj Rd; s with Taj view Rs 4800-7100, d with Taj view Rs 5200-7500; ✖ 🖳 🏊) Despite the evocative name, this is a set of high-rise executive rooms which are comfortable, cosy and equipped with all mod cons. The hotel boasts a gym, Ayurvedic massage, a bank, post office, shops and airline offices. Some parts of the hotel, however, are better than others (the tower wing has recently been refurbished).

Trident Hilton (Off map p132; ☎ 2331818; www.tri dent-hilton.com; Fatehabad Rd; d from US$130; ✖ 🖳 🏊) A tranquil, relaxed top-end choice, with particularly good reports of its pool and kids' club from travellers staying here with children. At the time of research, this hotel was about to cease to be part of the Hilton chain, so it's worth bearing in mind that the service, and the prices, could go up – or down.

Mughal Sheraton (Map p132; ☎ 2331701; mughal .sheraton@welcomgroup.com; Fatehabad Rd; s/d/ste US$150/160/400; ✖ 🖳 🏊) This sprawling red-brick luxury hotel is set amid tranquil gardens that include a tree planted by actor Peter O'Toole. Everything is shiny and elegant, and its Peshawri Restaurant (see p140) is especially recommended. Invigorate with a game of tennis or minigolf, and then have your fortune read by the in-house astrologer.

Amarvilas (Off Map p137; ☎ 2231515; www.oberoi hotels.com; Taj East Gate Rd; d from US$600, ste US$1350-3300; ✖ 🖳 🏊) A world-class hotel, considered the very best Agra – and, indeed, one of the best India – has to offer. Suffused with Mughal style, some of the most expensive rooms even have windows in the bathroom, so you can soak your aching feet while regarding the eternal Taj. If you're not flush enough to shell out for an overnight stay, stop in at the beautiful bar for a drink or two, and enjoy the splendour without the price tag.

EATING & DRINKING

Agra is historically famous for its rich, filling Mughlai fare, and simpler delicious local specialities can be found in the bazaars. *Peitha* is a square sweet made from pumpkin and glucose flavoured with rose-water, coconut or saffron, while *dalmoth* is Agra's famous version of *namkin* (prepackaged spicy nibbles).

From October to March look out for *gajak*, a spicy sesame-seed biscuit-strip.

Agra's drinking choices are fairly limited outside the top-end hotel-bars, of which **Amarvilas** (Off Map p132; drinks Rs150-250; ☾ 11am-11pm) is undoubtedly the best, with its exquisite terrace view of the Taj. There's a **beer shop** (Map p137; ☾ 10am-11pm) in Taj Ganj, which charges Rs 60 for a medium bottle of Kingfisher.

Taj Ganj Area

Taj Ganj has plenty of budget rooftop restaurants, where the meals may be basic and similar, but the views of the Taj range from good to fantastic. In general, keep an eye on hygiene: a quick peep into the kitchen can work wonders for your peace of mind. The places listed below are open from breakfast (around 7am to 8am) to dinner (10pm to 11pm) unless otherwise stated.

Joney's Place (Map p137; mains Rs 20-40; ☾ 5am-10.30pm) This tiny travellers' institution claims the best lassis in town, and is a good bet when the desire for hummus or a toasted sandwich strikes – especially useful for hungry early risers.

Stuff Makers (Map p137; Hotel Kamal; meals Rs 25-70) Join the crowd on the rooftop terrace with its fairy lights and great Taj views. The food is reliable, if uninspiring, and includes old favourites such as tasty honey-and-banana pancakes.

Shankara Vegis Restaurant (Map p137; meals Rs 25-70) This relaxed rooftop restaurant has no Taj view but does have plenty of hearty vegetarian favourites, prepared in a clean kitchen open to public view, as well as good music and a sublime lassis.

Hotel Sheela (Map p137; mains Rs 30-90) Hotel Sheela's shady garden café is one of the most reliable options in the neighbourhood, with consistently good reviews from travellers for its simple dishes and unusual, yummy fruit-and-nut lassis.

Yash Café (Map p137; meals Rs 30-95) A very laid-back joint with a '60s feel, Yash shows movies in the evening, offers a shower and storage space to day visitors, and cooks up good-value veg and nonveg thalis.

Shanti Lodge Restaurant (Map p137; meals Rs 50-100) A basic traveller-oriented restaurant but the food is reasonable and the rooftop Taj view is fantastic, making it a good place for breakfast before a day on your feet.

Sadar Bazaar

Lakshmi Vilas (Map p132; Taj Rd; meals Rs 30-60; 🍽) A clean, popular South Indian restaurant with all your *idli* (spongy, round savoury rice cake) and *uttapam* (a thick *dosa*-like pancake) favourites. Over 30 *dosa* varieties are available, including a 'family *dosa*', worth ordering if only because it's over a metre long.

Tourists Rest House (Map p132; Kutchery Rd; meals Rs 30-80) Nice, big breakfasts, great Indian dishes (including a winning *malai kofta*) and a lovely garden location makes this hotel-restaurant a cool, appealing retreat.

Park (Map p132; Sadar Bazaar; meals Rs 70-175; 🍽) A popular wood-panelled AC dining room with a long reputation among travellers, Park serves up Indian, Continental and Chinese food with some particularly tasty Mughlai dishes.

Dasaprakash (Map p132; Gwalior Rd; meals Rs 70-180; 🍽) Though not brimming with atmosphere, this efficient South Indian restaurant chain serves winning *dosas* (paper-thin lentil-flour pancakes) to loyal locals, along with generous thalis and indulgent ice-cream sundaes.

ourpick **Zorba the Buddha** (Map p132; Sadar Bazaar; meals Rs 80-150; 🕑 noon-3pm & 6-9pm, closed Jun; 🍽) Vases of flowers on neat little tables greet guests at this clean, quirky Osho-inspired bistro-style vegetarian restaurant. The healthy food and herbal teas are designed to nurture your soul as well as your body, while the ice creams make a nice finishing touch if you feel you've been all too worthy.

Other Areas

Only Restaurant (Map p132; the Mall; mains Rs 60-225; 🍽) This bamboo-lined, cosy restaurant is often packed with happy tour groups and has live music every evening from 7pm in the summer. Your best bets are the Mughlai dishes or tandoori options.

Peshawri (Map p132; Mughal Sheraton; 🕑 12.30-2.45pm & 7.30-11.30pm; mains from Rs 500; 🍽) One of the best, if priciest, North Indian dining options in the city, this restaurant serves particularly tasty tandoori and North-West Frontier barbeque dishes.

Esphahan (Off Map p137; Amarvilas; mains from Rs 550; 🍽) Though nonresidents have reported it hard to get a reservation, it's worth persisting if you're in the mood for top-of-the-range North Indian Avadhi cuisine in sumptuous surroundings. You can choose to dine at one of two sittings – 7pm or 9.30pm.

SHOPPING

Agra is well known for marble items inlaid with coloured stones, similar to the *pietra dura* work on the Taj. Sadar Bazaar (Map p132), Fatehabad Rd (Map p132), and the area around the Taj are all full of arts-and-craft emporiums of one kind or another. Be careful, though, as fake marble (usually soapstone, which you can spot by the ease with which it scratches) is common. Other popular buys include beautifully embroidered rugs and leather goods (Agra's tanneries are big shoe producers).

Away from the usual tourist trappings, the Kinari Bazaar (Map p132) is crowded and heady, vending to a largely local crowd. The smaller bazaar south of Taj Ganj is much calmer and tailors there will knock you up a pair of trousers for around Rs 200 or a shirt for Rs 100.

About a kilometre along the traffic-quiet road from Taj East Gate is Shilpgram (Off Map p137; 🕑 10am-10pm Oct-Mar), an open-air collection of stalls selling handicrafts and artworks that also has a café and bar. Every February a week-long festival also takes place here (see p131).

GETTING THERE & AWAY
Air

Agra's Kheria Airport is 7km from the city centre. Kingfisher Airlines (☎ toll free within India 18001800101; www.flykingfisher.com) flies daily from Delhi to Agra (1 hour), departing Delhi at 7.55am and Agra at 5pm. The return fare is approximately US$185; it's generally cheapest to reserve tickets online.

Bus

Most long-haul and deluxe buses connecting Agra with Delhi and Rajasthan depart from and arrive at **Idgah bus station** (Map p132; ☎ 2420324; Ajmer Rd). Hourly buses run to Delhi's Sarai Kale Khan bus station (Rs 105, five hours) via Mathura (Rs 30, 1½ hours). Hourly buses also depart from here to Jaipur (Rs 105, six hours) and frequent local buses head to Fatehpur Sikri (Rs 18, one hour) and Bharatpur (Rs 31, 1½ hours).

A few services also depart and arrive at **Agra Fort bus station** (Map p132; Power House bus station; ☎ 2364557). Buses leave here for Delhi (Rs 105, five hours) via Mathura (Rs 29, 1½ hours).

Official Rajasthan government deluxe buses (Map p132) depart hourly (on the half-hour) from outside Hotel Sakura (p138), and drop you off at the main bus station in Jaipur. They run from 6.30am to 2.30pm daily, and cost Rs 174. Tickets can be booked at the Hotel Sakura itself.

Train

Though Agra has six train stations, most travellers will only use either the **Agra Cantonment (Cantt) train station** (Map p132; ☎ 2421204) or the **Agra Fort train station** (Map p132).

The Agra Cantt is an important stop on the main Delhi–Mumbai line, with several trains daily from both New Delhi and Nizamuddin train stations. The fastest is the AC *Shatabdi Express* (chair/executive Rs 395/760, two hours) which runs daily except Fridays. It leaves New Delhi at 6.15am and departs from Agra for the return trip at 8.30pm, making it ideal for day-tripping.

A cheaper alternative is the daily *Taj Express* (2nd/chair car Rs 56/211, three hours). It leaves Delhi's Nizamuddin train station at 7.15am and departs from Agra for the return trip at 6.55pm, connecting with UP Tourism daily tours (see p133).

To Jaipur and Jodhpur, the *Marudhar Express* leaves Agra Fort at 6.15am on Monday, Wednesday and Saturday, reaching Jaipur (3AC/2AC Rs 330/473) at 11.30am, and Jodhpur (3AC/2AC Rs 622/892) at 6.20pm.

GETTING AROUND
To/From the Airport

For the short hop to Kheria Airport, taxis should charge about Rs 200 and autorickshaws Rs 100.

Autorickshaw

Just outside Agra Cantonment train station is the **prepaid autorickshaw booth** (Map p132; ⊙ 24hr). The official rates here are Rs 15 for a short 1km ride, Rs 30 to Sadar Bazaar and Rs 50 to Taj Ganj. A three-hour tour to the Taj Mahal and Agra Fort return costs Rs 160, a four-hour tour Rs 200 and an eight-hour tour Rs 300. A round trip including waiting time to Sikandra for Akbar's Mausoleum is likely to cost Rs 120. Autorickshaws are not allowed to go to Fatehpur Sikri or within the 'exclusion zone' around the Taj Mahal (see p134), so you'll need to take a bus or taxi.

Note, however, that it'll be nigh on impossible to find a driver willing to conform to these rates. Have your best haggling hat on, since you'll generally be quoted around 100% over the odds for any trip.

Autorickshaws to look out for are the green and yellow variety, which run on CNG (compressed natural gas) instead of petrol, and so are far less polluting to Agra's already strained environment.

Bicycle

Bicycles can be hired from **Raja Bicycle Store** (Map p137; per day Rs 50; ⊙ 8am-8.30pm) but you'll need nerves of steel and a desire to subject yourself to heat, dust and fumes in order to negotiate obstacle-course roads.

Cycle-rickshaw

Best for short distances, this environmentally friendly form of transport is cheaper than using autorickshaws and provides an income for some of the poorest employed sections of society. Rides should cost between Rs 20 and Rs 40, but can be excruciatingly slow and stinky due to Agra's traffic fumes.

Nowadays, it's possible to hire a brand new model of cycle-rickshaw, courtesy of an Indian NGO and the US Agency for International Development. Lighter and more comfortable for the hard-working driver to pedal, they can be rented from outside many of the top-end hotels; a city tour to the Taj, fort and Kinari Bazaar should cost around Rs 150.

Taxi

Outside Agra Cantonment train station is the **prepaid taxi booth** (⊙ 24hr). The cost to any five-star hotel is Rs 120 (AC Rs 150), while a three-hour tour costs Rs 300 (AC Rs 375) and a four-hour tour is Rs 450 (AC Rs 650). An eight-hour tour is Rs 650 (AC Rs 950), costing Rs 950 (AC Rs 1400) if it includes Fatehpur Sikri. A four-hour trip to Fatehpur Sikri costs Rs 700 (AC Rs 900). A return trip to the Keoladeo Ghana National Park at Bharatpur (p188) costs Rs 950 including waiting time. Further afield, one way to Delhi is Rs 2500, and Jaipur Rs 2700. As with autorickshaws, however, it may be hard to actually secure a ride for these prices, so you'll have to drive a hard bargain.

Other Transport

Environmentally friendly **electric buses** (Rs 5; ⊙ every 15min 6am-7pm) ply the route between the Taj Mahal west gate and Agra Fort, another good way of reducing your environmental impact on Agra.

AGRA

AROUND AGRA

FATEHPUR SIKRI

☎ 05613 / pop 28,750

This magnificent fortified ghost city, 40km west of Agra, was the Mughal Empire's short-lived capital between 1571 and 1585, during the reign of Akbar. Although brilliant and unusual from an architectural point of view, Akbar's city was erected in an area that suffered from water shortages and thus is said to have been abandoned shortly after his death, making the name 'Fatehpur', meaning 'city of victory', somewhat of an irony. The well-preserved palace buildings and the still-used mosque are the main points of interest.

Most people visit this World Heritage site as a day trip from Agra, but it's worthwhile staying in the nearby town if you have the time, since the red-sandstone palaces are at their most atmospheric at sunset. See p360 for details of Eid al-Fitr celebrations at the site.

Orientation & Information

The palace buildings lie on the top of a ridge, with the town of Fatehpur Sikri just to the south. The Jama Masjid and the ruins near it and behind the mint can be visited for free. Swarms of unofficial guides pester visitors, demanding a ridiculous fee of Rs 300, but if you want a guide it's best to hire an official one near a ticket office, which should cost Rs 50 to Rs 100. The purpose of many buildings is uncertain and you can safely assume that much of what guides will tell you is invented.

Sights

JAMA MASJID

The beautiful, expansive **Jama Masjid** (Dargah Mosque; ☉ sunrise-sunset), completed in 1571,

contains elements of Persian and Hindu design. The main entrance is through the impressive 54m-high **Buland Darwaza** (Victory Gate), perhaps the largest in Asia, built to commemorate Akbar's military victory in Gujarat. A Quranic inscription inside the archway quotes Jesus saying: 'The world is a bridge, pass over it but build no house upon it. He who hopes for an hour may hope for eternity', which seems appropriate considering the fate of the city.

Inside the courtyard is the superb white-marble **tomb of Shaikh Salim Chishti**, completed in 1581. Just as Akbar came to the saint four centuries ago hoping for a son, childless women still visit his tomb today and tie a thread to the jalis (marble lattice screens), among the finest in India.

PALACES & PAVILIONS

The first of the **palace buildings** (Indian/foreigner Rs 20/260, video Rs 25; ☉ sunrise-sunset) you enter from the south is the largest, the **Palace of Jodh Bai**. Constructed around a courtyard, it blends Hindu columns, Islamic cupolas and blue Persian roof tiles.

The **Palace of the Christian Wife** was used by Akbar's Goan Christian wife Mariam, and you can see the remains of the paintings that used to cover the inside. **Birbal Bhavan**, ornately carved inside and out, was probably used by two of Akbar's senior wives.

The function of the **Lower Haramsara** is controversial – it may have housed servants but looks more like stables for the horses, camels and elephants.

The most ornate structure is the amazing **Rumi Sultana**, whose surface is covered with intricate carving.

The whimsical **Panch Mahal** is a five-storey pavilion that was used by the court ladies.

SAVE THE BEARS

India's first sanctuary for 'dancing' bears was established by the **World Society for the Protection of Animals** (WSPA; www.wspa.org.uk) in 2002 with help from the UP Forestry Department and **Free the Bears** (www.freethebears.org.au). The 8-hectare Agra Bear Rescue Facility site is inside the Sur Sarovar Bird Sanctuary, 17km west of Agra and provides a refuge for more than 130 sloth bears, rescued from local Qalander gypsies who previously forced them to 'dance' in return for money from onlookers. This cruel entertainment is illegal in India but still enslaves some 800 bears, though ongoing efforts are being made to save them and re-educate the Qalanders; some young Qalander men are even employed to look after the bears at the facility. Visits to the sanctuary are limited so as not to disturb the bears during their rehabilitation period, but can be arranged through **Wildlife SOS** (☎ 011 246 21939 in Delhi; www.wildlifesos.com). Also see Animal Welfare, p83.

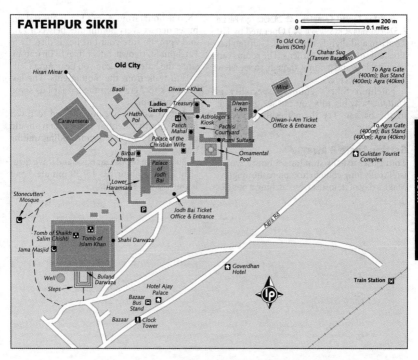

FATEHPUR SIKRI

Each of the storeys decreases in size until the top one consists of only a tiny kiosk. The lower floor has 84 columns, which are all different.

The **Treasury** has sea monsters, intended to protect the fabulous wealth once stored there, carved onto the ceiling struts, while the so-called **Astrologer's Kiosk** in front has its roof supports carved into a serpentine Jain style.

The **Diwan-i-Khas** (Hall of Private Audience) has an interior dominated by a magnificently carved stone column in the centre. The pillar flares to create a flat-topped plinth linked to the four corners of the room by narrow stone bridges, from where Akbar is believed to have debated with scholars who stood at the ends of the four bridges. Outside is the **Pachisi Courtyard** where Akbar is said to have played the game pachisi using slave girls as pieces.

The **Diwan-i-Am** (Hall of Public Audience) is where Akbar dispensed justice 'without harshness or ill-will', according to the information board.

Plenty of ruins are scattered behind the mosque, including the **caravanserai**, a vast courtyard surrounded by rooms where visit-ing merchants used to stay, and the bizarre 21m-high **Hiran Minar** tower that's decorated with hundreds of stone representations of elephant tusks. Badly defaced elephants still guard **Hathi Pol** (Elephant Gate), while the remains of the small **Stonecutters' Mosque** and a **hammam** (bath) are nearby.

Sleeping & Eating

Hotel Ajay Palace (☎ 282950; Agra Rd; d Rs 300, without bathroom Rs 200) Rooms in this small four-room guesthouse near the bus stand have squat toilets, but are neat and clean, and the place receives regular praise from travellers. The restaurant (meals Rs 20 to Rs 80) has the best food in town – try the fried eggplant, then finish off with the *kheer* (rice pudding).

Goverdhan Hotel (☎ 282643; www.hotelfatehpur sikriviews.com; Agra Rd; s Rs 250-600, d Rs 400-750; 🔀 💻) The Goverdhan proclaims, on its website, 'Cleanliness is Our Strength'; some rooms have decidedly odd décor, but are, as they are at pains to point out, clean. The restaurant serves up good Indian food cooked with filtered water, and in case you need to work up an appetite, there's a badminton court.

Gulistan Tourist Complex (☎ 282490; Agra Rd; s/d Rs 525/600, with AC Rs 850/950; ✺) Operated by UP Tourism and slightly run-down, Gulistan has a restaurant, bar, and gardens. The rooms can be quite dark and gloomy, though, so see a few before you decide.

Fatehpur Sikri's culinary speciality is *khataie,* tasty biscuits you can see piled high in the bazaar. Try them freshly baked in the evening.

Getting There & Away

Tour buses usually stop for 1½ hours, which isn't really long enough to explore thoroughly. Make a day of it, instead, by catching a bus (Rs 18, one hour) from Agra's Idgah bus station; buses depart every 30 minutes between 7am and 7pm. Be sure your bus heads directly to Fatehpur Sikri town, rather than to Bharatpur, since the latter will drop you near Agra Gate, a 1km walk from the monuments. The last bus back to Agra from the bazaar bus stand leaves at 7pm.

Autorickshaws are not allowed to travel from Agra to Fatehpur Sikri; a taxi should cost around Rs 700 return including waiting time.

Buses from the bazaar bus stand leave regularly for Bharatpur (Rs 15, 30 minutes) and Jaipur (Rs 80, 4½ hours).

Rajasthan

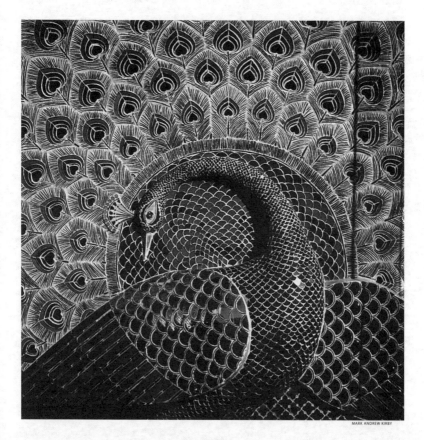

Jaipur

Jaipur's colourful, chaotic streets flow with a heady brew of old and new. Careering buses dodge dawdling camels, leisurely cycle-rickshaws frustrate swarms of motorbikes, and everywhere buzzing autorickshaws watch for easy prey. In the midst of this mayhem, the splendours of Jaipur's majestic past are islands of calm evoking a different pace and another world. Dusky pink and slightly soiled, Old Jaipur was painted a mock-sandstone hue to welcome the Prince of Wales in 1876, and though it doesn't look like it, it is given a fresh coat regularly. At its heart, the City Palace continues to house the royal family, the fascinating Jantar Mantar, the royal observatory, maintains a heavenly aspect, and the honeycomb Hawa Mahal gazes on the bazaar below.

Jaipur, the capital of Rajasthan, is an enthralling historical city and the gateway to India's most flamboyant and exciting state. It is also one of India's most vibrant and fastest-growing cities and an axis of the 'Golden Triangle', India's most popular tourist trail. Formidable fortifications surround the city, and just out of sight is the fairy-tale grandeur of not-to-be-missed Amber Fort.

However, it's not all fairy tales. Prepare your senses to be shaken and stirred as you come to grips with this mesmerising and, at times, frustrating metropolis. Jaipur suffers from overcrowding, traffic turmoil and pollution, and persistent touts can wear down your enthusiasm. But give this dishevelled romantic time to weave her magic and the appreciative guest will be tickled pink.

JAIPUR

HIGHLIGHTS

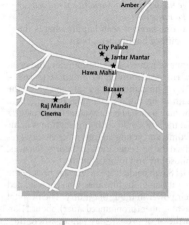

- Marvel at the maharaja high-life in the beautiful **City Palace** (p154), a maze of opulence
- Explore the stunning **Amber Fort** (p178), a mighty Rajput citadel rising from the rocks 11km from Jaipur
- Follow your stars among the outsized astronomical instruments at **Jantar Mantar** (p156)
- Hide like the harem at the **Hawa Mahal** (p157), the Palace of the Winds, a multiwindowed hive built for the women of the court
- Hunt and gather through the boisterous **bazaars** (p172) of the Old City
- Join the party and the painted pachyderms at one of Jaipur's colourful **festivals** (p148)
- Catch a Bollywood blockbuster at the swirling pink **Raj Mandir Cinema** (p172)

▤ AREA: 65 SQ KM	▤ POPULATION: 3.32 MILLION	▤ TELEPHONE CODE: 0141

FESTIVALS IN JAIPUR

Jaipur celebrates unique festivals, as well as numerous statewide and national festivals, with vigour and flair. It's worth visiting for any of these to catch the build-up, the dressing up and a few processions. For more information on festivals, see p358.

Makar Sankranti (14 Jan) This kite festival is worth catching. It's celebrated all over India, and heralds the transition of the sun into the northern hemisphere. The sky is full of kites, with special displays and kite fights – participants fiercely compete to cut down each others' kites (the strings are dipped in crushed glass) – anyone is fair game.

Jaipur Heritage International Festival (www.jaipurfestival.org; 21-30 Mar) In celebration of Jaipur's heritage, this festival aims to revive and conserve the regional culture and traditions. Performances are held throughout the Old City, in atmospheric venues from forts to temples. As well as the usual displays of folk, classical, traditional and contemporary dance, there are theatre, film, music and sporting events, as well as concerts, workshops, exhibitions and fashion shows. Contact the Indian National Trust for Art and Cultural Heritage (Intach; ☎ 2228275) for more details.

Elephant Festival (Mar) Takes place on the day before Holi. Elephants painted in amazing patterns and dressed in ribbons and jewellery (spot the females by their jangling anklets) lumber through the streets, along with camels, horses and dancers. Elephantine craziness includes matches of elephant polo at Chaughan Stadium in the Old City, elephant races, and a tug-of-war between elephants and humans.

Gangaur (Mar-Apr) Rajasthan's most important festival, especially for women, celebrates the love between Gan (Shiva) and his consort Gauri (Parvati). Parvati symbolises perfection in married life, so it's considered a good move for both unmarried and married women to worship during this festival. It commences on the day following Holi, the first day of Chaitra, and continues for 18 days. Newlywed women should observe the full 18 days. Unmarried women usually fast during this period. People make small terracotta images of Gan and Gauri to dress and worship. Some families have permanent wooden images of Gauri, which are freshly painted during Gangaur. The last three days are the climax of the festival. The terracotta and wooden images are dressed to impress in beautiful costumes and jewels. An elaborately garbed image of the goddess is carried on a palanquin from the Tripolia Gate, at the City Palace, through the streets of the Old City. The traditional dish to eat in Jaipur at this time is *ghewar*, a kind of sweet.

Teej (Jul-Aug) This is the swing festival, and heralds the onset of the monsoon month, Shravan. It's celebrated across Rajasthan in honour of the marriage of Gan and Gauri, but is at its best in Jaipur. It's another favourite with Rajasthani women, and a chance for them to get dressed up – traditionally they wear green and sing songs celebrating the onset of the rains. Flower-bedecked swings are hung from trees, and in Jaipur there are glittering processions through the streets for two days – floats feature gods and goddesses and wonderful costumes.

HISTORY

Je na dekkhyo Jaipario to kal main akar kaai kario?
If one has not seen Jaipur, what is the point of having been born?

Jaipur is named after its founder, the great warrior-astronomer Jai Singh II (r 1688–1744), who came to power at age 11 after the death of his father, Maharaja Bishan Singh. The maharaja had been assured by astrologers that the boy would achieve great things in his lifetime, and young Jai (meaning 'victory') received the best education in the arts, sciences, philosophy and military affairs.

Jai Singh could trace his lineage back to the Rajput clan of Kachhwahas, who consolidated their power in the 12th century. Their capital was at Amber (pronounced amer), about 11km northeast of present-day Jaipur, where they built the impressive Amber Fort (p178). The Kachhwahas had a talent for war and alliances of convenience, so their dominion spread, eventually encompassing a large area abutting the kingdoms of Mewar (in the Udaipur region) and Marwar (in the Jodhpur region).

The Kachhwaha clan recognised the expediency of aligning themselves with the powerful Mughal empire, and subsequently enjoyed the patronage of the Mughal emperors, which brought them great riches and influence. Raja Bihar Mal led an army for Humayun (second Mughal ruler of India), and was the first Rajput to be presented at Akbar's court. When Akbar visited the Muslim shrine at Ajmer, Bihar Mal presented him his daughter, who, as Akbar's wife, gave him his first son, later Emperor Jehangir. The next ruler, Bhagwan Das, also gave a daughter to be Jehangir's wife.

It's said that at 15 years of age, the prodigal Jai Singh – already king for four years – met the Mughal emperor Aurangzeb. When the emperor grasped the lad's hand, the youth retorted that, as the emperor had extended the traditional gesture of protection offered by a bridegroom to his new wife by taking his hand, it was incumbent on Aurangzeb to protect the young ruler and his kingdom in a similar fashion. Luckily Aurangzeb was impressed rather than peeved by such precocious behaviour, and conferred on Jai Singh the title 'Sawai', meaning 'one and a quarter', a title that was proudly borne by all of Jai Singh's descendants – there is still a quarter-sized flag flying above the full-sized version over the City Palace today.

Jai Singh did, however, severely peeve Aurangzeb's successor, Bahadur Shah, who came to power following Aurangzeb's death in 1707. Bahadur Shah's accession was contested by his younger brother, Azam Shah, and Jai Singh backed the wrong Shah. Bahadur responded by demanding his removal from Amber Fort, and installing Jai Singh's younger brother, Vijay, in his place. Jai Singh was unimpressed and eventually succeeded in dislodging his brother. Soliciting the support of other large Rajput states, Jai Singh formed a strong front against the Mughal ruler and eventually clawed his way back.

The kingdom grew wealthier and wealthier, and this, plus the need to accommodate the burgeoning population and a paucity of water at the old capital at Amber, prompted the maharaja in 1727 to commence work on a new city – Jaipur.

Northern India's first planned city, it was a collaborative effort using his vision and the impressive expertise of his chief architect, Vidyadhar Bhattacharya. Jai Singh's grounding in the sciences is reflected in the precise symmetry of the new city. The small villages that lay in the vicinity were incorporated into the new city, which was dissected by wide boulevards flanked by stalls of equal size that formed nine *mohallas* (rectangles) of varying size.

The city wasn't just an aesthetic triumph; its stout walls protected its inhabitants from would-be invaders, encouraging merchants and tradespeople to flock here, further serving to enhance the city's growth and prosperity. Jai Singh's interest in the arts, sciences and religion fostered their development, and the royal court became a booming centre of intellectual and artistic endeavour.

Following Jai Singh's death in 1744, power struggles between his many offspring laid the kingdom open to invasion by neighbouring Rajput kingdoms, which appropriated large tracts of territory. The kingdom maintained good relations with the British Raj, although the British gradually undermined the independence of the state, exercising increasing control over its administration.

During the first war of independence, the Indian Uprising of 1857, Maharaja Ram Singh conspicuously helped the British and, in so doing, raised his status with the imperial power. In 1876 Maharaja Ram Singh had the entire Old City painted pink (traditionally the colour of hospitality) to welcome the Prince of Wales (later King Edward VII). Today all residents of the Old City are compelled by law to preserve the pink façade. Maharaja Ram Singh also built Ramgarh Lake to supply water to the burgeoning city.

During the 19th and 20th centuries, the spacious and carefully planned city within Jai Singh's original city walls was bursting at the seams, and the city began to sprawl outwards, with no notion of the controlled planning at its conception.

In 1922 Man Singh II, Jaipur's last maharaja, took the throne on the death of his adoptive father, Maharaja Madho Singh II. Following Independence in 1947, the status of the princely state changed forever. In March 1949 Jaipur merged with the Rajput states of Jodhpur, Jaisalmer and Bikaner, becoming the Greater Rajasthan Union. Jaipur was honoured above the other former states when the title *rajpramukh*, meaning 'head of state', was conferred on Man Singh II, who was invested with administrative supervision of the new province. The title was later revoked, and Man Singh II was posted as Indian ambassador to Spain. In 1949 Jaipur became the capital of the state of Rajasthan.

Since 1950 the population has exploded from 300,000 to over three million, and it shows: unplanned urban sprawl has disfigured what was once one of India's most beautiful cities. Such massive growth breeds its own problems; overcrowding, pollution and traffic are the most obvious. The city is prosperous and attracts plenty of investment as a commercial, business and tourist centre.

In May 2008, 66 people were killed and hundreds injured in a series of blasts, which targeted busy markets and a Hindu temple in

JAIPUR

Jaipur's Old City. At the time of writing, the bombings and associated claims of responsibility were still being investigated. Islamic groups fighting against Indian rule in Kashmir are usually blamed for such attacks.

ORIENTATION

The walled 'Pink City' (Old City) is in the northeast of present-day Jaipur. The city's main tourist attractions are in the Old City, which is partially encircled by a crenellated wall punctuated at intervals by grand gateways. The major gates are Chandpol (*pol* means 'gate'), Ajmeri Gate and Sanganeri Gate. Broad avenues, over 30m wide, divide the Pink City into neat rectangles, each of which is the domain of a particular group of artisans or commercial activities (see Pink City Walking Tour, p162, for details about the locations of these).

There are three main interconnecting roads in the new part of town – Mirza Ismail (MI) Rd, Station Rd and Sansar Chandra Marg. Along or just off these roads are most of the budget and midrange hotels and restaurants, the main train station, the main bus station, many of the banks and the modern shopping strip. Panch Batti, midway along MI Rd, is a landmark intersection near the southwest corner of the Old City.

INFORMATION

Bookshops

Bookwise (Shop 110, Mall 21, Bhagwandas Marg; ☽ 10am-8.30pm Mon-Sat) An excellent selection of Indian and international fiction and nonfiction including glossy picture books focusing on Rajasthan. There's a branch in the Welcome Hotel Rajputana Palace Sheraton and the helpful manager will organise postage.

Books Corner (Shop No 82 MI Rd; ☽ 10am-8pm Mon-Sat) Stocks a range of books and magazines, including some French-language publications. Sells the informative *Jaipur Vision* (Rs 20) and *Jaipur City Guide* (Rs 30).

Corner Bookstore (Mall 21, Bhagwandas Rd; ☽ 10am-10.30pm) A small but focussed collection of fiction and nonfiction books secreted into a branch of the Barista coffee bar.

Crossword (1st fl KK Square, C11, Prithviraj Marg; ☽ 10.30am-9pm Mon-Sat) A modern bookstore boasting a vast selection of fiction and nonfiction books, maps, DVDs and music CDs.

Internet Access

Many places provide internet access including most hotels and guesthouses. However fast or slow, it'll set you back about Rs 20 per hour.

Mewar Cyber Café & Communication (Station Rd; per hr Rs 20; ☽ 24hr) Near the main bus station.

Media

Jaipur Vision and *Jaipur City Guide* are two useful, inexpensive booklets available at bookshops and some hotel lobbies that feature up-to-date listings, maps, local adverts and features. The redoubtable Mr Singh at the Pearl Palace Hotel publishes his free *Jaipur for Aliens* guide which is a handy traveller survival kit with everything from bus timetables to butter-chicken recipes.

Medical Services

At **Galundia Clinic** (☎ 2361040; dagalundia@doctor.com; MI Rd), **Dr Chandra Sen** (☎ 9829061040) is on 24-hour call; a normal consultation costs Rs 300 (however, reports suggest that he may recommend a number of consultations). Most hotels can arrange a doctor on site.

Good hospitals include the following:
Santokba Durlabhji Hospital (☎ 2566251; Bhawan Singh Marg)
Sawai Mansingh Hospital (☎ 2560291; Sawai Ram Singh Rd)

Money

There are plenty of places to change money, and masses of ATMs, most of which accept foreign cards, including **HDFC** (Ashoka Marg), **HSBC** (Sardar Patel Marg), **ICICI** (ground fl, Ganpati Plaza, MI Rd), **IDBI** (Sawai Jai Singh Hwy), and **Standard Chartered** (Bhagwat Bhavan, MI Rd), which are open 24 hours. Moneychangers are faster and more efficient than banks for exchanging currency.
Bank of Rajasthan (☎ 2381416; Rambagh Palace; ☽ 7am-8pm)
Thomas Cook (☎ 2360940; Jaipur Towers MI Rd & Sunil Sadan 2, MI Rd; ☽ 9.30am-6pm Mon-Sat) Two convenient branches; changes cash and travellers cheques.

Photography

Most photo labs around town, including those listed here, sell lithium batteries, memory sticks and compact flash cards, and will save your digital photos onto CD for around Rs 100.
Goyal Colour Lab (☎ 2360147; MI Rd; ☽ 10.30am-8.30pm Mon-Sat, 10am-4pm Sun)
Sentosa Colour Lab (☎ 2388748; ground fl, Ganpati Plaza, MI Rd; ☽ 10am-8.30pm Mon-Sat)

Post

DHL Worldwide Express (☎ 2362826; www.dhl.co.in; G8 Geeta Enclave, Vinobha Rd) This reliable international courier also has a small and friendly office inside the Standard Chartered Bank on MI Rd. Ensure that you ask to pay customs charges for the destination country upfront. Air freight for 10/25kg costs Rs 5685/10,176 to Australia, and Rs 6396/11,532 to Europe or the USA.

Main post office (☎ 2368740; MI Rd; ⏰ 8am-7.45pm Mon-Fri, 10am-5.45pm Sat) Efficient and has a parcel-packing wallah (from 10am till 4pm Monday to Saturday) in the foyer, who will pack, stitch and seal your parcels for Rs 10 to 100 per package, depending on size.

Telephone

There are numerous public call offices (PCOs) scattered around Jaipur, which are usually cheaper than the hotels for long-distance calls. The international reverse-charges operator can be reached on ☎ 186.

It is not unusual for telephone numbers to change in Rajasthan. Jaipur has tackled this problem with an excellent automated **changed telephone number service** (in English ☎ 1952, in Hindi ☎ 1951). For local telephone number inquiries call ☎ 197.

Tourist Information

The Tourism Assistance Force (police) is stationed at major tourist traps.

Foreigners' Regional Registration Office (FRRO; ☎ 2618508; City Palace Complex; ⏰ 10am-5pm Mon-Sat) Any applications for visa extensions should be lodged at the FRRO at least one week before the visa expires. It is somewhat hard to find behind the Hawa Mahal (so ask around), and the likelihood you'll get an extension on a tourist visa is slight – see p369 for more details.

Government of India tourist office (☎ 2372200; Khasa Kothi Circle; ⏰ 9am-6pm Mon-Fri) Next to Hotel Khasa Kothi. Provides brochures on places all over India.

RTDC Central Reservations Office (☎ 2202586; MI Rd; ⏰ 10am-5pm Mon-Sat) Handles bookings for RTDC hotels around Rajasthan, accommodation in the RTDC tourist village during the Pushkar Camel Fair (see Pushkar Camel Fair, p209) and reservations for the *Palace on Wheels* train (see the boxed text, p384). Behind RTDC Hotel Swagatam.

RTDC Tourist offices airport (☎ 2722647); Jaipur train station (☎ 2200778; platform 1; ⏰ 24hr); main bus station (☎ 2206720; platform 3; ⏰ 10am-5pm Mon-Fri); RTDC Tourist Hotel (☎ 2375466; ⏰ 8am-8pm Mon-Sat) Several obliging tourist offices around town.

Uttaranchal Tourism (☎ 2378892; ⏰ 10am-6pm Mon-Sat Jul-Apr, 10am-6pm daily May & Jun) Has an office in the RTDC Tourist Hotel compound.

Travel Agencies

There are plenty of travel agencies that can tailor local sightseeing trips, though your hotel can probably organise the same trips for a competitive price. For a half-day tour it costs around Rs 700/900 for a non-AC/AC car with driver; a full day costs Rs 900/1300. You can hire guides for Rs 800 per day. See p175 for rates on longer trips. The following agencies can arrange cars and jeep or camel safaris, make hotel reservations and book air tickets.

Crown Tours (☎ 2363310; Palace Rd) Opposite the Rajputana Palace Sheraton.

Indo Vacations (☎ 9414312872; www.indien-reise .com, in German; 312-6 Valmiki Rd, Raja Park)

Rajasthan Travel Service (☎ 2389408; www.rajas thantravelservice.com; ground fl, Ganpati Plaza, MI Rd)

DANGERS & ANNOYANCES

Travellers have reported problems with commission merchants in Jaipur. The town is notorious for gem scams – don't get involved in any get-rich-quick export schemes. So common they even have their own terminology, these *lapkas* (crooked touts) are involved in *dabbabazi* (the business of scamming tourists). They're particularly annoying around the City Palace, at train and bus stations, and at Amber Fort. Usually they'll leave you alone if you steadfastly ignore them, but if this doesn't work, you can report them to the tourist police stationed at these places. Often simply threatening to report them is enough to do the trick. For more information, see Gem Scams – A Warning, p154.

SIGHTS

The sights in and around Jaipur are well and truly on the tourist trail, but you can avoid the majority of the busloads of tourists (and the long queues) by visiting the City Palace and Jantar Mantar in the morning and Amber Fort in the afternoon.

The bustling Old City, often referred to as the **Pink City** for obvious reasons, was laid out by Jai Singh and his talented architect, Vidyadhar, according to strict principles of town planning set down in the *Shilpa Shastra*, an ancient Hindu treatise on architecture. At the centre of the grid is the **City Palace** complex, containing the palace itself, the administrative quarters, the **Jantar Mantar** (Jai Singh's remarkable observatory) and the *zenana mahals* (women's palaces).

Avenues divide the Pink City into neat rectangles, each specialising in certain crafts, as ordained in the *Shilpa-Shastra*. The main

JAIPUR

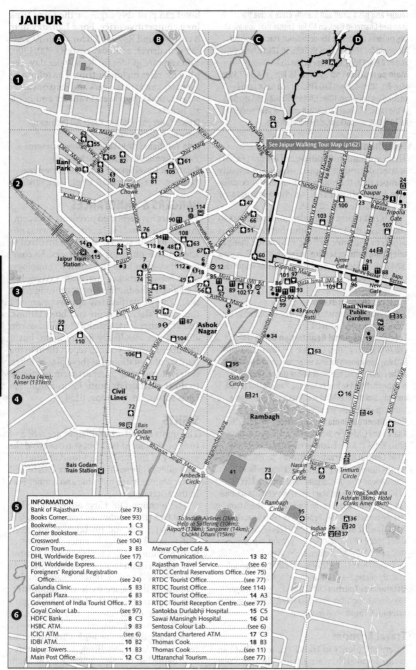

JAIPUR

See Jaipur Walking Tour Map (p162)

Bani Park

Jai Singh Chowk

Jaipur Train Station

Civil Lines

Bais Godam Circle

Bais Godam Train Station

Ashok Nagar

Statue Circle

Rambagh

Chandpol

Choti Chaupar

Tripolia Bazaar

Tripolia Gate

Ajmer Gate

New Gate

Bapu Bazaar

Ram Niwas Public Gardens

Panch Batti

Narain Singh Circle

Trimurti Circle

Rambagh Circle

Indian Circle

Ambedkar Circle

To Disha (4km); Ajmer (131km)

To Indian Airlines (2km); Help in Suffering (10km); Airport (12km); Sanganer (14km); Chokhi Dhani (15km)

To Yoga Sadhana Ashram (8km); Hotel Clarks Amer (8km)

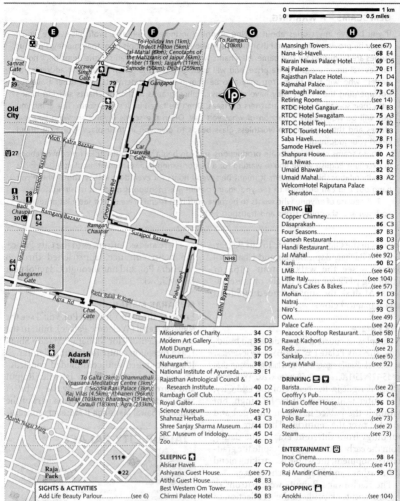

JAIPUR

GEM SCAMS – A WARNING

If you believe any stories about buying anything in India to sell at a profit elsewhere, you'll simply be proving (once again) that old adage about separating fools from their money. Precious stones are favourites for this game. Merchants will tell you that you can sell the items back home for several times the purchase price, and will even give you the (often imaginary) addresses of dealers who will buy them. You may also be shown written statements from other travellers documenting the money they have made, even photographs of the merchants shaking hands with their so-called business partners overseas. Don't be taken in, it's all a scam. The gems you buy will be worth only a fraction of what you pay. Often the scams involve showing you real stones and then packing up worthless glass beads to give you in their place. Don't let greed cloud your judgment.

These scams can be elaborate productions and can begin when touts strike up conversations in excellent English while you're waiting for a bus or eating in a restaurant, until you develop a friendly relationship with them. It might be several hours (or even days if they know where you hang out and can organise to see you again) before any mention is made of reselling items.

Tip: beware of anyone who wants to become your best friend in areas that see a lot of tourists, eg hotel and shopping strips and transport hubs.

---

bazaars in the Old City include Johari Bazaar, Tripolia Bazaar, Bapu Bazaar and Chandpol Bazaar – see the walking tour p162 or Shopping p172 for more details of these bazaars. At dusk the sunset-shaded buildings have a magical glow.

City Palace

A complex of courtyards, gardens and buildings, the **City Palace** (☎ 2608055; www.royalfamily jaipur.com; Indian/foreigner Rs 40/200, Indian/foreigner child aged 5-12 Rs 25/120, camera Rs 50, video Rs 200; ☽ 9.30am-4.30pm) is right in the centre of the Old City. The outer wall was built by Jai Singh, but within it the palace has been enlarged and adapted over the centuries. There are palace buildings from different eras, some dating from the early 20th century. Despite the gradual development, the whole is a striking blend of Rajasthani and Mughal architecture.

The Kachhwaha Rajputs were patrons of the arts and took pride in their collection of valuable artefacts. For a long time there was a private museum here, for viewing by visiting dignitaries, and in 1959 this became a public museum under Man Singh II. His successor, Maharaja Bhawani Singh, took a keen interest in its development and enlarged the museum substantially. Beyond the main courtyards is the seven-storeyed Chandra Mahal, which is still his residence and therefore not open to visitors.

The price of admission also gets you in to Jaigarh Fort (see p179, a long climb above Amber Fort). This is valid for two days.

There are two entrances to the City Palace: the main entrance, approached through Virendra Pol, and one through Udai Pol near Jaleb Chowk.

MUBARAK MAHAL

Entering through Virendra Pol, you'll see the **Mubarak Mahal** (Welcome Palace), built in the late 19th century for Maharaja Madho Singh II as a reception centre for visiting dignitaries. It's multiarched and colonnaded construction was cooked up in an Islamic, Rajput and European stylistic stew by the architect Sir Swinton Jacob. It now forms part of the **Maharaja Sawai Mansingh II Museum**, contain-

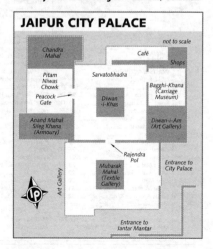

JAIPUR CITY PALACE

ing a collection of royal costumes and superb shawls, including Kashmiri *pashmina*. The most remarkable exhibit is Madho Singh I's clothing dating from 1760, including a loose quilted dress made from silk brocade woven with *zari* (gold embroidery). It has pale-yellow cotton lining and is almost 2m long, 3.5m around the chest and almost 7m around the hem. The maharaja was a cuddly 2m tall, 1.2m wide and 250kg. Guides will take great delight in telling you how much he supposedly ate for breakfast. Appropriately for such an excessive figure, he had 108 wives.

Also on display here is Maharaja Pratap Singh's more diminutive wedding dress – a red-and-gold piece with a massively pleated skirt dating from 1790. There are also several dresses with exquisite gold embroidery, dating from the 19th century, which were worn by royalty around Diwali.

RAJENDRA POL
North of the Mubarak Mahal is the grand **Rajendra Pol**, flanked by carved elephants with lotus flowers in their mouths – symbolising royalty – that date from 1931. The gate has brass doors and walls embedded with precious and semiprecious stones.

DIWAN-I-KHAS (SARVATOBHADRA)
Set between the Armoury and the Diwan-i-Am art gallery is an open courtyard known in Sanskrit as **Sarvatobhadra**. At its centre is a pink-and-white, marble-paved gallery that was used as the **Diwan-i-Khas** (Hall of Private Audience), where the maharajas would consult their ministers. Here you can see two enormous silver vessels (see p156). Overhead, a number of dusty crystal chandeliers serve as roosts for pesky pigeons despite the presence of an attendant with a pigeon-shooing stick.

DIWAN-I-AM
Within the lavish **Diwan-i-Am** (Hall of Public Audience) is the art gallery. Its great array of exhibits includes a touching collection of illustrated manuscripts showing everything from scenes of daily life to tales of the gods. The hall still has its beautifully preserved painted ceiling, with its barely faded, original semiprecious-stone colours, and an enormous crystal chandelier.

Exhibits include a copy of the entire Bhagavad Gita handwritten in tiny script,

and miniature copies of other holy Hindu scriptures, which were small enough to be easily hidden in the event that Mughal zealot Aurangzeb tried to destroy the sacred texts. There are Persian translations of the Ramayana and Mahabharata; the latter was made specially for Akbar, and has illustrations by the greatest Mughal painters. Some beautiful Sanskrit books are also on display, as are early manuscripts on palm leaf, and particularly fine miniature paintings from the Rajasthani, Mughal and Persian schools depicting religious themes. You will see various ornate howdahs, and exquisitely detailed paper cutouts that are incised with a thumbnail.

On the walls are some beautiful carpets, made in Lahore in the 17th century and probably bought to decorate the new fort-palace at Amber. One of the carpets is made from *pashmina* exquisitely decorated with a floral pattern.

THE ARMOURY
The Anand Mahal Sileg Khana – the Maharani's Palace – houses the **Armoury**, which has one of the best collections of weapons in the country.

Fearsome daggers are arranged over the entrance to say 'Welcome'. Many of the ceremonial weapons are elegantly engraved and inlaid belying their real purpose. They include two-bladed steel daggers that, at the flick of a catch, become scissors inside their victims; walking-stick swords; swords with pistols attached to their blades; and beautiful crystal-, ivory- and silver-handled daggers. There is also chain-mail armour, one complete set of which can weigh up to 35kg. Some pieces have a history attached to them, such as a sword inscribed for Shah Jahan, and a sword encrusted with rubies and emeralds that was presented by Queen Victoria to Maharaja Ram Singh, ruler of Jaipur from 1835 to 1880. Gun-lovers fear not, there is a fine array, including some that also serve as walking sticks; a gun the size of a small cannon for use on camel back; and double-barrelled pistols, which held bullets made of lead, dipped in poison and packed with gunpowder.

If bloody weaponry isn't your bag, however cunningly vicious and finely engraved, the 19th-century mirrored and gold-inlaid ceilings, decorated with a gorgeous floral pattern and women in various moods, are well worth a gaze.

JAIPUR

HUGE URNS OF HOLY WATER

Holding pride of place in the pink Diwan-i-Khas pavilion are two enormous silver *gangajalis* (urns), 1.6m tall and each weighing about 345kg. They were made for Maharaja Madho Singh II, a devout Hindu, so that he could take sufficient holy Ganges water to England for bathing when he visited for Edward VII's coronation in 1902. These enormous vessels each have a capacity of over 4000L, and have been listed in the *Guinness Book of World Records* as the largest sterling-silver objects in the world. They were beaten into shape from silver sheets – each made from 14,000 melted silver coins – without any soldering.

BAGGHI-KHANA – THE CARRIAGE MUSEUM

This **museum** houses a ramshackle collection of carriages and palanquins, featuring special covered versions for palace women, with the purpose of maintaining purdah (the custom among some Muslims and Hindus of keeping women hidden from men outside their own family). It's interesting also to see 19th-century European cabs adapted to Indian conditions, such as the small Victoria *bagghi* (carriage) given to the maharaja by the Prince of Wales in 1876 (the same year Jaipur was painted pink). An unusual piece is the *mahadol* – a palanquin with a single bamboo bar – usually used by priests and carried by bearers. Also on display here is the Thakurji ka Rath, a chariot used for carrying the state religious icon on special occasions.

PITAM NIWAS CHOWK & CHANDRA MAHAL

Located towards the palace's inner courtyard is **Pitam Niwas Chowk**. Here four glorious gates represent the seasons. The **Peacock Gate** depicts autumn, with zigzagging patterns and peacock motifs – around the doorway are five beautiful repeated peacock bas reliefs in all their feathered glory. The **Lotus Gate**, signifying summer, is just as splendid, and is covered in repeated flower and petal patterns. The **Green Gate** (or Leheriya, literally 'waves') representing spring is more subdued, but still beautiful with its simple green design, and winter is embodied by the **Rose Gate**, again with repeated flower patterns, but less colourful than the autumn or summer gates.

Beyond this *chowk* (square) is the private palace, the **Chandra Mahal**, where Iswari Singh – son of Jai – killed himself by a snakebite (see p158). This is where the royal family still lives, a seven-storeyed building with fantastic views over the city from the top floor. Flying above the building, you can see the one and a quarter flags that signify the presence of the maharaja. If he is away, the queen's flag will fly in its place.

GOVIND DEVJI TEMPLE

This early-18th-century Krishna **temple** is part of the City Palace complex, though outside the walls. It's decorated with a mixture of European and Indian designs – the chandeliers are European, the paintings Indian. The ceiling is decorated in gold. A popular place of worship, it's set in gardens and was situated so that the maharaja could see the deity from his palace, the neighbouring Chandra Mahal. The deity is unveiled seven times daily for *aarti* (worshipping ritual).

Jantar Mantar

Adjacent to the City Palace is **Jantar Mantar** (Indian/foreigner Rs 20/100; optional guide Rs 100; ⏰ 9.30am-4.30pm). The name is derived from the Sanskrit *yanta mantr* meaning 'instrument of calculation'. The building, begun by Jai Singh in 1728, is an observatory that resembles a collection of bizarre sculptures. Paying for the half-hour to one-hour guide is well worthwhile. Guides provide explanations of how each fascinating instrument works.

Jai Singh liked astronomy even more than he liked war and town planning. Before constructing the observatory, he sent scholars abroad to study foreign constructs. He built five observatories in total, and this is the largest and best preserved (it was restored in 1901). Others are in Delhi, Varanasi and Ujjain. No traces of the fifth, the Mathura observatory, remain.

Each construction within Jantar Mantar has a specific purpose, for example, measuring the positions of the stars, altitude and azimuth, and calculating eclipses.

The most striking instrument is the **Brihat Samrat Yantra** (King of the Instruments) sundial, a massive edifice with a staircase running to the top. It has a 27m-high gnomonic arm set at an angle of 27° – the same as the latitude of Jaipur. The shadow this casts moves up to 4m in an hour, and aids in the calculation of local and meridian time and various attributes of the heavenly bodies, including declination (the angular distance of a heavenly body from the celestial equator) and altitude. It's still used by astrologers and is the focus of a gathering during the full-moon in June or July, when it purportedly helps predict local monsoon rains, and subsequent success or failure of crops.

If you tour the *yantras* in a clockwise direction, to the left as you enter the compound is the **Laghu Samrat Yantra**, a small sundial of red sandstone and white marble, inclined at 27 degrees. It does not measure as precisely as the Brihat Samrat Yantra, but does calculate the declination of celestial bodies, and the shadow cast by its gnomon enables local time (which differs from 10 to 40 minutes from Indian Standard Time) to be determined. On either side are two quadrants and local time can be determined by the shadow cast on each quadrant (one for the morning, one for the afternoon). Nearby is the **Dhruva Darshak Yantra**, used to find the location of the Pole Star and the 12 zodiac signs.

The large circular object nearby, known as the **Narivalaya Yantra**, is actually two small sundials. The two faces of the instrument represent the northern and southern hemispheres, and enable calculation of the time within a minute's accuracy.

Two large disks suspended from the wooden beams nearby comprise the **Yantra Raj**, a multipurpose instrument that, among other things, can help determine the positions of constellations and calculate the date of the Hindu calendar. A telescope is at the centre. The similar-looking **Unnatansha Yantra** lies in the northeastern corner of the observatory complex. This metal ring is divided into four segments by horizontal and vertical lines. A hole where these lines intersect, in the centre of the instrument, aids in the calculation of the altitude of celestial bodies. Nearby is **Dakhinovrith Bhitti Yantra**, which serves a similar function to the Unnatansha Yantra.

West of the Brihat Samrat Yantra, near the southern wall of the observatory, you come to a cluster of 12 yellow instruments, the **Rashi Yantras**. Each *rashi* (individual instrument) represents one of the 12 zodiac signs. The gradient of each *rashi* differs in accordance with the particular sign represented and its position in relation to the ecliptic.

The **Jai Prakash Yantra**, resembling two huge slotted bowls, was the last instrument installed at the observatory and was invented by Jai Singh, after whom it was named. The instrument is used in celestial observations, but can also verify the calculations determined by other instruments at the observatory. Each of the two cavities is divided into six marble slabs, which are marked with minutes and seconds, and also with signs of the zodiac. The metal ring suspended in the centre represents the sun, and calculations can be made from the shadow cast by it on the marble slabs. This instrument may be used to calculate auspicious days for weddings, business negotiations and so on.

The two other sunken concave structures in the western section of the observatory compound comprise the **Kapali Yantra**. The eastern Kapali Yantra is inscribed with lines to which astronomers refer in their deliberations, and is used for graphical analysis. The western Kapali Yantra is used to determine the position of a celestial body. Between the two bowls stands the **Chakra Yantra**, a pair of metal wheels, which can revolve parallel to the earth's axis, and can be fitted with a brass tube in order to calculate the declination of celestial bodies.

Two other impressive instruments are the **Ram Yantras**, which look like miniature coliseums made of 12 upright slabs and 12 horizontal slabs. They are used in the calculation of the altitude and azimuth of celestial bodies. Between them is another circular instrument, the **Digansha Yantra**, with a pillar in the middle and two outer circles. It's used for calculating azimuths, particularly of the sun. It can also be used to determine the time of sunrise and sunset.

Hawa Mahal

Jaipur's most distinctive landmark, the **Hawa Mahal** (Palace of the Winds; admission incl museum Rs 5, camera Indian/foreigner Rs 10/50, video Rs 20/70; ⏰ 9am-4.30pm Sat-Thu) is an extraordinary, fairy-tale, pink-sandstone, delicately honeycombed hive that rises a dizzying five storeys. Constructed in 1799, the building is an amazing example of Rajput artistry, built to enable ladies of the royal household to watch the life and processions of the city. Inside it's barely a building at all, only around one room deep, with narrow, delicately scalloped walkways, under bulbous canopies. It's still a great

JAIPUR

THE RANI OF RAMBAGH

The life story of Gayatri Devi, the celebrated maharani of Jaipur, is an allegory of 20th-century Rajasthan, capturing the state's ambivalence towards its transition from princely rule to part of post-Independence, democratic India.

In her heyday, Gayatri Devi was an icon of royal glamour, adored by gossip columnists and dubbed one of the most beautiful women in the world by *Vogue* magazine. She was born in 1919, a princess from the small state of Cooch Behar (now in West Bengal). At the age of 19 she fell in love with Man Singh II, the last maharaja of Jaipur. Although Man Singh already had two wives, they were married in 1939 and settled down to the life of luxury enjoyed by Indian royalty of the time. There were polo matches, hunting jaunts, dinner parties and summers in England.

Man Singh converted his former hunting lodge, 3km southwest of the old city, into the magnificent Rambagh Palace for Gayatri Devi. Today the palace is surrounded by Jaipur's sprawling suburbs, but it was once a secluded retreat. Here the couple entertained some of the world's rich and famous, including Eleanor Roosevelt and Jackie Kennedy.

By this time, however, the Man Singhs were adjusting to their new role in post-Independence India. Rajasthan's ancestral rulers had been stripped of their powers, but many were still held in high regard by a large proportion of their former subjects. Banking on this support, Gayatri Devi, like many other royals, decided to enter politics. She stood against the Congress Party in the national elections in 1962 and enjoyed a stunning victory. In the 1967 and 1971 elections she retained her seat.

Indira Gandhi's Congress Party, however, was quick to act against the royals who were successfully challenging its hold on power. The privileges that the maharajas were promised following Independence (notably the privy purses paid to the royals from public funds) were abolished and investigations into their financial affairs were mounted. In the early 1970s Gayatri Devi was convicted of tax offences and served five months in Delhi's notorious Tihar Jail. On her release she penned her fascinating autobiography, *A Princess Remembers*. Now in her 90s, Gayatri Devi retains residential quarters at the Rambagh Palace, which, in 1958 was the first former palace in Rajasthan to be converted into a hotel (see p169).

---

place for people-watching from behind the small broken shutters, which are patterned by light. The top offers stunning views over Jantar Mantar and the City Palace one way, and over Siredeori Bazaar the other. The palace was built by Pratap Singh and is part of the City Palace complex.

There's also a small **museum** (9am-4.30pm Sat-Thu), with miniature paintings and some rich relics, such as ceremonial armour, which help evoke the royal past.

Entrance to the Hawa Mahal is from the back of the complex. To get here, return to the intersection on your left as you face the Hawa Mahal, turn right and then take the first right again through an archway.

Iswari Minar Swarga Sal

Piercing the skyline in this part of town is the unusual **Iswari Minar Swarga Sal** (Heaven-Piercing Minaret; Indian/foreigner Rs 5/10; 9am-4.30pm), near Tripolia Gate. The minaret was erected by Jai Singh's son Iswari, who later ignominiously killed himself by snakebite (in the Chandra

Mahal) rather than face the advancing Maratha army – 21 wives and concubines then did the necessary noble thing and committed *jauhar* (ritual mass suicide by immolation) on his funeral pyre. You can climb to the top of the minaret for excellent views over the old city. The entrance is around the back – take the alley 50m west of the minaret along Chandpol Bazaar.

New City

By the mid-19th century it became obvious that the well-planned city was bulging at the seams. During the reign of Maharaja Ram Singh (1835–80) the seams ruptured and the city burst out beyond its walls. Civic facilities, such as a postal system and piped water, were introduced. This period gave rise to a part of town very different from the bazaars of the Old City, with wide boulevards, landscaped grounds and florid buildings. The maharaja commissioned the landscaping of the **Ram Niwas Public Gardens**, on Jawaharlal Nehru (J Nehru) Rd, and the uproarious splendour of **Albert Hall**, built in honour of the Prince of Wales' 1876 visit, which now houses the Central Museum (right). It was designed by Sir Swinton Jacob, and combines elements of English and North Indian architecture. It was known as the pride of the new Jaipur when it opened in 1887. The gardens were in part a famine-relief project – to provide work for the unemployed.

These civic improvements were continued by Jaipur's last maharaja, Man Singh II, who is credited with the university, the Secretariat, residential colonies, schools, hospitals and colleges. Unfortunately the city has developed wildly outwards, in an unplanned urban sprawl, where private interests and political expediency have outweighed aesthetic considerations.

Opposite Albert Hall is Jaipur's **zoo** (Indian/foreigner Rs 10/100; 9am-5pm Wed-Mon), one of the oldest in India, and housing the usual motley array of disconsolate animals.

An old theatre houses Jaipur's **Modern Art Gallery** (admission free; 10am-5pm Mon-Sat), on the 1st floor of the Ravindra Manch building, a very peaceful place with some striking contemporary work – well worth a visit.

To the south, looming above J Nehru Rd, is the small, romantic fort of **Moti Dungri**. It has served as a prison, but today remains in the possession of the former royal family, and entry is prohibited.

Birla Lakshmi Narayan Temple (J Nehru Rd; admission free; 6am-noon & 3-8.30pm) is a large, splendid, modern marble edifice at the foot of Moti Dungri Fort. The wealthy industrialist Birla, born in Palani, Rajasthan, bought the land on which the temple now stands from the maharaja for a token Rs 1. Stained-glass windows depict scenes from Hindu scriptures. Ganesh, the protector of households, is above the lintel, and the fine quality of the marble is evident when you enter the temple and look back at the entrance way – Ganesh can be made out *through* the marble, which is almost transparent. The images of Lakshmi and Narayan were carved from one piece of marble. Many of the deities of the Hindu pantheon are depicted inside the temple, and on the outside walls great historic personages and figures from other religions are shown, including Socrates, Zarathustra, Christ, Buddha and Confucius. There is a small **museum** (J Nehru Rd; admission free; 8am-noon & 4-8pm) next to the temple. The collection includes Birla family household objects and clothing.

Just down the road is the popular **Ganesh Temple** (J Nehru Rd; photography prohibited; 5am-9pm Thu-Tue, 5am-11pm Wed). If you don't like crowds avoid the temple on Wednesdays (the auspicious day), when there are throngs of devotees. You can buy *ladoos* (sweet balls made from gram flour) to offer to Ganesh from the sweet stalls outside the temple.

Another construction that is funded by the wealthy Rajasthani industrialist, **Birla Planetarium** (Statue Circle; admission Rs 20; 11am-8pm, closed last Wed of month) is at the BM Birla Science & Technology Centre, near Statue Circle. All shows (35 minutes) are in Hindi. Next door there's a worthy **science museum** (2384224; admission Rs 10).

Other Museums

The **Central Museum** (2570099; Indian/foreigner Rs 5/30; 10am-4.30pm Sat-Thu) is housed in the spectacularly florid Albert Hall, south of the old city. It opened in 1887 but was closed and undergoing extensive renovation at the time of writing. When it reopens the grand old building will hopefully boast rejuvenated exhibits. The old array of tribal dress, models of yogis in various positions, dioramas, puppets, carpets, and musical instruments was looking a little tired.

Shree Sanjay Sharma Museum (2323436; 1670 off Chaura Rasta; Indian/foreigner Rs 35/80, photography prohibited; 10am-5pm) is a fascinating jumble of precious objects gathered by the parents of Shree Sanjay Sharma (who died as a boy) in his memory. It includes many rare manuscripts and some wonderful, historic Indian art from around the country. There's a set of 18th-century paintings of yoga postures showing which poses to strike if you're drowning, going deaf or suffering from gas. The collection also features elaborate locks, bookstands, drawings of temple architecture, beautiful royal games, 19th-century paper cut-outs, illustrated alchemy books and much more.

The collection of shoes is particularly fascinating: 18th-century atonement slippers (with only a toe hold), special acupressure slippers and one tiny 17th-century brass pair. All were used by sadhus or maharajas. On an upper floor is a room containing 125,000 manuscripts, dramatically shown off by the curator, but which seem to be slowly disintegrating and turning to dust in their cupboards. The

JAIPUR

museum is signposted (though not all that clearly) off Chaura Rasta.

The ramshackle, dusty treasure trove of the **SRC Museum of Indology** (Prachyavidya Path, 24 Gangwell Park; Indian/foreigner incl guide Rs 20/40; ☺ 8am-6pm) is another extraordinary private collection. It contains folk-art objects and other pieces – there's everything from a manuscript written by Aurangzeb and a 200-year-old mirrorwork swing from Bikaner to a glass bed (for a short queen). The museum is signposted off J Nehru Rd, south of the Central Museum. There are (long-term) plans to move the collection to a new building on Amber Rd, 6km from Jaipur.

Close to the Museum of Indology, in the Deaf, Dumb & Blind compound on J Nehru Rd, is the little **Dolls Museum** (admission by donation; ☺ 9.30am-4.30pm Mon-Sat). The collection includes dolls wearing traditional costumes from around India and the world, including two Irish leprechauns.

Nahargarh

Built in 1734 and extended in 1868, sturdy **Nahargarh** (Tiger Fort; ☎ 5148044; Indian/foreigner Rs 15/20, camera Rs 10/20, video Rs 20/70; ☺ 10am-5pm) overlooks the city from a sheer ridge to the north. An 8km-long road runs up through the hills from Jaipur, or the fort can be reached along a zigzagging 2km-long footpath, which starts northwest of the Old City. The views are glorious – it's a great sunset spot, and there's a restaurant that's perfect for a beer. The story goes that the fort was named after Nahar Singh, a dead prince whose restless spirit was disrupting construction. Whatever was built in the day crumbled in the night. He agreed to leave on condition that the fort was named for him.

The fort was built in 1734 by Jai Singh to increase the Amber defences, and was adapted in 1868 to its present form by Maharaja Ram Singh, to house the maharaja's numerous wives. You can visit the **Madhavendra Bhawan**, which has the nine apartments of Maharaja Ram Singh's nine other halves, with a separate suite for the king himself. There are bathrooms, toilets, boudoirs and kitchens.

Doors and windows had coloured panes, of which a few remain. Some of the boudoirs retain Belgian mirrors, and all are decorated with floral and bird motifs.

The rooms are linked by a maze of corridors – used so that the king could visit any queen without the others' knowledge.

You can even stay at the fort (see p166).

Royal Gaitor

The royal **cenotaphs** (admission free, camera Indian/foreigner Rs 5/10, video Rs 10/20; ☺ 9am-4.30pm), just outside the city walls, are an appropriately restful place to visit and feel remarkably undiscovered. Surrounded by a straggling village, the monuments bear much beautiful, intricate carving. Maharajas Pratap Singh, Madho Singh II and Jai Singh II, among others, are honoured here. Jai Singh II has the most impressive marble cenotaph, with a dome supported by 20 carved pillars.

The **cenotaphs of the maharanis of Jaipur** (Amber Rd) are between Jaipur and Amber.

Jal Mahal

Near the cenotaphs of the maharanis of Jaipur, on Amber Rd, is the red-sandstone **Jal Mahal** (Water Palace; ☺ closed to public), built in 1799 by Madho Singh as a summer resort for the royal family – they used to base duck-hunting parties here. It's accessed via a causeway, beautifully situated in the middle of the watery expanse of Man Sagar, which is variously full, dry or choked with hyacinths. Suffering from subsidence, much of the palace is waterlogged and its future is uncertain, though it is pitched to be developed for tourism, in a massive project partly funded by the government that will also mean a massive cleanup of the lake. The lake is home to a variety of migratory and resident birds.

Sisodia Rani Palace

Six kilometres from the city, on Agra Rd (leave by the Ghat Gate), are a pair of formal gardens that are enjoyable to wander around and take in a breath of fresh air. The first, grand formal **terraced gardens** (Indian/foreigner Rs 5/10; ☺ 8am-5pm), with fountains and statuary, were built in the 18th century for Maharaja Jai Singh's second wife, a Sisodian princess. They're overlooked by the **Sisodia Rani Palace** (☺ closed to public), whose outer walls are decorated with murals depicting hunting scenes and the Krishna legend. The nearby Vidyadharji-ka-Bagh are similar gardens currently closed to the public.

Regular local buses leave from Ghat Gate for the Sisodia Rani Palace (Rs 7). An autorickshaw will cost around Rs 250 return from the city centre to visit both.

Galta & Surya Mandir

Perched between the cliff faces of a rocky valley, **Galta** (Monkey Temple) is a desolate and barren, if evocative, place. You will find hundreds of monkeys living here – bold and aggressive macaques and more tolerable langurs. The macaques converge on the temple and you can purchase peanuts at the gate to feed to them. Be prepared to be mobbed.

The temple houses a number of sacred tanks, into which some daring souls jump from the adjacent cliffs. The water is claimed to be 'several elephants deep' and fed from a spring that falls through the mouth of a sculptured cow. The walls are decorated with frescoes, although very heavy rains destroyed many of the original paintings and the restored frescoes do not exhibit the same skill as the originals.

There are some original frescoes in reasonable condition in the chamber at the end of the bottom pool, including those depicting athletic feats, the maharaja playing polo, and the exploits of Krishna and the *gopis* (milkmaids).

On the ridge above Galta is the **Surya Mandir** (Temple of the Sun God), which rises 100m above Jaipur and can be seen from the eastern side of the city. A 2.5km-long walking trail climbs up to the temple from Suraj Pol, or you can walk up from the Galta side. There are hazy views over the humming city.

ACTIVITIES
Astrology
Dr Vinod Shastri is the medal-laden general secretary of the **Rajasthan Astrological Council & Research Institute** (☎ 2613338; Chandani Chowk, Tripolia Gate; ☽ consultations 9am-8pm), who will read your palm or prepare a computerised horoscope if you have your exact time and place of birth. Prices for basic readings and predictions start at around Rs 600 and quickly enter the stratosphere from there. Dr Shastri can be found in his shop near the City Palace. Though he should know when you're arriving, it's best to make an appointment.

Dr Shastri also conducts astrology lessons for (groups of) beginners (see p163).

Ayurvedic Clinics
Is Jaipur making your nerves jangle? **Kerala Ayurveda Kendra** (☎ 5106743; www.keralaayurvedakendra.com; F-30 Jamnalal Bajaj Marg; ☽ 8am-noon & 4-8pm) offers help through Ayurvedic massage and therapy. Treatments include *sirodhara* (Rs 1500), where medicated oil is streamed

steadily over your forehead for 1½ hours to reduce stress, tone the brain and help with sleep disorders. Massages (male masseur for male clients and female for female) cost from Rs 500 for 55 minutes.

Or try **Chakrapania Ayurveda** (☎ 2624003; www.chakrapaniayurveda.com; 8 Diamond Hill, Tulsi Circle, Shanti Path; ☽ 9am-2pm & 3-7pm Mon-Sat, 9am-1pm Sun), where you can get your body type analysed before having it massaged (from Rs 650) and you can have 30 to 45 minutes of *sirodhara* for Rs 600.

If you are seeking treatment for a specific ailment, you can visit the **National Institute of Ayurveda** (Madho Vilas), located close to Samrat Gate. This government hospital provides free Ayurvedic therapies, which include oil massages, steam baths and purification programmes. You first consult a doctor who will determine the appropriate treatment for you.

Beauty Parlours & Gyms
Jaipur has plenty of beauty parlours, which usually cater for both women and men.

Shahnaz Herbals (☎ 2378444; 50-55 Ashoka Marg, C-Scheme; ☽ 9.30am-7.30pm) is long standing and feels it, rather like stepping into a 1940s' beauty parlour. Here you can have manicures, pedicures and good massages (female masseurs for women). The head massage (Rs 1500) is a 15-minute massage, after which an electric tea cosy is placed on your head to warm the oils.

The **Add Life Beauty Parlour** (☎ 2388691; F143 Pt C, Ganpati Plaza, MI Rd; ☽ 8.30am-6pm), below Pizza Hut, is a much more contemporary place, offering gym membership and aerobics classes (Rs 1200 per month) for long-term visitors, as well as soothing massages (Rs 375 to Rs 625) and facials (Rs 250 to Rs 600).

Golf
Rambagh Golf Club (Bhawan Singh Marg; ☽ 6am-6.30pm), near the Rambagh Palace, has a scenic 18-hole course that was once part of the polo grounds. There are caddie charges and a small green fee; equipment is available.

Swimming
Many hotels will let you use their pool for a daily fee. Try the pools at the **Jai Mahal Palace Hotel** (p169; Rs 250), the **Mansingh Hotel** (p168; Rs 225), the **Narain Niwas Palace Hotel** (p168; Rs 150) or the **Hotel Palms** (p167; Rs 100).

PINK CITY WALKING TOUR

This walking tour will take you through Jaipur's bazaars passing the main attractions in the Old City. Allow about half a day for the tour (longer if you linger at the sights), and bring a hat, camera and plenty of water.

Entering the old city from **New Gate (1)**, turn right into **Bapu Bazaar (2)**, on the inside of the southern city wall. In stark contrast to most Indian cities, the Old City is made up of grids of streets such as this one, straight and wide and lined with uniformly sized shops. This bazaar also has an added and unusual advantage – it's mostly traffic-free. Brightly coloured bolts of fabric, leather *jootis* (traditional, pointy-toed shoes), trinkets and aromatic perfumes make the street a favourite destination for Jaipur's women. At the end

of Bapu Bazaar you'll come to **Sanganeri Gate (3)** on your right, but turn left here into **Johari Bazaar (4)**, the jewellery market, one of the city's main shopping strips. Johari Bazaar and the small lanes that dissect it are where you will find jewellers, goldsmiths and silversmiths. Of particular interest are the artisans doing *meenakari* (enamelling). This highly glazed and intricate work, in shades including ruby, bottle green and royal blue, is a speciality of Jaipur. On Johari Bazaar you can also find cotton merchants – cloth here is usually cheaper than at Bapu Bazaar. Interspersed with the uniform shop fronts are the grand pink *havelis* (mansions) of Jaipur's wealthy merchants.

Continuing north you'll pass the well-known **LMB Hotel (5**; p170), an ideal stop to rest the legs and partake of a cold drink or famous kulfi (pistachio ice cream), and then the **Jama Masjid (6)**, with its tall minarets. Beyond, the traffic congests around **Badi Chaupar (7)**, the Old City's major square – be extra careful crossing the road. To the north of the square is **Siredeori Bazaar (8)**, also known as Hawa Mahal Bazaar. The name is derived from the extraordinary **Hawa Mahal (9**; Palace of the Winds; p157), a

JAIPUR

> **WALK FACTS**
>
> **Start** New Gate
> **Finish** Ajmeri Gate
> **Distance** 4.5km
> **Duration** three to five hours

JAIPUR WALKING TOUR

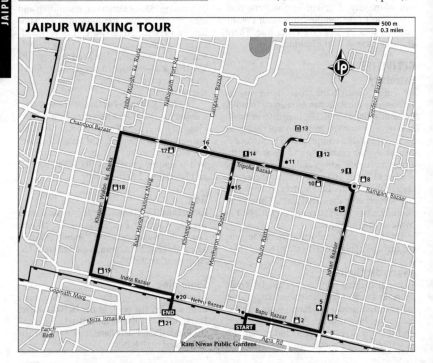

short distance to the north on the left side of the street. The building's exterior is most spectacular, but it's also worth going inside. You enter via the rear entrance, which you'll find if you head back to Badi Chaupar and turn right (west) into Tripolia Bazaar and right again down a small lane.

Back on **Tripolia Bazaar (10)**, continue west and you'll be confronted by stall after stall crammed with domestic kitchen utensils, textiles, trinkets and ironware. The stalls are closed on Sunday.

A few hundred metres along is the triple-arched **Tripolia Gate (11)**, after which the bazaar is named. This is the main entrance to the **Jantar Mantar (12**; p156) and **City Palace (13**; p154), but only the maharaja's family may enter here. The public entrance to the palace complex is via the less-ostentatious Atishpol (Stable Gate), a little further along.

After visiting the City Palace complex, head back to Tripolia Bazaar and resume your walk west. To your right you'll see the **Iswari Minar Swarga Sal (14**; Heaven-Piercing Minaret; p158), the highest structure in the old city and well worth the climb. Cross the road and you'll see a small archway directly opposite the minaret. If you head west from here, the next lane on the left is **Maniharon ka Rasta (15)**, the best place to buy lac (resin) bangles – it's packed by colourful stalls.

Back on Tripolia Bazaar, continue west to **Choti Chaupar (16)**, a busy spot where villagers from outlying regions come to trade their produce. Cross this square and you'll find yourself in **Chandpol Bazaar (17)**. Follow this road west until you reach a traffic light, where you turn left into the bustling **Khajane Walon ka Rasta (18)**. Here you'll find Jaipur's marble and stoneware carvers at work. Continue down Khajane Walon ka Rasta until you reach a broad road, just inside the city wall, **Indra Bazaar (19)**. Follow the road east towards **Ajmeri Gate (20)**, near the end of this tour. Further east is Nehru Bazaar, with further shopping opportunities, or go through the gate and across MI Rd to the large shopping emporium, **Rajasthali (21**; p172).

COURSES
Astrology
Dr Vinod Shastri at the **Rajasthan Astrological Council & Research Institute** (☎ 2613338; Chandani Chowk, Tripolia Gate; ☼ consultations 9am-8pm) offers lessons in astrology. The charge is Rs 3000 per

person (minimum of five people) for 15 one-hour lectures, given over a period of five days. More-advanced lessons are also available.

Block Printing & Pottery
You can do block-printing courses in nearby Sanganer village, around 16km south of Jaipur. **Sakshi** (☎ 2731862; Laxmi Colony; ☼ shop 8.30am-8.30pm, factory 9am-6pm) offers basic block-printing or blue-pottery courses (eight hours per day). You can also do two- to three-month courses. Costs depend on numbers of students; contact Sakshi for more details.

At **Kripal Kumbh** (☎ 2201127; B18A Shiv Marg, Bani Park) you can take free lessons in blue pottery (although it's not possible during the monsoon, from late June to mid-September). Advance bookings are essential. Here you will also find an excellent range of pottery for sale (see p173).

Meditation
Vipassana is one of India's oldest forms of meditation. The aim of this form is to achieve peace of mind and a content and useful life through a process of mental purification and self-examination.

Located in beautiful surrounds, **Dhammathali Vipassana Meditation Centre** (☎ 2680220) runs courses (for a donation) in meditation for both beginners and more-advanced students throughout the year. Courses are for 10 days, minimum, throughout which you must observe 'noble silence' – no communication with others. This serene meditation centre is tucked away in the hilly countryside near Galta, about 5km east of the city centre. Accommodation is in single rooms (some with private bathroom) and vegetarian meals are available. Courses are offered in Hindi, English, German, French, Spanish, Japanese, Hebrew, Italian, Korean, Portuguese, Mandarin and Burmese. Bookings are essential.

Music & Dance
Lessons in music and dance are available at **Maharaja Sawai Mansingh Sangeet Mahavidyalaya** (☎ 2611397; www.sangeetmahavidyalaya.org; Chandni Chowk, City Palace), behind Tripolia Gate. The sign is in Hindi – ask locals to point you in the right direction. Tuition is given in traditional Indian instruments, such as tabla, sitar and flute. It costs from Rs 500 per month in a small group for regular students. There is also tuition in *kathak*, the classical Indian

JAIPUR

dance. Classical Indian vocal tuition can also be undertaken. For details contact the school principal, Mr Shekhawat.

Yoga

There are several places in Jaipur that conduct yoga classes, including **Yoga Sadhana Ashram** (Bapu Nagar; ⊙ Wed-Mon), which nestles among trees off University Rd (near Rajasthan University). Classes incorporate breathing exercises, yoga asanas (poses) and exercise. Most of the classes are in Hindi, but some English is spoken in the 7.30am to 9.30am class.

Alternatively you could try the casual classes held at **Madhavanand Girls College** (☎ 2200317; C19 Behari Marg, Bani Park), next door to the Madhuban guesthouse. There are free daily classes, in Hindi and in English, from 6am to 7am.

TOURS

The **RTDC** (☎ 2202586; RTDC Tourist Hotel, MI Rd; ⊙ 10am-5pm Mon-Sat) offers half-/full-day tours of Jaipur and its surrounds for Rs 120/170. The full-day tours (9am to 6pm) take in all the major sights (including Amber Fort), with a lunch break at Nahargarh. The lunch break can be as late as 3pm, so have a big breakfast. Rushed half-day tours are confined to the city limits (8am to 1pm, 11.30am to 4.30pm and 1.30pm to 6.30pm) – some travellers recommend these, as you avoid the long lunch break. Fees don't include admission charges. Their Pink City by Night tour (Rs 200) departs at 6.30pm, explores several well known sights, and includes dinner at Nahargarh Fort. Tours depart from Jaipur train station (depending on demand), and pick customers up from the RTDC Hotel Teej, RTDC Hotel Gangaur and RTDC Tourist Hotel. You are not necessarily immune to prolonged stops at emporiums along the way. Book all tours at the **office** (⊙ 7am-8pm) at the RTDC Tourist Hotel.

Approved guides for local sightseeing can be hired through the **tourist office** (☎ 2375466; RTDC Tourist Hotel, MI Rd; ⊙ 8am-8pm Mon-Sat). A half-day tour (four hours) costs Rs 350. A full-day tour (eight hours) is Rs 450. An extra fee of Rs 100 to 150 for both tours is levied for guides speaking French, German, Italian, Japanese or Spanish.

Jaipur Virasat (☎ 2367678; www. jaipurvirasatfoundation.org; 9 Sardar Patel Marg, C-Scheme), a community group in association with the Indian National Trust for Art and Cultural Heritage (Intach), organises City Heritage Walks. The worth-

while two-hour guided walks, which are run by volunteers, take you through the walled city and focus on Jaipur architecture, local artisans and the homes of famous people. The walks are free (donations appreciated), and leave on Saturday from Albert Hall (the Central Museum) at 8.15am in winter (November to March) and 8am in summer (April to October). Bookings are essential.

SLEEPING

Prepare yourself to be besieged by autorickshaw drivers when you arrive by train or bus. If you refuse to go to their choice of hotel, many will either snub you or will double the fare. Some rickshaw drivers will openly declare their financial interest, which at least is honest.

To avoid this annoyance, go straight to the prepaid autorickshaw stands at the bus and train stations. Even better, many hotels will pick you up if you ring ahead.

From May to September, most midrange and top-end hotels offer bargain rates, dropping prices by 25% to 50%.

All of the rooms listed here have private bathrooms unless otherwise indicated. Prices quoted for midrange and top-end options exclude luxury taxes (officially 8% and applicable to rooms with rates over Rs 1000).

A recommended alternative to the hotels is the homestay programme run by **Jaipur Pride** (www.jaipurpride.com; r incl breakfast Rs 2500-6500). Currently there are about 40 homes participating in the project divided into three price categories. All are comfortable, friendly and offer an unsurpassed way to get under the skin of the city.

Budget

Although it's diminishing in size, there is a ghetto of cheap backpacker hotels at Chameliwala Market tucked into a network of alleys between MI Rd and Ashok Marg.

RTDC Tourist Hotel (☎ 2360238; MI Rd; dm Rs 50, s/d from Rs 200/300) Near the main post office and fronted by lawns, this government-run hotel has a certain faded appeal, though its courtyards feel like a cross between a colonial mansion and a prison yard. Rooms have high ceilings and are almost clean, but common areas are worse for wear. Still, it's OK for the price.

Retiring rooms (male-only dm Rs 60, s/d Rs 150/300, r with AC Rs 500; ⊠) Located at the train station.

Handy if you're catching an early-morning train. Make reservations on the inquiries number (☎ 131).

our pick **Hotel Pearl Palace** (☎ 2373700, 9414236323; www.hotelpearlpalace.com; Hari Kishan Somani Marg, Hathroi Fort; dm Rs 100, s Rs 300-750, d Rs 350-800; ⊠ 🖳) The delightful Pearl Palace continues to raise the bar for budget digs. Congenial hosts Mr and Mrs Singh are constantly upgrading and improving the accommodation, facilities and roof-top restaurant. There's a range of comfortable rooms to choose from – small, large, shared bath, private bath, some balconied, some with air-con or fan cooled, and all are spotless. This 'one-stop shop' offers all manner of services including free pick-up, money-changing and travel services, and it boasts one of Jaipur's best restaurants (see p169). Rightfully popular, advance booking is highly recommended.

RTDC Hotel Swagatam (☎ 2200595; Station Rd; dm Rs 100, s/d Rs 500/600, s/d with AC Rs 800/900; ⊠) The closest budget digs to the train station, this government budget hotel has a rather institutional feel and a neatly clipped lawn. Rooms are drab but spacious and acceptable.

RTDC Hotel Teej (☎ 2203199; www.rajasthantourism .gov.in; Collectorate Rd; dm Rs 100, s/d Rs 600/700, with AC Rs 990/1200; ⊠) Located opposite the Moti Mahal Cinema, Hotel Teej is set in a garden, and is better and more welcoming than many RTDC joints. The unexciting rooms are spacious, with high ceilings, and quite pleasant. The AC rooms are overpriced.

Ashiyana Guest House (☎ 2375414; Chameliwala Market; s/d from Rs 200/250, without bathroom Rs 150/200) A real budget choice, this is small, homey and family run. The grubby-mark-on-wall count is lower than at some other low-end places nearby. Rooms are petite and the hot water comes in buckets (though plumbing is planned!)

Jwala Niketan (☎ 5108303; C6 Motilal Atal Marg; s Rs 150-650, d Rs 200-700; ⊠) This quiet yet centrally located guesthouse has a range of good-value, clean but bland rooms. The host family lives on the premises and the atmosphere is decidedly non-commercial – almost monastic. There is no restaurant or room service other than a Rs 20 Indian breakfast.

Hotel Kailash (☎ 2577372; Johari Bazaar; s/d Rs 460/525, without bathroom Rs 250/275) This hotel, opposite the Jama Masjid, is one of the few places to stay within the old city, and is right in the thick of it. It's nothing fancy and the

undersized rooms are basic and stuffy despite the central air-cooling. Rooms at the back are quieter and management is buoyantly friendly and welcoming.

Devi Niwas (☎ 2363727; singh_kd@hotmail.com; Dhuleshwar Bagh, Sadar Patel Marg, C-Scheme; s/d Rs 250/400, s/d with AC & TV Rs 300/600; ⊠) This paying guesthouse is a genuine family affair in a spacious pale-yellow building nestled in the middle-class C-scheme. It has a homier feel than most with the extended family living downstairs. There are just seven rooms and happy guests have left their compliments on the walls. Food is home-cooked and tasty, and there's a small garden.

Evergreen Guest House (☎ 2361284; www.hotel evergreen.net; Chameliwala Market; s/d Rs 300/400; 🖳) This backpacker stalwart was morphing into the midrange Hotel Palms (same owners) at the time of research. The small section of backpacker rooms still remaining are accessed just off MI Rd, in the backpacking ghetto of Chameliwala Market. Even the management were a little unsure of the future of the remaining budget rooms, where cleanliness and service are erratic. The swimming pool has been commandeered by Hotel Palms.

Hotel New Pink City (☎ 2363774; off MI Rd; s/d Rs 400/600) Opposite the main post office, this is tucked off MI Rd, down a lane. The accommodation is fronted by a lawn and garden, and it's surprisingly peaceful considering its central location. Mosquitoes love the garden, the rooms are basic with bucket hot water, and reception is somewhat frosty. It's a popular marriage venue, so one to avoid in the wedding season (November to February).

Atithi Guest House (☎ 2378679; atithijaipur@hotmail .com; 1 Park House Scheme Rd; r Rs 550-950; ⊠ 🖳) This family-run guesthouse, set between MI and Station Rds, offers strikingly clean, simple rooms around a quiet courtyard. It's central but peaceful, a bit uninspiring but the service is friendly and helpful. There's a restaurant (guests only), room service and you can eat on the pleasant rooftop terrace. Rickshaw drivers don't like it here because the owner won't pay commission.

Karni Niwas (☎ 2365433; karniniwas@hotmail.com; C5 Motilal Atal Marg; s Rs 550-950, d Rs 650-1000; ⊠ 🖳) Tucked behind Hotel Neelam, this has clean, cool and comfortable rooms, often with balconies. There is no restaurant but there are relaxing plant-decked terraces to enjoy room service on. And being so central restaurants aren't far away. The owner shuns commissions for rickshaw drivers and free pick-up from the train or bus station is available.

Nahargarh (Tiger Fort; ☎ 5148044; d Rs 750) Nahargarh is a would-be romantic choice set high above the old city. There's only one very basic double room, in one of the fort's parapets behind the restaurant – the views from the bed are unparalleled. Unfortunately the condition of the room (broken windows, centuries of dust, dirty linen etc) and the mischievous monkeys make for a truly unforgettable stay. Bring your own mosquito protection, flashlight and bed sheet.

Midrange
BANI PARK

The Bani Park area is relatively green and restful (away from the main roads), about 2km west of the old city.

Jaipur Inn (☎ 2201121; www.jaipurinn.com; B17 Shiv Marg, Bani Park; s/d from Rs 750/950, ❄ ❑) Once a budget travellers' favourite, with a vast range of accommodation, this hotel has shrunk and now offers an eclectic mishmash of varying, overpriced rooms. Some are air-conditioned and some have balconies and you should inspect a few rooms before settling in. Plus points include the friendly manager and several common areas where travellers can make a coffee, pick-up wi-fi, or grab a meal. There's also free pick-up from the train or bus station and a rooftop restaurant.

Tara Niwas (☎ 2203762; www.aryaniwas.com; B-22-B Shiv Marg; s/d Rs 1200/1500; s/d per month from Rs 15,000/16,500; ❄) Run by the people behind Hotel Arya Niwas, Tara Niwas offers well furnished, long-stay apartments (minimum stay 15 days) at bargain prices. Some rooms have attached kitchenettes, and there's also a dining room. A new development by this company, Om Niwas (same website), features purpose-built serviced apartments in Bani Park for long-term visitors.

our pick **Madhuban** (☎ 2200033; www.madhuban .net; D237 Behari Marg, Bani Park; s Rs 1400-1900, d Rs 1500-2900; ❄ ❑ ❄) Madhuban is an elegant, heritage hotel/guesthouse run by the convivial Dicky and Kavita Singh (the family once ruled Patan, 70 miles northeast). It features a range of bright, spotless, antique-furnished rooms including a suite with a Jacuzzi. Most guests gravitate quickly to the peaceful lawn where they can drink tea, read a newspaper over breakfast, watch a puppet show at night or just

pat the dog. The brightly frescoed restaurant features a small, focussed menu and sits beside the petite courtyard pool, which is lit in the evening. Money-changing and travel services are available as is free pick-up from the bus or train station.

Umaid Bhawan (☎ 2206426; www.umaidbhawan.com; Behari Marg, via Bank Rd, Bani Park; s/d Rs 1400/1600, ste Rs 2000/2400; ❄ ❑ ❄) This mock-heritage hotel, behind the Collectorate, is situated in a quiet dead-end street and is extravagantly decorated in traditional style. The cascading stairways and numerous private balconies have you feeling you have entered a miniature Rajasthani painting. Rooms are stately, full of marble and carved-wood furniture. Free pick-up is available from the train or bus station and all taxes and breakfast are included in the tariff.

Hotel Meghniwas (☎ 2202034; www.meghniwas.com; C9 Sawai Jai Singh Hwy; s/d from Rs 1800/2000, ste Rs 3200; ❄ ❑ ❄) In a building erected by Brigadier Singh in 1950 and run by his gracious descendants, this very welcoming hotel has comfortable and spotless rooms, with traditional carved-wood furniture and leafy outlooks. There's a first-rate restaurant and an inviting pool set in a pleasant lawn area.

Jas Vilas (☎ 2204638; www.jasvilas.com; C9 Sawai Jai Singh Hwy, Bani Park; s/d Rs 2400/2800; ❄ ❑ ❄) This small but impressive hotel was built in 1950 and is still run by the same charming family. It offers 11 spacious rooms, most of which face the large sparkling pool set in a romantic courtyard. In addition to the relaxing courtyard and lawn, there is a cosy dining room and management will help with all onward travel planning.

Umaid Mahal (☎ 206426; www.umaidmahal.com; C-20, B/2 Behari Marg, Bani Park; s/d Rs 2500/3000; ❄ ❑ ❄) This extravagantly decorated hotel is run by the same family behind the popular Umaid Bhawan. It may not be a castle but it has plenty of front. Rooms are spacious, elaborate and regal, while downstairs a pool, bar and restaurant were under construction at the time of writing. Smokers have their own zenana-style screened balconies. Free pick-up is available from the train or bus station.

Shahpura House (☎ 2203069; www.shahpurahouse .com; D257 Devi Marg, Bani Park; s/d from Rs 2500/3000, ste Rs 3000/4000; ❄ ❑ ❄). Elaborately built and decorated in traditional style, this heritage hotel offers immaculate rooms, some with balconies, featuring murals, coloured-glass lamps, even ceilings covered in small mirrors (in the suites). This rambling palace boasts a durbar hall with huge chandelier and a cosy cocktail bar. There's an elegant rooftop terrace and an inviting swimming pool. It's another prime choice in the Bani Park area, though lacking the family-run feel you get in other hotels in this category.

OTHER AREAS

Rajasthan Palace Hotel (☎ 2611542; 3 Peelwa Garden, Moti Dungri Marg; r without/with AC Rs 500/1000; 🟦 🖳) This rather forgotten-feeling option has a quiet lawn area, a small pool and keen management. Apparently popular with the rickshaw drivers, as are other hotels in the vicinity. The high-ceilinged rooms are a bit shabby but pretty clean. The cheaper rooms may seem good value but you will want to carry mosquito protection.

Hotel Arya Niwas (☎ 2372456; Sansar Chandra Marg; www.aryaniwas.com; s from Rs 700, s/d with AC Rs 950/1300; 🟦 🖳) Just off Sansar Chandra Marg, behind a ugly high-rise tower, this is a very popular travellers' haunt with a good range of travel services. For a hotel of 92 rooms it is very well-run, though its size means it is not as personal as smaller guesthouses. The spotless rooms vary in layout and size so check out a few. There's an extensive terrace facing a soothing expanse of lawn for relaxing. The self-service vegetarian restaurant doesn't serve beer (so bring your own).

Chirmi Palace Hotel (☎ 2365063; www.chirmi.com; Dhuleshwar Bagh, Sardar Patel Marg; s/d from Rs 850/950, deluxe Rs 1350/1500; 🟦 🖳) Set in a grand 150-year-old *haveli*, Chirmi Palace is run by a traditional Rajput family. Rooms are atmospheric with high ceilings and make up in character what they lack in luxury and dust-free status. There are also a few cheaper rooms upstairs that might be worth investigating for those on a budget. The dining room is ornate and the pool is a summer-only affair.

RTDC Hotel Gangaur (☎ 2371641; www.rajasthan tourism.gov.in; Sanjay Marg; s/d from Rs 990/1200; 🟦) This, another RTDC option, is just off MI Rd and has a crazy-paving exterior and small lawn, but that's where any exception to the other government hotels ends – inside are lackadaisical staff and typically drab and functional rooms.

Hotel Diggi Palace (☎ 2373091; www.hoteldiggi palace.com; off Sawai Ram Singh Rd; r without/with AC Rs 1000/1800; 🟦 🖳) About 1km south of Ajmeri Gate, the splendid former residence of the *thakur* (nobleman) of Diggi is surrounded by beautiful, shaded lawns. Once a budget hotel, it remains a good-value heritage hotel although the more expensive rooms are substantially better than the cheaper options. The tariff includes all taxes and breakfast and there's free pick-up from the bus and train stations. The management also prides itself on using organic produce in the restaurant from the hotel's own gardens and farms. However it's a shame the staff can be grouchy towards independent travellers.

Nana-ki-Haveli (☎ 2615502; www.nanakihaveli.com; Fateh Tiba, Moti Dungri Marg; r without/with AC Rs 1200-1800, r with AC Rs 2200; 🟦) Found off Moti Dungri Marg is this tucked-away, tranquil place with attractive, comfortable rooms decorated with traditional flourishes (discreet wall painting, wooden furniture). It's hosted by a lovely family for whom nothing is too much trouble. It's a quiet, simple place fronted by a relaxing lawn and offers home-style cooking and discounted rooms in summer.

Jai Niwas (☎ 2363964; www.aryaniwas.com; 3 Jalupura Scheme, Gopinath Marg; r from Rs 1300, 4-bed ste Rs 1800; 🟦) Another option under the Arya Niwas umbrella, this modern bungalow is peaceful (fronted by a smart lawn), yet centrally located just off MI Rd. Rooms are functional, spacious and comfortable, if a little bland.

Hotel Palms (☎ 2362415; www.palmsthehotel.com; Ashok Marg, C-Scheme; d from Rs 1800; 🟦 🖳 🖳) With a grand front door facing Ashok Marg, this 'new' hotel features the bland, rather ordinarily renovated rooms of erstwhile backpacker hangout Evergreen Guest House. There's a shady garden courtyard and swimming pool, which nonguests can use for Rs 100.

LMB Hotel (☎ 2565844; info@lmbsweets.com; Johari Bazaar; s/d Rs 1925/2325, deluxe Rs 2325/2525; 🟦) In the old city above the renowned restaurant of the same name. The rooms offer a prime vantage point from where you can check out the mayhem of the bazaar. Standard rooms are large, but generally grubby and depressing. The renovated deluxe rooms are much brighter and cleaner though still overpriced.

Hotel Bissau Palace (☎ 2304391; www.bissau palace.com; outside Chandpol; s/d from Rs 2100/2400; 🟦 🖳) This is a worthy choice if you want to stay in a palace on a budget. It has heritage charm, and lots of antique furnishings and mementos, such as moustached photos and hunting paraphernalia. It feels a bit run down or past its prime, but it is atmospheric nonetheless.

It's only 10 minutes walk from Chandpol (a gateway to the Old City) where there is a very earthy produce market. There's a swimming pool, handsome wood-panelled library, and three restaurants (one on the rooftop offering splendid views, for guests only).

Rajmahal Palace (☎ 5105665; www.royalfamily jaipur.com; Sadar Patel Marg; s/d Rs 2300/2800, superior Rs 2850/3000, ste Rs 3500/3995; ❷ ⋑) In the south of the city, this place is a more modest, relaxed and dog-eared edifice than the other palace hotels (Rambagh or Jai Mahal). The superior rooms are comfortable, with cool marble floors and small patches of lawn to the front. Standard rooms are still good, though much less appealing. The suites are cavernous and impersonal. Built in 1729 by Jai Singh, it was also formerly the British Residency, and temporarily the home of Maharaja Man Singh II and the maharani after their residence, the Rambagh Palace, was converted into a luxury hotel.

Narain Niwas Palace Hotel (☎ 2561291; www.hotel narainniwas.com; Narain Singh Rd; s/d from Rs 2700/3800; ❷ ⋑) In Kanota Bagh, just south of the city, this genuine heritage hotel has a wonderful ramshackle splendour. There's a lavish dining room with liveried staff, an old-fashioned veranda on which to drink tea, and antiques galore. Settle into the wicker and time seems to stand still – or is it just that the service is a bit tardy. The high-ceilinged rooms are varyingly atmospheric and the bathrooms also vary greatly – so inspect before committing. You will find a large secluded pool and sprawling gardens out back. Rates include breakfast.

Alsisar Haveli (☎ 2368290; www.alsisarhaveli.com; Sansar Chandra Marg; s/d Rs 2750/3500; ❷ ⋑) Another genuine heritage hotel that has emerged from a gracious 19th-century mansion. Alsisar Haveli is set in beautiful, green gardens, and boasts a lovely swimming pool and a wonderful dining room. Its bedrooms don't disappoint either with elegant Rajput arches and antique furnishings. This is a winning choice, though again a little impersonal, perhaps because it hosts many tour groups.

Mandawa Haveli (☎ 2374130; www.mandawahotels .com; Sansar Chandra Marg; s/d from Rs 2900/3600; ❷ ⋑) Mandawa Haveli is a lovely heritage hotel, opposite the better known, Alsisar Haveli. Mandawa's management seems a little surprised to see a guest, but it is cheerful enough. The rooms are all spacious and elegantly if

simply furnished. Some boast beautiful double baths set under Rajput arches.

Top End

Jaipur has an impressive selection of luxury hotels, the best of which are the converted palaces of the maharajas and the *havelis* of lesser nobles.

Best Western Om Tower (☎ 2366683; ommljaipur@ yahoo.com; Church Rd, off MI Rd; s/d from Rs 4500/5000; ❷ ⋑) Resembling a piece of mislaid space junk, this tower, though modest by world standards, is a Jaipur landmark. Rooms are modern business bland, comfortable but hardly inspiring, and the bathrooms are space-capsule tiny. At least the views get better the higher you go. The pure-vegetarian revolving restaurant (see p171) has a certain fascination though not necessarily for the food.

Saba Haveli (☎ /fax 2630521; Gangapol; s/d Rs 4500/5500; ❷) Near Samode Haveli, in the northeastern part of the town, Saba Haveli is an authentic, friendly and idiosyncratic hotel positioned among a warren of narrow streets. It's another 200-year-old *haveli* that's in the process of being converted into a hotel. The process could take a while. The top floor is pretty much derelict and there were only a handful of renovated rooms in the fairly dilapidated building at the time we visited. In the low season (May to September) you'll get a hefty discount.

Chokhi Dhani (☎ 2225001; www.chokhidhani.com; Tonk Rd; hut/haveli ste Rs 5500/9900; ❷ ⋑) This is a mock-traditional Rajasthani village, 20km from Jaipur, with wonderful restaurants and entertainment in the evenings (see p172). Accommodation is in traditional-style mud huts with nontraditional interiors. These are well appointed, with a bedroom and sitting room decorated with mirrorwork. There are also eight big rooms in a *haveli*, all swathed in ruched satin. Additional features are the commodious pool and spacious grounds. It's popular with middle-class Indian families.

Mansingh Hotel (☎ 2378771; www.mansinghhotels .com; Sansar Chandra Marg; s/d from Rs 6500/7500; ❷ ▯ ⋑) Located just off Sansar Chandra Marg, the Mansingh is a very central and well-appointed business class hotel. It has comfortable though run-of-the-mill rooms, a coffee-shop beside the pool and rooftop bar and restaurant.

Mansingh Towers (☎ 2378771; s/d from Rs 7000/8000; ▯ ❷) Next door to Mansingh Hotel is the slightly swankier Mansingh Towers, which has a huge atrium and spacious rooms. All rooms have spa baths and you can use the pool

Samode Haveli (☎ 2632370; www.samode.com; Gangapol; s/d/ste €143/170/198, ste from €225/248; ❌ ▣ ☎) Tucked away in the northeast corner of the old city is this charming 200-year-old building, once the town house of the *rawal* (nobleman) of Samode, Jaipur's prime minister. The suites are astonishingly decorative, covered in twinkling mirrorwork, ornate paintings, tiny alcoves and soaring arches. They have large carved beds and most have private terraces. The standard rooms are more ordinary. The pool with its bar is a veritable oasis. The tariff, which includes breakfast, is much reduced from May to September.

Jai Mahal Palace Hotel (☎ 2223636; www.taj hotels.com; Jacob Rd; r from Rs 13,500, ste from Rs 20,000; ❌ ▣ ☎) Located south of the train station, this impressive hotel is set in 7 hectares of beautifully manicured Mughal gardens, which most of the swish rooms overlook. The 18th-century building was once the residence of Jaipur's prime minister and is now run as a hotel by the Taj Group. Tastefully furnished standard rooms are very comfortable and enhanced by miniature paintings. The suites are conservative and refined, with some exquisite antiques. There's a gorgeous circular pool set in the gardens.

Raj Palace (☎ 2634077-9; www.rajpalace.com; Chomu Haveli, Zorawar Singh Gate, Amber Rd; r US$350-450, ste from US$550; ❌ ☎) A former royal home, Raj Palace was built by Thakur Mohan Singhji of Chaumoo, then prime minister. The imposing building, just north of town on the Amber Rd, overlooks a splendid courtyard and has a range of individual and atmospheric rooms featuring splendid decoration and luxurious furnishings. There's also disabled access.

Rambagh Palace (☎ 2211919; www.tajhotels.com; Bhawan Singh Marg; s/d from Rs 35,000/36,500, ste from Rs 75,000; ❌ ▣ ☎) Now a Taj Group hotel, this splendid palace was once the Jaipur pad of Maharaja Man Singh II. Veiled in 19 hectares of gardens, there are fantastic views across the immaculate lawns. More-expensive rooms are naturally the most sumptuous. The maharani (see p158) still lives in separate quarters in the palace grounds. Nonguests can dine in the restaurant or drink tea on the veranda. At least treat yourself to a drink at the Polo Bar (p172).

Raj Vilas (☎ 2680101; www.oberoihotels.com; Goner Rd; r & luxury tents Rs 35,575, villas Rs 100,150; ❌ ☎)

About 8km from the city centre is Jaipur's most sophisticated and expensive hotel. It has 71 luxurious rooms, yet a boutique feel and attentive, unobtrusive service. Its terracotta domes are set in more than 32 shady orchard- and fountain-filled acres. Immaculate rooms, with sunken baths, are subtly decorated. Each of the three villas has its own pool. Guests ride around in golf buggies. Check the website for special offers.

Other plush options:

Holiday Inn (☎ 2672000; www.holidayinnjaipur.com; s/d from Rs 6000/6500; ❌ ▣ ☎) 1km north of the city on Amber Rd, this impressive, traditional-style building offers the usual comfortable Holiday Inn standards, and is good value if you ask for a discount. Breakfast is included.

Hotel Clarks Amer (☎ 2550616; www.hotelclarks.com; s/d from Rs 7500/8000; ❌ ▣ ☎) About 8km south of the city, this 200-room hotel is welcoming, plush and has everything you need for a very comfortable stay. It is also the contact point for homestays through Jaipur Pride (see p164).

Trident Hilton (☎ 2670101; www.trident-hilton.com; Amber Rd; r from Rs 8800; ❌ ▣ ☎) About 5km north of the city on the road to Amber Rd, the Trident Hilton is a slick and very well-managed international-class hotel. The well-appointed rooms offer balconies with lingering views of the Jal Mahal situated opposite. Disabled access.

WelcomHotel Rajputana Palace Sheraton (☎ 5100100; www.welcomgroup.com; Palace Rd; s/d from Rs 14,000/15,500; ❌ ▣ ☎) Ritzy and comfortable but parts are looking a little tired, and though it is staffed to the hilt it also feels a little impersonal. The exorbitant rack rate is heavily discounted if the hotel isn't full.

EATING

Despite its size, Jaipur doesn't have a huge array of quality restaurants. Apart from hotel restaurants (which are often the best option), there are a few traveller-friendly stalwarts as well as numerous veg and nonveg curry joints. As elsewhere in Rajasthan, many vegetarian restaurants don't serve beer. The locals tend to rock up after 9pm.

Restaurants

MI ROAD

Sankalp (☎ 5115553; MI Rd; dishes Rs 50-90; ❤ 9am-11pm) This popular South Indian chain restaurant serves up simply scrumptious South Indian staples, such as varieties of *dosas* (lentil-flour pancakes) and good-value thalis. It could also win the contest for the most waiters on MI Rd.

Surya Mahal (☎ 2362811; MI Rd; mains Rs 60-120; ❤ 9am-10.30pm) Near Panch Batti is this popular, good-value option specialising in South Indian vegetarian food; try the delicious *masala dosa*, and the tasty *dhal makhani* (black lentils and red kidney beans).

Handi Restaurant (☎ 2364839; MI Rd; mains Rs 60-180; ☿ noon-3pm & 6.30-11pm) Handi has been satisfying customers for years and has two outlets opposite the main post office. One is the original, tucked at the back of the Maya Mansions, offering scrumptious barbecued dishes and Mughlai cuisine. In the evenings it sets up a smoky kebab stall at the entrance to the restaurant. The pricier AC option is decorated with puppets and mirrors on the mud-covered walls. They share a kitchen and a no-alcohol policy.

Dasaprakash (☎ 2371313; Kamal Mansions, MI Rd; mains Rs 70-170; ☿ 11am-10.45pm) Part of a competent chain, Dasaprakash specialises in South Indian cuisine including several versions of *dosa* and *idli* (rice dumpling). Afterwards you can choose from a wonderful selection of over-the-top sundaes, including gems such as the Gold Rush: 'strike it delicious' (fudge, praline chocolate, coffee and a golden vein of butterscotch).

Natraj (☎ 2375804; MI Rd; mains Rs 85-200; ☿ 9am-11pm) Not far from Panch Batti is this classy vegetarian place, which has an extensive menu featuring North Indian, Continental and Chinese cuisine. Diners are blown away by the potato-encased vegetable bomb curry, and there's a good selection of thalis and South Indian food – the *dosa paper masala* is delicious. Slide into a booth or grab some takeaway Indian sweets.

Copper Chimney (☎ 2372275; Maya Mansions, MI Rd; mains Rs 100-220; ☿ noon-3pm & 6.30-11pm) Copper Chimney is casual, almost elegant and definitely welcoming with the requisite waiter army and a fridge of cold beer. It offers excellent veg and nonveg Indian cuisine, including aromatic Rajasthani specials. There is also Continental and Chinese food and a small selection of Indian wine, but the curry and beer combos are hard to beat. Take a seat behind the front window to watch the mayhem of MI Rd or settle further back.

Niro's (☎ 2374493; MI Rd; mains Rs 110-350; ☿ 10am-11pm) Established in 1949, Niro's is a long-standing favourite. Escape the chaos of MI Rd by ducking into its cool, clean, mirror-ceiling sanctum to savour veg and nonveg Indian, Chinese and Continental food. As usual, the Indian menu is the pick. Try the spicy *raj sula*

(barbecued lamb) and *began bharta* (aubergine) to an accompaniment of piped music.

ourpick Reds (☎ 4007710; 5th fl, Mall 21, Bhagwandas Marg; mains Rs 275-360; ☿ Sun-Fri 11am-midnight, Sat 11am-1.30pm) The Pink City's hippest nightspot (see p172) is Reds. Decked out in red-and-black sofas and overlooking the Raj Mandir cinema, Reds is also a smart restaurant, found just around the corner and far above the honking traffic of MI Rd. The Indian and Chinese is accompanied by great views and good service and there are special beer and food deals before 7pm. Speciality of the house is *Shahi Gilawat ka kebab*, a lamb kebab blessed with 36 aromatic and digestive spices that was created for the Nawab of Lucknow. Don't take the stairs – they don't reach the 5th floor – use the lift instead.

OLD CITY

Mohan (144-5 Nehru Bazaar; mains Rs 10-60; ☿ 9am-10pm) The name is in Hindi and it's on the corner of the street, a few steps down from the footpath. It's basic, cheap and grubby, but the curries and snacks are freshly cooked and very popular.

Ganesh Restaurant (☎ 2312380; Nehru Bazaar; mains Rs 35-85; ☿ 9.30am-11pm) Near New Gate is one of Jaipur's best-kept secrets. This pocket-sized outdoor restaurant is in a fantastic location – on the top of the old city wall. The cook is in a pit on one side of the wall, so you can check out your pure vegetarian food being cooked. Not much English is spoken, but if you're looking for a local eatery with fresh tasty food you'll love it. There's an easy-to-miss signpost, but no doubt a stallholder will show you the narrow stairway.

LMB (☎ 2560845; Johari Bazaar; mains Rs 55-170; ☿ 8am-11pm) Laxmi Misthan Bhandar, LMB to you and me, is a *sattvik* (pure vegetarian) restaurant in the old city that's been going strong since 1954. Though a welcoming AC refuge from frenzied Johari Bazaar, LMB is not the best eatery in town; however, travellers like to chalk up at least one meal in this institution with its singular décor and extensive sweet counter. The menu opens with a warning from Krishna about people who like *tamasic* (putrid and polluted food), which gets you into the *sattvik* mood. Try the Rajasthan thali followed by the signature kulfi with dry fruits and saffron.

Palace Café (☎ 2616449; City Palace; mains Rs 200-300; ☿ 9am-10pm) The courtyard café is ideal for a snack or main meal while exploring the Palace, whereas the AC buffet is usually booked by groups. The menu is predominantly Indian with some Rajasthani specialities and a few Continental options. The courtyard is very atmospheric in the evening when local musicians add to the romance.

OTHER AREAS

Peacock Rooftop Restaurant (☎ 2373700; Hotel Pearl Palace, Hari Kishan Somani Marg, Hathroi Fort; mains Rs 20-75; ☉ 8am-11pm) This rooftop restaurant at the popular Hotel Pearl Palace gets rave reviews for its excellent and inexpensive cuisine (Indian, Chinese and Continental) and sociable ambience. The mouth-watering food, attentive service, whimsical furnishings and romantic view towards Hathroi Fort make this a first-rate restaurant and the economical prices all the more unbelievable.

Four Seasons (☎ 2373700; D43A Subhas Marg; mains Rs 75-160; ☉ noon-3.30pm & 6.30-11pm) Four Seasons is one of Jaipur's best vegetarian restaurants and being pure vegetarian there's no alcohol. It's a vastly popular place on two levels, with a glass wall to the kitchens. There's a great range of dishes on offer, including tasty Rajasthani specialities and a selection of pizzas. Try a thali or the speciality *rawa masala dosa* (South Indian ground rice and semolina pancake with coconut, onions, carrots and green chillies).

OM (☎ 236683; Church Rd; mains Rs 110-300; ☉ noon-4pm & 7-11pm) Add Om to your list of revolving restaurants. This landmark, rocket-inspired tower boasts a showy, emphatically vegetarian (no alcohol) revolving restaurant at 56m. It spins at a cracking pace and, despite the odd bump and shudder, it's an amazing way to see the city. The menu of Indian, Continental and Chinese features several Rajasthani specialities – try the revolving thali. If you are lucky you will orbit past the centrally located stage featuring live *ghazal* singing.

Little Italy (☎ 4022444; 3rd fl, KK Square, C-11, Prithviraj Marg; mains Rs 165-200; ☉ noon-3.30pm, 6.30-11pm) Easily the best Italian restaurant in town, Little Italy is part of a small national chain that offers excellent vegetarian pasta, risotto and wood-fired pizzas in cool, contemporary beige surroundings – not a scalloped archway in sight! The menu is extensive and includes some Mexican items and first-rate Italian desserts. There is a lounge bar attached so you can accompany your vegetarian dining with wine or beer.

Geoffry's Pub (☎ 2360202; Park Plaza Hotel, Prithviraj Marg; mains Rs 180-285; ☉ noon-11.45pm) Settle into a booth of studded leather and panelled wood and select from a pub-inspired and sometimes-curious menu that includes Roast Lamb, Norwegian cheese steak and vodka pizza, as well as Italian, Chinese, Thai and Indian dishes. There's local beer on tap as well as international beers and wines to accompany your meal.

Quick Eats

Rawat Kachori (Station Rd; sweets Rs 10 or per kg Rs 120-300, lassis Rs 25) For great sweets head to this popular place. A delicious milk crown should fill you up for the afternoon.

Jal Mahal (MI Rd; ice creams Rs 12-110) Next door to Surya Mahal is this packed little takeaway ice-cream parlour, with some inventive concoctions.

Manu's Cakes & Bakes (Ashok Marg; mains Rs 30-90) Adjacent to the entrance to Hotel Palms, this small eatery has an ambitious menu including Mexican, Chinese, Indian. But wait; there's also falafel and toasted sandwiches as well as cakes and ice cream. The small roadside eatery is almost pleasant – depends on the heat and the traffic.

Kanji (Station Rd; sweets per kg Rs 130-330) Across the road from Rawat Kachori, Kanji also has a fabulous array of sweets.

DRINKING
Cafés

Barista (Mall 21, Bhagwandas Marg; coffees Rs 50-70) This smart, AC coffee bar is part of a chain that sells great espresso coffee and iced concoctions, as well as muffins, snacks and sandwiches. This branch, opposite that huge pink marshmallow – the Raj Mandir cinema, shares its space with a neat little bookshop.

Lassiwala (MI Rd) This famous, much-imitated institution, opposite Niro's, is a simple place that whips up fabulous, creamy lassis at Rs 10/20 for a small/jumbo. Will the real Lassiwala please stand up? It's the one that says 'Since 1944', directly next to the alleyway. Imitators spread to the right as you face it.

Indian Coffee House (MI Rd; coffee Rs 8-15) Set back from the street, down a grubby alley, this coffee house offers a very average cup of coffee in very average surroundings. Aficionados of Indian Coffee Houses will not be disappointed by the ambience. Cheap samosas and *dosas* grace the snack menu.

Bars

Many bars around town tend to be oppressive, all-male affairs; however, most upper-end hotel bars are good for casual drinking. Expect copies of Reds to crop up; these new kids on the block are effortlessly raising the bar.

Polo Bar (Rambagh Palace Hotel, Bhawan Singh Rd; 11am-1am) A spiffing watering hole adorned with polo memorabilia and arched, scalloped windows framing the neatly clipped lawns. A bottle of beer costs Rs 250 to Rs 300 and cocktails around Rs 450.

Steam (Rambagh Palace Hotel, Bhawan Singh Rd; 7pm-late Wed-Mon) The Rambagh's lounge bar is a relaxed and stylish haven with a steam engine and a DJ. Sip a cocktail, sample a pizza and lighten your wallet.

Geoffry's Pub (Park Plaza Hotel, Prithviraj Marg; noon-11.45pm) With coloured glass, dark wood and studded leather this English pub wannabe has local Golden Peacock on tap (Rs 105 a glass) and a good selection of international beer, wine and spirits available. One can also puff on a hookah or sip a cocktail. Meals are also available (see p171).

Reds (4007710; 5th fl, Mall 21, Bhagwandas Marg; 11am-midnight Sun-Fri, 11am-1.30pm Sat) Overlooking the Raj Mandir cinema and MI Rd with views to Tiger Fort, slick Reds is a great place to kick back with a drink or take a meal (see p170). Drop into one of the low-slung, red-and-black couches with a beer (bottled or draught), cocktail or mocktail and enjoy the sound system. Things heat up on Saturday and Sunday when the dance floor is cleared and the DJs pump out a mix of Hindipop and techno.

ENTERTAINMENT

Jaipur isn't a big late-night party town, although many hotels put on some sort of evening music, dance or puppet show. English-language films are occasionally screened at some cinemas in Jaipur – check the cinemas and local press for details.

Chokhi Dhani (2225001; Tonk Rd; adult/child aged 3-9 incl dinner Rs 250/150) Chokhi Dhani means 'special village' and this mock Rajasthani village, 20km south of Jaipur, lives up to its name. As well as the restaurants, where you can enjoy an oily Rajasthani thali, there is a bevy of traditional entertainment. You can wander around and watch traditional tribal dancers setting fire to their hats, children balancing on poles and dancers dressed in lion costumes lurking in a wood. You can also take elephant or camel rides. Children will adore it. It's hugely popular with middle-class Indian families.

Raj Mandir Cinema (2379372; Baghwandas Marg; admission Rs 37-91; screenings 12.30pm, 3.30pm, 6.30pm, 9.30pm) Just off MI Rd, Raj Mandir is *the* place to go to see a Hindi film in India. This opulent cinema looks like a huge pink cream cake, with a meringue auditorium and a foyer somewhere between a temple and Disneyland. It's a tourist attraction in its own right and is usually full, despite its immense size. Bookings can be made one hour to seven days in advance (10am to 6pm) at window Nos 7 and 8 – this is your best chance of securing a seat, although forget it in the early days of a new release. Alternatively, sharpen your elbows and join the queue when the current booking office opens 45 minutes before curtain up. Avoid the very cheapest tickets, which are very close to the screen.

Inox Cinema (2379372; www.inoxmovies.com; Crystal Palm complex, Bais Godam Circle; admission Rs 70-130) A modern three-screen multiplex with the latest Bollywood blockbusters and Hollywood offerings.

Polo ground (Ambedkar Circle, Bhawan Singh Marg) Maharaja Man Singh II indulged his passion for polo by building an enormous polo ground next to the Rambagh Palace, which is still a polo-match hub today. A ticket to a match also gets you into the lounge, which is adorned with historic photos and memorabilia. The polo season extends over winter, with the most important matches played during January and March – contact the **Rajasthan Polo Club** (2385380) for ticket details.

During Jaipur's Elephant Festival in March (see Festivals in Jaipur, p148) you can watch elephant polo matches at the Chaughan Stadium in the old city. Contact the Rajasthan Polo Club or **RTDC** (2202586; MI Rd; 10am-5pm Mon-Sat) for details.

SHOPPING

Jaipur is a shopper's paradise. You'll have to bargain hard though – shops have seen too many cash-rich, time-poor tourists. Shops around major tourist centres, such as the City Palace and Hawa Mahal, tend to be pricier. Also commercial buyers come here from all over the world to stock up on the amazing range of jewellery, gems, artefacts and crafts that come from all over Rajasthan.

For useful tips on bargaining, see The Art of Haggling, p364. At some shops, ie the government emporium and some upmarket stores, prices are (supposedly) fixed.

Most of the larger shops can pack and send your parcels home for you – although it'll be slightly cheaper if you do it yourself (see p150).

Jaipur is famous for precious and semiprecious stones. There are many shops offering bargain prices, but you do need to know your gems. The main gem-dealing area is around the Muslim area of Pahar Ganj, in the southeast of the old city. Here you can see stones being cut and polished in workshops tucked off narrow backstreets.

The city is still loosely divided into traditional artisans quarters. The Pink City Walking Tour (p162) will take you through some of these.

Bapu Bazaar is lined with saris and fabrics, and is a good place to buy trinkets. **Johari Bazaar** (⏲ closed part of Sun) and Siredeori Bazaar are where many jewellery shops are concentrated, selling gold, silver and highly glazed enamelwork known as *meenakari*, a Jaipur speciality. You may also find better deals for fabrics with the cotton merchants of Johari Bazaar.

Kishanpol Bazaar is famous for textiles, particularly *bandhani* (tie-dye). Nehru Bazaar also sells fabric, as well as jootis, trinkets and perfume. MI Rd is another good place to buy jootis. The best place for bangles is Maniharon ka Rasta, near the Shree Sanjay Sharma Museum.

Plenty of factories and showrooms are strung along the length of Amber Rd, between Zorawar Singh Gate and the Holiday Inn, to catch the tourist traffic. Here you'll find huge emporiums selling block prints, blue pottery, carpets and antiques; but these shops are used to busloads swinging in to blow their cash, so you'll need to wear your bargaining hat.

Rickshaw-wallahs, hotels and travel agents will be getting a hefty cut from any shop they steer you towards. Stay clear of friendly young men on the street trying to steer you to their uncle's/brother's/cousin's shop – commission is the name of their game too. Many unwary visitors get talked into buying things for resale at inflated prices, especially gems. Beware of these get-rich-quick scams.

Arts & Crafts

Kripal Kumbh (☎ 2201127; B18A Shiv Marg, Bani Park; ⏲ 9am-5pm) This is a showroom in a private home and a great place to buy Jaipur's famous blue pottery produced by, the late Mr Kripal Singh and his students. The renowned, multi-award-winning potter was an accomplished artist and there are some stunningly beautiful artworks for sale. Ceramics go for anything from Rs 20 (for a paperweight) to Rs 25,000 (for a large vase). You can also learn how to make blue pottery here (see p163). Touts may take you elsewhere, so make sure that you are taken to the right place (near the Jaipur Inn).

Rajasthali (MI Rd; ⏲ 11am-7.30pm Mon-Sat) The state-government emporium, opposite Ajmeri Gate, is packed with quality Rajasthani artefacts and crafts, including enamelwork, embroidery, pottery, woodwork, jewellery, colourful puppets, block-printed sheets, cute miniatures, brassware, mirror work and more, but it has an air of torpor that doesn't make shopping much fun. The best reason to visit is to scout out prices, before launching into the bazaar (things can be cheaper at the markets, after haggling, and you'll find more choice).

Juneja Art Gallery (www.artchill.com; 6-7 Laksmi Complex, MI Rd; ⏲ 10am-8pm Mon-Sat) This gallery, tucked in behind the brash Birdhichand Ghanshyamdas jewellery store has some striking pieces of contemporary art by Rajasthani artists (Rs 500 to Rs 50,000). There are regular shows of contemporary artists changing almost weekly and the new gallery 'Artchill' at Amber Fort should be open by the time you read this. It will feature works for sale as well as a display of masterworks.

Ayurvedic Remedies

Himalaya (MI Rd; ⏲ 10am-8pm Mon-Sat) For Ayurvedic preparations, try this place located just near Panch Batti, which exports internationally, and has been selling herbal remedies and beauty products for over 70 years. There are even treatments for your pet. The shampoos, moisturisers and beauty products are reasonable buys if you don't have anything more serious to treat.

Musical Instruments

Music N Sports (73 Chaura Rasta; ⏲ 10.30am-8pm Mon-Sat) This store sells a range of musical instruments, including sitars, tablas, hand cymbals, bamboo flutes, dancing bells on ankle cuffs

JAIPUR

and harmoniums. The helpful staff can recommend music teachers.

Shoes

Mojari (Bhawani Villa, Gulab Path, Chomu House, off Sadar Patel Marg; ☾ 11am-6pm Mon-Sat) Calling all foot fetishists! This shop sells fabulous footwear for around Rs 500. Named after the traditional decorated shoes of Rajasthan, Mojari is a UN-supported project that helps 3500 rural leatherworkers, traditionally among the poorest members of society. There is a wide range of footwear available, including embroidered, appliquéd and open-toed shoes, mules and sandals. There are also shoes featuring creative stitching, unusual cuts and decoration with bells, beads and sequins. The products meet export-quality standards, but are based on traditional leatherwork skills and design. You may have trouble finding your size. Mojari also has a small collection of covetable leather and felt bags.

Charmica (MI Rd; ☾ 10am-8pm Mon-Sat) Opposite Natraj restaurant, this small shop is the place for well-made but pricey *jootis*.

Tailors

New Jodhpur Tailors (9 Ksheer Sagar Hotel, Motilal Atal Rd; ☾ 9am-8.30pm Mon-Sat, 9am-5pm Sun) You can have a beautiful pair of jodhpurs made in preparation for your visit to the Blue City. Or you can just go for a made-to-measure suit or shirt.

Textiles

Anokhi (www.anokhi.com; 2nd fl, KK Square, C-11, Prithviraj Marg; ☾ 9.30am-8pm Mon-Sat, 11am-7pm Sun) Anokhi is a classy, upmarket boutique that's well worth visiting – there's a wonderful little café on the premises and an excellent bookshop in the same building. Anokhi sells stunning high-quality textiles, such as block-printed fabrics, tablecloths, bed covers, cosmetic bags and scarves, as well as a range of well-designed, beautifully made clothing that combines Indian and Western influences. The pieces are produced just outside Jaipur at an unusually ethical factory, built on the grounds of an organic farm. Anokhi provides excellent working conditions, including limited working hours, free health care and transport for its 200 workers, as well as a crèche and educational funding for their children.

Soma (5 Jacob Rd, Civil Lines; ☾ 10am-8pm Mon-Sat, 10am-6pm Sun) This is a chic boutique, which sells first-rate textiles, including bright, fresh block prints and lots of unique furnishings, as well as some lovely children's clothes.

GETTING THERE & AWAY

Air

It's possible to arrange flights to Europe, the USA and other places, such as Dubai, all via Delhi. For details of international airlines, see p373. It's best to compare ticket prices from travel agencies (see p151), with what the airlines supply directly and through their websites – the latter is where you will usually find the best price.

Offices of domestic airlines:

Indian Airlines (☎ 2743500; www.indian-airlines.nic.in; Nehru Place, Tonk Rd)

Jet Airways (☎ 2360450; www.jetairways.com; 1st fl, Umaid Nagar House, MI Rd; ☾ 9.30am-5.30pm Mon-Sat, 10am-3pm Sun) Opposite Ganpati Plaza.

Kingfisher Airlines (☎ 4030372; www.flykingfisher.com; Usha Plaza, MI Rd; ☾ 9.30am-5.30pm Mon-Sat, 10am-3pm Sun).

Bus

Rajasthan State Road Transport Corporation (RSRTC aka Rajasthan Roadways) buses all

---

DOMESTIC FLIGHTS FROM JAIPUR

There are plenty of domestic flights from Jaipur, mostly run by Indian Airlines and Jet Airways, who offer similar prices. Other airlines serving Jaipur include Deccan-Kingfisher, IndiGo, Go Air, SpiceJet, and JetLite who offer competitively priced flights: see p376 for more details.

Destination	Fare (US$)	Duration	Frequency
Ahmedabad	170	1hr	2 weekly
Delhi	75	40min	3 daily
Jodhpur	130	40min	daily
Kolkata (Calcutta)	300	2hr	1 daily
Mumbai (Bombay)	200	1½hr	5 daily
Udaipur	90	1¾hr	1 daily

BUSES FROM JAIPUR

Destination	Fare (Rs)	Duration (hr)	Frequency
Agra	124, AC 297	5½	at least hourly
Ajmer	71, AC 110	2½	10 daily
Bharatpur	102	4½	hourly
Bikaner	100, AC 141	8	hourly
Bundi	120, AC 178	5	5 daily
Chittorgarh	168, AC 272	7	every 2 hours
Delhi	270, AC 370-460	5½	at least hourly
Jaisalmer	341	15	1 daily
Jhunjhunu	105	5	half-hourly
Jodhpur	190, AC 282	7	every 2 hours
Kota	141, AC 210	5	hourly
Mt Abu	248, AC 432	13	1 daily
Nawalgarh	72	4	hourly
Pushkar	90	3	1 daily (direct)
Sawai Madhopur	91	6	4 daily
Udaipur	235, AC 358	10	hourly

leave from the **main bus station** (Station Rd), picking up passengers at Narain Singh Circle (you can also buy tickets here). There is a left-luggage office at the main bus station (Rs 10 per bag for 24 hours), as well as a prepaid autorickshaw stand.

Deluxe or private buses are far preferable to RSRTC Blue Line or Star Line or local buses, which stop in small villages and are usually crowded bone-rattlers with questionable safety records. Deluxe buses all leave from Platform 3, tucked away in the right-hand corner of the bus station, and seats may be booked in advance from the **reservation office** (☎ 5116032), which is within the main bus station.

For long journeys, the RSRTC Volvo and Gold Line buses are easily the most comfortable and safe AC services. Even the cheaper RSRTC Silver Line services get good reviews. The RSRTC Gray Line is a sleeper service, where you can lie down – theoretically ensuring better sleep than a chair service. Private companies also provide sleeper buses over long distances and are also usually cheaper. Private buses are generally not as reliable, however, when it comes to schedules and safe drivers. There is a cluster of private offices along Motilal Atal Rd, near the Polo Victory Cinema.

There are regular buses that travel to many destinations, including those that are outlined in the table (above). Numerous private agencies also operate direct services to these cities.

Car

There are no car-hire operators offering self-drive cars in Rajasthan. You'll have to hire a car in Delhi if you're mad enough to try this.

You can arrange car and driver hire directly with the driver at the taxi stand at the train station. Usually the drivers need only a day's notice for a long trip. A much easier way to do this is to utilise the services provided by your hotel. Most hotels will be able to contact drivers (with cars) that are known to the hotel. These drivers value the work they obtain through the hotels and that provides you with greater security and service standards. A reasonable price is non-AC/AC Rs 5/6 per kilometre, with a 250km minimum per day and an overnight charge of Rs 100 per night. See p379 for more information. Rates with the RTDC are from Rs 4.75/6 per kilometre (Rs 125/150 overnight charge) for a non-AC/AC car, with the usual 250km minimum per day.

Train

The efficient **railway reservation office** (☎ 135; ⏱ 8am-2pm & 2.15-8pm Mon-Sat, 8am-2pm Sun) is to your right as you exit Jaipur train station. It's open for advance reservations only. Join the queue for 'Freedom Fighters and Foreign Tourists' (counter 769). See the table (p176) for details of routes and fares.

For same-day travel, buy your ticket at the train station on platform 1, window 9. The railway inquiries number is ☎ 131.

There's a prepaid autorickshaw stand at the road entrance to the train station, as well as

MAJOR TRAINS FROM JAIPUR

Destination	Train No & name	Fare (Rs)	Duration (hr)	Departure
Agra	2308 *Howrah Jodhpur Exp*	157/385/520 (A)	4¾	2am
Ahmedabad	2958 *Ahmedabad SJ Rajdhani Exp*	890/1215/2055 (B)	9¼	12.45am (Wed-Mon)
	2916 *Ahmedabad Ashram Exp*	281/735/1013/1721 (C)	11	8.55pm
Ajmer	2015 *Shatabdi*	270/530 (D)	2	10.50pm (Thu-Tue)
Bikaner	4737 *Bikaner Exp*	178/654/1117 (E)	8½	10.10pm
	2468 *Intercity Exp*	119 (F)	7	3.50pm
Delhi	2016 *Shatabdi*	535/990 (D)	5	5.45pm
	2957 *Rajdhani*	530/715/1210 (B)	5½	2.30am
	2413 *Jaipur-Delhi Exp*	177/441/600/1018 (C)	5	4.35pm
Jaisalmer	4059 *Delhi-Jaisalmer Exp*	150/256/690/962 (G)	13	11.50pm
Jodhpur	2465 *Intercity Exp*	105/180/359/450 (H)	5½	5.40pm
	2461 *Mandore Exp*	180/450/612/1040 (C)	5½	2.35am
Sikar	0711 *Jaipur-S. Ganganagar Passenger*	80 (I)	3	8.40am
Sawai Madhoper	2956 *Jaipur-Mumbai Exp*	141/276/366/609 (C)	2	2.10pm
Udaipur	2965 *Jaipur-Udaipur Exp*	252/655/901/1524 (C)	9½	10.25pm

Fares: A – sleeper/2AC/3AC, B – 3AC/2AC/1AC, C – sleeper/3AC/2AC/1AC, D – AC chair car/executive chair car, E – sleeper/2AC/1AC, F – 2nd class, G – sleeper/2nd class/3AC/2AC, H – 2nd class/sleeper/AC chair car/3AC, I – sleeper.

a tourist information office and a cloakroom for left luggage on platform 1.

GETTING AROUND
To/From the Airport
There are no bus services from the airport, which is 12km southeast of the city. An autorickshaw/taxi costs at least Rs 150/250 for the 15km journey into the city centre, or there's a prepaid taxi booth inside the terminal.

Autorickshaw
There are prepaid autorickshaw stands at the bus and train stations. Rates are fixed by the government, which means you don't have to haggle. In other cases you should be prepared to bargain hard.

If you want to hire an autorickshaw for local sightseeing, it should cost about Rs 200/400 for a half/full day (including a visit to Amber but not Nahargarh); be prepared to bargain. This price is per rickshaw, not per person, and don't let drivers tell you otherwise. Make sure you fix a price before setting off to avoid a scene later. A slower, but cheaper, and more environmentally friendly option is to hire a cycle-rickshaw. Though it can be uncomfortable watching someone

pedalling hard to transport you, this *is* how they make a living.

Taxi
There are unmetered taxis available which will require negotiating a fare or there is the recommended **Pinkcity Radio Taxi** (☎ 5115100; flagfall Rs 20, per km Rs 8, 25% night surcharge 10pm-6am). It's a 24-hour service and taxis can hired for a four-hour block and used for sightseeing.

AROUND JAIPUR

Jaipur's environs take in some fascinating ancient sites and interesting towns and villages that make great day trips. A comprehensive network of local buses and the ease of finding a taxi or autorickshaw makes getting to these regions simple. It's also possible to join a tour run by the RTDC that includes a commentary on the various places visited. See p164 for more details.

AMBER
The formidable, magnificent, pink fort-palace of Amber (pronounced Amer), an ethereal example of Rajput architecture, rises from a rocky mountainside about 11km

northeast of Jaipur. Amber was the ancient capital of Jaipur state.

En route to Amber you can squeeze in visits to Royal Gaitor (p160), the Jal Mahal (p160) and the cenotaphs of the maharanis of Jaipur.

Amber was built by the Kachhwaha Rajputs, who originally hailed from Gwalior, in present-day Madhya Pradesh, where they reigned for over 800 years. They were adept at diplomacy through marriage, and it was a marital alliance between a Kachhwaha prince Taj Karan and a Rajput princess that resulted in the granting of the region of Dausa to the prince by the princess' father.

Taj Karan's descendants eyed the hilltop that Amber Fort was later built on, recognis-ing its virtue as a potential military strong-hold. The site was eventually prised from its original inhabitants, the Susawat Minas, and the Minas were granted guardianship of the Kachhwahas' treasury in perpetuity.

The Kachhwahas, despite being devout Hindus belonging to the Kshatriya (warrior) caste, realised the convenience of aligning themselves with the powerful Mughal empire. They paid homage at the Mughal court, ce-mented the relationship with marital alliances and defended the Mughals in their various skirmishes. For this they were handsomely rewarded. With war booty they financed con-struction of the fort-palace at Amber, which was begun in 1592 by Maharaja Man Singh, the Rajput commander of Akbar's army. It

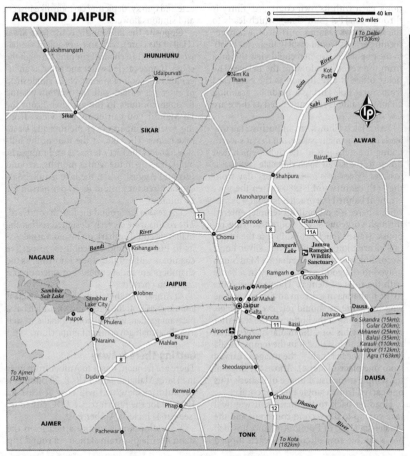

AROUND JAIPUR

was later extended and completed by the Jai Singhs before the move to Jaipur on the plains below.

Just beyond Amber Fort is the **Anokhi Museum of Handprinting** (Anokhi Haveli, Kheri Gate; ◷ 10.30am-5pm Tue-Sat, 11am-4.30pm Sun) which documents the art of hand-block printing and runs hands-on demonstrations. Of course there's a café and gift shop.

Sights
AMBER FORT
This magnificent **fort** (Indian/foreigner Rs 20/100, video camera Rs 200, guide Rs 200, audio guide Hindi/English/various European/various Asian Rs 100/150/200/250; ◷ 8am-7pm Aug-Mar, 7am-7pm Apr-Jul, last entry 5.30pm) is more of a palace, built from pale red sandstone and white marble, and divided into four main sections, each with its own courtyard. Entry is through **Suraj Pol** (Sun Gate), which leads to the **Jaleb Chowk** (Main Courtyard), where returning armies would display their war booty to the populace – women could view this area from the veiled windows of the palace. The ticket office is directly across the courtyard from Suraj Pol. Hiring a guide or grabbing an audio guide is recommended as there are few signs.

From Jaleb Chowk, an imposing stairway leads up to the main palace, but first it's worth taking the steps just to the right, which lead down to the small **Siladevi Temple** (photography prohibited; ◷ 6am-noon & 4-8pm). Every day from the 16th century until 1980 (when the government banned the practice) a goat was sacrificed here. It's a beautiful temple, entered through gorgeous silver doors featuring repoussé (raised relief) work. Before the image (an incarnation of Kali) lie two silver lions. According to tradition, Maharaja Man Singh prayed to the goddess for victory in a battle with the ruler of Bengal. The goddess came to the maharaja in a dream advising that if he won the battle he should retrieve her image, which was lying at the bottom of the sea. After vanquishing his foes, the maharaja recovered the statue and installed it in the temple as Sila Devi (*sila* means 'slab' – the image is carved from one piece of stone). Above the lintel of the temple is the usual image of Ganesh, this one carved from a single piece of coral.

Heading back to the main stairway will take you up to the second courtyard and the **Diwan-i-Am** (Hall of Public Audience), which has a double row of columns each topped by a capital in the shape of an elephant, and latticed galleries above. Here the maharaja held audience and received the petitions of his subjects.

The maharaja's apartments are located around the third courtyard – you enter through the fabulous **Ganesh Pol**, decorated with mosaics and sculptures. The **Jai Mandir** (Hall of Victory) is noted for its inlaid panels and multimirrored ceiling. Patterns made with coloured foil and paint are covered in glass. At night this would have been candlelit and the convex mirrors would have glittered brightly like stars. Regrettably, much of the decoration was allowed to deteriorate during the 1970s and 1980s, but restoration of varying quality proceeds. Carved marble relief panels around the hall are fascinatingly delicate and quirky, depicting cartoon-like insects and sinuous flowers.

Opposite the Jai Mandir is the **Sukh Niwas** (Hall of Pleasure), with an ivory-inlaid sandalwood door and a channel running through the room. It once carried water and acted as an ingenious air-cooling system. Not a single drop of water was wasted, with the overflow passing through conduits to the gardens. From the Jai Mandir you can enjoy fine views from the palace ramparts over picturesque **Maota Lake** below. The lake, at the foot of the hillside, reflects the fort's terraces and ramparts, but it dries up in the winter months. Around July and August, when the lake is full, boats can be hired for around Rs 50 per person for 15 minutes.

The **zenana** are around the fourth courtyard. The rooms were cleverly designed so that the maharaja could embark on his nocturnal visits to his wives' and concubines' respective chambers without the others knowing, as the chambers are independent but open onto a common corridor.

At Amber Fort there's also an **RTDC restaurant** (mains Rs 60-100), off the Jaleb Chowk, which has a pleasant garden, veg and nonveg thalis, as well as a Rajasthali government emporium.

Getting There & Away
There are frequent buses to Amber from near the Hawa Mahal in Jaipur (Rs 8, 25 minutes). An autorickshaw/taxi will cost at least Rs 150/450 for the return trip. RTDC city tours (see p164) include Amber Fort.

A good option is to hire a taxi from the stand near Jaipur train station – a round trip

THE AMBER ELEPHANTS & HELP IN SUFFERING

If an elephant has its own way, it will live in a hot, wet place, preferably close to a nice deep pool for bathing. Unfortunately, Rajasthan doesn't come up with the goods and the elephants that trundle tourists up the steep cobbled road to Amber Fort suffer greatly from the hot, dry days and freezing nights of their adopted desert state.

There are around 100 elephants working in rotation at Amber. Every day they have to walk to the fort from their compound, the Mahavaton-ka-Mohalla in Jaipur's old city – a distance of 11km each way. During the hot season temperatures at Amber can reach 45°C, and the elephants suffer from sunburn and cracked feet from walking on the hot bitumen roads. Elephants need to drink around 250L of water a day, most of which they drink while bathing. The Amber elephants used to do this at the lake below the palace – until the water level dropped. They also suffer from foot rot, abscesses and blindness caused by vitamin deficiencies.

Many of the mahouts (elephant keepers) are deeply concerned about the health and welfare of their elephants, but unfortunately some resort to metal prods (the *ankush*), which sometimes draw blood, to keep their elephants in line. Often this is linked to the poor conditions of the mahouts themselves – low wages mean that there's a high turnover of new recruits, and the important relationship between elephant and mahout never has a chance to develop.

If you're concerned about the elephants working the tourist trade at Amber, you can write a letter of support or make a donation to **Help in Suffering** (HIS; ☎ 2760803; www.his-india.org.au; Maharani Farm, Durgapura; ☤ 9am-5pm) which has a small office at the elephant mounting area below the fort. This organisation is lobbying the government to speed up its plans to build an elephant compound with bathing facilities close to Amber Fort, and to address the need for enforceable regulations to protect the animals, as well as better training and pay for the mahouts.

In addition to treating the elephants working at Amber, HIS also runs a rabies- and population-control programme for Jaipur's dogs, operates mobile clinics to rural areas, and rescues animals in trouble. It's possible to visit the Durgapura shelter, around 10km south of Jaipur, off the road to Sanganer, where happy dogs wander the grounds, and birds and animals of all descriptions convalesce. If you find an animal that is in need of some help, you can call HIS. Qualified vets can also volunteer here – see p370 for further details.

covering Amber Fort, Jaigarh and Nahagarh will cost around Rs 500, including waiting time (maximum five people). Try to arrive at Nahagarh in time for a sunset beer overlooking the city.

You can climb up to the fort from the road in about 10 minutes (cold drinks are available at the top). A seat in a jeep up to the fort costs Rs 200 return. Riding up on elephants is popular at Rs 550 per elephant carrying two passengers up – elephants return empty. In the mornings when most of the tour buses arrive, the queue for elephants is very long and you must be prepared to wait in the full blaze of the sun. Help in Suffering (see the boxed text, p179) is lobbying the government to speed up plans to build better facilities for these elephants.

JAIGARH

A scrubby green hill – Cheel ka Teela (Mound of Eagles) – rising above Amber, is topped by the imposing fortress of **Jaigarh** (Indian/foreigner Rs 25/75, camera or video Rs 50, admission free with City Palace ticket, car Rs 50, guide Rs 100; ☤ 9am-5pm). This massive fort was planned by Jai Singh I, but what you see today dates from the reign of Jai Singh II. It was only opened to the public in mid-1983 and thus has remained very much intact. Punctuated by whimsically hatted lookout towers, the fort was never captured and is a splendid example of grand 18th-century defences, without the palatial frills that are found in many other Rajput forts. It has water reservoirs, residential areas, a puppet theatre and the world's largest wheeled cannon, Jaya Vana.

During the Mughal empire Jaipur produced many weapons for the Mughal and Rajput rulers. This most spectacular example was made in the fort foundry, which was constructed in Mughal times. The huge cannon dates from 1720, has a barrel around 6m long, is made from a mix of eight different metals and weighs 50 tonnes. To fire it requires 100kg of gunpowder, and it has a range of 30km. It's debatable how many times this great device was used.

Sophisticated rainwater harvesting systems are in place at this fort. Complicated drainage channels, which fed three large tanks, are scattered throughout the fort. The largest has a capacity for 22.8 million litres of water. The fort served as the treasury of the Kachhwahas, and for a long time people were convinced that at least part of the royal treasure was still secreted in this large water tank. The Indian government even searched it to check, but found nothing. These tanks used to provide water for all the soldiers, residents and livestock that lived in the fort.

Within the fort is an **armoury** and **museum**, with the essential deadly weapons collection and some royal knick-knacks, including interesting photographs, maps of Jaigarh, spittoons and circular 18th-century playing cards. The structure also contains various open halls, including the **Shubhat Niwas** (Meeting Hall of Warriors), which has some weather-beaten sedan chairs and drums lying about.

The fort is a steep uphill walk (about 1km) from Amber and offers great views from the Diwa Burj watchtower.

Admission is free if you have a ticket to Jaipur's City Palace that is less than two days' old. Vehicles can drive up to the fort though your taxi driver will expect an extra 'hill fee' of Rs 150. There are cool drinks and snacks for sale inside the fort.

SANGANER & BAGRU

The large village of Sanganer is 16km south of Jaipur, and has a **ruined palace**, a group of **Jain temples** with fine carvings (to which entry is restricted) and two ruined **tripolias** (triple gateways). The main reason to visit, however, is to see its handmade paper and block-printing shops, workshops and factories (most shops can be found on or just off the main drag, Stadium Rd), where you can see the products being made by hand.

Best of all in Sanganer is walking down to the riverbank to see the brightly coloured fabrics drying in the sun. Though more and more of Sanganer's cloth is screen-printed, the time-honoured block printers of Sanganer are famous for their small floral prints, and the cloth produced here was traditionally used by the royal court. Traditional papermakers were also brought to the court at Amber in the 16th century, but moved to Sanganer in

the late 18th century due to water shortages. Later Gandhi's support helped develop the industry here.

Salim's Paper (☎ 2730222; www.handmadepaper.com; Gramodyog Rd; ⏰ 9am-5pm) is the largest handmade paper factory in India and claims to be one of the biggest in the world. It's well set up for visitors: you can take a free tour to see the paper production process. Significantly, the paper is not made from trees, but from scrap pieces of fabric, and often decorated with petals or glitter. You'll recognise lots of styles and designs, as the paper is exported all over the world. The 300 employees produce 40,000 sheets a day. There's also a beautiful range of tree-free paper products for sale in the showroom – great (and light) gifts for friends back home.

Another huge handmade paper manufacturer is **AL Paper House** (☎ 2731706; www.alpaperhouse.com; ⏰ 9am-5pm), near the tempo stand. This factory is also open to visitors.

For block-printed fabrics and blue pottery, there are a number of shops, including **Sakshi** (☎ 2731862; Laxmi Colony; ⏰ shop 8.30am-8.30pm, factory 9am-6pm). You can see the block-printing workshop here, and even try your hand at block printing. It also runs courses in block printing and blue pottery (see p163). There's a tremendous range of blue pottery and block-printed fabrics for sale.

About 20km west of Sanganer is the little village of **Bagru**, also known for its block-printing, particularly of colourful designs featuring circular motifs. You won't see as much here as in Sanganer, but it's more off the beaten track. The fabric is dyed with natural colours here and the printers' quarter – full of small family businesses – is a hive of activity.

Getting There & Away

Buses leave from the Ajmeri Gate in Jaipur for Sanganer every few minutes (Rs 8, one hour). To Bagru, there are daily buses from Sanganer (Rs 20, 1½ hours).

SAMODE
☎ 01423

The small village of Samode is spectacularly set among rugged hills, about 40km north of Jaipur. The only real reason to visit is if you can stay at the **Samode Palace** (admission Rs 100). If you want to be precise, it's not a palace, as it was owned by a nobleman rather than a ruler, but it's certainly palatial enough to get away with the title. Like the Samode Haveli in Jaipur, this building was owned by the *rawal* (nobleman) of Samode, and today it's also run by his descendants.

Mainly dating from the 19th century, it's a fantastical building nestling between the Aravalli hills and built on three levels, each with its own courtyard. The highlight is the exquisite Diwan-i-Khas, which is covered with original paintings and mirrorwork.

Above the palace is the overgrown Samode Fort – ask around and you'll find someone to let you in – where there are great views from the ramparts. This is also good walking country, with paths heading off into the countryside. Beneath the palace is a small village, where locals sell block-printed cloth and glass bangles.

Sleeping & Eating

Samode Bagh (☎ 40235; www.samode.com; s/d €100/110; 🍴 🏊) Also part of the Samode group, this luxurious tented accommodation (featuring private modern bathrooms) is a wonderful retreat. It's set in 8 peaceful hectares of land, surrounded by formal gardens and near a 150-year-old pavilion. Samode Bagh is 4km from Samode Palace. You can book through Samode Haveli in Jaipur.

Samode Palace (☎ /fax 240014/23; www.samode .com; s/d €143/170, ste €198-225; 🍴 🖳 🏊) Largely extended in the 19th century, this magnificent palace is a gloriously grand hotel decorated in no-holds-barred Rajput splendour, with a great courtyard swimming pool plus an infinity pool. The suites are particularly atmospheric and the room tariff includes breakfast. The palace admission fee for nonguests is deducted if you have a meal (Rs 250 to Rs 450) here. You can book through Samode Haveli in Jaipur. There are discounts from May to September and you should check the website for special offers.

Getting There & Away

There are a few direct buses to Samode from the main bus station in Jaipur (Rs 30, 1½ hours), or you can hire a taxi for around Rs 900 return.

RAMGARH

☎ 01426

This green oasis, about 35km northeast of Jaipur, has a pretty, though much shrunken lake, the **Jamwa Ramgarh Wildlife Sanctuary**. In 1982, when the lake was much fuller, some water-sports fixtures of the Asian Games took place here. The area around here has been scarred by mines – all are now closed as the area is protected. Panthers, hyenas, antelopes and wild boars once roamed the area, as the trophy-laden walls of Ramgarh Lodge testify, but loss of habitat, lack of water and hunting have, understandably, driven the wildlife to more welcoming areas. The scenery, with lush palms, huge banyans, remote villages, and small temples set into craggy rock, make it worth a visit to explore and walk in the area. There's a picturesque **polo ground** (in Jaipur for fixtures ☎ 0141-2374791) and the **Jamwa Maa Di Mandir**, an ancient Durga temple.

RTDC Jheel Tourist Village (☎ 52170; s/d Rs 300/400), further away from the lake, is very peaceful and offers accommodation in small round huts, which are a bit run down with peeling paint, but fine. The gardens are well kept with colonially trim lawns, and the views across to the remains of the lake are lovely. An extra bed costs Rs 100. There's a small dining area with veg thalis for Rs 55. Boating on Ramgarh Lake can be arranged when the water is high enough (Rs 125 per person per hour). They can also arrange jeep and camel safaris through the park.

Ramgarh Lodge (☎ 2552217; www.tajhotels.com; d with breakfast & dinner Rs 3700-4700, ste Rs 6700; 🍴 🏊), a one-time royal hunting lodge overlooking Ramgarh Lake, is spectacular, but it's one of those places with zillions of busy staff and immensely slow, offhand service, even when there are only a couple of guests. Inside the lodge are masses of glass-eyed stuffed beasts, the saddest of which is a bear holding a tray. Billiards, squash and tennis are available, as well as boating when the lake's water level is high enough. The pool (check it's full) has a great setting, and the most expensive rooms have fabulous views. Jeep safaris to the park cost Rs 1000 per jeep for one hour (maximum six people).

Buses travel between Jaipur (from the main bus station) and Ramgarh (Rs 13, one hour).

ABHANERI

About 95km from Jaipur on Agra Rd, this remote village surrounded by rolling wheat fields is the unlikely location for one of Rajasthan's most awe-inspiring step-wells, the **Chand Baori** (admission free; 🕐 sunrise-sunset).

With around 11 visible levels of zigzagging steps, this 10th-century water tank is an incredible, geometric sight, 20m deep. Flanking the *baori* is a small, crumbling **palace**, where the royals used to picnic and bathe in private rooms (water was brought up by oxen) – it's now inhabited by pigeons and bats. Next door is the **Harshat Mata Temple**, also dating from the 10th century, which was damaged by Muslim invaders, but retains some beautiful deep-relief sculptures in warm-orange sandstone. Both are thought to have been built by King Chand, ruler of Abhaneri and a Rajput from the Chahamana dynasty.

From Jaipur, catch a bus to Sikandra (1½ hours), from where you can hire a jeep for the 10km trip to Abhaneri (Rs 250 return, including a 30-minute stop). Alternatively, take a bus to Gular, from where it's a 5km walk to Abhaneri. If you have your own transport, this is a worthwhile stop between Jaipur and Bharatpur or Agra.

BALAJI

The extraordinary Hindu **exorcism temple** of Balaji, about 102km from Jaipur, is about 3km off the Jaipur to Agra road. People bring their loved ones who are suffering from possession here to have bad spirits exorcised through prayer and rituals. Most exorcisms take place on Tuesday and Saturday. At these times the street outside feels like it's hosting a Hindu rave, and the only people who can get inside the temple are the holy men and the victims – services are relayed to the crowds outside on crackly video screens. The possessed scream, shout, dance and shake their heads. It's an extraordinary experience.

If you wait until the service has finished, you will be able to look inside the temple. You may want to cover your head with a scarf as a mark of respect. No photography is permitted inside. The often-disturbing scenes at this temple may upset some. Believers say you shouldn't take items you buy from around the temple with you – they could bring you bad luck. The number of stands lining the way to the temple indicates that not everyone heeds these solemn warnings.

From the main bus station in Jaipur there are numerous buses to Balaji (local/express Rs 32/50, 2½/two hours).

SAMBHAR SALT LAKE

The country's largest salt lake, around 60km west of Jaipur, Sambhar Salt Lake's vast 230-sq-km wetland expanse once attracted flamingos, cranes, pelicans and many other waterfowl. According to myth, Sambhar is believed to have been given to local people by the goddess Shakambari some 2500 years ago. Her shrine, **Mata Pahari**, juts into the lake west of Jhapok. The people are certainly making good use of it – around 80 sq km of the lake is used for salt farming. On the eastern end, the lake is divided by a 5km-long stone dam. East of the dam are salt-evaporation ponds where salt has been farmed for the past 1000 years.

Also east of the dam is a railway line, built by the British (before Independence) which provides access from Sambhar Lake City to the saltworks. Water from the vast western section is pumped through gates to the other side when it is saline enough for salt extraction.

Sambhar was designated as a Ramsar site (recognised wetland of international importance) in 1990, because the wetland is a key wintering area for birds that migrate from northern Asia, some from as far as Siberia. Its privileged status, however, has not done it much good in recent years.

Usually the water depth fluctuates from a few centimetres during the dry season to about 3m postmonsoon. The specialised algae and bacteria growing in the lake provide striking water colours and support the lake ecology that, in turn, sustains the migrating waterfowl. Poor monsoons, however, have affected this environment, and the lake has almost completely dried up in places. Check locally about the current situation before heading out here, unless you have a particular interest in salt.

The best way to reach Sambhar from Jaipur is via train to Phulera Junction (Rs 25 in 2nd class, one hour and 10 minutes, two daily), 9km from the lake. From the station you can hire a jeep or rickshaw.

Eastern Rajasthan

Eastern Rajasthan includes the environs of Jaipur, the former fiefdoms of Alwar, Bharatpur and Deeg, the holy towns of Pushkar and Ajmer, and Rajasthan's most renowned wildlife sanctuaries. All the sights are easily accessible from Jaipur and the other corners of the 'Golden Triangle', Agra and Delhi.

Separating Eastern Rajasthan from the desert scapes of the west is the Aravalli Ranges. In the shadows of these hills lie Rajasthan's finest nature reserves – Ranthambhore, Sariska and Keoladeo Ghana – sadly much diminished from recent misfortune. Keoladeo's wetland lost its water supply in 2003, but hopes are held high for a wildlife-saving pipeline to lure back the exotic avian migrants every winter. Sariska Tiger Reserve has controversially, and hopefully only temporarily, lost its tigers to poaching. A plan to relocate villages and reintroduce tigers is underway; meanwhile, other wildlife – deer, antelope, monkeys and more appear to have proliferated in the absence of Shere Khan. South of Keoladeo is the knotted scarp hiding Ranthambhore National Park; an epic landscape with a cliff-hugging jungle fortress and abundant wildlife including elusive tigers.

Travellers of all description are pulled towards Pushkar, a pale blue pilgrimage town that hosts an extravagant annual camel fair. While Pushkar is a magnet for those who seek Hindu mysticism or a halt in their travels to rest, chill, and shop, in nearby Ajmer the extraordinary dargah of Khwaja Muin-ud-din Chishti is India's most important Muslim pilgrimage site.

EASTERN RAJASTHAN

HIGHLIGHTS

- Kick back in the pastel-hued pilgrimage town of **Pushkar** (p206), centred on its sacred ghats and enchanting lake

- Mingle with camels, converse with cameleers and catch the circus at the amazing **Pushkar Camel Fair** (p209)

- Spot a striped feline in the lush jungle and explore a magical cliff-top fortress at **Ranthambhore National Park** (p215)

- Observe abundant wildlife and explore temples, forts and a ghost city – in and around **Sariska Tiger Reserve** (p198)

- Merge with masses of pilgrims at India's most revered Muslim shrine – the **dargah** (p201) in Ajmer

- Cycle in peace while twitching for birds in the World Heritage–listed **Keoladeo Ghana National Park** (p188)

★ Sariska Tiger Reserve
★ Keoladeo Ghana National Park
★ Pushkar ★ Ajmer
★ Ranthambhore National Park
★

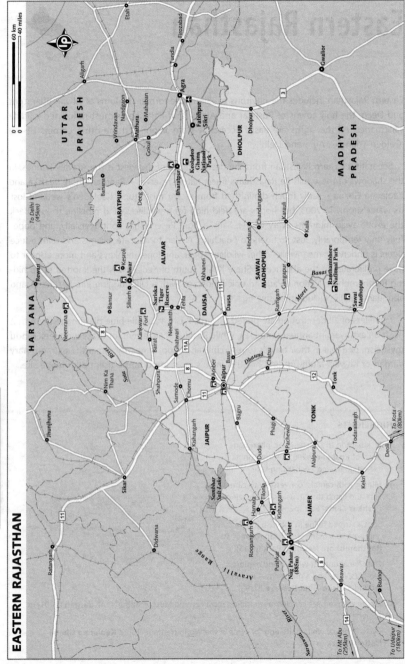

EASTERN RAJASTHAN

FESTIVALS IN EASTERN RAJASTHAN

For festivals celebrated statewide and nationwide, see p358.

Brij Festival (2-4 Feb; Bharatpur, p186) The Brij takes place over several days prior to Holi (so expect a bit of premature colour to be splashed around). It's known for the *rasalila* dance, which acts out the story of the love between Krishna and Radha, and is a good chance for everyone to get dressed up in colourful finery.

Alwar Utsav (Feb-Mar; Alwar, p194) A tourist carnival showcasing cultural activities with a procession, traditional music and dance, a flower show and craft displays.

Kaila Devi (Mar-Apr; Kaila, p219) One of eastern Rajasthan's bigger festivals, this huge event is held at the village of Kaila, 24km southwest of Karauli, in the month of Chaitra. The temple of Kaila Devi (also known as Lakshmi, the goddess of wealth) is 2km northwest of Kaila village, and thousands of pilgrims make their way here at this time of year bringing offerings. The devout will cover the distance to the temple wriggling prostrate along the ground, and the very devout won't eat or rest on the journey either. Masses of traders descend to make the most of the festival, selling crafts and souvenirs, and Mina tribespeople perform songs and dance.

Shri Mahavirji Fair (Mar-Apr; Chandangaon, p215) This huge Jain fair is held in honour of Mahavir, the 24th and last of the Jain *tirthankars* (great teachers), at the village of Chandangaon in Sawai Madhopur district. The Mahavirji temple contains an idol believed to have been dug out from a nearby hillside. Thousands of Jains congregate on the banks of the Gambhir River, to which an image of Mahavir is carried on a golden palanquin (litter) drawn by bullocks.

The Urs (Aug; Ajmer, p200) This is the anniversary of Sufi saint Khwaja Muin-ud-din Chishti's death, and signals a huge Muslim pilgrimage to Ajmer.

Ganesha Chaturthi (Aug-Sep; Ranthambhore, p215) Celebrated nationwide, Ganesh's birthday is particularly huge at Ranthambhore, which holds one of Rajasthan's most important Ganesh temples. Thousands of devotees make the pilgrimage here.

Pushkar Camel Fair (Oct-Nov; Pushkar, p206) Eastern Rajasthan hosts one of India's greatest festivals: a surreal, huge gathering of tribespeople, camels, livestock, horses, tourists, camera crews and touts.

History

Alwar is perhaps Rajasthan's most ancient kingdom, part of the Matsya kingdom since 1500 BC. It has been much coveted and fought over, due to its position on the strategic southwestern frontier of Delhi. The city of Alwar is believed to have been founded by a member of the Kachhwaha family from Amber, but control was wrested from the Kachhwahas by the Nikumbhas. They in turn lost the city to the Bada Gurjara Rajputs of Machari. It then passed to the Khanzadas, under Bahadura Nahara of Mewat, who converted from Hinduism to Islam to win the favour of Emperor Tughlaq of Delhi. At this time Alwar and Tijara were part of the kingdom of Mewat.

In 1427 descendants of Bahadura Nahara of Mewat bravely defended the fort at Alwar against the Muslims. Although the Mewati leader professed the Muslim faith, he chose to ally himself with the Rajputs as opposed to the Muslims of Mughal Delhi. The Mughals weren't at all happy about this and mounted military forays into the region, conquering it after great difficulty. Alwar was later granted to Sawai Jai Singh of Jaipur by Aurangzeb, but the emperor took back his generous gift

when he visited the city and saw the strategic virtues of its forts.

The Jats of Bharatpur threw their hat in and briefly overran the region, installing themselves in the Alwar fort. They were evicted by the Lalawat Narukas (the descendants of Naru, the Kachhwaha prince of Amber) between 1775 and 1782 under the leadership of the Naruka *thakur* (nobleman) Pratap Singh. His descendants were great patrons of the arts, commissioning the transcription of numerous sacred and scholarly texts, and encouraging painters and artisans to visit the Alwar court.

In 1803 the British invested the Alwar *thakur* with the title of maharaja as thanks for support in a battle against the Marathas. This friendly alliance was short-lived, however, since the maharaja of Alwar strongly resented British interference when a British Resident was installed in the city.

After Independence in 1947 Alwar was merged with the other princely states of Bharatpur, Karauli and Dholpur, forming the United State of Matsya, a name that reflected the fact that these states all comprised the ancient Matsya kingdom. In 1949 Matsya was merged with the state of Rajasthan.

EASTERN RAJASTHAN

Bharatpur is another ancient city, traditionally home of the Jats, who settled in this region before the emergence of the Rajputs. The relationship between the Jats, tillers of the soil, and the warrior Rajputs was, at best, uneasy. Marital alliances helped to reduce the friction, but they continually tussled over territory. The differences were only overcome when both groups turned to face the mutual threat posed by the Mughals.

It was Jat leader Suraj Mahl who built Deeg's beautiful palace and gardens, and commenced work on the Bharatpur Fort, which was completed in the late 18th century after nearly 60 years of toil. This was time well spent, as the British unsuccessfully besieged the fort for around six months, finally conceding defeat after substantial losses. The rulers of Bharatpur were the first to enter into an agreement with the East India Company.

The huge fort at Ranthambhore, founded in the 10th century by the Chauhan Rajputs, predates that at Bharatpur by many centuries. It's believed to be one of Rajasthan's oldest. Ranthambhore was held in reverence by the Jains, and several temples here were very important spiritually. Over the centuries Ranthambhore was subjected to numerous assaults by the Muslims.

The Mughal Emperor Akbar negotiated a treaty with Surjana Hada, a Bundi ruler who bought the fort of Ranthambhore from Jhunjhar Khan, and the fort passed to Jagannatha, under whose leadership the Jain religion flourished. Later, Aurangzeb took the fort, and it remained with the Mughals until the 18th century, when it was granted to the maharaja of Jaipur.

Ajmer was also founded by the Chauhans, three centuries earlier than Ranthambhore. In the late 12th century it was taken by Mohammed of Ghori, and remained a possession of the sultanate of Delhi until the 14th century. Another strategic jewel, it was fought over by various neighbouring states through subsequent centuries, but was mostly under Mughal rule. It was one of the few places in Rajasthan to be directly controlled by the British, from 1818.

BHARATPUR
☎ 05644 / pop 204,456

Bharatpur is famous for its Unesco World Heritage–listed Keoladeo Ghana National Park (p188), a wetland and significant bird sanctuary. Apart from the park, Bharatpur has a few historical vestiges, though it would not be worth making the journey for these alone. The town is dusty, noisy and not particularly visitor friendly. Bharatpur hosts the boisterous and colourful Brij festival (p185) just prior to Holi celebrations.

Orientation & Information
The fort is on an island in the centre of the old city, which was once surrounded by an 11km wall (now demolished). Keoladeo Ghana National Park lies 3km to the south of Bharatpur's centre. For tourist and other information, see p189.

Sights
LOHAGARH
Lohagarh, the early-18th-century Iron Fort, was so named because of its sturdy defences. Today still impressive, though also forlorn and derelict, it occupies the entire small artificial island in the town centre. The main entrance is the **Austdhatu (Eight-Metal) Gate** – apparently the spikes on the gate are made of eight different metals.

Maharaja Suraj Mahl, constructor of the fort and founder of Bharatpur, built two towers, the Jawahar Burj and the Fateh Burj, within the ramparts to commemorate his victories over the Mughals and the British. The fort also contains three much-decayed palaces within its precincts.

One of the palaces, centred on a tranquil courtyard, houses a seemingly forgotten **museum** (admission Rs 3, free Mon, camera/video Rs 10/20, no photography inside museum; ☒ 10am-4.30pm Sat-Thu). Downstairs is a Jain sculpture gallery that includes some beautiful 7th- to 10th-century sculpture, and most spectacularly, the palace's original hammam (bathhouse), which retains some fine carvings and frescoes. Upstairs, dusty cabinets contain royal toys, weapons – such as miniature cannons, some creepy animal trophies, and portraits and old photographs of the maharajas of Bharatpur. It's worth clambering up onto the roof for views across the city and other bird-inhabited palaces.

Jawahar Burj
This viewing point is a short walk to the northeast of the museum along a steep path that starts opposite the large water tank. It was

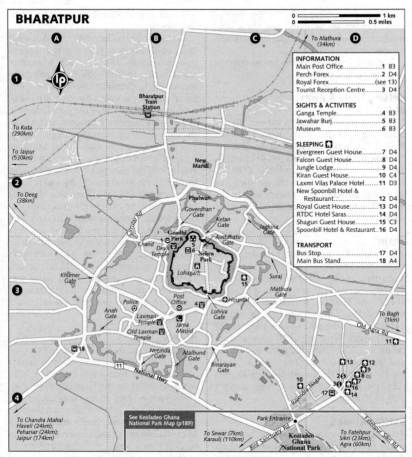

BHARATPUR

See Keoladeo Ghana National Park Map (p189)

INFORMATION

Main Post Office	1 B3
Perch Forex	2 D4
Royal Forex	(see 13)
Tourist Reception Centre	3 D4

SIGHTS & ACTIVITIES

Ganga Temple	4 B3
Jawahar Burj	5 B3
Museum	6 B3

SLEEPING

Evergreen Guest House	7 D4
Falcon Guest House	8 D4
Jungle Lodge	9 D4
Kiran Guest House	10 C4
Laxmi Vilas Palace Hotel	11 D3
New Spoonbill Hotel & Restaurant	12 D4
Royal Guest House	13 D4
RTDC Hotel Saras	14 D4
Shagun Guest House	15 C3
Spoonbill Hotel & Restaurant	16 D4

TRANSPORT

Bus Stop	17 D4
Main Bus Stand	18 A4

from here that the maharajas surveyed their city and it still has views. It's a peaceful, evocative place capturing the cool breezes in a series of pavilions, though unfortunately damaged and scarred with graffiti. The ceiling of one of the pavilions features badly deteriorating frescoes with hundreds of tiny scenes of daily life, elephants and chariots.

GANGA TEMPLE

Not far from the Lohiya Gate is this exquisite red-sandstone two-storey temple dedicated to the goddess Ganga, with elaborately carved stone terraces. Construction started in 1845 during the rule of Maharaja Balwant Singh, but it was not finished until 1937, five generations later, during the reign of Maharaja

Brijendra Sawai. Inside is a black-and-white chequered floor. There's a real sense of peace. However, you could shatter it if you go too close to the edges of the terrace on which the temple stands, overlooking the busy streets below – they're not stable.

Sleeping

Shagun Guest House (Map p187; ☎ 232455; rajeev shagun@hotmail.com; s/d Rs 90/100, without bathroom Rs 75/80) It doesn't get much more basic than this – the only reasonable choice in Bharatpur city. Right in town, down a lane inside Mathura Gate, you will find yourself well off the tourist trail with a little tree-shaded courtyard and friendly locals keen for a chat. Though basic and a bit grubby, the beds do have mosquito nets, there is hot water, home-cooked meals are available, and the affable owner is knowledgeable about the park and conducts village tours.

For additional accommodation options near the park, see p191.

Getting There & Away

BUS

There are regular buses to various places, including Agra (local/express Rs 38/55, 1½ hours), Fatehpur Sikri in Uttar Pradesh (Rs 25, one hour), Jaipur (Rs 99, 4½ hours), Deeg (Rs 25, one hour) and Alwar (Rs 50, four hours). Buses leave from the main bus stand, but also drop off and pick up passengers at the bus stop at the crossroads by the tourist office.

TRAIN

The *Janata Express* (9023/4) departs from Delhi (2nd class/sleeper Rs 67/121) at 1.45pm and arrives in Bharatpur at 5.40pm. It leaves Bharatpur at 8.05am, arriving in the capital at 12.40pm. There are several trains that run to Sawai Madhopur (sleeper/3 air-con Rs 141/326), including the *Golden Temple Mail* (2904) which departing at 10.45am and arriving at 1.05pm, which travels on to Kota and Mumbai. To Agra (2nd class/ AC chair car Rs 49/197), the *Jaipur Gwalior Express* (2987) departs at 9.05am arriving at Agra Fort at 10.15am.

Getting Around

An auto- or cycle-rickshaw from the bus stand to the tourist office and most of the hotels should cost around Rs 25 (Rs 35 from the train station). An excellent way to zip around is by hiring a bicycle, which can be done at many of the hotels or at the park entrance – see p190 for further details.

KEOLADEO GHANA NATIONAL PARK

This famous bird **sanctuary** (Indian/foreigner Rs 25/200, video Rs 200; ☾ 6am-6pm Apr-Sep, 6.30am-5pm Oct-Mar) was initially recognised as one of the world's most important bird-breeding and feeding grounds. In a good monsoon season over one-third of the park was submerged, and it hosted a staggering 364 species within its 29 sq km. You could spot hundreds of different species within a few days. The marshland patchwork was a wintering area for aquatic birds, including visi-

tors from Afghanistan, Turkmenistan, China and Siberia.

In recent years, however, Keoladeo has suffered greatly from poor management and poor monsoons, and less water has meant fewer birds. In 2003 the Panchana Dam located on the Gambhir River became operational and the park ceased to receive its usual monsoon water. In 2004 the park lodged an appeal for a higher allocation of water from the dam (it barely receives enough to cover evaporation in a few small dams), but came up against fierce opposition from land holders. In 2007 the park was a dismal echo of its former glory: it was mostly dry and invaded by thousands of cattle (from neighbouring farms) that were grazing the grasslands that occupied the former wetlands. In early 2008 it was announced that the flood waters from the Yamuna River via the Govardhan drain will be piped to the park. This *may* solve the problem. However, it could take several years to happen and the piped water may not supply the fish and the algae that are needed to support the extensive migratory bird populations.

History

Keoladeo originated as a royal hunting reserve in the 1850s. Before then Maharaja Suraj Mahl, the founder of Bharatpur, built the Ajun Bund on the Gambhir River converting a low-lying swamp into a reservoir. During the late 1800s further earthworks increased the water capacity and a network of canals and sluice gates diverted monsoon run-off into a series of impoundments. In so doing a wetland ecosystem was created which, albeit artificial, was the perfect habitat for an astonishing variety of birds (as well as turtles, pythons and fish). It is named Keoladeo (one of Shiva's many incarnations) after the small temple that is located in the park.

Keoladeo continued to supply the maharajas' tables with fresh game until as late as 1965. A large tablet near the small temple in the park records that 12 November 1938 was a particularly bad day to be a duck – 4273 were shot by the then viceroy of India, Lord Linlithgow, and his party.

A fence was built around the forests of the wetlands in the latter part of the 19th century to stop feral cattle from roaming through. Between 1944 and 1964 forestation poli-

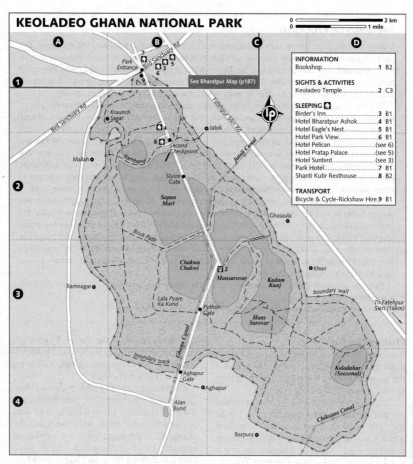

KEOLADEO GHANA NATIONAL PARK

INFORMATION	
Bookshop	**1** B2

SIGHTS & ACTIVITIES	
Keoladeo Temple	**2** C3

SLEEPING	
Birder's Inn	**3** B1
Hotel Bharatpur Ashok	**4** B1
Hotel Eagle's Nest	**5** B1
Hotel Park View	**6** B1
Hotel Pelican	(see 6)
Hotel Pratap Palace	(see 5)
Hotel Sunbird	(see 3)
Park Hotel	**7** B1
Shanti Kutir Resthouse	**8** B2

TRANSPORT	
Bicycle & Cycle-Rickshaw Hire	**9** B1

cies were pursued by means of the planting of acacias.

The post-Independence period was one of great turmoil. Poor local communities were keen to divert the canals, which feed the swamplands, for irrigation and to convert the wetlands into crop lands. Although this tension still exists, the conservationists won the day, and in 1956 the region was made a sanctuary, although hunting was not prohibited until 1972. In 1982 Keoladeo was declared a national park and it was listed as a World Heritage site in 1985.

Orientation & Information

Keoladeo Ghana National Park is 3km south of Bharatpur's centre and easily accessed by cycle-rickshaw.

A lot of places offer internet access for around Rs 40 per hour.

Bookshop (Map p189; 6am-5pm) At the second checkpoint, 1.5km from the main gate inside the park. This tiny place has a selection of titles on Indian animal and birdlife, and also sells postcards.

Main post office (Map p187; 10am-1pm & 2-5pm Mon-Sat) Near Gandhi Park.

Perch Forex (Map p187; 2224195; New Civil Lines; 5am-11pm) Cash travellers cheques, get credit-card advances or change money here.

Royal Forex (Map p187; New Civil Lines; 6am-10pm) Moneychanger that has expanded into the hotel and internet café business.

Tourist Reception Centre (Map p187; 222542; 10am-5pm Mon-Sat, closed 2nd Sat of month) About 700m from the park entrance; has a map of Bharatpur (Rs 10).

THE BIRDS OF KEOLADEO

During the monsoon period (July to August), and for a month or so following the monsoon, the park should be home to vast colonies of birds that have come here to breed and feed on the fertile wetland. However, since it lost most of its water supply in 2003 fewer and fewer migratory birds have returned to Keoladeo. With the promise of water being delivered by pipe, it is hoped that the park will return to its days of glory when it was a frenzy of feathered activity.

The wintering migratory birds would arrive in October and usually stay until around the end of February; these intervening months are the best time to visit. Some of the species that would nest at this time included storks, moorhens, herons, egrets and cormorants. In October and November the park would become full of ducks and geese. Pelicans would arrive later, when the fish are bigger and make for a more substantial meal. The most famous winter visitor was once the rare Siberian crane, though these haven't been seen since 2002, and that was only one pair. Saras cranes are the tallest birds in the park, and were seen in 2008. They have a fascinating breeding ritual whereby the male and female dance in front of each other and make trumpeting calls.

The migratory flocks have mostly left by the end of March. At the beginning of April, when the waters begin to recede, there is still a substantial population of birds of prey, some kingfishers and smaller birds, such as robins, wagtails and mynahs. Many of these birds feed at the few pools teeming with fish that remain in the park during the dry summer months. During the height of summer, when the waters have all but disappeared, the sanctuary is carpeted in dry grasslands that afford habitat to a variety of fauna, such as deer (spotted, sambar, bluebull), jackals, jungle cats, blackbucks, hares and mongoose.

Pythons are most commonly seen in the winter, when they emerge from underground for a sun bath.

The best times for bird-spotting are the early morning and evening.

Visiting the Park

If the park receives sufficient water and *if* these flows mimic natural seasonal patterns, and *if* the migratory flocks return, then the best time to visit is from October to February.

Admission entitles you to one entrance per day; if you want to spend the day inside the park, get your hotel to provide a packed lunch. Carry drinking water, as bird-watching is thirsty work. There is a bookshop and a snack bar near the Keoladeo Temple. You can also get a bite to eat at the Hotel Bharatpur Ashok (see p192) in the park.

One narrow road (no motorised vehicles are permitted) runs through the park, and countless embankments thread their way between the shallow dam. Walking or cycling along them affords unique opportunities to observe the rich birdlife at close quarters.

GUIDES & CYCLE-RICKSHAWS

Hiring an experienced ornithologist guide will cost Rs 70 per hour for up to five people and Rs 120 per hour for more than six people. Guides can be hired at the park entrance. Many hotels are run by qualified guides or will arrange guides for you, who charge the same rate. All registered guides provide a good service, but you may find a guide who speaks better English by arranging one through your hotel. If you want a guide who speaks another European language, it's also best to enquire at your hotel.

Government-authorised cycle-rickshaws (recognisable by the yellow plate bolted onto the front) only are allowed inside. You don't pay an admission fee for the drivers, but they charge Rs 50 per hour. Some are very knowledgeable. However, these cycle-rickshaws can only travel along the park's larger tracks.

BICYCLES

It's a good idea to take a rickshaw or guide on your first visit, then strike off on your own later. You get a scrappy but adequate map free with your ticket. An excellent way to see the park is by hiring a bike (Rs 25 per day), at the park entrance. You must leave your passport or a Rs 1000 deposit. At the time of writing you were no longer allowed to bring in a bike that you had hired outside of the park. This rule may change and most of the hotels are holding onto their hire bikes in the hope that it does. Having a bike is a wonderfully quiet way to travel, and allows you to avoid bottlenecks, which occur at the nesting sites of the larger birds.

EASTERN RAJASTHAN

The southern reaches of the park are virtually devoid of *humanus touristicus*, and so are better than the northern part for serious bird-watching.

Sleeping & Eating

Don't be pressured by touts at Bharatpur train or bus stations. The following places are all within easy walking distance (within 1km) of the bird sanctuary. All can arrange park guides and offer binocular (around Rs 50 per day) and bike hire. Room tariffs fluctuate according to the season. All of the rooms listed in this chapter have private bathrooms, unless otherwise noted. Guests usually eat in the hotel they are staying at and most places offer a thali for between Rs 60 and Rs 90. One thing to note is the quality of Bharatpur's water during these dry times – it's very salty. If you want a decent cup of tea or coffee get the kitchen to boil bottled water.

BUDGET

The cluster of guesthouses from the Spoonbill to the New Spoonbill are all run by different branches of the same family.

Hotel Pelican (Map p189; ☎ 224221; Bird Sanctuary Rd; r Rs 75-300) This funky little hotel with old car windscreens for windows has an overgrown garden and very relaxed management. There is quite a variety of rooms: from a pokey little cheapie to a couple of good-value doubles. The rooms upstairs are brighter.

Royal Guest House (Map p187; ☎ 230283; rinkesh btp@yahoo.com; s/d from Rs 150/200; 🖳) One of the park's newest hotels though the ultrakeen management have run a moneychanging business here for years. There are just five rooms, all clean and fresh, and a rooftop restaurant was on the plans when we visited. Guests are welcome to use the kitchen for self catering, and the attached internet café (guests/nonguests Rs 20/40) is the fastest in town.

Hotel Park View (Map p189; ☎ 9887493558; Bird Sanctuary Rd; s/d Rs 150/250) One of the closest hotels to the park, its basic rooms are small and cell-like. You will need to bring your own mosquito protection for the room and the small garden restaurant.

Evergreen Guest House (Map p187; ☎ 225917; s Rs 150-200, d Rs 200-250) This is a more basic, less outstanding option, with just two rooms. Nevertheless it is a good cheapie that satisfies customers, with the option of rooftop or garden dining and delicious home cooking. The owner also offers classes in Indian cooking.

Kiran Guest House (Map p187; ☎ 223845; www .kiranguesthouse.com; 364 Rajendra Nagar; d Rs 150-600, s without bathroom Rs 60; 🔀) Managed by eager-to-please brothers, this guesthouse delivers great value with seven simple, spacious, clean rooms and a pleasant rooftop where you can eat tasty home cooking. It's on a quiet road not far from the park. Nature guiding and free pickup from the Bharatpur train and bus stations are offered.

Spoonbill Hotel & Restaurant (Map p187; ☎ 223571; www.hotelspoonbill.com; s/d from Rs 150/200 to Rs 600/700; mains Rs 30-150; 🔀) The original Spoonbill has a variety of different rooms – all good-value and clean, if a bit shabby. The best room is superspacious and has a balcony. The place is run by a businesslike retired major and his son who also conducts birdwatching tours. The hotel has excellent food, with curd from the family cow and Rajasthani delicacies such as *churma* (sugar, cheese and dried fruit fried in butter), the royal dish of Rajasthan. There's often a campfire in winter.

Falcon Guest House (Map p187; ☎ 223815; falcon guesthouse@hotmail.com; s/d downstairs Rs 150/200 upstairs Rs 300/400, r with AC Rs 600-1200; veg thali Rs 60; 🔀) In the same area as the Spoonbill, the Falcon may well be the pick of this bunch. It is a well-kept, snug place to stay, run by the affable Mrs Rajni Singh. Her husband, Tej, is an ornithologist and he's happy to answer any bird-related questions. There are a range of comfortable, good-sized rooms, though more money gets you a softer mattress and private balcony. Flavoursome home-cooked food is served in the garden restaurant.

Jungle Lodge (Map p187; ☎ 225622; r Rs 200-400, r with AC summer only Rs 600; 🔀) Surrounded by an overgrown garden, the simple rooms, which could do with more ventilation, face onto a shady veranda. The owner is a naturalist, and the family is welcoming. Tasty home-cooked meals are available.

New Spoonbill Hotel & Restaurant (Map p187; ☎ 223571; www.hotelspoonbill.com; s/d from Rs 250/350 to Rs 650/750; mains Rs 30-150; 🔀 🖳) Run by the major's son, this newer place has simple but smart rooms, each with a small terrace. The larger rooms are great, with lots of windows. The dining room looks onto the garden.

Shanti Kutir Resthouse (Map p189; ☎ 200753; s/d Rs 415/600; breakfast Rs 25, lunch & dinner Rs 50) This erstwhile hunting lodge inside the park has a few rooms available at the behest of the park director. No forward booking is available but you can ring the director and take a punt on there being a vacancy. Simple meals are also available.

MIDRANGE

Hotel Pratap Palace (Map p189; ☎ 225093; www.hotel pratappalace.net; Bird Sanctuary Rd; ordinary s/d Rs 300/400, deluxe Rs 850/1050, with AC Rs 1300/1450; 🔀 🖵 🐾) This grand-looking hotel offers spacious but slightly faded rooms. The budget rooms aren't bad value though the standard at all levels is variable, so look at a few. The refreshing pool is available for nonguests for Rs 100 per person.

RTDC Hotel Saras (Map p187; ☎ 223700; cnr Fatehpur Sikri & Bird Sanctuary Rds; s/d Rs 550/650, with AC from Rs 800/900; 🔀) In typical RTDC fashion this hotel offers spacious, bleak rooms running off an echoing hallway. Its best features include its acceptable cleanliness and central location at the crossroads just by the tourist office and the bus stop.

Hotel Eagle's Nest (Map p189; ☎ 225144; Bird Sanctuary Rd; s/d Rs 600/800, with AC Rs 800/1000; 🔀 🖵) This smart option has 12 spacious and comfortable rooms (only two with air-con) with private balconies and a large multicuisine restaurant. Guided tours by a naturalist can be arranged and there are binoculars for hire.

Hotel Sunbird (Map p189; ☎ 225701; www.hotel sunbird.com; Bird Sanctuary Rd; s/d Rs 1000/1250, deluxe Rs 1400/1800; mains Rs 40-260; 🔀) Another well-run and popular place next door to Birder's Inn. Rooms are clean and comfortable and upstairs there's an appealing restaurant with a good range of dishes including tasty veg (Rs 150) and nonveg (Rs 200) thalis and cold beer. Packed lunches and guided tours are available.

Birder's Inn (Map p189; ☎ 227346; www.thebird ersinn.com; Bird Sanctuary Rd; s/d Rs 1100/1400; mains Rs 50-250; 🔀 🖵) The Birder's Inn is rightly a popular base for exploring the park. The atmospheric thatched restaurant is great place for a meal though there are plans for it to become the reception area and for a new restaurant to be constructed. The older front rooms are airy, spacious, and nicely decorated with good bathrooms, while the new rooms, under construction at the time of writing, were expected to boast bath tubs and LCD TVs. The in-house naturalist welcomes

guests and conducts tours (half day/full day Rs 400/700). The hotel can even arrange pick-up from Delhi airport.

Park Hotel (Map p189; ☎ 233192; thepark@yahoo .com; Bird Sanctuary Rd; d Rs 1500) Modern and clean, the Park offers spacious motel-style rooms with gleaming tiled floors and windows that overlook the surrounding manicured lawns There is also a bright and airy restaurant offering the usual Chinese, Continental and Indian dishes.

Chandra Mahal Haveli (Off Map p187; ☎ 05643-264336; www.chandramahalhaveli.com; Peharsar; s/d Rs 1650/2050, r with terrace Rs 2600, s/d ste Rs 2100/2400; 🔀) This is an old converted Muslim *haveli*, in Peharsar village 23km from Bharatpur on the way to Jaipur, about 1.5km off the Jaipur–Agra Hwy. The grand building, dating from 1850, has charming, simple rooms set around an inner courtyard. Ask for a room with a balcony view over the surrounding countryside. It's a good option if you are travelling by car. It's very peaceful and you can visit carpet weavers in the surrounding village.

Hotel Bharatpur Ashok (Map p189; ☎ 222722; www.bharatpurashok.com; s/d Rs 2500/2700; 🔀 🖵) This lodge, run by the Indian Tourism Development Corporation (ITDC), is 1km inside the park and 8km from the Bharatpur train station. It's looking a little faded, and service is typically lax. However, the comfortable, quiet rooms have balconies with swing seats and there's a bar downstairs. The multicuisine restaurant's handy if you want something to eat while within the park (nonguests are welcome).

TOP END

Laxmi Vilas Palace Hotel (Map p187; ☎ 223523; www.laxmivilas.com; Kakaji-ki-Kothi, Old Agra Rd; s/d/ste Rs 3300/3600/4600; 🔀 🖵 🐾) This is a heritage hotel, about equidistant between the national park and the town centre, owned by the younger son of Maharaja Jaswant Singh. Arched ceilings and heavy old furniture make for exquisite, atmospheric rooms, set around a courtyard. A new 'palace' with another 20 rooms was being constructed next door at the time we visited. It's also a busy lunch stop for tour groups travelling between Jaipur and Agra.

Bagh (Off Map p187; ☎ 225415; www.thebagh.com; Old Agra Rd; s/d US$130/150, ste US$150/170; 🔀 🖵 🐾) A picturesque hotel 2km from town, the Bagh has 23 elegant rooms spread out in separate pavilions nestled in a former royal orchard. The standard rooms are not much smaller than the suites and boast cool marble floors, antique furnishings and wonderful bathrooms. Décor is traditional but the cool clean lines have a contemporary feel. The 4-hectare garden is over 200 years old and has masses of birds if you're feeling too lazy to go to the park.

Getting There & Around

For travel details, see p188.

DEEG

☎ 0564 / pop 40,826

Deeg is a small, rarely visited, dusty tumult of a town. At its centre stands an incongruously glorious palace edged by stately formal gardens, famous for their coloured-water fountains (switched on for festivals). Nearby are mighty fortifications. It's about 36km north of Bharatpur, and is an easy day trip (there's nowhere good to stay) from Bharatpur, or from Agra or Mathura, both in the adjacent state of Uttar Pradesh.

Built by Suraj Mahl in the mid-18th century, Deeg was formerly the second capital of Bharatpur state and was the site of a famous battle in which the maharaja's forces withstood a combined Mughal and Maratha army of 80,000 men. Eight years later the maharaja even had the temerity to attack the Red Fort in Delhi, carrying off masses of booty, including an entire marble building, which can still be seen in the palace grounds.

Sights

SURAJ MAHL'S PALACE

One of India's most beautiful and carefully proportioned buildings, the **palace** (Indian/foreigner Rs 5/100; ◷ 9.30am-5.30pm) is splendidly preserved. Photography is not permitted in some of the bhavans (buildings).

Built in a mixture of Rajput and Mughal architectural styles, the 18th-century, mostly two-storey **Gopal Bhavan** is three and four storeys high in places. Downstairs is a lower storey that becomes submerged during the monsoon as the water level of the adjacent tank, **Gopal Sagar**, rises – but this hasn't happened for many years. The eastern façade is fronted by imposing arches to take full advantage of the early-morning light. It was used by the maharajas until the early 1950s, and contains many original furnishings, includ-

ing faded, spilling sofas, huge punkas that are over 200 years old, chaise longues, a stuffed tiger, elephant-foot stands, and fine porcelain from China and France. In an upstairs room at the rear of the palace is an Indian-style marble dining table – a stretched oval-shaped affair raised just 20cm off the ground. Guests sat around the edge, and the centre was the serving area. In the maharaja's bedroom is an enormous, 3.6m by 2.4m wooden bed with silver legs. On either end of Gopal Bhavan are two low stone tables used for washing and dressing dead bodies. One is made from a single piece of black granite, and was brought from the Red Fort in Delhi. The other one is white marble and found inside a small Hanuman temple.

Two large tanks lie alongside the palace, the aforementioned Gopal Sagar to the east and **Rup Sagar** to the west. The well-maintained gardens and flowerbeds, watered by the tanks, continue the extravagant theme with over 2000 fountains. Many of these fountains are in working order and coloured waters pour forth during the monsoon festival in August.

The Keshav Bhavan (Summer or Monsoon Pavilion) is a single-storey edifice with five arches along each side. Tiny jets spray water from the archways and metal balls rumbled around in a water channel imitating monsoon thunder. An arcade runs around the interior of the pavilion over a canal with hundreds of fountains, many of which are functional and are turned on for local festivals. The fountains are powered by water pressure when plugs are pulled from a rooftop reservoir. Deeg's massive walls (which are up to 28m high) and 12 vast bastions, some with their cannons still in place, are also worth exploring. You can walk up to the top of the walls from the palace.

Other bhavans (in various states of renovation) include the marble **Suraj Bhavan**, probably stolen from Delhi and reassembled here, the **Kishan Bhavan** and, along the north side of the palace grounds, the **Nand Bhavan**.

LAXMI MANDIR

This ancient **temple** is presided over by a *mataji* (a female priest). There are alcoves on three sides enshrining images of Durga, Hanuman and Gada, and a small shrine to Shiva to one side. The temple is on Batchu Rd, 20 minutes' walk from the palace.

EASTERN RAJASTHAN

Sleeping

Few travellers stay in Deeg, and with the recent closure of the RTDC hotel, there is only one very basic option available. The **Tourist Hotel** (s/d Rs 100/150) adjacent to the bus stand has nothing to recommend it, and Deeg can easily be visited as a day trip from Bharatpur. Bus travellers may still find themselves in the Tourist Hotel.

Getting There & Away

The roads to Deeg are rough and the buses crowded. Frequent buses run to and from Alwar (Rs 34, 2½ hours) and Bharatpur (Rs 25, one hour, half-hourly). One direct bus travels to Agra (Rs 60) and one express bus goes to Mathura (Rs 22, 1½ hours).

ALWAR

☎ 0144 / pop 260,245

Sprawling, dusty Alwar has a rambling and remarkable palace with an above-average museum packed with royal booty, testifying to its former importance as capital of a Rajput state. Alwar is perhaps the oldest of the Rajasthani kingdoms, forming part of the Matsya territories of Viratnagar in 1500 BC. It became known again in the 18th century under Pratap Singh, who pushed back the rulers of Jaipur to the south and the Jats of Bharatpur to the east, and who successfully resisted the Marathas. It was one of the first Rajput states to ally itself with the fledgling British empire, although British interference in Alwar's internal affairs meant that this partnership was not always amicable.

Not many tourists come here, so there is a refreshing lack of hustle, and you will find some colourful bazaars as well as the rustic palace. It is usually quiet but Alwar comes to life during the annual three-day festival of Alwar Utsav (p185). It is the nearest town to Sariska Tiger Reserve, where you'll find the grand hunting lodge that is another relic of Alwar's royal past.

Orientation

The city palace and museum are found in the northwest of the city, a steep 1km north of the bus stand. There's a collection of budget hotels a short distance to the east of the bus stand. The train station is on the eastern edge of town, and the main post office is about midway between it and the bus stand.

Information

ICICI ATM Next door to the State Bank of Bikaner & Jaipur.
Om Cyber Zoné (18 Ram Kuteer, Company Bagh Rd; per hr Rs 40; ☒ 7am-10pm)
State Bank of Bikaner & Jaipur (Company Bagh Rd; ☒ 10am-2pm Mon-Fri, 10am-noon Sat) Near the bus stand. Changes travellers cheques and major currencies.
Tourist Reception Centre (☎ 2347348; Nehru Rd; ☒ 10am-5pm Mon-Sat) Located near the train station, this helpful centre has maps of Alwar and booklets on Rajasthani culture.

Sights

BALA QILA

This imposing **fort**, with its 5km ramparts, stands 300m above the city, its fortifications hugging the steep incline. Predating the time of Pratap Singh, it's one of the few forts in Rajasthan built before the rise of the Mughals, who used it as a base for attacking Ranthambhore. Babur and Akbar have stayed overnight here, and Prince Salim (later Emperor Jehangir) was exiled in Salim Mahal for three years. Now in ruins, unfortunately, the fort houses a radio transmitter station and can only be visited with permission from the superintendent of police. However, this is easy to get: just ask at the superintendent's office in the City Palace complex. You can walk up to the fort entrance or take a rickshaw (it's a very steep couple of kilometres by foot and 7km by rickshaw).

CITY PALACE COMPLEX

Below the fort sprawls the colourful and convoluted **City Palace**, or Vinay Vilas Mahal, with massive gates and a tank reflecting a symmetrical series of ghats and pavilions. Today most of the complex is occupied by government offices, overflowing with piles of dusty papers and soiled by pigeons and splatters of *paan* (a mixture of betel nut and leaves for chewing). The curious can peer through the offices at the once splendid rooms and marvel at their neglect. Just outside the palace you will find clerks busily clacking away on typewriters for their lawyer bosses (who have outdoor 'offices' here).

Hidden away within the City Palace is an excellent government **museum** (admission Rs 3; ☒ 10am-4.30pm Sat-Thu). Its eclectic exhibits evoke the extravagance of the maharajas' lifestyle: stunning weapons, stuffed Scottish pheasants, royal ivory slippers, erotic miniatures, royal vestments, a solid silver table,

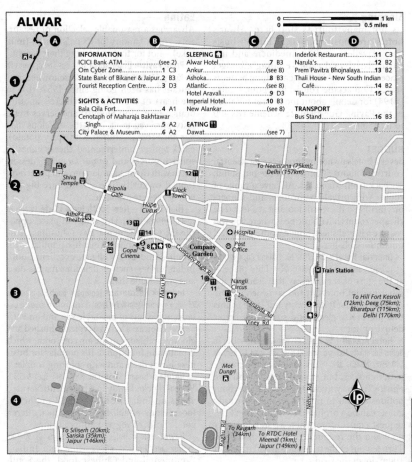

ALWAR

INFORMATION
ICICI Bank ATM.....................(see 2)
Om Cyber Zone.......................**1** C3
State Bank of Bikaner & Jaipur..**2** B3
Tourist Reception Centre.........**3** D3

SIGHTS & ACTIVITIES
Bala Qila Fort........................**4** A1
Cenotaph of Maharaja Bakhtawar
    Singh..............................**5** A2
City Palace & Museum.............**6** A2

SLEEPING
Alwar Hotel...........................**7** B3
Ankur...................................(see 8)
Ashoka.................................**8** B3
Atlantic................................(see 8)
Hotel Aravali.........................**9** D3
Imperial Hotel.......................**10** B3
New Alankar..........................(see 8)

EATING
Dawat..................................(see 7)

Inderlok Restaurant................**11** C3
Narula's................................**12** B2
Prem Pavitra Bhojnalaya.........**13** B2
Thali House - New South Indian
    Café.................................**14** B2
Tija.....................................**15** C3

TRANSPORT
Bus Stand.............................**16** B3

and stone sculptures, such as an 11th-century sculpture of Vishnu. There are also some striking 'widescreen' paintings of Imperial processions. Somewhat difficult to find in the Kafkaesque tangle of government offices, it's on the top floor of the palace, up a ramp from the main courtyard. However, there are plenty of people around to point you in the right direction and from there you can follow the signs.

CENOTAPH OF MAHARAJA BAKHTAWAR SINGH

This double-storey edifice, resting on a platform of sandstone, was built in 1815 by Maharaja Vinay Singh in memory of his father. To gain access to the **cenotaph**, take the steps on the far left when facing the palace. The cenotaph is also known as the Chhatri of Moosi Rani, after one of the mistresses of Bakhtawar Singh who performed *sati* (self-immolation) on his funeral pyre – after this act she was promoted to wifely status. Every day several women can be seen paying homage to the maharani by pouring holy water over raised sculpted footprints of the deceased royal couple. You will discover fine carving on the interior of the cenotaph (shoes should be removed), but unfortunately the paintings on the ceiling have almost disappeared. It is located alongside a beautiful tank, which is lined by a row of ghats and temples that also act as houses for local families.

EASTERN RAJASTHAN

Sleeping

As not many tourists stop here, Alwar's hotels are mostly aimed at budget business travellers, and are mediocre and not particularly good value. Finding a budget place is not a problem, but anything better is scarce. Contact the Tourist Reception Centre (p194) for details about the houses involved in the Paying Guest House Scheme (Rs 400 to Rs 1500).

BUDGET

Several hotels owned by brothers ring a central courtyard about 500m east of the bus stand, set back from Manu Rd. All have a range of rooms with private bathrooms and numerous tariffs, so it's worth looking at a few. The cheaper rooms have basic beds where you will require a hostel sheet. Single women may feel uncomfortable here.

Imperial Hotel (☎ 2701730; 1 Manu Rd; s/d from Rs 100/300, deluxe d Rs 400-800; 🔀) This place is at the start of the laneway that leads to the other budget hotels. It too is owned by one of the brothers. It has musty but large rooms that are pretty clean, and somewhat better deluxe options.

Hotel Aravali (☎ 2332883; www.hotelaravali.co.in; Nehru Rd; dm Rs 100, s/d from Rs 450/500, with AC from Rs 850/950; 🔀 🖥 🛉) This is one of the town's better choices, but nevertheless is a bit like *Fawlty Towers* without the humour. Its room options stretch to midrange, though rowdy guests can be a problem. If the hotel isn't full request a quiet room. There's a summer-only pool and the restaurant's not all that great. Turn left out of the train station and it's about 100m down the road.

RTDC Hotel Meenal (☎ 2347352; Topsingh Circle; s/d Rs 500/600, with AC Rs 700/800; 🔀) This is a respectable option with bland and tidy rooms typical of the chain. It is located about 1km south of town, so it's quiet and leafy, though it's a long way from the action.

MIDRANGE

Alwar Hotel (☎ 2700012; www.hotelalwar.com; 26 Manu Rd; s/d from Rs 900/1150, ste Rs 1750; 🔀) Set back from the road in a neatly manicured garden, this well-run hotel has spacious, renovated and comfortable rooms. This is easily the best option in town, and staff can be helpful with general information and sightseeing advice. The Alwar also boasts one of the town's better multicuisine restaurants, (right).

Eating

Alwar has a reasonable selection of restaurants, and is famous for its *palang torh* (milk cake) – not for those watching their weight.

Prem Pavitra Bhojnalaya (Old Bus Stand; mains Rs 20-40; 🕒 11am-10.30pm) Alwar's renowned restaurant has been going since 1957. It is in the heart of the old town (there's another branch near Moti Dungri) and serves fresh, tasty pure veg food – try the delicious *aloo parathas* (bread stuffed with spicy potato), *palak paneer* (unfermented cheese cubes in spinach purée) and *gaajar ka halva* (dessert made with carrots, cardamom and pistachios, topped by curd). The servings are big and half-serves are available.

Thali House – New South Indian Café (mains Rs 20-45; 🕒 9am-10pm) This dimly lit place, opposite the Gopal Cinema, has a shuffling, half-hearted atmosphere, but it's popular with families and offers cheap, excellent South Indian dishes, such as delicious masala dosa and good value thalis.

Inderlok Restaurant (Company Bagh Rd; mains Rs 25-90; 🕒 noon-3pm & 7-11pm) This main road restaurant has lots of palatable veg and unusual *paneer* choices. There's a typically hushed and gloomy ambience in the air-con room, which is plain and functional. It's popular for business-lunch deals and with courting couples.

Narula's (mains Rs 50-120; 🕒 11am-3pm & 5.30-10.30pm) Tucked away in a basement, Narula's whips up Indian, Chinese and Continental food. A long-established restaurant, it offers a good choice of veg and nonveg dishes.

Dawat (Alwar Hotel, Manu Rd; mains Rs 50-100; 🕒 Tue-Sun) Dawat serves first-rate Indian, Continental and Chinese food; the South Indian selection is particularly good. It's slightly gloomy in the restaurant but you can eat in the pleasant garden.

Tija (Nangli Circle) This small café is a town favourite and teenager meeting point. A great place to grab a coffee (hot/cold Rs 15/20) or one of its excellent lassis (yogurt and iced water drinks, Rs 15).

Getting There & Away

BUS

From Alwar there are numerous buses to Sariska (Rs 18, 1½ hours, half-hourly 5.15am to 8.30pm), which go on to Jaipur (Rs 78, four hours), via Bairat (Rs 27). There are also frequent (bumpy) services to Bharatpur (Rs 50, four hours) for Keoladeo

Ghana National Park, and Deeg (Rs 34, 2½ hours). Buses to Delhi take two different routes (Rs 88, via Tijara/Ramgarh four/five hours, half-hourly).

The following are cookie-cutter similar and cheek by jowl around a quiet courtyard. **Ankur** (☎ 2333025; s/d from Rs 300/500; 🔀) occupies two hotels and has passable rooms. **Atlantic** (☎ 2343181; s/d from Rs 300/500, with AC Rs 700/850) has plain, possibly cleaner rooms. **New Alankar** (☎ 3202966; s/d from Rs 300/400, with AC Rs 500/750) offers the newest, freshest rooms at the time of writing. **Ashoka** (☎ 2346780; s/d from Rs 300/500) offers passable rooms, though the cheaper rooms are far less appealing than the pricier ones.

CAR
A return taxi to Sariska Tiger Reserve (including a stop at Siliserh) will cost you around Rs 900.

TRAIN
The *Shatabdi Express* (2015/6) passes through Alwar. It departs for Ajmer (AC chair class/1st class Rs 435/830, four hours) at 8.39am and stops at Jaipur (Rs 320/605) at 10.45am. For Delhi, it departs at 7.30pm (Rs 335/640, 2½ hours). The *Mandore Express* (2461) departs Alwar at 9.45pm, arriving in Jodhpur (2 AC/3 AC Rs 793/578, 465km) at 8am.

Getting Around
There are cycle-rickshaws and autorickshaws. A cycle-rickshaw from the train station to the town centre should cost about Rs 20. You can hire bicycles near the train station (Rs 40 per day).

AROUND ALWAR
Siliserh
For a breath of fresh air, this former royal retreat, 20km southwest of Alwar (off the road to Sariska Tiger Reserve), is one of the state's lesser known secrets. Uninhabited forested hills encircle a tranquil 10.5 sq km lake and perched above the lake is the erstwhile hunting lodge – a cream-coloured confection with cupolas, balconies and courtyards. It was built by the Alwar Maharaja Vinay Singh in 1845, and is now a governmet-run hotel. Apart from the **Lake Palace** (admission Rs 30) there's not much else here except for some touristy waterborne activities and cheap restaurants. You can get a water view by hiring a decidedly unseaworthy

paddleboat (per 30min Rs 80), or putt-putting around on a **motorboat** (per 15min Rs 400).

The **RTDC Hotel Lake Palace** (☎ 0144-2886322; s/d Rs 1075/1525, with AC Rs 2000/2600, ste Rs 3100/3700; 🔀), in the palace, has wonderful lake views and a relaxed atmosphere. You will have to overlook the erratic cleanliness and service and very ordinary food typical of a government hotel. The admission charge can be offset by buying a meal at the restaurant.

GETTING THERE & AWAY
A tempo from Alwar will cost you about Rs 15, or you can hire a taxi for around Rs 400.

Kesroli
☎ 01468
This pleasant small town, 12km from Alwar, has a rambling 14th-century fort (with seven turrets) – now a hotel – still keeping a watch over bucolic agricultural scenery. The fort ramparts offer views across the fields, where the working villagers make splashes of colour.

The fairy-tale **Hill Fort Kesroli** (☎ 01468-289352; www.neemranahotels.com; r Rs 2000-5500; breakfast/lunch /dinner Rs 200/300/400) is an authentic stone fortress perching on a rocky knoll that would set any kid's imagination flying. True to form it is a bit haphazard, with mysterious passageways, changing floor levels and 22 very different, character-loaded rooms. It's an isolated, self-sufficient place set in tranquil countryside, with bike rides and car excursions available to break any self-imposed siege.

Many guests will be from small tour groups, but plenty of independent travellers rest their weary feet here for a couple of stress-free days. From Alwar you can take a taxi or an autorickshaw to the fort. It is run by the folks at the Neemrana Fort Palace (below).

Neemrana
☎ 01494
This small village lies about 75km north of Alwar on the main Delhi–Jaipur Hwy, a short distance to the south of the Haryana border. The reason to visit is the magnificent fortress palace, 2km away from Neemrana village. Dating from 1464, it was from here that the Rajput Maharaja Prithviraj Chauhan III reigned, and it's now one of Rajasthan's oldest luxury hotels.

The magnificent **Neemrana Fort Palace** (☎ 01494-246007; www.neemranahotels.com; s/d/ste

EASTERN RAJASTHAN

from Rs 1500/2500/3500; ✗ ✆) surmounts a fortified rugged plateau. The fort rises an amazing 10 levels, set in 25 acres among the folded Aravalli Hills. Rooms are decorated in a mixture of Rajput and colonial styles, and are massively varied – you should try to get one with a balcony or terrace. The fort layout is fascinatingly complex, with hidden courtyards and terraces, and corridors that resemble mazes.

GETTING THERE & AWAY

Buses on the main Delhi to Jaipur route generally stop at Behror, 14km from Neemrana (from where it's a further 2km to the hotel). A taxi from Behror to the hotel will cost about Rs 300.

SARISKA TIGER RESERVE
☎ 0144

Enclosed within the dramatic, shadowy folds of the Aravallis, the **Sariska Tiger Reserve** (Indian /foreigner Rs 25/200, car/jeep Rs 125, video Rs 200; ☉ ticket sales 7am-3.30pm Oct-Mar, 6am-4pm Apr-Sep, park closes at sunset) is a tangle of remnant semideciduous jungle and craggy canyons sheltering streams and lush greenery. It covers 866 sq km (including a core area of 498 sq km), and is home to peacocks, monkeys, majestic sambars, nilgai, chital, wild boars and jackals.

Although Project Tiger has been in charge of the sanctuary since 1979, there has been a dramatic failure in tiger protection. In 2004 there were an estimated 18 tigers in the park; however, reports in 2005 called this into question, after an investigation by the World Wild Fund for Nature (WWF). That report prompted the federal government to investigate what has happened to the tigers of Sariska. See opposite for more details.

Tigers or no tigers, Sariska is in any case a fascinating sanctuary to visit – and with visitor numbers at an all time low and deer numbers at a high, the wildlife-viewing experience is exceptional. Unlike most national parks, it opens year-round, although the best time to spot wildlife is November to March, and you'll see most wildlife in the evening. During July and August your chance of spotting wildlife is minimal, as the animals move on to higher ground, and the park is 'open' primarily for temple pilgrimage rather than wildlife viewing.

In early 2008 it was proposed to stop private car access into the park and to end the free access to Indians between 8am and 3pm Tuesday and Saturday (during summer) for visiting the Hanuman temple. As we go to print these proposals hadn't been acted on.

Sights

Besides wildlife, Sariska has some fantastic sights within the park or around its peripheries, which are well worth seeking out. If you take a longer tour, you can ask to visit one or more of these. A couple of them are also accessible by public bus.

KANKWARI FORT

Deep inside the sanctuary, this imposing small jungle fort, 22km away from Sariska, offers amazing views over the plains of the national park, dotted with red mud-brick villages. This is the inaccessible place that Aurangzeb chose to imprison his brother, Dara Shikoh, Shah Jahan's chosen heir to the Mughal throne, for several years before he was beheaded.

HANUMAN TEMPLE

You can visit a small Hanuman temple, deep in the park surrounded by an unsightly cement building painted pink. Its recumbent idol, adapted from a rock, is painted orange with a couple of eyes and is shaded by silver parasols. People give offerings of incense and receive tiny parcels of holy ash. From the temple there is a pleasant walk, for over a kilometre to **Pandu pol**, a gaping natural arch. The rough trail follows an ephemeral stream beneath sheer ravine walls which merge at the 'gateway'. There is a deep green pool below the arch and the track becomes a steep slippery climb best left alone.

NEELKANTHESHWAR TEMPLE

Around 35km from Sariska is an ancient temple complex, up a dramatically winding road that allows fantastic views. This 8th-century complex sits on a small plateau ringed by low hills where the old defensive wall is still visible. It's said that the temples remained preserved because bees chased Aurangzeb away when he tried to attack them. The main temple is dedicated to Shiva (photography prohibited). The small podlike shrines outside the temple are priests' graves. A little bit further away,

EASTERN RAJASTHAN

THE CASE OF THE MISSING TIGERS

News splashed across the press in spring 2005 that the tigers were gone, presumed poached. The distressing news from Sariska followed a report from the WWF, who had searched areas previously frequented by tigers and found that there was no evidence to indicate any recent tiger activity. They found that no tigers had been sighted in these areas since August 2004. The WWF concluded that something had happened to the last tigers between then and December 2004. Furthermore, it was suggested that previous estimations of numbers of tigers in the park were exaggerated.

Though notorious interstate poachers and poor local villagers have since been brought before courts and poachers have been jailed, the prime minister's inquiry into the crisis suggested fundamental management changes before tigers could be reintroduced to the reserve. Several recommendations and extra funding was proposed covering relocation of villages within the park, restricting access and increasing the protection force. While poaching is the most likely cause of the ultimate extinction of the last of Sariska's tigers, the WWF report highlighted the issues of widespread woodcutting and grazing within park boundaries and the low morale among park staff. And it's not only tigers at risk here – sambars have also been targeted for their antlers. The underlying problem – the inevitable interplay between India's poorest tribal and village populace with rare and phenomenally valuable wildlife on their doorstep – remains largely unresolved. Of the 11 villages within the core area of the park, four have been earmarked for urgent relocation. By early 2008 only one of these four villages, Bhagani, had been relocated.

As things stand, Sariska Tiger Reserve is a sad indictment of tiger conservation in India, from the top government officials down to the underpaid forest guard. Tragically it seems it will inevitably be repeated in future interactions between the soaring populations of *Homo sapiens* and the dwindling numbers of *Panthera tigris* and their diminishing habitat.

through a tangle of vegetation (ask locals to point out the right path), is a Jain temple built from orange-red sandstone, with a huge stone statue of the 23rd *tirthankar*, known locally as Nogaza.

BHANGARH

Around 55km from Sariska, beyond the inner park sanctuary and out in open countryside, is this deserted, well-preserved, notoriously haunted city. It was founded in 1631 by Madho Singh, and had 10,000 dwellings, but was suddenly deserted about 300 years ago for reasons that remain mysterious. However, the favoured explanation is that a magician who loved the queen found his love unrequited and cursed the city. The buildings today, in their wonderful setting of unspoilt countryside, are largely restored, which gives a remarkable sense of the city and its town planning. Temples and *chhatris* (cenotaphs, literally 'umbrellas') dot the surrounding area.

After you enter the main gate, there is a *haveli*, once a grand house, to the right. Beyond it, you can walk through the market area's well-defined and ordered bazaars up to the ruined, evocative palace for striking views. Within the complex are two well-preserved, ornate Shiva temples. One has its lingam (phallic image of Shiva) still intact, and lies alongside a green-shaded tank.

Bhangarh can be reached by a bus that runs twice daily through the sanctuary (Rs 29) to nearby Golaka village. Check what time the bus returns, otherwise you risk getting stranded.

Tours

While it was possible to take private cars into the park when we visited, there was a proposal to stop this before any introduction of tigers. In any case private cars are limited to sealed roads. The best way to visit the park is by jeep, which can explore off the main tracks. For diesel/petrol jeeps you'll be quoted Rs 700/800 for three hours, or Rs 2000/2500 for a full day. They can take up to five people. It's worth paying the extra for a petrol jeep, as the diesel vehicles are noisier and can scare away the animals. On the days when admission is free for Indians (Tuesday and Saturday in summer) the park gets very crowded; however, it is also proposed that free entry will be discontinued in the future. Guides are available (Rs 100 for three hours; maximum five people). It's also possible to arrange guided treks.

EASTERN RAJASTHAN

Bookings can be made at the **Forest Reception Office** (☎ 2841333; Jaipur Rd), directly opposite the Hotel Sariska Palace, which is where buses will drop you.

Sleeping & Eating

RTDC Hotel Tiger Den (☎ 2841342; dm Rs 50, s/d Rs 1075/1525, with AC Rs 1775/2350; 🛏) Hotel Tiger Den is a quasi-Soviet block, backed by a rambling garden that's also used as a rubbish tip. Rooms are drab and a bit run-down, but they have balconies and occupy a pleasant setting. Bring a mosquito net or repellent. Various tours of the reserve can be organised at reception here.

Sariska Tiger Heaven (☎ 224816; r Rs 2500, with AC Rs 3200; 🛏 🍽) This is an isolated place about 3km west of the bus stop at Thanagazi village; free pick-up is on offer. Rooms are set in stone-and-tile cottages and the cement tree stumps in the neatly clipped lawn complete the picture. Rooms have big beds and windowed alcoves, and are set in 5 acres. It's a tranquil, if overpriced and overstaffed, place to stay. Staff can arrange jeeps and guides to the park.

Alwar Bagh (☎ 2885231; www.alwarbagh.com; r & tent Rs 2800, ste Rs 3500; breakfast/lunch/dinner Rs 150/300/300; 🛏 🍽) This is a very peaceful option located in the village of Dhawala, between Alwar (14km) and Sariska (19km). It can arrange pick-up and drop-off from Alwar and can also arrange tours of Sariska. The bright new hotel boasts traditional styling, spotless rooms and romantic tents, an organic orchard, a garden restaurant and a sparkling swimming pool.

Hotel Sariska Palace (☎ 6451322; r Rs 6600, ste from Rs 17,400; mains Rs 330-400, set breakfast/lunch/dinner Rs 350/650/900; 🛏 🍽) Near the park entrance is this imposing former hunting lodge of the maharajas of Alwar. There's a pot-holed driveway leading from opposite the Forest Reception Office. Rooms have LCD TVs, soaring ceilings and soft mattresses. Those in the annexe by the swimming pool have newer interiors and good views. The Fusion Restaurant here serves expensive Indian and Continental dishes and guests can help themselves to the buffet. It's set in 20 hectares, and it's possible to take short horse and camel rides around the grounds.

Amanbagh (☎ 065-68873337; www.amanresorts.com; r from US$650; 🛏 💻 🍽) Set some way away, isolated among the folds of the Aravalli range, is this vastly opulent hotel. It's a lush walled compound that was once a site for the hunting camps of the maharaja of Alwar. Amanbagh means 'peaceful garden'. The splendid rooms have domed ceilings and huge baths – it's like walking into a movie set – and the most expensive have a private pool. The resort is just 10km from Bhangarh.

Getting There & Away

Sariska is 35km from Alwar, a convenient town from which to approach the sanctuary. There are frequent buses from Alwar (Rs 18, one to 1½ hours, at least hourly) and on to Jaipur (Rs 67). Buses stop in front of the Forest Reception Office.

AJMER

☎ 0145 / pop 485,197

Ajmer is a bustling chaotic city around 130km southwest of Jaipur. Situated beside the tranquil lake of Ana Sagar, and surrounded by barren Aravalli hills, Ajmer is Rajasthan's most important place in terms of Islamic history and heritage. It contains one of India's most important Muslim pilgrimage centres – the shrine of Khwaja Muin-ud-din Chishti, a venerated Sufi saint who founded the Chishtiya order, the prime Sufi order in India today. As well as some superb examples of early Muslim architecture, Ajmer is also a significant centre for the Jain religion, possessing an amazing golden Jain temple. However, most travellers just use Ajmer as a stepping stone to nearby Pushkar, a supremely sacred town to Hindus and former hippy hang-out. With Ajmer's combination of high-voltage crowds, commerce and traffic, most travellers choose to stay in laid-back Pushkar, and visit on a day trip.

Ajmer gets very busy during Ramadan, and the anniversary of the saint's death – the Urs (see p185).

History

Ajmer has always had great strategic importance. Located on the major trade route between Delhi and the ports of Gujarat, it was fought over for centuries. Its significance was such that its rulers, from the time of the Turks until the East India Company, tried to keep Ajmer under direct control.

The city was founded in the 7th century by Ajaipal Chauhan, who constructed a hill fort and named the place Ajaimeru (Invincible Hill). Ajmer was ruled by the Chauhans until the late 12th century, when Prithviraj Chauhan lost it to Mohammed of Ghori. It became part of the sultanate in Delhi and remained so until 1326. Ajmer then entered a tumultuous period when it was continually fought over by surrounding states, including the sultans of Delhi and Gujarat, and the rulers of Mewar (Udaipur) and Marwar (Jaipur).

Later in its history, Ajmer became a favourite residence of the great Mughals. One of the first contacts between the Mughals and the British occurred in Ajmer when Sir Thomas Roe met Emperor Jehangir (who lived here for three years) in 1616.

In 1659 Aurangzeb battled and won here against his brother Dara Shikoh, changing the course of succession and signalling the end of the Mughal empire.

The city was subsequently taken by the Scindias and, in 1818, was handed over to the British, becoming one of the few places in Rajasthan controlled directly by the British rather than being part of a princely state. The British set up Mayo College here in 1875, a prestigious school in an overexcited building, exclusively for the Indian nobility. Today it's open to all boys (whose parents can afford the fees). Other monuments that stand as reminders of Ajmer's colonial past are the Edward Memorial Hall, Ajmer Club and Jubilee Clock Tower.

Orientation

The main bus stand is close to the RTDC Hotel Khadim on the east side of town. Most of the hotels are west of the train station. Northwest of the main post office is Naya Bazaar (known for its silver jewellery and tie-dyed fabrics) and Agra Gate. Further north is the large artificial Lake Ana Sagar.

Information

Ajmer has several ATMs, including an IDBI ATM on Jaipur Rd.

Bank of Baroda (Prithviraj Marg; 🕙 10am-3pm Mon-Fri, 10am-12.30pm Sat) Changes travellers cheques and does credit-card advances and has an ATM.

JLN Hospital (☎ 2625500; Daulat Bagh)

Main post office (Prithviraj Marg; 🕙 10am-1pm & 1.30-6pm Mon-Sat) Less than 500m from the train station.

Satguru's Internet (60-61 Kutchery Rd; per hr Rs 20; 🕙 8am-10pm)

State Bank of Bikaner & Jaipur ATM (Kutchery Rd)

State Bank of India (☎ 2627048; 🕙 10am-2pm & 2.30-4pm Mon-Fri, 10am-1pm Sat) Opposite the Collector-

ate, changes travellers cheques and currency and has an ATM.

Surya Tours & Travels (☎ 2631731; 🕙 8am-6pm Mon-Sat) In the forecourt of the RTDC Hotel Khadim, this helpful travel agent can arrange transport and tickets.

Tourist office RTDC Hotel Khadim (☎ 2627426; 🕙 8am-noon & 3-6pm Mon-Sat); train station (🕙 10am-2pm & 2.30-5pm Mon-Sat)

Sights
ANA SAGAR

This large lake, created in the 12th century by damming the River Luni, is set against a blue-grey hilly spine that merges into its surface. On its bank is a park, the **Subash Bagh & Dault Bagh**, containing a series of marble pavilions erected in 1637 by Shah Jahan. There are good views towards Ajmer from the hill beside the Dault Bagh, particularly at sunset. It's a popular place for an evening stroll, though you may get quite a lot of attention. Pedalos and motorboats can be hired from the Fun N Joy Boat Club.

DARGAH OF KHWAJA MUIN-UD-DIN CHISHTI

> The dargah was packed. Tens of thousands of devotees from all over India and beyond were milling around. Ecstatics and madmen were shrieking to themselves, beating their foreheads against the stone railings on the tomb. Blind beggars stumbled around with their alms bowls. Women discreetly suckled young babies under the folds of their saris.
>
> *William Dalrymple,* City of Djinns

Situated at the foot of a hill and in the old part of town is the **dargah of Khwaja Muin-ud-din Chishti** (www.dargahajmer.com; 🕙 5am-9pm winter, 4am-9pm summer), India's most important Muslim pilgrimage site.

This is the tomb of a Sufi saint Khwaja Muin-ud-din Chishti, who came to Ajmer from Persia in 1192 and died here in 1236. The tomb gained its significance during the time of the Mughals – many emperors added to the buildings here. Construction of the shrine was completed by Humayun, and the gate was added by the nizam (ruler of Hyderabad). Akbar used to make the pilgrimage to the dargah from Agra every year.

You have to cover your head in certain parts of the shrine, so remember to take a

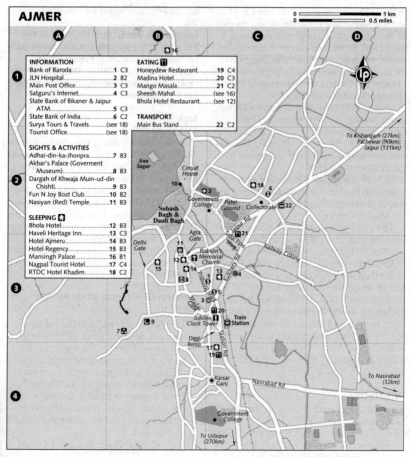

AJMER

0 — 1 km
0 — 0.5 miles

INFORMATION
Bank of Baroda.............................1 C3
JLN Hospital..................................2 B2
Main Post Office..........................3 C3
Satguru's Internet........................4 C3
State Bank of Bikaner & Jaipur
  ATM...5 C3
State Bank of India......................6 C2
Surya Tours & Travels...........(see 18)
Tourist Office........................(see 18)

SIGHTS & ACTIVITIES
Adhai-din-ka-Jhonpra..............7 B3
Akbar's Palace (Goverment
  Museum)...............................8 B3
Dargah of Khwaja Muin-ud-din
  Chishti....................................9 B3
Fun N Joy Boat Club.................10 B2
Nasiyan (Red) Temple.............11 B3

SLEEPING
Bhola Hotel...............................12 B3
Haveli Heritage Inn..................13 C3
Hotel Ajmeru.............................14 B3
Hotel Regency...........................15 B3
Mansingh Palace........................16 B1
Nagpal Tourist Hotel................17 C4
RTDC Hotel Khadim..................18 C2

EATING
Honeydew Restaurant.............19 C4
Madina Hotel.............................20 C3
Mango Masala...........................21 C2
Sheesh Mahal......................(see 16)
Bhola Hotel Restaurant......(see 12)

TRANSPORT
Main Bus Stand.........................22 C2

To Kishangarh (27km);
Pachewar (90km);
Jaipur (131km)

To Nasirabad (32km)

To Udaipur (270km)

Ana Sagar
Circuit House
Subash Bagh & Dault Bagh
Government College
Patel Ground
Collectorate
Agra Gate
Delhi Gate
Robson's Memorial Church
Railway Colony
Madar Gate
Jubilee Clock Tower
Train Station
Diggi Bazaar
Kaisar Ganj
Government College
Station Rd
Nasirabad Rd

scarf or cap, although there are plenty for sale at the colourful bazaar leading to the dargah, along with floral offerings and delicious Muslim toffees.

Following a fatal bomb blast in October 2007, security is extremely tight adding to the usual bottleneck of pilgrims at the entrance. The first gate is the Nizam Gate, built in 1915 up some steps to protect it from the rains. The green and white mosque, **Akbari Masjid**, on the right was constructed by Akbar in 1571 and is now Moiniua Usmania Darul-Uloom, an Arabic and Persian School for religious education. The second gate was built by Shah Jahan, and is often called the Nakkarkhana because it has two large *nakkharas* (drums) fixed above it.

In an inner court there is another mosque, built by Shah Jahan. Of white marble, it has 11 arches and a Persian inscription running the full length of the building.

The third gate, Buland Darwaza, dates from the 16th century. It's tall – about 28m high – and whitewashed, and leads into the dargah courtyard.

Flanking the entrance of the courtyard are the *degs*, large iron cauldrons (one donated by Akbar in 1567, the other by Jehangir in 1631) for offerings for the poor. Sometimes someone will sponsor a cauldron and they will be filled with porridge to be distributed to the needy (one *deg* feeds around 70 people). In the past this gave rise to a specialist profession, known as 'looting the *degs*' – people wearing protec-

EASTERN RAJASTHAN

tive clothes would dive into the cauldrons to distribute the food. Today it's more boringly distributed using large ladles.

The saint's tomb has a marble dome, and the tomb inside is surrounded by a silver platform. Pilgrims believe that the saint's spirit will intercede on their behalf in matters of illness, business or personal problems, so the notes and holy string attached to the railings around are thanks or requests.

At the entrance, *khadims* (Muslim holy servants or mosque attendants) wielding donation books will ask you for cash (there are 4000 *khadims* in Ajmer!). It's likely you'll be asked for still more money inside, where you might be blessed with the edge of the tomb blanket. If you don't want to give, just be firm about it or give a small amount.

Despite the hustle, it's a fascinating shrine with a sense of profound significance. It's good to visit in the evening, when it's decorated in twinkling lights and there are Qawwali singers, who sing verses in praise of the Prophet and saints. These verses can have a powerful effect – it's said that Khwaja Sahib once heard a verse devoted to the Prophet and was so ecstatic that he fainted and was unconscious for seven nights and days.

Pilgrims and Sufis come from all over the world on the anniversary of the saint's death, the Urs (when William Dalrymple visited). The anniversary is celebrated in the seventh month of the lunar calendar, Jyaistha (the dates are variable, so check with the tourist office). The saint retired to his cloister for a long meditation, and when it was opened six days later he was dead, hence the festival lasts six days. It's an interesting time, but the crowds can be suffocating – praying people line the streets all the way down from the dargah. Many pilgrims also come here in the month of Ramadan.

ADHAI-DIN-KA-JHONPRA & TARAGARH
Beyond the dargah, on the town outskirts, are the extraordinary ruins of the **Adhai-din-ka-Jhonpra** (Two-and-a-Half-Day Building) mosque. According to legend, construction in 1153 took 2½ days. Others say it was named after a festival lasting 2½ days. It was built as a Sanskrit college, but in 1198 Mohammed of Ghori seized Ajmer and converted the building into a mosque by adding a seven-arched wall covered with Islamic calligraphy in front of the pillared hall.

Although in need of restoration, it's an exquisite piece of architecture, with soaring domes, pillars and a beautiful arched screen, largely built from pieces of Jain and Hindu temples.

About 3km and a steep 1½-hour climb beyond the mosque, the ancient **Taragarh** (Star Fort) commands a superb view over the city (accessible by car). Built by Ajaipal Chauhan, the town's founder, it saw lots of military action during Mughal times and was later used as a British sanatorium.

NASIYAN (RED) TEMPLE
This marvellous Jain **temple** (Prithviraj Marg; admission Rs 5, camera Rs 15; ⊙ 8am-4.30pm) was built in 1865. It's also known as the Golden Temple, due to its amazing display – its double-storey temple hall is filled with a huge golden diorama depicting the Jain concept of the ancient world, with 13 continents and oceans, the intricate golden city of Ayodhya, flying peacock and elephant gondolas, and gilded elephants with many tusks. The hall is decorated with gold, silver and precious stones. It's unlike any other temple in Rajasthan and is worth a visit. Children will like it, too.

AKBAR'S PALACE
Not far from the main post office, Akbar built this imposing building in 1570 – partly as a pleasure retreat, but mainly to keep an eye on pesky local chiefs. This is just part of the impressive fortifications originally built by Akbar. It saw life as an arms magazine during the British rule, and is still known locally as the 'Magazine'. It houses the **government museum** (admission Rs 3; ⊙ 10am-4.30pm Sat-Thu), with a small collection of old weapons, miniature paintings, ancient rock inscriptions and stone sculptures that date back to the 8th century.

Sleeping
Commission rackets are ingrained in Ajmer: you'll be accosted by cycle-rickshaws and autorickshaw drivers the minute you step off the bus or train. On top of this, the hotels here offer poor service and soulless atmosphere – it's a far better idea to stay in nearby Pushkar.

A good alternative to hotels is to stay in one of the homes participating in Ajmer's Paying Guest House Scheme, which gives you the opportunity to stay with an Indian family. Rates range from around Rs 200 to Rs 800

THE INCLUSIVE SAINT

Born in eastern Persia sometime in 1138 or 1139, Khwaja Muin-ud-din Chishti was orphaned in his early teens and lived on the proceeds of his ancestral orchards. According to legend, a holy man passed his garden and when Khwaja rushed out to greet him, the holy man gave him some food that enlightened him. Khwaja then renounced all worldly goods, became a fakir (Muslim holy man) and began to wander in search of knowledge. He visited Samarkand and Bukhara, great centres of Islamic learning, and absorbed all he could from great Central Asian Sufis – theirs was an Islam with an emphasis on devotion, mysticism and miracles. He then settled in Baghdad, and later made a pilgrimage to Medina for the haj, where he heard a divine voice telling him to go to Hindustan. Now in his 50s, he wandered to India, arriving in Ajmer in around 1190, where he settled on a hill by Ana Sagar. His beliefs and life of meditation and fasting – it's said he only ate one chapati every eight days – had brought him great renown, and people flocked to him to hear his teachings. Even Mohammed of Ghori took time off raiding temples to pay his respects to the holy man.

His preachings were notably generous and inclusive. He spoke to Hindus as much as to Muslims, emphasising that theirs were different approaches along the same path. Hindus could relate to many aspects of Sufism (for example, holy men renouncing everything except faith bears considerable resemblance to Hindu practice). He preached against discrimination and differentiation between believers of different faiths.

In 1236 he died, aged 97, and was buried in his simple brick cell, now covered by its elaborate shrine. In tribute to his teachings and beliefs, it is regarded as a holy place by people of many different faiths.

per night depending on the facilities provided. The tourist office (p201) has details about these guesthouses.

BUDGET

RTDC Hotel Khadim (☎ 2627490; dm Rs 100, s/d from Rs 350/450, with AC Rs 990/1200; ✷) This unexciting option is near the bus stand and has reasonable, though dreary budget rooms that aren't bad value.

Nagpal Tourist Hotel (☎ 2429503; Station Rd; s Rs 225-400, d Rs 500, s/d with AC Rs 900/950; ✷) Nagpal is friendly though a typical low-budget business hotel with uninspiring rooms. The non-air-con rooms are not all that clean but the air-con rooms are much better and almost worth the increased expense. It's in a good location next to the recommended Honeydew restaurant (opposite) and near the train station.

Bhola Hotel (☎ 2432844; Agra Gate, Prithviraj Marg; s/d Rs 250/350) Opposite the church, southeast of Agra Gate, this hotel is friendly and one of the better budget options, though being near the road it is a bit noisy. There are five nondescript but tolerably clean rooms. It has a vegetarian restaurant (opposite) serving a decent thali.

Hotel Ajmeru (☎ 2431103; Khailand Market; s/d from Rs 450/550, with AC Rs 800/1100; ✷) This welcoming hotel with a veg restaurant can be found just past the narrow Kotwali Gate off Prithviraj Marg. It was undergoing extensive renovation when we visited; expect bland, comfortable, freshly painted rooms with TVs and phones.

MIDRANGE & TOP END

Haveli Heritage Inn (☎ 2621607; Kutchery Rd; r Rs 500-1600) Set in an old and modest *haveli*, this is a welcoming city-centre oasis and arguably Ajmer's best choice. The high-ceilinged rooms are quite large and clean though a bit worn and run-down. There's a pleasant, grassy courtyard and the hotel is infused with a family atmosphere, complete with home-cooked meals.

Hotel Regency (☎ 2620296; s/d from Rs 550/600, with AC from Rs 825/875) Although a typically insipid business hotel with overpriced rooms, the Regency is close to the dargah, and a good base for exploring the alleys of old Ajmer. Rooms are serviceable but dreary.

Mansingh Palace (☎ 2425956; Circular Rd; s/d from Rs 4000/4500; ✷ ♨) This modern place, overlooking Ana Sagar, is Ajmer's only top-end hotel. It's rather out of the way, but has attractive and comfortable, though overpriced, rooms, some with views and balconies. The hotel has a shady garden, a bar and an acceptable restaurant, the Sheesh Mahal (opposite).

Eating

Ajmer has a few good options, and there is also a flourishing trade in ice creams and cakes.

Bhola Hotel Restaurant (☎ 2432844; Agra Gate, Prithviraj Marg; mains Rs 15-50; 🕒 11am-10pm) This place (see opposite) has a gloomy but surprisingly appealing and good-value veg restaurant at the top of a seedy staircase. Tasty thalis cost Rs 50.

Mango Masala (☎ 2422100; Sadar Patel Marg; mains Rs 35-90; 🕒 11am-11pm) With dim, barlike lighting and nursery school décor, this no-alcohol veg restaurant is where Ajmer's teens hang out. There's an imaginative menu of pizzas, Chinese, and North and South Indian vegetarian food – tasty and freshly cooked. There are also cakes, ice cream, ice-cream sodas and mocktails.

Madina Hotel (Station Rd; mains Rs 40-55; 🕒 9am-11pm) Handy if you're waiting for a train (it's opposite the station), this simple, open-to-the-street eatery cooks up cheap veg and nonveg fare, with specialities such aschicken Mughlai and *rumali roti* (huge paper-thin chapati).

Honeydew Restaurant (☎ 2622498; Station Rd; mains Rs 40-110; 🕒 9am-11pm). The Honeydew offers a great selection of veg and nonveg Indian, Chinese and Continental food in a pleasant, relaxed atmosphere. It has long been Ajmer's best, and is the restaurant of choice for Mayo College students' midterm treat. It's just near the Nagpal Tourist Hotel.

Sheesh Mahal (mains Rs 80-160; 🕒 noon-3pm & 7-10.30pm) This upmarket restaurant, located in the Mansingh Palace, offers Indian, Continental and Chinese dishes as well as a buffet when the tour groups pass through. The service is slick and the food is palatable and it boasts a bar.

Getting There & Away

BUS

There are frequent buses going from Ajmer to Pushkar (local/express/starline Rs 6/7/8, 30 minutes), which leave from the main bus stand. Regular RSRTC buses go to and from the places listed in the table and beyond. The inquiry number is ☎ 2429398.

In addition, there are private buses to these destinations – many companies have offices on Kutchery Rd. If you book your ticket to one of these destinations through an agency in Pushkar, they should provide a free transfer to Ajmer to start your journey.

BUSES FROM AJMER

Destination	Fare (Rs)	Duration (hr)
Bikaner	131	8
Bundi	91	5
Chittor	110	5
Delhi	205	9
Jaipur	69/AC	
	114	2½
Jodhpur	109	6
Kota	106	6
Udaipur	150	8

TRAIN

There are no tourist quotas for many Ajmer trains, so book early; go to booth 5 at the train station's **reservations office** (🕒 8am-2pm & 2.15-8pm Mon-Sat, 8am-2pm Sun). **Surya Tours & Travels** (☎ 2631731; 🕒 8am-6pm Mon-Sat) in the forecourt of the RTDC Hotel Khadim can arrange tickets.

Ajmer is a busy station on the Delhi–Jaipur–Ahmedabad–Mumbai line. The *Shatabdi Express* (2016/5, Thursday to Tuesday) runs between Ajmer and Delhi (AC chair/1st class, Rs 645/1200, four hours) via Jaipur (Rs 300/575). It leaves Delhi at 6.10am and arrives in Ajmer at 1pm. Going the other way, the train leaves Ajmer at 3.50pm, arriving in Jaipur at 5.35pm and in Delhi at 10.40pm. There's also the 2957 *Rajdhani Express* to Delhi (3 AC/2 AC/1 AC, Rs 660/895/1530, seven hours), which leaves Ajmer at 12.35am.

The *Delhi-Ahmedabad Mail* (9105/6) departs from Ajmer at 8.28pm and arrives in Delhi (sleeper/3 AC/2 AC Rs 200/531/740) at 6.30am. Heading for Gujarat, the train leaves Ajmer at 7.40am and arrives in Ahmedabad (sleeper/3 AC/2 AC Rs 215/574/800) at 5.35pm.

The *Ajmer Udaipur City Express* (2992) leaves at 6.15am, arriving in Udaipur (2nd class/AC chair Rs 103/346) at 11.40am via Chittorgarh (Rs 80/266; 9.20am).

Getting Around

There are plenty of autorickshaws (anywhere in town should cost around Rs 25), as well as cheaper cycle-rickshaws and tongas.

AROUND AJMER

Kishangarh

☎ 01463 / pop 116,000

Kishangarh is 27km northeast of Ajmer and was founded in the early 17th century by Kishan Singh, a Rathore prince. Since the 18th century the town of Kishangarh has been associated with one of India's most famous schools of miniature painting. Among its renowned works is the *Bani Thani* painting by Kishangarh master Nihal Chand – a sensual, graceful portrayal of Krishna's consort, Radha, depicted with exaggeratedly slanting, almond-shaped eyes – you'll see this reprinted all over Rajasthan. Today local artists are trying to revive this magnificent school of painting by making copies of the originals on surfaces such as wood, stone and cloth (the originals were done on paper). Kishangarh is also famous for painted wooden furniture.

Kishangarh town is divided into the charming old city and the less-charming new part, which is mainly commercial. Pollution is steadily increasing, along with the growing number of dusty marble factories and textile mills.

SLEEPING

Phool Mahal Palace (☎ /fax 01463-247405; www .royalkishangarh.com; s/d Rs 2400/2800; 🖭 🖭) This romantic heritage building on the shores of Gundalao Lake was built in 1870 as a 'monsoon palace'. The lake fills after the monsoon rains and the palace, with its looming backdrop of Kishangarh Fort, is very picturesque. Nevertheless the waters have taken their toll and the rambling hotel is rather musty and insect prone. Fresh frescoes brighten the otherwise drab and overpriced rooms.

Roopangarh Fort (☎ /fax 01497-220444; www.royal kishangarh.com; s/d Rs 2750/3300, ste Rs 4900; 🖭) About 25km out of town, Roopangarh Fort has been converted into an evocative hotel. Roopangarh was the capital of this province for about 100 years and was never conquered, despite being repeatedly attacked by its neighbouring states. The fort was founded in 1653 by Maharaja Roop Singh, the fifth ruler of Kishangarh, who was inspired to make this site his capital after watching a mother sheep gallantly protect her lambs from a pack of hungry wolves. Rooms are large, and decorated with lots of traditional furniture. The road to the fort passes through a timeless village, where it seems life has been the same for centuries. The hotel can arrange village tours, bird-watching, and camel, horse or jeep safaris, and if you stay here you can view the maharaja's private collection of miniatures. The fort itself is well endowed with fine paintings.

GETTING THERE & AWAY

Frequent daily buses go between Ajmer and Kishangarh (Rs 18).

Tilonia
☎ 01463

In Tilonia village, located about 25km northeast of Kishangarh and 7km off the Ajmer to Jaipur road, is the inspiring **Barefoot College** (☎ 01463-288204; www.barefootcollege.org); see opposite. This NGO is run by and for villagers, and uses their skills for development work in the area to address problems of water supply, housing, education, health and employment. Part of the complex is devoted to an impressive showroom where goods made by villagers are on sale – it's a fantastic place to pick up high-quality, reasonably priced souvenirs, including everything from textiles to furniture and leather goods. Other great gifts include bell *totas* (colourful strings of stuffed birds), painted ceramic bowls and wooden toys. All proceeds go towards maintaining and developing rural projects.

GETTING THERE & AWAY

The easiest way to get to Tilonia is to hire a taxi, which should cost around Rs 600 return from Ajmer or Pushkar. From Ajmer you can take a Harmara bus (Rs 23) and ask to be dropped off at Tilonia. There are also buses from Kishangarh (Rs 10). The Barefoot College centre is about 1km from the bus stop.

Pachewar
☎ 01437

This little village, about 90km east of Ajmer, has a lake that attracts migratory birds in winter. It has an imposing fort, once ruled by the Khangarot Rajputs. Thakur Anoop Singh Khangarot captured the fort of Ranthambhore from the Marathas and annexed it to his family allies in Jaipur. To reward him, Maharaja Sawai Madho Singh I of Jaipur granted him the Pachewar territory in 1758.

Pachewar Garh (☎ 01437-28756, in Jaipur 0141-2601007; s/d Rs 1800/2200, with AC Rs 2100/2500; 🖭) is the impressive 300-year-old fort. The spacious rooms are furnished with antiques, and some are splendidly decorated with frescoes. The hotel can also arrange village safaris.

PUSHKAR
☎ 0145 / pop 14,789

Pushkar has a magnetism all of its own, and is quite unlike anywhere else in Rajasthan. It's a prominent Hindu pilgrimage town and devout Hindus should visit at least once in their lifetime. The town curls around a holy lake,

BAREFOOT COLLEGE

Barefoot College is an NGO mixing radical change with respect for traditional knowledge. The college emphasises that it values people without qualifications, degrees, certificates or the usual signals of expertise. It values people who are dispossessed and deprived, and invests in their training in order to benefit the community in which they live. It teaches people new respect for themselves and for their capabilities, as well as humility and openness to new knowledge.

The entire complex is solar powered, and Barefoot has been instrumental in bringing solar power to many communities. It's even pulled women out of purdah to teach them how to become solar-power engineers. Other major projects are the installation of hand pumps and the implementation of rainwater harvesting projects. Local people, including significant numbers of women, have been trained to maintain the systems.

Barefoot makes great use of puppet shows in poor rural areas, and has trained puppeteers to communicate with semiliterate communities, with shows on health, education and human rights. Use of a medium such as puppetry is typical of its work, as it is appropriate to the environment, based on the long Rajasthani tradition of storytelling and education through puppet theatre. Barefoot communicators also include screen-printers, photographers and filmmakers, who help get similar messages across with more modern means.

Officially known as the Social Work & Research Centre, Barefoot College was set up in 1972 and since then has pioneered many creative ideas like this to promote self-reliance in poor communities. Other programmes include night schools that give working adults and children access to education, and a variety of schemes that promote the work of low-caste artisans on fair-trade principles.

The organisation is largely supported by the government and international donors. However, the handicrafts section employs around 300 women – often homebound and unable to pursue other work because of the tradition of purdah – who are able to support their families through their skills. You can support the college's efforts and check out the project by visiting the craft showroom at Tilonia.

said to have appeared when Brahma dropped a lotus flower. It also has one of the world's few Brahma temples (p210). With 52 sky-blue bathing ghats and 400 milky temples, the town literally hums with regular *pujas* (prayers) generating an episodic soundtrack of chanting, drums and gongs, and devotional songs.

Besides pilgrims, travellers have long discovered Pushkar's charms, and small, whitewashed budget guesthouses almost outnumber the temples and *dharamsalas* (pilgrims guesthouses). Many visitors reach here and grind to a satisfied halt, experimenting variously with spirituality, bhang (marijuana) and facial hair. Time can slip by very easily in Pushkar.

The result of this magnetism is a muddle of religious and tourist scenes. The main street is one long bazaar, selling anything to tickle a traveller's fancy, from hippy-chic tie-dye to didgeridoos. Despite the commercialism and banana pancakes, the town remains enchantingly small and authentically mystic. You can help preserve the spiritual balance by respecting tradition and dressing appropriately and abiding by local restrictions (no

alcohol, meat or eggs, and no public displays of affection).

Pushkar is world famous for its spectacular camel fair (p185), which takes place here in the Hindu lunar month of Kartika (October/November). If you're anywhere nearby at the time, you'd be crazy to miss it.

During this period the town is jam-packed with tribal people from all over Rajasthan, pilgrims from all over India, and filmmakers and tourists from all over the world. And there are plenty of camels and other livestock (it's best to arrive a few days before the official start to see serious trading).

Pushkar is only 11km from Ajmer but separated from it by Nag Pahar, the Snake Mountain.

Orientation

The pastel town surrounds the deep green Pushkar Lake, with its many bathing ghats and fabulous temples. Pushkar town remains small despite the constant stream of visitors, and it's a twisting maze of narrow streets filled with interesting little shops, food stalls, hotels

EASTERN RAJASTHAN

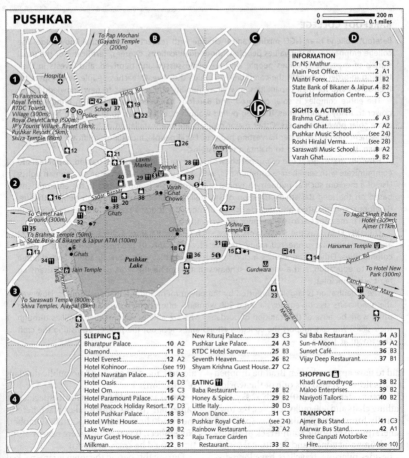

PUSHKAR

0 ———— 200 m
0 ———— 0.1 miles

INFORMATION
Dr NS Mathur.................................**1** C3
Main Post Office..........................**2** A1
Mantri Forex..................................**3** B2
State Bank of Bikaner & Jaipur.**4** B2
Tourist Information Centre......**5** C3

SIGHTS & ACTIVITIES
Brahma Ghat.................................**6** A3
Gandhi Ghat.................................**7** A2
Pushkar Music School................(see 24)
Roshi Hiralal Verma...................(see 28)
Saraswati Music School............**8** A2
Varah Ghat....................................**9** B2

SLEEPING 🏠
Bharatpur Palace....................**10** A2
Diamond..................................**11** B2
Hotel Everest...........................**12** A2
Hotel Kohinoor....................(see 19)
Hotel Navratan Palace...........**13** A3
Hotel Oasis..............................**14** D3
Hotel Om.................................**15** C3
Hotel Paramount Palace........**16** A2
Hotel Peacock Holiday Resort.**17** D3
Hotel Pushkar Palace..............**18** B3
Hotel White House..................**19** B1
Lake View................................**20** B2
Mayur Guest House.................**21** B2
Milkman..................................**22** B1

New Rituraj Palace.................**23** C3
Pushkar Lake Palace...............**24** A3
RTDC Hotel Sarovar...............**25** B3
Seventh Heaven.....................**26** B2
Shyam Krishna Guest House..**27** C2

EATING 🍴
Baba Restaurant.....................**28** B2
Honey & Spice........................**29** B2
Little Italy...............................**30** D3
Moon Dance...........................**31** C3
Pushkar Royal Café.............(see 24)
Rainbow Restaurant..............**32** A2
Raju Terrace Garden
 Restaurant............................**33** B2

Sai Baba Restaurant...............**34** A3
Sun-n-Moon...........................**35** A2
Sunset Café............................**36** B3
Vijay Deep Restaurant..........**37** B1

SHOPPING 🛍
Khadi Gramodhyog................**38** B2
Maloo Enterprises.................**39** B2
Navjyoti Tailors.....................**40** B2

TRANSPORT
Ajmer Bus Stand....................**41** C3
Marwar Bus Stand.................**42** A1
Shree Ganpati Motorbike
 Hire.................................(see 10)

and temples. Fortunately, there is very little motorised traffic in the main bazaar, making it a pleasurable place to explore at leisure – though watch out for idiots on motorbikes. The town is very tourist-friendly and most people speak some English, so you should have no problem finding your way around.

Information

Cash and travellers cheques may be changed at places along Sadar Bazaar Rd, but check the commission first. There's an ATM near the Brahma temple. Many places also offer (slow) internet services for Rs 20 per hour.
Hospital (☎ 2772029) North of the post office.
Main post office (🕙 9am-5pm Mon-Sat) Just south of the hospital.

Mantri Forex (Sadar Bazaar; 🕙 9am-10pm Mon-Sat) Changes cash and travellers cheques and provides internet.
State Bank of Bikaner & Jaipur (☎ 2772006; 🕙 10am-4pm Mon-Fri, 10am-12.30pm Sat) Changes travellers cheques and currency.
Tourist Information Centre (☎ 2772040; 🕙 10am-5pm Mon-Sat) Sells a town map (Rs 10).

Dangers & Annoyances

Priests – some genuine, some not – will approach you near the ghats and offer to do a *puja* (prayer) for which you'll receive a 'Pushkar passport' (a red ribbon around your wrist). Others proffer flowers (to avoid trouble, avoid taking any flowers that you are offered). In either case you'll be asked to add up your family members whose happiness is *surely* worth multiple Rs 100. You could always try denying your family, or massively exaggerating their number to get a reduction on bulk purchase. However, you can choose to avoid encouraging these pushy, unprincipled 'priests' altogether – they can become unpleasantly aggressive. At least don't be bullied and agree on a price beforehand. The priests will suggest anything from Rs 101 to Rs 1001 (they add the 1 for luck), and beyond! An offering of Rs 11 or Rs 21 is enough, though you'll probably have trouble getting one of these priests to accept this. Be prepared for an earful of abuse if you don't give the priest as much as they want, and try not to let this spoil your visit to the lake.

You can try reporting people to the tourist office if they get you down. If enough people make a fuss, the tourism authorities may address the problem.

On the other hand, flowers are offered at the Brahma Temple, where there are simply donation boxes. Here you can offer flowers and sacred sweets for the happiness of your friends, family and everyone you've ever known – and still have change for a *masala* chai.

During the camel fair, Pushkar is besieged by pickpockets working the crowded bazaars.

You can avoid the razor gang by not using thin-walled daypacks and by carrying your daypack in front of you.

Sights
TEMPLES
Pushkar boasts hundreds of temples, though few are particularly ancient, as they were mostly desecrated by Aurangzeb and subsequently rebuilt. Most famous is the **Brahma Temple**, said to be one of the few such temples in the world as a result of a curse by Brahma's consort, Saraswati (see p210). The temple is marked by a red spire, and over the entrance gateway is the *hans* (goose symbol) of Brahma. Inside, the floor and walls are engraved with dedications to the dead.

The one-hour trek up to the hilltop **Saraswati Temple** overlooking the lake is best made before dawn, though the views are fantastic at any time of day. The sunrise views over town from the closer **Pap Mochani (Gayatri) Temple**, reached by a track behind the Marwar bus stand, are also well worth the 30-minute climb.

About 8km southwest of the town (past the turn-off to Savitri) is a collection of **Shiva temples** near Ajaypal, which make a great trip by motorbike (or bike if you're fit and start

PUSHKAR CAMEL FAIR

Come the month of Kartika, the eighth lunar month of the Hindu calendar and one of the holiest, Thar camel drivers spruce up their ships of the desert and start the long walk to Pushkar in time for Kartik Purnima (full moon). Each year around 200,000 people converge here, bringing with them some 50,000 camels, horses and cattle. The place becomes an extraordinary swirl of colour, sound and movement, thronged with musicians, mystics, tourists, traders, animals, devotees and camera crews.

Trading begins a week before the official fair (a good time to arrive to see the serious business), but by the time the RTDC mela starts, business takes a back seat and the bizarre sidelines (snake charmers, children balancing on poles) jostle onto centre stage. Even the tourist board's cultural programme is bizarre: moustache contests, turban tying contests, or seeing how many people can balance on a camel.

It's hard to believe, but this seething mass is all just a sideshow. Kartik Purnima is when Hindu pilgrims come to bathe in Pushkar's sacred waters. The religious event builds in tandem with the camel fair in a wild, magical crescendo of incense, chanting and processions to dousing day, the last night of the fair, when thousands of devotees wash away their sins and set candles afloat on the holy lake.

Although fantastical, mystical and a one-off, it must be said that it's also crowded, touristy, noisy (light sleepers should bring earplugs) and tacky. Those affected by dust and/or animal hair should bring appropriate medication. However, it's a grand epic, and not to be missed if you're anywhere within camel-spitting distance.

It usually takes place in October or November:

2008	2009	2010	2011
5-13 Nov	25 Oct-2 Nov	13-21 Nov	2-10 Nov

DREAMER OF THE UNIVERSE

According to one Indian saying, GOD stands for Generation, Operation, Destruction, and the Hindu trinity of Brahma, Vishnu and Shiva are respectively responsible for these three tasks. Of the three, Brahma, the Creator, is the most mysterious. Unlike Vishnu and Shiva, he is rarely worshipped, although reality itself is Brahma's dream. Each of his lifetimes spans 311,040,000,000,000 human years and corresponds to a great cycle of the universe, at the end of which it is destroyed by Shiva. Then Brahma is reborn to dream it all again.

Brahma is usually depicted with four bearded faces facing the four directions, and four hands, each holding one of the four books of the Vedas (Books of Knowledge). His vehicle is the swan and his consort is Saraswati, the Goddess of Education.

According to legend, the sacred lake of Pushkar sprang up at the spot where Brahma dropped a lotus flower from the sky. Pushkar takes its name from this incident – *push* means 'flower' and *kar* means 'hand'. Brahma wanted to perform a *yagna* (self-mortification) at the lake on a full-moon night, a ceremony that required the presence of his consort. But Saraswati was late. Irritated, Brahma quickly married a convenient milkmaid named Gayatri, and when Saraswati arrived she discovered Gayatri seated in her own honoured place beside Brahma. Saraswati was understandably furious and vowed that Brahma would be forgotten by the people of the earth. It was a profound curse and the gods pleaded with her to reconsider. Finally she relented, decreeing that he could be worshipped, but only in Pushkar. Since then, the Brahma temple at Pushkar has remained one of the only temples in the world dedicated to Brahma and allegedly the only one in India. Meanwhile, Saraswati and Gayatri receive their *pujas* at separate temples, at opposite ends of the town.

---

early in the day), through barren hills and quiet villages. Be warned: the track is hilly and rocky. Another Shiva temple is about 8km north, tucked down inside a cave, which would make for a good excursion.

GHATS

Fifty-two bathing ghats surround the lake, where pilgrims bathe in the sacred waters. If you wish to join them, do it with respect; remember, this is a holy place. Remove your shoes and don't smoke, kid around or take photographs.

Some ghats have particular importance: Vishnu appeared at **Varah Ghat** in the form of a boar, Brahma bathed at **Brahma Ghat** and Gandhi's ashes were sprinkled at **Gandhi Ghat** (formerly Gau Ghat).

Activities

REFLEXOLOGY

Dr NS Mathur (☎ 9828103031; Shri Raghu Nathji Temple; ☼ 10.30am-6.30pm) provides back, hand and foot reflexology (from Rs 200), which will most certainly take your mind off any pains you might have had. The doctor also teaches reiki.

Courses

MUSIC

The **Saraswati Music School** (☎ 2773124; Mainon Ka Chowk) teaches classical tabla (drums), flute,

singing and *kathak* (classical dance). Birju, who's been playing for around 20 years, charges from Rs 350 for two hours, and, for an intensive bout, you can live in for Rs 500 a night. He often conducts evening performances (8pm to 9.30pm), and also sells instruments.

Pushkar Music School (☎ 5121277; Pushkar Lake Palace, Parakrama Marg) teaches classical sitar, tabla, harmonium, dancing and more, for Rs 150 per hour in a peaceful lakeside location. It is affiliated to the Hidden Light Foundation (www.hidden-light.org).

YOGA & HEALING

For reiki, yoga and shiatsu, Reiki Master Roshi Hiralal Verma is based at Baba Restaurant (p213). Costs depend on the duration and nature of your session.

Dr NS Mathur (see left) is also a teacher of reiki (I/II Rs 1500/2500), and his daughter teaches yoga and provides beauty treatments.

Tours

HORSE & CAMEL SAFARIS

Lots of people in Pushkar offer horse or camel safaris, which are a good way to see the lovely landscape – a mixture of desert and the rocky hills – around town. They're far removed from the camel-crazy hype of Jaisalmer. A safari here is entirely different from one over in the west of the state – don't expect iconic sweeping dunes; it's more of a chance to have a rural ramble and visit some little-known spots. It's best to ask your hotel, a travel agent or other travellers to recommend somebody who organises good trips.

For camels, the prices per hour/three hours are quoted at about Rs 100/300, or Rs 500 per day for two or more days. Horses per hour/day can be similarly hired for around Rs 200/500.

Most organisers are happy to tailor-make a safari and they have good suggestions about places of interest in and around Pushkar. If you want to get off the beaten track, you can arrange a safari all the way to Jaisalmer, a journey of about four weeks. Camel safaris are a splendid way to experience the rugged beauty of the countryside.

Sleeping

Owing to Pushkar's status among backpackers, there are far more budget options than midrange though many have a selection of midrange-priced rooms. The explosion in visitor numbers over recent years has seen an explosion in budget hotels – most are basic, clean, whitewashed and well run, though few are legally registered businesses. They can be small and windowless, so to avoid a cell, ask to see a few rooms. There are a couple of choice upmarket options here, too.

At the time of the camel fair, prices multiply five to 10 times; it's best to book several weeks, even months, ahead.

BUDGET
Hotel Om (☎ 2772672; www.hotelompushkar.com; r Rs 70-500; 🖳 🖳) Near the Vishnu temple, Om has a peaceful garden with an unappealing, undercover pool, and views over surrounding hills and the gurdwara (Sikh temple). Rooms are basic, air-cooled and a bit overpriced.

Milkman (☎ 2773452; vinodmilkman@hotmail.com; Mali Mohalla; r Rs 300-600, without bathroom Rs 80-100; 🔀) Milkman is a cosy guesthouse in a back-street location with a relaxing rooftop retreat. The varying rooms are all brightly decorated with paintings and though some rooms are small and doorways are low, the bright colours, cleanliness and friendly family keep this place cheerful.

RTDC Hotel Sarovar (☎ 2772040; dm Rs 100, s/d Rs 400/500, with lake view Rs 600/700, with AC Rs 990/1200; 🔀 🖳) This hotel is set in spacious grounds

and has a great position along the eastern shore of the lake. It has more character than most RTDC places, with colonnades, arches and domes, but the rooms are generally bland and the service apathetic.

Hotel Paramount Palace (☎ 2772428; d Rs 150-300, without bathroom Rs 100-120, with balcony Rs 450-700) Perched on the highest point in town overlooking an old temple, this welcoming hotel has fine views. The most expensive rooms (106, 108, 109) have lovely balconies, stained glass and are good value; smaller rooms can be dingy. There's a dizzyingly magical rooftop terrace.

Mayur Guest House (☎ 2772302; mayurguesthouse@ hotmail.com; Holin Ka Chowk; r Rs 200-700, s without bathroom Rs 100) A pleasant blue-washed place, with neat, unspectacular rooms around a tiny leafy courtyard. Upstairs rooms have balconies and there's a cheerful welcome and more views from the rooftop.

Hotel Kohinoor (☎ 9414494249; Mali Mohala; r Rs 150-300) This is a simple guesthouse, more or less operating as the cheap alternative to the nearby, and related, Hotel White House at mela time. There are 11 small but spotless rooms with attached bathrooms. They vary in size so check a few.

Hotel Everest (☎ 2773417; r Rs 150-500; 🖳) This welcoming budget hotel is secreted in the quiet laneways north of Sadar Bazaar and is convenient to the bazaar and the mela ground. It is run by a friendly father-and-son team who can't do too much for their appreciative guests. The rooms are simple, variable in size and spotless and the beds are comfortable. The roof is a pleasant retreat for meals or just relaxing with a book.

Lake View (☎ 2772106; Sadar Bazaar; r Rs 300-400, without bathroom Rs 200) Lake View is a long-standing place, wonderfully located above the ghats, with superb views over the lake from the restaurant. Rooms are simple and run-down, but some doubles (usually those with shared bathroom) have balconies facing the water.

Hotel Oasis (☎ 2772100; www.hoteloasispushkar.net; Ajmer Rd; r from Rs 200, with AC from Rs 750; 🔀 🖳 🖳) Right near the Ajmer bus stand is this big hotel, which is very popular with Israeli tourists. It has large, bare rooms, which open onto long walkways overlooking the central pool. The best rooms are upstairs. Occasional loud techno might put some off.

Bharatpur Palace (☎ 2772320; r Rs 200-800; 🔀) This rambling old building occupies one of the best spots in Pushkar, on the upper levels of the western ghats. Room No 1 is the most romantic place to wake up: it's one room surrounded on three sides by the lake. It's possible to lie in bed with the doors open and have the lake and ghats laid out before you. Even without an attached bathroom, it's a bargain at Rs 600 (Rs 3000 during the camel fair). Room No 9 is also good, with three doors opening onto the lake. There's a variety of rooms with or without bathrooms, hot water and air-con.

Hotel Navaratan Palace (☎ 2772145; www .pushkarnavaratanpalace.com; s/d from Rs 250/300, with AC from Rs 500/600; ✲ ⚛) Located close to the Brahma Temple, this hotel has a lovely enclosed garden with a fabulous pool (Rs 50 for nonguests), when it is clean and operational, and children's playground. The rooms are clean, small and crammed with carved wooden furniture.

Hotel White House (☎ 2772147; hotelwhitehouse@ hotmail.com; r without balcony Rs 350-450, with balcony Rs 550-650) This place is indeed white with spotless and airy rooms. There is also good traveller fare and fine views from the plant-filled rooftop restaurant. It is efficiently run by a tenacious businesslike mother-and-son team who plan to add rooms that have air-con. Checkout is 10am and the front door is closed at 10pm.

Hotel Peacock Holiday Resort (☎ 2772093; r from Rs 350-550, with air-con Rs 800-900; ✲ ▯ ⚛) Located around 500m southeast of Sadar Bazaar, Hotel Peacock has a congenial host and a cooling pool (Rs 75 for nonguests) that is set in a leafy courtyard. The cheapest rooms are rather shabby and overall the place has a well worn feel and is due for a makeover.

Some other good cheap options that are recommended:

New Rituraj Palace (☎ 2772875; Bamdev Marg; tents Rs 100, r Rs 150-400) This place, tucked away behind an untidy garden, has very basic rooms. At camel fair time tents are erected directly outside rooms and the place gets very crammed.

Shyam Krishna Guest House (☎ 2772461; r Rs 200-400, s/d without bathroom Rs 125/200) Serene, lovely old building run by Brahmins with simple, bare rooms and pleasant lawn.

Diamond (☎ 9828462343; Holi ka Chowk; r Rs 250-350, s without bathroom Rs 150) In a quiet part of town, Diamond has tiny rooms around a small tranquil courtyard.

MIDRANGE & TOP END

Several of these have a few budget-priced rooms and some are located a few kilometres out of town.

JP's Tourist Village Resort (☎ 2772067; s Rs 300-1000, d Rs 500-1500; ⚛) About 3km out of town, JP's has whimsical small, reed-roofed cottages with elaborate wooden furniture. In the shady, rambling gardens are a tree house (for the brave), a pint-sized pool and a restaurant. It's popular with families, with lots of exploring potential and kids' play equipment.

ourpick Seventh Heaven (☎ 5105455; www .inn-seventh-heaven.com; Chotti Basti; r Rs 400-1275; ✲) You enter this lovingly converted *haveli* through heavy wooden doors into an incense-perfumed courtyard, centred with a marble fountain and featuring a fair-trade shop. There are just 12 individually decorated rooms on three levels, with traditionally crafted furniture and comfortable beds. All the rooms have their own character and vary in size from the downstairs budget rooms to the spacious 'Asana' suite. On the roof you'll find the excellent restaurant as well as sofas and swing chairs for relaxing with a book. This popular place is professionally run by the laid-back Anoop, and early booking (two-night minimum, no credit cards) is recommended.

Hotel New Park (☎ 2772464; www.newparkpushkar .com; Panch Kund Marg; r from Rs 500, with AC Rs 750-1200; ✲ ⚛) This is an excellent, modern hotel, located among fields of red roses in a quiet locale on the outskirts of town. Smart, modern rooms with balconies overlook the fields against a backdrop of hills and there's a pleasant rooftop restaurant sharing the view.

Pushkar Lake Palace (☎ 51210771; Parikrama Marg; r with/without AC Rs 1000/600; ✲ ⚛) This is a quiet, modern hotel, located close to the lake with a smashing little restaurant, the Pushkar Royal Cafe (opposite). The nonair-con rooms are nothing special but are clean and adequate. It is when you add the friendly service, the location and the good food that this hotel excels. Another bonus is the on-site Pushkar Music School (p210).

Jagat Palace Hotel (☎ 2772953; www.hotelpushkar palace.com; Ajmer Rd; s/d Rs 2662/3267; ✲ ⚛) This is a lovely heritage hotel in new but traditional-designed buildings resembling a palace. It offers romantic bedrooms with carved wooden furniture and lovely bathrooms. Balconies overlook large, lush gardens and a gorgeous, secluded-feeling pool (Rs 300 for nonguests) with mountain views. There are tempting packages and low-season discounts.

Pushkar Resorts (☎ 2772944; www.pushkarresorts .com; Motisar Marg; s/d from Rs 3495/3945; ⚿ ⚿) This sprawling resort, about 5km out of town, is set in an orchard and has a pool shaded by palms. There are four clusters of 10 modern and comfortable cottages, and some have been renovated beautifully. However, those awaiting renovation are showing their age. One aspect of its popularity is that it is outside the city limits and so has meat and alcohol on the menu.

Hotel Pushkar Palace (☎ 2773001; www.hotelpush karpalace.com; s/d from Rs 6050/7260) Once belonging to the maharaja of Kishangarh, and in a romantic lakeside setting, this place is let down by frosty reception and unhelpful staff. Rooms have carved wooden furniture and beds, but aren't as appealing as those at its sister hotel, the Jagat Singh. There's a pleasant outdoor eating area overlooking the lake. Only the suites look directly onto the lake; other rooms open onto a lakeside walkway. If you want to stay here, ask for a discount.

Tourist Village

During the camel fair, the RTDC and many private operators set up a sea of tents near the fairground. It can get rather cold at night, so bring something warm. A torch (flashlight) may also be useful. You're advised to book ahead. These all have private bathroom.

RTDC Tourist Village (☎ 2772074; s/d huts from Rs 700/800, tents s/d from Rs 6000/6500) This option has various permanent huts and semipermanent tents that are usually booked out by tour groups well in advance. Full payment must be received two months in advance. Rates include all meals.

Royal Desert Camp (☎ 2772957; www.hotelpushkar palace.com; tents s/d Rs 2420/2662) Further away from the fairground than Royal Tents, but another good option. You can book at Hotel Pushkar Palace (above).

Royal Tents (www.jodhpurheritage.com; tents US$250) Owned by the maharaja of Jodhpur, these are the most luxurious tents. The rates include meals. Reservations for the Royal Tents should be made in advance through Jodhpur's Balsamand Palace (☎ 0291-2571991).

Eating

Pushkar has plenty of atmospheric eateries with lake views and menus reflecting the back-

packer presence. Strict vegetarianism, forbidding even eggs, limits the range of ingredients, but the cooks (sometimes) make up for this with imagination.

Little Italy (☎ 2772366; mains Rs 20-60; ☱ 10am-11pm) This superb garden restaurant has excellent thin-crust, wood-fired pizzas and imported pasta with tasty sauces. As well as homemade pesto and gnocchi, there are some Indian and Israeli dishes.

Pushkar Royal Cafe (Pushkar Lake Palace; ☎ 51210771; Parakrama Marg; mains Rs 20-100; ☱ 8am-10pm) This rooftop restaurant has a wonderful view across the lake to the northern ghats and the lights of Sadar Bazaar. The jovial cook is keen and traveller fare includes imported pasta and tasty pizzas and there's a filling and tasty thali. Deserts include a wonderful apple crumble and icecream.

Sai Baba Restaurant (mains Rs 20-110; ☱ 7am-10pm) In a relaxing garden, this restaurant offers lots of Indian, Chinese and Italian dishes. There are regular mesmerising dance displays in the evenings with whirling nomadic dancers (but not during the camel fair).

Honey & Spice (Laxmi Market; mains Rs 25-70; ☱ 8am-10pm) Run by a friendly couple who learned their skills in Europe, this tiny restaurant has delicious South Indian coffee, homemade banana cakes, soups and vegetable stew.

Baba Restaurant (☎ 2772858; mains Rs 25-70; ☱ 8am-10pm) Tucked away, east of Sadar Bazaar, and open to the street, Baba has good pizzas and Israeli food and a chilled atmosphere.

Sun-n-Moon (☎ 2772823; dishes Rs 25-90; ☱ 8am-10pm) Popular with neo-hippies, the Sun-n-Moon has a lovely, quiet courtyard surrounding a bodhi tree and a shrine, and populated with contented tortoises. There are pizzas, pasta and apple pie, and breakfast for the homesick includes hash browns and hot chocolate, while for others there are sustaining lassis and masala chai.

Vijay Deep Restaurant (mains Rs 30-60; ☱ 10am-10pm) A cosy local joint with a dirt floor near the Marwar bus stand, it has a simple menu of spicy Indian dishes, and is a good choice if you want to get away from the tourist scene.

Raju Terrace Garden Restaurant (Sadar Bazaar; mains Rs 35-80; ☱ 10am-10pm) This relaxed rooftop restaurant serves lots of dishes for the homesick (for example, shepherd's pie, pizza and baked potatoes) and oddly bland Indian food. It's on a pleasant terrace that's filled with pot plants and fairy lights and has great views of the lake.

Moon Dance (☎ 2772606; mains Rs 35-100; ✆ 8am-10.30pm) This has tables in an inviting garden, and an area with low tables and floor cushions to lounge around on. It feels a bit like it's been made from a backpacker-restaurant kit, and the food, including Indian, Mexican and many Italian dishes, is reasonable.

Rainbow Restaurant (☎ 51210771; mains Rs 45-100; ✆ 11am-11pm) On a small rooftop with an attractive view over the lake, the Rainbow is a bit cramped with slow and surly waiters, but stick it out and you can eat great curries, pasta, pizza and other traveller fare. The falafel and hummus with fresh pita bread is delicious. Desserts include apple pie and ice cream and you can get a decent cup of tea.

Sunset Café (mains Rs 50-110; ✆ 7.30am-midnight) Right on the eastern ghats, this café has sublime lake views. It offers the usual traveller menu plus there's a German bakery serving OK cakes. The lakeshore setting is perfect at sunset and gathers a crowd.

Shopping

Pushkar's Sadar Bazaar is lined with enchanting little shops and is a good place for picking up gifts. Many of the textiles come from the Barmer district south of Jaisalmer. There's plenty of silver and beaded jewellery catering to foreign tastes, and some old tribal pieces, too. Coloured glass lamps are another appealing buy (you can ponder over trying to get them home intact), as are embroidered and mirrored wall hangings. The range of Indian-music CDs makes this an excellent place for buying some local tunes.

Bookshops in the main bazaar sell a tremendous range of secondhand novels, and they'll usually buy them back for around 50% of the price you paid.

Pushkar is also good for getting clothes made. One reliable place with reasonable prices is **Navjyoti Tailors** (Sadar Bazaar). Also recommended is **Maloo Enterprises** (Varah Ghat Chowk), opposite the post office. **Khadi Gramodhyog** (Sadar Bazaar) sells traditional hand-weaves – mainly men's shirts, scarves and shawls.

As Pushkar is touristy, you'll have to haggle. Ignore 'last-price' quotes that aren't negotiable – take your time and visit a few shops.

Getting There & Away

There are two bus stations in Pushkar. Ajmer Bus Station on Ajmer Rd is where most gov-

ernment buses to/from Ajmer stop. There are frequent buses to/from Ajmer (local/express/Star Line Rs 6/7/8) and the last bus leaves Ajmer bus station around 9pm. The other bus station, Marwar, to the north of town, has government and private buses to Ajmer and major destinations in Rajasthan. It operates 24 hours. Local travel agencies sell tickets for private buses – shop around for the best price. Buses generally stop for an hour or more in Ajmer. Be warned that some buses (particularly those travelling via Jodhpur) may involve a change of bus *and* an extra fare. Destinations include Agra (ordinary/sleeper, Rs 150/210, nine hours), Bundi (Rs 98, four hours), Delhi (ordinary/sleeper, Rs 160/220, 10½ hours), Jaipur (Rs 100, four hours), Jaisalmer (ordinary/sleeper, Rs 240/340, 10½ hours), Jodhpur (Rs 120, five hours) and Udaipur (Rs 180, eight hours). Government bus fares are slightly cheaper (and the buses less comfortable).

For around Rs 50, some agencies will book train tickets for services ex-Ajmer (including free transfer to Ajmer).

For cars, the road toll to Ajmer is Rs 25 which is raised to Rs 35 during the camel fair.

Getting Around

There are no autorickshaws, but it's a breeze to get around on foot. Another good option is to hire a bicycle (Rs 30 per day) or a motorbike (Rs 150 to Rs 250 per day). Try **Shree Ganpati Motorbike Hire** (☎ 2772830; Brahma Rd) whose bikes have an all-Rajasthan tourist permit. A wallah can carry your luggage on a hand-drawn cart to/from the bus stand for around Rs 10.

TONK

This town, 95km south of Jaipur, on the way to Ranthambhore National Park, was built in the mid-17th century. The colourful bazaar and the beautifully painted mosque are worth a look, though the town is regularly the focus of Hindu–Muslim tension and is very much off the tourist trail.

The town of Tonk was originally ruled by a tribe of Afghani Pathans, and their prosperous Muslim descendants have left a legacy of fine mansions, a testament to the wealth they accumulated when they ruled as nawabs from this region. Tonk also served as an important administrative centre during the era of the Raj, and the British have left behind some well-preserved colonial buildings.

Worth seeking out is the early-19th-century **Sunehri Kothi** (Najar Bagh Rd), which is decorated with exquisite coloured Belgium glass, inlay work and gilding. However it is all much in decay with amateurish renovation attempts. You must sign in at the small office opposite the entrance and the guide will expect a tip. A contrasting but equally beautiful sight is the imposing **Jama Masjid**, Rajasthan's finest mosque. Delicately frescoed inside and out with interlocking patterns, ferns and flowers, and sinuous gold decoration, it's hung with dusty glass chandeliers and busy with elderly men praying. This important place of worship was begun in 1246 by the first nawab of Tonk, Nawab Amir Khan, and completed by his son in 1298.

At the **Arabic & Persian Research Institute** (☉ 10am-5pm Mon-Fri) a rare collection of old Arabic and Persian manuscripts and books is housed, dating from the 12th to the 17th century.

About 22km out of town, by Ranthambhore Rd, is a huge elephant carved out of a single block of stone. This is **Hathi Bhata**, carved in 1200 – the date is given in script on the elephant's right ear. Beside the elephant are 64 plate-sized depressions in the rock. This is where worshippers sit and eat at festival times. The flickering firelight from the open kitchen must make the hathi an impressive sight.

Getting There & Away

Many local buses from Jaipur's main bus stand pass through Tonk (Rs 49, 2½ hours) en route to Kota. There are also numerous buses between Tonk and Sawai Madhopur for Ranthambhore National Park (Rs 67, two hours).

RANTHAMBHORE NATIONAL PARK

☎ 07462

Near the railway town of Sawai Madhopur, this **park** (☉ Oct-Jun) has tremendously dramatic scenery – wild jungle hemmed in by steep crags, crossed by a system of lakes and rivers, and scattered with crumbling temples, pavilions and *chhatris*. The 10th-century Ranthambhore Fort stands on a rocky outcrop looking like a set from an adventure epic. The park was a hunting ground for maharajas till 1970 – 15 years after it had become a sanctuary. You can still see numerous hides where the Jaipur maharajas mounted their elaborate big-game shoots (shikars) inviting royalty and bigwigs from all over the world.

In 1955 this game park was declared a wildlife sanctuary, and in 1973 became one of nine sanctuaries selected as part of the Project Tiger programme. In 1980 the central area was designated a national park, and the Project Tiger reserve was expanded over subsequent years. The reserve and park now covers 1334 sq km.

Ranthambhore is where you are most likely to spot a tiger on safari in India. Traffic into the park is restricted, and the tigers are so used to being observed that they are not scared away by jeeps and canters (large, open-topped trucks seating 20).

The park is one of Project Tiger's greatest conservation successes, though here the project's difficulties have also become apparent, such as when government officials were implicated in tiger poaching and when tiger numbers have been questioned.

Just as in Sariska Tiger Reserve (p198), which lost its tigers to poaching in 2004, Ranthambhore also witnesses the struggle between local villagers and authorities over livestock. Villagers compete for land in both the national park and its buffer zones. They need land for cultivation, grazing and woodfelling. There are 332 villages in and around Ranthambhore, with around 150,000 cows. Most of the villages are directly dependent on the park for fodder. Although it is illegal to graze stock within the core national park area, some villagers have been compelled to break the law as overgrazing has left them with no grazing grounds at all. Despite efforts of education within the local villages, the relationship between the villagers and park authorities remains strained.

According to a recent census, the park has around 26 to 30 tigers, a drop from 2004 figures (39 to 41 individuals), thought to be the result of poaching. Seeing one is a matter of luck; you should plan on two or three safaris to improve your chances. There are also more than 300 species of birds in the park. Other animals inhabiting Ranthambhore include the endangered caracal, also a member of the cat family, the leopard and the jungle cat; several members of the dog family, such as hyenas, foxes and jackals; the sloth bear; and varieties of deer, including the chital (spotted deer) and the sambar, India's largest deer. There are also two species of antelope: the chinkara (Indian gazelle) and the nilgai. However, the park is also worth visiting for its scenery, particularly if you walk up to the fort.

Ranthambhore is very popular on the tourist trail, which has led to pressure on resources around the park, and there can be difficulties getting a place in a jeep or canter. A large and colourful Jain festival, the Shri Mahavirji Fair (p185), is celebrated in the village of Chandangaon, within the Sawai Madhoper district.

Orientation
It's 10km from Sawai Madhopur to the first gate, and another 3km to the main gate and Ranthambhore Fort. Accommodation is stretched out along the road from the town to the park.

Information
The post office is on the street that runs parallel to, and north of, the main bazaar in Sawai Madhopur.

Bank of Baroda ATM (Bazariya Market) Situated 200m northwest of the train station.

Project Tiger office (☎ 223402; Ranthambhore Rd) The office is 500m from the train station. Don't expect much in the way of information.

Ranthambhore Art Gallery (☎ 221137; Ranthambhore Rd) Sells a small range of wildlife books.

State Bank of Bikaner & Jaipur ATM (Train Station) East of the entrance in the train station building.

State Bank of Bikaner & Jaipur (☒ 10am-2pm Mon-Fri, 10am-noon Sat) The place to change cash or travellers cheques, also with an ATM. It's in the old city (a local bus runs there for Rs 4, or a return rickshaw costs Rs 60).

Tiger Track (☎ 222790; Ranthambhore Rd; per hr Rs 60; ☒ 7am-10.30pm) Near Ankur Resort. Offers internet access and a good range of books.

Tourist Reception Centre (☎ 220808; Train Station; ☒ 10am-5pm Mon-Sat) This friendly office has a good, although not to scale, map of Sawai Madhopur and the park.

Sights
RANTHAMBHORE FORT
In the heart of the national park, this ancient fort (admission free; ☒ 6am-6pm) is believed to have been built by the Chauhan Rajputs in the 10th century, only a few years before the invasion of India by Mohammed of Ghori. According to tradition, the fort was erected over the site at which two princes were engaged in a boar hunt. The boar eluded the princes and dived into a lake. Not to be thwarted, the princes prayed to Shiva to bring back the boar. This Shiva deigned to do, on condition that the princes build a fort in his honour at the spot.

However, it is ever-popular Ganesh who rules the roost at the fort, and a temple to him overlooks its southern ramparts – often busy with pilgrims. The temple hosts the annual Ganesha Chaturthi festival (see p185). Traditionally, when a marriage is to take place, invitations are forwarded to Ganesh before any other guests. The temple at the fort receives hundreds of letters each week addressed to the elephant god, some of which include money to enable him to cover his fare. There are two other Hindu temples inside the fort: the others are dedicated to Shiva and Ramlalaji. All three date from the 12th and 13th centuries and are constructed with impressive blocks of red Karauli stone. Built from the same stone are a number of cenotaphs that can be seen in the precincts of the fort.

The fort is believed to be the site of the first *jauhar* (ritual mass suicide by immolation) in Rajput history. In the early 14th century the ruler of the fort, Hammir Deva, was engaged in a protracted battle with the Muslim forces. Although Hammir repulsed the Muslim invaders, the women who were installed in the fort for their safety heard that he had succumbed on the battlefield. In Rajput style, preferring death to dishonour, they committed mass suicide. When confronted with the grisly news, the victorious Hammir beheaded himself before the image of Shiva in the temple at the fort.

From a distance, the fort is almost indiscernible on its hilltop perch – as you get closer, it seems almost as if it is growing out of the rock. It covers an area of 4.5 sq km, and affords peerless views from the disintegrating walls of the Badal Mahal (Palace of the Clouds), on its northern side. The ramparts stretch for over 7km, and seven enormous gateways are still intact.

Tours
The best time to visit is between October and April; the park closes during the monsoon (July–September). Safaris take place in the early morning and late afternoon. The mornings can be very chilly in the open vehicles, so bring some warm clothes.

The only way to travel into the core of the park is by jeep or canter safari. A good network of seven gravel tracks crisscrosses the park and on each safari, vehicles divide among the trails. The canters and jeeps are

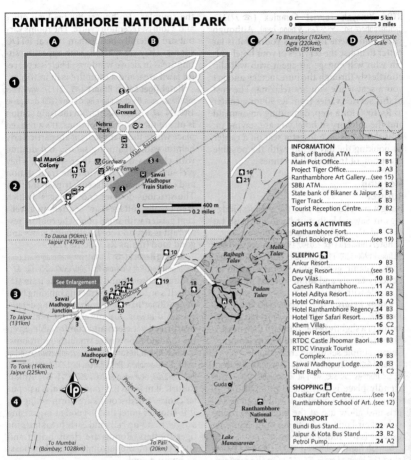

RANTHAMBHORE NATIONAL PARK

To Bharatpur (182km);
Agra (220km);
Delhi (351km)

Indira
Ground

Nehru
Park

Bal Mandir
Colony

Gurdwara
Shiva Temple

Sawai
Madhopur
Train Station

To Dausa (90km);
Jaipur (147km)

Rajbagh
Talav

Malik
Talav

Padam
Talav

See Enlargement

Sawai
Madhopur
Junction

To Jaipur
(131km)

Sawai
Madhopur City

To Tonk (140km);
Jaipur (225km)

Project Tiger Boundary

Guda

Ranthambhore
National
Park

To Mumbai
(Bombay; 1028km)

To Pali
(20km)

Lake
Manasarovar

INFORMATION	
Bank of Baroda ATM................1	B2
Main Post Office.....................2	B1
Project Tiger Office..................3	A3
Ranthambhore Art Gallery...(see 15)	
SBBJ ATM.............................4	B2
State bank of Bikaner & Jaipur..5	B1
Tiger Track............................6	B3
Tourist Reception Centre..........7	B2

SIGHTS & ACTIVITIES	
Ranthambhore Fort..................8	C3
Safari Booking Office.........(see 19)	

SLEEPING	
Ankur Resort..........................9	B3
Anurag Resort...................(see 15)	
Dev Vilas.............................10	B3
Ganesh Ranthambhore............11	A2
Hotel Aditya Resort...............12	B3
Hotel Chinkara......................13	A2
Hotel Ranthambhore Regency..14	B3
Hotel Tiger Safari Resort........15	B3
Khem Villas..........................16	C2
Rajeev Resort........................17	A2
RTDC Castle Jhoomar Baori....18	B3
RTDC Vinayak Tourist Complex.............................19	B3
Sawai Madhopur Lodge..........20	B3
Sher Bagh.............................21	C2

SHOPPING	
Dastkar Craft Centre............(see 14)	
Ranthambhore School of Art..(see 12)	

TRANSPORT	
Bundi Bus Stand....................22	A2
Jaipur & Kota Bus Stand.........23	B2
Petrol Pump..........................24	A2

EASTERN RAJASTHAN

open-topped. If you've ever been on safari in Africa you might be thinking this is risky, but the tigers appear unconcerned by garrulous tourists toting cameras only metres away from where they're lying. No-one has been mauled or eaten – yet!

You have as much chance of seeing a tiger from a jeep or canter, though sometimes canter passengers can be rowdy, which obviously isn't a great advantage when spotting wildlife. Alternatively, the higher canter provides a better view and you have 20 sets of eyes scouring the country for those hidden stripes.

Demand outstrips supply because the number of motorised vehicles is restricted – only 20 jeeps and 20 canters are allowed inside

per session. An extra 10 canters are allowed at Diwali and Christmas. Under the current system, seats in canters and two jeeps are allocated on a first-come-first-served basis. Seats on the 18 other jeeps can be booked in advance at www.rajasthantourism.gov.in.

A guide is compulsory and is included in the canter ticket price, but will cost an extra Rs 150 if you go by jeep.

Safaris take 3½ hours. The price for a canter is Rs 285/460 for Indians/foreigners; and a jeep is Rs 391/566. A camera is free, while video is Rs 200.

From October to February, both canters and jeeps leave at 7am and 2.30pm. From March to June, they leave at 6.30am and 3.30pm. Bookings can be made at the

RTDC Vinayak Tourist Complex (☎ 221333; Ranthambhore Rd; ⏱ 5-7am & noon-2pm). Although you could queue for tickets yourself it is far better to utilise the services of your hotel wallah who will engage an agent who will slip effortlessly through the bureaucracy and get you a seat while you are relaxing. The cost of this service varies from Rs 90 for a canter to Rs 1000 for a jeep, depending on demand and the category of hotel you are staying in. You should be able to get a seat on a canter by booking the day before with the possible exception of Indian holiday times.

Sleeping
BUDGET
Budget travellers will find the cheapest lodgings in Sawai Madhopur itself, but it isn't a particularly inspiring place to stay.

Hotel Chinkara (☎ 220340; 13 Indira Colony, Civil Lines; s/d from Rs 200/300) This place is quiet, with large, dusty, quaint, good-value rooms. It's run by a cheery family and home-cooked meals are available with notice.

Rajeev Resort (☎ 221413; 16 Indira Colony, Civil Lines; s/d from Rs 200/300; ❄) Rajeev Resort has decent rooms of a slightly better standard than nearby Chinkara's, but the staff are less welcoming. Cheap, simple set meals are available.

Hotel Aditya Resort (☎ 9351244510; Ranthambhore Rd; s/d from Rs 250/300, with AC Rs 500/600; ❄) This friendly place is way ahead of anything in town. The keen young staff will organise safaris and allow use of the big air-con room without air-con for a hefty discount. Nothing it seems is too much trouble.

Ganesh Ranthambhore (☎ 220230; 58 Bal Mandir Colony, Civil Lines; d from Rs 400; ❄) On the western side of the overpass, this is the most appealing of the options in the town centre. Rooms are adequately clean and more airy and light than most of the pokey options in Sawai Madhopur. Rooms have passable bathrooms, and tasty meals are available in the restaurant.

MIDRANGE & TOP END
All of the following places offer fixed-price meals, and some also offer an à la carte selection. All of these places can help with safari bookings – though some are better than others – and some will close when the park is closed.

RTDC Vinayak Tourist Complex (☎ 221333; Ranthambhore Rd; s/d Rs 700/800, with AC Rs 990/1200; ❄) You're well placed for tour reservations here –

the complex also houses the booking office and a tourist reception centre. The rooms vary but are generally better than typical RTDC rooms. They are spacious with appealing sitting areas in alcove windows. There's a peaceful lawn area, and a campfire is lit in winter.

Hotel Tiger Safari Resort (☎ 221137; www.tiger safariresort.com; Ranthambhore Rd; d from Rs 800, cottages Rs 1300; ❄ ❄) About 4km from the train station is one of the best-value options. It's a relaxed place where the management are particularly helpful with organising safaris and dealing with clueless would-be tiger-spotters. They pick-up and drop-off from the train station and can organise sightseeing trips to the fort. The spacious doubles and 'cottages' (which aren't really cottages) are centred on a well-kept garden with small pool. The rooftop restaurant is airy and cool, with good views and good food (mains Rs 35 to Rs 125).

Anurag Resort (☎ 220451; www.anuragresort.com; Ranthambhore Rd; s/d from Rs 1200/1500; ❄ 🖥 ❄) Anurag is also around 3km from the train station. It's an attractive terracotta building built in neo-Rajasthani style with scalloping details, set amid lawns. Rooms are tiny, plain and overpriced yet clean and comfortable. Even the top-end rooms have smallish bathrooms.

Hotel Ankur Resort (☎ 220792; ankurswm@sanchar net.in; Ranthambhore Rd; s/d from Rs 1200/1800, with AC Rs 1600/2200, new wing Rs 2000/2600; ❄ ❄) Ankur Resort, 3km from the train station, is a popular choice, and discounts are worth asking for. It is another hotel that is good at organising safaris, wake-up calls and early breakfasts for tiger spotters. Rooms are clean, bright and attractive, and the surrounding gardens boast an inviting pool.

RTDC Castle Jhoomar Baori (☎ 220495; Ranthambhore Rd; standard s/d Rs 1775/2375, ste Rs 3400/4025; ❄) This is a stunningly set hilltop former royal hunting lodge, about 7km from the train station (you can spot it from the train). The multi-chamber rooms are loaded with character, although they're a bit shabby in true RTDC style. Open-rooftop areas add appeal. The tariff includes breakfast.

Hotel Ranthambhore Regency (☎ 221176; www .ranthambhore.com; Ranthambhore Rd; room only Rs 3000; s/d incl meals from US$120/150; ❄ 🖥 ❄) This is a professionally run place which caters to tour groups. It has immaculate, well-appointed rooms which would rate as suites in most hotels. The central garden is a virtual oasis and the impressive pool is inviting.

ourpick Khem Villas (☎ 252099; www.khemvillas
.com; Ranthambhore Rd; s/d homestead Rs 6000/7000, tents Rs
9000/11,500, cottage Rs 12,000/14,000 incl all meals & taxes;
⊠) This splendid option has been created
by the Singh Rathore family – the patriarch
Fateh Singh Rathore is lauded as the driving
force behind the conservation of the tiger at
Ranthambhore. His son Goverdhan, and his
daughter-in-law Usha, run this impressive
eco-lodge. The accommodation ranges from
rooms in the colonial-style bungalow to luxury tents to sumptuous stone cottages. Privacy
is guaranteed – you can even bathe under the
stars; and socialising is relaxed – join the tiger
talk at sunset drinks while the jungle sounds
switch from the day shift to the night shift.

Sher Bagh (☎ 252120; www.sherbagh.com;
Ranthambhore Rd; s/d Rs 12,000/13,325 incl all meals &
taxes; ☾ Oct-Apr) A tented camp: here luxurious
tents – based on the design for the maharaja
of Jodhpur last century – are set on manicured lawns in an isolated woodland near
the park. Each of the 12 tents has a veranda
and gorgeous ensuite bathrooms with sunken
marble showers.

Sawai Madhopur Lodge (☎ 220541; Ranthambhore
Rd; r from Rs 13,500; ⊠ ⊠) This Taj Group lodge,
3km from the train station, once belonged to
the maharaja of Jaipur. It's luxurious, with a
pool (Rs 400 for nonguests), a tennis court
and more than 4.5 hectares of lovely, well-kept
gardens. The bar boasts half a tiger and a billiard table. The rooms are in bungalows with
spiffing colonnaded verandas and are surrounded by serene lawns. The faded but restful rooms feature new marble bathrooms.

Dev Vilas (☎ 252168; www.devvilas.com; Ranthambhore
Rd; s/d incl all meals r or tent US$200/225; ⊠ ⊠) This
well-appointed hotel is modelled on a grand
Indo-Saracen hunting lodge, albeit one with
wheelchair accessibility in mind. It is set on
out-of-the-way acres and has a luxurious pool
in its neat garden. The tents are lavish and
private, while the marble-floored lodge rooms
are truly elegant.

Shopping
Dastkar Craft Centre (☎ 252051; Ranthambhore Rd;
☾ 10am-8pm) About 3km from the train station,
this place is worth a visit. The organisation
helps to empower low-caste village women,
who gain regular income through selling
their textile and embroidery work. Many
attractive handicrafts are on sale, including
saris, scarves, bags and bedspreads. You can

visit the workshops located beyond the park
entrance, near Sher Bagh Hotel.

Ranthambhore School of Art (☎ 222892;
Ranthambhore Rd) This place aims to promote
conservation through art, and sells signature photo-realistic wildlife watercolours
and prints with 20% of the proceeds going
towards conservation.

Getting There & Away
BUS
Buses to Jaipur (Rs 91, six hours, four daily)
via Tonk, and to Kota (Rs 80, five hours) via
Bundi (Rs 56, 3½ hours) leave from the Bundi
bus stand near the petrol station close to the
overpass. Travelling to Bharatpur by bus invariably involves a change in Dausa (on the
Jaipur–Bharatpur road). Buses to Dausa (Rs
55, five hours), leave from the roundabout
near the main post office. The train is preferable for all routes. The inquiries number
is ☎ 2451020.

TRAIN
The train station has a **computerised reservation office** (☾ 8am-8pm Mon-Sat, 8am-2pm Sun)
for bookings.

The *Golden Temple Mail* (2903/4) leaves
Sawai Madhopur at 12.40pm, stopping at
Bharatpur (sleeper/3 AC Rs 141/316) at
3.08pm, arriving in Delhi (Rs 192/484) at
7pm. From Delhi, it leaves at 7.50am, stopping at Bharatpur at 10.40am and arriving
at 1.05pm. To Kota, there are about seven
trains daily, the most convenient of which is
the *Avadh Express* (9037/8). It leaves Sawai
Madhopur at 9.15am and arrives in Kota
(sleeper/3 AC Rs 121/238) at 11am. Going
the other way, it leaves Sawai Madhopur
at 4.25pm, arriving in Agra (Rs 130/335)
at 9.50pm.

Getting Around
Bicycle hire is available in the main bazaar
(around Rs 25 per day). Autorickshaws are
available at the train station; the journey to
Ranthambhore Rd will cost around Rs 25.

KARAULI
☎ 07464 / pop 66,200
Karauli was founded in 1348 and is the home
of Shri Madan Mohanji, the deity of Lord
Krishna, and has some important Krishna
temples which attract many pilgrims. Around
23km from Karauli is the massively popular

temple of Kaila Devi – during the Navratri celebrations in March/April and September/October, thousands of devotees flood the town en route to the temple (see p185).

Completely off the tourist trail, the area is also famous for its red-sandstone quarries and for its lac (resin) bangles. Nearby is the rugged **Kaila Devi Game Sanctuary** (25km away), home to chinkaras, wild boars, antelope, jackals and leopards.

The mainly 17th-century **old city palace** (Indian/foreigner Rs 50/100; ☼ sunrise-sunset) was constructed over different periods; the oldest part has existed for 600 years. The Durbar Hall has some particularly fine paintings. Occupied by the Karauli royal family until around the 1950s, the palace is run-down and worn, but very atmospheric with great views from the roof. It's worth getting the guard to guide you around for a tip. There's a **Krishna temple** (☼ 5-11.30am & 4-8pm) in the compound.

Around 40km from town, along a pot-holed road, is a tragically ruined fort, **Timangarh**. Built around 1100 and reconstructed in 1244, this once mighty fort overlooks a lake filled with water lilies. It was deserted 300 years ago, but was destroyed by looters over the last 50 years. You'll need to hire a taxi to get here, and one that can manage the track – the return journey will cost you around Rs 500.

Bhanwar Vilas Palace (☎ 07464-20024, 2290763; www.karauli.com; s/d from Rs 1750/2000; ✵ ▨), owned by Maharaja Krishna Chandra Pal (whose family hail back to Krishna), is closer to a large country manor than a palace. A back-in-time place, it features a billiard room, shady verandas, rambling grounds and classic cars in the garages. Rooms are comfortable here and at the neighbouring Bhumendra Vilas. Excursions to nearby points of interest, including the old city palace, can be organised.

The town is 182km southeast of Jaipur, situated between Bharatpur (110km) and Sawai Madhopur (104km). There are buses running between Jaipur and Karauli (Rs 65, five hours).

The nearest train stations are Gangapur City (31km) and Hindaun (30km), both on the main Delhi–Mumbai (Bombay) Line, where almost all the trains running between Mumbai and Delhi stop.

Southern Rajasthan

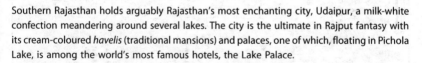

Southern Rajasthan holds arguably Rajasthan's most enchanting city, Udaipur, a milk-white confection meandering around several lakes. The city is the ultimate in Rajput fantasy with its cream-coloured *havelis* (traditional mansions) and palaces, one of which, floating in Pichola Lake, is among the world's most famous hotels, the Lake Palace.

In the south of the region are Rajasthan's two finest forts, Chittorgarh (Chittor), sprawling over an enormous hilltop plateau, and remote Kumbalgarh, perched at 1100m, with breathtaking views over the dense Aravalli Hills fading into a pale blue horizon. Here, too, are two Jain temple complexes where artistic virtuosity reached dizzy peaks. Ranakpur, deep in an Aravalli valley, has a hall of 1444 pillars, each one different; Dilwara, on a hilltop near Mt Abu, sports marble carving so delicate that it's almost transparent. Mt Abu is Rajasthan's only hill station; a cool holiday destination for locals, it's still largely undiscovered by foreign tourists.

If you're keen to get off the well-beaten track, Bundi, though definitely discovered, is an enchanting town, painted Brahmin blue and overlooked by a palace; nearby Kota holds another fine palace. Jhalawar, meanwhile, is really off the trail, with its mighty, forgotten fort and nearby city of temples. Serene Jaisamand, a vast blue-reflecting hill-ringed expanse, is Asia's biggest artificial lake. The region offers some exhilarating activities too. You can trek or ride the beautiful countryside near Udaipur, Mt Abu or Kumbalgarh, cycle about Bundi, or take a boat trip down the crocodile habitats of the Chambal River.

HIGHLIGHTS

- Explore the vast forts of busy **Chittorgarh** (p236) and remote **Kumbalgarh** (p259), whose architectural magnificence reflect nobler times

- Mess about on the river at **Kota** (p228), by taking a leisurely Chambal River boat cruise

- Indulge in **Udaipur** (p240), an ice-cream cake of a city, with dreamy lakes overlooked by shadowy hills

- Examine the exquisite, mind-blowing carving in the Jain temples at **Mt Abu** (p265) and **Ranakpur** (p261)

- Kick back in endearing **Bundi** (p223), a blue-painted small town, overlooked by a ramshackle fort and a magical palace

★Bundi

★Kumbalgarh   ★Kota
Ranakpur ★Chittorgarh

★Mt Abu ★Udaipur

lonelyplanet.com

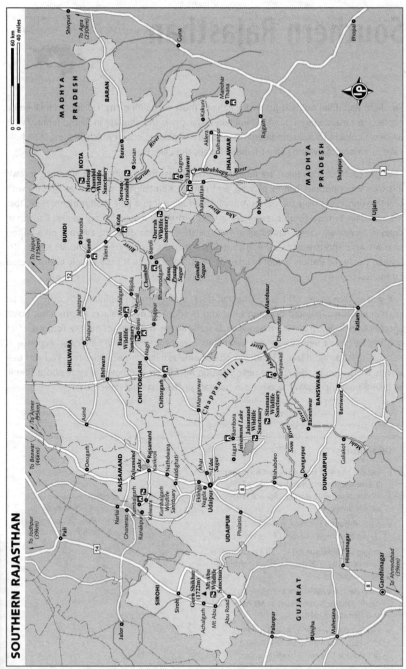

SOUTHERN RAJASTHAN

History

The kingdom of Mewar (the area encompassing Chittorgarh and Udaipur) has dominated the history of the south, which is splattered with bloodshed and vast doses of valour.

Chittorgarh, Mewar's former capital, was sacked three times between 1303 and 1568, each defeat ending in immense carnage, with the impossibly noble Rajputs (a Hindu warrior caste that formerly ruled western India) reliably choosing death before dishonour. While the men died in battle, the women committed *jauhar* (collective self-sacrifice), throwing themselves into the flames of huge pyres. After the third attack, Mewar's ruler, Maharaja Udai Singh II, wisely decided to give up Chittorgarh as a bad job and establish his new capital in Udaipur.

Udaipur, shielded by thick forests and the Aravalli Hills, was far less vulnerable than exposed Chittorgarh. But this didn't stop invaders from trying their luck, and Udaipur also had its share of battles. These power struggles ended in the early 19th century when the British signed an alliance pledging to protect the Mewar rulers.

The rulers of the Mewar region, the illustrious Sisodia Rajput clan, claim descent from the sun, and you'll see the symbol of the sun repeated in their palaces and forts. Their dynasty is believed to be one of the oldest in the world, reigning in unbroken succession for over 1400 years. Staunchly defying foreign domination of any kind, they were the only Hindu princes who refused to intermarry with the once-influential Mughal emperors. For them, honour, heritage and independence were paramount, even if that meant deprivation and suffering.

Other princely states in southern Rajasthan, such as Kota and Bundi, were formed long after the Mewar region, with the remote royal state of Jhalawar created as recently as 1838.

BUNDI

☎ 0747 / pop 100,000

A captivating small town with narrow lanes of Brahmin-blue houses, lakes, hills, bazaars and a temple at every turn, Bundi is dominated by a fantastical palace – faded-parchment cupolas and loggias rising from a mighty fortress mounted on a crag. Though it's becoming increasingly popular with travellers, the town remains the perfect place to relax and write that novel (as Rudyard Kipling did, in a fragile lakeside icing-sugar house) before the crowds really descend in earnest. A visit in August or September might reward you with a glimpse of the cheerful festival of Kajli Teej (p224), celebrating the arrival of the monsoon, while October to November sees Bundi Utsav (p224), a cultural festival complete with music and fireworks, blaze through Bundi's quiet streets

Bundi's crumbling storybook palace houses the famous Bundi murals (see the boxed text, p232), along with legions of bats; dusk heralds the extraordinary sight of streaming clouds of them exiting the palace and taking to the skies as this still-sleepy town closes down for an early night.

History

The Hadoti Chauhans, who claim descent from the sacred fires of Mt Abu, conquered this area in the 12th century, wresting it from the Mina and Bhil tribes and claiming it as capital of their new kingdom, after being pushed south from their stronghold at Ajmer by Mohammed of Ghori.

In 1624 Kota, the land grant of the ruler's eldest son, was made into a separate state at the instigation of the Mughal emperor Jehangir. Bundi's importance dwindled with the rise of Kota during Mughal times, but it maintained its independence until it was incorporated into the state of Rajasthan after Independence in 1947.

Orientation

Bundi is small and easily navigable, and it's easy to find your way to the palace on foot through the bazaar. Once you pass through the city gates, there are only two main roads through town, and the palace is visible from many points. The bus stand is at the Kota (southeast) end of town, and the train station is about 2km south of town, across National Hwy 12.

Information

Along with the Ayurvedic Hospital, there's a conventional government hospital in the south of town, near the bus stand. Mukesh Mehta, at the Haveli Braj Bhushanjee (p228), is a terrific source of tourist information; his brother's website, www.kiplingsbundi.com, is also useful.

Ayurvedic Hospital (☎ 2443708; ☼ 9am-1pm & 4-6pm Mon-Sat, 9am-1pm Sun) Opposite the Haveli Braj

FESTIVALS IN SOUTHERN RAJASTHAN

There's a flurry of colourful festivals in the south, while statewide and nationwide festivals (see p358) are also celebrated with aplomb.

Baneshwar Fair (Baneshwar, p264; Jan-Feb) This large tribal event, honouring both Lord Shiva and Vishnu (worshipped as Mavji) is celebrated by thousands of Bhil people, the fair site lying at the confluence of the Mahi, Som and Jakham Rivers. Festivities include acrobatic and cultural programmes, and a silver image of Mavji is paraded through the village on horseback and doused in the river. The river is thought holiest at this time, so many people bathe along with the idol.

Holi (Udaipur; Feb-Mar) Udaipur is the place to be for this joyful festival, which marks the end of winter and the beginning of spring. The Udaipur royal family hosts an elaborate function at the City Palace to celebrate Holi, with an evening horse procession, a band, local nobility in traditional attire and, of course, the royal family. After performing an ancient religious ceremony, the royal family lights a huge sacred fire, Holika Dahan, signifying the triumph of good over evil. Afterwards, you'll get the chance to rub shoulders with nobility at a cocktail and dinner reception held in the Zenana Mahal (Royal Ladies' Palace) at the City Palace. Tickets, costing Rs 4000 per person, can be obtained at the Shiv Niwas Palace Hotel (p253).

Gangaur (Mt Abu; Mar-Apr) Gangaur, celebrated across Rajasthan, has some interesting adaptations in this region. Essentially a festival for women, it's dedicated to the goddess Gauri (Parvati). Wives pray for their spouses, and unmarried women pray for good husbands. The Garasia tribes of the Mt Abu region celebrate Gangaur for an entire month, with an image of Gauri carried aloft from village to village, accompanied by singing and dancing. In Bundi, Kota and Jhalawar, unmarried girls collect poppies from the fields during Gangaur and make them into wreaths for the goddess; in Nathdwara the Gangaur procession lasts for seven days, the goddess dressed differently each day.

Mewar Festival (Udaipur; Mar-Apr) Udaipur's colourful take on Gangaur, this festival also welcomes the onset of spring. People dressed in traditional costumes sing and dance in a lively procession that goes through the town to Gangaur Ghat on Pichola Lake. Idols of Gauri and Shiva, representing the 'perfect couple', are carried in procession and set afloat on the lake in boats. There are also free cultural programmes.

Summer Festival (Mt Abu; Apr-May) Mt Abu registers the coolest temperatures in the state at this scorching time of the year; the festival includes classical and traditional folk-music programmes, as well as boat races on Nakki Lake and fireworks.

Kajli Teej (Bundi; Aug-Sep) The traditional Rajasthani festival of Teej, marking the onset of the monsoon, is celebrated somewhat differently in Bundi. Here it's observed on the 3rd day of the month of Bhadra. A palanquin (a covered litter) bearing the goddess Teej is carried through the streets from Nawal Sagar lake to Azad Park. The celebrations are a good chance to see local artists perform, and are merged with the festival of Janmastami, Krishna's birthday.

Bundi Utsav (Bundi; Oct-Nov) This cultural festival showcases the colourful traditions of the region with a procession, classical raga (free compostion) performances, magic and fireworks.

Dussehra (Kota;Oct-Nov) Kota is the place to be at the end of this festival, when enormous effigies, some around 20m high, are filled with crackers and set alight. The festival – an India-wide celebration – celebrates the story of Rama's victory over Ravana (see p48).

Ghans Bheru Festival (Bharodia; Oct-Nov) Held on the day after Diwali (see p360) in the village of Bharodia, about 10km northeast of Bundi, the festival honours the Hindu god Ghans Bheru. While almost unknown to most tourists, this colourful festival attracts thousands of villagers from the district, who converge on the village to celebrate a prosperous harvest.

Chandrabhaga Fair (Jhalrapatan, p234; Nov-Dec) This huge cattle fair takes place on the last day of the Hindu month of Kartika on the banks of the holy Chandrabhaga River near Jhalrapatan. Attracting villagers from across Rajasthan, it includes livestock trading and colourful stalls, while pilgrims bathe in a sacred part of the river known as Chandrawati.

Bhushanjee, this charitable hospital prescribes natural plant-based remedies. There are medicines for all sorts of ailments, from upset tummies to arthritis, and many of them are free.

Cyber Dream (per hr Rs 60; 9am-9pm) One of the increasing number of places to check your email.

Pandey Forex (9am-4pm Mon-Fri) A good place to change money, about 300m south of the palace.

SBBJ ATM (outside Chogan Gate) This frequently out-of-service ATM machine accepts international cards.

Shri Balaji.com (Nahar ka Chuhata; per hr Rs 60; 9am-9pm) An alternative to Cyber Dream.

Tourist office (☎ 2443697; Lanka Gate Rd; ☽ 10am-5pm Mon-Fri) Near Raniji-ki-Baori. You can get a free map here.

Sights

BUNDI PALACE

An extraordinary, decaying edifice, the **palace** (Indians/foreigners Rs 10/50, camera/video Rs 50/100; ☽ 7am-5pm) is actually a series of smaller *mahals* (palaces) which have fabulous, fading turquoise-and-gold murals. It's reached from the bazaar's northwestern end. Previously shut up and left to the bats, the entirety is now open to the public, and knowledgeable guides hang around the ticket office to illuminate your tour of a place so fairy tale–esque that Kipling called it 'the work of goblins rather than of men'.

Entering through the huge Elephant Gate (built in 1607), visit the Chhatra Mahal (palace), built in 1644, which houses some of Bundi's finest murals: one room features well-preserved paintings of Krishna – one for each month of the year. The Phool Mahal was built in 1607 and murals here include an immense royal procession. Dating from the same time, the Badal Mahal (Cloud Palace) houses Bundi's very best murals, including a wonderful Chinese-inspired ceiling, divided into petal shapes and decorated with peacocks and Krishnas.

To get to yet more murals at the **Chitrasala** (Umed Mahal; admission free; ☽ 7am-6pm), a small palace built by Rao Umed Singh in the 18th century, exit through the Elephant Gate and walk uphill to the entrance. Above the garden courtyard are several rooms covered in beautiful paintings. There are some great Krishna images, including a detail of him sitting up a tree playing the flute after stealing the clothes of the *gopis* (milkmaids). The back room to the right is the Sheesh Mahal, badly damaged but still featuring some beautiful inlaid glass, while back in the main courtyard there's an image of 18th-century Bundi itself.

TARAGARH

Built in 1354, the ramshackle, vine-strewn **Taragarh** (Star Fort; admission free) is a rewarding place to ramble around. With its overgrown vegetation and resident monkeys (pick up a stick on the walk up to the fort, to ward them off), the fort is so far beguilingly uncommercialised.

The views from the top are magical, especially at sunset. Inside the ramparts are huge reservoirs carved out of solid rock and the Bhim Burj, the largest of the great bastions, upon which is mounted a famous cannon; a trench alongside it provided shelter for the artillery.

Taragarh is reached by a steep road leading up the hillside to its enormous gateway. Take the path up behind the Chitrasala, then head east along the inside of the ramparts and left up the steep stone ramp just before the Dudha Mahal, a small disused building 200m from the palace. It's also possible to take an autorickshaw to the top.

There are splendid views of the palace and Taragarh from the south side of Nawal Sagar lake.

BAORIS & WATER TANKS

Bundi has around 60 beautiful *baoris* (stepwells; see the boxed text on p260), some right in the town centre. The most impressive, **Raniji-ki-Baori** (Queen's Step-Well), is 46m deep and decorated with sinuous carvings, including the avatars of Lord Vishnu. Built in 1699 by Rani Nathavatji, wife of Rao Raja Singh, it's one of the largest of its kind anywhere. The **Nagar Sagar Kund** is a pair of matching step-wells just outside the Chogan Gate to the old city.

Visible from the fort is the square artificial lake of **Nawal Sagar**, which tends to dry up if the monsoon is poor. At its centre is a temple to Varuna, the Vedic god often associated with rain.

Opposite the **Abhaynath Temple**, one of Bundi's oldest Shiva temples, is the 16th-century tank **Bhora-ji-ka-Kund**, which attracts a variety of bird life after a good monsoon, including kingfishers and hummingbirds. The **Dhabhai Kund**, south of the Raniji-ki-Baori, is another imposing tank.

OTHER ATTRACTIONS

It's great to amble around the bazaars of the old city. Just outside the walls, the **sabzi (vegetable) market**, between Raniji-ki-Baori and Nagar Sagar Kund, is particularly vibrant. There are more than 200 temples here, and you can pick up a self-guided map at Haveli Braj Bhushanjee (p228).

Bundi's other attractions are out of town and best visited by bike (bikes are available for rent at many guesthouses throughout town) or autorickshaw. **Jait Sagar**, to the north, is a picturesque lake flanked by hills and strewn with pretty lotus flowers during the monsoon and winter months. On the lake's southern

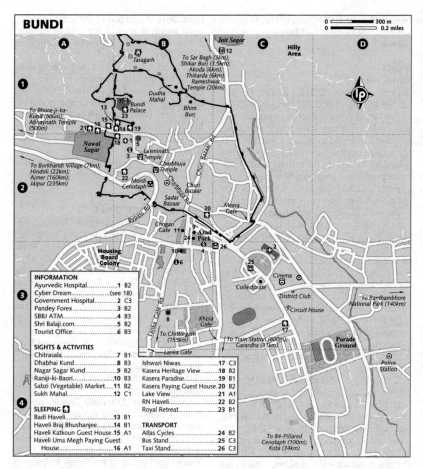

BUNDI

0 — 300 m
0 — 0.2 miles

INFORMATION
Ayurvedic Hospital	1 B2
Cyber Dream	(see 18)
Government Hospital	2 C3
Pandey Forex	3 B2
SBBJ ATM	4 B3
Shri Balaji.com	5 B2
Tourist Office	6 B3

SIGHTS & ACTIVITIES
Chitrasala	7 B1
Dhabhai Kund	8 B3
Nagar Sagar Kund	9 B2
Raniji-ki-Baori	10 B3
Sabzi (Vegetable) Market	11 B2
Sukh Mahal	12 C1

SLEEPING
Badi Haveli	13 B1
Haveli Braj Bhushanjee	14 B1
Haveli Katkoun Guest House	15 A1
Haveli Uma Megh Paying Guest House	16 A1
Ishwari Niwas	17 C3
Kasera Heritage View	18 B2
Kasera Paradise	19 B1
Kasera Paying Guest House	20 B2
Lake View	21 A1
RN Haveli	22 B2
Royal Retreat	23 B1

TRANSPORT
Atlas Cycles	24 B2
Bus Stand	25 C3
Taxi Stand	26 C3

shore, the stately **Sukh Mahal** (10am-5pm) is a small summer palace surrounded by terraced gardens where Rudyard Kipling once stayed and wrote part of *Kim*. On the opposite side of the lake, the neglected **Sar Bagh** contains 66 rarely visited royal cenotaphs, some with terrific, intricate carvings – the most spectacular is that of Chattar Sal Singh. If the gate is locked, knock on the caretaker's hut near the gateway, and tip him for the trouble of opening up. **Shikar Burj** is a small former royal hunting lodge (once there were tigers, deer and boars here). Next to a water tank, on the road that runs along the north side of the Jait Sagar, it is a good place for a picnic.

South of town is the **84-Pillared Cenotaph**, which is set in gardens. Particularly stunning when lit up at night, it was built to honour the son of the maharaja's ayah (nurse) about 600 years ago.

There are some lovely bike excursions from Bundi. Cycle 6km north of Bundi to reach **Akoda**, a merchant's village, and **Thikarda**, which has various potteries. If you're in Bundi around Diwali time (October to November), head 10km northeast to the small village of Bharodia to witness the spectacular Ghans Bheru festival (p224), held on the day after Diwali itself. About 20km north are a Shiva cave temple and a waterfall at **Rameshwar**. Around 7km west of Bundi is rural **Borkhandi Village**. Twenty-two kilometres towards Jaipur is **Hindoli**, home to a huge lake and a ruined hilltop fort.

SOUTHERN RAJASTHAN

About 33km south of Bundi, at the village of **Garardha**, you can see some ancient rock paintings, believed to be about 15,000 years old, flanking the river. There's a curious depiction of a man riding a huge bird, as well as some hunting scenes. It's best to come here with a local guide; contact Haveli Braj Bhushanjee (p228) for more information. A half-day trip in a jeep costs around Rs 600 return.

Activities

The **Ayurvedic Hospital** (☎ 2443708; ⏱ 9am-1pm & 4-6pm Mon-Sat, 9am-1pm Sun), opposite the Haveli Braj Bhushanjee, prescribes natural plant-based remedies and offers various Ayurvedic treatments. Many remedies are for free, and you can usually drop in without an appointment.

Sleeping & Eating

Bundi's guesthouses are largely charming and family run, and make the best places to eat in town. Many will provide a free pick-up service from the train or bus station if you call and book in advance. Accommodation in town is mainly budget, with some midrange options and currently no top-end choices.

BUDGET

Lake View (☎ 2442326; lakeviewbundi@yahoo.com; r Rs 250, without bathroom Rs 150) This guesthouse, set in the modest, slightly scruffy 200-year-old Meghwahanji Haveli, is overseen by a kindly old man and his assorted younger relations. It occupies a lovely lakeside spot, with some of its seven rooms sporting lake views and stained-glass windows. Most travellers, though, plump for the cheaper rooms downstairs next to a small garden. Good home-cooked meals (dishes around Rs 30) are available.

RN Haveli (☎ 2443278; r Rs 250, without bathroom Rs 150-200; 🖳) Behind Laxminath Temple, this is consistently voted one of the best budget options in town, and is an atmospheric, antique-adorned choice despite being a little bit run down. It's staffed by an energetic mother–daughter combination, who cook up fabulous vegetarian home-cooked cuisine (though beers aren't available) and can arrange upbeat jaunts across town.

Royal Retreat (☎ 2444426; royalretreatbundi@yahoo.com; s Rs 150-350, d Rs 300-500) In the palace compound, and once the palace's dyeing and printing works, Royal Retreat has four attractive rooms with air-coolers and tiled floors arranged around a hushed, open-air

courtyard. The restaurant serves good food and beer. However, it's lackadaisically staffed and can feel rather disconnected from the Bundi vibe, particularly if you happen to be the only guests.

Haveli Uma Megh Paying Guest House (☎ 2442191; r Rs 200-500) A good option with low prices, this peaceful guesthouse is run by friendly brothers, and has a range of rooms with wall paintings and alcoves and some with lake views. It has an excellent lakeside garden restaurant (dishes Rs 35 to 70) that's just right for candlelight dinners.

Kasera Paying Guest House (☎ 2446630; Charbhuja Rd; d Rs 300, without bathroom Rs 250) The same family from Kasera Heritage View watches over this small-scale guesthouse near Chogan Gate in the main bazaar. It offers small budget rooms, set in a delightful small *haveli*, and a good little rooftop restaurant (dishes Rs 30 to 35).

Ishwari Niwas (☎ 2442414; in_heritage@indiatimes.com; 1 Civil Lines; r Rs 250-800) Family-run Ishwari Niwas has royal associations. The graceful old colonial building has variable rooms with murals – some rooms have high ceilings – all arranged around a large, peaceful courtyard. The location, however, is not the best as it's away from the old city, past the bus stand. Sightseeing excursions can be arranged.

Kasera Heritage View (☎ 2444679; r Rs 300-1000) Popular and operated by a charming young couple, the Kasera has a rooftop restaurant that's perfectly placed for gazing at the palace, and 11 nice rooms in an old *haveli* (if you can, take the room with the palace-view balcony or another overlooking the mosque).

Haveli Katkoun Guest House (☎ 2444311; raghunandansingh@yahoo.com; r Rs 350-850) Run by retired Major Singh and his gentle family, this hassle-free place has six comfortable, spotless rooms off a calm, leafy garden. The rooms upstairs open onto a communal balcony with views. The popular garden restaurant provides tasty home-cooked food (and beer), making it one of the livelier eating options in town, and free pick-up from the bus and train stations is on offer.

MIDRANGE

Kasera Paradise (☎ 2444679; www.kaseraparadise.com; r Rs 500-1800; ✷) The amiable couple at Kasera Heritage View opened this second, smarter hotel in a 16th-century *haveli* that had lain empty for 80 years. The spacious rooms have smartly tiled bathrooms and the décor features coloured glass, murals, pretty bedspreads and sparkling chandeliers. There's a fabulous rooftop with city and palace views.

Haveli Braj Bhushanjee (☎ 2442322; www.kiplingsbundi.com; r Rs 800-2650; ❄) This rambling 250-year-old *haveli* has a warren of 24 appealing, characterful rooms, directed by the helpful Braj Bhushanjee family (descendants of Bundi's former prime ministers). It's an enchanting place with splendid rooftop views. There's an unrivalled range of accommodation: rooms have views and are old and atmospheric or modern, beautifully muralled and decorated with antique furniture and miniatures. The vegetarian meals and snacks, though relatively expensive (mains from around Rs 200), are delicious, and the place has recently tried to make itself eco-aware, with rainwater conservation and solar hot-water heating. Free pick-up from the bus stand and train station is available. Staff will arrange cycle and walking tours, and even camel safaris. Its attached Badi Haveli hotel round the back has slightly lower rates but offers the same basic experience.

Getting There & Away

BUS

Bus journeys to and from Bundi are bone-rattlers, although the road to Udaipur seems to be very slowly improving. Express buses run to Ajmer (Rs 80, four hours, hourly), Kota (Rs 22, one hour, half hourly), Chittorgarh (Rs 95, four hours, four daily), Udaipur (Rs 155, eight hours, two daily), Jodhpur (Rs 160, 10 hours, three daily), Bikaner (Rs 190, 10 hours, three daily), Jaipur (Rs 90, five hours, hourly) and Pushkar (Rs 90, five hours, three daily). A private sleeper bus also runs to Udaipur from Bundi; enquire at the bus stand at the southern end of town.

There are also buses to Bijolia (Rs 24, 1½ hours, 10 daily), Keshraipatan (Rs 16, 1½ hours, 10 daily), Menal (Rs 24, two hours, four daily), and Shivpuri (Rs 125, eight hours, two daily).

TRAIN

The train station is about 2km south of the old city. At the time of research, no useful services were running, making it more practical to travel by bus.

Getting Around

Taxis can be hired at the stand near Raniji-ki-Baori. A rickshaw to the train station costs Rs 40; a half-day city/outside city tour should cost around Rs 90/150; and a trip out to Akoda and Rameshwar costs around Rs 250 return. For local sightseeing, expect to pay around Rs 50 per hour for an autorickshaw.

Bicycles are an ideal way to get around this area. They are available at many guesthouses and at **Atlas Cycles** (Azad Park; per hr/day Rs 5/25). You can also hire motorbikes locally – ask around at the guesthouses.

KOTA

☎ **0744 / pop 695,899**

Busy, clamorous Kota lacks the charm of many Rajasthan towns, and so has remained untouristy: foreign tourists still attract curious stares – both from locals and from each other – on the street. However, it has a spectacular palace with an excellent museum and lovely murals, and the Chambal River runs through the town, offering opportunities for scenic boat trips.

Kota serves as an army headquarters and has the dubious distinction of being Rajasthan's industrial centre (mainly producing chemicals) and home to one of Asia's largest fertiliser plants. The nearby nuclear plant made headlines in 1992 when it was revealed that levels of radioactivity were way above safe levels. Growing industrialisation, moreover, has led to increased pollution, with black smoke belching from two huge chimneys on the opposite side of the river. Fortunately, leafy parks and an artificial lake provide much-needed breaths of fresh air.

Kota is well known for its beautiful saris, which are woven in the nearby village of Kaithoon. Known as *kota doria* saris, they are made of cotton or silk in an assortment of colours, many with delicate golden-thread designs. In case you're in the mood to shop for one, head to any of the town's bazaars, where you'll find a wide selection for sale. The miniature paintings of Kota are also famous – check them out in the marvellous City Palace. If you happen to hit Kota in October or November, check whether you're in town during the Dussehra festival, during which massive effigies are built then spectacularly set aflame (p224).

History

Building of the city began in 1264 following the Hadoti Chauhan defeat and beheading of Koteya, a Bhil chieftain who gave the city his name. The foundation stone of the fort was

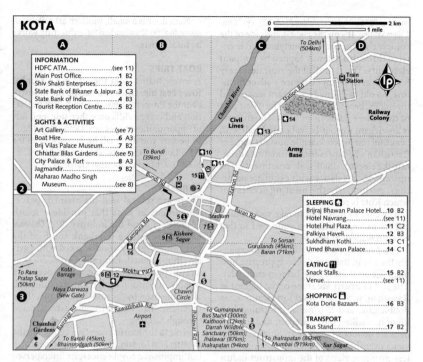

KOTA

laid, rather gruesomely, on the very spot he lost his head.

Kota didn't reach its present size until well into the 17th century, when Rao Madho Singh, a son of the ruler of Bundi, was made ruler of Kota by the Mughal emperor Jehangir. Kota remained a separate state until it was integrated into Rajasthan after Independence. Subsequent rulers have all added to the fort and palaces, each contributing to making Kota a flourishing centre of art and culture.

Orientation

Kota is strung out along the east bank of the Chambal River. The train station lies to the north; the RTDC Hotel Chambal, a number of other hotels and the bus stand are in the middle; and Chambal Gardens, the fort and the Kota Barrage are to the south.

Information

There are numerous ATMs, including HDFC ATMs next to Hotel Phul Plaza, and on platform 1 of the railway station.
Main post office (10.30am-1.30pm & 2-6pm Mon-Sat) Centrally located.

Shiv Shakti Enterprises (per hr Rs 50; 10am-10pm) Offers internet access.
State Bank of Bikaner & Jaipur (Industrial Estate) Changes travellers cheques and currency.
State Bank of India (Chawni Circle) Changes travellers cheques (Amex only) and currency.
Tourist reception centre (2327695; 10am-5pm Mon-Sat, closed 2nd & 4th Sat of month) In the grounds of the RTDC Hotel Chambal.

Sights & Activities
CITY PALACE & FORT

Beside the Kota Barrage, overlooking the river, the **City Palace and Fort** (9am-5pm) make up one of the largest such complexes in Rajasthan. The palace itself was the former residence and centre of power; the treasury, courts, arsenal, soldiers and various state offices were all located here. Some of its buildings are now used as schools. Entry is from the south side through the **Naya Darwaza** (New Gate).

There are several palaces within the fort, including Madho Singh Mahal, Raj Mahal, Bada Mahal, Chhatra Mahal and the ruined Jhala Haveli. Inside, too, is the excellent **Maharao Madho Singh Museum** (2385040; Indian/

foreigner Rs 10/100, camera/video Rs 50/100; ☾ 10am-4.30pm Sat-Thu). It's on the right-hand side of the complex's huge central courtyard and is entered through a gateway topped by rampant elephants. You'll find all the stuff necessary for a respectable Raj existence – silver furniture, an old-fashioned ice-cream maker and ingenious, beautiful weapons. The oldest part of the palace dates from 1624. Downstairs is an elegant durbar (royal court) hall with beautiful mirrorwork, while upstairs some of Rajasthan's best-preserved miniatures decorate the elegant, small-scale apartments. The upstairs rooms dance with exquisite paintings, particularly the hunting scenes for which Kota is renowned.

The curator may offer to take you around, but try to look around on your own so that you can wander at leisure.

After visiting the museum it's worth exploring the rest of the complex to appreciate how magnificent it must have been in its heyday. The fort ramparts are some of the highest in Rajasthan, with three-level fortifications, six double gates and 25 towers. Unfortunately, a lot of it is falling into disrepair, and the gardens are no more, but there are some excellent views over the old city and the Chambal and less-inspiring views of the monstrous industrial complex across the river, pollution from which is believed to be contributing to the deterioration of the fort, including the fading away of exterior murals.

JAGMANDIR

Between the City Palace and the tourist reception centre is the picturesque artificial lake **Kishore Sagar**, constructed in 1346. In the middle of the lake, on a small island amid palm trees, is the enchanting little tangerine palace of Jagmandir. Built in 1740 by one of the maharanis of Kota, it's a sight that seems to mock the frantic streets on either side of the lake. The palace, sadly, is closed to the public.

BRIJ VILAS PALACE MUSEUM

Near Kishore Sagar, this small **government museum** (admission Rs 3; ☾ 10am-5pm Sat-Thu) is also housed in a palace. It has a collection of miniature paintings, and some interesting 9th- to 12th-century stone idols and other sculptural fragments (mainly from Baroli and Jhalawar), such as Vishnu reclining on a serpent with Lakshmi (Vishnu's consort) at his feet.

Next door is a small, modern **art gallery** (admission free; ☾ 10am-5pm Mon-Sat) exhibiting works by local artists.

BOAT TRIPS

A lovely hiatus from the city is a Chambal River **boat trip**. Once you escape the industry near the town, it's beautiful, with lush vegetation and craggy cliffs on either side, and lots of opportunities to spot birds and crocodiles – so be sure you don't fall in. It costs Rs 25 for a 1½ hour trip and Rs 50 for a 3½-hour trip. Boats start from Chambal Gardens.

GARDENS

There are several well-maintained, peaceful gardens in Kota that provide a splash of greenery amid the industry. The **Chambal Gardens** are on the riverbank south of the fort, with a murky pond stocked with gavials (thin-snouted, fish-eating crocodiles) as a centrepiece, which you can walk over on a wobbly suspension bridge. Once common all along the river, by the mid-20th century these crocodiles had been virtually exterminated through hunting.

Next to the tourist reception centre are the **Chhattar Bilas Gardens**, a collection of overgrown but impressive royal cenotaphs interspersed with carved elephants.

Sleeping & Eating

Budget accommodation in Kota is lacklustre, but the city's reasonably well served for top-end hotels (where it's always worth asking for a discount). Understandably, however, most travellers prefer to base themselves in the more atmospheric town of Bundi. Mosquitoes can be a problem at some hotels in Kota, so come armed with repellent.

A few hotels have good restaurants, or you can graze on offerings from the early-evening snack stalls on the footpath outside the main post office.

BUDGET

Hotel Phul Plaza (☎ 2329351; s/d from Rs 375/475, with AC Rs 600/800; ✸) Next door to Hotel Navrang, this option is a clean, no-nonsense business hotel with ordinary rooms and overpriced suites. Rooms at the front are a bit noisy. There's a good vegetarian restaurant, serving a wide range of dishes.

Hotel Navrang (☎ 2323294; s/d from Rs 500/600, with AC Rs 800/1000; ✸) Better than the exterior suggests, the Navrang's rooms are worn but comfortable and arranged around a modern internal courtyard. Some have more character than others, so try to look at a few first. There's also a good veg restaurant, Venue (dishes Rs 35 to 60), open from 11am to 11pm.

Sukhdham Kothi (☎ 2320081; s Rs 560-920, d Rs 680-1200) Sukhdham Kothi is atmospheric, comfortable and over 100 years old and was once the home of the British Resident's surgeon. It's set in pretty gardens and is a friendly, family-run place. The inviting rooms have antique furniture, and some open onto terraces.

MIDRANGE & TOP END

Palkiya Haveli (☎ 2387497; Mokha Para; s/d Rs 900/1100; ☒) This is an exquisite *haveli* that has been in the same family for 200 years. It's a plant-filled oasis with impressive murals and six appealing rooms. The family is charming and helpful, and the food is excellent. The *haveli* is very close to the City Palace.

Brijraj Bhawan Palace Hotel (☎ 2450529; s/d from Rs 1700/2350) On an elevated site high above the Chambal River, this charismatic hotel is named after the current maharaja of Kota, Brijraj Singh, who lives with his family in part of the palace. Built in 1830 by the British East India Company, this was once the British Residency, and has attractive rooms opening onto riverside terraces. Some rooms, such as 4, are huge, with dizzyingly high ceilings. Queen Mary chose this for a snooze in 1911. There are well-maintained gardens, a croquet lawn and an intimate dining room (for guests only), which, unlike most palaces, is homy rather than grand.

Umed Bhawan Palace (☎ 2325262; s/d deluxe from Rs 2400/2900) Surrounded by sprawling gardens off Station Rd, this gracious palace is stuffily Edwardian and lacks the sparkle and intimacy of Sukhdham Kothi or the

Brijraj Bhawan Palace. Still, it's fancy and comfortable, and sports a restaurant, bar and billiard room.

Shopping

The Kota Doria Bazaars around Rampura Rd sell a wide range of *kota doria* (gold-woven saris), or you can hunt them down at their source in nearby Kaithoon (12km south of Kota, Rs 4 by bus, Rs 100 return in a rickshaw), where you'll find the widest selection and best quality. **Hamid Bihari** (Kota Saree Wala, Kaithoon; ☽ 10am-7pm), in Kaithoon near the police station, opposite Taileyan Mandirwhich, sells exquisite pieces, which you can see being woven upstairs. Prices range from Rs 600 to 2600.

Getting There & Away

BUS

There are plenty of express bus connections (see the table, above).

There are also buses for Delhi (Rs 280, 11 hours) and Mt Abu (Rs 290, 12 hours). Buses leave for Jhalawar (Rs 45, two hours) every half-hour.

TRAIN

Kota is on the main Mumbai–Delhi line so there are plenty of trains to choose from. There's a daily train to Agra which leaves at 7.45am, arriving in Agra at 1.35pm (Rs 115), and four daily trains to Delhi (Rs 630/883/1547 in 3AC/2AC/1AC, 6¼ to 10 hours). To Mumbai, there are two daily Rajdani services, which depart Kota at 9.05pm and 9.55pm (Rs 981/1390/2443 in 3AC/2AC/1AC, 12¼ hours). Seven daily trains run to Jaipur (Rs 408/562/965 in 3AC/2AC/1AC, four to five hours) and the daily *Mewar Express*, 2963, departs at 1.10am for Udaipur (Rs 473/656/1145 in 3AC/2AC/1AC, six hours).

BUSSES FROM KOTA

Destination	Fare (Rs)	Duration (hr)	Frequency
Ajmer	105	6	half-hourly
Bikaner	290	12	3 daily
Bundi	22	¾	half-hourly
Chittorgarh	95	6	5 daily
Jaipur	130	6	half-hourly
Jodhpur	195	11	3 daily
Udaipur	170	6	6 daily

THE MINI-MASTERPIECES OF KOTA & BUNDI

Some of Rajasthan's finest miniature work was produced around Bundi and Kota, the ruling Hada Rajputs being keen artistic patrons, and their influence and finances have left an exquisite legacy. The style combined the dominant features of folk painting – intense colour and bold forms – with the Mughals' concern with naturalism. See p61 for more on the development of miniature painting.

All the regions of Rajasthan produce paintings of individual character, but here they are even more distinctive. The schools were initially similar, but developed markedly different styles, though both usually have a background of thick foliage, cloudy skies and scenes lit by the setting sun. When architecture appears it is depicted in loving detail. The willowy women sport round faces, large petal-shaped eyes and small noses – forerunners of Bollywood pin-ups. Themes are often passionate, as well as being courtly or religious.

The paintings of the Bundi school are notable for their blue hues, with a palette of turquoise and azure unlike anything seen elsewhere. Bundi Palace in particular hosts some wonderful examples.

In Kota you'll notice the painters' penchant for hunting scenes, and for depicting the local foliage and fauna. Their dense woodland-packed paintings are unique, providing a vivid and detailed portrayal of hunting expeditions in Kota's once thickly wooded surrounds. Kota City Palace has some of the best-preserved wall paintings in the state.

Getting Around

Minibuses link the train station and bus stand (Rs 4). An autorickshaw should cost Rs 30 for this journey; there's a prepay place at the station. Cycle-rickshaws are, as always, a cheaper option (around Rs 20).

AROUND KOTA
Wildlife Sanctuaries

The thickly forested, wildly beautiful 250-sq-km **Darrah Wildlife Sanctuary** (Indian/foreigner Rs 20/100; ☺ 10am-5pm) is about 50km from Kota. Once a royal hunting ground, there are spotted deer, wild boars, bears, sambars, leopards and antelopes. The sanctuary is sometimes closed during the monsoon (usually from early July to mid-September). You need to get permission to visit from the local forest ranger, or contact the **District Forest Office** (☎ 0744-2321263) in Kota. If all else fails, ask at the Kota **tourist reception centre** (☎ 0744-2327695), where they should be able to provide you with information and costs for a trained accompanying guide.

About 45km east of Kota, flanking the main canal of the Chambal and Parvan Rivers, are the **Sorsan grasslands**. Covering 35 sq km, these grasslands are rich with insects during the monsoon and attract a good variety of resident and migratory birds, including the great Indian bustard – a reluctant flier more commonly seen stalking through the grasslands on its sturdy legs. Other, often fantastically named, birds of Sorsan include mynahs, orioles, quails, partridges, bulbuls, chats, drongos, shrikes, robins and weavers. Flocks of migrants, such as warblers, flycatchers, larks, starlings and rosy pastors, winter at Sorsan between October and March. The nearby canal and lakes attract waterfowl, such as bar-headed and greylag geese, common pochards, common teals and pintails.

You can hire a jeep with a driver to reach these parks from Kota for around Rs 5 per km. Ask at the tourist reception centre for details.

Baroli

One of Rajasthan's oldest temple complexes is at Baroli, 45km southwest of Kota on the way to Rana Pratap Sagar, the second dam on the Chambal River. Set in a peaceful rural area, many of these 9th-century temples were vandalised by Muslim armies, but much remains. The main edifice is the **Ghateshvara Temple**, which features impressive columns and a finely carved *sikhara* (temple spire). It's one of the best-preserved temples here, with figures including a dancing Shiva, Vishnu and Brahma. Inside it are five Shiva lingams – one of which looks like an upturned pot (*ghata*), hence the temple name. **Trimurti**, a ruined temple to the southeast, contains a three-headed Shiva.

Many of the sculptures from the temples are displayed in the Brij Vilas Palace Museum in Kota.

There are buses from Kota (Rs 25, 1½ hours, hourly) – tell the driver you want to be dropped off at Baroli. The buses leave from the Gumanpura bus stand, near the petrol pump.

Bhainsrodgarh

Near Baroli is picturesque Bhainsrodgarh, a 14th-century fort that was never besieged by enemies. Perched on a ridge overlooking the Chambal River, it's still occupied by descendants of a feudal family. Although you can't go inside, the views from outside at the top are superb. You need permission to visit – enquire at Kota's **tourist reception centre** (☎ 0744-2327695). You can reach Bhainsrodgarh by autorickshaw from Baroli (about Rs 150 return).

JHALAWAR

☎ 07432 / pop 48,049

Jhalawar is a quiet, sprawling town that sees few visitors but has some charming sights in the surrounding area, part of their appeal being that they are so seldom visited. Seven kilometres to the south is Jhalrapatan, the ancient walled City of Temple Bells, which has some beautiful temples, and 10km northeast is Gagron, a forgotten fort towering over the confluence of two rivers.

Jhalawar was once the capital of a small princely state created in 1838 by Zalim Singh, the charismatic regent of Kota. Singh signed a treaty with the British on behalf of the young Kota prince, and in return received Jhalawar to rule in his own right.

Situated 87km south of Kota, it stands at the centre of an opium-producing region, evidence of which you'll see during winter, when fields are carpeted with picturesque pink and white poppies.

Information

Though no banks in Jhalawar will currently change money, there's an SBBJ ATM in the Jhalawar Fort building.

Tourist office (☎ 230081; ⏳ 10am-5pm Mon-Sat) At the RTDC Hotel Chandrawati.

Sights & Activities

In the town centre is **Jhalawar Fort** (admission free; ⏳ 10am-5pm Mon-Sat), built by Maharaja Madan Singh in 1838. A run-down and sprawling cream-and-terracotta building, today it houses government offices and dusty rooms filled with piles of ledgers. Try, nevertheless,

to get a look in at the Zenana Khas room, which still has fine murals and mirrors, and at the Aina Mahal room, where indications of past glory compete with whirring institutional fans. Nearby there's also the small **government museum** (admission Rs 3; ⏳ 10am-5pm Mon-Sat), which has a curious collection comprising 8th-century sculptures, gold coins, weapons, old paintings, a handwritten copy of the Quran and a leopard-skin coat. The 1920s **Bhawan Natyashala**, inside the fort, was used for Parsi theatre, with a unique design including special underground constructions that allowed horses and carriages onto the stage.

Also interesting to visit is the **Government College Library** (⏳ 10am-1pm & 2-5pm), round the corner from the Hotel Dwarika. Topped by a *chhatri* (cenotaph, literally 'umbrella'), the great old building houses 70,000 books; edifying mottoes, including 'Books are the lighthouses erected in the great sea of time', adorn the walls.

Sleeping & Eating

Attracting only a smattering of tourists, Jhalawar has limited and uninspiring accommodation.

Purvaj Hotel (☎ 231355; r Rs 150-450) Near the clock tower is this simple, extremely run-down, 200-year-old *haveli*. Rooms are basic but cheap, and the building has more character than the other hotels in Jhalawar, with good views from the roof. Solo female travellers might prefer to stay elsewhere since the area can feel a bit deserted at night and in the early morning.

RTDC Hotel Chandrawati (☎ 512080; Jhalrapatan Rd; s/d Rs 300/350, with AC Rs 600/700) Also housing the tourist office, this is a pleasant compound with bare rooms around a leafy courtyard. 'Deluxe' rooms are overpriced, but there's a passable restaurant (dishes Rs 15 to 40).

Hotel Dwarika (☎ 232626; Hospital Rd; s/d Rs 300/350, deluxe Rs 400/450, with AC Rs 750/850) The best of the bunch, this hotel has rooms that are all almost exactly the same, except that the deluxe and air-con rooms have the luxury of hot water.

Rupali Dhani (Hospital Rd; dishes Rs 15-40; ⏳ 9am-11pm) Set opposite Hotel Dwarika, this is a friendly garden restaurant dishing up tasty Chinese, South Indian and veg dishes. The sign outside is in Hindi, but 'garden restaurant' is written in English.

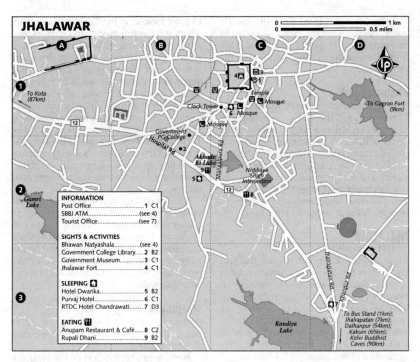

JHALAWAR

INFORMATION
Post Office..........................1 C1
SBBJ ATM..........................(see 4)
Tourist Office.....................(see 7)

SIGHTS & ACTIVITIES
Bhawan Natyashala............(see 4)
Government College Library....2 B2
Government Museum............3 C1
Jhalawar Fort.....................4 C1

SLEEPING 🏠
Hotel Dwarika....................5 B2
Purvaj Hotel.......................6 C1
RTDC Hotel Chandrawati.......7 D3

EATING 🍴
Anupam Restaurant & Café.....8 C2
Rupali Dhani.......................9 B2

Anupam Restaurant & Café (Patan Rd; dishes Rs 35-65; 🕙 9am-11pm) Another decent choice, this offers tasty veg and nonveg food in a small indoor restaurant.

Getting There & Away
There are regular buses between Jhalawar and Kota (Rs 43, two hours). The bus stand is 1km south of town.

Getting Around
If you plan to visit the historic sites outside of town, it's best to hire a jeep or taxi. Many of the roads are in a state of bumpy disrepair. Expect to pay Rs 5 per kilometre. The tourist office should be able to arrange jeep or taxi hire for you; otherwise, ask at your hotel. To travel anywhere in town by autorickshaw should cost Rs 20.

AROUND JHALAWAR
Jhalrapatan
Seven kilometres south of Jhalawar on the Kota road is Jhalrapatan (City of Temple Bells), on the banks of the holy Chandrabhaga River. This walled town once had more than

100 temples, although far fewer remain. The best known is the huge 10th-century **Surya Temple** (🕙 7am-noon & 5-10pm) at the centre, a spacious, high-ceilinged building that contains magnificent sculptures and one of the best-preserved idols of Surya (the sun god) in India. It has a glorious, high stupa with very intricate, almost organic carving. There's also the 12th-century **Shantinath Jain Temple** – colourful, brightly painted and restored with intricately carved statues, an inlaid black-and-white marble floor, and two huge stone elephants – and **Sheetaleshvara Temple**, a fine example of Gupta architecture. If you are visiting during November or December, you should look out for the huge Chandrabhaga Fair (p224), a lively cattle fair that consumes the town.

About 3km outside Jhalrapatan, the enchanting, peaceful 7th-century **Chandrabhaga Temple** is set in beautiful, lush, well-kept gardens on the banks of the Chandrabhaga River. Ghats (steps) along the riverbank neighbour some hidden-away erotic carvings.

There are regular daily buses from Jhalawar to Jhalrapatan (Rs 7, 15 minutes). An autorickshaw from Jhalawar will cost around Rs 100 return.

Gagron Fort

Don't miss a trip to the spectacular **Gagron Fort** (admission free; ☼ sunrise-sunset), 10km from Jhalawar, while you're in the area. It's set high above the confluence of the Kalisindh and Ahu Rivers and has big, big views, as the rivers surround the building on three sides, while on the fourth is a deep moat. Though not as famous as the forts at Chittorgarh, Jodhpur and Jaisalmer, the huge fort occupies a prominent place in the annals of Rajput chivalry and has been fought over for centuries. It was established in the 8th century, changed hands many times, and was the site of a huge *jauhar* in 1443. Later, it was conquered by the Mughal emperor Akbar.

For the best view of the fort itself, head to Changari, the little village on the outcrop opposite.

Near the fort walls there's the small village of **Gagron** and the **shrine of the Sufi saint Mitthesah**, constructed in 1423. The gate to the shrine was built by Akbar in 1580 and many pilgrims still come here during Ramadan.

An autorickshaw here should cost around Rs 150 return, but beware – the road is in a sorry state.

Other Attractions

The Jhalawar environs' other attractions are further out of town and difficult to reach without your own transport (a jeep is best as the roads are rough). About 54km (1½ hours) southeast of Jhalawar, at **Dalhanpur**, temple ruins near the Chhapi River include some carved pillars with erotic figures. Take care not to damage the fragments of pillars and statues that have fallen over. About 30km from Dalhanpur, at **Kakuni**, are the ruins of an old township on the Parvan River. Ruined 9th- to 12th-century temples are scattered around the area, one of which includes a huge idol of Ganesh. Beyond Kakuni is the large **Fort of Manohar Thana**, once of great strategic importance. There are several small temples within its walls, and a reforestation programme has filled the compound with vegetation and bird life.

There are ancient **Buddhist caves** and **stupas** atop a desolate hill near the town of **Kolvi**, about 90km south of Jhalawar. It's only a short climb to the top, where you'll find several enormous figures of Buddha. A narrow path winds past large stupas and numerous bat-filled meditation chambers. These 35 remarkable caves are believed to date back to the 5th century, and some contain weathered sculptures of Buddha, now sadly neglected and deteriorating.

BUNDI TO CHITTORGARH (CHITTOR)

If you're travelling by taxi from Bundi to Chittorgarh, there are various attractions worth stopping off at along the way.

Bijolia, a large town 16km northeast of Menal, was once a famous pilgrimage centre with 100 temples. Most of these were destroyed by Mughal invaders, and today only three are left standing. One of them, **Hajaresvara Mahadeva**, is devoted to Shiva, with delicate carving and a high lingam (phallic symbol) surrounded by lots of small lingams.

Menal, 48km from Bundi, is a complex of crumbling Shiva temples built in the Gupta period, with some striking statuary and a domed pavilion that affords superb views. Menal was once the retreat of Prithviraj Chauhan of Delhi, and there are a few ruined palaces. To the northwest of Menal, **Mandalgarh** is the third fort of Mewar to be built by Rana Kumbha (the others are the great fort of Chittorgarh and the fort at Kumbalgarh). The vast, sprawling ruins afford good views.

Bassi

The town of Bassi, about 30km northeast of Chittorgarh and well off the tourist trail, is famous for its woodcarvers, who create brilliantly coloured religious pieces (see Kavads, p236). There's also the **Bassi Wildlife Sanctuary** to explore, with its leopards, antelopes, wild boars and many birds; hotels here can arrange jeep safaris to the sanctuary with a day or so's notice.

Twenty kilometres southwest of Bassi, on the Chittorgarh road, is **Nagri**, one of Rajasthan's oldest towns. Hindu and Buddhist remains from the Mauryan to the Gupta periods have been found here, along with many old copper coins and sculptures, now gracing museum collections in Chittorgarh and Udaipur.

SLEEPING & EATING

There are a couple of top-end accommodation choices around Bassi, which are far better bets than the dingy Chittorgarh options.

SOUTHERN RAJASTHAN

KAVADS

The artisans of Bassi are famous for their brightly painted woodcarvings, and in particular the amazing folding boxes known as kavads. Carved from mango wood, these portable temples – usually painted in traffic-stopping reds or yellows – are made of a number of hinged doors that open outwards, each one covered in colourful pictures that illustrate the great Indian epics. They were the tools of professional bards, known as Kavadia Bhatts, who traditionally travelled from village to village chanting the tales of the Mahabharata (a Vedic epic poem of the Bharata dynasty), a skill that was handed down through the generations. As the stories unfolded, so did the boxes. At the climax of the tale, the last door opened to reveal the supreme deities – usually Rama, Lakshmana and Sita or Krishna. Somewhere near the bottom of the kavad there was always a slot where the audience could show their appreciation by depositing coins. Today, you can buy these magical boxes at the source in Bassi, or in shops in Udaipur.

Castle Bijaipur (www.castlebijaipur.com; s/d Rs 1550/1850; ❄ 🛋) The adorable Castle Bijaipur is a fantastically set 16th-century palace, apparently plucked from the whimsy of Udaipur and dropped into the rural village of Bijaipur, 18km south of Bassi. It's a great place to settle down with a good book, compose a fairy-tale fantasy or just laze around. Rooms are romantic and luxurious, there're a pleasant garden courtyard, and an airy restaurant serving Rajasthani food. Reservations should be made through Chittorgarh's Hotel Pratap Palace. The friendly owners can arrange horse or jeep safaris to places of interest around Bijaipur, such as the nearby Bhil tribal village, or a visit to their cool jungle property, Thanderiberi.

Bassi Fort Palace (☎ 01472-225321; www.bassifortpalace.com; s/d Rs 1700/1900, ste Rs 2000/2100, deluxe tents Rs 1300) This glorious meringue of a place is in the town's 450-year-old fort (which was never defeated) and set amid verdant hills. In case you need a spot of luck, ask for directions for the tree known as *kalp vraksha*, which is set in the grounds and is said to grant wishes. It's a peaceful spot with 16 lovely rooms arranged around a garden, or you can opt for the swish tented camp beside a lake in the wildlife sanctuary.

GETTING THERE & AWAY

Frequent buses travel daily from Chittorgarh to Bassi (Rs 15, 30 minutes), passing through Nagri on the way. A jeep taxi to Bassi costs around Rs 350. There are also buses from Chittorgarh to Bijaipur (Rs 20, 1½ hours), or you can get a return taxi for around Rs 350.

CHITTORGARH (CHITTOR)

☎ 01472 / pop 96,028

Chittorgarh holds a special place in the hearts of many Rajputs. Its fort is the greatest in

Rajasthan and has a history that epitomises Rajput romanticism, chivalry and tragedy. Three times Chittor was under attack from a more powerful enemy; each time, soldiers realised the odds were impossible and chose death before dishonour, performing *jauhar*. The men donned the saffron martyrs' robes and rode out from the fort to certain death, while the women and children immolated themselves on a huge funeral pyre.

The only real reason to come to Chittor is to see the fort – the town itself is quite grotty and not of much interest. An increasing number of industries are based in and around Chittorgarh, scarring the landscape around the fort and making the fort best visited on a day trip, or as a stop between Bundi and Udaipur.

History

Chittor is first mentioned in the Mahabharata, which tells that Bhim, one of the Pandava heroes, struck the ground here so hard that water gushed out to form a large reservoir. Its fort, founded by Bappa Rawal of Sisodia, dates back to the 8th century. The fort's first defeat came in 1303, when Ala-ud-din Khilji, the Pathan king of Delhi, besieged it, apparently in order to capture the beautiful Padmini, an adventure culminating in disaster and *jauhar* (see Death Before Dishonour, p240).

In 1535 Bahadur Shah, the sultan of Gujarat, besieged the fort again with the age-old aim of laying claim to some new territory. Once again, the medieval dictates of chivalry determined the outcome; this time it's thought that some 13,000 Rajput women and 32,000 Rajput warriors died following the declaration of *jauhar*.

The final sacking of Chittor came just 33 years later, in 1568, when the Mughal emperor Akbar took the town. Once again, the odds were overwhelming. The women performed *jauhar*, and 8000 orange-robed warriors rode out to die. On this occasion, Maharaja Udai Singh II fled to Udaipur, where he re-established his capital. In 1616 Jehangir returned Chittor to the Rajputs; no attempts were made to resettle, though the fort was restored in 1905.

Orientation

The fort is roughly fish-shaped, and stands on a 28-sq-km site on top of a 180m-high hill that rises abruptly from the surrounding plain. Until 1568 the town of Chittor was

contained within the fort walls, but today's modern town, known as Lower Town, clatters and sprawls to the west of the hill. A river separates it from the bus stand and the railway line.

Information

You can change money at the State Bank of Bikaner & Jaipur, a short distance north of the post office. There is also an SBI ATM in town.

Maharir Cyber Café (Collectorate Circle; per hr Rs 25; 9am-10pm) Internet access.

Main post office (10am-1pm & 2-6pm Mon-Sat) Less than 1km south of the bus stand.

Tourist reception centre (☎ 241089; 10am-1.30pm & 2-5pm Mon-Sat) Near the train station.

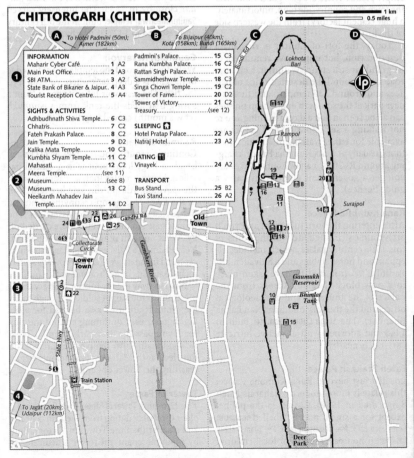

CHITTORGARH (CHITTOR)

INFORMATION		
Maharir Cyber Café	1	A2
Main Post Office	2	A3
SBI ATM	3	A2
State Bank of Bikaner & Jaipur	4	A3
Tourist Reception Centre	5	A4

SIGHTS & ACTIVITIES		
Adhbudhnath Shiva Temple	6	C3
Chhatris	7	C2
Fateh Prakash Palace	8	C2
Jain Temple	9	D2
Kalika Mata Temple	10	C3
Kumbha Shyam Temple	11	C2
Mahasati	12	C2
Meera Temple	(see 11)	
Museum	(see 8)	
Museum	13	C2
Neelkanth Mahadev Jain Temple	14	D2

Padmini's Palace	15	C3
Rana Kumbha Palace	16	C2
Rattan Singh Palace	17	C1
Sammidheshwar Temple	18	C3
Singa Chowri Temple	19	C2
Tower of Fame	20	D2
Tower of Victory	21	C2
Treasury	(see 12)	

SLEEPING		
Hotel Pratap Palace	22	A3
Natraj Hotel	23	A2

EATING		
Vinayek	24	A2

TRANSPORT		
Bus Stand	25	B2
Taxi Stand	26	A2

Sights

FORT

All Chittor's attractions are within the **fort** (Indian/foreigner Rs 5/100; ☼ sunrise-sunset). A zigzag ascent of more than 1km leads through seven gateways to the main gate on the western side, the **Rampol** (*pol* means 'gate'; the former back entrance).

On the climb you pass two **chhatris**, memorials between the second and third gates. These mark the spots where Jaimal and Kalla, heroes of the 1568 siege, fell during the struggle against Akbar. Jaimal had already been fatally wounded but was carried out by Kalla to fight on to the death. The main gate on the eastern side of the fort is known as the **Surajpol**, and offers fantastic views across the empty plains. There are also good views over the town and countryside (and, unfortunately, a huge cement factory) from the western side of the fort.

Today, the fort of Chittor is virtually a deserted ruin, but impressive reminders of its grandeur still stand. Within it, a circular road runs around the deserted ruins of palaces and around 130 temples, and there's a deer park at the southern end. The main sites can all be seen in half a day (assuming you're not walking – see opposite) and guides are available for either walking or autorickshaw tours, usually at Rana Kumbha Palace, charging around Rs 200 for a few hours. Make sure you get a government guide (they carry a guide licence).

Rana Kumbha Palace

After entering the fort, turn right and you'll arrive almost immediately at the ruins of this 15th-century **palace**, which includes elephant and horse stables and a Shiva temple. Padmini's *sati* is said to have taken place in a now-blocked cellar. Across from the palace is the museum and archaeological office, and the treasury building (Nau Lakha Bhandar). The **Singa Chowri Temple**, built in 1448 and adorned with attractive intricate carving, is nearby.

Fateh Prakash Palace

Located just beyond Rana Kumbha Palace, this **palace** is more modern (Maharaja Fateh Singh died in 1930). Closed to the public, except for a small, poorly labelled **museum** (admission Rs 3, free admission Mon; ☼ 10am-4.30pm Sat-Thu), it houses a school for local children

(around 4000 villagers still live within the fort's walls).

Tower of Victory

The glorious **Tower of Victory** (Jaya Stambha), symbol of Chittor, was erected by Rana Kumbha between 1458 and 1468 to commemorate his victory over Mahmud Khilji of Malwa in 1440. It rises 37m in nine exquisitely carved storeys, and you can climb the 157 narrow stairs (the interior is also carved) to the 8th floor, from which there's a good view of the area. Hindu sculptures adorn the outside; its dome was damaged by lightning and repaired during the 19th century.

Close to the tower is the **Mahasati** area where there are many *sati* (suicide by immolation) stones here – 13,000 women committed *jauhar* close by in 1535. The intensely carved **Sammidheshwar Temple**, built in the 6th century and restored in 1427, is nearby.

Gaumukh Reservoir

Walk down beyond the temple and at the edge of the cliff is a deep **tank** where you can feed the fish. The reservoir takes its name from a spring that feeds the tank from a *gaumukh* (cow's mouth) carved into the cliffside.

Padmini's Palace

Continuing south, you reach **Padmini's Palace**, beside a large lotus pool with a central pavilion. Legend relates that, as Padmini sat in this pavilion, Ala-ud-din saw her reflection in the lake. This glimpse convinced him to destroy Chittor in order to possess her. The bronze gates to this pavilion were carried off by Akbar and can now be seen in Agra Fort. Near Padmini's Palace is a small prison where captured invaders were kept; former prisoners include sultans of Malwa and of Gujarat.

Not far away are the former military training grounds for Rajput soldiers, though today the grounds are used as a helipad for visiting dignitaries. Continuing around the ring road, you pass the deer park, Bhimlat Tank, Adhbudhnath Shiva Temple, the Surajpol and the Neelkanth Mahadev Jain Temple before reaching the Tower of Fame.

Tower of Fame

The 22m-high **Tower of Fame** (Kirti Stambha) is older (probably dating from the 12th century) and smaller than the Tower of Victory. Built by a Jain merchant, the tower is dedicated to

Adinath, the first Jain *tirthankar* (one of the 24 revered Jain teachers) and is decorated with naked figures of various other *tirthankars*. A narrow stairway leads through the seven storeys to the top; though the staircase is usually locked, the gatekeeper may open the door for some baksheesh.

Rattan Singh Palace

While Padmini's Palace was the summer abode of the Chittor royals, the **winter palace** takes the name of her husband, Rattan Singh. It overlooks a small lake and, although run down, is an interesting place to explore.

Other Buildings

Close to the Fateh Prakash Palace is the **Meera Temple**, built during the reign of Rana Kumbha in the ornate Indo-Aryan style and associated with mystic-poetess Meerabai. She consumed poison sent by an enemy, but survived due to the blessings of Krishna. The larger temple in this same compound is the **Kumbha Shyam Temple** (Temple of Varah).

Across from Padmini's Palace is the **Kalika Mata Temple**, an 8th-century sun temple damaged during the first sack of Chittor and then converted to a temple for the goddess Kali in the 14th century. At the fort's northern tip is another gate, the **Lokhota Bari**, while at the southern end is a small opening once used for hurling criminals into the abyss.

Sleeping & Eating

Hotel standards in Chittor are generally disappointing; cleanliness and service are usually below average and many of the cheaper places have miserable bathrooms. If your budget stretches to top end, you're far better off staying in Bassi and visiting Chittor on a day trip.

Hotel Pratap Palace (☎ 243563; hpratap@hotmail .com; s/d Rs 1150-1500, deluxe r Rs 1250-1600, superdeluxe Rs 1800-2100; 🕃) Deservedly one of the most popular places to stay, the cheaper rooms are reasonable value, though nothing special, and the more expensive rooms have window seats and leafy outlooks. Next to a pleasant garden area there's a restaurant with good food. Village safaris and visits to the owners' castle in Bijaipur (p235) can be arranged.

Hotel Padmini (☎ 241718; hotel_padmini@rediffmail .com; s/d Rs 800/1000, with AC Rs 1250/1500; 🕃) Out of town near the Bearch River, Padmini has a garden with horses and kids' play equipment. The hotel is owned by a marble magnate, and thus is lined with his favourite stone. Some rooms have balconies looking out to the distant fort, though this is about their biggest asset.

Natraj Hotel (☎ 241009; Gandhi Rd; s without bathroom Rs 60-125, d Rs 90-250) Near the bus stand, this place has cheery reception staff who'll usher you through to small, dark rooms – still, it's an adequate option if you're counting the rupees while waiting for your bus or train.

Vinayek (Collectorate Circle; dishes Rs 15-60; 🕒 7am-11pm) Vinayek serves up North Indian veg dishes as well as Chinese and South Indian food. It's in a gloomy basement, but enlivened by its popularity and sweets counter.

Retiring rooms can be found at the train station. Doubles are Rs 100 or Rs 200 with AC. A simple but tasty vegetarian thali is available for a bargain Rs 20.

Getting There & Away

If you're coming from Bundi, it's possible to catch the early morning train to Chittor, spend three or four hours seeing the fort and then catch a bus on to Udaipur, or vice versa.

BUS

Express buses serve Delhi (Rs 350, 14 hours, two daily), and regularly go to Ajmer (Rs 125, five hours), Jaipur (Rs 175, eight hours), Udaipur (Rs 50/70 local/express, three/2½ hours) and Bundi (Rs 95, five hours), among other places.

TRAIN

The No 2966 *Udaipur–Jaipur Super Express* leaves Chittor at 9.40pm and arrives in Jaipur (sleeper Rs 357) at 7am.

For Udaipur (Rs 38 in 2nd class), the No 2965 *Chetak Express* leaves at 5.40am, arriving at 9am. Check at the station for details of other services to Ajmer, Bundi and Delhi: at the time of research, services were being scaled back.

Getting Around

It's about 6km from the train station to the fort (less from the bus stand) and 7km around the fort itself, not including the long southern loop out to the deer park. Autorickshaws charge around Rs 200 from the bus or train station to go around the fort, and back (including waiting time). You'll have to haggle, and make sure it's clear that you're going to visit the sights and have time to look around. A rickshaw between the bus and train stations should cost Rs 30.

DEATH BEFORE DISHONOUR

History has been kept alive by bards and folk songs in Rajasthan, and thus historical fact often merges with myth; this is the story told of the first sack of Chittor.

By the turn of the 14th century, much of North India had been conquered by the Mughals who ruled from Delhi. However, the *rana* (king) of Chittor, Rattan Singh, like many Rajput rulers, had managed to resist the invaders.

The jewel of the kingdom was Padmini, Rattan Singh's wife. Although she never left the zenana (women's quarters) uncovered, word had spread of her beauty, and Padmini was admired far beyond the sturdy walls of the fortress, even as far away as Delhi. The rumours aroused the curiosity of the Pathan king of Delhi, Ala-ud-din Khilji, and he decided to confirm them for himself.

In 1303 Ala-ud-din amassed his armies around Chittorgarh and sent word to Rattan Singh that he wanted to meet Padmini. Knowing his forces were no match for the sultan's armies, the *rana* reluctantly agreed, but set a number of conditions. The sultan was required to enter the fort unarmed; once inside, Ala-ud-din was not permitted to meet Padmini in person, but was only able to gaze upon her reflection in a mirror, while she sat well out of his reach inside a pavilion built (just to be sure) in the middle of a lotus pool.

But this glimpse was enough. Ala-ud-din was mesmerised and resolved to possess her at any cost. As Rattan Singh escorted him to the gate, Ala-ud-din gave an order to his forces lying in wait. The *rana* of Chittor was taken hostage and the ransom demanded for his return was Padmini herself.

The court was thrown into panic, until Padmini came up with a plan. She sent word that she agreed to Ala-ud-din's terms and soon a long train of 150 beautiful curtained palanquins, befitting great ladies of the court in purdah (the custom of keeping women in seclusion), trundled slowly out of the fort. The palanquins were Chittor's Trojan Horse – as soon as they had made their way into the sultan's camp, four armed Rajput warriors leaped out of each palanquin and rescued their leader.

The sultan was furious and laid siege to the fort, patiently waiting as the Rajputs slowly starved. It was clear the sultan could not be defeated, but the Rajputs couldn't consider the dishonour of surrender. Instead, a funeral pyre was lit in an underground tunnel. Padmini and all the ladies of the court put on their wedding saris and threw themselves into the fire as their husbands watched. The men then donned saffron robes, smeared sacred ashes on their foreheads and rode out of the fort to certain death.

Although it's clear that Ala-ud-din Khilji did lay siege to Chittor in 1303, and that the Rajput women indeed committed the horrific act of *jauhar,* it's also rumoured that the beautiful Padmini may have been invented by a 16th-century bard.

UDAIPUR

☎ 0294 / pop 389,317

> The most romantic spot on the continent of India
>
> *Colonel James Tod,* Annals & Antiquities of Rajasthan

A cupola-crowned city of cream, rose and honeysuckle hues, Udaipur – considered by many as the most romantic city in India – sits prettily on Pichola Lake, at the centre of which lies the Lake Palace, the creamiest, most wedding cake–like building of them all. A few years ago, when the monsoon rains were poor, there were fears that this magnificent, shimmering body of water might dry up altogether. Now the rains have finally returned and when

the lake is full, the palace once again seems to float, a grandiose piece of architectural frippery, as insubstantial as icing sugar.

The city sits in a valley surrounded by the ochre- and purple-shaded Aravalli Hills, dominated by the huge lakeside City Palace and overlooked by Sajjan Garh (Monsoon Palace), perched high on a peak as if plucked from a miniature painting. Udaipur is at its best if you step from the tourist epicentre into the jumbled streets of the old city, wander around the lake or find a rooftop to while away a dreamy afternoon. It's also surrounded by some dramatic countryside – folded peaks dotted with tiny villages – so it's rewarding to venture outside the city on foot or horseback, or by motorbike.

Udaipur is also a centre for arts, crafts and dance, and has a renowned school of miniature painting. West of the city is Shilpgram (p247), a village specially constructed to showcase the best of the region's arts. Here, you can see puppet shows and whirling dance displays, serenaded by some of the state's best musicians. The city is also a great place to shop, with miniature paintings, jewellery, brightly woven textiles, woodcarvings, handmade paper and puppets galore. If you're in Udaipur between February and March, moreover, you might be lucky enough to experience the festival of Holi, Udaipur-style, when the town comes alive in a riot of colour (p224). March to April, meanwhile, brings the procession-heavy Mewar Festival (p224) – Udaipur's own version of the springtime Gangaur festival – to town.

Although Colonel Tod's description (in *Annals & Antiquities of Rajasthan*) can still be trotted out, the old city around Lal Ghat is nowadays rife with rampant commercialism – every building is a hotel, shop, restaurant, travel agent or (most commonly) all four rolled into one. The city suffers, too, from mountains of plastic waste, ever-taller hotels competing for the best view and endless mediocre restaurants serving up a standard menu. And, like most Indian cities, Udaipur has more than its fair share of urban and industrial sprawl, along with the inevitable accompanying pollution, a discouraging first impression when you arrive at the city's train or bus station. Ignore it, though, and hurry on to the old city, where an utterly different world – despite the tourist trappings – still awaits.

History

Udaipur was founded in 1568 by Maharaja Udai Singh II following the final sacking of Chittorgarh by the Mughal emperor Akbar. According to legend, Udai Singh II found the site of his new capital some years before the last assault on Chittor, after coming across a holy man meditating on a hill near Pichola Lake, who advised the maharaja to establish his capital on that very spot. Since the site is surrounded by forests, lakes and the protective Aravalli Hills, the old man's advice was sound: the new capital of Mewar had a much less vulnerable location than Chittor.

Maharaja Udai Singh II died in 1572 and was succeeded by his son, Pratap, who bravely defended Udaipur from subsequent Mughal attacks and gallantly fought at the Battle of Haldighati in 1576. The Mewar rulers were fiercely independent; unlike many other rulers in Rajasthan, they refused to be controlled by foreign invaders, even though they were constantly under attack. After struggling against the Mughals, Udaipur then had to deal with the Marathas (central Indian people who controlled much of India at various times and fought the Mughals and Rajputs).

An end to all the bloody battles and instability came with British intervention in the early 19th century, when a treaty was signed that pledged to protect Udaipur from invaders – protection that lasted right up until 1947. At Independence, along with all the other princely states, Udaipur surrendered its sovereignty and became part of a united India.

Orientation

The old city, bounded by the meagre remains of a city wall, is on the east side of Pichola Lake. The train station and bus stand are both just outside the city wall to the southeast. Udaipur's aesthetically challenging urban sprawl ranges out beyond.

Information

A good website, with tourist and cultural information, can be found at www.udaipurplus.com.

BOOKSHOPS

Numerous places clustered around Lal Ghat purvey and exchange books. It's a good place to buy nonfiction and fiction about India, though books here can be more expensive than elsewhere in India. Novels, guidebooks and books about Rajasthan are widely available.

INTERNET ACCESS

You can surf the internet at plenty of places, particularly around Lal Ghat, though connections can sometimes be unbearably slow. Most places charge between Rs 30 and Rs 50 per hour. There are several reasonably swift internet options:

BA Photo N Book Store (Map p245; 69 Durga Sadan; per hr Rs 30; ⊙ 9.15am-11pm)

iWay (Map p245; Jagdish Temple Rd; per hr Rs 30; ⊙ 8am-11pm)

Mewar International (Map p245; 35 Lal Ghat; per hr Rs 30; ⊙ 9am-11pm)

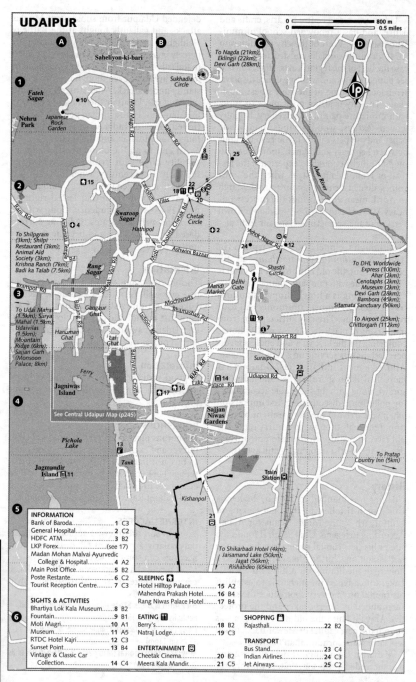

UDAIPUR

INFORMATION	
Bank of Baroda	1 C3
General Hospital	2 C2
HDFC ATM	3 B2
LKP Forex	(see 17)
Madan Mohan Malvai Ayurvedic	
College & Hospital	4 A2
Main Post Office	5 B2
Poste Restante	6 C2
Tourist Reception Centre	7 C3

SIGHTS & ACTIVITIES	
Bhartiya Lok Kala Museum	8 B2
Fountain	9 B1
Moti Magri	10 A1
Museum	11 A5
RTDC Hotel Kajri	12 C3
Sunset Point	13 B4
Vintage & Classic Car	
Collection	14 C4

SLEEPING	
Hotel Hilltop Palace	15 A2
Mahendra Prakash Hotel	16 B4
Rang Niwas Palace Hotel	17 B4

EATING	
Berry's	18 B2
Natraj Lodge	19 C3

ENTERTAINMENT	
Cheetak Cinema	20 B2
Meera Kala Mandir	21 C5

SHOPPING	
Rajasthali	22 B2

TRANSPORT	
Bus Stand	23 C4
Indian Airlines	24 C3
Jet Airways	25 C2

MEDICAL SERVICES
General hospital (Map p242; ☎ 2528811; Chetak Circle) For medical emergencies.

Madan Mohan Malvai Ayurvedic College & Hospital (Map p242; ☎ 2431900; Ambamata Temple Rd; ☯ 10am-5pm) Prescribes natural medicines and conducts free courses in Ayurveda. This government-run hospital was opened in 1944 and specialises in joint pain, paralysis and neurological disorders.

MONEY
There are lots of ATMs around, including an HDFC ATM (Map p245) near the main post office and a UTI ATM (Map p242) near Jagdish Temple. Three of the many places to change money are:

Bank of Baroda (Map p242; ☎ 2420671; ☯ 10am-2.30pm Mon-Fri, to 12.30pm Sat) About 200m southeast of Delhi Gate. Changes cash and gives credit-card advances.

LKP Forex (Map p242; ☎ 2423358; Lake Palace Rd; ☯ 9.30am-7pm Mon-Sat) Next to the Rang Niwas Palace Hotel. Changes numerous currencies.

Thomas Cook (Map p245; ☎ 2419746; City Palace Complex; ☯ 10am-1.30pm & 2-5pm) Changes travellers cheques and foreign currency.

POST
DHL Worldwide Express office (Off Map p242; ☎ / fax 2412979; 380 Ashok Nagar Rd; ☯ 9.30am-7.30pm Mon-Sat) Situated east of town. Has a free collection service within Udaipur and can arrange air freight around the world.

Main post office (Map p242; Chetak Circle; ☯ 10am-4pm Mon-Fri, to 3pm Sat) North of the old city (but note that the poste restante office is at Shastri Circle).

Post office (Map p245; ☯ 10.30am-1pm & 1.30-4.30pm Mon-Sat) Outside the City Palace Museum.

TOURIST INFORMATION
Apart from the tourist reception centre listed below, smaller tourist information counters operate at both the train station and the airport. The bimonthly *Out and About in Udaipur* magazine (Rs 10) contains lots of useful listings, and can be found at most Udaipur bookshops.

Tourist reception centre (Map p242; ☎ 2411535; Fateh Memorial Bldg; ☯ 10am-5pm Mon-Sat, closed 2nd & 4th Sat of month) Situated in not the most convenient position, near Surajpol and less than 1km from the bus stand, this place dishes out a limited amount of brochures and information. It can also arrange official guides for tours of the city; a four- to eight-hour tour should cost between around Rs 250 and 500.

TRAVEL AGENCIES
Udaipur has scores of small travel agencies (concentrated in the tourist-laden old city), all promising the best deals in town. It's definitely worth shopping around for the best price, as most will try to match or better the prices quoted to you by other agencies.

Dangers & Annoyances
If you have trouble with hotels, taxi or autorickshaw drivers (in the latter two cases, note down their vehicle registration number), contact the **police** (☎ 2412693) or report it to the **tourist reception centre** (☎ 2411535).

Sights
PICHOLA LAKE
Limpid and large, Pichola Lake (Map p242) reflects the cool grey blue mountains on its rippling mirrorlike surface. It was enlarged by Maharaja Udai Singh II, following his foundation of the city, by flooding Picholi Village, which gave the lake its name. The lake is now 4km long and 3km wide, but remains shallow and dries up in severe droughts, when you can walk to Jagniwas and Jagmandir, its two major islands, and camels and buffalo graze around the exposed foundations of the seemingly shipwrecked Lake Palace.

The lake is allegedly home to a handful of crocodiles, believed to reside near uninhabited sections of the shore (making it an unappealing option for swimming and wading); occasionally, the waters get choked up with water hyacinths.

The City Palace extends for a long stretch along the lake's east bank. South of the palace, a pleasant garden runs down to the shore. To the palace's north, you can wander along the waterfront to some interesting bathing and dhobi (laundry) ghats, where the slip-slap noises of the dhobi-wallahs (washerpeople) echo across the quiet waters.

Boat rides (Map p245; adult/child per 30min Rs 130/70, per 1hr Rs 250/130; ☯ 9.30am-5pm) leave half-hourly from the City Palace jetty (aka Bansi Ghat), when the lake water is high enough. The half-hour ride involves a quick trip around the lake, while the longer trip includes a 20-minute visit to Jagmandir Island. Note that nonguests have to pay Rs 25 to enter this area. If you're part of a group, you can also hire a whole boat for around Rs 2000 for the hour's trip

---

THE ULTIMATE SACRIFICE

In Udaipur a royal servant named Panna Dhai has been immortalised for the most extraordinary loyalty to the royal family that you could possibly imagine.

In 1535 Prince Udai Singh II was just a baby when his father, Vikramaditya, maharaja of Mewar, was assassinated by a character named Banbir. Banbir wanted control of the kingdom, and he was determined to eliminate anyone that stood in his way, including the young heir to the throne – Udai Singh himself. One night, Banbir managed to break into the prince's bedroom, planning to kill the baby boy.

Udai Singh's devoted *dhai* (wet nurse), Panna Dhai, was, however, one step ahead of him. At the time, Panna was also breastfeeding her own infant son, Chandan. Having already suspected Banbir's wicked intentions, she had placed, as a precaution, her Chandan in the prince's own cradle. When Banbir demanded to know which child was the prince, Panna Dhai pointed to the prince's cradle where her own son slept. Banbir whipped out his sword and slaughtered the child.

Soon after the murder, Panna Dhai hid the prince in a basket and fled to the fort at Kumbalgarh. She told the nobles and people of Mewar what had happened, and the prince was promptly crowned, ensuring the unbroken lineage of the Mewar dynasty.

The current maharaja of Udaipur has ensured the memory of Panna Dhai lives on with a special award at the annual Maharaja Mewar Foundation Awards ceremony. The Panna Dhai Award is given to an individual who 'ventures beyond the call of duty and sets an example in society of permanent value through sacrifice'.

Jagniwas Island

The world-famous Lake Palace Hotel island of Jagniwas (Map p245) is about 1.5 hectares in size, almost entirely covered by the opulent palace built by Maharaja Jagat Singh II in 1754. Once the royal summer palace, it was converted into the **Lake Palace Hotel** in the 1960s by Maharaja Bhagwat Singh and was, during the conversion, greatly extended. It remains the ultimate in the world's luxury hotels, with gleaming courtyards, fountains, restaurants and a swimming pool, and has been largely responsible for putting Udaipur on the international tourist map. You may also remember it from that classic Bond movie, *Octopussy*, along with the Shiv Niwas Palace and the Monsoon Palace. It is a magical place. Casual visitors, however, are discouraged; nonguests can only come over to experience its atmosphere over lunch or dinner (see p255). Hotel launches cross to the island from the City Palace jetty – note that nonguests have to pay Rs 25 to enter this area.

Jagmandir Island

The palace on Jagmandir Island (Map p242) was built by Maharaja Karan Singh in 1620, added to by Maharaja Jagat Singh during his reign between 1628 and 1652, and has changed very little in the four centuries since. It's said that the Mughal emperor Shah Jahan (then Prince Kharrim) derived some of his inspiration for the Taj Mahal from this palace after staying here in 1623 and 1624 while leading a revolt against his father, Jehangir. European women and children were later sheltered here by Maharaja Sarup Singh during the 1857 Indian Uprising. Flanked by a row of enormous stone elephants, the island has an impressive *chhatri* carved from grey bluestone, and fantastic views across the lake to the city and its golden palace. There's a small **museum** here in the main building, detailing the history of the island; apart from this, there are gardens to wander, filled with fragrant frangipani trees, flowers and neat courtyards, all tended by the island's only residents, three gardeners still in royal employ.

CITY PALACE & MUSEUMS

Surmounted by balconies, towers and cupolas towering over the lake, the imposing **City Palace** (Map p245) is Rajasthan's largest palace, with a façade 244m long and 30.4m high. Construction was begun by Maharaja Udai Singh II, the city's founder, and it later became a conglomeration of structures (including 11 separate smaller palaces) built and extended by various maharajas, though it still manages to retain a surprising uniformity of design. There are fine views over the lake and the city from the palace's upper terraces.

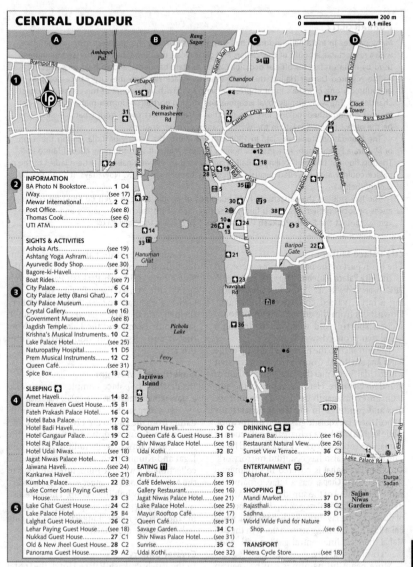

CENTRAL UDAIPUR

0 — 200 m
0 — 0.1 miles

INFORMATION
BA Photo N Bookstore..............1 D4
iWay..............................(see 17)
Mewar International................2 C2
Post Office.......................(see 8)
Thomas Cook......................(see 6)
UTI ATM...........................3 C2

SIGHTS & ACTIVITIES
Ashoka Arts......................(see 19)
Ashtang Yoga Ashram...............4 C1
Ayurvedic Body Shop..............(see 30)
Bagore-ki-Haveli..................5 C2
Boat Rides.......................(see 7)
City Palace.......................6 C4
City Palace Jetty (Bansi Ghat)...7 C4
City Palace Museum................8 C3
Crystal Gallery..................(see 16)
Government Museum................(see 8)
Jagdish Temple....................9 C2
Krishna's Musical Instruments...10 C2
Lake Palace Hotel................(see 25)
Naturopathy Hospital.............11 D5
Prem Musical Instruments.........12 C2
Queen Café.......................(see 31)
Spice Box.........................13 C2

SLEEPING
Amet Haveli......................14 B2
Dream Heaven Guest House.........15 B1
Fateh Prakash Palace Hotel.......16 C4
Hotel Baba Palace................17 D2
Hotel Badi Haveli................18 C2
Hotel Gangaur Palace.............19 C2
Hotel Raj Palace.................20 D4
Hotel Udai Niwas................(see 18)
Jagat Niwas Palace Hotel.........21 C3
Jaiwana Haveli..................(see 24)
Kankarwali Haveli...............(see 21)
Kumbha Palace....................22 D3
Lake Corner Soni Paying Guest
  House...........................23 C3
Lake Ghat Guest House............24 C2
Lake Palace Hotel................25 B4
Lalghat Guest House..............26 C2
Lehar Paying Guest House........(see 18)
Nukkad Guest House...............27 C1
Old & New Jheel Guest House......28 C2
Panorama Guest House.............29 A2

Poonam Haveli....................30 C2
Queen Café & Guest House.........31 B1
Shiv Niwas Palace Hotel.........(see 16)
Udai Kothi.......................32 B2

EATING
Ambrai...........................33 B3
Café Edelweiss..................(see 19)
Gallery Restaurant..............(see 16)
Jagat Niwas Palace Hotel........(see 21)
Lake Palace Hotel...............(see 25)
Mayur Rooftop Café..............(see 17)
Queen Café......................(see 31)
Savage Garden....................34 C1
Shiv Niwas Palace Hotel.........(see 31)
Sunrise..........................35 C2
Udai Kothi......................(see 32)

DRINKING
Paanera Bar.....................(see 16)
Restaurant Natural View.........(see 26)
Sunset View Terrace..............36 C3

ENTERTAINMENT
Dharohar........................(see 5)

SHOPPING
Mandi Market.....................37 D1
Rajasthali.......................38 C2
Sadhna...........................39 D1
World Wide Fund for Nature
  Shop...........................(see 6)

TRANSPORT
Heera Cycle Store...............(see 18)

Entering the palace from the north, you'll come through the Baripol (Great Gate; 1600) and the three-arched Tripolia Gate (1725). To the left, seven arches commemorate the seven times maharajas were weighed here and their weight in gold or silver distributed to the lucky locals. The ticket office is here too, where guides can be hired for Rs 100 to Rs 150 (maximum of five people).

In the large rectangular courtyard set outside the museum, there are a number of pricey handicraft shops, a **World Wide Fund for Nature** (WWF; Map p245; 9.30am-5.30pm) shop, a Thomas Cook office, a post office and banks.

SOUTHERN RAJASTHAN

DURBAR GLITZ

Many palaces in India have a durbar hall (royal court). Usually the grandest room in the place, with a respectable amount of chandeliers and gilt overlay, the durbar hall was dressed to impress, used by India's rulers for official occasions, such as state banquets, and to hold meetings.

The restored Durbar Hall at the Fateh Prakash Palace Hotel in the City Palace complex is undoubtedly one of India's most impressive, vast and lavish, with some of the country's hugest chandeliers. The walls display royal weapons and striking portraits of former maharajas of Mewar (a most distinguished-looking lot). The illustrious Mewar rulers come from what is believed to be the oldest ruling dynasty in the world, spanning 76 generations.

The foundation stone was laid in 1909 by Lord Minto, the viceroy of India, during the reign of Maharaja Fateh Singh. As a mark of honour to Lord Minto, it was originally named Minto Hall. The top floor of this high-ceilinged hall is surrounded by viewing galleries, where ladies of the palace could watch in veiled seclusion what was happening below. Nowadays, it's the Crystal Gallery (below).

The hall still has the capacity to hold hundreds of people and can even be hired for conferences or social gatherings. If you find yourself in need of just such an imposing and expansive venue, contact the **Fateh Prakash Palace Hotel** (☎ 2528019; www.hrhindia.com).

City Palace Museum

The main part of the palace is now preserved as the **City Palace Museum** (Map p245; adult/child Rs 50/30, camera/video Rs 200; ◷ 9.30am-4.30pm), housing a large, varied collection of artefacts. Downstairs from the entrance is an armoury section sporting old weapons, including a lethal two-pronged sword.

The entrance to the museum leads up to the **Rajya Angan** (Royal Courtyard), the very spot where Udai Singh met the sage who told him to found his city here. Here, the rooms of the museum are extravagantly decorated with mirrors, tiles and paintings. In the **Manak Mahal** (Ruby Palace) there is exquisite glass- and mirrorwork, while **Krishna Vilas** has a remarkable collection of miniatures (no photography is permitted here). The **Moti Mahal** also has beautiful mirrorwork, and the **Chini Mahal** is covered in ornamental tiles. The **Surya Chopar** has a huge, ornamental sun – the symbol of the sun-descended Mewar dynasty. **Mor Chowk** (Peacock Sq) holds mosaics of peacocks, the favourite Rajasthani bird, while **Bhim Vilas** has a striking striped floor. In the **Bari Mahal** there's a fine central garden with good views over the old city.

More beautiful paintings can be seen in the **Zenana Mahal**, which opens onto **Laxmi Chowk**; there's a beautiful white pavilion in the centre of this square. Take note of the large tiger-catching cage, which worked rather like an oversized mousetrap, near the Zenana Mahal entrance.

Palace ladies once used the gallery to observe the grand **Durbar Hall** (above).

Inside the separate palace enclosure, entered from the south of Badi Chowk, are the Shiv Niwas and Fateh Prakash Palace Hotels (p253), the Sunset View Terrace (p256), the Gallery Restaurant (p255), the Crystal Gallery (below), and the boat wharves for trips out to Jagmandir Island and the Lake Palace. Note that it costs Rs 25 for nonguests to enter this area.

Government Museum

Inside the city palace complex, there's also a **government museum** (Map p245; admission Rs 3; ◷ 10am-4.30pm Sat-Thu). There are inscriptions dating from the 2nd to the 17th centuries, and some wonderful sculpture dating from the 5th century onwards, including pieces from Jagat and Kumbalgarh. It also has a splendid collection of jewel-like miniature paintings of the Mewar school. Stranger exhibits include a stuffed monkey holding a lamp. There are also regal maharaja portraits in profile, documenting the palace's rulers along with the changing fashions of the moustache.

Crystal Gallery

In the Fateh Prakash Palace Hotel, the **Crystal Gallery** (Map p245; adult/child Rs 325/165; ◷ 10am-1pm & 3-8pm) houses rare crystal that Maharaja Sajjan Singh ordered from F&C Osler & Co in England in 1877. The maharaja died before it arrived, and all the items stayed forgotten and packed up in boxes for 110 years. The extraordinary, extravagant collection includes crystal chairs, sofas, tables and even beds. There's an exquisite antique jewel-studded carpet that has to be seen to be believed. The rather hefty admission fee includes a soft drink, tea or coffee in the Gallery Restaurant (see p255), where a nice high tea is served daily. Admission also includes entry to the grand Durbar Hall (opposite). No photography is permitted.

JAGDISH TEMPLE
Only 150m north of the City Palace entrance, this busy, fantastically carved Indo-Aryan **temple** (Map p245; 5am-2pm & 4-10.30pm) was built by Maharaja Jagat Singh in 1651. It enshrines a black stone image of Krishna as Jagannath, Lord of the Universe; there's a brass image of the Garuda (man-bird vehicle of Vishnu) in a shrine in front of the temple, and the temple's steps are flanked by elephants. You can donate money, which is used to feed the hungry, between 11am and noon.

BAGORE-KI-HAVELI
This gracious 18th-century **haveli** (Map p245; admission Rs 25; 10am-5.30pm), set on the water's edge in the Gangaur Ghat area, was built by a former prime minister and has been carefully restored. There are 138 rooms set around courtyards, some arranged to evoke the period during which the house was inhabited, and others housing cultural displays, including – intriguingly enough – the world's biggest turban. The *haveli* also houses an interesting art gallery, featuring contemporary and folk art, and an eclectic selection of world-famous monuments lovingly carved out of polystyrene. The upper courtyard makes an atmospheric setting for the fabulous Rajasthani dance performances at 7pm (see p256).

FATEH SAGAR
North of Pichola Lake, this lake (Map p242) – which dries up if the monsoon has been poor – is ringed by hills and is a popular hangout for lovestruck locals. Overlooked by a number of hills, it was originally built in 1678 by Maharaja Jai Singh but reconstructed by Maharaja Fateh Singh after heavy rains destroyed the dam. A pleasant drive winds along the east bank. In the middle of the lake is **Nehru Park**, a garden island. An autorickshaw from the old city costs Rs 30 (one way).

MOTI MAGRI
Overlooking Fateh Sagar, atop Moti Magri (Pear Hill; Map p242), is a statue of the Rajput hero Maharaja Pratap, who frequently defied the Mughals while riding his beloved horse, Chetak (see Haldighati, p258 for more about this noble quadruped). The path to the top passes a pleasant **Japanese Rock Garden** (Map p242; adult/child Rs 20/10; 7.30am-7pm). Car/rickshaw/motorcycle/bicycle entry costs Rs 20/10/5/1.

BHARTIYA LOK KALA MUSEUM
The interesting collection exhibited by this small **museum** (Map p242; 2529296; Indian/foreigner Rs 20/35, camera/video Rs 10/50; 9am-6pm) and foundation for the preservation and promotion of local folk arts includes a dusty collection of dresses, turbans, dolls, masks, musical instruments, paintings and – its high point – puppets. Diverting **puppet shows** (Indian/foreigner Rs 30/50), a good reason to visit if you're travelling with children, are staged at intervals throughout the day (depending on demand), with a one-hour performance at 6pm.

SAHELIYON-KI-BARI
In the north of the city, the **Saheliyon-ki-Bari** (Garden of the Maids of Honour; Map p242; admission Rs 5; 9am-7pm) was built by Sangram Singh II in 1710. This small, quaint ornamental garden was laid out for the enjoyment of 48 women attendants who came as part of a princess's dowry and has beautiful, well-maintained fountains (water shortages permitting; you may have to pay to see them turned on), kiosks, marble elephants and a delightful lotus pool.

SHILPGRAM
A crafts village 3km west of Fateh Sagar lake, **Shilpgram** (Off Map p242; admission Rs 25, camera/video Rs 10/50; 11am-7pm), was inaugurated by Rajiv Gandhi in 1989. Set in dusty, rolling countryside, it's contrived but remains interesting. There are displays of traditional mud huts with glittering mirrored interiors from Rajasthan, Gujarat, Goa and Maharashtra. Best, though, are the excellent demonstrations by traditional performers and artisans (crafts are on sale, though they might not be of the highest quality). There are always splendid groups ready to perform as you approach (you'll be expected to proffer a tip if you stay to watch), though it can feel deserted of visitors on a weekday and even more so out of season. The best reason to visit is if you're in town for the festival here

in December: it's a fantastic spectacle, often with hundreds upon hundreds of artisans in attendance. Check with the tourist reception centre (p243) for details.

Shilpi Restaurant (Off Map p242; dishes Rs 50-112; ☼ 11.30am-10.30pm), next to the crafts village site, is a pleasant open-air restaurant serving good veg and nonveg Indian, Continental and Chinese food. It also has a **swimming pool** (admission Rs 100; ☼ 11am-8pm).

Some people walk or cycle out to Shilpgram; a return autorickshaw trip (including a 30-minute stop) between the old city and Shilpgram costs Rs 100.

AHAR

About 2km east of Udaipur, at Ahar (Off Map p242), are more than 250 restored **cenotaphs** (Off Map p242) of the maharajas of Mewar, forming a spectacular city of snowy domes built over 350 years. Around 19 former maharajas were cremated here, and the most striking cenotaph is that of Maharaja Amar Singh, who ruled from 1597 to 1620. Nearby you can visit the remains of an ancient city – the Sisodias' capital – and a **museum** (Off Map p242; admission Rs 5; ☼ 10am-5pm) housing some accompanying artefacts, including a collection of earthen pottery, sculptures and other archaeological finds. Some pieces date back to 1700 BC, and there's a beautiful 10th-century metal figure of Buddha. Photography is not permitted. Not many tourists make it out here, but the sites, despite being rather unkempt these days, make it worth the trip. A return trip by autorickshaw should cost around Rs 80, including waiting time.

SAJJAN GARH (MONSOON PALACE)

Perched on top of a distant mountain range like a fairy-tale castle, this melancholy, neglected late-19th-century palace (Off Map p242) was constructed by Maharaja Sajjan Singh. Originally an astronomical centre, it became a monsoon palace and hunting lodge. Now government owned, it's open to the public after lengthy closure, but there's not much to see but neglect. You pay Rs 80/20 per person/rickshaw at the foot of the hill to enter the Sajjan Garh Wildlife Sanctuary. The main reason to visit is for the breathtaking views, particularly at sunset. Autorickshaw return trips cost Rs 150 (including waiting time).

OTHER ATTRACTIONS

The maharajas' **Vintage & Classic Car Collection** (Map p242; ☎ 2420979; Lake Palace Rd; admission Rs 100; ☼ 9-11am & 2-6pm) makes a fascinating diversion. Housed in the former state garage are 22 splendid vehicles, including a 1938 Cadillac complete with purdah system, the beautiful 1934 Phantom Rolls Royce used in *Octopussy*, a homely little Morris Minor Traveller from 1959, and the Cadillac convertible that whisked Queen Elizabeth II to the airport in 1961.

Sunset Point (Map p242; admission Rs 5) is a lovely, easy-to-reach sunset spot, with dazzling views over Pichola Lake, Jagmandir Island and off toward the Monsoon Palace. There's a musical fountain here (drought permitting), which plays each evening.

The huge **fountain** (Map p242) in the middle of Sukhadia Circle, north of the city, is illuminated at night. **Sajjan Niwas Gardens** (Map p242), near the Vintage & Classic Car Collection, has a rose garden, pleasant lawn, and a zoo.

Almost 5km beyond Shilpgram, 7.5km west from town, is the mammoth artificial lake **Badi ka Talab** (Tiger Lake). Flanked by hills, it's a great place to head for some relaxation and a picnic. Crocodiles apparently lurk in parts of the lake, so swimmers beware. Near the lake there's a small **Shiva and Hanuman temple**. An autorickshaw to the lake should cost Rs 100/200 one-way/return (with a one-hour wait).

Activities

See p243 for information about boat rides.

AYURVEDA

Madan Mohan Malvai Ayurvedic College & Hospital (Map p242; ☎ 2431900; Ambamata Temple Rd; ☼ 10am-5pm) prescribes natural medicines and conducts free courses in Ayurveda.

HORSE RIDING

Kumbha Palace (p252) arranges highly recommended riding excursions, for both beginners and experienced riders, around Udaipur. A half-/full-day excursion costs Rs 700/1300 (including lunch and water) and takes you wandering on four legs through hills and local villages.

Pratap Country Inn (p252) also runs horse safaris, as does tour operator **Princess Trails** (☎ 09829042012; www.princesstrails.com), which is a German-and-Indian-owned company that

THE ULTIMATE SLICE OF WEDDING CAKE

Getting married? If you want to play the ultimate game of prince and princess, you couldn't do much better than Udaipur, with its palaces already dressed in white for the day. The city has become a favourite wedding venue for foreigners – many have travelled thousands of miles to take the plunge in this dreamy destination.

Plump in the middle of Pichola Lake, the gorgeous Lake Palace Hotel, itself resembling a huge, elaborate wedding cake, was once the exclusive summer residence of Udaipur's maharajas, but today is accessible to anyone who can afford the rather hefty prices. There are several sumptuous venues to choose from within the palace: if you're a bit of a Bond fiend, then the Lily Pond, which starred in *Octopussy*, may appeal to you. For those wanting to get hitched on the waters of the lake itself, there's the Gangaur Boat, a graceful old royal barge belonging to the maharaja of Udaipur.

Arrangements for these, and several other sorts of weddings, can be made by staff at the Lake Palace Hotel itself. Most kinds of wedding ceremonies are possible: if you intend to be married by a Christian priest, you must send a Certificate of No Impediment (issued by a church in your country of residence) to the hotel at least a month prior to your wedding date. If you opt for a Hindu ceremony, the hotel can advise you on where to find traditional Rajasthani wedding clothes and on the conventions and etiquette surrounding such an event.

Whatever your wedding preferences, you're advised to make reservations for the big day at least six months ahead: bear in mind that the best and most pleasant time to get married is during the cooler months between November and March. For prices and further information, contact the food and beverages manager at the **Lake Palace Hotel** (☎ 2528800; lakepalace.udaipur@ tajhotels.com; Post Box 5, Udaipur 313001, Rajasthan).

The Lake Palace isn't the only location offering weddings to intrepid travellers. It's also possible to arrange your event at the beautiful, opulent Shiv Niwas Palace Hotel (see p253), where venues include the poolside, the lawns and the top terrace. For a big bash, there's the Fateh Prakash Palace Hotel's grand Durbar Hall (see Durbar Glitz, p246), while its Sunset View Terrace is perfect for more intimate gatherings. Otherwise, you could go for evocative Jagmandir Island, with its fantastic colonnaded terrace overlooking the lake – here there are venues that can accommodate from 30 to 500 people. There are also various courtyards within the City Palace itself. For these venues, you must contact the sales and marketing manager, HRH Group of Hotels at the **City Palace** (☎ 1600-332933; www.hrhindia.com; Udaipur 313001, Rajasthan). Check out more details on the website. If at all possible, it's worth visiting all the venues you're considering before making a choice.

---

offers mostly multiday excursions on thoroughbred Marwari steeds.

MASSAGE

The **Ayurvedic Body Shop** (Map p245; ☎ 5120802; 39 Lal Ghat; head/full-body massage Rs 100/500, 15min back massage Rs 200; ☷ 10.30am-9pm) offers Ayurvedic massages and has some good products on sale, such as oils, moisturisers, shampoos and soaps.

You can also indulge in a massage at the **Naturopathy Hospital** (Map p245; ☎ 2422700; cnr Battiyanni Chotta & Lake Palace Rd; 30min massage Rs 50; ☷ 8am-2pm Mon-Sat, 8-11am Sun), though 'indulge' may be the wrong word. You'll be rubbed down vigorously by one or two masseurs in a room of uncertain cleanliness. It may not be relaxing, but it's certainly an invigorating experience – and it's cheap too.

TREKKING

Exploring the surrounding countryside and villages on foot is a fantastic way to see rural and tribal life while taking in some beautiful scenery. Piers at **Mountain Ridge** (☎ 3291478; www .mountainridge.in; Sisarma) can organise a knowledgeable guide for you; others are loosely attached to guesthouses, so enquire at your hotel or seek out recommendations from fellow travellers.

Courses

See opposite for information on courses in Ayurveda.

COOKING

Spice Box (Map p245; ☎ 5100742; spicebox2001@yahoo .co.in; 38 Lal Ghat) offers recommended hands-on cooking lessons (Rs 400 to 500 for four hours), in which you learn to cook a selection of dishes and then eat the results.

Queen Café (Map p245; ☎ 2430875; 14 Bajrang Rd) A four-hour introductory cooking lesson – encompassing a grand 14 dishes – costs Rs 900 and is a fantastic, fragrant way to chop and sizzle away the afternoon.

MUSIC

Bablu at **Prem Musical Instruments** (Map p245; ☎ 2430599; 28 Gadia Devra) gives sitar, tabla and flute lessons (Rs 100 per hour). He also sells and repairs those instruments and can arrange performances. Krishna at **Krishna's Musical Instruments** (Map p245; 37 Lal Ghat) also offers recommended lessons.

PAINTING

Ashoka Arts (Map p245; Hotel Gangaur Palace) runs painting lessons (Rs 150 for two to three hours, including materials).

YOGA

Ashtang Yoga Ashram (Map p245; ☎ 2524872; Raiba House), inside Chandpol, is a friendly hatha yoga centre with yoga classes every morning at around 8am. The teacher has 20 years' experience, and payment is by donation (proceeds go to the local Animal Aid hospital).

Tours

Five-hour **city tours** (per person excl admission charges Rs 90, minimum 5 people) leave at 8am from the RTDC Hotel Kajri (Map p242) and take in the main sights. There are also **excursions** (per person excl admission charges incl veg lunch Rs 330) to Ranakpur and Kumbalgarh. Contact the tourist reception centre (p243) for more information.

Sleeping

Staying close to the lakeshore is undoubtedly the most romantic Udaipur option. West of Jagdish Temple and close to the shores of the lake, the Lal Ghat area is crowded with places offering masses of choice. Otherwise, opt for the quieter and less-tourist-filled Hanuman Ghat on the other side of the lake, which often has even better views. Always make sure to ask for a lake-facing room, though, not surprisingly, these will be more expensive. In the low season, prices plummet – so it's well worth bargaining.

The hotel room commission racket operates in Udaipur with a vengeance, so if you're unlucky enough to get an autorickshaw driver who insists that the hotel of your choice has burnt down or suddenly closed, firmly decline his kind alternative offer. To attempt to bypass rapacious rickshaw drivers altogether, try to use the police-supervised prepaid autorickshaw stands outside the train and bus stations. Some unscrupulous drivers will still try to take you to the hotel of their choice, but remember: they don't get reimbursed until you hand over the receipt at the end of your journey.

If you're heading for Lal Ghat to begin an accommodation search, ask to be deposited at Jagdish Temple, a good place to start looking. An autorickshaw from the bus stand to Jagdish should cost about Rs 30. See Dangers & Annoyances (p243) for info on what to do if you have trouble with hotels or rickshaw drivers.

BUDGET

Udaipur pioneered the Paying Guest House Scheme in Rajasthan. Expect to pay Rs 100 to Rs 300 per night. The tourist reception centre has a list detailing all the places and services offered.

Lal Ghat Area

Lalghat Guest House (Map p245; ☎ 2525301; lalghat@ hotmail.com; 33 Lal Ghat; dm Rs 75, s/d Rs 250-350, s without bathroom Rs 125, d without bathroom Rs 150-200; 🖳) This mellow guesthouse by the lake was one of the first to open in Udaipur, and, though looking a little worn around the edges, it's still a sound choice. The rooftop areas have superb lake views and are a serene place to sunbathe, and there's a back terrace overlooking the ghats. Accommodation ranges from spruce, end-to-end dorm beds (with curtained-off beds) to their top range room, which sports arched windows and thick walls (Rs 350). Rooms in the older part of the building generally have a lot more character. All the rooms have fans and mosquito nets, and there's a small kitchen for self-caterers.

Hotel Gangaur Palace (Map p245; ☎ 2422303; Gangaur Ghat Rd; r Rs 100-400) This whitewashed, elaborate, faded *haveli* is set around a courtyard. The pricier rooms are atmospheric though basic, with wall paintings, window seats and private bathrooms; the cheaper rooms are simple and share a bathroom, but are fine. Rooms with a lake view are the most expensive. The hot water is a bit iffy. In case you need help with where to go from here,

---

KEEPING UDAIPUR GREEN

Slowly, Udaipur guesthouse proprietors are realising that it pays to be green, not only for the future of their city but also to attract eco-conscious travellers. You'll probably notice solar panels on lots of hotel rooftops, and the maharaja himself has been investing in high-tech solar-powered autorickshaws to do his bit towards a cleaner future for the environmentally hard-pressed city.

Much of the new green movement has been instigated by **Shikshantar** (☎ 2451303; www .swaraj.org/shikshantar) a community group advocating a 'no waste' Udaipur, which has created a 'green leaf' rating for hotels, based on 14 different criteria, including energy usage and waste management. Check out their website for current ratings.

In order to do your bit towards keeping Udaipur the treasure it is today, consider cutting to a minimum the amount of plastic you consume. Some hotels, for example, offer filtered water to refill mineral water bottles; also try to carry a bag with you for your shopping, rather than picking up numerous plastic bags en route. Look out for recycling points for plastics you do use; consider walking instead of taking autorickshaws when and where you can; and even the old 'don't change your bath towels every day' mantra of top-end hotels is sure to help a little bit.

---

there's a palm reader working here from 2pm to 5pm, who charges Rs 50 to 100.

Lake Corner Soni Paying Guest House (Map p245; ☎ 2525712; 27 Navghat Rd; s/d from Rs 140/180, without bathroom from Rs 100/140) Tucked away close to the City Palace is this simple courtyard-centred guesthouse. It's run by a lovely elderly couple and is imbued with a family atmosphere, though the rooms themselves are a little shabby. Mr Soni offers Hindi lessons, the home cooking is excellent, and there's a great view from the rooftop.

Nukkad Guest House (Map p245; 56 Ganesh Ghat Rd; r from Rs 150-250) Staying at the Nukkad means renting one of 10 simple rooms – some with attached bathroom – in an extremely friendly family house. There's terrific home-cooked food on offer and a nice rooftop. Follow the signs for the guesthouse from Jagdish Temple.

Lehar Paying Guest House (Map p245; ☎ 2417651; 86 Gangaur Ghat Rd; d Rs 150-700) Run by a redoubtable matriarch, this place has five squeaky-clean rooms in an old building, some of which (usually the costlier ones) are decorated with wall paintings and coloured glass. The very best room has its own little courtyard and is considerably more comfy than the others.

Hotel Udai Niwas (Map p245; ☎ 5120789; www .hoteludainiwas.com; Gangaur Ghat Rd; r Rs 200-1000;) A bright new hotel occupying a narrow space off Ganguar Ghat, Udai Niwas has excellent, spotless rooms that feel much more luxurious than their price range would suggest. They're painted white and decorated with puppets and wall hangings – the cheapest rooms are a real bargain. Staff are nice and helpful, and there's

a good travel agency and internet café. The hotel claims the highest rooftop in Udaipur – we're unsure if building so high should be encouraged, but for views alone this is a very good choice.

Old & New Jheel Guest House (Map p245; ☎ 2421352; 56 Gangaur Ghat; d Rs 250-800) Both Old and New Jheel are right down by the ghat. Old Jheel Guest House is in an old *haveli*, and accommodation ranges from basic back rooms to one with a small balcony and three lake-facing windows. Nearby New Jheel has breezy rooms and a brilliant position over the lake. Room 201 is the best, with windows on three sides. Both the Jheels get good reviews from readers.

Hotel Badi Haveli (Map p245; ☎ 2412588; Gangaur Ghat Rd; r Rs 300-550) In an old whitewashed building around a leafy courtyard, the Badi Haveli offers clean, basic rooms; the costlier ones are furnished with wall paintings, coloured glass and alcoves, and some have views. See a variety of rooms on offer before you take your pick.

Poonam Haveli (Map p245; ☎ 2410303; poonam haveli@hotmail.com; 39 Lal Ghat; r Rs 400-1050;) A fairly modern place decked out in traditional style, Poonam has 16 rooms, all of which get positive reports from readers. Boasting big beds, the rooms are plain, fresh and large, some decorated with mirrorwork and some with lake views. The '007' room has arches as elegant as a raised eyebrow.

Lake Ghat Guest House (Map p245; ☎ 2521636; 4/13 Lal Ghat; d Rs 600-800) Some of the smart, biggish rooms have views, others have balconies, and all are decorated with stained glass. The rooms are set around a small atrium filled with hanging plants; there are splendid views from up on the roof, and a good restaurant (veg dishes around Rs 60).

Hanuman Ghat Area
Directly across the water from Lal Ghat, Hanuman Ghat, with its local vibe and handful of excellent choices, is a more peaceful place to stay.

Panorama Guest House (Map p245; ☎ 2431027; krishna2311@rediffmail.com; Hanuman Ghat; r Rs 80-150) Another good choice that's smart, well kept and quietly set, overlooking a small local square. The spotless rooms have wall paintings and either a private bathroom or a view, and there's a relaxing rooftop.

Queen Café & Guest House (Map p245; ☎ 2430875; 14 Bajrang Rd; r without bathroom Rs 170-220) Run by a Jain family, Queen has just two comfortable, quiet and unadorned rooms in a homy and atmospheric family house. The home cooking (veg dishes Rs 15 to 35) is excellent, and fantastic cooking lessons are offered here (see p249).

Dream Heaven Guest House (Map p245; ☎ 2431038; 22 Bhim Permashever Rd; r Rs 180-520) An excellent choice and deservedly popular. With a handful of spick-and-span rooms featuring wall hangings and paintings, this is a popular place to come to a halt. Some rooms have views and some have a splendid balcony. The food at the rooftop restaurant (veg and nonveg dishes Rs 20 to 50), which overlooks the lake and shows Udaipur at its best, is fresh, tasty and highly recommended – the perfect place to chill out on a pile of cushions.

Other Areas
Kumbha Palace (Map p245; ☎ 2422702; Battiyanni Chotta; r Rs 100-400, ranch cottages d Rs 1000-1200) This excellent place is run by a Dutch–Indian couple. Quietly tucked away, not far from Jagdish Temple, Kumbha Palace has nine simple rooms (some with bathroom, some without), backed by a lush lawn, and a very good restaurant. The owners run highly recommended horse-riding excursions (p248). Free pick-ups from the bus or train stations are on offer. You can also stay overnight in the hotel's rural cottages at Krishna Ranch, set in beautiful countryside 7km from Udaipur, or arrange much longer trips. A 24-hour safari including accommodation at the ranch costs Rs 2200.

Pratap Country Inn (Off Map p242; ☎ 2583138; s/d Rs 500/600) about 7km southeast of Udaipur,

this is a serene, though shabby, secluded country retreat at Titaradi Village. Its best selling point is not so much its quiet location or its very standard rooms, but the good-value horse-riding safaris that can be arranged from here. The hotel offers free transport from the train or bus station, with prior arrangement.

MIDRANGE
Lal Ghat Area
Jaiwana Haveli (Map p245; ☎ /fax 2521252; 14 Lal Ghat; r Rs 700-2000; ▨) This modern, spacious, but rather impersonal place has unfussy, well-kept rooms decorated with block-printed fabrics. Views from the rooms (especially the corner ones) are made a little bit frustrating due to the slightly tinted windows, but there are vast views from the rooftop.

Hotel Baba Palace (Map p245; ☎ 2427126; www.hotel babapalace.com; s Rs 750, d Rs 1200-1400, deluxe r with AC Rs 1400-2600; ▨ ▣) This newish hotel has sparkling if not especially exciting rooms (though they do have great views) and an unusual location eye-to-eye with Jagdish Temple.

Jagat Niwas Palace Hotel (Map p245; ☎ 2420133; mail@jagatniwaspalace.com; 23-25 Lal Ghat; r with AC Rs 1350, deluxe r Rs1895, ste Rs 4999; ▨) On the lakeshore, this wonderful hotel consistently receives good reports. In two converted *havelis*, rooms are charming and evocative, with carved wooden furniture and cushioned window seats; splash out on one with a lake view. The hotel also has a highly recommended rooftop restaurant (p254).

Kankarwa Haveli (Map p245; ☎ 2411457; 26 Lal Ghat; r Rs 1450-2200) This option, in an old *haveli*, is set right next to Jagat Niwas Palace Hotel. Whitewashed rooms give a sublime simplicity, but the service isn't always spot on. The pricier rooms overlook Pichola Lake, and there are home-cooked meals on request.

Lake Palace Road Area
Mahendra Prakash Hotel (Map p242; ☎ 2419811; r Rs 700-2500; ▨ ▣) Spacious gardens, well-furnished rooms, a cheery atmosphere and friendly staff are the name of the game at Mahendra Prakash. The restaurant overlooks a step-well, and there's a great pool (Rs 150 for nonguests).

Rang Niwas Palace Hotel (Map p242; ☎ 2523890; www.rangniwaspalace.com; Lake Palace Rd; s Rs 770-1800, d Rs 1000-2300, s/d ste Rs 2700/3300; ▨ ▣) A converted 19th-century palace in scenic gardens, Rang

Niwas boasts a tiny pool (Rs 125 for nonguests). Rooms (some are small) have carved wooden furniture, and some feature balconies with swing seats for relaxing on. The garden is soothing and the staff are usually very friendly.

Hotel Raj Palace (Map p245; ☎ 2410364; rajpalaceudr@ yahoo.com; 103 Battiyanni Chotta; d Rs 950-1150, ste from Rs 1250) The Raj Palace is housed in a 300-year-old *haveli* that feels a mite more tired than old. There are comfortable doubles; the more expensive they are, the more cushioned alcoves and pillars you get. There's a leafy courtyard restaurant, which is a great place to chill out with a beer, and the staff are friendly and efficient.

Hanuman Ghat

Amet Haveli (Map p245; ☎ 2431085; regiudr@datainfosys .net; s/d/ste 2200/2700/3300) This 350-year-old heritage building on the lakeshore is a romantic choice. The beautiful rooms have window seats and small stained-glass, shuttered windows. One of Udaipur's most scenic restaurants, Ambrai (p254), is next door. Breakfast costs an additional Rs 200.

Other Areas

Mountain Ridge (Off Map p242; ☎ 3291478; www .mountainridge.in; Sisarma; d incl half-board from Rs 1900; ⛱) Out in the Udaipur countryside, perched high above Sisarma Village, this place offers rest and respite, with three double rooms and a nice pool with a view. Treks around the region can be organised from here, there's yummy food available, and, in winter, a fire roars away merrily in the fireplace.

Shikarbadi Hotel (Off Map p242; ☎ 2583201; www .hrhindia.com; d/ste from Rs 2800/3500; 🅿 ⛱) This option is 4km south of town on the Ahmedabad road. Once a royal hunting lodge, it's set in wilderness in the Aravalli foothills, amid relaxing gardens with pristine lawns. Some rooms have exposed stone walls, others are whitewashed, but all have refreshing rural outlooks, and some have balconies. A stud farm on the premises offers short horse rides (Rs 250 for 40 minutes). In case you need them, there's also a private airstrip and a polo field. Sip tea while you watch the wild boars gorge at 4pm each day (not far from the pool area).

TOP END
Central Udaipur

Udai Kothi (Map p245; ☎ 2432810; www.udaikothi.com; s/d/ste Rs 4600/5200/6000; 🅿 ⛱) This hotel is in a

new building, but designed with lots of traditional froth (cupolas, icing-sugar stucco etc). It has a wonderful rooftop terrace, where you can dine well (p254) or swim in Udaipur's *only* rooftop pool (Rs 200 for nonguests), and there's a Jacuzzi with a view. Book a table for dinner beside the pool for highly romantic eating (a full meal costs around Rs 400 per person). Rooms are beautifully appointed and decorated with summery, pretty prints, and the hotel is full of thoughtful touches, such as bowls of floating flowers.

Shiv Niwas Palace Hotel (Map p245; ☎ 2528016; www.hrhindia.com; d/d with terrace/ste from US$175/445/547; 🅿 🖳 ⛱) Once the maharaja's guest quarters, Shiv Niwas has some incredibly lavish, over-the-top rooms, filled with fountains and silver furniture. The marble pool (Rs 500 for nonguests) is gorgeous. The cheapest (palace) rooms are unexciting and not really great value – for one notch higher, go for a terrace room – or, for an all-out splurge, there are some extravagant, technicolour suites; the mirrored, antique-heavy imperial suites even come complete with small fountains and, of course, the ubiquitous dreamy four-poster bed. The hotel has an atmospheric restaurant (above), a bar and an Ayurvedic massage centre.

Fateh Prakash Palace Hotel (Map p245; ☎ 2528019; www.hrhindia.com; d from US$298; 🖳) Built in the early 20th century when Maharaja Fateh Singh reigned, the hotel has palatial suites. The cheapest double rooms are not in the main palace wing, but all have a lake view. Far more ornate rooms furnished with traditional pieces are available (some with a lake view). The intimate Gallery Restaurant (p255) has wonderful views across the lake.

Lake Palace Hotel (Map p245; ☎ 2528800; www.taj hotels.com; d from US $550, ste US$3500-4700; 🅿 🖳 ⛱) Overblown it might be. Overpopular? That, too. But this romantic palace, seemingly floating in the lake, remains extraordinary, with its open-air courtyards, lotus ponds and a small, mango tree-shaded pool. Rooms are hung about with breezy silks and filled with carved furniture. The cheapest rooms (still coming in at well over a sobering US$500) overlook the lily pond or terrace; the most opulent suite will make you feel like a maharaja.

Other Areas

our pick **Devi Garh** (Off Map p242; ☎ 02953289211; Delwara; www.deviresorts.com; d/ste from US$275/740; 🖳 🖳 ⛱) Think of every conceivable

21st-century luxury, all parcelled up within a gorgeous 18th-century palace, and you've pretty much got Devi Garh. The pool, the spa, the trekking, the kite flying (kites are available at reception): you name it, they've thought of it, and they do it impeccably. Rooms, as you might expect, are the ultimate Rajasthan fantasies; the food is outstanding (if inevitably pricey) and the gliding staff will cater to your every sybaritic whim.

Udaivilas (Off Map p242; ☎ 2433300; www.oberoi hotels.com; d from US$475, ste with pool from US$2200; ❌ ▣ ❋) Lying 1.5km west of Udaipur, Udaivilas' sea-of-butter sculptured domes are a recent addition to the Udaipur skyline. It's a luxury boutique hotel that doesn't spare the glitz or gold leaf, and suites even come equipped with private pools. The hotel houses two excellent restaurants (see opposite).

Eating

Udaipur has scores of sun-kissed rooftop cafés, many with mesmerising lake views, as well as the ultimate in fine dining at top-end hotels.

Many budget restaurants have nightly 7pm screenings of contemporary movies or *Octopussy* – in case you'd forgotten this was partly filmed in Udaipur.

LAL GHAT AREA

Café Edelweiss (Map p245; Gangaur Ghat Rd; snacks Rs 20-80; ❤ 7.30am-7.30pm) There's a morning magnetism to Edelweiss, and something rather European that attracts travellers in droves to this bright, open-fronted cubbyhole bakery. You can sit in the comfortable chairs to drink real coffee and eat cakes (the apple pie, squidgy chocolate cake and sticky cinnamon rolls all deserve special mention) along with other savoury snacks. The same owners run Savage Garden (above).

Sunrise (Map p245; cnr Lal Ghat & Gangaur Ghat Rd; dishes Rs 30-90; ❤ 8am-10pm) Set up high on top of a family house, this is the place to come for tasty, filling breakfasts, or for nice Indian dishes at other times of the day. Run by a friendly family, it also makes a terrific location for a spot of people-watching over those perfectly turned scrambled eggs.

Mayur Rooftop Café (Map p245; 155 Jagdish Temple Rd; dishes Rs 40-100; ❤ 8am-11pm) Open-air Mayur with *de rigueur* scalloped arches has a great view into Jagdish Temple. The Western and Chinese options on the menu aren't really anything special, but the café is worth visiting

for the location and its good-value vegetarian thalis (Rs 55). This is one of the places to head to if you're in need of a good dose of *Octopussy*.

Jagat Niwas Palace Hotel (Map p245; ☎ 2420133; 23-25 Lal Ghat; mains around Rs 120 ❤ 9am-10pm) With great views over the lake from its well-padded window seats, this rooftop restaurant is a good bet for a romantic evening dinner: the fish dishes are fresh, well cooked and come recommended by quite a few travellers. It's worthwhile booking in advance for a good table, from which to enjoy the live sitar music and indulgent desserts.

HANUMAN GHAT AREA

Queen Café (Map p245; ☎ 2430875; 14 Bajrang Rd; ❤ 8am-10pm) This guesthouse-café, which also offers great cooking lessons (p249), makes a fabulous lunch stop on a busy sightseeing day. With delicious vegetarian cuisine cooked up by its lovely owners, there are plenty of fragrant curries to choose from, including some delicious varieties incorporating pumpkin and coconut. The chocolate desserts, too, come highly recommended – and each of these dishes comes in at just below the Rs 50 mark.

Ambrai (Map p245; Hanuman Ghat; dishes Rs 90-170; ❤ 12.30-3pm & 7.30-10.30pm) This outdoor restaurant has a superb location, and is a great place for a long, languid lunch. Unusually for restaurants in Udaipur, it sits at water level, looking directly across at the Lake Palace, Lal Ghat and the City Palace. It feels like a French park, with its wrought-iron chairs and dusty ground. The ambience is brilliant, and the North Indian food – especially the tandoori dishes – extremely tasty.

Udai Kothi (Map p245; dishes Rs 100-270) The glorious terrace restaurant set high up in the hotel of the same name (p253) has tables and cushioned alcoves around the edge of the rooftop pool and is especially romantic in the evening. Highly recommended are any of the several tandoori dishes on offer. Musicians play every evening from around 8pm between October and April.

OTHER AREAS

our pick Natraj Lodge (Map p242; New Bapu Bazaar; thalis from Rs 50; ❤ 10am-3pm & 6.30-11pm) Famous throughout town for its delicious all-you-can-eat Gujarati thalis, this place has been filled to the brim for two decades with devout locals, who arrive to chow down on its huge portions

---

UDAIPUR'S TOP FIVE ROMANTIC EATS

If you're taking your beloved out for a candlelight treat or lavish lunch, Udaipur has a whole slew of places fit to pop the question or simply indulge in the food, views and, of course, each other's company. Here are five of the best.

Jagat Niwas Palace Hotel (p253) Rooftop views of the lake, live music and delicious food.

Ambrai (opposite) Water-level garden with wonderful views.

Udai Kothi (opposite) Glamorous rooftop terrace with poolside seating.

Savage Garden (below) Lashings of flair, deep-blue walls, alcoves and unusual Indo-Western fusion dishes.

Udai Mahal (below) *Haute cuisine* in surroundings of bygone opulence.

---

of cheap, fresh food. The veg thali, for example, includes a whopping selection of rice, dhal, roti, pickles and at least five different vegetable dishes, all for a decent Rs 50. The only drawback is that the place is rather hard to find, tucked away in a backstreet. Your best bet is to corner a local and ask for directions: it's definitely worth the hunt.

Berry's (Map p242; Chetak Circle; dishes Rs 50-270; 9am-11pm) A calm and fairly refined restaurant with an impressive brass door and lots of international options on the menu (including tasty burgers), Berry's is enhanced by white tablecloths and a burbling fish tank. It's a better place for dinner than for lunch, as tables are full then and the atmosphere is at its best; for dinner, the Indian menu is recommended over the Chinese and Italian dishes.

Savage Garden (Map p245; 22 Inside Chandpol; dishes Rs 100-170; 11am-10pm) Tucked away in the backstreets (but well signposted) near Chandpol, Savage Garden continues to receive rave reviews from backpackers, particularly for its winning line in soups, nice fresh salads, and unusual fusion pasta dishes, which feature spaghetti and penne topped with Indian-spiced sauces. It's unusually atmospheric, set as it is in a 250-year-old *haveli* with peacock-blue walls, and laid out with bowls of flowers and tables in alcoves or in a pleasant courtyard. Staff are quick and courteous, and there's a great bar for a cold beer after a day seeing Udaipur's fairy-tale sights.

Shiv Niwas Palace Hotel (Map p245; dishes around Rs 400; 6.30-10.30am, 12.30-2.30pm & 7.30-10.30pm) Most captivating in the evening, this formal restaurant in Shiv Niwas Palace Hotel (p253) has indoor seating, but it's best out in the pleasant open-air courtyard by the pool. Indian classical music is performed nightly. You can take your pick from an extensive buffet or the regular menu, though the romantic ambience, rather than the food, is the main reason to come here.

Surya Mahal (Off Map p242; dishes around Rs 600; noon-10pm) For a big romantic splash, it's worth heading to Udaivilas' Surya Mahal, (p253) a 1930s-style place serving delicious Thai, Continental and loosely fusion cuisine in high-ceilinged opulence. If you're in the mood for a picnic with a difference, the restaurant can also arrange a picnic basket lunch, to be eaten on a gondola in the middle of a lake.

Udai Mahal (Off Map p242; dishes around Rs 700; 7-10pm) Udai Mahal, also in Udaivilas, is a candlelight treat, specialising in refined Rajasthani and North Indian food. Like everything at Udaivilas, this is opulence at its best, both in location and cuisine.

Lake Palace Hotel (Map p245; 2528800; 7.30-10.30pm) In the hotel of the same name (p253), this is Udaipur's most famous dining experience, but one that has left a few too many travellers feeling that it's overpriced and overhyped. The sumptuous buffet lunch costs a weighty Rs 2000 (including boat crossing), while a three-course dinner comes in at Rs 3000. Reservations are essential – at least a day before you wish to dine (reservations can be taken at the desk on the City Jetty) – and dress is smart casual. For something especially unusual, enquire about the tiny floating pontoon on Pichola Lake, which holds lunch or dinner for US$75 per person (maximum four people). If you don't want a waiter hanging around, you can request a cordless phone to be left in case you need anything. Be sure to wear something warm here, though, if you're dining at night in winter.

Gallery Restaurant (Map p245; high tea Rs 255; 2528019; high tea 3-6pm) In the palace enclosure (admission Rs 25), at the Fateh Prakash Palace Hotel (p253), this elegant little restaurant has beguiling views across Pichola Lake. You can eat within Durbar Hall itself or out on the terrace in the sunshine. Ignore the main meals: the reason to come here is for the best cream teas in town; they include sandwiches and biscuits, as well as the all-important combination of scones, jam and cream.

Drinking

There are plenty of good places for a beer in Udaipur: most guesthouses have a roof terrace serving up cold Kingfishers, while the top-end places have predictably plush options, though not all allow nonguests during the evening.

Paanera Bar (Map p245; ⊗ 11am-11pm) At the Shiv Niwas Palace Hotel (p253), this is a relaxingly plush poolside bar equipped with soft sofas and the inflated drinks tariffs you'd expect of a top-end joint.

Sunset View Terrace (Map p245; City Palace; admission Rs 25; ⊗ 11am-11pm) On a terrace overlooking Pichola Lake, this is *the* place to be at sunset – it's perfect gin-and-tonic territory. The food is overpriced and nothing special, so stick closely to drinks, and get here just before 7.30pm to nab a table for the live music that's performed every night.

Entertainment

Dharohar (Map p245; Gangaur Ghat; adult/child Rs 60/30, camera/video Rs 10/50; ⊗ 7pm) Don't miss out on this: against the wonderful backdrop of Bagore-ki-Haveli are staged mesmerising Rajasthani dances, including traditional Mewari, Bhil and western Rajasthani dances, by talented performers who can whirl better than most dervishes.

Meera Kala Mandir (Map p242; ☎ 2583176; Sector 11, Ahmedabad Rd; admission Rs 60) Rather touristy one-hour Rajasthani folk dance and music performances take place here at 7pm Monday to Saturday from August to April. An autorickshaw from Jagdish Temple costs Rs 30.

Cheetak Cinema (Map p242; Chetak Circle) This is one of a number of cinemas in Udaipur, if you feel like taking in the latest Bollywood hit. Tickets for performances cost about Rs 60. Check out screening times at the box office (open all day).

Shopping

Udaipur offers glorious shopping potential, with masses of little shops selling jumbles of things from cloth lanterns to exquisite antique jewellery.

The town is known for its local crafts, particularly miniature paintings in the Rajput–Mughal style: shops line Lake Palace Rd and cluster around Jagdish Temple. The miniatures are painted on cloth, marble,

wood, paper and even leaves, and Udaipur is known as one of the best places in the state to buy them. There are also many leather- and cloth-bound books of handmade paper (from Jaipur) for sale, in every design imaginable. Silver jewellery, carpets, block-printed fabrics, marble items, wooden figures and papier-mâché are other popular buys. Shops along Lake Palace Rd also sell small, beautiful, brightly painted wooden Hindu gods, perfect for portable presents. Be prepared, however, to bargain hard, as most places will probably quote you an initially ridiculous price: as a general rule, aim to pay around 50% of the opening asking price.

Interesting and less tourist-focused bazaars spread out from the clock tower (Map p245). Bara Bazaar sells silver and gold, as well as saris and fabrics. Traditional shoes are sold at Mochiwada, and more silver at Battiyanni. Colourful Mandi Market, a sprawling bazaar, is the centre for an aromatic assault of brightly coloured loose spices.

Sadhna (Map p245; www.sevamandir.org; Mangi Kee Baudi, Kasaron Ki; ⊗ 10am-7pm) This is the outlet for Seva Mandir, an NGO set up in 1969 to help rural women. The small shop sells attractive and individual fixed-price textiles such as clothes, cushion covers and bags; profits go to the artisans and towards community development work.

Rajasthali (Chetak Circle (Map p242; ⊗ 10.30am-7pm Mon-Sat); Jagdish Temple (Map p245; ⊗ 10am-6.30pm) This fixed-price government emporium is worth dropping into to gauge handicraft prices.

Getting There & Away

AIR

There are daily **Indian Airlines** (Map p242; ☎ 2410999; www.indian-airlines.org; Delhi Gate; ⊗ 10am-1pm & 2-5pm Mon-Sat, 10am-2pm Sun) flights to Delhi (US$115). The airline also has direct flights that go to Jodhpur (US$75; three times per week), Jaipur (US$90; daily except Sunday) and Mumbai (US$138; daily). **Jet Airways** (Map p242; ☎ 2561105; www.jetairways.com; Blue Circle Business Centre, Madhuban), which is located near the main post office, close to Chetak Circle, and **Kingfisher** (☎ toll free 18001800101; www.fly kingfisher.com) have similar flights for similar prices. See p376 for more information on flying within Rajasthan.

It's strongly advisable to make flight bookings well in advance during the busy tourist season; it's usually cheapest to book online.

BUS

Frequent **Rajasthan State Road Transport Corporation** (RSRTC; ☎ 2484191; www.rsrtc.gov.in) buses travel from Udaipur to other regional centres, as well as to Delhi and Ahmedabad. If you use these buses, take an express as the ordinary buses take an incredibly long time, making innumerable detours to various towns off the main route, and can be very uncomfortable, rattling and overcrowded. For long-distance travel it's best to use deluxe or express buses, but you'll need to book ahead. Destinations served by express and deluxe buses are listed in the table below. Where only one price is given, there are only express, and no deluxe, buses.

Private buses operate to Ahmedabad (Rs 150/200/150 in ordinary/AC/sleeper, six hours), Mumbai (Rs 400/600 in ordinary/sleeper, 16 hours), Delhi (Rs 200/350 in ordinary/sleeper, 14 hours), Mt Abu (Rs 100 in ordinary, five hours) and Jodhpur (Rs 100/150 in ordinary/sleeper, six hours).

TAXI

Many drivers will show you a list of 'official' rates to places such as Mt Abu, Chittorgarh and Jodhpur, but shop around (Rs 5 per km is a good starting point) for the most competitive rate. Remember that taxis will charge you return fares even if you're only going one way. For useful tips on hiring a taxi and driver, see p380.

TRAIN

The daily No 2964 *Nizamuddin Mewar Express* (Rs 210/591/853/1509 sl/3AC/2AC/1AC/) departs Udaipur for Delhi at 6.35pm, arriving the next morning at Nizamuddin station at 6.10am. The daily No 2966 *Udaipur City*

Jaipur Express leaves Udaipur at 9.35pm and arrives at Jaipur (Rs 142/399/576 sl/3AC/2AC) at 7.10am, stopping at Kota at an inconvenient 2.15am along the way. More services may be running in the near future; to check, the train enquiries number is ☎ 2527390.

Getting Around

TO/FROM THE AIRPORT

The airport is 25km east of town. A taxi will cost at least Rs 250; there's no airport bus.

AUTORICKSHAW

These are unmetered, so you should agree on a fare before setting off – the standard fare anywhere in town is around Rs 30 to 35. There are prepaid autorickshaw stands at the bus and train stations. It costs Rs 200 to hire an autorickshaw for a day of local sightseeing.

Udaipur's autorickshaw drivers are keen on the hotel commission malarkey, so be extra vigilant that you're being taken to where you really want to go.

BICYCLE & MOTORCYCLE

A cheap and environmentally friendly way to buzz around is by bike; many guesthouses can arrange bikes to rent, costing around Rs 30 per day. Motorbikes, meanwhile, are great for exploring the surrounding countryside. **Heera Cycle Store** (Map p245; ☎ 2523525; ⏲ 7.30am-9pm), near Hotel Badi Haveli, hires out bicycles/mopeds/motorcycles for Rs 30/150/350 per day.

NORTH OF UDAIPUR

Eklingji & Nagda

The interesting village of Eklingji – only 22km and a short bus ride north of Udaipur – has a fascinating ancient temple complex

BUSES FROM UDAIPUR		
Destination	**Fare (express/deluxe, Rs)**	**Approximate duration (hr)**
Agra	121/170	6
Ahmedabad	150	6
Ajmer	131/180	8
Bundi	155	7
Chittorgarh	70/68	3/2½
Delhi	300/470	14
Jaipur	191/231	9
Jodhpur	135/150	8
Kota	170	8
Mt Abu	105	6

EXPLORING AROUND UDAIPUR

Around Udaipur lie huge, rugged hills – cut through by narrow roads snaking across an expansive landscape – that open up to impressive views across the countryside. It makes a fantastic excursion to ramble out into the rural areas, stopping along the way at small villages and little-visited temples. The best way to travel like this is by motorbike, since you can explore completely at your leisure. If you're not keen on motorbikes, try to find a willing and knowledgeable autorickshaw driver who'll be able to stop at all the right places.

Heading north, you could spend a day visiting **Madar Lakes**, around 15km from the city; head to Madar Village, from which there are two tracks, leading to **Little Madar Dam** or **Great Madar Dam**, each with splendid views across the expanse of water. Venturing west out of Udaipur, head towards the village of Sisarma (where the excellent Mountain Ridge guest house is based; see p253), then head onwards towards the tiny village of Dhar, from which the road leads to the **Ubeshwarji**, a revered Shiva shrine that attracts many pilgrims. Leaving Ubeshwarji, the road continues on through a remote hill pass; seek out local help along this road to get directions to **Kailashwarji**, a magnificent waterfall that plunges 50m, straight out of *The Jungle Book*. The small villages and temples you hit on the way may not be spectacular, but it's an adventure – and the journey, as they say, is the destination.

---

attracting lots of pilgrims but few tourists. The **Shiva temple** (admission free, ☿ 4-6.30am, 10.30am-1.30pm & 5-7.30pm), with its 108 small shrines, was originally built in AD 734, although its present form dates from the 15th-century rule of Maharaja Raimal. Constructed from sandstone and marble, the walled complex has an elaborately pillared hall under a large pyramidal roof and features a four-faced Shiva image of black marble. Note, though, that opening hours change quite regularly, so you might have to wait an hour or two if you arrive at the wrong time of day. Avoid the temple on Monday (an auspicious day for devotees), as it can get very crowded; the maharaja of Udaipur himself pays a private visit to the temple on Monday evening. Guides are available at the temple; bank on paying around Rs 50 to 100 to engage their services. Photography is not permitted.

Several kilometres further on from Eklingji, at Nagda, are some 10th-century temples. The 11th-century **Jain temple of Adbudji** remains very fine, despite damage at the hands of the Mughals, and contains a 15th-century black-marble idol of *tirthankar* Shanti Nath. About 500m away are a pair of **Saas-Bahu Temples** (the name meaning 'mother-in-law–daughter-in-law') dating from the 9th century and featuring some fine, intricate carvings, including a number of erotic figures. You can reach these temples by hiring a bicycle in Eklingji. There's a bike-hire shop in the village; a day's rental should cost around Rs 30. There are also some small temples submerged in the nearby lake; after a poor monsoon they're completely exposed.

GETTING THERE & AWAY
Local buses travel from Udaipur (Rs 10, 30 minutes) to Eklingji every hour from 5am to 10pm.

Haldighati
This **battlefield site** (Rs 30; ☿ 8am-8pm), 40km north of Udaipur, is where Maharaja Pratap defied the superior Mughal forces of Akbar in 1576. The site is marked by a small *chhatri* that commemorates the warrior's horse, Chetak. Although badly wounded and exhausted, this loyal steed carried Maharaja Pratap to safety before collapsing and dying. There's not a lot to see, but the historic site attracts many Indian visitors. Haldighati can be reached by bus from Nathdwara (Rs 12, 30 minutes); the site is 2km southeast of the town.

Nathdwara
☎ 02953
The 18th-century Krishna temple of **Sri Nathji** (admission free, ☿ 5-5.30am, 7.15-7.45am, 9.15-9.45am, 11.30am-noon, 3.30-4pm, 4.30-5pm & 6-6.30pm) stands at Nathdwara, 48km north of Udaipur. It's another place that draws many pilgrims but sees few tourists; photography is not permitted. The shrine has special significance for Vaishnavites (followers of Vishnu or of his incarnations). The black-stone Krishna image housed in the temple was brought here from Mathura in 1669 to protect it from the destructive impulses of the

Mughal ruler Aurangzeb. According to legend, the getaway vehicle, a wagon, sank into the ground up to the axles as it was passing through Nathdwara. The priests realised that this was a sign from Krishna that the image did not want to travel any further; accordingly, the Sri Nathji Temple was built on the spot.

Attendants treat the black-stone image like a delicate child, waking it up in the morning, washing it, dressing it, offering it specially prepared meals and putting it to sleep, all at precise times throughout the day. It's a very popular pilgrimage site, and the temple opens and closes around the image's daily routine. It gets very crowded from 3.30pm to 4pm when Krishna gets up after a siesta.

Nathdwara is also well known for its *pichwai* paintings, which were produced after the image of Krishna was brought to the town in the 17th century. These bright screen paintings, with their rather static images, were usually created on handspun fabric and intended to be hung behind the idol – they usually show Sri Nathji decked out in different outfits. As with many other schools of painting, numerous inferior reproductions of the *pichwai* paintings are created specifically for the lucrative tourist market.

SLEEPING & EATING

RTDC Hotel Gokul (☎ 230917; Lal Bagh; dm/s/d Rs 50/450/600, superdeluxe d Rs 800; 🍴) Considering it's a Rajasthan Tourism Development Corporation (RTDC) establishment, this small hotel is surprisingly good. It's set in quiet gardens, around 4km from the temple. A bar and a restaurant are on site.

RTDC Hotel Yatrika Mangla (☎ 231119; dm/s/d Rs 70/350/450) The Yatrika Mangla is only around 1km from the temple, so it's more convenient than Gokul, though plainer and less appealing.

GETTING THERE & AWAY

There are frequent daily buses from Udaipur to Nathdwara (Rs 28, one hour). If you're coming by car, it costs Rs 10 to park at the temple.

Kankroli & Rajsamand Lake

At Kankroli, 66km north of Udaipur, there's a beautiful **temple** devoted to Dwarkadhish (an incarnation of Krishna), which is similar to the temple at Nathdwara; the opening hours are similarly erratic.

Nearby is the large **Rajsamand Lake**, created by a dam constructed in 1660 by Maharaja Raj Singh (r 1652–80). There are numerous ornamental arches and beautifully carved *chhatris* set along the huge *bund* (embankment), which is 335m long and 13m high, along with several interesting old inscriptions.

There are frequent RSRTC buses from Udaipur (Rs 25, 2½ hours).

Kumbalgarh
☎ 02954

About 84km north of Udaipur, **Kumbalgarh** (Indian/foreigner Rs 5/100; 🕐 9am-6pm) is a fantastic, remote fort, fulfilling romantic expectations and vividly summoning up the chivalrous, warlike Rajput era. Built by Rana Kumbha in the 15th century, the isolated fort is perched at an amazing 1100m, from where endless views melt into blue distance. The journey to the fort, a trip along twisting roads through the Aravalli Hills, is a highlight in itself.

Kumbalgarh was the most important Mewar fort after Chittorgarh, and the rulers, sensibly, used to retreat here in times of danger. Here, a baby prince of Mewar was hidden from an assassin (see The Ultimate Sacrifice, p244). Not surprisingly, Kumbalgarh was only taken once in its entire history, and even then it took the combined armies of Amber, Marwar and Mughal emperor Akbar to breach its strong defence and they only managed to hang onto it for two days.

The fort's thick walls stretch some 36km; they're wide enough in some places for eight horses to ride abreast and they enclose around 360 temples, as well as palaces, gardens, *baoris* and 700 cannon bunkers. Renovated in the 19th century by Maharaja Fateh Singh, it's worth taking a leisurely walk in the large compound, which has some interesting ruins and is very peaceful.

If you stay in Kumbalgarh, you can trek from your hotel to the fort, a dramatic way to approach it. It's a steep climb up to the entrance, so don't forget to buy your ticket first, near the start of the road from the car park. It costs Rs 25 to park a car.

Nearby there's also the large, densely wooded **Kumbalgarh Wildlife Sanctuary** (Indian/foreigner Rs 10/100; 🕐 sunrise-sunset), known for its leopards and wolves. The scarcity of water holes between March and June makes this the best time to see animals. Wildlife includes chowsingha (four-horned deer), leopards,

THE STEP-WELLS OF RAJASTHAN

Ten wells equal one *vapi*, 10 *vapis* equal one pond
Ten ponds equal one son and 10 sons equal one tree

Vedic verse

Step-wells, or *baoris* as they are also known, are widespread throughout Rajasthan, and you will find them located in the south, not only the more famous examples at Bundi – where there are several dozen – but also at smaller, more out-of-the-way locations such as within the atmospheric, remote fort remains at Kumbalgarh and in quiet, pastoral Narlai. The term *baori*, when used to describe a well of this kind, usually means it has some sort of connection to the religious community.

Building a step-well is lauded in the ancient Hindu scriptures as an act of great merit, the wealthy having built wells to gain kudos and good karma. Although the distinctions have become blurred, there are several other terms used to describe these wells, including *kund*, which generally refers to a structural lake/tank, and *vapi* (also known as a *vav* or *wav*), a water supply accessed via a series of steps.

In addition to their essential function as a water supply in arid areas, step-wells were frequently attached to temples and shrines, enabling devotees to bathe and purify themselves. Many formed part of a larger complex that included accommodation for weary travellers, constructed in far-reaching trails along caravan routes. The more elaborate *baoris* have intricate pillars; steps built in artistic configurations; and rooms, corridors, galleries and platforms cut into the various levels. The spiritual and life-giving properties of step-wells, and their pivotal role in daily life, meant that many were adorned with carvings and statues of gods and goddesses, with Ganesh, Hanuman, Durga and Mahishasura the most commonly represented deities. The presence of these wells served to transform the everyday necessity of collecting water into a social occasion, and women would dress to impress in their finest outfits just to go out for the day's supply – the equivalent of going grocery shopping today in your best evening wear.

sloth bears and various bird species. You need a permit from the forest department in nearby Kelwara to enter (ask at your hotel for advice). All hotels can arrange three-hour horse or jeep safaris. **Shivika Lake Hotel** (☎ 285078; www .shivikalakehotel.com) in Ranakpur arranges jeep tours at a cost of Rs 700 per person, which also covers admission fees.

SLEEPING
Thandiberi Forest Guest House (d Rs 350) This is a plain and basic guesthouse but it's situated within the sanctuary. Bookings should be made in advance through the deputy chief wildlife warden (☎ 0294-2453686) in Udaipur.

Kumbhal Castle (☎ 242171; s/d Rs 800/980, deluxe Rs 1400/2000) The modern Kumbhal Castle, 3km from the fort, has plain but pleasant modern white rooms featuring curly iron beds, bright bedspreads and window seats, shared balconies and good views.

Aodhi Hotel (☎ 242341; www.hrhindia.com; s/d from Rs 3500/4000, ste from Rs 5000; ❄ 🖥 🐾) About 5km from the fort is this appealing, blissfully tranquil

hotel with an inviting pool and winter campfires. It's an ideal place to read a book or play a leisurely game of cards, though the rooms themselves are very much on the kitsch side (especially the tiger- and parrot-themed suites). A jeep safari from here costs Rs 1200, a three-hour visit to the sanctuary is Rs 4000 (maximum of five people), and trekking is around Rs 1000 per day for five people. Nonguests can dine in the restaurant, where good standard Indian fare is the pick of the options on offer, or have a drink in the cosy Chopal Bar.

GETTING THERE & AWAY
Several RSRTC buses go to/from Udaipur (Rs 35, 3½ hours); some leave from the bus stand (Map p242) and others from Chetak Circle (Map p242). Some services stop in Kelwara, 7km away, and some at the Aodhi Hotel, from where it's a 5km walk; check with your bus driver before boarding in Udaipur. There's one direct bus from the RSRTC bus stand, which leaves at 12.45pm and takes four hours, dropping passengers off at the Aodhi Hotel.

SOUTHERN RAJASTHAN

Hiring a taxi from Udaipur means you can visit both Ranakpur and Kumbalgarh in a day. Many travellers ask around to make up a group and share the expense (taxis take four to five people and cost Rs 1200 for a round trip).

Ranakpur
☎ 02934

In a remote and plunging wooded valley, reached down a twisting road, **Ranakpur** (admission free, camera/video Rs 50/100; ☺ Jains 6am-7pm, non-Jains noon-5pm) is one of India's biggest and most important Jain temples. The main temple called the **Chaumukha Mandir** (Four-Faced Temple), is dedicated to Adinath and was built in 1439. It's an incredible milk-white marble building, a complicated series of 29 halls supported by a forest of 1444 pillars, no two of which are alike. The interior is completely covered in knotted, lovingly wrought carving. The pale interior has a marvellously calming sense of space and harmony. Remember that shoes, cigarettes and all leather articles must be left at the entrance.

Within the complex are two other Jain temples, dedicated to **Neminath** (22nd *tirthankar*) and **Parasnath** (23rd *tirthankar*), and a nearby **Sun Temple**. About 1km from the main complex is **Amba Mata Temple**.

The complex is well worth a visit and makes a convenient stop between Jodhpur and Udaipur. It's 90km from Udaipur and is, for those with the time, a great place to kick back for a few days. You can visit Kumbalgarh and its nearby wildlife sanctuary from here, and trek into the hills. One four-hour trek leads to a Parshurama Shiva Temple in a cave. Guided trekking trips cost around Rs 500 for a day and can be arranged through Shivika Lake Hotel.

SLEEPING & EATING

If you don't mind the discomfort of an old mattress on a concrete floor, you can stay at the temple complex itself for a bargain Rs 10, along with the legions of Jain pilgrims. For an extra Rs 20, you'll get a simple vegetarian dinner, served daily at 5pm. Aside from this, however, accommodation in the area is all fairly pricey.

Shivika Lake Hotel (☎ 285078; www.shivikalakehotel.com; r Rs 600-1600; ✗ ☐ ☑) Offering small, cosy cottages with pretty décor, and set amid leafy gardens, Shivika Lake is a welcoming, rustic place to stay. Five tents with private bathrooms are also available. The warm,

knowledgeable family arranges forest safaris (a three-day safari costs around Rs 1950 per person per night, all included) and guides for short or longer treks. The hotel has a good restaurant (dishes Rs 40 to 100) and a nice, refreshing pool.

Ranakpur Hill Resort (☎ 286411; www.ranakpurhillresort.com; Ranakpur Rd; s/d/tent Rs 1500/2000/1800; ✗ ☐ ☑) This is a smart, traditional-style place, with plenty of frills and a pleasant pool in the garden, around which are ranged the simple but well-decorated tented rooms. The rooms are well adorned and have nice, new bathrooms, and the beds are extra comfy.

Fateh Bagh (in Udaipur ☎ 0294-2528008; www.hrhindia.com; Ranakpur Rd; s/d Rs 3000/3500, ste from Rs 5000; ✗ ☐ ☑) It might amaze you to know that this palatial building carved from peachy sandstone is at not its original site: the original palace, built by Rawla Koshilav near Jodhpur in 1802, was transferred here piece by piece and reconstructed – 65,000 pieces were moved in total. The result is an impressive and opulent small hotel, with rooms decorated comfortably in antique pieces and local crafts. The deluxe suites are particularly impressive: novel features include a swing bed in the honeymoon suite.

GETTING THERE & AWAY

A good number of buses run to Ranakpur from Udaipur (Rs 45, three hours, hourly), and stop right outside the temple, but it's hard to visit both Ranakpur and Kumbalgarh by public transport in a day. A taxi taking in both from Udaipur costs around Rs 1200.

There are express buses to/from Mt Abu (Rs 90, five hours) and Jodhpur (Rs 95, five hours).

All the accommodation listed in Ranakpur is too far from the bus stop to be able to walk there. Jeeps can sometimes be hired at the bus stop (ask at the shop), or call your hotel and see if you can be picked up.

Narlai
☎ 02934

Quiet yet spectacular, Narlai makes a nice base for exploring the various attractions in the countryside around Udaipur. Opposite the Rawla Narlai hotel is a mammoth granite rock that's dotted with caves and temples; the village is also home to a good *baori* and several old temples and offers lots of opportunities for quiet walks.

Rawla Narlai (☎ 282425, in Delhi ☎ 011-26221419; www.ajitbhawan.com; r Rs 2400-2900, ste Rs 3000) was once the hunting lodge of the rulers of Narlai. This is the main reason to stay in Narlai: it's a beautifully maintained place, with 26 appealing, antique-furnished rooms. These are often decorated with frescoes, stained glass and hanging baubles and lead onto balconies and porches that face the huge granite outcrop opposite. Sumptuous Indian dinners can be eaten poolside, or, if you're in the mood, opt for the 'themed dinner' which involves a magic show, a countryside bullock-cart ride, and local traditional entertainment, all while you tuck into your thali.

There are buses from Udaipur (Rs 62, two hours) and Jodhpur (Rs 110, four hours).

Ghanerao
☎ 02934

About 12km from Narlai is little Ghanerao, dominated by a castle that has been converted into yet another charismatic hotel. **Mahavira Temple**, a 10th-century Jain temple devoted to the founder of Jainism, is also worth visiting. Splendidly set among woodland, it's flanked by two mighty elephants, and its walls are richly carved with warriors, horses and gods riding chariots.

Ghanerao Royal Castle (☎ 284035; www.ghaeraoroyalcastle.com; s/d/ste Rs 2000/2500/3000) is the place to stay in town. Carved from red sandstone, this creaky old place has bags of atmosphere in its ambling corridors, courtyards, frescoes, and marble pavilion in a central courtyard where palace musicians used to perform. Though it can seem a little deserted in anything but the high, high season, this only adds to the abandoned-castle experience, especially in the evenings, when eerie shadows play in its courtyards. The whitewashed rooms are a little bare but comfortable, with arches, antiques, coloured glass and tall ceilings. Near the castle are cenotaphs of former rulers.

To get to Ghanerao, take an RSRTC bus from Udaipur to Sadri (Rs 75) or Desuri (Rs 75), then a jeep taxi (about Rs 80) from there.

SOUTH OF UDAIPUR
Rishabdeo
☎ 02907

The village of Rishabdeo, about 65km south of Udaipur, is a significant pilgrimage centre with a magical atmosphere, making it well worth a visit. The village is home to a 15th-century **Jain temple** (admission free; ☀ 7am-9.30pm) dedicated to Rishabdeo, a reincarnation of Mahavira, the 24th and last of the Jain *tirthankars*. Mahavira founded Jainism around 500 BC and is also worshipped as a reincarnation of Vishnu. The temple features a beautiful silver image of Rishabdeo and some lovely carvings, including 52 images of idols. Two large, glossy, black-stone elephants flank the temple's entrance, two more are beyond them, and another huge one is inside. The interior is multipillared and decorated with carvings in white marble. A short walk through a lane lined with small shops leads you there.

RTDC Hotel Gavri (☎ 230145; dm Rs 50, s/d from Rs 600/700, with AC Rs 900/1000; ✗) is about 500m from the temple. The rooms are functional, if thoroughly unspectacular, and there are pleasant lawns surrounding the building.

There are buses going to Rishabdeo from Udaipur (Rs 35, 1½ hours).

Bambora
☎ 0294

About 45km to the southeast of Udaipur, the sleepy village of Bambora has a dramatic 250-year-old fort that has been converted into another impressive hotel.

Karni Fort (☎ 2398220; s/d from Rs 2200/3000; ✗ ▣) is in the middle of nowhere, dramatically plumped on a hilltop. Inside the fort walls the main building rises up like a grand country house. All rooms are light, bright and colourfully decorated; the best come with stunning panoramic views. There's a good restaurant, an old underground 'secret' passageway, and an alluring marble swimming pool with four water-spurting marble elephants and a central pavilion, set in the hilly garden. Staff are extremely helpful, and a range of jeep and trekking options are on offer.

Jaisamand Lake
☎ 0294

A startlingly vast tract of water 48km southeast of Udaipur, Jaisamand Lake lies between wooded hills, surveyed by yje Udaipur maharanis' summer palaces. At 88 sq km, the artificial lake is one of Asia's largest, created by damming the Gomti River and built in the 17th century by Maharaja Jai Singh (who, on the day of its inauguration, went for a leisurely stroll distributing gold – his own weight of it, in fact – to the locals) and is today around 14km long and 9km wide in places. There are beautiful marble *chhatris* around the 330m-long, 35m-high embankment, fronted by carved elephants, and today busy with a scattering of people waiting for boats and small boys selling food with which to feed the teeming fish. The small hilltop palace is Rothi Rani; the larger palace, near the dam, is Hawa Mahal.

The lake features a variety of bird life, and the small nearby **Jaisamand Wildlife Sanctuary** (Indian/foreigner Rs 10/80, camera Rs 200; 10am-5pm) is home to leopards, deer, wild boars and crocodiles. The forests here used to be a favourite hunting ground of the former rulers of Mewar, and elaborate hunting expeditions would frequently take place. It costs Rs 65/3 to take a car/bicycle inside; it's not, however, well set up for visitors, with no information or guides available.

There are boats available for lake tours – a small/medium/large circuit of the lake costs Rs 30/50/100. This lake could be great for bird-watching, but if you take a boat out you'll find the engine noise a hindrance; see if you can negotiate a price for taking the boat out then sitting for an hour or two, engine cut, to watch the birds emerge.

SLEEPING

Forest Guest House (r Rs 450) Run by the wildlife sanctuary, this guesthouse has large double rooms and fantastic views over the lake. It has a dilapidated air, though, and the bathrooms are a little dirty, but the location is worth it. You must contact the deputy chief wildlife warden (0294-2453686) in Udaipur for reservations.

Jaisamand Island Resort (2431401; www.lakend .com; s/d/ste from Rs 2200/3300/4400;) Modern and imposing but somewhat rough around the edges, this hotel is in a wonderful, secluded island location, 20 minutes by boat across the lake. Rooms are comfortable but they're run down, rather dark and hence overpriced. However, all have great views over the water. The swimming pool has a brilliant setting, right beside the water's edge. Discounts are often available. A return boat ride to the resort costs Rs 150 (nonguests are welcome to visit). The only dining option for guests is at the hotel restaurant, which serves up reasonable Indian, European and Chinese dishes; mains are between Rs 150 and Rs 450.

GETTING THERE & AWAY
There are frequent buses from Udaipur (Rs 25, 1½ hours, hourly).

Sitamata Wildlife Sanctuary
If you want to get away from it all, this is the place to visit. Lying 90km southeast of Udaipur, Sitamata Wildlife Sanctuary covers 423 sq km of mainly deciduous forest, which is known for its ancient teak trees. Wildlife includes deer, sambars, leopards, caracals, flying squirrels and wild boars. Few tourists make it out this way, which is part of its charm. If you're in search of picturesque countryside, peace and plenty of fresh air, this place is ideal.

Fort Dhariyawad (02950-220050; s/d Rs 1700/1950, deluxe r from Rs 2335) is in the Sitamata sanctuary area, 120km from Udaipur. It's housed in a 16th-century fort founded by Prince Sahasmal, second son of Maharaja Pratap, and offers great all-round creature comforts, though the beds aren't the comfiest. The restaurant here serves tasty Indian food, and meals can be taken in the enchantingly lit gardens. Jeep safaris can be arranged to places of interest in the area, and the owners can also arrange tented accommodation for the Baneshwar Fair (p264).

There are RSRTC buses from Udaipur to Dhariyawad (Rs 60, 3½ hours).

Dungarpur
 02964
About 110km south of Udaipur, attractive Dungarpur, the City of Hills, was founded in the 13th century when Rawal Veer Singh Dev took over this area from the Bhils. It's set in the foothills of the Aravalli Hills, and the landscape is wild and stony, dotted with cacti and hardy trees.

The town's wonderful, deserted, crumbling old palace, **Juna Mahal** (admission Rs 100; 9am-5pm), was built in stages between the 13th and 18th centuries, on a 450m-high rocky peak, and is filled with old frescoes and paintings. The fascinating murals include the Kamasutra, hidden discreetly in a cupboard, and there are willow-pattern plates embedded in the walls. The Aam Khas (main living room) has impressive mirrorwork and glass inlays. The former royal hunting lodge, on a nearby hilltop, has sensational views over the town and its many temples. Get your ticket to Juna Mahal from Udai Bilas Palace.

Also of interest is the **Rajmata Devendra Kunwer State Museum** (admission Rs 5, free Mon; ☺ 10am-5pm Sat-Thu), near the hospital, which has a sculpture gallery featuring pieces from as far back as the 6th century, including a black-stone Shiva. There are also some interesting old photographs of the area.

The multilayered **Deo Somnath Temple**, about 25km north of town, dates back to the 12th century and is worth a visit for its beautiful, harmonious architecture. Note the amazing centuries-old banyan tree opposite the temple.

SLEEPING

Hotel Pratibha Palace (☎ 230775; Shastri Colony; d Rs 150-200) This is the best budget hotel in town. It has tiny rooms that are nothing flash but aren't bad value for money.

Udai Bilas Palace (☎ 230808; www.udaibilaspalace .com; s/d/ste Rs 3500/4450/5300; ❄ ⊠ ☒) Set on the sparkling Gaib Sagar River, this fantastical 18th-century palace (with beautifully carved balconies built of *pareva*, Dungarpur's blue-stone) has been partly converted into a hotel by Maharaja Kumar Harshvardhan Singh. It's built around the astonishing Ek Thambia Mahal (One-Pillared Palace), and the rooms retain their original Art Deco and 1940s furnishings (some have balconies facing the lake). The previous maharaja's penchant for hunting is underlined by the stuffed beasts that watch your progress around the hotel, including in the long dining hall, where the exquisite ceiling is made from Burmese teak. The gorgeous outdoor pool is so designed that it seems to merge with the lake as you swim. Bicycle hire and bird-watching excursions can be organised for guests. Meals, which take the form of lavish buffets, can be eaten either indoors or poolside; breakfast comes in at Rs 300, lunch at Rs 500 and dinner costs Rs 575 per person.

GETTING THERE & AWAY

Frequent RSRTC buses travel to and from Udaipur (Rs 60, three hours, hourly).

Galiakot

About 50km southeast of Dungarpur is the important Muslim pilgrimage centre of Galiakot. This small town is famous for the **tomb of the saint Fakruddin**, who spread the word of Mohammed in the 10th century. Each year, thousands of local and international Bohra Muslim pilgrims flock here to pay homage to the saint at his white-marble shrine.

There are daily express buses from Udaipur (Rs 65, three hours).

Baneshwar

The town of Baneshwar lies at the confluence of three holy rivers: the Mahi, Som and Jakham. In January/February the week-long **Baneshwar Fair** is held at the Baneshwar Temple, about 80km from Dungarpur. The fair honours Vishnu incarnated as Mavji – there's a nearby Vishnu temple believed to have been built where Mavji meditated – and the event attracts thousands of Bhil tribal people. Music, dance and fairground rides go on alongside the rituals of the festival.

There are regular buses from Dungarpur (Rs 10, one hour) to Baneshwar.

MT ABU

☎ 02974 / pop 22,045 / elev 1200m

According to one legend, Mt Abu is as old as the Himalaya range itself, named after Arbuda, a mighty serpent who saved Nandi, Shiva's revered bull, from plunging into an abyss. According to another, it was in Mt Abu that the four Rajput fire clans, the Chauhans, Solankis, Pramaras and Pratiharas, were created by Brahmin priests from a seething pit of fire.

The town is certainly unlike anywhere else in Rajasthan, a green, serene and welcome retreat during summer from the scorching temperatures and arid beige terrain elsewhere. The state's only hill station, it lies close to the Gujarat border, reached by way of a winding road through massive wooded hills (a haven for bears, langurs, hyenas and the like), the rolling alpine slopes a revelation after so many baking desert plains. Gujarat and Rajasthan's favourite holiday getaway, Mt Abu is a particular hit with honeymooners and middle-class Gujarati families; unlike the hill stations of northern India, you won't find many Western travellers here. The beautiful landscape around the town, though – home to some rare plant life, including graceful exotic orchids – makes it well worth exploring, and there are several excellent short treks that start from here.

Mt Abu's cool climate is, inevitably, what draws most visitors to the town. Try to avoid arriving in Diwali (October to November) or the following two weeks, though, when prices soar and the place is packed. Equally, like most hill stations, it's best to avoid Mt Abu in summer, when hordes of people come to escape the heat, though this might be exactly why you're also making your way into town. This is also when the Summer Festival hits town, with music, fireworks and boat races (p224). If you are visiting in the cooler months, you will find that everyone is wrapped up in shawls and hats to keep warm; remember to pack something woolly to avoid winter chills in poorly heated hotel rooms. If you visit here in spring, you may come across the local variation of the Gangaur festival (p224), that is celebrated by Garasia tribespeople.

Sadly, tourism has taken its toll on the surrounding natural environment, with large tracts of vegetation having been cleared to make way for the many hotels that continue to crop up. As with all Rajasthan's destinations, trying to minimise your consumption of plastics and other waste will help to safeguard the town, and its surroundings.

Orientation

Mt Abu sprawls along a 1220m-high plateau that's about 22km long by 6km wide, and 27km from the nearest train station (Abu Rd). The main part of town extends north from the station along Abu Rd and surrounds picturesque, central Nakki Lake.

Information

There's an SBBJ ATM near Hotel Samrat International, and a State Bank of India ATM right next to the tourist reception centre.

Bank of Baroda (☺ 10am-3pm Mon-Fri, to 12.30pm Sat) Changes travellers cheques and currency, and does credit-card advances.

Main post office (Raj Bhavan Rd; ☺ 9am-5pm Mon-Sat) At the northern end of town.

Shree Krishna Cyber Café (per hr Rs 40; ☺ 8am-10pm) Internet access; located in the main Market.

Tourist reception centre (☎ 235151; ☺ 10am-5pm Mon-Sat, closed 2nd Sat of month) Opposite the main bus stand and below the railway ticket reservation office. Offers a free map of town, though the maps aren't especially accurate, useful or illuminating.

Sights

NAKKI LAKE

Scenic Nakki Lake, the town's focus, is one of its biggest attractions. It's so named because, according to legend, it was scooped out by a god

using his *nakh* (nails). Some Hindus thus believe it to be a holy lake, but you're more likely to see people pedalling in a pedalo than bathing in it. It's a pleasant stroll around the perimeter – the lake is surrounded by hills, parks and strange rock formations. The best known, **Toad Rock**, looks just like a toad about to hop into the lake. The 14th-century **Raghunath Temple** stands beside the lake.

Nakki Lake is the heart of all activity in Mt Abu. At the edge, by the town centre, there's a carnival of juice and food stalls, ice-cream parlours, balloon vendors and souvenir shops. You'll probably have to plough through the persistent photographers eager to take a happy snap of you by the water. The honeymoon market is catered for by aphrodisiac vendors, with potions that allegedly 'make big difference'.

To enter into the spirit of things, you can do as the honeymooners do and hire a **pedalo** (2-/4-person boat per 30min Rs 50/100), or, for the especially romantically inclined, a gondola-like **shikara loveboat** (2-person boat per 30min Rs 100). Those travelling with small children will doubtless be pressured into purchasing a **pony ride** (per hr Rs 50) from the stand one road back from the lake, for a slow but scenic stroll along the water's edge.

VIEWPOINTS

Sunset Point is a popular and lovely place from which to watch the brilliant setting sun, though distinctly unromantic unless you find that being thrust red roses, bags of peanuts, or Polaroid cameras gets you into a loving mood. Hordes stroll out here every evening to catch the end of the day, the food stalls and all the usual jolly hill-station entertainment. It's a 1km-walk from the road to the viewpoint. Other viewpoints include **Honeymoon Point** – another good sunset point – and **The Crags** (Ganesh Temple). You can follow the white arrows along a path to the summit of **Shanti Shikhar**, west of Adhar Devi Temple, where there are panoramic views.

The best view over the lake is from the terrace of the maharaja of Jaipur's former **summer palace**, which has been converted into Jaipur House (p268).

DILWARA TEMPLES

These remarkable **Jain temples** (admission free, donations encouraged; ☺ Jains sunrise-sunset, non-Jains noon-6pm) are Mt Abu's main attraction and feature

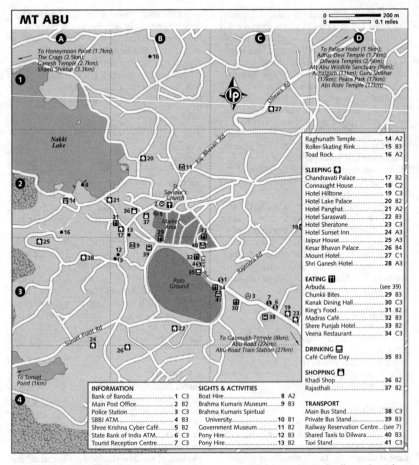

MT ABU

0 ——— 200 m
0 ——— 0.1 miles

To Honeymoon Point (1.7km);
The Crags (2.5km);
Ganesh Temple (2.7km);
Shanti Shikhar (3.3km)

To Palace Hotel (1.5km);
Adhar Devi Temple (1.7km);
Dilwara Temples (2.5km);
Mt Abu Wildlife Sanctuary (8km);
Achalgarh (11km); Guru Shikhar
(17km); Peace Park (17km);
Atri Rishi Temple (17km)

Nakki Lake

St Saviour's Church

Market Area

Polo Ground

Sunset Point Rd

To Sunset Point (1km)

To Gaumukh Temple (8km);
Abu Road (27km);
Abu Road Train Station (27km)

Raghunath Temple	14	A2
Roller-Skating Rink	15	B3
Toad Rock	16	A2

SLEEPING
Chandravati Palace	17	B2
Connaught House	18	C2
Hotel Hilltone	19	C3
Hotel Lake Palace	20	B2
Hotel Panghat	21	A2
Hotel Saraswati	22	B3
Hotel Sheratone	23	C3
Hotel Sunset Inn	24	A3
Jaipur House	25	A3
Kesar Bhavan Palace	26	B4
Mount Hotel	27	C1
Shri Ganesh Hotel	28	A3

EATING
Arbuda	(see 39)	
Chunkii Bites	29	B3
Kanak Dining Hall	30	C3
King's Food	31	B3
Madras Café	32	B3
Shere Punjab Hotel	33	B2
Veena Restaurant	34	C3

DRINKING
Café Coffee Day	35	B3

SHOPPING
Khadi Shop	36	B2
Rajasthali	37	B2

TRANSPORT
Main Bus Stand	38	C3
Private Bus Stand	39	B3
Railway Reservation Centre	(see 7)	
Shared Taxis to Dilwara	40	B3
Taxi Stand	41	C3

INFORMATION
Bank of Baroda	1	C3
Main Post Office	2	B2
Police Station	3	C3
SBBJ ATM	4	B3
Shree Krishna Cyber Café	5	B2
State Bank of India ATM	6	C3
Tourist Reception Centre	7	C3

SIGHTS & ACTIVITIES
Boat Hire	8	A2
Brahma Kumaris Museum	9	B3
Brahma Kumaris Spiritual University	10	B1
Government Museum	11	B2
Pony Hire	12	B3
Pony Hire	13	B2

some of India's finest temple decoration. It's said that the artisans were paid according to the amount of dust they collected, encouraging them to carve ever more intricately. Whatever their inducement, there are two temples in which the marble work is dizzyingly intense, a collection of delicate milky kaleidoscopes, with icing-like carving so fine it looks like you could break it off and eat it. No photography is permitted.

The older of the temples is the **Vimal Vasahi**, on which work began in 1031 and which was financed by a Gujarati minister named Vimal. Dedicated to the first *tirthankar,* Adinath, it took 14 years and allegedly cost Rs 180.5 million to build. The central shrine has an image of Adinath himself, while around the

courtyard are 52 identical cells, each enclosing a cross-legged Buddha-*tirthankar* – the crucial difference between these statues and those of Buddha is that their eyes are always open. Forty-eight beautifully carved pillars form the courtyard entrance, in front of which stands the **House of Elephants**, featuring a procession of elephants marching to the temple entrance, some of which were damaged long ago by marauding Mughals.

The later **Luna Vasahi Temple** is dedicated to Neminath, the 22nd *tirthankar*, and was built in 1230 by the brothers Tejpal and Vastupal for a mere Rs 125.9 million. Like Vimal, the brothers were both Gujarati government ministers. The marble carving here took 2500 workers 15 years to create, and its most notable feature is its intricacy and delicacy, which is so fine that, in places, the marble becomes almost transparent. In particular, the many-layered lotus flower that dangles from the centre of the dome is an astonishing piece of work. It's difficult to believe that this huge lacelike filigree started life as a solid block of marble. The temple remains incredibly well preserved, employing several full-time stone masons to maintain the work.

There are three other temples in the enclosure – **Bhimashah Pittalhar** (built between 1315 and 1433), sporting a 4-tonne five-metal statue of Adinath; **Mahaveerswami** (1582), a small shrine flanked by painted elephants; and the three-storey **Khartar Vasahi**. None, however, competes with the ethereal beauty of Luna Vasahi and Vimal Vasahi.

As at other Jain temples, leather articles (belts as well as shoes) have to be left at the entrance, and menstruating women are warned away.

You can stroll out to Dilwara from Mt Abu in less than an hour, or hop aboard a shared taxi.

BRAHMA KUMARIS SPIRITUAL UNIVERSITY & MUSEUM

The white-clad people you'll see around town around town are students of the **Brahma Kumaris Spiritual University** (www.bkwsu.com). This organisation teaches that all religions lead to God and are equally valid, and that the principles of each should be studied. The university's aim is the establishment of universal peace through 'the impartation of spiritual knowledge and training of easy raja yoga meditation'. The headquarters are here in Mt Abu, and many followers come each year to attend courses at the university.

For many the teachings are intensely powerful; there are over 4500 branches in 70 countries. It even has consultative status on the Economic and Social Council of the UN. For others, it gives off a spooky New Age–sect vibe and non-believing locals of Mt Abu might try to warn you away. You can decide for yourself by paying a visit to the university's **Universal Peace Hall** (☎ 238268; 8am-6pm), where free tours are available, including an introduction to the philosophy of the Brahma Kumaris. If you want to find out more, you can attend a daily morning meditation class (held at the museum) or take an introductory course (seven lessons), including yoga tuition for a minimum of three days, though a course of seven days is recommended. If

you come out hooked, there's a further six-month advanced course to set you on target for spiritual enlightenment. There's no fee for any of these activities.

The organisation also runs the **Peace Park** (admission free; 8am-6pm), 17km north of town, and a **museum** (☎ 223260; admission free; 8am-8pm) in the town centre, the entrance of which is labelled 'Gateway to Paradise'. The museum outlines the university's teachings through the means of wonderfully kitsch light-up dioramas, and attempts answers to teasers such as 'How can world peace be established?' in a manner of which old Walt himself would have been proud.

OTHER ATTRACTIONS

The small, seldom-visited **government museum** (Raj Bhavan Rd; admission Rs 3; 10am-4.30pm Sat-Thu) features a diorama illustrating local tribal life, some hill dwellers' artefacts, and a few miniature paintings. The highlight is the sculpture gallery, with works from the ancient town of Chandravati, 7km from Mt Abu, dating from the 6th to the 12th centuries. Note the sculpture of the snake goddess Vish Kanya breastfeeding a snake – something not to attempt at home.

About 3km north of town, 365 steps lead to the ancient **Adhar Devi Temple**, which is built in a natural cleft in the rock. You have to stoop to get through the low entrance to the temple, which holds atmospheric devotional services at dawn. There are splendid views over Mt Abu from up here.

Activities

The town has a **roller-skating rink** (per 15/30 min incl skate hire Rs 15/25; 9am-10pm). Beware the honeymooners on wheels for the first time, whizzing uncontrollably at high speed towards you.

TREKKING

There are many good treks to be undertaken from Mt Abu; see p268 for details.

HORSE RIDING

You can hire ponies at the stand not far from the lake, and at various places dotted around the town. One-hour rides cost Rs 50.

Tours

The RTDC has five-hour tours of Mt Abu's main sites, leaving from the bus stand at 8.30am and 1.30pm (later in summer). Tours cost Rs 65, excluding admission and camera

---

TREKKING FROM MT ABU

Unused by most local holidayers who remain firmly enchanted with the pedalo-and-pony attractions of the town, Mt Abu's hiking trails are many and various, leading you in just a few minutes out into untouched wilderness. Here, you'll find tranquillity, solitude, wild flowers and birdlife in abundance – as well as the odd snake, leopard or bear. Though deforestation was, until recently, threatening to scar the landscape, stringent new laws on wood gathering seem to have worked wonders, and regrowth can already be seen.

Since many hiking and trekking routes are unmapped, it's best to employ the services of a guide. This is especially important these days if you're travelling alone, as the tourist police actively discourage – or even forbid – solo hiking after a group of tourists were seriously assaulted some years ago by bandits. A guide will also be able to point out the manifold medicinal plants you'll encounter along the way, used to make Ayurvedic remedies. You'll also doubtless see the troublesome human-introduced lantana plant, which has overrun many hillsides, threatening indigenous species that have been growing here for millennia.

There are a few good guides in Mt Abu; contact Mahendra Dan (aka Charles) at Mount Abu Treks (☎ 91-9414154854; www.mount-abu-treks.blogspot.com), who runs a whole range of tailor-made whole- and half-day treks, with overnight journeys also possible. Alternatively, join one of the treks organised by Lalit at the Shri Ganesh Hotel, who takes groups out for three- to four-hour jaunts each morning. Routes vary and the level of difficulty depends on the fitness of the group.

---

fees. The afternoon tour finishes at Sunset Point. Make reservations at the **enquiries counter** (☎ 235434) at the main bus stand.

Sleeping

Mt Abu town centre seems to largely consist of hotels, and new ones spring up each year. The high season lasts from mid-April to June, during and after Diwali (October to November, when you need to book way ahead, prices become ridiculous, and you can't move for crowds – not a good time to visit) and from Christmas to New Year.

During the low season, discounts of up to 70% are available, and midrange accommodation can be an absolute steal. Most places are definitely open to a bit of bargaining, and the rates become more appealing the longer you plan to stay.

Hot water can be erratic at the budget places, and service, at all but the choicest top-end places, can be a bit lacklustre when things are busy. The Paying Guest House Scheme, which gives you the opportunity to live with a local family and is a great way to circumvent uninspiring hotel choices, operates in Mt Abu, costing around Rs 100 to Rs 500 per person, per night. Contact the tourist reception centre for details.

BUDGET

our pick **Shri Ganesh Hotel** (☎ 237292; lalit_ganesh@yahoo.co.in; dm Rs 50, r Rs 150-250, without bathroom Rs 60-200; 🖳) Up the hill towards the old summer palace of the maharaja of Jaipur, this serene place is the most popular spot to stay, and deservedly so. It has a peaceful rooftop, friendly management, loads of helpful local info, a guest kitchen and good home cooking. There's yoga on the roof in the mornings. Lalit Ganesh takes travellers trekking (above), and his Irish wife, Beverley, offers cooking lessons. If you stay in the dorm, you'll have to pay Rs 50 for a shower. Call ahead for pick-up from the bus or train station.

Hotel Saraswati (☎ 238887; r Rs 250-700) Popular and efficient, Saraswati is a reasonably appealing place in a peaceful setting behind the polo ground, and is one of the best, after Shri Ganesh, of the budget bunch. There's a range of rooms, which go from just passable to pretty decent; see a few of the 36 on offer before you decide (and plump, if you can, for one with a balcony). The rooms in the annexe are mostly in better condition than the others. The restaurant serves fantastic Gujarati thalis. Note that prices frequently double at the weekend.

Chandravati Palace (☎ 238219; d Rs 300-800) Down a quiet side street, this is a pleasant small guesthouse with basic but extremely clean and bright modern rooms. The best ones have spacious balconies and hill views.

Hotel Panghat (☎ 238886; d Rs 350-600) Well situated and overlooking the lake, this hotel is in the heart of the action. The rooms are plain and uninspiring, but are compensated by a great rooftop with a view, and unusually friendly and obliging staff.

MIDRANGE

Most places offer low-season discounts of 30% to 50%.

Mount Hotel (☎ 235150; Dilwara Rd; s/d Rs 500/1000) Once a British army officer's house, this is a lovely, homy place. The seven rooms are outfitted with wooden furnishings that give off a distinctly Swedish vibe. It's in a tranquil location, on the road to the Dilwara Temples, with a small lawn.

Hotel Sunset Inn (☎ 235194; Sunset Point Rd; s/d Rs 800/1000) On the western edge of Mt Abu, the popular, modern Sunset Inn is efficiently run and friendly, with a good vegetarian restaurant and good-sized, clean, but (like most hotels in Mt Abu) overpriced rooms. It's set in pleasing small gardens.

Hotel Sheratone (☎ 238366; d from Rs 1000) The spelling isn't quite right…a cunning attempt to cash in on a famous name. Rooms, though lacking in anything approaching character, have balconies and views across the trees. Marble staircases add to the general feel of attempted grandeur done on the cheap, but it's clean and the management is very keen to please.

Hotel Lake Palace (☎ 237154; www.savshantihotels .com; d/ste from Rs 1800/1980; 🔄) In an excellent lakeside location, spacious, friendly Lake Palace overlooks a small garden. It's classier than most on the lake, with appropriately high prices. Rooms, though simple and unspectacular, are clean, uncluttered, and some have semiprivate lakeview terrace areas. It's popular with Brahma Kumaris students; beware the rainy season, however, when rooms can get rather damp and gloomy.

Kesar Bhavan Palace (☎ 238647; Sunset Point Rd; r/ste from Rs 2000/2850; 🔄 🔄) This heritage property, originally the 19th-century home of the Sirohi royal family, is perched high up among trees and has beautiful views of rolling hills, which extend to the windows of some of the suites' bathrooms. The well-thought-out, comfortable, marble-floored rooms all have balconies, most rooms are fitted out with dark wooden antique furniture, and the suites are split-level. The hotel also tries, honourably, to reduce its environmental impact: there's water recycling to water the gardens, solar hot-water heating, and a no-plastic-bag policy in place.

Hotel Hilltone (☎ 238391; www.hotelhilltone.com; s/d from Rs 2400/3000; 🔄 🔄) Hotel Hilltone is a central, modern holiday complex, a second – and equally badly spelled – Mt Abu attempt at emulating a certain famous international chain. Rooms are tidy and comfortable, with two curious 'cave suites' incorporating carved rock walls. There's a small pool, a sauna, a children's playground, a good restaurant and a cocktail bar.

Palace Hotel (Bikaner House; ☎ 238673; www.palace hotelbikanerhouse.com; Delwara Rd; r deluxe from Rs 2500, ste from Rs 4000; 🔄) Near the Dilwara Temples is this huge palace, built in 1893 by Sir Swinton Jacob. Once the summer residence of the maharaja of Bikaner, the sprawling building resembles a Scottish stately manor, with tree-shaded gardens, a private lake, two tennis courts and a restaurant. There are 35 well-decorated rooms; the ones in the old wing have the most character – some are huge and feel very much like you've stepped into a little piece of Britain, a theme firmly continued in the grand old dining room with its hearty full English breakfasts.

Connaught House (☎ 238560; Rajendra Rd; d Rs 3500-3800; 🔄) Owned by the maharaja of Jodhpur and seemingly staffed by Raj retainers, Connaught House is delightful, a stuck-in-time colonial bungalow on the southeastern edge of town. It's more like an English cottage than a hotel, with lots of sepia photographs, dark wood, slanted ceilings, gorgeous shady gardens and marmalade for breakfast. Attractive newer rooms in a separate block have great views over the hills, though far less character. Delicious meals are available but should be ordered in advance.

TOP END

There are quite a few top-end choices in town, but the three listed here are the most atmospheric: all vestiges of old India or, in the case of Connaught House and the Palace Hotel, old England. Prices drop quite substantially in the low season and climb equally steeply during the busiest times of year.

Jaipur House (☎ 235176; www.royalfamilyjaipur.com; s/d junior ste Rs 2000/2800, other ste Rs 4500-6500; 🔄) Perched on a hilltop overlooking the lake, this old summer palace was built by the maharaja of Jaipur in 1897. Opulent suites overlook the town from a suitably lofty height. If you're not really a suite person, there are rooms in the former servants' quarters that verge on the simple (but aren't any cheaper). The restaurant and bar are open to nonguests; the restaurant's food is nothing to write home about, but the bar makes a terrific venue for imbibing the views while sipping a G&T.

Eating

Most holidaymakers here are Gujarati – tough customers when it comes to cuisine, hence the profusion of good-quality places to eat in the town.

our pick **Kanak Dining Hall** (dishes Rs 25-65; ☽ 8am-11pm) A popular option, the excellent all-you-can-eat Gujarati thalis (Rs 60) are without doubt some of Mt Abu's best. Sit indoors in the extremely popular, bustling dining hall or outside under a canopy.

Veena Restaurant (veg dishes Rs 25-70; ☽ 7am-11pm) Veena, near the taxi stand, also draws crowds for its excellent Gujarati thalis and traditional Indian fare; the freshly brewed coffee makes a good way to round off a button-popping meal. As at Kanak, you can eat outside, which you might want to do given the Bollywood soundtrack and garish lighting indoors.

King's Food (dishes Rs 25-90; ☽ 7.30am-11.30pm) This busy, open-to-the-street fast-food joint is good for a light bite. It has the usual have-a-go menu, including Chinese, Punjabi and South Indian food, and good lassis, as well as filling breakfasts and nice Indian dinner-sized curries.

Madras Café (Lake Rd; dishes Rs 30-80; ☽ 7am-11pm) The laid-back Madras Café has pleasant indoor, outdoor and rooftop seating. It's a pure-veg place serving an assortment of South Indian and Punjabi dishes, as well as pizzas. Try the delicious, substantial mixed-fruit lassi. You can watch bread being baked in the outside oven and round it all off with an ice-cream sundae.

Chunkii Bites (Shopping Complex, Lake Rd; dishes Rs 35-70; ☽ 7am-11.30pm) This place (whose catch-phrase is a snazzy 'bite to live long') is a good spot to grab a cheap snack. Grubby but cheerful, it has loud music and regional delicacies such as *bhelpuri* (a popular Mumbai snack) and Delhi *chaat* (snacks such as samosas and potato patties seasoned with spices and served with chutney).

Arbuda (Arbuda Circle; dishes Rs 35-80; ☽ 6am-11pm) Across the road from Chunkii Bites and set on a sweeping, curved, open-air terrace that's filled with chrome chairs, Arbuda special-

ises in Punjabi and South Indian food – the dosas are divine – and serves up some mean vegetarian curries, though even their pizzas are pretty decent.

Shere Punjab Hotel (dishes Rs 35-200; ☽ 8am-midnight) Shere Punjab, in the market, has bargain Punjabi and Chinese food. For the devil-may-care carnivore, there's brain fry or brain masala, but there are also some more conventional options, such as chicken curry, and a long list of vegetarian options for those frightened off by the sight of all that brain.

Drinking

Most of the more upmarket hotels have bars serving local and imported drinks; the prices are predictably high, but the heritage hotels more than justify this with their quaint and antiquated atmosphere.

Café Coffee Day (Hotel Maharaja International; snacks Rs 30-80; ☽ 8.30am-11pm) Every now and then, it's not a crime to be gasping for an over-priced, oversized latte or a cup of unadulterated Darjeeling tea. This popular coffee-shop chain also serves satisfyingly squidgy cakes, to consume while guiltily ensconced in a nice, deep armchair.

Jaipur House (☎ 235176; www.royalfamilyjaipur.com) The outdoor terrace of this heritage hotel has superlative views across Mt Abu, Nakki Lake and the surrounding countryside, and is the perfect place for a sunset tipple, watching the town's twinkling lights flicker to life.

Shopping

Around Nakki Lake are lots of bright little shops and stalls flogging all sorts of kitsch curios. In the evening the town comes to life, and this is a fine time to do some leisurely browsing and people-watching.

There's an expensive branch of **Rajasthali** (Raj Bhavan Rd; ☽ 9.30am-9pm), the government crafts emporium, which has some very eager sales staff. Alternatively, you may like to try the fixed-price **khadi shop** (Raj Bhavan Rd; ☽ 10am-1pm & 3.30-9pm), which sells all things woven.

Getting There & Away

As you enter Mt Abu there's a toll gate – bus and car passengers are charged Rs 10, plus Rs 21 for a car (keep change handy).

BUS

From 6am to 9pm, buses make the exciting 27km mountain road climb from Abu Road train station up to Mt Abu (Rs 24, one hour, half-hourly). Buses leave from outside the main bus stand, next to the ticket booth. Some RSRTC buses go all the way to Mt Abu, while others terminate at Abu Road.

The bus schedule from Mt Abu is extensive, and for many destinations you will find a direct bus faster and more convenient than going down to Abu Road and waiting for a train.

RSRTC buses (☎ 235434) go to Jaipur (Rs 230/250 in express/deluxe, 11 hours, one nightly), Ajmer (Rs 175/211 in express/deluxe, seven hours, one nightly), Udaipur (Rs 98 in express, five hours, four daily), Jodhpur (Rs 144 in express, six hours, one daily), and Ahmedabad (Rs 104 in express, 6½ hours, three daily). Buses that belong to private bus companies, offering similar services at similar prices, depart from the private bus stand.

There are lots of travel agencies around town offering bus tickets. Shop around for the best price.

TAXI

A taxi for up to six people into town from Abu Road costs about Rs 300. Some drivers claim that this is only as far as the bus stand and ask an extra fee (as much as Rs 50) to take you to your hotel; make the total price clear before you depart Abu Road. To hire a jeep for sightseeing costs about Rs 500/1000 per half-day/day (bargain hard and you may bring it down). Many hotels can arrange jeep hire, or you can hire your own in the town centre.

TRAIN

Abu Road, the railhead for Mt Abu, is on the line between Delhi and Mumbai via Ahmedabad. In Mt Abu, above the tourist office, there's a **railway reservation centre** (☼ 8am-2pm), which has quotas on most of the express trains.

Several trains per day run from Abu Road to Ahmedabad; the No 2916 *Ashram Express* departs Abu Road at an early-morning 3.50am but arrives conveniently swiftly at Ahmedabad at 7.40am (Rs 196/283/501 3AC/2AC/1AC). The daily No 9223 *Tawi Express* runs from Abu Road to Jodhpur (Rs 115/465 Sl/2AC), departing Abu Road at 3.17pm and arriving at 8.15pm. For other services, check up-to-date information at the reservation centre.

Getting Around

Buses from the main bus stand go to the various sites in Mt Abu, but it takes a little planning to get out and back without too much hanging around; check return times at the bus stand before you leave. For Dilwara you can take a shared taxi (jeeps, which leave when full from opposite the Madras Café and cost Rs 6 per person, or Rs 40 all to yourself). Alternatively, it makes a pleasant 4km walk to the temples.

There are no autorickshaws in Mt Abu, but it's easy to get around on foot. Unique to the town is the *baba-gari*, a porter-pulled handcart, which will cart your luggage for Rs 15 or even one/two people for Rs 30/40.

AROUND MT ABU
Mt Abu Wildlife Sanctuary

This beautiful 290-sq-km **sanctuary** (Indian/foreigner/jeep Rs 10/40/100; ☼ 8am-5pm), on a large plateau 5.5km northeast of Mt Abu, is home to leopards, sambars, foxes, wild boars, bears, crocodiles and birdlife. It's about a 1km walk from the Dilwara Temples.

Achalgarh

The fascinating, atmospheric Shiva temple of **Achaleshwar Mahandeva**, 11km north of Mt Abu in Achalgarh, boasts a number of diverting features, including what's said to be a toe of Shiva, as well as a brass Nandi bull (Shiva's vehicle). Where the Shiva lingam would normally be there's a deep hole, believed by devotees to extend all the way down to the underworld.

Just outside the temple, beside the car park, three stone buffaloes stand around a tank, while the figure of a king shoots at them with his bow and arrows. A legend tells that the tank was once filled with ghee, but demons, in the form of the buffaloes, arrived from the skies to pollute the holy ghee – until, that is, the king managed to shoot them. A path leads up the hillside to the hilltop group of colourful Jain temples, which have fantastic views out over the plains.

Guru Shikhar

At the end of the Mt Abu plateau, 15km north of the town itself, is 1722m-high **Guru Shikhar**, Rajasthan's highest point. A road goes almost all the way to the summit and the **Atri Rishi Temple**, complete with a priest and fantastic, huge views. A popular spot, it's visited as part of the RDTC tour; if you decide to go it alone, a jeep will cost Rs 400 return.

Gaumukh Temple

Down on the Abu Road side of Mt Abu, 8km southeast of the town, a small stream flows from the mouth of a marble cow, giving the shrine its name (*gaumukh* means 'cow's mouth'). There's also a marble figure of the bull Nandi. The tank here, Agni Kund, is said to be the site of the sacrificial fire made by the sage Vasishta, from which four of the great Rajput clans were born. An image of Vasishta is flanked by figures of Rama and Krishna.

To reach the temple you must take a path consisting of 750 steps down into the valley – a nd then trudge those same 750 steps back up again.

ABU ROAD

This station, down on the plains 27km from Mt Abu, is the rail junction for Mt Abu. The train station and bus stand are conveniently located right next to each other on the edge of town.

Although there are RSRTC buses from Abu Road to cities such as Jodhpur, Jaipur, Udaipur and Ahmedabad, there's little point in catching them from here since services are all available from Mt Abu itself, along with alternative private bus company services to the same destinations. The **railway retiring rooms** (d Rs 150) at the station have rock-bottom prices with suitably rock-hard mattresses, but are convenient if you're catching a very early train. Note that you may be asked to show an onward ticket to be able to bed down here for the night.

Northern Rajasthan (Shekhawati)

Far less visited than most other parts of Rajasthan, the extraordinary Shekhawati region is most famous for its painted *havelis* (traditional, ornately decorated residences), smothered with dazzling, often cartoonlike murals. What makes the region all the more astonishing is that these works of art are largely found in tiny towns, connected to each other by single-track roads that run through bleak, arid countryside, where women's colourful clothes seem to flicker like beacons as they move across the barren fields.

Today it seems curious that such care, attention and financing was lavished on these out-of-the-way houses, but from the 14th century onwards, Shekhawati's towns were important trading posts on the caravan routes from Gujarati ports. Most buildings, though, date from the 18th and 19th centuries, when the local merchants moved to places with richer pickings, and sent all their money back to build grand edifices to house their families and impress the neighbours.

Part of what makes the artwork on Shekhawati's *havelis* so fascinating is the manner in which their artists combined traditional subjects, such as mythology, religious scenes and images of the family, with contemporary concerns, including brand-new inventions and accounts of current events, many of which these isolated painters rendered straight from their imagination. As a whole these kaleidoscopic images present a unique document of life, and all its concerns, a century and more ago. While it's impossible to detail all the beautiful homes you may stumble across on your journey through Shekhawati, this chapter includes a selection of highlights. Look out, too, for forts, *baoris* (step-wells), *chhatris* (cenotaphs) and mosques, all ripe for the discovery.

HIGHLIGHTS

- Gaze at glorious technicolour *havelis* (merchants' houses) in **Parsurampura** (p282), **Ramgarh** (p290) and **Mukundgarh** (p284).

- Head out on an ecologically minded tour from **Nawalgarh** (p280), exploring unchanged rural villages.

- Explore the derelict Khetri Mahal in **Jhunjhunu** (p286) – all arches, columns and architectural whimsy.

- Take in Sone ki Dukan Haveli, featuring lavish paintings using real gold, in sleepy, back-in-time **Mahansar** (p289)

- Take time out in the beautifully restored Haveli Nadine Prince in **Fatehpur** (p292), lingering over lunch in its cool café.

Mahansar ★   ★ Jhunjhunu

Fatehpur ★   ★ Mukundgarh

Nawalgarh ★   ★ Parsurampura

★ Ramgarh

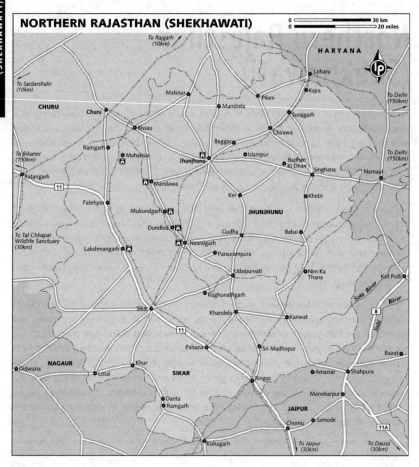

NORTHERN RAJASTHAN (SHEKHAWATI)

History

A rich but lawless land on the trade route between the ports of the Arabian Sea and the fertile Ganges Valley, this region was, in its early history, dominated by the Shekhawats, with portions (principally Jhunjhunu and Fatehpur) held by the Muslim Kayamkhani Nawabs (Muslim ruling princes or landowners). The Shekhawati *thakurs* (noblemen), like other Rajasthani rulers, were once most noted for their penchant for arguing among themselves. Unlike other areas of Rajasthan, the region was thus never combined into a single principality, but remained a conglomeration of separate, quarrelsome feudal domains that were mainly run by the same family.

The name 'Shekhawati' can be traced to a 15th-century Rajput Kachhwaha chieftain by the name of Rao Shekha. As the Mughal empire declined after the death of the emperor Aurangzeb in 1707, his descendants, who had already installed themselves in the area to the east of the Aravalli Hills, encroached to the north and west.

The *thakurs* of the region retained a nominal loyalty to the Rajput states of Jaipur and Amber, which in turn honoured them with the hereditary titles of *tazimi sardars* (hereditary nobles entitled to be received at a ceremonial reception held by the chief). The Rajputs, however, never really trusted the *thakurs* – for example, when Jaipur was built in the 18th century, the Shekhawats were offered land *outside* the city walls to build their houses. Despite not being allowed in the inner circle, it was probably exposure to the courts of Jaipur and Amber that encouraged the *thakurs* to commission the very first murals to decorate their *havelis*.

By 1732 two of these *thakurs* – Sardul Singh and Shiv Singh – had overthrown the nawabs of Fatehpur and Jhunjhunu and carved out their territories in the region. Their descendants, particularly the sons of Sardul Singh, installed themselves in surrounding villages, filling their pockets with heavy taxes imposed on the poor farmers of the area and duties levied on caravans carrying goods from the ports of Gujarat. But for the merchants travelling on the Shekhawati route, this trail was nevertheless a cheap option – the Rajput states on either side imposed even greater levies and the arid region soon became busy with trade, attracting more and more merchants. The riches, inevitably, also attracted dacoits (bandits), imbuing the area with a distinctly lawless, Wild West flavour.

The rise of the British Raj could potentially have been a death blow for Shekhawati, since the British ports in Bombay (Mumbai) and Calcutta (Kolkata) were able to handle a far higher volume of trade than those in Gujarat. Moreover, pressure from the British East India Company compelled Jaipur state to reduce its levies, so it was no longer necessary for traders to travel with their goods through Shekhawati. But Shekhawati merchants had received a good grounding in the practices and principles of trade, and were reluctant to relinquish a lucrative source of income.

Towards the end of the 19th century, Shekhawati's men thus emigrated en masse from their desert homes to the thriving trading centres emerging on the ports of the Ganges. Their business acumen was unparalleled, and soon some of the richest merchants residing in Calcutta were those who hailed from the tiny region of Shekhawati. Some of India's wealthiest industrialists of the 20th century, such as the Birlas, were originally Marwaris, as the people of Shekhawati later became known.

Information

BOOKS

For a full rundown on the history, people, towns and buildings of the area, try tracking down a copy of *The Painted Towns of Shekhawati* by Ilay Cooper, which, though currently out of print, can be picked up at secondhand bookshops in the region.

Another good book, available locally, is *Shekhawati Painted Townships* by Kishore Singh, which is well photographed and has lots of background information.

Apani Dhani (p281) in Nawalgarh has a good reference library of books on the region, in English and French, available for use by guests and those dropping by for a meal.

Activities & Tours

A number of operators offer camel or horse-riding safaris in the Shekhawati region. These are a relaxing way to see rural life and birdlife, fitting in well with the pace of life outside the towns. In Nawalgarh you have a wide choice of trekking, horse riding, camel safaris or tours by bicycle (p280). In Dundlod experienced riders can go horse riding (p284) on fine Marwari horses, or you can take a camel or jeep safari. Camel safaris are on offer at Mahansar's **Narayan Niwas Castle** (☎ 01595-264322) and camel and jeep safaris at Mukundgarh, while you have the choice of camel, jeep or horse trips at Mandawa (p295), or camel, jeep or bicycle trips at Jhunjhunu (p287).

There are also several places where, inspired by all this artwork, you can undertake courses in painting or local crafts (p280). In

---

FESTIVALS IN NORTHERN RAJASTHAN

Shekhawati has a couple of festivals to its name, but also celebrates statewide and nationwide festivals with fervour (see p358).

Shekhawati Festival (www.shekhawatifestival.com; statewide; Feb) Promoted by the Rajasthan Tourism Development Corporation (RTDC), the official programme includes safaris, tours of the region, competitions and fireworks, but remains a small and locally flavoured affair, for the moment at least.

Bissau Festival (Bissau; Sep/Oct) Ten days before the festival of Dussehra, Bissau hosts dramatic mime performances of the Ramayana. The actors wear costumes and locally made masks, and the performances take place in the bazaar at twilight.

SEEING SHEKHAWATI RESPONSIBLY

Though the tourist boom has not quite caught up here yet, it probably won't be too much longer in coming, bringing with it, as it has in many other parts of Rajasthan, seemingly unavoidable concerns for the culture and environment. For those lucky enough to visit the region before the tourist buses descend en masse, there are a number of things you can do to reduce your impact. Since many gorgeous *havelis* have, for decades, been plundered or left to fade away, responsible tourism can play a positive role in the preservation of the region's masterpieces, generating the will among locals to preserve and cherish its heritage.

Currently, only a few *havelis* are open as museums or specifically for display, and consequently many are either totally or partially locked up. They are frequently still owned by the family who built them a century or more ago, but these people often no longer reside in this dusty, out-of-the-way corner of the state, either employing a *chowkidar* (caretaker) or renting the place out to tenants. While the caretakers and tenants are often tolerant of strangers wandering into their front courtyard, be aware that these are private places, and that tact should be used. Some may ask for a little baksheesh to let you in; Rs 20 or Rs 30 is usually a good price to pay for a glimpse of hidden treasures.

- Local custom dictates that shoes should be removed when entering the inner courtyard of a *haveli*. Remember that most are private homes and you should ask permission politely before entering or taking photos.

- On your travels you'll doubtless find antique shops filled temptingly with beautiful items ripped from *havelis* – usually doors and window frames, and smaller pieces of carving or painted surfaces. Under no circumstances purchase any of these items – by doing so, you will be actively encouraging the desecration of the region's greatest treasure.

- Flashes from cameras can damage the paintings. In many instances, there may not be an express prohibition on flash photography, but even so, refrain from flashing away.

  As in other parts of Rajasthan, try to limit your consumption of plastic products – especially plastic mineral water bottles and plastic carrier bags – as much as possible. The less waste you generate, the smaller the piles of plastic bottles blotting the landscape.

- In many towns, it's easy to get around by bike or on foot, rather than plumping for the pollution-heavy autorickshaw option whose fumes will, in time, erode Shekhawati's murals. Where you can, use your feet or pedal power to see the sights.

- Water is a critical issue in Shekhawati and every drop is precious (see p80). Consider washing with a bucket rather than using the shower, even if your hotel has one installed; equally, think carefully before staying in a hotel with a swimming pool.

- Camel and horse safaris are a popular way to visit the local villages. When on safari, ensure that your rubbish is carried away and insist on kerosene fires instead of using scarce sources of wood.

- It's possible in some places to stay in village homes, a good way to meet locals and gain an insight into their way of life: Ramesh Jangid from Nawalgarh has some interesting homestay programmes (p280). He is also the president of **Les Amis du Shekhawati** (Friends of Shekhawati; www.apanidhani.com) – to read more information about the society and its endeavours to protect the paintings of Shekhawati, see p370.

- French artist Nadine Le Prince's restored *haveli* (p292) in Fatehpur is now a cultural centre. Local and French artists work here, and the centre publicises the plight of the *havelis*: it's worth a visit.

Jhunjhunu you can also take cooking courses (p287) of various lengths.

Getting Around

The Shekhawati region is crisscrossed by narrow, dusty roads and all towns are served by government or private buses and jam-packed shared jeeps. Old 1950s snub-snouted Tata Mercedes buses ply the routes, with turbaned villagers riding 'upper class' (on the roof). Buses may be busy but they are less crowded than jeeps, and generally a little bit safer. Many of the roads are in poor condition, so be prepared for an occasionally bumpy journey.

Though several towns are served by trains, services are currently slow and unreliable, so bus or jeep is definitely the better bet.

To zip from town to town more speedily and in greater comfort, hire a taxi for the day. The usual rate for a non-AC taxi is Rs 3.5 to 5 per kilometre with a minimum of 250km per day. Around four or five people can travel in one car, so having a larger group will keep costs down.

Another means of getting around the area is by bicycle – you can hire bikes in most of the major places – but be prepared for a bumpy, dusty ride. The best way to explore the towns themselves is on foot. Some of the larger towns also offer transport in autorickshaws and tongas (two-wheeled horse carriages).

NAWALGARH
☎ 01594 / pop 56,482

Nawalgarh is a small and lively town almost at the very centre of the region, and thus makes a great base for exploring. It has a fine bunch of *havelis*, a colourful, mostly pedestrianised bazaar and some excellent accommodation options.

The town was founded in 1737 by Nawal Singh, one of the five sons of the Rajput ruler Sardul Singh. The arrival of merchants from Jaipur increased the town's prosperity, and some of India's most successful merchants, such as the wealthy Goenka family (which built many *havelis*), hailed from Nawalgarh. The town is built in a depression where a number of rivers terminate; the accumulated silt carried by these rivers was used to make the bricks (some of the best preserved in Shekhawati) for local *havelis*.

Orientation & Information

Nawalgarh is quite compact, and most of its *havelis* are centrally located and easy to reach on foot. The train station and bus stands are all at the western end of town, while accommodation is concentrated in the north and west.

There are several internet cafés around town; they change frequently but all charge Rs 30 to 50 per hour. Ask at your hotel if you have any trouble locating one. The **State Bank of Bikaner & Jaipur** (SBBJ; Bala Qila complex) changes currency and travellers cheques, and there's an SBBJ ATM near the post office, though it's not always working.

The best sources of information on Nawalgarh and its painted *havelis* are Ramesh Jangid at **Apani Dhani** (☎ 222239; www.apanidhani .com) and his son Rajesh at **Ramesh Jangid's Tourist Pension** (☎ 224060). Both father and son are involved in the preservation of Shekhawati's *havelis* and in educational programmes to raise local awareness about their rich cultural legacy. They also run ecologically minded tours through their agency Alternative Travels, mainly in Rajasthan but also to Gujarat, Uttar Pradesh, Madhya Pradesh, Tamil Nadu, Kerala and Karnataka. See the website www .apanidhani.com for more details.

Sights
BALA QILA

The fort of Bala Qila was founded in 1737, but today its modern additions largely obscure the original building, and it houses a fruit-and-vegetable market and two banks. The **Sheesh Mahal** in the southeastern quarter of the fort, though, is one room that retains mirrorwork and beautiful paintings on its ceiling, depicting map-like street scenes of both Jaipur and Nawalgarh from the mid-19th century. The grand but rather spooky room was once the dressing room of the maharani of Nawalgarh. To find it, climb a small greenish staircase in the southeastern corner of the fort to the 2nd floor. The room is hidden behind a sweet shop, where you will be asked for Rs 10 or Rs 20 to be allowed through.

HAVELIS

To the west of Bala Qila is a group of six *havelis*, known as the **Aath Havelis**, erected around 1900. *Aath* means 'eight', and they were so named because originally eight *havelis* were planned. The paintings are not technically as proficient as some others in this town, but they are interesting because they illustrate the transition in painting styles over the decades. As you approach the group through the gate from the road, for example, the first *haveli* to the left has older paintings on the front of the side external wall, while newer paintings, with synthetic colours, are at the rear. The front section depicts a steam locomotive, and the back section features some monumental pictures of elephants, horses and camels. There are lots of eclectic, lively subjects to peruse, including barbers, trains and false windows.

Opposite this group of *havelis* is the beautifully preserved **Murarka Haveli**, which has some fine paintings, including miniatures above the entrance depicting the Krishna (the most

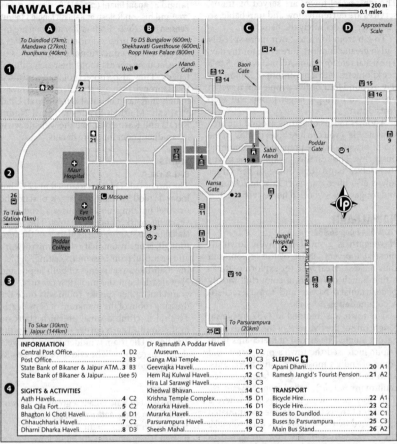

NAWALGARH

INFORMATION		
Central Post Office	1	D2
Post Office	2	B3
State Bank of Bikaner & Jaipur ATM	3	B3
State Bank of Bikaner & Jaipur	(see 5)	
SIGHTS & ACTIVITIES		
Aath Havelis	4	C2
Bala Qila Fort	5	C2
Bhagton ki Choti Haveli	6	D1
Chhauchharia Haveli	7	C2
Dharni Dharka Haveli	8	D3

Dr Ramnath A Poddar Haveli		
Museum	9	D2
Ganga Mai Temple	10	C3
Geevrajka Haveli	11	C2
Hem Raj Kulwal Haveli	12	C1
Hira Lal Sarawgi Haveli	13	C3
Khedwal Bhavan	14	C1
Krishna Temple Complex	15	D1
Moraka Haveli	16	D1
Murarka Haveli	17	B2
Parsurampura Haveli	18	D3
Sheesh Mahal	19	C2

SLEEPING		
Apani Dhani	20	A1
Ramesh Jangid's Tourist Pension	21	A2
TRANSPORT		
Bicycle Hire	22	A1
Bicycle Hire	23	C2
Buses to Dundlod	24	C1
Buses to Parsurampura	25	C3
Main Bus Stand	26	A2

celebrated of the Hindu deities) legends. The *haveli* is nowadays rented out for weddings. Unless there's an event going on, the courtyard is, sadly, likely to be locked; you can still catch a glimpse, though, through a gap in the gate.

About 10 minutes' walk to the north is the **Hem Raj Kulwal Haveli**, built in 1931; this *haveli* remains lived-in, but you'll be allowed entry for the customary baksheesh. Here, above the entrance, are portraits of the Kulwal family, of Mahatma Gandhi and Jawaharlal Nehru, and of a European lady putting on her make-up. Kaleidoscopic architraves surround the windows, and the outer courtyard features a triumphant train. An ornate silver door adorned with mini-

ature peacocks leads to the inner courtyard, which features paintings depicting mostly religious themes, though most are obscured by soot from decades of smoky kitchen fires. Opposite is the household's guesthouse, built in the same year, which looks as if it's strayed from Brighton (England).

Nearby is the still-inhabited **Khedwal Bhavan**, which features beautiful mirrorwork above the entrance to the inner courtyard, and fine blue tilework. A locomotive is depicted above the archway, and a frieze along the north wall shows the Teej festival (spot the women on swings). On the west wall is a large locomotive crossing a bridge and underneath are portraits of various English people. On the outside north wall is the story of Dhola

THE ARCHITECTURE OF THE HAVELI

The Persian term *haveli* means 'enclosed space', but the architecture of the *haveli* did much more than simply enclose space; it in fact provided a comprehensive system that governed the everyday lives of its inhabitants.

Most *haveli*s have a large wooden gate (usually locked) as their main entrance, in which is set a smaller doorway that gives access to the outer courtyard. Often a huge ramp leads from the street to this grand gate, up which a prospective groom would have been able to ascend in appropriate grandeur on horse- or elephant-back. Above the entrance you can usually see one or more small shield-shaped devices called *torans*. These are wrought of wood and silver, and often feature a parrot – the bird of love. In a mock show of conquest, the groom was required to pierce the *toran* with his sword before claiming his bride.

The doorway leads into an outer courtyard known as the *mardana* (men's courtyard). To one side there's usually a *baithak* (salon) in which the merchant of the household could receive his guests. In order to impress visitors, this room was generally the most elaborately crafted and often featured marble or mock-marble walls. Here, you'll frequently see images of Ganesh, god of wealth and good fortune, and this was where the merchant and his guests reclined against bolsters and were fanned by manually operated *punkahs* (cloth fans) as they discussed their business. Opposite the *baithak* is often a stable and coach house for accommodating camels, horses or elephants called a *nora*.

The outer *mardana* leads into the second, inner women's courtyard, known as the *zenana*, where the women of the household spent the majority of their lives in strict purdah (seclusion). Between the two courtyards there was often a small latticed window, through which they could peep out at male guests. Sometimes, there was also a screened-off balcony, known as the *duchatta*, above the *mardana* for them to spy on proceedings. Entry into the inner courtyard was restricted to women, family members and, occasionally, privileged male guests.

The *zenana* was the main domestic arena – the walls today are often smoke-stained by countless kitchen fires. Rooms off this courtyard served as bedrooms or storerooms, and staircases led to galleries on upper levels, which mostly comprised bedrooms – some of which were roofless, for hot nights. The courtyard arrangement, together with thick walls, provided plenty of shade to cool the inner rooms, a vital necessity in this sun-scorched land. The *haveli* thus provided everything for the women and there was no need for them to venture into the outside world – and in Shekhawati these were spectacularly gilded cages.

In the wealthiest of families, there were far more than two simple courtyards, some *haveli*s enclosing as many as eight, with galleries up to six storeys high. This meant plenty of wall space to house the elaborate murals that wealthy Shekhawati merchants were so fond of commissioning.

Maru (p292), painted in two frames. In the first frame, soldiers chase the fleeing camel-borne lovers. Maru fires arrows at the assailants while Dhola urges the camel on. Above this is a smaller painting of an English woman with an infant.

To the northeast of the Baori Gate is **Bhagton ki Choti Haveli**, where you need to pay the caretaker around Rs 40 to be allowed in. On the external west wall is a locomotive and a steamship. Above this, elephant-bodied *gopis* (milkmaids) dance. Adjacent to this, women dance during the Holi festival.

Above the doorway to the inner courtyard is a detailed picture of the marriage of Rukmani, at which Krishna cheated the groom Sisupal of his prospective wife. The walls of the salon resemble marble, painted black with decorative incisions. The inner chamber upstairs contains the family quarters, also elaborately painted. A room on the west side is home to a strange picture of a European man with a cane and pipe and a small dog on his shoulder. Adjacent, a melancholy English woman plays an accordion.

About 200m east is the **Morarka Haveli** (admission Rs 40; 8am-6.30pm). This has well-presented original paintings, preserved for decades behind doorways blocked with cement. The inner courtyard hosts some gorgeous Ramayana scenes, and look out for the slightly incongruous image of Jesus on the uppermost storey, beneath the eaves in the southeast corner of the courtyard.

On Dharni Dharka Rd is the **Parsurampura Haveli**, which dates from the early 20th century and belongs to a merchant from Parsurampura. Demonstrating the change in style that came with the influence of magazines and Western art, the grandiose paintings, with religious and secular themes, are almost *too* perfect.

In the street behind this *haveli* is the **Dharni Dharka Haveli**, which dates from 1930. There's an ornate painted carving above the arches and there are portraits of Gandhi, Nehru in an automobile, and Krishna and Radha (favourite mistress of Krishna when he lived as a cowherd) on a swing.

A short distance south of the fort are a number of interesting buildings, including the **Chhauchharia Haveli**, behind Jangit Hospital, with paintings dating from the last decade of the 19th century. These include a hot-air balloon being optimistically inflated by several Europeans blowing vigorously through pipes, and a man who at first glance appears to be exposing himself – though closer examination reveals that he is, in all innocence, holding out his finger. The elaborate floral motifs over the enormous doorway have been restored with oil paints.

To the southwest of the fort is the **Hira Lal Sarawgi Haveli**, famous for its different representations of cars. Other entertaining pictures on its external walls include an English couple sitting stiffly on a bench, a tractor with a tip-tray – an exciting new invention – and a woman trying to distract a sadhu (holy man) with an erotic dance. A short distance north is the **Geevrajka Haveli**, which has fine paintings on the ceiling of the entrance depicting various Hindu deities.

Dr Ramnath A Poddar Haveli Museum (admission Rs 85, camera Rs 30; ☾ 8.30am-5.30pm), built in the 1920s on the eastern side of town, is one of the region's few buildings to have been brightly and thoroughly restored. The building also now partly houses a secondary school upstairs, funded by the Poddars. The paintings of this *haveli* are defined in strong colours, as they must have looked when new, though some people object to the fact that many have been repainted rather than restored. Note the trompe l'oeil windows on the façade, the fresco subjects, including religious scenes, trains, cars and the British people, and the curious panel that depicts a bull's head when viewed from one side and an elephant's head

when looked at from the other. On the ground floor are several reasonably interesting displays, including one room with examples of different schools of Rajasthani painting and another with dolls in the wedding dress of different castes.

GANGA MAI TEMPLE
Several hundred metres to the south of the Nansa Gate is this fine temple, dedicated to the goddess Ganga, and decorated with mirrorwork around the inner sanctum. The courtyard is surrounded by four aisles, each formed by five archways topped by floral motifs. There are some good, small paintings above the *mandapa* (chamber before the inner sanctum of a temple). The temple was built by the wealthy Chhauchharia merchants in 1868. Devotees arrive here to worship at dawn and dusk.

Courses
Apani Dhani (☎ 222239) and **Ramesh Jangid's Tourist Pension** (☎ 224060) both arrange enjoyable lessons and workshops in Hindi, tabla drumming, cooking and local crafts such as *bandhani* (tie-dyeing); tell them exactly what you're interested in and chances are they'll be able to arrange a workshop for you.

Tours
Ramesh Jangid at **Apani Dhani** (☎ 222239) and his son Rajesh at **Ramesh Jangid's Tourist Pension** (☎ 224060) are keen to promote rural tourism, in part by organising homestays with families in small Shekhawati villages. Numbers are kept to a minimum (a maximum of two couples at a time per host family), and an English-speaking interpreter is provided. They also organise three-day treks in the Aravalli Range, camel safaris around Rajasthan, and informative guided tours around the painted *havelis*, including walking tours and trips by bicycle.

Treks start at Rs 1800/1500/1250 per person per day for up to two/three/four people. Treks include food, accommodation, transfers and a guide, and involve such excursions as walks along a dried-up river bed (you can have your luggage carried for you between picnics and nightly encampments), and visits to ashrams and temples en route.

Prices for jeep tours to the villages of Shekhawati from Nawalgarh are as follows: a three-hour trip taking in Dundlod and Parsurampura is Rs 1500 for up to four people;

a five-hour trip taking in Mandawa, Dundlod and Fatehpur is Rs 1800 for up to four people; a seven- to eight-hour trip visiting Bissau, Churu, Ramgarh and Mahansar is Rs 2000. Guided walking tours of Nawalgarh cost Rs 350 and take two to three hours. Camel-cart tours cost from Rs 1500 per person, per day.

The **Roop Niwas Palace** (☎ 222008; www.roop niwaskothi.com) specialises in high-end horse and camel excursions, the horse riding mostly on Rajasthan's gorgeous Marwari horses. Horse rides cost Rs 500 for one hour; for more elaborate overnight excursions, including accommodation in luxury tents, costs start at around US$200 per person per day. Camel rides cost Rs 450/900/1800 for one hour/half-day/full day. It offers themed package rides of a week or more; full details can be found on its website at www.royalridingholidays.com.

Sleeping & Eating

DS Bungalow (☎ 222703; s/d Rs 350/400, bigger r Rs 450/500) Run by a nice, friendly couple, this is a quiet, comfortable place with simple air-cooled rooms, a little out of town on the way to Roop Niwas Palace. It's backed by a garden with a pleasant outdoor mud-walled restaurant. The home cooking is excellent; a full dinner comes in at around Rs 250.

Ramesh Jangid's Tourist Pension (☎ 224060; s/d from Rs 400/450) Near the Maur Hospital, this pension is well known, so if you get lost, just ask a local to point you in the right direction. The guesthouse, run by genial Rajesh, Ramesh's son, offers homely, clean accommodation in spacious rooms with big beds. Some rooms have furniture carved by Rajesh's grandfather, and the more expensive rooms also have murals created by visiting artists. Scrumptious pure veg meals, made with organic ingredients, are available (including a delectable vegetable thali for Rs 80). The family also arranges all sorts of tours around Shekhawati.

Shekhawati Guesthouse (☎ 224658; www.shek hawatirestaurant.com; s/d/tr Rs 400/500/600) Next door to DS Bungalow, this is a clean, family-run place with six rooms (the best of which are the cottages in the back garden) and a lovely garden restaurant in a thatched bungalow, which offers home cooking made from organic produce. They'll make you a great (also organic) packed lunch for a day of sightseeing for Rs 125. Free pick-up from the bus or train station can be arranged, as can cooking lessons.

our pick **Apani Dhani** (☎ 222239; www.apanidhani .com; s/d from Rs 700/950) This ground-breaking, award-winning ecofarm is a delightful and relaxing place. Rooms are in traditional, cosy mud-hut bungalows, enhanced by thatched roofs and comfortable beds, around a bougainvillea-shaded courtyard. The adjoining organic farm supplies delicious ingredients, and alternative energy is used wherever possible, including solar cookers and water heaters, compost toilets and biogas. It's on the west side of the Jaipur road. Multilingual Ramesh Jangid runs the show, and is also president of Les Amis du Shekhawati, an organisation aiming to preserve the *havelis*. Tours around the area, via bicycle, car or foot, are available.

Roop Niwas Palace (☎ 222008; www.roopniwaskothi .com; s/d/ste Rs 2000/2300/3000; 🏊) About 1km north of the fort is this converted palace, with a dusty, back-to-the-Raj feel, grand grounds, a billiard room and comfortable old-fashioned rooms that are eclectically decorated. This was once the rural retreat of the *thakur* of Nawalgarh, Nawal Singh (1880–1926). Note that this is one of Shekhawati's swimming pool–equipped hotels. The hotel also runs fabulous camel and horse excursions (opposite).

Getting There & Away

BUS

There are RSRTC buses between Nawalgarh and Jaipur (Rs 62, 3½ hours, every 15 minutes), and several morning services each day to Delhi (Rs 170, eight hours) and Jodhpur (Rs 190, nine hours, six daily). There's also a daily deluxe bus to Jaipur departing at 8am (Rs 112, 3 hours) and several private services, most of which drop you an inconvenient 5km outside Jaipur. There are also private services that go to Ajmer (Rs 105, six hours).

Buses for destinations in Shekhawati leave every few minutes, while shared jeeps leave according to demand (Rs 12 to Sikar, Rs 18 to Jhunjhunu). Private buses run to Fatehpur (Rs 26, hourly) and Mandawa (Rs 15, every 45 minutes).

TRAIN

At the time of research, train services to/ from Nawalgarh were erratic and unreliable. It might be worth checking for up-to-date information at the train station, but generally it's quicker and more convenient to travel here by bus.

Getting Around

Bicycles can be hired from various places on the Dundlod road and near Bala Qila for around Rs 50 per day. If you're staying at Apani Dhani or Ramesh Jangid's Tourist Pension, bicycle hire can also be organised.

A shared autorickshaw from the train or bus station to the main market costs Rs 5; you can wave them down anywhere along this route. To hire an autorickshaw or a horse-drawn tonga from either the bus or train station to the fort costs about Rs 30.

PARSURAMPURA

☎ 01594

This sleepy little village, 20km southeast of Nawalgarh, is home to some of Shekhawati's best-preserved and oldest paintings. The **Shamji Sharaf Haveli**, just south of the bus stand, dates from the end of the 18th century and is decorated with a mixture of Hindu gods and Europeans. Pictures include a grandmother having her hair dressed, a woman spinning yarn and an intriguing image of a European woman in patent-leather shoes carrying a parasol. A frieze shows a marriage celebration – on one side is a priest presiding over the ceremony – while the opposite wall depicts Europeans in a car. Above the lintel are some well-preserved portraits, and below, portrayals of Ganesh, Vishnu, Krishna and Radha. Saraswati (wife of Hindu god Brahma) is riding a peacock in the right-hand corner.

Beautiful paintings featuring the lives of the gods ring the interior of the dome of the **Chhatri of Thakur Sardul Singh** cenotaph, 50m south of the *haveli*, which dates from the mid-18th century. The exquisite work here is reminiscent of miniature painting and its antiquity is evident in the use of muted, russet colours – these are natural rather than artificial pigments, which came later. Images include those of the *thakur* and his five sons, graphic battle scenes from the Ramayana, and the love story of Dhola Maru (p292), a common Romeo-and-Juliet-style theme employed by the painters of Shekhawati. To visit the cenotaph you must obtain the key from the caretaker, Sri Banwari Lal (nicknamed Maharaj), who sits in the little booth under the peepul tree outside the gate of the Shamji Sharaf Haveli. Maharaj is a Brahmin priest, and it's almost entirely through his efforts that the *chhatri* is so well maintained. He is responsible for the pretty flower beds of roses

and jasmine that surround the *chhatri*, and there's a toilet here. A small donation would be welcome – it'll be put to good use.

Also to be found in Parsurampura is the small **Gopinathji Mandir**, on the left just before you leave the village on the road to Nawalgarh. The temple was built by Sardul Singh in 1742 and it's believed that the same artist responsible for the paintings on the Chhatri of Thakur Sardul Singh executed the fine paintings here. According to local lore, the artist had half completed the work when the son of Sardul Singh chopped his hands off because he wanted the artist's work to be exclusive to his father's *chhatri*. Not to be deterred, the valiant artist completed the work with his feet. Perhaps this accounts for some of the subject matter, which includes a lurid vision of the various torments of hell.

Getting There & Away

There are numerous buses to Parsurampura from Nawalgarh, which depart from the Parsurampura bus stand. The trip can take up to one hour (due to multiple stops en route) and costs Rs 12. You'll probably have to fight for a seat, or for cooler but dustier and more precarious roof space.

DUNDLOD

☎ 01594

Dundlod is a peaceful, back-in-time village lying about 7km north of Nawalgarh. Its small fort was built in 1750 by Keshri Singh, the fifth and youngest son of Sardul Singh. Major additions were made in the early 19th century by his descendant Sheo Singh, who resettled in the region despite attempts on his life by Shyam Singh of Bissau (Shyam Singh also murdered his father and brother in an attempt to claim the region for himself). Members of the wealthy Goenka merchant family also settled here, and their prosperity is, as usual, evident in their richly painted *havelis*.

Sights

The **Dundlod Fort** (admission Rs 20; ☼ sunrise-sunset) was built and frequently modified over 200 years, and features a blend of Rajput and Mughal art and architecture. Inside, it combines a mix of European and Rajput decorative elements; the Diwan-i-Khas (Hall of Private Audience) has a mustard-coloured colonnade, stained-glass windows, fine Louis XIV antiques and an impressive collection of

SHEKHAWATI'S OUTDOOR GALLERIES

In the 18th and 19th centuries, shrewd Marwari merchants lived frugally far from home while piling up money in India's new commercial centres. They sent the bulk of their vast fortunes back to their families in Shekhawati to construct grand *havelis* (traditional, ornately decorated mansions) – to show their neighbours how well they were doing and to compensate their families for their long absences. Merchants competed with one another to build ever more grand edifices – homes, temples, step-wells – which were richly decorated, both inside and out, with painted murals.

The artists responsible for these acres of decoration largely belonged to the caste of *kumhars* (potters) and were both the builders and painters of the *havelis*. Known as *chajeras* (masons), many were commissioned from beyond Shekhawati – particularly from Jaipur, where they had been employed decorating the new capital's palaces – and others flooded in from further afield to offer their skills. Soon, there was a cross-pollination of ideas and techniques, with local artists learning from the new arrivals.

Haveli walls, particularly at the entrance, in the courtyards and sometimes within some of the rooms, were frequently painted by the *chajeras* from the ground to the eaves. Often the paintings mix depictions of the gods and their lives with everyday scenes featuring modern inventions, such as trains and aeroplanes, even though these artists themselves had never seen them. Hence, Krishna and Radha are seen in flying motorcars and Europeans can be observed inflating hot air balloons by blowing into them.

As well as the *havelis*, the temples (for example Gopinathji Mandir in Parsurampura) are sometimes painted, and the characteristic village or town *chhatri* (for example, the one in Dundlod) and its adjacent quadruple-towered and domed well are painted too.

These days most of the *havelis* are still owned by descendants of the original families, but not inhabited by their owners, for whom small-town Rajasthan has lost its charm. Many are occupied just by a single *chowkidar* (caretaker), while others may be home to a local family. Though they are pale reflections of the time when they accommodated the large households of the Marwari merchant families, they remain a fascinating testament to the changing times in which they were created. Only a few *havelis* have been restored; many more lie derelict, crumbling slowly away.

rare books. Above the Diwan-i-Khas is the *duchatta* (women's gallery) from where the women in purdah could view the proceedings below through net curtains. The zenana features walls of duck-egg blue, and opens out onto the reading room of the *thakurani* (noblewoman). This room has a hand-carved wooden writing table, which bears Oriental dragon motifs. Parts of the fort have been transformed into a hotel and you can also take horse-riding, camel or jeep tours from here.

The beautiful **Chhatri of Ram Dutt Goenka** and the adjacent well were built by Ram Chandra Goenka in 1888. They are about five minutes' walk southeast of the fort. If there's no caretaker in sight, ask to borrow the key from the Ram Chandra Goenka Haveli (p284). The interior of the dome has floral motifs extending in banners down from its centre, and is encircled by a frieze depicting Krishna dancing with the *gopis*, interspersed with peacocks and musicians. Paintings around the inner base of the dome illustrate a battle scene from the Mahabharata (an epic poem of the Bharata

dynasty), a marriage celebration and Vishnu reclining on a snake.

Nearby **Bhagirath Mal Goenka Haveli** is often locked, but you can see some fine mirrorwork above the windows on the upper courtyard walls. Portraits in circular frames nestle under the eaves. The *haveli* opposite is interesting, because the work is unfinished, so it's possible to see how the artist sketched the drawings before adding colour. Pictures include an elephant, a camel and rider, and a horse.

In a small square to the right just before the fort entrance is **Satyanarayan Temple**, which was built by Hariram Goenka in 1911. On the temple's west wall is a long frieze, with endearing pictures showing Europeans on sturdy bicycles and in cars, and a long train with telegraph lines above it (all very cutting-edge for the day). The portraits under the eaves meanwhile show nobles at leisure, reading and sniffing flowers. One fine moustached and turquoise-turbaned fellow has a bird in his hand, while another painting shows a woman admiring herself in a mirror.

A short distance to the south of the temple is the stunning restored 1875–85 **Seth Arjun Das Goenka Haveli** (admission Rs 30; ☉ 8am-7pm). As with all restored *havelis*, the bright colours, which is how they would have been in their original form, are something of a shock after becoming used to the discrete tones of murals faded with age. The interior offers a good illustration of the merchants' lives, beginning with their reception room, cooled by huge punka fans swinging from ropes. Above the window arches, mirrors are arranged in florets.

Well-preserved paintings can be seen on the east wall of nearby **Jagathia Haveli**, with a particularly animated train station scene – in one carriage, a man appears to be in a passionate embrace with his wife, but look closer and you can see he is furiously beating her. Another man hurries along on a bicycle, parallel to the train, pursued by a dog. Just south of here, the outer courtyard of the **Ram Chandra Goenka Haveli** is painted a soft yellow colour, featuring florets and birds.

Tours
Dundlod Fort (☎ /fax 252519, in Jaipur 0141-2211276; www.dundlod.com) has around 60 horses stabled at its Royal Equestrian and Polo Centre – India's largest Marwari horse-breeding centre. They organise upmarket horse safaris, which cost from Rs 9000 per person per day, for experienced riders only. You can ride for three to 12 days, covering about 25km to 30km per day, and along various routes, for example around Shekhawati, to local fairs, in the Aravalli hills, or to other areas of Rajasthan such as Pushkar or Nagaur.

Sleeping & Eating
Dundlod Fort (☎ /fax 252519, in Jaipur 0141-2211276; www.dundlod.com; s/d/ste from Rs 2600/3000/3800; ☒ ☒) Still run by the extremely friendly and welcoming family of Dundlod's founder, a descendant of Sardul Singh, the fort has grand and imposing communal rooms, but the rooms themselves are rather shabby. The suites are better restored than the rest of the rooms on offer, and the restaurant's food is fresh and tasty.

Getting There & Away
It's possible to walk all the way from Nawalgarh to Dundlod, although it's a hot walk along a busy, dusty road. For a quieter stroll, you can walk through the fields, ex-cept for the last stretch towards Dundlod. Ask a local for directions. Alternatively, for just a few rupees you can catch one of the many local buses that ply the route every 15 minutes. Buses depart from the bus stand in Nawalgarh.

MUKUNDGARH
☎ 01594
About 5km north of Dundlod, Mukundgarh is a crafts centre, renowned for its textiles, brass and iron scissors and betel-nut cutters. It's a charming, quiet town with little tourist development and some interesting painted *havelis,* including Kanoria, Ganriwal and Saraf Havelis.

Saraf Haveli (admission Rs 40) is open whenever there's a caretaker around. The atmospheric house was built in 1909, though it took eight years to complete. The main entrance is on an elevated platform almost 3m high, and is big enough for an elephant. One of the biggest *havelis* in the whole of Shekhawati, it has eight courtyards, though not all may be open for viewing. Rooms retain old family pictures and punkas, while the paintings in the main courtyard are fine though faded and those in the second courtyard feature religious stories.

Mukundgarh Fort (☎ 7252397, in Delhi 011-6372565; fax 011-6814954; s/d from Rs 1000/2000, Maharaja ste Rs 6000; ☒ ☒) is an impressive fort dating from the 18th century, although it's a little run down and some of the 46 rooms are beset by damp patches. Newer rooms are better, though less atmospheric, and the bathrooms are clean and modern. The Maharaja suite can accommodate up to eight people, though this isn't much use unless you're travelling with a group of good friends. Camel or jeep safaris can be arranged (a two-hour trip on a camel cart costs Rs 400 per person) and the staff and management are accommodating and friendly.

JHUNJHUNU
☎ 01592 / pop 100,476
Shekhawati's most important commercial centre, Jhunjhunu has a different atmosphere from the smaller towns, with lots of traffic, concrete and hustle and bustle as befits the district headquarters. Though it's not the most exciting or inspiring of Shekhawati destinations, it does have a few appealing *havelis* and a bustling, colourful bazaar.

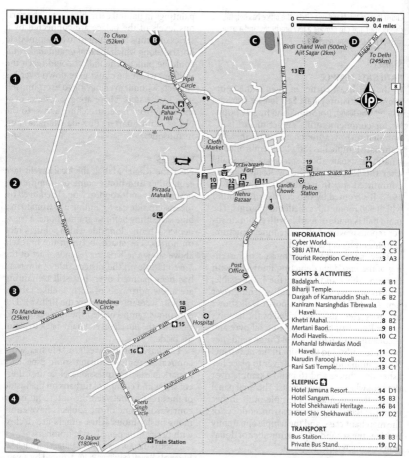

JHUNJHUNU

INFORMATION
Cyber World.....................................1	C2
SBBJ ATM..2	C3
Tourist Reception Centre............3	A3

SIGHTS & ACTIVITIES
Badalgarh.......................................4	B1
Bihariji Temple..............................5	C2
Dargah of Kamaruddin Shah........6	B2
Kaniram Narsinghdas Tibrewala	
Haveli......................................7	C2
Khetri Mahal.................................8	B2
Mertani Baori................................9	B1
Modi Havelis................................10	C2
Mohanlal Ishwardas Modi	
Haveli.....................................11	C2
Narudin Farooqi Haveli..............12	C2
Rani Sati Temple.........................13	C1

SLEEPING
Hotel Jamuna Resort...................14	D1
Hotel Sangam...............................15	B3
Hotel Shekhawati Heritage........16	B4
Hotel Shiv Shekhawati...............17	D2

TRANSPORT
Bus Station...................................18	B3
Private Bus Stand.......................19	D2

The town was founded by the Kayamkhani Nawabs in the middle of the 15th century, and remained under their control until it was taken by the Rajput ruler Sardul Singh in 1730. It was in Jhunjhunu that the British based their Shekhawati Brigade, a troop formed in the 1830s to try to halt the activities of the dacoits, local petty rulers who had discovered that an easy way to become wealthy was to pinch other people's money.

Jhunjhunu has numerous impressive *chhatris*, as well as some remnants of forts and a palace. Unfortunately, though, many of the fine frescoes that once adorned the town's architecture have been whitewashed out of existence. The town is also notorious for its Rani Sati Temple – enormously popular with locals and dedicated to a young bride who burned to death on her husband's funeral pyre in 1595.

Information

Laxmi Kant Jangid (owner of the Hotel Shiv Shekhawati and Hotel Jamuna Resort) is a knowledgeable, government-approved guide. He provides free guided tours around Jhunjhunu and can arrange car tours of surrounding towns.

Cyber World (per hr Rs 30; 9am-8pm Mon-Sat, 11am-8pm Sun) A cramped place near Nehru Bazaar.

SBBJ ATM (Paramveer Path) No banks in Jhunjhunu currently exchange money; you can try this ATM but it's rather unreliable.

Tourist reception centre (232909; 10am-5pm Mon-Sat, closed every 2nd Sat) Out of the centre at the

Churu Bypass Rd, Mandawa Circle, the office has helpful, cheery staff and can provide a few brochures, and a basic map of the town and region.

Sights

RANI SATI TEMPLE

In the northeast corner of town is the enormous, multistorey **Rani Sati Temple** (admission free, ☼ 4am-10pm), notorious and hugely popular for commemorating an act of *sati* (self-immolation) by a merchant's wife in 1595. Rani Sati Temple has long been embroiled in a national debate about *sati* (p43), especially after the 19-year-old widow Roop Kanwar committed *sati* in nearby Sikar district in 1987. It's fronted by two courtyards, around which 300 rooms offer shelter to pilgrims. The main hall is made of marble with elaborate silver repoussé work before the inner sanctum. (Photography is permitted.)

There's a tile-and-mirror mosaic on the ceiling of the *mandapa* depicting Rani Sati, with Ganesh, Shiva and Durga (the Inaccessible; a form of Devi, Shiva's wife) watching over her. A relief frieze on the north wall shows her story. Her husband is killed by the nawab's army; Rani Sati mounts the funeral pyre and is consumed by flames while Durga sends her power to withstand the pain. In the next panel Rani commands a chariot driver to place her ashes on a horse and to build a temple over the spot where the horse halts. The final panel shows the ostentatious temple built in her honour. Rani Sati is the patron goddess of the merchant class, and the temple apparently receives the second-highest number of donations of any temple in India.

KHETRI MAHAL

A series of small laneways at the western end of Nehru Bazaar (a short rickshaw drive north of the bus station) leads to the imposing **Khetri Mahal** (admission Rs 20), a small palace dating from around 1770 and one of Shekhawati's most sophisticated and beautiful buildings. It's believed to have been built by Bhopal Singh, Sardul Singh's grandson, who founded Khetri. Unfortunately, it now has a desolate, forlorn atmosphere, with the architecture – though doorless and windowless – remains a superb open-sided collection of intricate arches and columns, the unpainted lime plaster giving off a rosy cast.

In the private chamber of the *thakur* are two small alcoves that retain fragments of paintings in natural earth pigments. The various levels of the palace are connected by a series of ramps (big enough to accommodate horses) along which the *thakur* and *thakurani* could be pulled. The *thakur* could reach the rooftop, where he could gaze down over his subjects without even having to exert himself up a single step. There are good views over the town from here, stretching across to the old Muslim quarter, Pirzada Mahalla, and its mosques.

HAVELIS

Near the Khetri Mahal, the **Modi Havelis** face each other and house some of Jhunjhunu's best murals and woodcarving. The *haveli* on the eastern side has a painting of a woman in a blue sari sitting before a gramophone; a frieze depicts a train, alongside which soldiers race on horses. The spaces between the brackets above show the Krishna legends. Part of the *haveli* façade on the eastern side of the road has been painted over, but still remaining are a few portrayals of fairly lifelike rabbits (rabbits were introduced by the British). The enormous ramp enabled the bridegroom to ride into the *haveli* on elephant-back to claim his bride.

The *haveli* on the western side has some comical pictures, featuring some especially remarkable facial expressions. Note the different styles and colours of turbans on the inside of the archway between the outer and inner courtyards. Some of the subjects have enormous bushy moustaches; others are decked with perky little pencil-style numbers.

A short distance away is **Kaniram Narsinghdas Tibrewala Haveli** (admission Rs 10), fronted by a vegetable market. On the west wall of the first courtyard is a frieze depicting two trains approaching each other: the left-hand one is a passenger train and the right a goods train filled with livestock – these trains look like they have come straight from the artist's imagination.

A short distance west is **Narudin Farooqi Haveli**. In accordance with Islamic style, only floral motifs are depicted (there are no animal or human representations) and blue is the predominant colour. Unfortunately, the arches leading to the salons off the first courtyard have been sealed off with concrete.

On the north side of Nehru Bazaar is **Mohanlal Ishwardas Modi Haveli** (admission Rs 10), which dates from 1896. A train runs merrily across the front façade. Above the entrance to the outer courtyard are scenes from the life of Krishna – in the centre Krishna has stolen the clothes of the *gopis,* who stand waist deep in water as he hides up a tree. On a smaller, adjacent arch are British imperial figures, including monarchs and robed judges. Facing them are Indian rulers, including maharajas and nawabs.

Around the archway, between the inner and outer courtyards, there are some glass-covered portrait miniatures, along with some fine mirror-and-glass tilework. In the second half of the antechamber, Krishna dances with the *gopis* while angels fly overhead. The inner courtyard shows the hierarchy of the universe, with deities in the upper frieze, humans in the middle band, and animal and floral motifs below.

OTHER ATTRACTIONS

Northwest of Khetri Mahal, **Badalgarh** (originally called Fazalgarh after its constructor, Nawab Fazal Khan) is a mighty 16th-century fort, dating from the period of the nawabs. It belongs to the Dundlod family but is currently closed to the public, awaiting renovation.

On the northwest side of town, about 1km from Nehru Bazaar, is **Birdi Chand Well,** surmounted by four imposing minarets (two minarets generally symbolise the presence of a step-well), which are covered in fading paintings. As water is such a precious commodity in the desert, wells were sacred, and it's common to see a temple at a well – there's a small one here devoted to Hanuman (the Hindu monkey god). To the west of the well is an old inn where caravans would once have halted. A couple of kilometres further north is the picturesque lake **Ajit Sagar,** built in 1902.

The **Mertani Baori,** to the northwest of the fort, is Shekhawati's most impressive step-well, named after the woman who commissioned it, Mertani, the widow of Sardul Singh. Built in 1783, it has been restored and is about 30m deep, with sulphuric waters said to cure skin diseases. An English official reported in 1930, however, that the water here was so poisonous that anyone who drank it died a couple of hours later. On either side of the well, steps lead to a series of cool resting rooms for visitors.

To the south of Kana Pahar Hill is the **Dargah of Kamaruddin Shah,** a complex consisting of a madrasa (Islamic college), a mosque and a *mehfilkhana* (concert hall in which religious songs are sung). Fragments of paintings depicting floral motifs remain around the courtyard, particularly on the eastern and northern sides (although many have been whitewashed).

A short distance northwest of Jorawargarh Fort is the fine **Bihariji Temple,** which dates from approximately 1776 and is dedicated to Krishna. It has some fine, though worn, murals. On the inside of the dome, Krishna and the *gopis* are rendered in natural pigments – their circular dance, called the *rasalila,* suits the form of the dome and so is a popular theme here.

Courses

If you are interested in tuition in traditional Shekhawati painting, contact Laxmi Kant Jangid at the Hotel Shiv Shekhawati or Hotel Jamuna Resort.

Laxmi also runs hands-on cookery courses at Hotel Jamuna Resort; these cost around Rs 500 per day. One-day decorative art workshops are also available, and cover henna painting, textiles (including *bandhani* – tie-dyeing) and fresco painting; the Jamuna Resort also offers free daily yoga classes.

Tours

Camel and jeep safaris can be arranged (along with packed lunch or snacks) at Hotel Shiv Shekhawati or Hotel Jamuna Resort. The hotel also arranges three- to five-day bicycle packages around the region. The tours cost US$70 per person per day (including all accommodation, meals and jeep transfers), cover 90km to 110km and start and end in Jhunjhunu. Routes include Alsisar–Malsisar–Bissau, Mandawa–Fatehpur–Ramgarh–Mahansar, and Mukandgarh–Nawalgarh–Dundlod–Churi. Hotel Shiv Shekhawati also arranges full- and half-day excursions in the area. Costs are Rs 1000/1500 per person for a half-/full-day tour.

Sleeping & Eating

Hotel Sangam (☎ 232544; Paramveer Path; s/d from Rs 350/400) This impersonal hotel, in the bus-station area, has large, passable but shabby doubles tiled in grey and blue; singles are small but still not too bad. Budget rooms are at the front and could be noisy; it's better to take one at the back.

Hotel Jamuna Resort (☎ 232871; s/d from Rs 600/800, d with AC from Rs 1200; 🛏 🐾) Operated by Laxmi Kant Jangid (who also runs Hotel Shiv Shekhawati), Jamuna Resort has air-con rooms either vibrantly painted with murals or decorated with traditional mirrorwork. There's a pool (Rs 50 for nonguests), also set in the serene garden. The hotel also has a large meeting hall and brand-new kitchens – all set up for the cooking courses.

Hotel Shekhawati Heritage (☎ 237134; Paramveer Path; www.hotelshekhawatiheritage.com; s/d from Rs 400/500, with AC from 700/800; 🛏) Near Hotel Sangam, this place, with kindly management, is the pick in this area. The clean, bright rooms have leafy outlooks and those with air-con are blissfully chilly, even in the hottest of weather.

Hotel Shiv Shekhawati (☎ 232651; www.shivshek hawati.com; Khemi Shakti Rd; d Rs 800-1200; 🛏) East of the centre, Shiv Shekhawati is a modern place built around a central inner courtyard, with plain but squeaky-clean rooms. It's 600m from the private bus stand in a quiet area on the eastern edge of town. The affable owner, Laxmi Kant Jangid (usually at Hotel Jamuna Resort), is a wealth of knowledge on the villages of Shekhawati.

Getting There & Away

BUS

Regular buses run between Jhunjhunu and Jaipur (Rs 80, four hours), Churu (Rs 25/30 in local/express, around 1½ hours, hourly) and Bissau (Rs 20, 1½ hours, hourly). Numerous buses go to Mandawa (Rs 15, one hour), to Nawalgarh (Rs 20, one hour) and to Baggar (Rs 8, 40 minutes) from 6.30am.

Buses leave for Delhi from 5am (Rs 130, seven hours, hourly). There are also buses to Jodhpur (Rs 180, 10 hours), Ajmer (Rs 142, seven hours) and Bikaner (Rs 95, five hours). A private bus stand on Khemi Shakti Rd runs a number of similar services.

TRAIN

At the time of writing, there were no useful train services in or out of Jhunjhunu. Check in at the station to see if the situation has since changed, though buses are invariably faster.

Getting Around

For local sightseeing, you'll pay about Rs 50 per hour for an autorickshaw. A rickshaw from the train or bus station to the Hotel Shiv Shekhawati costs about Rs 25.

BAGGAR

☎ 01592

This small, peaceful village has few *havelis* to nose around, but the main reason to stay here is because of its great hotel. It's about 15km northeast of Jhunjhunu.

Piramal Haveli (☎ 01592-221220; www.neemrana hotels.com; r Rs 1500-2000) has just eight rooms so advance bookings are essential. This is a gorgeous, colonial-style, grand old 1920s house – somewhere between Tuscan villa and Rajasthani mansion – built by a merchant who traded in opium, cotton and silver in Bombay. The house is appointed with original furniture and kitsch paintings featuring gods in motor-cars. The *haveli* serves up terrific vegetarian thalis for dinner (Rs 250); afterwards, sip a strong drink on the porch with a peaceful game of backgammon.

BISSAU

☎ 01595 / pop 21,133

Pint-sized Bissau lies about 32km northwest of Jhunjhunu. Founded in 1746 by Keshri Singh, the last of Sardul Singh's sons, it has one of Shekhawati's fiercest histories. The town prospered under Keshri, but fell into brigandry during the rule of his grandson Shyam Singh. It is said that the merchants of Bissau, who had been encouraged to set up in the town by Keshri, packed up and left when Shyam extracted vast sums of money from them. The *thakur* then resorted to a life of crime, embarking on raids with dacoits to neighbouring regions. The British called on the Shekhawati Brigade to restore order in the anarchic town, but by the time the expedition was mounted Shyam Singh had expired and his heir, Hammir Singh, had driven out the brigands and encouraged the merchants to return. The British were impressed by the town's prosperity and left without a single shot being fired. Look out for the Bissau Festival (p275), which hits the town for tens days annually, in either September or October, when locals perform scenes from the Ramayana.

Sights

On the façade of the **Chhatri of Hammir Singh** (1875), near the private bus stand, you can see British folk in fancy carriages, including one carriage shaped like a lion and another like a hybrid lion-elephant. The *chhatri* is now multipurpose, being both a primary school, with lessons held under the dome and even in the sandy courtyard, and a storage place for fodder. On the external back wall is a portrayal of Dhola Maru (p292); unusually, the bard who features in the love story is also depicted.

Walking north from the bus stand, take the first right and on the left-hand side at the next intersection is the **Haveli of Girdarilal Sigtia**. The paintings on the external walls have been destroyed, but the rooms retain some vibrant murals in bright oranges, blues, reds and greens. A room in the northeast corner of the *haveli* shows Shiva (with the unusual addition of a moustache) with the Ganges flowing from his hair. Note the orange handprints on the outer courtyard wall; these are a custom peculiar to Shekhawati, signifying the birth of a male child.

On the opposite side of this lane is the **Motiram Jasraj Sigtia Haveli**, now a junior school. On the north wall, Krishna has stolen the *gopis'* clothes; the maidens have been modestly covered by the artist in the coils of snakes, although one reptile can be seen slinkily emerging from between a *gopi's* legs.

Getting There & Away
There are daily buses from Bissau to Jhunjhunu (Rs 20, 1½ hours) every 30 minutes and to Mahansar (Rs 8, 20 minutes), Mandawa (Rs 18, 1½ hours) and Churu (Rs 12, 30 minutes).

Getting Around
Bicycles can be hired for around Rs 40 per day from the shops near the Chhatri of Hammir Singh. Bicycles are an excellent way to tour this region, and are particularly good for the 6km trip to Mahansar.

MAHANSAR
☎ 01595
A turn-off to the left as you leave Bissau on the Churu road leads 6km to the quaint, slow-moving and untouristed village of Mahansar, a dusty place with lots of rural charm where donkeys outnumber motorised vehicles. Because of its inaccessibility – set in the middle of vast tracts of arid field and sand – it has remained untouched and, as such, makes a good place to stay to explore the area.

Mahansar was founded by Nawal Singh in 1768, and the town prospered for several decades, with gemlike *havelis* financed by the wealthy Poddar clan, until one of the Poddars lost his livelihood when two shiploads of opium sank without a trace. The town is nowadays famous for homemade liquor, known as *daru*, which resembles Greek ouzo; imbibe with care as it's extremely potent.

Sights
The **Raghunath Mandir**, dating from the mid-19th century, is a temple that resembles a *haveli* in its architecture. It has fine floral arabesques beneath the arches around the courtyard and a grand façade. There are good views across the small town from the *chhatri*-ringed upper floor.

A short distance to the northeast of the Raghunath Mandir is **Sone ki Dukan Haveli** (admission Rs 100; ◷ 7am-5pm). (Ask at neighbouring shops if it's locked up.) The name means 'gold shop', due to the striking paintings, which use a shimmering amount of gold leaf – unusual for Shekhawati. The scenes from the Ramayana in the southern section of the ceiling in the first chamber are particularly intense, with their glorious quantities of gold leaf. The lower walls are richly adorned with floral and bird motifs, a fantasy of butterflies, fruit-laden trees and flowers. Painted in gold script on panels on the west wall of this chamber are the names of the gods. On the north side of the ceiling, the life of Krishna is portrayed. A golden river connects the holy cities of Vrindavan, where Krishna spent his childhood, and Mathura, where he lived as a king. Lakshmi, Vishnu's consort (and Hindu goddess of wealth), is also featured, as are portraits of women playing different instruments.

About 10 minutes' walk from the bus stand, past the fort on the right-hand side of Ramgarh Rd, is the **Sahaj Ram Poddar Chhatri**. Some archways have been bricked in, but there are still some well-preserved paintings on the lower walls of this well-proportioned and attractive building.

Sleeping & Eating
Narayan Niwas Castle (☎ 01595-264322; r from Rs 800) is the only place to stay in this remote village. It is located in the old fort, about 100m north of the bus stand. This is a proper creaky Rajasthani castle dating from 1768 that feels evocatively uncommercial. Rooms are dusty but charakterful, some (including rooms 1 and 5) with antique furniture and paintings covering the walls. It's run by the down-to-earth *thakur* of Mahansar and his wife, an elderly

---

THE COLOURS OF SHEKHAWATI

Shekhawati's colourful paintings were a vivid response to its incredibly parched and arid landscape, serving at once to educate, entertain and depict the concerns of the day.

Originally the colours used in the region's murals were all ochre based, the ochre colour obtained from the urine of cows fed on mango leaves – a practice discontinued after it was deemed cruel to the poor mango-eating cows. Other colours were obtained from stones and minerals: copper, lead, gold, indigo and lapis lazuli were all used, though since the lapis used for blue tones – a staple in the decoration of Muslim temples in the area – was extremely costly, most blues were created from synthetic dyes imported from overseas. In the 1860s, further artificial pigments were introduced from Germany, and colours began to change from the subtle tones of natural colours to the brasher, brighter effect of artificial hues: you'll still be able to make out the difference between the natural and the artificial on Shekhawati's *havelis* today.

To create the meandering fresco images, artists engaged in a painstaking process: first, the wall was covered in several layers of plaster (with clay often gathered from ant hills), to which were added various ingredients such as lime and hessian. The final layer was then of lime dust mixed with buttermilk and jaggery (coarse brown sugar made from the sap of the date palm). The painters worked on the plaster while it was still wet, which accounts for the brilliance of the colours. Once completed, the works were polished with agate and rubbed with dry coconut to seal them; some were also set with semi-precious stones. After the turn of the 20th century, the artists instead began to paint on dry plaster, allowing greater intricacy but losing the original urgency.

The early paintings are strongly influenced by Mughal decoration, with floral arabesques and geometric designs (according to the dictates of Islam, the Mughals never created a representation of an animal or human). The Rajput royal courts were the next major influence; scenes from Hindu mythology were prevalent – usually featuring Krishna and Rama (seventh incarnation of Vishnu) – and were used as moral teachings in which good prevailed over evil. Many such moralistic themes were employed near the *havelis'* front doors, in order to be edifying and instructive to the townspeople outside.

Other major themes included history, folk tales, animals, landscapes and eroticism (many of these works have since been prudishly defaced or destroyed). With the arrival of Europeans, walls were embellished with paintings of the new technological marvels that the Shekhawati merchants had been exposed to in centres such as Calcutta. Pictures of trains, planes, telephones, gramophones and bicycles appeared – often painted direct from the artist's imagination.

The advent of photography and exposure to European art had yet another dramatic influence on Shekhawati art. Previously, subjects were depicted two-dimensionally, with little emphasis on anatomical accuracy or shading for perspective. With the influence of photography, artists sought a more faithful rendering of their subjects.

The paintings of Shekhawati are thus an extraordinary synthesis of Eastern and Western influences, the cultural collision perfectly illustrated in paintings showing Krishna playing a gramophone for Radha, or the two of them flying off in a Rolls Royce.

---

couple who know lots about the local area and can tell interesting stories about bygone days. The food is sumptuous and a few glasses of the castle's own hooch before bedtime will be sure to have you seeing ghosts of Rajputs flitting by.

Getting There & Away

Regular bus services go between Mahansar and Ramgarh (Rs 8), Churu (Rs 10), Fatehpur (Rs 15) and Bissau (Rs 6, 20 minutes). Change at Bissau for buses to Jhunjhunu.

RAMGARH

Sixteen kilometres south of Churu and 20km north of Fatehpur is Ramgarh, which was founded by a disaffected group from the wealthy Poddar family in 1791, and has the biggest concentration of painted *havelis* in the region. The Poddars defected from nearby Churu in a fit of pique after the local *thakur* imposed an extortionate wool levy. They set about building extravagant homes for themselves, and Ramgarh thus has a splendid, albeit uncared-for and faded, artistic legacy.

It prospered until the late 19th century, but remains pretty snoozy today.

The town is easy to explore on foot. The bus stand is at the western edge of town; in the northern section of town, about 600m from the bus stand, there's a concentration of *havelis*, as well as the main Shani Mandir temple and the Ganga Temple. At the time of writing, there was nowhere to stay here, so it's necessary to visit on a day trip from elsewhere.

Sights

The imposing **Ram Gopal Poddar Chhatri**, to the south of the bus stand, was built in 1872. The main dome of the *chhatri* is surrounded by a series of smaller domes; on the west side of the main dome's outer rim, one of the projecting braces bears a picture of a naked woman stepping into her *lenga* (skirt), while another woman shields her with the hem of her skirt from a man's gaze. The drum of the main dome is brightly painted and has well-preserved paintings in blues and reds depicting the battle from the Ramayana. The building on the north side of the *chhatri* was where family members paying homage to their dead ancestor could rest. Unfortunately, the *chhatri* is in a sorry state – the northeast corner of the building is badly water damaged. To enter the compound, you will need to find the caretaker, who'll ask for about Rs 50.

A short distance north of the town wall, on the east side of the road, is the fine **Ganga Temple**. It was built by one of the Poddar clan in 1845, and is an imposing building with large elephant murals on its façade, with plenty of images of the local favourite, Krishna. The right side of the façade is deteriorating and the foundations are crumbling. The temple only opens for morning and evening *puja* (prayers).

About 20m further north, on the left-hand side, is a **Ganesh Temple**. It has a densely painted forecourt and a series of interesting paintings between the brackets under the eaves, mostly featuring birds and religious themes.

From here, a road heads east to the spectacular tiny **Shani Mandir** (Saturn Temple). This was built in 1840, and despite a crude exterior, has a richly ornamented interior, completely covered in fantastic mirrorwork. In the chamber before the inner sanctum are some fine murals worked in gold, and the overall effect is dazzling. Subjects include Krishna and Radha and events from the Mahabharata. To the south (left) of the inner sanctum there's a painting on the ceiling featuring the marriage of Shiva and Gauri (aka Parvati, another form of Devi). Unfortunately, the ceiling in the chamber on the right-hand side of the inner sanctum is badly damaged by damp.

Heading back to the main Churu Gate, continue past the gate for about 50m, then turn left to reach a group of **Poddar havelis**. Popular motifs include soldiers, trains and an unusual design, peculiar to Ramgarh, of three fish arranged in a circle. One *haveli* has a painting of women carrying water in pitchers, and there's a novel portrayal of the Dhola Maru legend (p292) on the west wall of another: while Maru fires at the advancing assailants, Dhola nonchalantly smokes a hookah.

Getting There & Away

There are buses to Nawalgarh (Rs 25, 2½ hours), Bissau (Rs 8, 45 minutes), Fatehpur (Rs 12, 45 minutes) and Mandawa (Rs 16, 1½ hours) from the bus station at the western edge of town. For other destinations, change at Fatehpur or Mandawa.

FATEHPUR

☎ 01571 / pop 78,471

A scruffy, workaday small town, Fatehpur is chock-full of wonderful but slowly disintegrating *havelis* on either side of the main street. Though many are still in a shocking state of disrepair, it's hoped that the grand restoration of Haveli Nadine Prince, now a wonderful gallery and cultural centre, will help rescue the area's other beautiful buildings by refocusing attention on the area. Currently, though, Fatehpur is poorly developed for tourists, making it a better stop-off than overnight stay.

Established in 1451 as a capital for Muslim nawabs, Fatehpur was their stronghold for centuries before it was taken over by the Shekhawati Rajputs in the 18th century. Curiously, it was even ruled by an Irish sailor-turned-mercenary, George Thomas, in 1799, before he lost it to the maharaja of Jaipur. The wealth of the later merchant community here (which included the rich Poddar, Choudhari and Ganeriwala families) is illustrated in the number of vibrant, grandiose *havelis*, fine *chhatris*, wells and temples interspersed along the dusty town streets.

THE LEGEND OF DHOLA MARU

One of the most popular paintings to be seen on the walls of the Shekhawati *havelis* depicts the legend of Dhola Maru, Shekhawati's own, happier answer to *Romeo and Juliet*.

Princess Maru hailed from Pugal, near Bikaner, while Dhola was a young prince from Gwalior. When Maru was two years old, there was a terrible drought in her homeland, so her father, the maharaja, shifted to Gwalior, where his friend, Dhola's father, ruled. He remained there for three years, returning to Pugal when he learned that the drought was over. But before he left, as a token of friendship between the two rulers, a marriage alliance was contracted between their children, Maru and Dhola. After 20 years, however, the promise was forgotten and Princess Maru was contracted to marry someone else.

Wedding plans would have proceeded as normal, except that a bard, who'd travelled from Pugal to Gwalior, sang at the royal court of the childhood marriage of Dhola and Maru. In this way Dhola came to hear of the beautiful and virtuous Maru, with whom he immediately, sight unseen, fell in love and resolved to meet. Of course, when Maru laid eyes on him she returned his affections and they decided to elope at once.

Her betrothed, Umra, heard of their flight and gave chase with the help of his brother, Sumra. They pursued the camel-borne lovers on horseback as the brave Maru fired at them with arrows, though this proved of little use against the brothers, who were armed with guns. Nevertheless, they were able to elude the brothers, taking shelter in a forest where Dhola was promptly bitten by a snake and succumbed on the spot. Maru, thus thwarted by death, wept so loudly for her lost lover that her lamentations were heard by Shiva and Gauri who, luckily, were walking nearby. Gauri beseeched Shiva to restore the dead Dhola to life and thus the loving couple was reunited.

Sights

Without doubt the main sight in town is the **Haveli Nadine Le Prince** (☎ 233024; www.cultural-cen tre.com; adult/child Rs 100/50; ☾ 10am-7pm), an 1802 *haveli* that has been brightly restored to its former glory. There's a finely carved lintel with Ganesh sculpted over the centre.

French artist Nadine Le Prince spent three years having the *haveli* restored (after it had lain empty for nearly 40 years), and turned it into a gallery and cultural centre. Inside, the grand hall retains the original woodcarv-ing and has a ceiling lined with real gold. Charming features include a couple's winter room with specially designed steep steps to deter children, and niches for musicians in the dining room.

There's a gallery displaying art by French artists working here, as well as a tribal art gallery, which shows some beautiful, deli-cate work by local artists. Its Art Café is a cool retreat from a hot day and serves tasty snacks.

Just south of this *haveli* is the small **Chauhan Well**, which dates from the early 18th century and was built by the Rajput wife of a Muslim nawab. There's some painting around the windows and a couple of the pavilions, and the minarets retain fragments of geometric and floral designs.

West from the Haveli Nadine Le Prince is the **Jagannath Singhania Haveli**, dating from 1855. It has a fantastic ornately painted interior, but is often locked. There are some interest-ing paintings on its façade, including that of Krishna and Radha framed by four elephants, and, above this, some British men with guns.

Further south is the **Geori Shankar Haveli**, an atmospheric and still-inhabited ruin with fine mirror mosaics on the ceiling of the antecham-ber, religious paintings in the outer courtyard, and elephant statues on the roof. You'll prob-ably be asked for a donation to enter.

Nearby, on the same road, is the **Mahavir Prasad Goenka Haveli** (admission Rs 20), which was built in 1885 and is considered by some to have the best paintings in Shekhawati, com-bining a perfect synthesis of colour and de-sign. The rooms on the 1st floor are most dazzling: stepping into one is like entering a jewellery box – it glimmers with mirrorwork, colour and gold. One of the rooms shows elaborate Krishna illustrations. Unfortunately, the *haveli* is often locked, though you can usually enter the first courtyard; restoration work here is currently ongoing.

The **Jagannath Singhania Chhatri**, on the east side of the Churu–Sikar road (enter through a gateway behind the *chhatri*), has well-tended, pretty gardens. This imposing building has

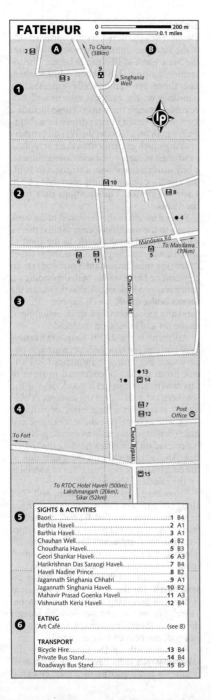

FATEHPUR

relatively few paintings, some of hunting scenes and some which appear to be unfinished. There's a small Shiva shrine here at which villagers still pay homage. Opposite is the small, still-used Singhania well.

Near the private bus stand is a large **baori**, built by Sheikh Mohammed of Nagaur in 1614, which for centuries provoked legends of bandits hiding in its depths. There's a path to the *baori* from a lane opposite the private bus stand. Unfortunately, today the *baori* is in a shocking state of disrepair – even dangerous (don't get too close to the edges) – and appears to have a new incarnation as a rubbish dump. It was obviously a feat of some magnitude to dig to this depth, and around the sides there's a series of arched galleries, mostly collapsed. On the south side, a *haveli* has half fallen into the well, and its courtyard paintings are exposed. The minarets of the *baori* stand as sad testament to its former grandeur.

Diagonally opposite the *baori*, on the south side of the private bus stand, the **Harikrishnan Das Saraogi Haveli** features a colourful façade with iron lacework on the upper verandas and shops at street level. There's a vibrantly coloured outer courtyard. Spot the woman smoking a hookah and, in the inner courtyard, a camel-drawn cart juxtaposed with a motorcar.

Adjacent, to the south, is the **Vishnunath Keria Haveli**. The outer courtyard has some wonderful pictures on either side of the inner courtyard door that show the marriage of religion and technology. Radha and Krishna can be seen in strange gondola-like flying contraptions, one with an animal's head, the other with the front part of a vintage car, and both featuring angel-like wings. On the north wall of the outer courtyard is a portrait of King George and Queen Victoria. The paintings in the southeast corner of the inner courtyard have, like many others, been badly damaged by smoke from the kitchen fire. In this courtyard, the sun god Surya is seen in a carriage being drawn by horses. On the southern external wall, pictures include Queen Victoria, a train, a holy man and Krishna playing a gramophone to Radha.

Sleeping & Eating

RTDC Hotel Haveli (☎ 230293; dm Rs 70, s/d from Rs 300/400, with AC Rs 700/900; ✷) If you find that you really must stay in town for the night, this is probably your best option, about 500m south of the Roadways bus stand on the Churu–Sikar road. Rooms are dark and shabby but it's friendly and there's the requisite gloomy dining hall (dishes Rs 30 to 75) serving reasonable food.

Art Café (Haveli Nadine Le Prince; dishes Rs 35-100) You'll have to pay to get into the *haveli,* but this is a good option for a light lunch. It's a cosy arched place with low tables, serving food such as omelettes, toast and rum-blazed bananas, as well as some Indian snacks.

Getting There & Around
At the private bus stand, on the Churu–Sikar road, buses leave for Jhunjhunu (Rs 22, one hour), Mandawa (Rs 15/18 in local/express, one hour), Churu (Rs 20, one hour), Ramgarh (Rs 12, 45 minutes) and Sikar (Rs 24/30 in local/express, one hour/45 minutes).

From the Roadways bus stand, which is further south down this road, buses leave for Jaipur (Rs 75, 3½ hours, every 15 minutes), Delhi (Rs 160, seven hours, six daily) and Bikaner (Rs 102, 3½ hours, hourly).

Bicycles (Rs 5/40 per hour/day) can be hired near the private bus stand.

MANDAWA
☎ 01592 / pop 20,717
No longer the quiet little market town of former years, Mandawa is nowadays Shekhawati's most frequented destination on the tourist trail. As such, you can expect more hassle from would-be guides and souvenir vendors than elsewhere in the region, though compared to some of Rajasthan's most visited destinations, it's still fairly relaxed. The gorgeous painted *havelis,* moreover, make up for a lot.

Settled in the 18th century, and fortified by the dominant merchant families, the town's fort was built by Sardul Singh's youngest son in 1760, though inhabited much later, and has some fine frescoes in what is nowadays an upmarket hotel.

Information
Deshnok Money Changer (☉ 24hr) Changes cash and travellers cheques, and offers cash advances against MasterCard and Visa. Also offers slowish internet access, for Rs 50 per hour.

State Bank of Bikaner & Jaipur (☉ 10am-4pm Mon-Fri, to 1pm Sat) In Binsidhar Newatia Haveli; changes travellers cheques and currency.

Sights
Binsidhar Newatia Haveli, on the northern side of the Fatehpur–Jhunjhunu road, now houses the State Bank of Bikaner & Jaipur. The interior paintings have been whitewashed, but there are fantastically entertaining paintings on the external eastern wall (accessible through the bank). These include a European woman in a car driven by a chauffeur; a man on a bicycle; the Wright brothers evoking much excitement in their aeroplane as women in saris point with astonishment; a boy using a telephone; a strongman hauling along a car; and a bird-man flying by in a winged device. The paintings date from the 1920s.

Several *havelis* to the northwest of the bank belong to the wealthy Goenka family: there's **Hanuman Prasad Goenka Haveli,** to the right of which is a composite picture that shows either Indra (the most important Vedic god) on an elephant or Shiva on his bull, depending on which way you look at it. Across the road is the **Goenka Double Haveli,** which has two entrance gates and monumental pictures, including of elephants and horses, on the façade.

Adjacent is the 1930s **Murmuria Haveli** – here you can see how European art and images were beginning to influence local artists. From the sandy courtyard in front of this *haveli,* you can get a good view of the southern external wall of the adjacent double *haveli:* it features a long frieze depicting a train, with a crow flying above the engine and much activity at the railway crossing. Nehru is depicted on horseback holding the Indian flag. Above the arches on the south side of the courtyard are two paintings of gondolas on the canals of Venice.

From here a road leads south, and 50m along you can take a short detour to the right to see the impressive **Harlalka Well,** marked by four pillars and its old pulley and camel ramp. Nearby is the **Jhunjhunwala Haveli** (admission Rs 20), which has an impressive gold leaf–painted room to the right of the main courtyard.

About 50m southeast is the **Mohan Lal Saraf Haveli.** On the south wall, a maharaja is depicted grooming his bushy moustache. There's fine mirror- and mosaic-work around the door to the inner courtyard, and Surya, the sun god, can be seen over the lintel.

Further south on the same street is the **Lakshminarayan Ladia Haveli.** The west wall features a faded picture of a man enjoying

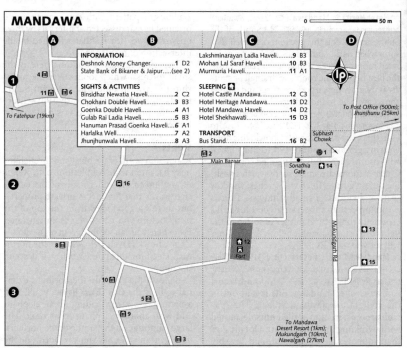

MANDAWA

0 ——————— 50 m

INFORMATION	
Deshnok Money Changer	1 D2
State Bank of Bikaner & Jaipur	(see 2)

SIGHTS & ACTIVITIES	
Binsidhar Newatia Haveli	2 C2
Chokhani Double Haveli	3 B3
Goenka Double Haveli	4 A1
Gulab Rai Ladia Haveli	5 B3
Hanuman Prasad Goenka Haveli	6 A1
Harlalka Well	7 A2
Jhunjhunwala Haveli	8 A3

Lakshminarayan Ladia Haveli	9 B3
Mohan Lal Saraf Haveli	10 B3
Murmuria Haveli	11 A1

SLEEPING	
Hotel Castle Mandawa	12 C3
Hotel Heritage Mandawa	13 D2
Hotel Mandawa Haveli	14 D2
Hotel Shekhawati	15 D3

TRANSPORT	
Bus Stand	16 B2

To Fatehpur (19km)

To Post Office (500m);
Jhunjhunu (25km)

Main Bazaar

Sonathia
Gate

Subhash
Chowk

Mukundgarh Rd

Fort

To Mandawa
Desert Resort (1km);
Mukundgarh (10km);
Nawalgarh (27km)

a hookah, and a good procession frieze. Between the wall brackets, *gopis* emerge from the tentacles of a sea monster upon whose head Krishna dances. Other pictures include that of Rama slaying Ravana (demon king of Lanka, now Sri Lanka).

Unfortunately, many of the erotic images in the **Gulab Rai Ladia Haveli**, a short distance to the east, have been systematically defaced by prudish souls. In the last pair of brackets on the first half of the southern wall, a woman is seen giving birth, attended by maidservants. There's an erotic image in the fifth niche from the end on this wall, but don't draw too much attention to it, or it may suffer the same fate as the other erotic art. There's also something untoward happening in a train carriage on this wall.

About 50m south past this *haveli* is the grand **Chokhani Double Haveli** (admission Rs 10; ☼ dawn to dusk) dating from 1910, and so called because it was built in two adjoining wings for the families of two brothers. The paintings inside include floral arabesques and peacocks above the archways, as well as the Krishna legends and some mournful British soldiers.

Activities

You can organise camel and horse rides at the Hotel Castle Mandawa or the Mandawa Desert Resort. A one-hour camel ride costs around Rs 600 and a half-/full-day trip is Rs 900/1300. Both places can also organise horse and jeep safaris on request.

Another possibility is the Hotel Heritage Mandawa, which organises half-/full-day camel rides and longer safaris, as well as jeep hire or guide hire for around the same prices. The Hotel Shekhawati, too, offers camel rides, along with jeep and horse tours, at good prices.

Sleeping & Eating

Hotel Shekhawati (☎ 223036; hotelshekwati@sify.com; r Rs 400-900; ✖ ▯) Near Mukundgarh Rd, the only real budget choice in town is run by a retired bank manager and his son (who's also a registered tourist guide). Bright, naive and somewhat lurid murals painted by artistic former guests give the rooms a splash of colour. Tasty meals are served on the peaceful rooftop, and competitively priced camel, horse and jeep tours can also be arranged.

Hotel Heritage Mandawa (☎ 223742; www.hotel heritagemandawa.com; r Rs 700-2500; ☒) South of the Subhash Chowk is this gracious old *haveli*. The somewhat dark, sometimes clashingly decorated rooms are set around tranquil courtyards; the best bets are the rooms with small upstairs areas. Nightly music performances and puppet shows are held in the little garden.

Hotel Mandawa Haveli (☎ 223088; http://hotel mandawa.free.fr; s/d/ste 1200/1750/2950; ☒) Close to Sonathia Gate and Subhash Chowk, this hotel is set in a glorious, restored 19th-century *haveli* with rooms surrounding a painted courtyard. Cheaper rooms are small, so it's worth splashing out on a suite, filled with arches, window seats and countless small windows. There's a rooftop restaurant serving good food; it's especially romantic at dinner time, when the lights of the town twinkle below. A set dinner will set you back Rs 375.

Mandawa Desert Resort (☎ 223151; in Jaipur 0141-2371194; www.castlemandawa.com; s/d Rs 2500/3000, cottages Rs 3600/4800; ☒ ☒) A top-end resort run by Castle Mandawa, this is laid out in the style of a Rajasthani village. The spacious rooms, in mud-walled huts decorated with twinkling mirrorwork, are a lot plusher than your average village home and have big bathrooms. It's in a pretty spot but all feels a bit contrived.

Hotel Castle Mandawa (☎ 223124; www.castlemand awa.com; s/d from Rs 2050/2650, deluxe Rs 3900/4800, ste from Rs 7500; ☒ ☒) Mandawa's large upmarket hotel in the old town's converted fort attempts a slightly twee medieval atmosphere but is still a swish and generally comfortable choice. Some rooms are far better appointed than others (the best are in the tower, with four-poster and swing beds), so check a few before you settle in.

Getting There & Away

There are buses to Nawalgarh (Rs 15, 45 minutes), Fatehpur (Rs 12/16 in local/express, one hour), Bissau (Rs 15/18 in local/express, 1½ hours) and Ramgarh (Rs 22, 1½ hours). Direct buses also run to Jaipur (Rs 75, four hours) – change at Fatehpur – and Bikaner (Rs 70, 3½ hours). A taxi between Mandawa and Fatehpur costs Rs 300 (one way), or you can take a crammed share jeep for Rs 15.

LAKSHMANGARH
☎ 01573 / pop 47,288
Off the tourist track, 20km south of Fatehpur, is this unusual town, laid out in an easy-to-

explore grid pattern, with a main north–south oriented bazaar dissected at intervals by three busy *chaupars* (town squares formed by the intersection of major roads).

The most imposing building here is the small fortress, which looms over the township to its west, built by Lakshman Singh, raja (king) of Sikar, in the early 19th century after the prosperous town was besieged by Kan Singh Saledhi.

Sights
About 50m north of the bus stand through the busy bazaar, a wide cobblestone path wends its way up to the eastern side of the **fort**. A sign warns that the fort is private property, but there's a good view from the top of the ramp before you get to the main entrance. From here you can see the layout of the double Char Chowk Haveli, below and to the northeast. Head for this point when you descend the ramp.

Beneath the eaves on the northern external wall of the **Char Chowk Haveli**, you'll find a picture of a bird standing on an elephant and with another elephant in its beak. The large paintings on the façade of the northern *haveli*, meanwhile, have mostly faded, and the paintings in the outer downstairs courtyard are covered by blue wash. The murals in the inner courtyard, however, are well preserved, and the walls and ceiling of a small upstairs room on the east side of the northern *haveli* are completely covered with paintings. It has some explicit erotic images, but it's ill-lit, so you'll need a torch to see them properly.

In the same building, a room in the northwest corner retains floral swirls and motifs on the ceiling with scenes from the Krishna legends interspersed with inlaid mirrors. The black-and-white rectangular designs on the lower walls create a marbled effect. No-one lives in the *haveli*, but the caretaker may open it for you (for baksheesh). The front façade is disintegrating at the lower levels, with the plaster crumbling and the bricks exposed. The southern *haveli* is still inhabited by about 30 people.

About 50m east of this *haveli* is the large **Radhi Murlimanohar Temple** (1845), which retains a few paintings beneath the eaves and some sculptures of deities around the external walls.

If you take the road west from the temple, on the corner of the second laneway on the right is the **Chetram Sanganeeria Haveli**. The lower paintings on the west wall are badly damaged; the plaster has peeled away and concrete rendering has been applied. But you can still spot a woman on a swing suspended from a tree, a man dancing on a pole while balancing some knives, folks enjoying a ride on a Ferris wheel, a man ploughing fields with oxen, and men sawing timber.

A little to the south of the temple is the busy **bazaar**, flanked by shops whose overhanging balconies have three scalloped open arches between two blank arches, which have lattice friezes. The shops were constructed during the mid-19th century by a branch of the Poddar family known as the Ganeriwala, who hailed from the village of Ganeri.

Located on the northeast corner of the clock tower square, about 100m south of the temple via the busy bazaar, is the **Rathi Family Haveli**. On the west wall, a European woman in a smart red frock sews on a treadle machine. The European influence is much in evidence here, with painted roses and a Grecian column effect. On the south side of this *haveli* are ostentatious flourishes and the British Crown flanked by unicorns. On the east side are some blue-eyed British soldiers and a railway station (with a sign saying 'a railway station' in case it wasn't clear enough).

There's a busy set of chai stalls on the west side of the *haveli*, a good place to sit down and admire these extraordinarily over-the-top paintings.

Getting There & Away
There are many buses to/from Sikar (Rs 16), Fatehpur (Rs 15) and Nawalgarh (Rs 15).

Getting Around
A bicycle shop just south of Radhi Murlimanohar Temple hires out bikes for around Rs 20 per day.

CHURU
☎ 01562 / pop 97,627
Situated across the border in Bikaner district, Churu is not technically part of Shekhawati but it has a Shekhawati heart. It was once a centre of trade and commerce, and the many rich merchant families who hailed from here left a legacy of fine painted *havelis*. About 95km to the southwest of Churu is the small Tal Chhapar Wildlife Sanctuary, home to a substantial population of blackbucks and other mammals and birds.

Sights
You'll need help (ask a local) to find the **Malji ka Kamra**, which is north of the bus stand, down a lane on the west side of the main bazaar. It's worth the effort to find this place: it's an extraordinary edifice covered in pale-blue stucco and perched on green pillars like a wedding cake, though nowadays a rather stale one. Statues on the façade include a bored-looking woman dressed in a sari (with a handbag and wings), turbaned men, and angels. Built in 1925, its days of glory are long gone.

A short distance to the northwest (within easy walking distance) is the five-storey **Surana Double Haveli**, packed with hundreds of rectangular windows and achieving something of a Georgian effect. On the lower levels of the west wall are fragments of paintings, including processions and peacocks. The *haveli* is beyond an archway at the end of a narrow laneway.

A further 100m to the northwest is the **Surajmal Banthia Haveli**, which was built in the 1920s. It's best known for its infamous picture of a laconic Christ enjoying a cigar, on the external north wall, rather incongruously juxtaposed beside a British lady. Across the lane to the north is a **haveli** with what may well be the most bizarre paintings on any of the *havelis* of Shekhawati – beneath the eaves on the eastern side is a series of inverted paintings of naked men fondling rabbits.

Sleeping & Eating
Not many travellers choose to stay in Churu, but if you do find yourself here for a night there's one reasonable hotel; note that English can be a problem.

Hotel Deluxe (☎ 251114; d Rs 350) faces the private bus stand and offers small, basic rooms. There's a restaurant downstairs that cooks up unassuming vegetarian fare at modest prices, with main dishes going for around Rs 25.

Getting There & Away
The Roadways bus stand is 500m west of the private one. Regular services to destinations in Shekhawati from the private bus stand include Fatehpur (Rs 20, one hour), Jhunjhunu (Rs 25/30 in local/express, around 1½ hours) and Sikar (Rs 40, two hours). From the Roadways bus stand there are services to Delhi (Rs 175, six hours) and Jaipur (Rs 115, five hours).

AROUND CHURU

Tal Chhapar Wildlife Sanctuary

This little-known, small grassland sanctuary, which lies about 95km southwest of Churu and 210km northwest of Jaipur, covers 70 sq km of ponds, sand, scrub and salt flats. It has healthy populations of blackbucks, elegant antelopes with long spiralling horns, as well as fast, graceful chinkaras (Indian gazelles), wolves and smaller mammals such as desert foxes. The sanctuary lies on the migration route of a number of bird species, most notably harriers, which descend here during September.

Other wintering birds include various types of eagle (tawny, imperial, short-toed, steppe), and the demoiselle crane. Throughout the year there are populations of crested larks, ring and brown doves and skylarks.

It's best to visit the sanctuary in August or September. There's a **forest resthouse** (☎ 01562-250938; d Rs 300) near the sanctuary entrance at Chhapar – it's easy to find, so no need for further instructions – offering basic double rooms. For a day trip, a taxi from Churu should cost Rs 1000 for a return journey, including waiting time.

Western Rajasthan

Rama, hero of the Ramayana, fuming with rage at the sea god who policed the straits between India and Lanka (Sri Lanka), resolved to fire a destructive arrow into the sea. However, in the nick of time, the sea god appeased the irate god, and Rama switched his aim. He fired the arrow into the northwest, creating the parched arid lands of western Rajasthan, represented today by the Thar Desert, which embraces the romantic citadels of Jodhpur and Jaisalmer.

The vast desert, extending into Punjab, Haryana and Gujarat, and into Pakistan, is not all barren and sandy. In fact it's the world's most populous arid zone. Desert culture, from the down-to-earth villages to the majestic forts, is vibrant and resilient, and such a vital ingredient of Rajasthan's allure. The towns of this region are powerfully evocative. Jodhpur, the Blue City, spreads out like an inland sea from beneath the glare of mighty Mehrangarh – a fort of impressive proportions. Jaisalmer, the Golden City, arises f rom the drifting sands of the Thar like an enormous sand castle. Bikaner, with no allotted colour, has narrow medieval bazaars, and its fort, Junagarh, has some of Rajasthan's most opulent interiors. Barmer, in the far southwest, is the colourful centre of handicraft production with treasures galore for adventurous shoppers.

The west is where you can ride a camel over a sand dune and into the sunset, camp under a desert sky and meet villagers in radiant robes. It's as if the romance of the great caravans has been preserved in the desert air.

HIGHLIGHTS

- Listen to a city's secrets from the soaring ramparts of magnificent **Mehrangarh** (p304), above Jodhpur's blue building blocks

- Marvel at the overworked stone carving of Jaisalmer's lavish **Havelis** (p326) – delicate yet powerful symbols of wealth

- Explore the ancient **Jaisalmer Fort** (p324) – the world's biggest sand castle

- Jump on a camel and embark on a **camel safari** from Jaisalmer (p330), Khuri (p336), Bikaner (p343) and Osiyan (p317) – the best way to experience the desert, and you get to sleep under the stars

- Spot a white rat at **Karni Mata Temple** (p348) in Deshnok where rodents run riot, gnawing sweets, slurping milk and scampering over your feet

- Watch the skies over Khichan for the graceful **demoiselle cranes** (p318) flying in for a free feed

★ Bikaner
★ Deshnok
★ Khichan
★ Jaisalmer
★ Osiyan
★ Khuri
★ Jodhpur

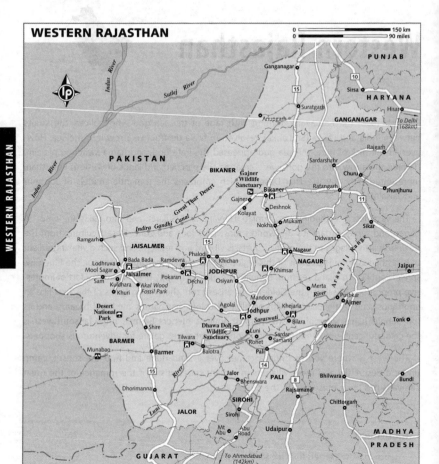

History

The district of Jodhpur was for a long time the ancient kingdom of Marwar, the largest kingdom in Rajputana and the third largest in India, after Kashmir and Hyderabad.

The region's history is hazy until the 3rd century BC. The indigenous inhabitants were subjugated by the Aryans during their invasion of northern India between 1500 and 200 BC. In 231 BC Chandragupta Maurya's empire came to power, spreading across northern India from its capital at present-day Patna, in Bihar. Subsequent centuries saw a bit of pass the parcel until the Rathore Rajputs, who hailed from Kannauj in present-day Uttar Pradesh, came out on top. This is when the state of Marwar

emerged. The Rathores originally settled at Pali, southeast of present-day Jodhpur, shifting to Mandore in 1381. In 1459 Rao Jodha, the Rathore leader, moved the capital about 9km to the south and founded the city of Jodhpur.

Jaisalmer was founded in the 12th century, after the Bhati Rajput capital at Lodharva had been destroyed by Mohammed of Ghori. After experiencing great unrest in the medieval period, Jaisalmer enjoyed a heyday from the 16th century to the 18th century, when it was a stop on an international trade route.

Meanwhile, the Muslims were entrenched at Nagaur. Mohammed Bahlim, the governor of Sind, erected a fort there in 1122, having subdued the local Hindu chief, Ajayaraja.

The rule of Nagaur fell variously to Ajayaraja (again), the sultanate of Delhi, the Rathores, an independent local dynasty led by Shams Khan Dandani, the Lodi sultans of Delhi and the Mughals under Akbar. In 1572 Akbar granted it to Raisimha, the chief of Bikaner. In the early 18th century Nagaur was acquired by the maharaja of Jodhpur.

The desert city of Bikaner was founded by one of the sons of Rao Jodha, founder of Jodhpur, following a schism in the ruling Rathore family.

After Independence, the desert kingdoms retained their autonomy for some time. The territory was strategic, owing to its proximity to Pakistan, and the various rulers were enticed to join India. The forces stationed along the border underscore the area's longstanding embattled character.

JODHPUR
☎ 0291 / pop 846,400

Jodhpur is dominated by the huge fort of Mehrangarh, which glowers from its perch on a rocky ridge. The fort is Rajasthan's finest – an awesome stone structure with a delicate palace peering over the top of its dizzying walls. Beneath the fort sprawls Jodhpur – a mass of blue building-block houses. The city is blue, really blue, and it is at its bluest in the old city which is surrounded by a 10km-long, 16th-century wall. Inside is a tangle of winding, glittering streets, scented by incense, roses and sewers, with shops selling everything from trumpets and temple decorations to snuff and saris. Traditionally, blue signified the home of a Brahmin, but non-Brahmins have got in on the act, too. As well as glowing with a mysterious light, the blue tint is thought to repel insects.

FESTIVALS IN WESTERN RAJASTHAN

Western Rajasthan's colourful festivals, usually featuring camels, splash colour against the desert. (For details of statewide and nationwide festivals, see p358.)

Bikaner Camel Festival (Jan–Feb; Bikaner, p338) Organised by the Department of Tourism, this festival sees decorated camels and best-breed competitions, camel dances and tugs-of-war, processions, and races.

Jaisalmer Desert Festival (Jan–Feb; Jaisalmer, p320) Light-hearted and tourist-focused festival featuring camel races and dances, folk music, traditional ballads, puppeteers, turban-tying contests and the famous Mr Desert competition. Many events take place on the Sam sand dunes, which provide a spectacular backdrop for the festivities.

Nagaur Fair (Jan–Feb; Nagaur, p316) A week-long cattle and camel fair – more about trading and more authentic than most. The fair attracts thousands of people from far and wide – and, this being Rajasthan, it does have its share of song, dance, camel fashion and trinket traders.

Jambeshwar Fair (Feb–Mar; Mukam, Bikaner, p338) This honours the founder of the Bishnoi sect (p315) and draws pilgrims from across India. At Guru Jambhoji's temple in Mukam, people offer grain which is used to feed birds around the temple.

Barmer Thar Festival (Mar; Barmer, p337) Cultural shows, dancing and puppetry.

Mallinath Fair (Mar–Apr; Tilwara, near Barmer, p337) One of Rajasthan's biggest cattle fairs, this 14-day event revolves around animal trading, bullock, camel and horse races, and masses of local colour. Traders come from Rajasthan, Gujarat and Madhya Pradesh. It's believed that local hero Mallinath (you can see his statue at Mandore gardens; p313) used to trade here, the origin of the fair. People make offerings to his shrine and, when their wish is answered, offer miniature horse figures, which can be bought at the fair.

Karni Mata Fair (Apr–May & Sep–Oct; Deshnok, p349) Devotees throng to the Karni Mata Temple, where rats are worshipped as the reincarnations of local people. The bigger fair is the one held in spring.

Ramdevra Fair (Aug–Sep; Ramdevra, p319) Ramdev Temple is the focus of this festival, which is celebrated by both Hindus and Muslims to commemorate Ramdev, a saint who helped the downtrodden. Female performers with 13 small cymbals attached to their costumes dance the *terahtal* (a traditional dance) while balancing pitchers of water on their heads.

Marwar Festival (Oct–Nov; Jodhpur, above) Celebrates the rich cultural legacy of Marwar (Jodhpur) and honours the region's heroes. The festival features lots of regional folk artists, the great art of turban tying and a moustache competition. It's held over two days, one of which coincides with the full moon.

Kolayat Fair (Nov; Bikaner, p338) This is a kind of mini-Pushkar, with sadhus instead of camels (the holy men are a lot less well groomed) and very few tourists. As in Pushkar, devotees take a dip in the holy lake at the full moon.

JODHPUR'S JODHPURS

Jodhpurs are baggy-tight aristocratic riding breeches – a fashion staple, worn by
self-respecting horsey people all around
the world. Usually a pale cream colour,
they're loose above the knee and tapered
from knee to ankle. It's said that Sir Pratap
Singh, a virtuoso horseman, designed the
breeches for hunting and polo, and also
brought them to a wider public by wearing them on trips abroad.

Jodhpur is overcrowded, cluttered with
traffic, over polluted and a very hectic place.
It feels less developed than the cities of the
east. Be prepared for some hassle, particularly
around the clock tower and up to the fort.
You can escape this by diving into the heart
of the old city (west of the clock tower), with
its tangle of medieval bazaars. Jodhpur hosts
the colourful Marwar Festival (p301) which
celebrates, primarily through folk music, the
erstwhile kingdom's rich heritage.

History

Driven from their homeland of Kannauj by
Afghans serving Mohammed of Ghori, the
Rathores fled west to the region around Pali,
a short distance to the south of Jodhpur. An
expedient marriage between the Rathore
Siahaji and the sister of a local prince enabled
the Rathores to take root in the region. They
prospered to such a degree that they managed
to oust the Pratiharas of Mandore, 9km to the
north of present-day Jodhpur.

By 1459 it became evident that more secure
headquarters were required. The rocky ridge
9km to the south of Mandore was an obvious
choice for the new city of Jodhpur. The natural
fortifications afforded by its steep flanks were
greatly enhanced by a fortress of staggering
proportions (see p304).

Founded by Rao Jodha, from whom it
takes its name, the city lay on the vital trade
route between Delhi and Gujarat. It grew out
of the profits of opium, sandalwood, dates
and copper, and controlled a large area. The
Rathore kingdom was once cheerily known
as Marwar (the Land of Death) due to its
harsh topography and climate.

A war for independence and struggles
for succession dominated the 17th and 18th
centuries. However, the 19th century saw

the commencement of competent rule by
Sir Pratap Singh (of riding pants fame; see
left), followed by Maharaja Umaid Singh.
Thus Jodhpur – Rajasthan's largest kingdom – was reasonably stable when it came
to Independence in 1947.

Orientation

The Tourist Reception Centre, train stations and bus stand are all outside the old
city. High Court Rd runs from Raika Bagh
train station, past the Umaid gardens, and
round beside the city wall towards the main
(Jodhpur) train station and the main post
office. Trains from the east stop at the Raika
Bagh station before heading on to the main
station, which is handy if you're staying at a
hotel on the eastern side of town.

Watch out in Jodhpur for similarly named
places – some businesses take on remarkably
unoriginal names, closely resembling a thriving local business, in order to confuse travellers (this doesn't only happen in the hotel
business – check out the number of clone-
named spice and omelette shops around the
clock tower).

Information

There are ATMs all over the city, including
a UTI ATM near Sojati Gate, SBBJ near the
Tourist Reception Centre, and ICICI and
IDBI ATMs on Airport Rd.

Bank of Baroda (Map p303; Sojati Gate) Issues cash
advances against Visa and MasterCard.

International Tourist Bureau (☎ 2439052;
🕐 5am-11.30pm Mon-Sat) At the main train station, the
bureau provides help for foreign passengers. It's a handy
place to hang around while waiting for a train. There
are comfortable armchairs and a shower and toilet here.
Unattended luggage must be deposited in the train station
cloakroom (Rs 10 per piece for 24 hours).

LKP Forex (Map p303; ☎ 2512066; shop No 1, Maha-
reer Palace) Changes cash and travellers cheques. Opposite
Circuit House.

Main post office (Map p303; Station Rd; 🕐 10am-5pm
Mon-Fri, 10am-1pm Sat) Less than 500m north of the
main train station.

Rathi's Media Centre (Map p303; Mohanpura Overbridge; 🕐 7am-9pm) Stocks a reasonable range of
magazines and books in English, including novels and
recent releases.

Reliance Webworld (Map p303; Nai Sarak; per hr Rs
30; 🕐 10.30am-11pm) One of many cheap internet
places.

JODHPUR

0 _____ 1 km
0 _____ 0.5 miles

INFORMATION
Bank of Baroda.............................**1** B3
ICICI ATM...................................**2** C4
IDBI ATM....................................**3** C4
LKP Forex...................................**4** C3
Main Post Office.........................**5** B3

Rathi's Media Centre...................**6** B3
Reliance Webworld......................**7** B3
Saji Sanwri Internet Cafè.......(see 35)
SBBJ ATM.............................(see 10)
Sarvodaya Bookstall....................**8** B3
State Bank of India......................**9** C2
Tourist Reception Centre...........**10** C3
UTI ATM................................(see 1)

SIGHTS & ACTIVITIES
Clock Tower..............................**11** B2
Jaswant Thada..........................**12** B1
Rajasthan Sangeet Natak Akademi
    Folk Art Museum..................**13** C3
Sadar Club................................**14** C6
Sadar Government Museum.......**15** C3
Umaid Bhawan Palace &
    Museum.............................**16** D4
Zoo...**17** C3

SLEEPING 🏠
Ajit Bhawan.............................**18** C3

Blue House...............................**19** A2
Cosy Guest House......................**20** A2
Devi Bhawan.............................**21** D5
Durag Niwas Guest House...........**22** C3
Durag Villas Guest House......(see 22)
Ganpati Guest House..................**23** B2
Govind Hotel.............................**24** B3
Hotel Haveli..............................**25** B3
Hotel Kalinga............................**26** B3
Inn Season................................**27** B4
Karni Bhawan............................**28** D5
Madho Niwas............................**29** C5
Newton's Manor........................**30** C5
Pal Haveli.................................**31** B2
Park Plaza................................**32** C5
Ranbanka Palace.......................**33** C3
Ratan Vilas...............................**34** C5
Saji Sanwri Guest House.............**35** A2
Shahi Guest House.....................**36** A2
Shivam Paying Guest House.........**37** B2
Singhvi's Haveli.........................**38** A2
Taj Hari Mahal Palace.................**39** A5
Tourist Guest House...................**40** B3
Umaid Bhawan Palace...........(see 16)

EATING 🍴
Agra Sweets..............................**41** B3
Hotel Priya & Restaurant............**42** B3
Indique................................(see 31)
Jharokha..............................(see 25)
Kalinga Restaurant.................(see 26)
Mid Town.................................**43** B3
Omelette Shop..........................**44** B2
On the Rocks........................(see 48)
Pokar Sweets........................(see 42)
Pushpa Bhojnalya Dining Hall....**45** A3
Shri Mishrilal Hotel...................**46** B2
Sweet Shops............................**47** A3

SHOPPING 🛍
Anokhi....................................**48** C4
Antique Shops..........................**49** D3
Handloom House.......................**50** B3
MV Spices................................**51** B2

TRANSPORT
Indian Airlines..........................**52** C4
Jet Airways...............................**53** B5
Railway Booking Office...............**54** C4
Roadways Bus Stand..................**55** C3
Taxi Stand................................**56** B3

See Mehrangarh Map (p304)

Mehrangarh

Navchokiya

To Maha Mandir (2km);
Balsamand Lake (5km);
Mandore (7km);
Osiyan (65km);
Khimsar (95km);
Nagaur (135km)

Sadar
Market

Umaid
Gardens

Raika Bagh
Train Station

To Ajmer (205km);
Jaipur (336km)

Nai Sarak

Ranchodji
Temple

MG Rd

Mohanpura
Overbridge

High Ct Rd

Jodhpur
Train
Station

Chopasni Rd

To Dhawa Doli
Wildlife Sanctuary (40km);
Barmer (150km)

Station Rd

Ratanada Rd

Circuit
House

Palace Rd

Airport Rd

Old Loco
Shed Rd

Bhatia
Circle

Ratanada
Circle

To Rohet (40km);
Sardar Samand (66km);
Bhenswara (130km);
Udaipur (260km);
Mt Abu (326km)

Umaid Bhawan Rd

Rotary
Circle

Residency Rd

Panc
Batti
Circle

To Airport (200km)

Bhagat
ki Kothi
Train
Station

Saji Sanwri Internet Cafe (Map p303; Ghandi St; per hr Rs 40; ☺ 9am-11pm) Modern, cool and fast internet café encompassing all digital services.

Sarvodaya Bookstall (Map p303; ☺ 8.30am-10.30pm) Off Station Rd, opposite Ranchodji Temple. Sarvodaya has English-language newspapers and magazines, a good range of books and maps on Rajasthan, and a few Western novels.

State Bank of India (Map p303; ☎ 2543649; ☺ 10am-4pm Mon-Fri, 10am-1pm Sat) Changes currency and travellers cheques. Located about 1km north of the Tourist Reception Centre.

Tourist Reception Centre (Map p303; ☎ 2545083; ☺ 10am-5pm Mon-Sat) In the RTDC Hotel Ghoomar compound. Offers a free map and can arrange city tours and Bishnoi village excursions.

Sights
MEHRANGARH

Still run by the maharaja of Jodhpur, **Mehrangarh** (Map p304; www.Mehrangarh.org; Indian/foreigner admission Rs 20/250, incl camera & audio guide; ticket sales ☺ 9am-5pm) is an enchanting place to visit. Following the lines of a 125m hill, the fort's height becomes apparent as you approach. It's a mesmerising, formidable feat of construction. The battlements are 6m to 36m high. As the building materials were chiselled from the rock on which the fort stands, the structure merges with its base. The fort was added to over the centuries by Jodhpur's maharajas. A winding road leads up to the entrance from the city, 5km below.

Cast off your audio-tour prejudices, as this tour (in multiple languages requiring a deposit of credit card/passport/Rs 2000) is terrific. The mix of history, information and royal reminiscing make it entertaining and engaging. It's a real treat to wander around at your leisure, taking a fix of information when you feel like it. However, if you prefer a real person, guides are available for Rs 150.

The fort's seven *pols* (gates) include the **Jayapol**, built by Maharaja Man Singh in 1806 following his victory over the rulers of Jaipur and Bikaner. This is the main entrance to the fort. Beyond it is the ticket office, where there's a lift (Rs 15) that will whisk disabled or weary travellers to the top of the fort. The walls at the entrance are still scarred by cannonball hits, showing that this was a fort that earned its keep. To the left, just beyond the ticket office, is the **Chhatri of Kiratsingh Sodha**. This cenotaph was built over the site where a soldier fell defending Jodhpur against Jaipurians in 1806.

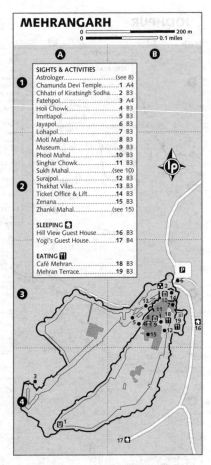

MEHRANGARH

SIGHTS & ACTIVITIES		
Astrologer	(see 8)	
Chamunda Devi Temple	1	A4
Chhatri of Kiratsingh Sodha	2	B3
Fatehpol	3	A4
Holi Chowk	4	B3
Imritiapol	5	B3
Jayapol	6	B3
Lohapol	7	B3
Moti Mahal	8	B3
Museum	9	B3
Phool Mahal	10	B3
Singhar Chowk	11	B3
Sukh Mahal	(see 10)	
Surajpol	12	B3
Thakhat Vilas	13	B3
Ticket Office & Lift	14	B3
Zenana	15	B3
Zhanki Mahal	(see 15)	
SLEEPING 🏠		
Hill View Guest House	16	B3
Yogi's Guest House	17	B4
EATING 🍴		
Café Mehran	18	B3
Mehran Terrace	19	B3

Built in the 16th-century, **Imritiapol** is arranged at the top of a slope, after a sharp turn, in order to stop onslaughts by an enemy's elephants. The **Fatehpol** (Victory Gate), at the southwestern side of the fort, was erected by Maharaja Ajit Singh to commemorate his defeat of the Mughals.

The next gate is the **Lohapol** (Iron Gate), again built at the top of the slope, just beyond a bend. Its iron spikes were a further elephant deterrent. Beside the gate are 15 tiny handprints, the *sati* (self-immolation) marks of Maharaja Man Singh's widows, who threw themselves on his funeral pyre in 1843 – the last *sati* widows of the Jodhpur dynasty. The handprints still attract devotional attention, and are usually covered in red powder and paper-thin silver.

Inside the fort is a stone-latticed network of courtyards and palaces, all beautiful examples of Rajput architecture. **Surajpol** leads to the museum. Through the gate you'll find **Singhar Chowk**, where coronations take place. The small marble seat has been used for coronations from the 17th century.

The **museum** holds a splendid collection of Indian royal trappings, showing the wealth and power of the Marwars, including Rajasthan's best collection of elephant howdahs (seats for carrying people on an elephant's back – essential for glittering processions). Some feature the most exquisite repoussé (raised relief) silverwork. There are also maharajas' palanquins, including covered palanquins for the women in purdah (seclusion). Apparently one of these sent the British media into a frenzy when the maharajas visited – the press were all desperate to get a picture of the hidden queen. One photographer caught a picture of her foot, but there was such an outcry when it was published that all the newspapers in which it was printed had to be recalled. Perhaps the finest palanquin is that presented to Jaswant Singh I by the Emperor Shah Jahan; it's exquisitely worked in silver and gold, and has a natty little parasol to beat the heat. The museum also has some splendid miniatures and, as you might expect, the armoury is impressive – each weapon is a work of art. Also on display is some wonderful ephemera, such as 19th-century ivory-inlaid ladies' dumbbells and camel-bone carpet weights.

Within the complex are numerous small palaces with evocative names, such as the **Sukh Mahal** (Pleasure Palace). Upstairs is the **Phool Mahal** (Flower Palace), in which traditional dances were performed. It was also used as a durbar hall (see p246) by former maharajas. The fine paintings adorning the walls of this palace were executed by a single artist, who took 10 years to create them using a curious concoction of gold leaf, glue and cow's urine. The artist passed away before the work was finished, which is evident in the bare patch to the left of the hallway. The gold ceiling is embellished with over 80kg of gold plate, and around it the various maharajas of Jodhpur are depicted. Stained glass further adds to the room's opulence.

Also on view is **Thakhat Vilas**, the private chamber of Maharaja Thakhat Singh (r 1843-73), who had no less than 30 maharanis and numerous concubines. The beautiful ceiling is distractingly adorned with lac painting and hung with Christmas baubles.

Nearby, in the zenana (women's apartments), the **Zhanki Mahal** has cradles of infant princes, including that of the current maharaja – a motorised version. From the zenana the women would peep at palatial goings-on through the latticed windows, the screens of which are said to feature over 250 different designs.

Next is an impressive marble-floored courtyard called **Holi Chowk**; this is where the maharaja and friends would celebrate Holi. On its right is the early 17th-century **Moti Mahal** (Pearl Palace), where royal women would hold meetings. The walls are coated with crushed seashell *chunam* (lime paste). The five alcoves along the western wall and the other tiny alcoves were for oil lamps. The gold-painted ceiling is embellished with glass tiles.

At the southern end of the fort, cannons look out from the ramparts over the sheer drop to the old town beneath. There are magical, stupendous views, and you can clearly hear the voices and city sounds swept up by the air currents. Aldous Huxley noted this in *Jesting Pilate – An Intellectual Holiday* (George H Doran Co, 1926):

From the bastions of the Jodhpur Fort one hears as the Gods must hear from Olympus – the Gods to whom each separate word uttered in the innumerable peopled world below, comes up distinct and individual to be recorded in the books of omniscience.

The peaceful **Chamunda Devi Temple**, dedicated to the goddess Durga (the Inaccessible, a form of Devi) in her wrathful aspect, stands at the southwest end of the fort. This is a lovely place to sit in the window alcoves overlooking the city below.

Just near Surajpol is **Café Mehran** (Map p304; meals Rs 70-180; ⏰ 9am-5pm), offering snacks and some simple meals. A restaurant, Mehran Terrace (p310), which is spectacularly situated on the fort ramparts, is only open in the evenings.

JASWANT THADA

This flamboyant milk-white marble **memorial** (Map p303; admission Rs 20, camera Rs 25; ⏰ 9am-5pm) to Maharaja Jaswant Singh II is about 1km from the fort. It's a peaceful spot away from the hubbub of the city, and the view across to

WESTERN RAJASTHAN

the fort is superb. The cenotaph, built in 1899, was followed by the royal crematorium and the three other cenotaphs that stand nearby. There are carved wooden doors and marble jali (lattice) work over the windows. Brought 240km from Makrana, the marble used to build the monuments is now translucent in places. Look out for the memorial to a peacock that flew into a funeral pyre.

CLOCK TOWER & MARKETS
The **clock tower** (Map p303) is an old city landmark, surrounded by the chaotic and vibrant Sadar Market. The market's lines of shops are an impressive example of 19th-century town planning and a wonderful place to ramble. Narrow alleys bustle with commerce and tiny hole-in-the-wall outlets. Heading westwards from here, you go deep into the old city's commercial heart, with crowded alleys and bazaars selling vegetables, spices, sweets, silver and handicrafts.

RAJASTHAN SANGEET NATAK AKADEMI FOLK ART MUSEUM
This national academy, established in 1938, has the task of preserving the traditional folk art, dance, drama and music of Rajasthan. You might need to rustle someone up to open the little **museum** (Map p303; ☎ 2544090; www.sange etnatakakademi.org; Town Hall, High Court Rd; admission Rs 5; ❤ 10am-5pm Tue-Sun), but it's well worth the effort. There are beautiful puppets, an amazing array of traditional instruments and other exhibits on the performing arts. Unfortunately, there's not much information in English. The academy also organises regular performances of music, dance and theatre.

UMAID GARDENS & SADAR GOVERNMENT MUSEUM
The pleasant **Umaid gardens** contain the **Sadar Government Museum** (Map p303; admission Rs 5; ❤ 10am-4.30pm Sat-Thu), which feels charmingly frozen somewhere in the 19th century. The ill-labelled exhibits in dusty cabinets include weapons and 6th- to 10th-century sculptures, as well as the obligatory moth-eaten stuffed animals.

There's also a desultory **zoo** (Map p303; Indian/foreigner Rs 7/50; ❤ 10am-5pm Wed-Mon) in the grounds.

UMAID BHAWAN PALACE & MUSEUM
Take a rickshaw or taxi to this hill-top **palace** (Map p303), sometimes called the Chittar

Palace because local Chittar sandstone was used to build it. Building began in 1929 and the 365-room edifice was designed by the British Royal Institute of Architects president for Maharaja Umaid Singh, and took over 3000 workers 15 years to complete, at a cost of around Rs 11 million. The building is mortarless, and incorporates 100 wagon loads of Makrana marble and Burmese teak in the interior. The impressive central dome sits 30m above the sky-blue inner dome. It was built surprisingly close to Independence, after which the maharajas and their grand extravagances were a thing of the past. Apparently the construction of this over-the-top palace was motivated as a royal job-creation programme during a time of severe drought – very philanthropic.

Umaid Singh died in 1947, four years after the palace was completed; the current maharaja, Maharaja Gaj Singh II (known as Bapji), still lives in part of the building. The rest has been turned into a suitably grand hotel (see p310).

Most interesting in the **museum** (admission Rs 50; ❤ 9am-5pm) are the photos showing the elegant Art Deco design of the palace interior. The museum also has beautifully crafted weapons; an array of stuffed leopards; an enormous banner presented by Queen Victoria to Maharaja Jaswant Singh Bahadur in 1877; and a fantastic clock collection, including specimens shaped like windmills and lighthouses. Attendants will ensure that you don't stray into the hotel, but you can peer at the soaring domed central hall. Alternatively, you can visit the hotel to eat at one of its restaurants (see p311). Look out for some of the maharaja's highly polished classic cars displayed on the lawn in front of the museum.

Activities
ASTROLOGY
Astrologer **Mr Sharma** (Map p304; ☎ 9414130200; ❤ 9am-5.30pm) has been studying astrology for over 30 years. Don't wear nail polish if you intend to get a reading, as the nails are used to ascertain your state of health. Mr Sharma charges around Rs 300 for a basic consultation at his office in the Moti Mahal section of the fort. He can also offer a private consultation, for which you'll need a booking.

GOLF
There's a golf course at **Sadar Club** (p303; ❤ 1-11pm), south of Jodhpur in Ratanada. The

brown grounds offer some challenging shots for golfers. Expect to pay around Rs 200 for 18 holes, including equipment hire. Popular with the British during the Raj, the club is about 100 years old, but has been revamped over the last few years. However, it still has a sense of history: you can see the damage inflicted on part of the building when it was bombed during the first war between India and Pakistan.

Tours

The Tourist Reception Centre runs **city tours** (Rs 100, min 4 persons, admission fees extra; ☑ 9am-1pm & 2-6pm), taking in the Umaid Bhawan Palace, Mehrangarh, Jaswant Thada and Mandore gardens (see p313). There's no guide, just a driver and vehicle.

Jodhpur is known for its interesting village safaris, which visit the nearby villages of the Bishnoi, a people whose belief in the sanctity of the environment and the need to protect trees and animals dates from the 15th century. See p314 for more information.

It's a well-worn trail, visiting potters and *dhurrie* (rug) weavers, so it can feel touristy – it depends how good your guide is. However, you have the chance to meet the local people as they go about their daily lives, have a traditional lunch at one of the villages and stop at a few crafts outlets. Visitors are sometimes invited to share *amal* (an opium preparation), which is traditionally offered to guests. Just about every hotel can organise these excursions; all charge around Rs 400 to Rs 500 per person (minimum of two people) for a half-day tour, including lunch. Recommended hotel-run tours include **Singhvi's Haveli** (Map p303; ☎ 2624293), **Durag Niwas Guest House** (Map p303; ☎ 2512385), **Durag Villas Guest House** (Map p303; ☎ 2512298) and **Govind Hotel** (Map p303; ☎ 2622758). **Deepak Dhanraj** (☎ 9314721655; www.bishnoivillagesafari.com) is also a good option.

Shivam Paying Guest House (Map p303; ☎ 2610688) arranges recommended trips to villages around Osiyan (see p317), 65km north of Jodhpur, where you can take a camel or jeep safari and stay overnight in a village.

Cosy Guest House (Map p303; ☎ 2612066) and the **Govind Hotel** (Map p303; ☎ 2622758) can also arrange trips out to Osiyan.

Sleeping

As usual, if a rickshaw driver is clamouring to take you somewhere, it's because he is going to receive a commission (up to 50% for the budget hotels). For anywhere near the clock tower, you can avoid this by getting dropped at the tower and walking the rest. Some rickshaw drivers ask 'which clock tower?' to confuse you. There's only one.

Staying around the clock tower is convenient for the fort and shopping district, and there's a cluster of mainly budget guesthouses here, but it's also where you'll encounter the most hassle. The places around Navchokiya in the old city are quieter.

Prices everywhere fluctuate according to how many tourists are around. If it's busy, prices will often go up, while at quiet times you can get big discounts.

Like most tourist centres in Rajasthan, there are far more budget choices than midrange options. However, the quality of accommodation in all categories is good, with an excellent range of atmospheric options.

A number of families are registered with the Paying Guest House Scheme in Jodhpur. Costs per double room per night range from Rs 200 to Rs 1500. Inquire at the Tourist Reception Centre (see p302).

BUDGET

Cosy Guest House (Map p303; ☎ 2612066; www.cosyguesthouse.com; Navchokiya; rooftop Rs 60, tents Rs 150, d Rs 300-650, s/d without bathroom Rs 200/250; ⛶ 🖥) This is a great, unpretentious choice in a quiet corner of the old city. It's a 500-year-old blue house, with several levels of rooms and rooftops and a genial owner, Mr Joshi. Options include rooms with bathroom, a single room without bathroom but with a fantastic view from the doorway and its own flight of steps, and tents on the roof. The rooftop restaurant has great views and vegetarian food. Ask the rickshaw-wallah for Navchokiya Rd, from where the guesthouse is signposted or give the hotel a call and you will be met.

Govind Hotel (Map p303; ☎ 2622758; www.govindhotel.com; Station Rd; dm Rs 70, s 150, r Rs 350-900; 🖥) This is a friendly, central place, well set up for travellers and with helpful management. Opposite the main post office, it's a five-minute walk from the train station, which is great if you've got an early-morning departure. The rooms vary; those at the back are the quietest, though some have no external window. Otherwise, rooms range from basic to smart, and there's a rooftop restaurant with espresso coffee and fort views (if you ignore the billboard). The owners don't pay commissions.

Hill View Guest House (Map p304; ☎ 2441763; s Rs 150, d 200-250) A family house perched high up on the way to, and in the shadow of, the fort, this option is very enthusiastically run (you'll be made to feel part of the family). Rooms are basic, clean and simple, all with bathrooms, and the terrace has a great view over the city. Simple, tasty vegetarian food is on offer.

Blue House (Map p303; ☎ 2621396; bluehouse36@ hotmail.com; Moti Chowk; s Rs 150, d Rs 250-1500; ✷) Certainly blue, this haphazard old house has a variety of individually decorated rooms and some very steep stairs. Run by a friendly Jain family, some rooms are incongruously opulent for this part of town: top of the range has a bed and a bathtub of carved sandstone! Beware of competitors with similarly named hotels.

Tourist Guest House (Map p303; ☎ 2541235; udaibedi@hotmail.com; Rallaram Bldg, High Court Rd; s/d from Rs 200/250 to 500/600) This is a friendly choice outside the old city and thus outside the tourist scene. Don't be put off by the battered exterior and hectic High Court Rd, as this is a really nice place to stay. Run by a lovely family who won't pay rickshaw commissions, it has simple, basic clean rooms and offers tasty home-cooked inexpensive vegetarian fare.

Durag Niwas Guest House (Map p303; ☎ 2512385; www.durag-niwas.com; 1 Old Public Park; s/d from Rs 200/250, r Rs 650; ✷) This is a cool blue house run by a friendly family who are well-informed and helpful. Good home-cooked veg dishes are available, and there's a cushion-floored, sari-curtained area on the roof for hanging out. The basic rooms vary and some are in need of maintenance. The more expensive rooms come with air-con.

Yogi's Guest House (Map p304; ☎ 2643436; r Rs 350-1200, s/d without bathroom Rs 200/250; ▣) At the base of the fort walls is Yogi's, a popular travellers' hangout that's moving upmarket with many refurbished rooms, though there are still plenty of budget options. Set in the 500-year-old Rajpurohitji-ki-Haveli, the rooms are smart, spacious and clean. However, the service can be erratic and the ticket-booking service is best avoided. There's a lovely rooftop restaurant with a fort view and good food. The guesthouse is well signposted off the lanes leading to the fort.

ourpick Saji Sanwri Guest House (Map p303; ☎ 2440305; www.sajisanwri.com; Kapara Bazaar; s without bathroom Rs 200, d Rs 350-1300; ✷ ▣) An energetic mother-and-son team run this rambling 32-room, character-filled guesthouse in the heart of the old city. A high degree of care and thought for their guests is very apparent, and the varied rooms are all spotless and comfortable. There's a modern internet café on site (opening onto Gandhi St) and all travel ticketing services are available. There's an early checkout of 9am but you can make use of the sitting room and store luggage until your departure.

Singhvi's Haveli (Map p303; ☎ 2624293; Navchokiya, Ramdevji ka Chowk; r Rs 200-1800) This 500-plus-year-old, red-sandstone *haveli* is in a peaceful corner of the oldest part of the city. Run by a friendly Jain family, it's a wonderful and welcoming place to stay. Rooms are atmospheric, ranging from basic, good-value options to the multimirrored Sheesh Mahal or the magnificent Maharani Suite with 10 windows and a fort view. The romantic rooftop restaurant serves home-cooked meals (and there are eggs for non-Jain guests). You can even visit the fort via the Fatepol entrance and experience a whole other (and uncrowded) side of the fort.

Shivam Paying Guest House (Map p303; ☎ 2610688; shivamgh@hotmail.com; Makrana Mohalla; d from Rs 250-600, r without bathroom Rs 150) Near the clock tower is this cosy option where you'll get no hassles. Run by a helpful family, it has comfortable rooms on several floors, reached by steep staircases. Bathrooms have been shoe-horned into this old building, and there's a lovely rooftop restaurant, where the home-cooking is excellent.

Ganpati Guest House (Map p303; ☎ 2631686; Makrana Mohalla; s Rs 250, d Rs 300-900; ✷) This fully renovated guesthouse is run by the family at the nearby Shivam Paying Guest House and has been designed to avoid the nuisances that the old buildings present. Clean, bright, airy rooms have modern bathrooms and there is a pleasant all-veg rooftop restaurant.

Durag Villas Guest House (Map p303; ☎ 2512298; www.duragvillas.com; 1 Old Public Park; r Rs 250-950; ✷) As this guesthouse is next door to Durag Niwas, the competition here seems fierce. However, it is also a friendly place with simple, good-value rooms accessed via very steep stairs and set around a small, tranquil, leafy courtyard.

Shahi Guest House (Map p303; ☎ 9828583883; www .shahiguesthouse.com; Ghandi St; r Rs 400-1200; ✷) This architecturally intriguing 350-year-old *haveli* has six very distinct and individual rooms surrounding a peaceful inner courtyard. It's in a very central position in the old city yet the solid walls keep it quiet and cool. It's very atmospheric and relaxing and upstairs there's a pleasant rooftop restaurant with fort views.

Hotel Haveli (Map p303; ☎ 2614615; www.hotelhaveli.net; Makrana Mohalla; r Rs 400-1500; ❄ ☐) This 250-year-old building inside the walled city is a popular, efficient and friendly place, previously known as Haveli Guest House. Rooms vary greatly and many have semi-balconies and fort views. Interiors have been brightly renovated in traditional Rajasthani style, and the management have rented a building across the road (with equally pleasant rooms) to take the overflow from the original. The rooftop veg restaurant, Jharokha (see p310), has exceptional food and views.

MIDRANGE
Madho Niwas (Map p303; ☎ 2512486; Airport Rd, Ratanada; s/d Rs 800/1000, deluxe Rs 1100/1350; ❄ ☐) This stately, rambling house built in the 1940s, is run by Dalvir Singh and is a relaxed place to stay, with a quiet lawn area. More rooms and a larger swimming pool were under construction when we visited. It's around 3km from the centre of town, but is good value, with comfortable rooms and tasty food. The hotel can also arrange a stay at Ravla Bhenswara (p315), outside Jodhpur.

Devi Bhawan (Map p303; ☎ 2511067; www.devibhawan.com; 1 Ratanada Area; r Rs 950-1500; ❄ ☐ ☐) Devi Bhawan is a delightful green oasis, with appealing rooms and a cottage. Though it's a bit out of the way, it's great value and you'll have no hassles here whatsoever. There's a noon checkout, a good restaurant (veg thali Rs 120) and bar and shady grounds with a pool.

Newtons Manor (Map p303; ☎ 2430686; www.newtonsmanor.com; 86 Jawahar Colony, Ratanada; r Rs 995-1195; ❄ ☐) Newtons Manor, 3km southeast of the town centre, is a lovely, colonial-style family home chock-full of Victoriana. It has elegant rooms crammed with antique furniture, and TV and fridge. There's a lovely billiard room and pleasant outdoor area. Scrumptious home-cooked meals are available and a free pick-up service is offered.

Ratan Vilas (Map p303; ☎ 2614418; www.ratanvilas.com; Old Loco Shed Rd, Ratanada; r Rs 995-1950; ❄) This attractive, quiet, colonial villa is fronted by a clipped lawn, and the homey sitting room

gives the place a relaxed bygone-days atmosphere. Rooms are spotless, wonderful home-cooked meals are available, including breakfast in the sunny courtyard, and management say they are planning to build a swimming pool. If you're interested in getting authentic jodhpur trousers made, ask here – allow at least a week for your jodhpurs to be stitched.

Inn Season (Map p303; ☎ /fax 2616400; www.innseasonjodhpur.com; r with/without AC Rs 1500/1000, ste Rs 3500; ❄ ☐) Near the taxi stand, this is an Art Deco bungalow with spacious, tidy rooms and a lovely suite. All rooms have wireless internet access but for old-fashioned fun there's an old radiogram and a German record player with an eclectic collection of classic records. The restaurant serves excellent Indian and Continental food.

Hotel Kalinga (Map p303; ☎ 2627338; www.kalingahotel.com; s/d Rs 1600/2100; ❄) This hotel is convenient, as it's close to the main train station, however management are more in tune with travelling salesmen than tourists. It's a dull, almost seedy, business hotel, with musty, overpriced but well appointed rooms with TV and fridge.

Karni Bhawan (Map p303; ☎ 2512101; www.karnihotels.com; Palace Rd, Ratanada; s/d from Rs 1850/2300; ❄ ☐ ☐) This place is a remodelled 1940s bungalow with a pleasant garden-restaurant with campfire, and an inviting pool. Its rooms are spacious and clean with solid colonial furnishings, and some are mildly themed (such as one based on Holi). The kitchen prides itself on its succulent regional cuisine which can be enjoyed in the restaurant, by the pool or under a thatched roof in the re-created *dhani* (traditional village).

Pal Haveli (Map p303; ☎ 2439615; www.palhaveli.com; Gulab Sagar; r Rs 2500-4000; ❄ ☐) This stunning *haveli* was built by the Thakur of Pal in 1847. There are 20 charming, spacious rooms, elaborately decorated in traditional heritage-style surrounding a cool central courtyard. Be aware that at the time of writing management was planning to upgrade all rooms to the more expensive category. The family still lives here and can show you their small museum. There are two restaurants serving excellent food and the rooftop Indique (p311) boasts unbeatable views.

TOP END
Ajit Bhawan (Map p303; ☎ 2511410; www.ajitbhawan.com; Airport Rd; tent Rs 4000, r Rs 5500-9000; luxury tent &

ste Rs 10,000-15,000; 🍴 🍸) This is a superb place to stay, and it's deservedly popular with travellers. Despite its location on a dusty main road, the hotel is a city oasis; the gracious heritage building is set well back from the road, amid verdant gardens and attention to detail is obvious. Behind the main building are private thatch-roofed cottages with traditional furnishings. There's a whimsical swimming pool (Rs 500 for nonguests) with a waterfall and you can swim beneath the restaurant.

Park Plaza (Map p303; ☎ 5105000; www.sarovarhotels.com; 5 Airport Rd; s/d from Rs 5000/5500, ste Rs 9,000; 🍴 🖵 🍸) A modern, functional business hotel with an incongruous British-style wood-panelled bar and restaurant, Geoffrey's. The standard rooms are well-appointed and comfortable without any heritage trappings. Room rate includes breakfast and airport transfer.

Ranbanka Palace (Map p303; ☎ 2512801; www.ranbankahotels.com; Airport Rd; r Rs 5000-6500, ste Rs 8500-12,500) In a beautiful sandstone building, built for Maharajadhiraj Ajit Singh (younger brother of Maharaja Umaid Singh), this is right next to higher profile and related Ajit Bhawan. Rooms have soaring ceilings and old colonial furniture and those facing the pool and garden are the best. Rooms are airy but devoid of charisma.

Taj Hari Mahal Palace (Map p303; ☎ 2439700; www.tajhotels.com; 5 Residency Rd; r from Rs 11,000, ste Rs 17,500; 🍴 🖵 🍸) Run by the Taj Group, this is a luxurious modern hotel built with traditional Rajasthani flourishes. It is centred on a courtyard with a big, inviting swimming pool. Cheaper rooms look out on the garden, while the pricier ones have a pool view. Prices drop by up to two-thirds in the low season.

Umaid Bhawan Palace (Map p303; ☎ 2510101; www.tajhotels.com; r Rs 28,000-42,000, ste Rs 87,000-144,000; 🍴 🖵 🍸) This massive 20th-century Art Deco palace, also home to a museum (see p306), is constructed from honey sandstone and white marble and is a Jodhpur landmark. It's so immense it feels rather like a parliament building or a university – that is, it's not all that cosy. The hotel is managed by the professional Taj Group. It has luxurious rooms of course and numerous sporting facilities, including a magnificent indoor swimming pool. There are lush lawns and several restaurants (see right) for grazing.

Eating

While you're in Jodhpur, try a glass of *makhania* lassi, a thick and filling saffron-flavoured edition of that most refreshing of drinks.

RESTAURANTS

Pushpa Bhojnalya Dining Hall (Map p303; Jalori Gate; mains Rs 15-45; 🕙 10am-10.30pm) A small local eatery in a busy section of town, this is indeed a good restaurant with tasty Rajasthani regional cuisine. Try the hearty *dal batti* (baked balls of wholemeal flour served with dhal) or the Kashmiri *paneer* with apple, cashew and banana.

Mid Town (Map p303; ☎ 2637001; Station Rd; mains Rs 18-70; 🕙 7am-11pm) Mid Town has downstairs and rooftop eating areas, though the rooftop was under renovation at the time we visited. This clean restaurant with good veg food, including some Rajasthani specialities, has some particular to Jodhpur, such as *chakki-ka-sagh* and roti (wheat dumpling cooked in rich gravy), *bajara-ki-roti pachkuta* (*bajara* wheat roti with local dry vegetables) and *kabuli* (vegetables with rice, milk, bread and fruit).

Jodhpur Coffee House (Map p303; High Court Rd; mains Rs 20-40; 🕙 9am-10.30pm) This stuck-in-time place has been going since 1954, and feels like it might not have changed much since then. A calm contrast after the busy street, the pale-blue restaurant is a bit street soiled with a utility-furniture feel, and offers inexpensive thalis and South Indian food.

Hotel Priya & Restaurant (Map p303; ☎ 2547463; 181-182 Nai Sarak; mains Rs 25-40; 🕙 6am-midnight) Partially open to the hubbub of Nai Sarak, this popular, friendly eatery has a cheerful sense of chaos. It's usually packed with locals, has good service, and serves reliable North and South Indian cuisine. The thalis are tasty, and there are sweets, too.

Kalinga Restaurant (Map p303; Station Rd; dishes Rs 25-100; 🕙 8am-10.30pm) This restaurant, at the hotel of the same name (see p309), is smart and popular, with a dimly lit ambience typical of an Indian bar. Offering tasty veg and non-veg Indian, Chinese and Continental food, it's a good place to kill time while waiting for a train.

Jharokha (Map p303; ☎ 2614615; Makrana Mohalla; mains Rs 60-90; 🕙 7am-10.30pm) On the rooftop of Hotel Haveli (see p309), this pleasant restaurant offers tasty Indian and Continental food with excellent city and fort views. The vegetarian dishes extend from pizza and pasta to dosas and thalis.

On the Rocks (Map p303; ☎ 5102701; Airport Rd; mains Rs 85-285; ☺ lunch 12.30-3pm, dinner 7-11pm, bar 12.30-11pm, happy hour 4-6pm) This leafy place next to the Ajit Bhawan hotel (same owner) is very popular with locals and tour groups. The garden restaurant has plenty of shade trees, a small playground and is candlelit in the evening. It serves Chinese and tasty Indian cuisine, with lots of barbecue options and very rich and creamy curries. There's also a partly open-air bar and an excellent bakery.

Indique (Map p303; ☎ 2439615; www.palhaveli.com; Gulab Sagar; mains Rs 90-160; ☺ 7am-11pm) On the rooftop of Pal Haveli (see p309), this wonderful restaurant offers tasty Indian dishes, including the outstanding silver thali (veg/nonveg Rs 250/300). It also has excellent views over the old city, the clock tower, Gulab Sagar and Mehrangarh Fort.

Mehran Terrace (Map p304; ☎ 2548790; Mehrangarh; veg/nonveg thalis Rs 540/600; ☺ 7.30-10pm) Dining with cannons under the stairs on one of the fort's terraces is unsurpassably romantic. The open-air restaurant is overlooked by floodlit palace buildings resembling a stage, complete with live music and traditional dancing. Perched 140m above the city, when you look over the ramparts, the sparkling metropolis is spread out below – an amazing sight. Sit at one of the well-spaced, candlelit tables and enjoy the rich (and constantly re-filled) Rajasthani thalis. You will need to book ahead.

Umaid Bhawan Palace (☎ 2510101) Located at the hotel of the same name (see opposite), this place has a selection of elegant eateries including the very grand Marwar Hall, which is used for functions but worth a look. **Risala** (mains Rs 650-1750; ☺ lunch 1-3pm, dinner 7.30-11pm), celebrating the famous Jodhpur Lancers (Risala means cavalry), is a casual fine-dining experience with Indian and international dishes including New Zealand lamb and local Rajasthani specialities. Behind Risala on the colonnaded western verandah is the **Pillars** (mains Rs 650-1750; ☺ 6.30am-11pm), a breezy coffee shop and informal à la carte eatery sharing the menu from Risala. There are sublime views across the lawn towards Mehrangarh. For liquid refreshments you could pull up an elephant-foot stool at the **Trophy Bar** (☺ 11am-3pm & 6-11pm) and discuss the finer points of pig sticking.

QUICK EATS

Omelette Shop (Map p303; Sadar Market; mains Rs 10-15) Just through the entrance gate into Sadar Market on the northern side of the square, this shop claims to go through 15,000 eggs a day – the egg man has been doing his thing for over 30 years. Three tasty, spicy boiled eggs cost Rs 10, and a two-egg omelette with chilli, coriander and four pieces of bread is Rs 15.

Shri Mishrilal Hotel (Map p303; clock tower) This place is on your right as you enter Sadar Market. It's nothing fancy, but whips up the best lassis in town. A delicious glass of impossibly thick, creamy *makhania* lassi costs Rs 15 and will do you for lunch.

Agra Sweets (Map p303; MG Rd, opposite Sojati Gate) There are good lassis (Rs 12) here, as well as delectable Jodhpur specialities, such as *mawa ladoo* (a milk sweet made with sugar, cardamom and pistachios wrapped in silver leaf; Rs 6) and the baklava-like *mawa kachori* (Rs 12).

Pokar Sweets (Map p303; cnr Nai Sarak & High Court Rd) This place has a huge selection of sweet treats. You can pick out a box of six for around Rs 30.

There's an inviting cluster of **sweet shops** (Map p303) in the old city, on the way to Cosy Guest House. The cool, quiet refreshment room on the 1st floor of the train station has a strangely timeless ambience and has surprisingly palatable thalis.

Shopping

Take care while shopping in Jodhpur. If a rickshaw driver, friendly man on the street, or hotel recommends a shop to you, it's almost certain that they're getting a commission.

The usual Rajasthani handicrafts are available, with shops selling textiles and other wares clustered around the clock tower (you'll need to bargain hard). However, Jodhpur is famous for antiques. The greatest concentration of showrooms is along Palace Rd, near Umaid Bhawan Palace. These shops are well known to Western antique dealers, so you'll be hard-pressed to find any bargains. Also remember that the trade in antique architectural fixtures may be contributing to the desecration of India's cultural heritage. However, most of these warehouse-sized showrooms deal in antique reproductions, catering for a growing number of overseas export houses, and can make you a piece of antique-style furniture. The showrooms are fascinating places to wander around, and they're definitely the spot to head if you want a life-size wooden giraffe or two.

Make sure you find out how much customs charges will be in your home country. Restrictions also apply to the export of Indian items over 100 years old; see p365.

Around the clock tower are various spice shops targeting tourists, with prices to match, and there have been complaints about quality. However, **MV Spices** (Map p303; ☎ 5109347; www .mvspices.com; 209B Vegetable Market; ⌚ 10am-9pm) still gets good reports from travellers for its genuine spices and excellent service. If you would like to buy spices at local prices, head westwards from the clock tower towards Navchokiya. You'll pass a square overlooked by a temple; beyond are some small spice shops. Heading this way into the old city you'll come across little cubbyhole shops selling such things as hand-carved wooden printing blocks, miniature gods, musical instruments and *bandhani* (tie-dye) saris.

Handloom House (Map p303; Nai Sarak) On the main drag is this busy department store, thronged with locals. Alongside many questionable clothes are mountains of good-quality fixed-price *bandhani*, silk saris and woollen shawls.

Anokhi (Map p303; Airport Rd) The local branch of this culturally and environmentally aware textile company sells high-quality block-printed and other fabrics. Contemporary and traditional designs feature colourful embroidery and beadwork.

Getting There & Away

AIR

Several domestic airlines have flights from Jodhpur. **Kingfisher** (☎ 1800 2333131; www.fly kingfisher.com) flies daily to Agra (US$80) via Jaipur (US$50) and to Jaisalmer (US$45) and Udaipur (US$40). **Jet Airways** (Map p303; ☎ 5102222; www.jetairways.com; Residency Rd) has an office in Jodhpur and flies daily to Delhi (US$60) and Mumbai (US$85). **Indian Airlines** (Map p303; ☎ 2510757; Airport Rd) also has an office in Jodhpur and daily flights to Delhi and Mumbai.

Jodhpur **airport** (☎ 2512617) is just 5km from the city centre.

BUS

There are numerous (at least daily) Rajasthan State Road Transport Corporation (RSRTC)

Silver Line buses to Ajmer (Rs 133, 4½ hours), Bikaner (Rs 123, 5½ hours), Delhi (Rs 345, 14 hours), Jaipur (Rs 188, 7½ hours), Jaisalmer (Rs 168, 5½ hours), Pushkar (Rs 96 5 hours), Mt Abu (Rs 178, 5½ hours), and Udaipur (Rs 173, 5½ hours). RSRTC buses leave from the Roadways bus stand and ideally you should book tickets a day ahead.

Private buses have a union with fixed prices including Jaisalmer (Rs 120, 5½ hours, half-hourly), Udaipur (Rs 130, 5½ hours, seven daily), Jaipur (sitting/sleeping Rs 140/200, 7½ hours, half-hourly), Ajmer (Rs 100, 4½ hours, half-hourly), Bikaner (sitting/sleeper Rs 120/160, 5½ hours, half-hourly), Mt Abu (sitting/sleeper Rs 150/200, 5½ hours), Delhi (sitting/sleeper Rs 200/320, 12½ to 14 hours, five daily) and Ahmedabad (sitting/sleeper Rs 200/240, 10 to 12 hours, six daily). Private buses have ticket offices opposite the main train station and in the street leading to the Ranchodji Temple. Private buses leave from various locations in Sardapura, 1km southwest of the main train station.

The main highway between Jodhpur and Jaisalmer goes via Agolai, Dechu and Pokaran, but it's more interesting to go on the less frequently travelled route via Osiyan and Phalodi (for Khichan), which meets the main route at Pokaran.

TAXI

There's a taxi stand outside as you exit the main train station. The usual rules apply – a good price to aim for is Rs 5 per kilometre (for a non-AC car), with a minimum of 250km per day. The driver will charge you at least Rs 100 for overnight stops and will charge for his return journey.

TRAIN

The computerised **booking office** (Map p303; Station Rd; ⌚ 8am-8pm Mon-Sat, 8am-1.45pm Sun) is between the main train station and Sojati Gate. Demand for tickets is heavy, so come here soon after you arrive. There are tourist quotas on trains from here. Reserve your tickets at window 788. At the main train station there's an International Tourist Bureau (see p302).

To Jaisalmer, the *Delhi–Jaisalmer–Barmer Express* (4059/60) departs at 6.10am arriving in Jaisalmer (sleeper/3AC Rs 157/411) at 1pm. The *Jodhpur–Jaisalmer Express* (4809/10) departs every night at 11.25pm, arriving in Jaisalmer at 5.30am. The latter originates in Jodhpur so the departure time is more reliable.

To Delhi, the *Mandore Express* (2461/2) leaves Jodhpur at 7.30pm, stops at Jaipur (sleeper/3AC Rs 180/450) at 1am, arriving in Delhi (sleeper/3AC Rs 276/720) at 6.30am. The *Ranthambhore Express* (2466) departs at 5.55am and arrives at Jaipur (sleeper/3AC Rs 180/450) at 10.35am, and Sawai Madhopur (sleeper/3AC Rs 220/561) at 1.15pm. There are several daily trains to Bikaner, including the *Ranakpur Express* departing at 10.05am and arriving in Bikaner (sleeper/3AC Rs 148/386) at 4pm.

The weekly *Thar Express* (aka *JU MBF Link Express*, 4889, see p376) runs between Jodhpur and Karachi. In Jodhpur it leaves from Bhagat ki Kothi station every Saturday at 1.00am and reaches Munabao on the border at 7.00am. From Munabao you change to a Pakistan train (assuming you have a Pakistan visa).

Getting Around
TO/FROM THE AIRPORT
The journey to/from the airport costs about Rs 70/180 in an autorickshaw/taxi.

AUTORICKSHAW
Most autorickshaw journeys in town should cost no more than Rs 45. A day's sightseeing costs around Rs 250.

TAXI
There's a taxi stand near the main train station. To hire a taxi for sightseeing in Jodhpur, expect to be quoted around Rs 600/900 per half/full day. To Mandore, a taxi costs about Rs 250, including a one-hour wait. To Osiyan the fare is Rs 800 return, including a three-hour stay there.

AROUND JODHPUR
Maha Mandir & Balsamand Lake
About 2km northeast of the city is the **Maha Mandir** (Great Temple), which is quite an adventure to seek out. This edifice is supported by 84 pillars and protected by defensive bastions. There's a splendid altar in the centre of the temple, covered by a golden canopy. On the walls are pastel paintings of fantastic yoga contortions. The temple also houses a local school.

The picturesque **Balsamand Lake** is 3km further north. A refreshing escape from Jodhpur,

this artificial lake is the oldest in Rajasthan – it was built in 1159 – and has a picturesque summer palace on its banks.

Striking **Balsamand Palace** (☎ 2572321; s/d/ste Rs 5400/6050/14850; 🖳 🖳), a deep-red sandstone building with elaborately carved balconies, sits at the edge of the lake. It offers comfort in a lush and serene setting not too far from Jodhpur. The attractive rooms are in the former stables. All have a private terrace with exposed stone walls and serene views.

Mandore
Situated 9km north of the centre of Jodhpur, Mandore was the capital of Marwar prior to the founding of Jodhpur. It was founded in the 6th century, and passed to the Rathore Rajputs in 1381. Few traces of the ancient seat of power remain, but the lush gardens and domed *chhatris* (cenotaphs, literally 'umbrellas') make the place an appealing and relaxing excursion from Jodhpur (it's thronged with local tourists at weekends).

Its **gardens**, stepped with rock terraces, contain a variety of dark-red cenotaphs of Jodhpur's rulers. These include the soaring **Chhatri of Maharaja Dhiraj Ajit Singh** (1793), which combines Buddhist and Jain elements in its architecture. It's an enormous edifice with carved elephants, a pillared forechamber, fine sculpture and *amalaka* (disk-shaped flourishes with fluted edges). You can climb to the third storey up a peculiar set of staircases. The memorial also marks the spot where 64 queens and concubines committed *sati* on Ajit Singh's death in 1724.

Opposite is the 1720 **Chhatri of Maharaja Dhiraj Jaswant Singh I**, an enormous octagonal pavilion with a vast dome. It achieves a remarkable symmetry, with a gallery supported by huge pillars, and sculptures of Krishna and the *gopis* (milkmaids). The rest of the cenotaphs all date to the 17th century.

At the rear of the complex is the small **government museum** (admission Rs 5; ⏰ 10am-4pm Sat-Thu), which is housed in the Abhay Singh Palace and shows relics of Mandore, including sculpture and inscriptions.

To the left is the 18th-century **Hall of Heroes**. This is a fantastically bright array of 15 solemn Hindu deities and local Rajput heroes carved out of a rock wall, coated with fine plaster and luridly painted. The **Shrine of 33 Crore Gods** is painted with figures of deities and spirits (one crore equals 10 million).

SLEEPING

Mandore Guest House (☎ 0291-2545210, 2571620; www.mandore.com; s/d Rs 500/850, with AC Rs 700/900; ⚟) Delightful rounded mud-walled cottages are set in a leafy garden here, and there's good home-cooked food. The guesthouse is also connected with a local NGO working to address problems faced by disadvantaged people of Rajasthan and provide medical services. The NGO has short-term volunteer programmes (see p370).

GETTING THERE & AWAY

There are many buses throughout the day between Jodhpur and Mandore (Rs 8), which is on the main road between Jodhpur and Nagaur. Catch one on High Court Rd.

Mandore is also included on the Tourist Reception Centre's city tours (p307).

You could get a rickshaw to take you there and back for around Rs 200.

Bishnoi Villages

A number of Bishnoi and other traditional villages are strung along and off the Pali road, located to the southeast of Jodhpur. Various operators, including the RTDC in Jodhpur, conduct jeep safaris to the villages – see p307 for details. A tour is essential to visit this region. Some of these villages are tiny, and they're reached along tracks that can barely be made out in the sand (and that you'll be hard-pressed to find on any maps). Unfortunately, the increase in tourism is starting to cause tension in some villages. Remember that you are visiting a private community, and make sure you ask before taking photographs.

Many villagers live in handmade thatched huts, in the traditions of their ancestors. Tours usually include a meal cooked over the fire in one of the villages.

Many visitors are surprised by the density, and fearlessness, of the wildlife around the Bishnoi villages. The relationship between the villagers and the animals has been nurtured for hundreds of years. The 1730 sacrifice of 363 villagers to protect the khejri trees (opposite) is commemorated in September at **Khejadali** village, where there is a memorial to the victims fronted by a small grove of khejri trees.

At **Guda Bishnoi**, the locals are traditionally engaged in animal husbandry. There's a small artificial lake where migratory birds,

such as demoiselle cranes and mammals, such as blackbucks and chinkaras, can be seen, particularly at dusk when they come to drink. The lake is full only after a good monsoon (July and August).

The village of **Salawas** is a centre for weaving *dhurries*, though many villages also practise this craft. Today a cooperative of 48 weavers runs the efficient **Roopraj Dhurry Udyog** (☎ 0291-2896658; rooprajdurry@sify.com) in Salawas, through which all profits go to the artisan. A beautiful 1.3ft x 5ft *dhurrie* can take about one month to complete, depending on the intricacy of the design (there are more than 100 traditional designs) and the number of colours used, and costs about Rs 3000. The coordinator, Roopraj, will happily answer any questions you may have about this craft.

These days, chemical rather than natural dyes are used. *Dhurries* are usually of cotton, but sometimes camel or goat hair, or silk, is used. After the weaving is completed, the *dhurries* are sometimes stonewashed to give an antique effect. The *dhurrie* weavers can arrange post by sea or air (shipping costs around Rs 1200 for one piece).

Also in Salawas, several families, mostly of the Muslim community, are engaged in block printing. The hand-woven, block-printed cloth is known as *fetia*. A single bed sheet costs around Rs 400, and a double sheet is about Rs 500, depending on the design.

At the villages of **Zhalamand**, **Salawas** and **Kakani**, potters can be seen at work, using hand-turned wheels.

Sardar Samand Lake

The route to this charming and remote wildlife refuge, located about 66km southeast of Jodhpur, passes through a number of colourful little villages. Blackbucks, chinkaras and birdlife, including flamingos, pelicans, ducks, cranes, egrets and kingfishers, may be spotted.

Built in 1933 as the maharaja of Jodhpur's summer palace and hunting lodge, **Sardar Samand Palace** (☎ 02960-245003; www.jodhpurheritage.com; s/d Rs 3600/5000; ⚟) is a grey-stone building with a single domed turret. Rooms are comfortable and have great views. There is a restaurant and a lakeside swimming pool, and it's a world away from the clamour of Jodhpur. Village safaris are available.

The only way to get here is by taxi (around Rs 700 round trip).

THE TWENTY NINE

Sar santey rookh rahe to bhi sasto jaan. (A chopped head is cheaper than a felled tree.)

Bishnoi saying

The Bishnoi are among the world's most dedicated conservationists. They hold all animal life sacred, in particular the endangered blackbuck (Indian antelope). The Bishnoi sometimes bury dead blackbuck and mark their graves with stones, and the women are said to suckle blackbuck fawns that have been orphaned. They believe that they will be reincarnated as antelope. They also have a long history of protecting the sacred khejri tree – sometimes with their lives. The men are recognisable by their large white turbans, while women usually wear red (or purple for mourning) and a large nose ring, a skirt with a white dot and a red dupatta (long scarf for women) with a green border.

The sect was founded in the 15th century, when a severe drought was crippling the desert regions near Jodhpur. A villager named Jambeshwar had a vision that the drought had been caused by humans meddling with the natural order. He laid down 29 tenets for conserving nature, including not killing animals, not felling trees and not using wood for funeral pyres (they bury their dead unlike the majority of Hindus). Other commandments include taking early morning baths, not taking opium or cannabis or drinking alcohol, not indulging in unnecessary discussions, and not wearing blue (it's thought this was to save the indigo plant). Jambeshwar became known as Guru Jambhoji, and his followers became known as the Bishnoi (meaning '29') after the principles they followed.

In 1730 the most famous Bishnoi act of self-sacrifice occurred. The maharaja of Jodhpur sent woodcutters into Bishnoi villages to cut down khejri trees for his lime kilns. A woman named Amritdevi clung to one of the trees and refused to be removed, crying 'A chopped head is cheaper than a felled tree'. The axeman cut her head off. One by one, other Bishnoi villagers followed Amritdevi's lead, and each in turn was killed by the axemen until 363 people lay dead. The maharaja, hearing of the carnage, declared a conservation zone around the Bishnoi villages, prohibiting tree felling or poaching in the area.

Today the site at Khejadali is a quiet grove of khejri trees, and a temple commemorates the sacrifice. The Bishnoi continue to live by their strict code and to defend native wildlife. In 1996 a Bishnoi villager named Nihal Chand Bishnoi was shot and killed by poachers near Bikaner as he tried to save the lives of some chinkaras (Indian gazelles). In October 1998 Bollywood superstar Salman Khan was arrested for killing two blackbucks near a Bishnoi village. The authorities were allegedly alerted to the crime by the villagers, who chased Khan from the scene and presented the dead blackbucks as evidence. Khan eventually faced court and has spent short terms in jail, in 2006 and 2007, between appeals and bail hearings, before the case was buried into the black hole of bureaucracy in late 2007. Reports from the Bishnoi suggest that the high profile of the case has resulted in a reduction in poaching activity. Today around 90% of the blackbucks in Rajasthan live under Bishnoi protection.

A festival near Bikaner celebrates Jambeshwar, the sect's founder, in around January or February (see p301).

Rohet

In this small village, 40km south of Jodhpur, the former local ruler has converted his 350-year-old manor into a heritage hotel. **Rohet Garh** (☎ 02936-268231; www.rohetgarh.com; s/d from Rs 3450/4500, ste Rs 4950; 🅿 🏊) is a heritage hotel with lots of character and relaxing gardens. Bruce Chatwin wrote *The Songlines* here, and William Dalrymple began *City of Djinns* in the same room (No 15). It's surprising that they were so diligent, as there's a gorgeous colonnaded pool and the rooms are lovely. The hotel has a stable of Marwari horses and can organise horse rides from one-day to six-day treks.

From Jodhpur, there are local daily buses to Rohet (Rs 18), or you can get a taxi for around Rs 800.

Bhenswara

Bhenswara, which translates as 'the place where buffaloes were kept', is about 130km south of Jodhpur, on the banks of the Jawai river.

Ravla Bhenswara (☎ 02978-222080; s/d from Rs 1995/2595, ste Rs 3000; ✹ ☎), an unpretentious rural manor, is perfect if you want a respite from travelling. This place is run by a nice young couple, Shiv Pratap Singh and Uma Kumari, who give the hotel a cosy appeal. The quaint rooms are decorated with lots of personality. Jeep village safaris and village bullock cart rides can be organised (there's a minimum of two people). The hotel owners can arrange a visit to the nearby **Jalor Fort**. The climb up to the fort takes about 45 minutes (carry water, as the ascent can be a hot one).

The closest bus route goes to Jalor (Rs 80 from Jodhpur), where you should catch a taxi to Bhenswara.

Dhawa Doli Wildlife Sanctuary

This sanctuary is about 40km southwest of Jodhpur, on the road to Barmer, and has populations of blackbucks, partridges, desert foxes and nilgais. There's no accommodation here, but it's possible to take a half-day tour from Jodhpur (make enquiries at the RTDC Tourist Reception Centre) for Rs 800, or if you have your own transport you could stop en route to Barmer. The forest office is in a small group of village huts – you'll have to ask on the way – and the family there will help you look for wildlife. It's best to visit before about 11am or a few hours before sunset.

Khejarla

This 400-year-old **fort** (☎ 02930-258311; s/d Rs 2200/2700, ste 4500; ✹ ☎) is 85km east of Jodhpur en route to Ajmer. Its extraordinary carved window frames, made of deep-red sandstone, are bunched on the front of its stern fortifications. Rooms are whitewashed and rustic rather than swish.

Village safaris can be arranged, as well as a visit to an old step-well (ask Dalip Singh about the ghost).

Khimsar

About 95km northeast of Jodhpur, **Khimsar Fort** (☎ 01585-262345; www.welcomeheritagehotels.com; s/d Rs 5400/6000, ste Rs 6000; ✹ ☎) dates back to 1523. The zenana was added in the 18th century, and a new wing built in the 1940s. The palatial building has been converted into an upmarket hotel, with lush, well-appointed rooms. The hotel also boasts a sauna, yoga centre, pool

(with nearby hammock to laze away the day), a good restaurant and pleasant gardens. It's possible to arrange a jeep safari, or a horse or camel ride. Ayurvedic massage costs around Rs 825 for one hour.

A local bus from Jodhpur costs Rs 50, while a taxi costs about Rs 800.

NAGAUR

☎ 01582 / pop 88,313

Lying 135km northeast of Jodhpur, Nagaur is home to the massive 12th-century ruins of **Ahhichatragarh** (Fort of the Hooded Cobra; Indian/foreigner Rs 15/50, camera/video Rs 25/100, parking Rs 15, guide Rs 100; ☼ 9am-1pm & 2-5pm), which are being restored (the project partly financed by the Getty Foundation). The 1 sq km fort complex is protected by vast double walls that encompass a Rajput-Mughal palace and an ingenious water recycling system. The frescoes appear not as elaborate as elsewhere in Rajasthan and, though there is much restoration activity going on, this vast complex is a carcass stripped bare. Years of army occupation ensured many frescoes were whitewashed over and anything that could be shifted was carted away. Just outside the fort but within the walls of the old city are several **mosques**, including one commissioned by Akbar for a disciple of the Sufi saint Khwaja Muin-ud-din Chishti (see p204). The minarets of **Akbari Masjid** can be seen from the fort's ramparts.

Nagaur also hosts a colourful fair, which is a smaller and even more camel-focused version of Pushkar Camel Fair – see p301. During this time a tourist information office is set up at the festival grounds.

Sleeping & Eating

Hotel Bhaskar (☎ 240100; Station Rd; s/d from Rs 200/300; mains Rs 25-70) This friendly, central place has worn out and grim rooms, but it's conveniently near the train station and a veg curry won't ruin the budget.

Hotel Sujan (☎ 240283; Nakash Gate; s/d Rs 200/350, r with AC Rs 600; mains Rs 25-45; ✹) Just beyond Naksar Gate, in the old city walls, the Hotel Sujan has gloomy hallways, and rather grimy rooms. The basic restaurant does veg curries.

Hotel Mahaveer International (☎ 243158; Vijai Vallabh Chowk; r Rs 350-550, with AC Rs 950-1500; mains Rs 85-175; ✹) About 1km from the fort, this hotel has uninspiring but comfortable rooms aimed at business travellers. Inspect rooms in the old and new wing before deciding. There's a relatively clean (for Nagaur) and cool vegetarian restaurant and a bar.

Fabulous, 4 sq metre royal tents are available in the fort grounds from November to March. Tents with private bathroom cost from Rs 11,500 during fair time. Bookings are essential; contact **Balsamand Palace** (☎ 0291-2571991).

During Nagaur's fair, the **RTDC** (s/d Rs 6500/7500) also has accommodation. For details, contact the general manager at **Central Reservations** (☎ 0141-2202586; www.rajasthantourism .gov.in; RTDC Hotel Swagatam Campus, Jaipur, 302006).

Getting There & Away

Nagaur is connected by express bus to Jodhpur (Rs 70, three hours) and Bikaner (Rs 69, 2½ hours).

JODHPUR TO JAISALMER

The most direct route by road to Jaisalmer is the southern route via Agolai, Dechu and Pokaran. But, if you have time, it's more rewarding to take the lesser-travelled northern route, which goes via Osiyan and Phalodi and meets up with the main route at Pokaran. The exquisite temples at Osiyan, the spectacular demoiselle cranes at Khichan and the important pilgrimage site of Ramdevra, all lie on or just off this northern route, which numerous buses ply every day.

Osiyan

This ancient Thar Desert town, 65km north of Jodhpur, was an important trading centre between the 8th and 12th centuries. Known as Upkeshpur, it was dominated by the Jains, whose wealth left a legacy of exquisitely sculptured, well-preserved temples. Today it receives lots of pilgrims at certain times, but not that many tourists, and it's a good place for a taste of the desert if you can't make it to Jaisalmer. The village of Osiyan is inhabited mostly by Brahmins – most of the houses here are painted blue (traditionally a Brahmin practice), as in Jodhpur.

SIGHTS

The finely carved ancient temples of Osiyan rival the Hoysala temples of Karnataka and the Sun Temple of Konark in Orissa.

About 200m north of the bus stand is the hilltop **Sachiya Mata Temple** (☉ 6am-7.15pm) – Sachiya Mata (Mother of Truth) is the ninth and last incarnation of the goddess Durga. This temple receives crowds of pilgrims,

both Hindu and Jain. People usually come here after the marriage of their children, but crowds come for Navratri (nine nights of worship in March or April and October or November). A long flight of steps, under fancifully decorated arches, takes you to the forechamber. Before the *mandapa* (pavilion in front of a temple), and beyond the impressive *torana* (gateway), are sandstone statues of various incarnations of Durga that were excavated by archaeologists and installed here. The main temple is flanked by nine smaller temples, each dedicated to an incarnation of the goddess. Abutting the sides of the main temple is a series of ancient temples contemporary with this one.

Five minutes' walk from Sachiya Mata Temple, directly opposite the entrance, is **Mahavira Temple** (admission Rs 5, camera/video Rs 40/100; ☉ 6am-8.30pm), which was dedicated to the last of the Jain *tirthankars* (great teachers). This is a more spacious temple than Sachiya Mata, featuring an open-air pavilion-style *mandapa* supported by carved pillars. As at the Sachiya Mata Temple, the drum of the dome features sculptures of *apsaras* (heavenly nymphs). There is also a beautiful *torana* before the temple, decorated with very intricate sculptural work.

The image of Mahavira is glistening with piercing eyes. According to legend it's over 2000 years old, was found buried underground, and is made of sand and milk and coated in gold. In the right-hand corner there's an ancient frieze, which retains fragments of colour. Interestingly, there is much restoration and replacement of stone carvings, however, the friezes are not being painted with the traditional vegetable-dye paints apparently because tourists prefer unpainted carvings.

Among the other temples in Osiyan are those dedicated to Surya, Shiva and Harihara. The temples are ruined, but they have some beautiful carving. The damaged 9th-century Katan *baori* (step-well) has more fine, worn sculptural work.

TOURS

Gemar Singh (☎ 0291-272313; www.hacra.org) lives in a village outside Osiyan and arranges homestays, camping, desert walks and horse or camel safaris from Jodhpur to Osiyan and surrounding Rajput and Bishnoi villages. Gemar Singh's safari's get rave reviews from readers. It costs around Rs 800 per person per day, with a minimum of two people.

WESTERN RAJASTHAN

SLEEPING & EATING

Few travellers overnight in Osiyan, which accounts for the lack of accommodation.

Guest House (☎ 02922-274331, 9414440479; s/d Rs 250/300) Prakash Bhanu Sharma, a personable Brahmin priest, has basic accommodation that is geared for pilgrims, located directly opposite the Mahavira Temple. Expect simple rooms with shared bathroom and bucket hot water, though Prakash is planning to build a bigger and better guesthouse. Prakash can arrange jeep excursions and camel safaris, and is also a knowledgeable guide to the temples. You can usually find him sitting at the gateway to the temple, or ask any of the village children, who will happily track him down for you.

Camel Camp (in Jodhpur ☎ /fax 0291-2437023; www .camelcamposian.com; tents Rs 8500) This place offers upmarket but rather overpriced accommodation in tents that are located on a secluded sand dune that overlooks Osiyan. The tariff includes all meals, as well as entertainment and a camel ride at sunset. Additional camel safaris can be arranged. Bookings are essential.

Four kilometres beyond Osiyan, heading to Phalodi, is **Osian Desert Café** (mains Rs 110-225), a highway stop that has been built for tour groups and takes some beating for tasty food and cold drinks, including beer, in clean comfortable surroundings.

GETTING THERE & AWAY

There are regular buses from Jodhpur (Rs 30, 1½ hours, half-hourly), and buses also serve Phalodi (Rs 35, two hours) for Khichan.

There's also train 4059 from Jodhpur which departs Jodhpur at 6.20am and arrives at Osiyan (sleeper/3AC Rs 121/213) at 7.37am and then departs for Jaisalmer (sleeper/3AC Rs 135/350). On the return journey train 4060 departs Jaisalmer at 4pm, stops in Osiyan at 9pm and arrives Jodhpur at 10pm.

A return taxi from Jodhpur costs Rs 800.

Khichan & Phalodi

Morning and afternoons in the winter months, the tiny village of Khichan hosts a fabulous feast for huge flocks of graceful demoiselle cranes (below). Khichan is about 10km east of Phalodi, a town about 135km from Jodhpur and 165km from Jaisalmer.

Phalodi surrounds an old desert citadel, a crumbling 15th century fort, that gradually rose to prominence during the 18th century when Jain business families trading in salt built impressive *havelis*. As well as the beautiful *havelis* (some over 250 years old), they built colourful and gaudy Jain temples, including the domed **Shri Parashnath temple** (admission free, camera Rs 20), glistening with gold and Belgian glass. The most prominent *haveli*, **Dadha Haveli**, is now the Lal Niwas hotel and houses a small

---

THE DEMOISELLE CRANES OF KHICHAN

From late August or early September to the end of March you can witness the extraordinary sight of over 7000 demoiselle cranes (*Anthropoides virgo*) wintering near Khichan. Morning and afternoon, the birds circle overhead, then make a dramatic descent for the grain Khichan's villagers spread for them. Brought to France from the Russian steppes, the cranes were tagged 'demoiselle' by Marie Antoinette because of their grace. Here they're known as kurjas.

Brown-grey birds with a black chest and throat, demoiselle cranes stand about 76cm high, and have a long neck and a short beak. In traditional Marwari songs, women beseech the cranes to bring back messages from their loved ones when they return from distant lands. The flock consumes a phenomenal 600kg of grain each day, which is distributed at the Birds Feeding Home. All the grain is funded by (very welcome) donations.

The feeding of the cranes dates back some 150 years. The grain is spread at night, ready for the birds to feed at sunrise (about 7am), and again around 4pm, in time for the birds' return in the afternoon. The sight of these wonderful birds in such large numbers descending on the feeding ground is truly awe-inspiring – the noise of the assembly is amazing. It shouldn't be missed if you're in the area. Please keep a distance from the birds and refrain from making a noise, so as not to scare them.

The demoiselle cranes also winter in Pakistan and Africa. To migrate they must cross the Himalayas from their breeding range, which extends over a wide belt spanning eastern Europe, Central Asia and eastern China.

museum (admission Rs 40; � 9am-4pm) containing coins, documents and arms.

SLEEPING & EATING
Note that all options are in Phalodi.

Hotel Sunrise (☎ /fax 02925-222257; s/d Rs 200/250, without bathroom Rs 100/150) Directly opposite the Roadways bus stand, this place has basic, barely acceptable rooms and a restaurant.

Hotel Chetnya Palace (☎ 02925-223945; Station Rd; s Rs 150-700, d Rs 200-750; ❄) Opposite the local bus stand, this place has very worn and grim rooms and only the AC rooms have running hot water. The restaurant is equally challenging.

Lal Niwas (☎ 02925-223813; www.welcomeheritage hotels.com; Dadha St; s/d Rs 2400/2650, ste 2750/3100; ❄ 🖥) This is a splendid, carved, deep-terracotta *haveli* in the old part of town, with balconies, courtyards and a tangle of passages. All the rooms are different, decorated in the traditional style with heavy wooden furniture. The family suite is fantastic, especially if you have kids, as it has a number of rooms divided by carved arches. A multicuisine restaurant and a bar are on site, and the management act as the defacto information office for the region and can organise tours to Kichan.

GETTING THERE & AWAY
There are regular buses to/from Jodhpur (Rs 86, 3½ hours), Jaisalmer (Rs 72, 3½ hours) and Bikaner (Rs 84, 3½ hours).

Phalodi is on the Jodhpur–Jaisalmer line and has daily rail connections with Jodhpur (sleeper/3AC Rs 121/251, 2½ hours) and Jaisalmer (sleeper/3AC Rs 121/276, four hours).

GETTING AROUND
There are daily buses between Phalodi and Khichan (Rs 5, 15 minutes). A return autorickshaw to Khichan will cost Rs 70.

Ramdevra
This desolate and windswept desert village lies 10km north of Pokaran. While it has an important temple dedicated to deified local hero Ramdev, who lived in the Middle Ages, it's not the most salubrious place to visit or stay and there's little English spoken.

SIGHTS
Ramdev Mandir
Ramdev was born in Tanwar village to a Rajput family and was opposed to all forms of untouchability, believing that all human beings are equal. He took samadhi (an ecstatic state involving conscious exit from the body) in 1458. The 1931 **temple** built in his honour has a brightly coloured façade, but isn't especially thrilling architecturally. However, the devotional activities of the hundreds of pilgrims who pay homage here are enthralling (Ramdev is worshipped by both Hindus and Muslims). The temple's at its busiest during the festival devoted to the saint in August or September (p301). The streets outside are lined with *dharamsalas* (pilgrims guesthouse), tea shops and souvenir-wallahs. Devotees place model horses in the temple in honour of the holy man's trusty steed, who carried him around when he was doing his good works.

You'll probably be assailed by people with receipt books demanding donations, both as you enter the temple complex and within the temple itself, even by men who 'guard' your shoes.

SLEEPING & EATING
Hotel Sohan Palace (☎ 02996-237025; s/d Rs 200/500) Near the temple and the bus stand, Hotel Sohan is not much of a palace. It has basic pilgrim rooms and no meals are available.

Hotel Ramdev & Dining Hall (☎ 02996-235069; r Rs 500-800; ❄) A better option is this modern place, with clean comfortable rooms and good food, on the road to Pokaran about 1km from the temple.

GETTING THERE & AWAY
Most buses between Phalodi and Pokaran pass through Ramdevra – the trip from Phalodi to Ramdevra costs Rs 30. Jeep taxis leave when full and travel along the main street to Pokaran (Rs 5, 20 minutes).

Pokaran
☎ 02994
At the junction of the Jaisalmer, Jodhpur and Bikaner roads, 110km from Jaisalmer, is this desert town, site of another fort – a grand edifice the colour of dark plums. If you wander through the town look for the famous red-clay pottery products including animals, lamps, statues and more.

Pokaran became notorious in 1998 as the site of India's controversial nuclear tests (p320).

The bus stand is on the Jodhpur road at the southern edge of town. The fort is 1.5km to the

---

NUCLEAR SABRE-RATTLING

In May 1998 India detonated five nuclear devices in the Pokaran area. These included miniature devices to be used for missile warheads and a 43-kiloton device that was almost three times more powerful than the Hiroshima bomb. India also conducted its first nuclear test here, in 1974.

The 1998 tests led to heightened tension between India and neighbouring Pakistan. Hundreds of thousands of Hindu loyalists celebrated the controversial decision to hold the tests with parties in the street. The US was less impressed, immediately imposing sanctions, suspending aid and recommending the freezing of international development loans. Japan withdrew its ambassador. Pakistan also swiftly responded to India by detonating its own nuclear devices, igniting global concern about a nuclear arms race in south Asia. The rupee plummeted and visitors were scared away – Jaisalmer was rendered a virtual ghost town.

In late September 2001 the US lifted the sanctions against India. Analysts saw this as a reward for India's support in the 'war against terror' after the 9/11 attacks on the United States.

Worth seeking out is director Anand Patwardhan's award-winning 2002 documentary *War & Peace*. This fascinating, dark and funny film examines the nuclear standoff, the patriotism that followed and the human cost. It was banned in India for two years.

Less controversial missiles continue to be tested at the site.

---

northeast of the bus stand. There is a State Bank of Bikaner & Jaipur ATM in the bazaar.

SIGHTS
Pokaran Fort & Museum
The red-sandstone **Pokaran Fort** (admission Rs 50, camera or video Rs 30; ⏲ 7am-7pm) is an evocative place overlooking a tangle of narrow streets lined by balconied houses. Built from the 14th to the 17th century, it once had charge of 108 villages. Part of it is now a heritage hotel. There's a small museum with an assortment of weaponry, some brocaded clothes, old wooden printing blocks and various games belonging to former rulers of Pokaran, including dice and dominoes. There are also 15 'living' temples or shrines; that is, the villagers still attend them, scattered around the fort, including a small shrine to Durga.

A stop at Pokaran breaks the long journey between Jodhpur and Jaisalmer. There's not a huge amount to see, but it's a great place to relax and escape the touts. Many travellers stop here for lunch, too.

SLEEPING & EATING
RTDC Motel Godawan (☎ 222275; s/d Rs 500/600, with AC Rs 700/800) About 3km west of the bus stand, this place offers rooms and huts. A lot better than many other RTDC hotels, it also has a restaurant.

Fort Pokaran (☎ 222274; www.fortpokaran.com; r from Rs 3000, ste Rs 7000; breakfast/lunch/dinner Rs 250/450/450; ✷ ▣) The impressive sandstone fort offers 19 individual, atmospheric rooms that have

been expertly restored yet unchanged as much as possible – many rooms boast their original floors, antique furniture, and teak and mirror ceilings. Of course there are modern amenities for nontraditional comforts, and there's a superb swimming pool. The restaurant specialises in regional cuisine which you can enjoy in the grand dining room or beside the pool. It's a wonderfully peaceful place to stay, and jeep safaris can be arranged from here.

GETTING THERE & AWAY
There are regular RSRTC buses to Jaisalmer (Rs 37, two hours). There are also buses to Bikaner (Rs 98, five hours) and to Jodhpur (Rs 65, three hours).

Pokaran is on the Jodhpur–Jaisalmer line and has daily rail connections with Jodhpur (sleeper/3AC Rs 121/306, four hours) and Jaisalmer (sleeper/3AC Rs 121/238, three hours).

JAISALMER
☎ 02992 / pop 58,286
Jaisalmer is a breathtaking sight. A magical, multiturreted sand castle on the 80m-high Trikuta (Three-Peaked) Hill rises mirage-like from the horizontal desert plain. Known as the Golden City, it seems to have sprung from a chivalrous tale or an overly imaginative miniature illustration. No place better evokes ancient desert splendour and exotic trade routes. Jaisalmer celebrates its desert culture with an action-packed festival in winter (see p301).

Ninety-nine huge bastions encircle the narrow streets of the fort, which is still inhabited. Elaborate houses, splendid temples, magnificent gateways and a beautiful palace are all carved out of the same warm-yellow sandstone. Once the inhabitants worked for the maharajas, but today they mainly run guesthouses, or shops and stalls swaddled in the kaleidoscopic mirrors and embroideries of Rajasthani cloth. Despite the commercialism of the Italian restaurants, internet cafés and camel-safari culture, it's impossible not to be enchanted.

There's still a sense of community within the straitened streets, with families pouring out of the close-knit web of houses, and cows blocking the narrowest corners. Spreading from the fort is the old city, containing lavish sandstone *havelis,* and all around lie the scrub, dunes, wind turbines and villages of the Thar Desert.

History

Since the city was founded in 1156, Jaisalmer history has been derived from the tales and songs of the bards. The succession of maharajas of Jaisalmer trace their lineage back to a ruler of the Bhatti Rajput clan, Jaitasimha. The Bhatti Rajputs trace *their* lineage back to Krishna.

The 13th and 14th centuries were a tempestuous time, as rulers relied on looting for want of other income, and Jaisalmer was repeatedly attacked as those looted sought revenge. In the 14th century the emperor of Delhi, Ala-ud-din Khilji, mounted an expedition to Jaisalmer to retrieve treasure that the Bhattis had taken from a caravan train en route to the imperial capital. He laid siege to Jaisalmer Fort for nine years. When defeat was imminent, *jauhar* (ritual mass suicide) was declared: the women of Jaisalmer committed themselves to the flames, while the men donned saffron robes and rode out to certain death. Jaitasimha's son Duda, a hero of the Bhattis, perished in the battle.

Duda's descendants continued to rule over the desert kingdom. In 1541 Lunakarna of Jaisalmer fought against Humayun when he passed through Jaisalmer en route to Ajmer. The relationship between the Jaisalmer rulers and the Mughal empire was not always hostile, and various marriages were contracted between the two parties to cement their alliance. Later Jaisalmer notables include Sabala Simha, who won the patronage of the Muslim Emperor Shah Jahan (r 1627-58) when he fought with distinction in a campaign at Peshawar. Although not the legitimate heir to the *gaddi* (throne), Shah Jahan invested Sabala Simha with the power to rule Jaisalmer, and he

ARRIVAL IN JAISALMER

If you're arriving in Jaisalmer by bus, you'll notice that the number of passengers suddenly swells about an hour before arrival. Your new companions are touts, not wanting to miss the chance of a captive audience. All foreigners will be asked to pay a tourist tax of Rs 20.

In the past few years, local authorities have introduced policies designed to keep the touts at bay. Most carriages on the overnight train carry at least a couple of soldiers to try to ensure you get a good night's sleep, and soldiers also patrol the train station platforms in Jodhpur with varying degrees of vigilance. Perhaps the most surreal experience is stumbling out of the train in the predawn light to find a small army of hotel owners kept behind a barricade about 20m from the station exit, holding up their signs and champing at the bit. Once you cross that line, you're on your own.

Don't believe anyone who offers to take you 'anywhere you like' for just a few rupees. Take with a fistful of salt claims that the hotel you want to stay in is 'full', 'closed' or 'no good any more', or has suffered some other inglorious fate. Don't listen to people outside your chosen hotel telling you 'their' hotel is full. They have probably followed your rickshaw on a motorbike and are pretending to be associated with the hotel. Go inside to the reception where you may well find a vacancy.

Also watch out for hotel representatives who offer you amazingly cheap rooms. They often just want you to join their camel safari and will throw you out if you don't fancy it – some even become aggressive. If the hotel of your choice has a representative waiting for you, by all means accept the free ride. Alternatively, take a rickshaw and hope you get an honest driver (they do exist) – pay no more than Rs 30.

WESTERN RAJASTHAN

JAISALMER

400 m
0.2 miles

INFORMATION
Bank of Baroda..........................(see 37)
Bhatia News Agency..........................1 C1
Byas & Co..........................2 C1
Centrum..........................(see 7)
Main Post Office..........................3 B2
Police Station..........................4 B2
State Bank of Bikaner & Jaipur.....5 C3
Sumit Cyber Cafe..........................(see 34)
Suresh Photo Studio..........................6 C1
Thomas Cook..........................7 C1
Tourist Reception Centre..........................8 D3

SIGHTS & ACTIVITIES
Boat Hire..........................(see 16)
Desert Culture Centre &
Museum..........................9 D3
Government Museum..........................10 A2
Jaisalmer Folklore Museum..........................11 E3
Nathmal-ki-Haveli..........................12 C2
Patwa-ki-Haveli..........................13 D2
Salim Singh-ki-Haveli..........................14 D2
Satyam Tours..........................15 C1
Thar Safari..........................(see 15)
Tilon-ki-Pol..........................16 E3

SLEEPING
Artist's Hotel..........................17 C1
Hotel Dhola Maru..........................18 E1
Hotel Golden City..........................19 D3
Hotel Haveli..........................20 D3
Hotel Jaisal Palace..........................21 C2
Hotel Moonlight..........................22 B2
Hotel Nachana Haveli..........................23 C2
Hotel Pleasant Haveli..........................(see 24)
Hotel Ratan Palace..........................24 C1
Hotel Renuka..........................25 C1
Hotel Swastika..........................26 A1
Jawahar Niwas Palace..........................(see 13)
Killa Bhawan Lodge..........................27 C2
Mandir Palace Hotel..........................28 C1
Narayan Niwas Palace..........................29 D2
Residency Centrepoint Paying Guest
House..........................30 A2
RTDC Hotel Moomal..........................31 C3
Shahi Palace..........................32 B2
Shree Narayan Villas..........................33 C3

EATING
Chandan Shree Restaurant..........................34 C1
Desert Boys Dhani..........................35 B2
Kalpana Restaurant..........................34 C1
Kanishka Restaurant..........................35 B2
Natraj Restaurant..........................(see 14)
Saffron..........................36 C2
Trio..........................37 C2

SHOPPING
Gandhi Darshan Emporium..........................38 B2
Khadi Gramodyog Bhavan
(Seemagram)..........................39 C3
Rajasthali..........................40 B2
Zila Khadi Gramodan
Parishad..........................41 C1

TRANSPORT
Bicycle Hire..........................42 C1
Bus Stand..........................43 C3
Crown Tours..........................44 B2
Private Bus Stand..........................45 C3
RSRTC Bus Stand..........................46 F3
Shiva Bikes..........................47 D3
Taxi & Jeep Stand..........................48 B2

To Rang Mahal (1km);
Gorbandh Palace Hotel (1km);
Amar Sagar (7km);
Mool Sagar (9km);
Lodhruva (15km);
Kuldhara (25km);
Kanoi (42km);
Desert National Park
& Sanctuary (42km);
Sam Sand Dunes (42km)

To Himmatgarh
Hotel (200m);
Vyas Chhattris (200m);
Bada Bagh (6km)

To Desert
Moon (400m)

Ramgarh Rd

Sam Rd

Hanuman
Chowk

Hanuman Circle Rd

Hospital

To Rahwada (2km);
Hotel Rawla Kot (2km);
Akal Wood Fossil Park (17km);
Pokaran (110km);
Ramdevra (120km);
Khichan (150km);
Jodhpur (285km);
Barmer (153km)

To Akal Wood
Fossil Park (17km);
Barmer (153km)

Train
Station

Barmer Rd

Jethwai Rd

Gadi
Sagar

City View & Sunset Point

Gandhi
Chowk

Sadar Bazar

Bhatia
Market

Amar
Sagar
Gate

Gopa
Chowk

First
Fort
Gate

See Jaisalmer Fort Map (p325)

To Lilu
Guest
House (500m)

Shiv Rd

To
Airport (2km)

annexed areas that now fall into the administrative districts of Bikaner and Jodhpur.

The Jaisalmer rulers continued to line their coffers with illicit gains won through cattle rustling as well as through more orthodox methods, such as imposing levies on the caravans that passed through the kingdom on their way to Delhi. They were renowned for their valour in battle and for their treachery, as they fought to enlarge and secure their territories.

Religion and the fine arts flourished under the rulers of Jaisalmer. Although professing Hinduism, they were tolerant of Jainism, encouraging the construction of the beautiful temples that now grace the old city within the fort walls. Sculptural depictions of both Hindu and Jain deities and holy men stand side by side on the walls of these fine buildings. The visionary rulers commissioned scholars to copy precious sacred manuscripts and books of ancient learning that may otherwise have been lost during Muslim raids.

From the 16th to the 18th century Jaisalmer's strategic position on the camel-train routes between India and Central Asia brought it great wealth. The merchants and townspeople built magnificent houses and mansions, all carved from wood and golden-yellow sandstone. These merchant *havelis* can be found elsewhere in Rajasthan (notably in Shekhawati), but nowhere are they quite as exquisite as in Jaisalmer. Even the humblest of shops and houses display something of the Rajput love of the decorative arts in its most whimsical form.

The rise of shipping trade and the port of Mumbai saw the city decline. At Independence, Partition and the cutting of trade routes through to Pakistan seemingly sealed the city's fate, and water shortages could have pronounced the death sentence. However, the 1965 and 1971 wars between India and Pakistan revealed Jaisalmer's strategic importance, and the Indira Gandhi Canal to the north brings revitalizing water to the desert.

Today tourism rivals the military base as the pillar of the city's economy. And wind farms have proliferated around the city. The presence of the Border Security Force means that the regular sound of war planes disturbs the tranquillity of this desert gem. Being so reliant on the tourist dollar, Jaisalmer is in a vulnerable position. When tensions run high along the border, the city suffers.

Orientation

This old city was once completely surrounded by an extensive wall, much of which has, sadly, been torn down for building material. Some of it remains, however, including the city gates and, inside them, the massive fort that rises above the city and is the essence of Jaisalmer. The fort is entered via the First Fort Gate. Within its walls is a warren of narrow, paved streets complete with Jain temples and the old palace of the former ruler – it's small enough that you'll never get lost for long.

The main market, Bhatia Market, and most of the city's attractions and important offices surround the fort to the north.

Information
BOOKSHOPS
Bhatia News Agency (Map p322; Bhatia Market; ☾ 9am-9pm) This well-stocked place has an excellent selection of new books (especially novels), as well as some secondhand books (in several languages), which can be bought or swapped. Day-old newspapers are also available.

INTERNET ACCESS
There are internet cafés inside and outside the fort. The cost is around Rs 40 per hour.
Sumit Cyber Cafe (Map p322; Gandhi Chowk; ☾ 9am-10pm) Has a minimum charge of Rs 20.

MEDICAL SERVICES
Dr Dube (☎ 9414149500; consultation Rs 500) A recommended doctor who will visit your hotel.

MONEY
Bank of Baroda (Map p322; ☎ 252402; Gandhi Chowk; ☾ 10am-2pm Mon-Fri) Next to Trio restaurant, this bank changes Amex travellers cheques, issues cash advances on Visa and MasterCard and has an ATM.
Centrum (Map p322; ☎ 251878; Gandhi Chowk) Similar services to Thomas Cook.
State Bank of Bikaner & Jaipur (Map p322; ☎ 252430) Near the bus stand. Changes travellers cheques and major currencies.
Thomas Cook (Map p322; ☎ 253679; Gandhi Chowk; ☾ 9.30am-9.30pm) A reliable moneychanger, changing travellers cheques and cash, and providing credit-card advances.

PHOTOGRAPHY
Byas & Co (Map p322; Court Rd, Bhatia Market; ☾ 9am-9pm) Sells photographic supplies and batteries and develops pictures.
Suresh Photo Studio (Map p322; Kuchery Rd; ☾ 9am-8.30pm) About 50m to the east of Byas, Suresh offers

GOLDEN CITY BLUES

Jaisalmer's fort is one of the most endangered monuments in the world. About 120L of water per head per day pumps through the city's aged plumbing system – 12 times the original capacity – and all this water is causing the fort to slowly self-destruct. Since 1993, three of the 12th-century bastions have collapsed. As the group 'Jaisalmer in Jeopardy' puts it: what happens when you tip a bucket of water over a sand castle?

Another mortal enemy is thoughtless building work. Ironically, the fort's inhabitants may be destroying their own livelihood by not taking conservation measures seriously.

For information on saving Jaisalmer, contact **Jaisalmer in Jeopardy** (☎ /fax 020-73524336; www .jaisalmer-in-jeopardy.org; 3 Brickbarn Close, London SW10 0TP), a British charity established in 1996 to preserve the city's heritage. It's part of the **Jaisalmer Conservation Initiative** (☎ 011-24631818; www.intach.org; 71 Lodi Estate, Delhi 110 003), a wider initiative by the Indian National Trust for Art and Cultural Heritage (Intach) to conserve and restore Jaisalmer's heritage. Donations are put to good use on a number of projects.

Travellers can do their bit for sustainable tourism by staying outside the fort. Tourists and tourist-related industries are substantial water users. You can also help by showing an interest in conserving Jaisalmer's heritage and encouraging locals to take pride in it. Many people are simply unaware of how important this is for the city's future.

---

similar services. In a small shop opposite it also sells an excellent range of B&W prints of Jaisalmer from the early 20th century (Rs 85-350).

POST
Main post office (Map p322; Hanuman Circle Rd; ☯ 10am-5pm Mon-Sat) West of the fort.
Post office (Map p325; ☯ 10am-3pm Mon-Sat) Inside the fort, this post office only sells stamps.

TOURIST INFORMATION
Tourist Reception Centre (Map p322; ☎ 252406; Gadi Sagar Rd; ☯ 10am-5pm) Provides various brochures, including a map of Jaisalmer (Rs 10). It is 1km southeast of the First Fort Gate.

Sights
JAISALMER FORT
Built in 1156 by the Rajput ruler Jaisala and reinforced by subsequent rulers, **Jaisalmer Fort** (Map p325) was the focus of a number of battles between the Bhattis, the Mughals of Delhi and the Rathores of Jodhpur. The lower of the fort's three layers of wall is composed of solid stone blocks, which reinforce the loose rubble of Trikuta Hill. The second wall snakes around the fort, and between this and the third, or inner wall, the warrior Rajputs hurled boiling oil and water, and massive round missiles on their unwitting enemies below.

The Jaisalmer standard, which features a *chhatri* against a red-and-yellow background, flies above the structure.

You enter the fort through a forbidding series of massive gates leading to a large courtyard, and it's inside the walls that Jaisalmer's unique quality becomes clear: it is a living fort – about 25% of the city's population resides within its walls. It's an extraordinary, resonant experience to wander around the lanes inside this animated museum. It's packed with houses, temples, handicraft shops and beauty parlours, and honeycombed with narrow, winding lanes, all of them paved in stone. It's also quiet – vehicles cannot drive beyond the main courtyard. The fort walls provide superb views over the old city and surrounding desert – it's fantastic to stroll around the outer fort ramparts at sunset. The fort looks especially magical when it's lit up at night under a clear sky full of stars.

Sadly, the tourist trade is threatening the fort. Tourist numbers and government indifference have placed it on the World Monuments Watch list of 100 endangered sites worldwide (see above).

Maharaja Mahal
Towering over the fort's main courtyard is the former maharaja's elegant seven-storey palace, now the **Fort Palace Museum** (Map p325; admission inc audio guide & camera Rs 250; video Rs 150; ☯ 8am-6pm Apr-Oct, 9am-6pm Nov-Mar). The square was formerly used to review troops, hear petitions and present extravagant entertainment for important visitors.

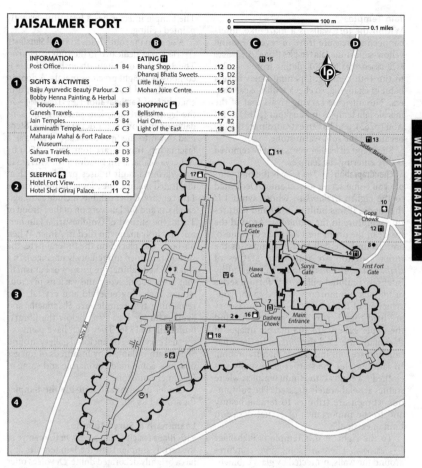

JAISALMER FORT

0 — 100 m
0 — 0.1 miles

INFORMATION
Post Office...........................1 B4

SIGHTS & ACTIVITIES
Baiju Ayurvedic Beauty Parlour.2 C3
Bobby Henna Painting & Herbal
  House...............................3 B3
Ganesh Travels.....................4 C3
Jain Temples........................5 B4
Laxminath Temple.................6 C3
Maharaja Mahal & Fort Palace
  Museum............................7 C3
Sahara Travels......................8 D3
Surya Temple.......................9 B3

SLEEPING
Hotel Fort View...................10 D2
Hotel Shri Giriraj Palace.........11 C2

EATING
Bhang Shop.........................12 D2
Dhanraj Bhatia Sweets...........13 D2
Little Italy...........................14 D3
Mohan Juice Centre..............15 C1

SHOPPING
Bellissima..........................16 C3
Hari Om.............................17 B2
Light of the East..................18 C3

Part of the palace is open to the public – floor upon floor of small rooms, giving you a fascinating sense of how such buildings were designed to spy on the outside world. Highlights are the mirrored and painted Rang Mahal, a small gallery of finely wrought 15th-century sculptures, and the spectacular 360-degree views from the rooftop.

On the eastern wall of the palace is a sculpted pavilion-style balcony. Here drummers raised the alarm when the fort was under siege. The doorways connecting the rooms of the palace are quite low. This isn't a reflection on the stature of the Rajputs, but was deliberately done to force those walking through to adopt a humble, stooped position, in case the room they were entering contained the maharaja.

In the **Diwan-i-Khas** (Hall of Private Audience), on the east side of the palace, there's a display of stamps from the former Rajput states. The room affords fine views out over the entrance ramp to the fort and the town spread beneath it. From here you can clearly see the numerous round rocks piled on top of the battlements, ready to be rolled onto advancing enemies. There's a small **Diwan-i-Am** (Hall of Public Audience), with lower walls lined with porcelain tiles.

The adjacent room is lined with blue and white tiles. Upstairs, close to the maharaja's private chamber on the east side of the palace, is a room with some exquisite stone-panel friezes that on first glance appear to have been carved from wood.

Jain Temples

Within the fort walls is a maze-like, interconnecting treasure trove of seven beautiful yellow-sandstone **Jain temples** (Map p325; admission Rs 20, camera/video Rs 50/100), dating from the 12th to the 16th century. Opening times have a habit of changing, so check with the caretakers. The intricate carving rivals that of the marble Jain temples in Ranakpur (p261) or Mt Abu (p265), and has an extraordinary quality because of the soft, warm stone.

Shoes and all leather items must be removed before entering the temples.

Chandraprabhu (🕒 7am-noon) is the first temple you come across as you enter. Dedicated to the eighth *tirthankar*, whose symbol is the moon, it was built in 1509 and features fine sculpture in the *mandapa*. Around the inside of the drum are 12 statues of Ganesh, and around the hall that encompasses the inner sanctum are numerous statues of *tirthankars*. The *mandapa* is supported by intensely sculpted pillars that form a series of *toranas*. No mortar was used in the construction of this temple; blocks of masonry are held together by iron staples. Around the upper gallery are 108 marble images of Parasnath, the 23rd *tirthankar*. In the inner sanctum are four images of Chandraprabhu. In Jain temples the statues are usually unclothed – a contrast to Hindu temples, where statues are elaborately dressed. The voluptuous women are tributes to female beauty and to the importance of carnal desire in human existence.

To the right of this temple is **Rikhabdev** (🕒 7am-noon). There are some fine sculptures around the walls, protected by glass cabinets, and the pillars are beautifully sculpted with *apsaras* and gods. This temple has a lovely, tranquil atmosphere. On the south side of the inner sanctum, a carving depicts a mother with a child who is reaching up for the fruit she is holding just out of reach. Behind the sanctum is a depiction of the Hindu goddess Kali, flanked by a Jain sculpture of an unclothed woman – a chance to compare the elaborately garbed Hindu statue with its less prim Jain equivalent.

Behind Chandraprabhu temple is **Parasnath** (🕒 11am-noon), which you enter through a beautifully carved *torana* culminating in an image of the Jain *tirthankar* at its apex. There is a voluptuous carving of an *apsara* balancing sets of balls on her raised forearm.

The temple interior has a beautiful, brightly painted ceiling.

A door to the south leads to small **Shitalnath** (🕒 11am-noon), dedicated to the 10th *tirthankar*. The depiction of Shitalnath enshrined here is composed of eight precious metals. A door in the north wall leads to the enchanting, dim chamber of **Sambhavanth** (🕒 11am-noon) – in the front courtyard, Jain priests grind sandalwood in mortars for devotional use. Steps lead down to the **Gyan Bhandar** (🕒 10-11am), a fascinating, tiny library founded in 1500 by Acharya Maharaj Jin Bhadra Suri. This small underground vault houses priceless ancient illustrated manuscripts, some dating from the 11th century. Other exhibits include astrological charts and the Jain version of the Shroud of Turin: the Shroud of Gindhasuri, a Jain hermit and holy man who died in Ajmer. When his body was placed on the funeral pyre, the shroud remained miraculously unsinged. In a small locked cabinet are images of Parasnath that are made of ivory and various precious stones, including emerald and crystal. The remaining two temples are **Shantinath**, and **Kunthunath** (🕒 11am-noon), below the library, both built in 1536. They each have plenty of sensual carving. The enclosed gallery around Shantinath is flanked by hundreds of images of saints, some made of marble and some of Jaisalmer sandstone.

Guides are available outside the temples for around Rs 50.

Laxminath & Surya Temple

This **Hindu temple** (Map p325), in the centre of the fort, is simpler than the Jain temples and has a brightly decorated dome. Devotees offer grain, which is distributed before the temple. There're a repoussé silver architrave around the entrance to the inner sanctum, and a heavily garlanded image enshrined within.

There's also a small Hindu temple devoted to Surya, the sun god, inside the fort.

HAVELIS

Outside the fort walls, Jaisalmer has some incredibly fine sculpted sandstone buildings built by wealthy merchants in the 19th and 20th centuries; some are in excellent condition. An admission fee is charged at some of the *havelis*, but most of them reserve their most stunning decoration for the outside – showing that building was much about status for these merchants.

Patwa-ki-Haveli

The biggest fish in the *haveli* pond is **Patwa-ki-Haveli** (Map p322; admission Indian/foreigner Rs 10/50; 8am-7.30pm), which towers over a narrow lane, its intricate stonework like honey-coloured lace. It is divided into five sections and was built between 1800 and 1860 by five Jain brothers who made their fortunes in brocade and jewellery. It's at its most impressive from the outside, though one of the sections has been restored internally into a **museum** (Map p322; admission Indian/foreigner Rs 30/50, camera/video Rs 20/40; 8am-7.30pm). There are displays of turbans, household items and postcards, and there are remnants of original painting and fine mirrorwork. There's a superb view of the fort from the roof.

Salim Singh-ki-Haveli

This 300-year-old private **haveli** (Map p322; admission Rs 15, camera/video incl guide Rs 15/50; 8am-7pm May-Sep, 8am-6pm Oct-Apr) has a distinctive shape. It's narrow for the first floors, and then the top storey spreads out into a mass of carving, with graceful arched balconies surmounted by pale blue cupolas. The beautifully arched roof has superb carved brackets in the form of peacocks. There is one remaining stone elephant before the *haveli*. Elephants are a traditional sign of welcome commonly found in front of all respectable palaces and grand mansions. Amazingly, the building is constructed with no mortar or cement – the stones are connected with visible iron joints.

Salim Singh was a notorious prime minister of Jaisalmer. His father had been prime minister before him, and was murdered. When Salim Singh was old enough, he took revenge on the perpetrators of his father's death by murdering them in turn. His was a stern, unpleasant rule, and his ill treatment of the local Paliwal community led them to abandon their 84 villages in the Jaisalmer region and move elsewhere. You can visit Kuldhara, one of the deserted villages – see p335. Salim Singh was eventually murdered on the orders of the maharaja.

The admission fee to Salim Singh-ki-Haveli includes a free guided tour.

Nathmal-ki-Haveli

This late-19th-century **haveli** (Map p322; admission Rs 20; 8am-7pm) also used to be a prime minister's house and is still an inhabited private house. It has an extraordinary exterior drip-ping with carving. The entrance fee allows you to venture to the 1st floor where the beautiful paintings used 1.5kg of gold. A doorway is surrounded by 19th-century British postcards, and there's a picture of Queen Victoria. The left and right wings were the work of two brothers, whose competitive spirit apparently produced this virtuoso work – the two sides are similar, but not identical. Sandstone elephants keep guard out the front.

GADI SAGAR

This soupy green reservoir, south of the city walls, was once the water supply of the city and, befitting its importance in providing precious water to the inhabitants of this arid place, it is surrounded by many small temples and shrines. The tank was built in 1367 by Maharaja Gadsi Singh, taking advantage of a natural declivity that already retained some water. It's a waterfowl favourite in winter. Between 8am and 9pm you can paddle around for 30 minutes in a paddleboat for Rs 50 or in a 2-seater Kashmiri *shikara* (gondola-like boat) for Rs 100.

The attractive **Tilon-ki-Pol** (Map p322) gateway that straddles the road down to the tank is said to have been built by a famous prostitute. When she offered to pay to have it constructed, the maharaja refused permission on the grounds that he would have to pass under it to go down to the tank, and he felt that this would be beneath his dignity. While he was away, she built the gate anyway, adding a Krishna temple on top so the king could not tear it down.

VYAS CHHATRIS

The **Vyas Chhatris** (Off Map p322; admission Indian/foreigner Rs 10/20, camera/video Rs 20/30) is an atmospheric assemblage of golden sandstone *chhatris* forming a peaceful and picturesque sunset point from which to view the fort. Enter from Ramgarh Rd opposite Himmatgarh Palace hotel.

MUSEUMS

Next to the Tourist Reception Centre is the **Desert Culture Centre & Museum** (Map p322; 252188; admission Rs 20; 10am-5pm), which has interesting information on Rajasthani culture, as well as textiles, old coins, fossils, traditional Rajasthani musical instruments and a *karal* (opium-mixing box), among other things. Its aim is to preserve cultural heritage and conduct research on local history. There're nightly, one-hour, English commentary **puppet shows** (admission Rs 30, camera/video Rs 20/50; 6.30pm, 7.30pm).

Related to the Desert Culture Centre is the small **Jaisalmer Folklore Museum** (Map p322; admission Rs 20, camera/video Rs 20/50; 8am-6pm), which has an eclectic and dusty collection of camel ornaments, printing blocks and camel-hide opium bottles. Both museums were founded by NK Sharma, a local historian and folklorist, who has written several booklets including the informative *Jaisalmer, the Golden City*, available for Rs 100 at the museums. The hill nearby is a tremendous place to soak up the sunset.

Close to the RTDC Hotel Moomal is the small **government museum** (Map p322; admission Rs 3, free Mon, photography prohibited; 10am-4.30pm Sat-Thu), which houses a limited but well-captioned collection of fossils, some dating back to the Jurassic era (160 to 180 million years ago). Other exhibits include examples of ancient script, coins, religious sculptures (some from the 11th century), puppets and textiles. There's even a stuffed great Indian bustard, the state bird of Rajasthan, which thrives in the Thar Desert but is declining in numbers elsewhere.

Activities
MASSAGE
After a long camel trek you can soothe your jangled body with a spot of Ayurvedic massage and herbal healing. Many places also offer henna painting.

Bobby Henna Painting & Herbal House (Map p325; 254468; 10am-8pm) Seving women only, Bobby is an energetic lady who also runs an outlet for rural women's handicrafts (see p333). Bobby will decorate your hands with henna (Rs 50 to 100) and provide a herbal massage (full body Rs 250, Ayurvedic Rs 300).

Baiju Ayurvedic Beauty Parlour (Map p325; 255730; 10am-8pm), located near Maharaja Mahal (king's palace) in the fort, offers facials (Rs 200) and Ayurvedic massage (Rs 400), as well as manicures, pedicures and waxing. It's female run, so women will feel comfortable here.

Tours
Few travellers visit Jaisalmer without venturing into the desert on a camel. For details, see p330.

The Tourist Reception Centre runs sunset tours to the Sam sand dunes (Rs 150 per person, minimum four people) at 3pm, returning after sunset. On request, the tours to Sam may stop at Kanoi, 5km before the dunes, from where it's possible to get a camel to the dunes in time for sunset (around Rs 200).

Another tour visits Amar Sagar (p335), Lodhruva (p335) and Bada Bagh (p335). It departs at 8am and costs Rs 550 per car.

Sleeping
Staying within the fort is romantic, but authorities are urging tourists to make an ethical choice and stay outside the walls, as pressure on the fort infrastructure is contributing to subsidence (see p324). Lonely Planet has taken the decision not to recommend *any* hotels within the fort. We have a commitment to sustainable and responsible travel, and we want to make sure we communicate this commitment to travellers and operators. When we become aware that travel is having an impact on cultures, peoples and the environment (rural or built), we do have a responsibility to live up to the commitment we have made. Our aim is to provide information and encourage travellers to make an ethical decision when visiting Jaisalmer.

The World Monuments Fund has listed the fort as an endangered site. We appreciate that local business owners take considerable care to repair and maintain their buildings. However we still can't encourage readers to stay there if we know that despite the best efforts of locals the actions of travellers are seriously harming the fort.

Rates fluctuate a lot. If there's a festival on, rooms are expensive and scarce, but at slow times most places offer big discounts. You'll get massive discounts between April and August, but you'd also be crazy to come during this time, as Jaisalmer becomes hellishly hot. Often guesthouses here are rented by the management, so they can alter in quality from one year to the next according to who's in charge.

Like many Rajasthan tourist centres, there are a lot more budget choices than midrange options, but some of the budget choices are of a very decent standard. (Unfortunately, a few budget hotels are really into the high-pressure selling of camel safaris; see p321.) This being such an important stop on the tourist route, there's a large choice of top-end hotels.

Be aware that many hotels in Jaisalmer have a 9am checkout time.

BUDGET

Most of the rock-bottom places are pretty similar in standard – clean and reasonable, but watch out for the safari hard-sell. Check the midrange options for dormitories and cheap single rooms. The Paying Guest House Scheme has only a handful of participants in Jaisalmer. Contact the **Tourist Reception Centre** (Map p322; ☎ 252406; Gadi Sagar Rd; ☿ 10am-5pm) for details.

Hotel Shri Giriraj Palace (Map p325; ☎ 252268; r Rs 125-150, without bathroom from Rs 80) Just off Bhatia Market, this hotel has cheap rooms with tiny attached bathrooms in an old building. The upstairs restaurant has fort views and checkout is at 9am.

Hotel Golden City (Map p322; ☎ /fax 251664; www .hotelgoldencity.com; s/d Rs 125/175, d with AC Rs 450-650; ✦ ✦) This hotel is in the southern section of the walled city, off Gadi Sagar Rd, and has a range of clean, basic rooms from smaller budget options to larger ones with a balcony. All have satellite TV. Nonguests can use the pool for Rs 100.

Hotel Fort View (Map p325; ☎ 252214; Gopa Chowk; r Rs 150-400) Close to the fort entrance is this friendly option. The cheapest rooms have a separate bathroom and some of these rooms are tiny. The better rooms have attached showers with hot water and rooms 26 and 31 have fort views. There's a popular top-floor fort-facing restaurant, but the 9am checkout is not so popular.

Hotel Haveli (Map p322; ☎ 252552; jaisalmer_haveli@ yahoo.co.in; s Rs 150, d Rs 200-750; ✦) Located opposite a State Bank of India branch, this modest hotel has clean, inexpensive and unexciting rooms with TVs. The better rooms are found on the top floor.

Hotel Renuka (Map p322; ☎ 252757; hotelrenuka@ rediffmail.com; s Rs 250-300, without bathroom Rs 150, d without AC Rs 300-400, d with AC Rs 600; ✦ ✦) Renuka has bright, clean rooms – the best have balconies and bathrooms. The hotel has a roof terrace with great fort views and a restaurant.

Hotel Swastika (Map p322; ☎ 252483; swastikahotel@ yahoo.com; Chainpura St, Gandhi Chowk; s/d from Rs 150/300, d with AC Rs 600; ✦) This place is well run, efficient and clean, and you'll receive no hassles. Rooms are simple and unfussy with no frills; some have balconies. Management offer free pick-up from the bus and train stations.

Artist's Hotel (Map p322; ☎ 252082; artisthotel@yahoo .com; Artist Colony, Suly Dungri; s Rs 180, d Rs 300-600) This Austrian-managed operation help support local musicians with school fees and emergency money. The surrounding 'musicians' colony has a village atmosphere, and there are great fort views from the roof (where there are regular concerts). Rooms vary, as do the bathrooms, but are clean and comfortable.

Hotel Ratan Palace (Map p322; ☎ 252757; s/d Rs 300/400) The same friendly family that runs the Hotel Renuka (left) operate Ratan Palace. All rooms here have bathrooms. It is a newer building than Renuka, with spacious, bright rooms.

Residency Centrepoint Paying Guest House (Map p322; ☎ /fax 252883; s/d Rs 400/450) Near the Patwa-ki-Haveli, this friendly, family-run guesthouse has five clean, spacious doubles in a lovely 250-year-old building. Rooms vary in size – budget by price but midrange in quality – and No 101 has a wonderful antique balcony. The rooftop restaurant has superb fort views and offers home-cooked food.

MIDRANGE

RTDC Hotel Moomal (Map p322; ☎ 252392; dm Rs 100, s/d Rs 600/700, with AC Rs 1300/1500; ✦) West of the walled city, the exterior here is more impressive than the interior. There are ordinary (and musty) rooms in the main complex and air-cooled thatched huts in the grounds. There is also a bar and a restaurant.

Hotel Pleasant Haveli (Map p322; ☎ 253253; pleasant haveli@yahoo.com; Gandhi Chowk; dm Rs 200; d without/with AC Rs 1500/2500; ✦ ✦) This place is new, with just four doubles when we visited but more are on the way. The spacious rooms in raw sandstone with colour-themed soft furnishings look fabulous. Room rates include breakfast.

our pick Shahi Palace (Map p322; ☎ 255920; www.shahi palacehotel.com; r Rs 350-1750; ✦ ✦) Shahi Palace is a brilliant, peaceful place to stay, offering stunning value and free pick-up from the transport stations. It has lovely rooms with window seats, raw sandstone walls, colourful embroidery, and carved stone or wooden beds. The elegant rooftop restaurant is also fantastic, with veg and nonveg dishes, cold beer and a superb sunset fort view. The hotel is just off Shiv Rd. This popular hotel has expanded into two new buildings nearby. At the time of writing the **Star Haveli** and **Oasis Hotel** with a similar range of rooms and tariffs, were to be contacted through the Shahi Palace phone number.

JAISALMER CAMEL SAFARIS

Steering your own camel through the deserts around Jaisalmer is the most evocative and enjoyable way to experience Rajasthan. The best time to go is from October to February.

Before You Go

Competition between safari organisers is cut-throat, and standards vary. None of the hotels have their own camels – these are independently owned – so the hoteliers and the travel agencies are just go-betweens. Furthermore, there is a union of camel drivers and the rates they charge the hotels and agents is fixed.

If you're offered a cut-price safari you can be sure corners are going to be cut somewhere – probably with food and time in the desert. Beware of operators who claim (and charge for) three-day safaris when you return directly after breakfast on the third day.

The realistic minimum price for a safari is about Rs 600 per person per day including overnight. For this you can expect breakfasts of porridge, tea and toast, and lunches and dinners of rice, dhal and chapatis. Blankets are also supplied. Usually you must bring your own mineral water. Of course, you can pay for greater levels of comfort, such as tents, stretcher beds, better food and beer, but take care: some travellers have paid extra for promised upgrades, only to find out afterwards that their safari was much the same as for people who paid less.

However much you decide to spend, ensure you know where you'll be taken and check that what has been promised is in place before leaving Jaisalmer. Attempting to get a refund for services not provided is a waste of time. Take care of your possessions, particularly on the return journey. It's wise to look after your own bag rather than have drivers keep an eye on it. Any complaints you do have should be reported, either to the **Superintendent of Police** (☎ 252233) or the **Tourist Reception Centre** (☎ 252406).

If you're on your own, it's worth getting a group together. Organisers will make up groups, but four days – or even two – are a lot to spend with a stranger you don't get on with. Usually each person is assigned their own camel, but check this, as some agencies might try to save cash by hiring fewer camels. This means you'll find yourself sharing your camel with a camel driver – definitely not an advisable option for female travellers, and not much fun for men either.

What to Take

A wide-brimmed hat (or I-am-Lawrence-of-Arabia turban), long trousers, toilet paper, sunscreen and a water bottle (with a strap) are recommended. Women should also consider wearing a sports bra, as a trotting camel is a bumpy ride. It can get cold at night, so if you have a sleeping bag, bring it along even if you're told that lots of blankets will be supplied. During summer rain is not unheard of – so come prepared.

our pick **Desert Moon** (Off Map p322; ☎ 250116, 9414149350; www.desertmoonguesthouse.com; Achalvansi Colony; s Rs 500-700, d Rs 650-1000; ❷) Near the Vyas Chhatris sunset point, Desert Moon is a new guesthouse in a peaceful location, about a 10-minute walk from Gandhi Chowk. The guesthouse is run by a friendly Indian-Kiwi couple who can help organise good-value camel safaris and who offer free pick-up from the train and bus stations. The rooms are cool, clean and comfortable with polished stone floors and sparkling bathrooms. At the time of writing there were just five rooms, and though another five are on the way, booking is recommended. The rooftop restaurant has fort and *chhatri* views and offers simple vegetarian fare.

Hotel Jaisal Palace (Map p322; ☎ 252717; www.hotel jaisalpalace.com; s/d from Rs 600/750; ❷) This is a well-run, good-value hotel though some rooms are smallish and characterless and checkout is at 9am. Those on the south side have fort-facing balconies. The chair-swing on the roof terrace is a great place to soak up the view.

Fifu Guest House (Off Map p322; ☎ 254317; www .fifutravel.com; Bera Rd; r Rs 750-1500; ❷ ▣) Set 250m south of town, a little bit away from the hub-bub, Fifu has comfortable, bright sandstone rooms with colourful furnishings, though there are lots of stairs to negotiate. There's a wonderful rooftop with a stunning fort view, and secluded terraces that act as common areas where you can have a drink and soak

Which Safari?

Several independent camel safari agencies have been recommended. **Ganesh Travels** (Map p325; ☎ 250138; ganeshtravel45@hotmail.com), inside the fort, is owned by camel drivers and is a well-thought-out operation that gets good reports. **Sahara Travels** (Map p325; ☎ 252609; www.mrdesert jaisalmer.com), by the First Fort Gate, also gets good reviews. It's run by Mr Bissa, Mr Desert, who graces lots of Rajasthan Tourism posters. **Satyam Tours** (Map p322; ☎ 250773; ummedsatyam@yahoo .com; Gandhi Chowk) and **Thar Safari** (Map p322; ☎ /fax 250227; tharsafari@yahoo.com; Gandhi Chowk) offer variations on the usual circuit.

Remember that no place is perfect – recommendations here should not be a substitute for doing your own research. The best way to go about this is to ask other travellers who've recently been desert-bound. Many hotels run good safaris, such as the Desert Moon (opposite), and again it's advisable to ask around about these, too.

Whoever you go for, insist that all rubbish is carried back to Jaisalmer.

In the Desert

Don't expect dune seas: the Thar Desert is mostly barren scrub, sprinkled with villages and ruins. You often see tiny fields of millet, and children herding flocks of sheep or goats, whose neckbells ring in the desert silence. It's a nice change from the sound of belching camels.

Camping out at night, huddling around a tiny fire beneath the stars and listening to the camel drivers' songs, is magically romantic.

The reins are fastened to the camel's nose peg, so the animals are easily steered. Stirrups make the journey a lot more comfortable. At resting points, the camels are unsaddled and hobbled. They limp away to browse on nearby shrubs while the camel drivers brew chai or prepare food. The whole crew rests in the shade of thorn trees.

Most safaris last three to four days; if you want to get to the most interesting places, this is a bare minimum unless a significant jeep component is included.

The traditional circuit takes in Amar Sagar (p335); Lodhruva (p335); Mool Sagar (p335); Bada Bagh (p335); and the Sam sand dunes (p336), as well as various abandoned villages along the way.

However, more and more travellers are opting for 'nontouristic' safaris on offer by agencies and hotels. You are driven in a jeep for around 30km or so, and then head off on your steed, avoiding the major sights and other groups.

If you're really pressed for time, you could opt for a half-day camel safari (which involves jeep transfers).

The camel drivers will expect a tip or gift at the end of the trip; this tops up their meagre wage, so don't neglect to give them one (unless you're heartily dissatisfied, of course).

For a more off-the-beaten-track safari option, see p343

up the atmosphere. The tariff includes all taxes, and management also run a guesthouse in Khuri.

Shree Narayan Villas (Map p322; ☎ 254444; shree narayanvillas@rediff.com; Malka Prol Rd; s/d from Rs 1400/1500, with AC Rs 1900/2000; ⊠) This hotel is not to be confused with its neighbour, the Narayan Niwas Palace. It has rather overpriced rooms, comfortable but neglected. A discount should be forthcoming unless some serious renovations have occurred.

Hotel Moonlight (Map p322; ☎ 252717; www .moonlighthotelresort.com; Hanuman Circle Rd; s/d from Rs 1450/2150; ⊠ 🖵) This is a new hotel developed by the people from Hotel Jaisal Palace. The Moonlight boasts extravagantly-carved

sandstone interiors and the rooms are decorated with a certain confidence. Some rooms have their own fridge while all have TV and telephone. Checkout is at noon.

Killa Bhawan Lodge (Map p322; ☎ 253833; www .killabhawan.com; r without/with AC Rs 1600/2200; ⊠) Situated behind Patwa-ki-Haveli, this B&B operation is managed by the same group that run a luxury operation within the fort. There are six big and beautifully decorated rooms and there is a pleasant rooftop restaurant. As well as breakfast, all taxes are included in the tariff and there is complimentary tea and coffee available all day.

Hotel Nachana Haveli (Map p322; ☎ 251910; nachana _haveli@yahoo.com; Gandhi Chowk; d Rs 1950-2300, ste Rs

3300; 🏊) Housed in a charming 280-year-old sandstone *haveli*, this hotel has interesting architecture, and a caravanserai ambience. The comfortable rooms, some with grand Rajput furnishings, are located around a courtyard.

Narayan Niwas Palace (Map p322; ☎ 252408; www .narayanniwas.com; Malka Prol Rd; s/d from 2050/3550; 🏊 🆒) North of the fort, this grand 19th-century building counts among its former guests Britain's Princess Anne. Rooms are big and tidy, and there's an odd indoor swimming pool with pillars and shadows and a neat little bar. The rooftop has a superb view of the fort and the old city. However, the hotel is a tad impersonal and geared towards groups.

Hotel Dhola Maru (Map p322; ☎ 252863; www.hotel dholamaru.com; Jethwai Rd; s/d Rs 2500/3000; 🏊 🆒) This option, to the northeast of the walled city, is a couple of kilometres from the fort entrance and along with the inconvenient location it lacks a fort view. Rooms are clean and comfortable but rather bland. There's an extraordinary little bar, which has incorporated tree roots and saddle-shaped bar stools into its décor, and a clover-shaped pool.

Mandir Palace Hotel (Map p322; ☎ 252788; www.wel comeheritagehotels.com; Gandhi Chowk; r Rs 2800/3200; 🏊) Just inside the town walls is this royal palace – the erstwhile royal family still lives here. It's so named because it contains many mandirs (temples). The intricate stone latticework is exquisite. Some rooms are atmospheric, with antique furnishings, but the newer ones have less character and the service can be tardy.

Rang Mahal (Off Map p322; ☎ 250907; www.hotel rangmahal.com; s/d from Rs 3000/3500, ste Rs 9000; 🏊 🆒) About 2km west of Hanuman Chowk is this dramatic, traditional-style building with big bastions and impressive rooms. The bland unwelcoming lobby suggests this place usually caters for big groups. The fort view rooms and suites are divine, and there's a spectacular pool (Rs 165 for nonguests).

Jawahar Niwas Palace (Map p322; ☎ 252208; jawahar niwas@yahoo.co.in; Bada Bagh Rd; s/d Rs 3000/3900; 🏊 🆒) Located about 1km west of the fort, this stunning sandstone palace stands rather incongruously in its own sandy grounds. Rooms are elegant and spacious with soaring ceilings and the generous bathrooms have a relaxing bath tub. Those rooms upstairs at the front have the best fort views. There are sumptuous common areas to curl up with a book, a grand dining room, and a fabulously large pool.

Himmatgarh Palace (Off Map p322; ☎ 252002; him matgarh@sancharnet.in; Ramgarh Rd; s/d from Rs 3050/3550; 🏊 🆒) This group-oriented hotel is about 1.5km northwest of Hanuman Chowk opposite the entrance to the Vyas Chhatris. The rooms are clean, functional and bland though all have a fort view. There is a vast lawn and terrace for watching the sun set on the fort with a drink in your hand. Or you could plunge into the star-shaped pool (Rs 200 for nonguests).

TOP END

Fort Rajwada (Off Map p322; ☎ 253233; www.fort rajwada.com; Jodhpur-Barmer Link Rd; s/d from Rs 4400/5900; 🏊 🆒) About 3.5km east of the old city, this modern place was built according to the ancient Indian design principles of *vaastu*, which is similar to feng shui. All materials in the hotel are natural. An opera designer created the traditional interior, so it's suitably dramatic. Carved sandstone balconies, taken from royal *havelis* in Jaisalmer, have been installed in the foyer.

Hotel Rawal-Kot (Off Map p322; ☎ 252638; www .tajhotels.com; Jodhpur-Barmer Link Rd; r Rs 5500, 2-night package s/d Rs 8500/10,500; 🏊 🆒) Next to Fort Rajwada is another plush top-end choice. The hotel is a grand, impressively carved sandstone faux fort surrounding a courtyard embellished with manicured gardens. The spacious rooms are decorated in traditional style with very untraditional but well stocked minibars and other luxuries. Check out the good-value two-night package which includes breakfast, taxes and a half-day tour.

Gorbandh Palace Hotel (Off Map p322; ☎ 253801; www.hrhindia.com; Sam Rd; r/ste Rs 6000/7000; 🏊 🆒) Adjacent to Rang Mahal is another grand modern hotel with traditional design elements and aimed at tour groups. Constructed of local sandstone, the friezes around the hotel were sculpted by local artisans. You won't be writing home about the rooms, but they are comfortable, and there's a superb pool (Rs 200 for nonguests).

Eating

With so many tourists visiting Jaisalmer, there are plenty of choices where you can kick back and enjoy a good meal, often with a view. Nonetheless, you may find standards and service at some restaurants sloppy.

Chandan Shree Restaurant (Map p322; Hanuman Circle Rd; mains Rs 20-100, thalis Rs 40-100; ☯ 7am-11pm)

Always busy, this is a popular dining hall, usually packed with locals, churning out tasty, spicy, all-you-can-eat South Indian, Gujarati, Rajasthani, Punjabi and Bengali thalis. We wouldn't recommend the Chinese and pizza, however.

Kalpana (Map p322; ☎ 252469; Gandhi Chowk; mains Rs 35-130; ⏱ 8pm-10.30pm) Perched above an old gateway overlooking hectic Gandhi Chowk, this is an inexpensive place for a snack or simple meal of veg and no-veg curries and OK pizzas.

Natraj Restaurant (Map p322; ☎ 252667; mains Rs 40-225; ⏱ 8am-11pm) This is an excellent place to eat, and the rooftop has a satisfying view of the upper part of the Salim Singh-ki-Haveli next door, and across the south of town. The veg and nonveg food, including tandoori and curries, as well as Chinese and Continental dishes, is consistently excellent, as is the service. And we must mention the scrumptious desserts such as fried ice cream, apple pie and banana split.

Desert Boys Dhani (Map p322; ☎ 254336; Seemagram Campus; mains Rs 50-90; ⏱ 9am-11pm) This is a walled-garden restaurant with tables scattered across its dusty lawns, as well as traditional cushion seating under cover. It's a pleasant place to eat excellent, good-value Indian veg dishes.

Kanishka (Map p322; ☎ 254500; Sam Rd; mains Rs 50-130; ⏱ 8am-11pm) This restaurant is tucked away off the road and features a pleasant garden and terrace where you can enjoy the inexpensive vegetarian offerings. Less pleasant is the windowless AC dining room – though no doubt it is at its best in summer. The Rs 130 thali is excellent and there are snacks and curries for lighter meals.

Trio (Map p322; ☎ 252733; Gandhi Chowk; mains Rs 65-180; ⏱ 7.30am-10.30pm) With a romantic setting under a tented roof, this popular, long-running Indian, Chinese and Continental restaurant offers reliably good veg and non-veg dishes. The thalis and tandoori items are excellent, and the restaurant has a lot more atmosphere than most places in town. Traditional musicians play in the evening, and there's a great fort view.

Saffron (Map p322; ☎ 251910; Gandhi Chowk; mains Rs 70-155; ⏱ 6.30am-10.30pm) Operated by the heritage Hotel Nachana Haveli, the veg and non-veg food here gets excellent reports. Choose from Italian, Chinese, Indian and more. The restaurant has a great setting on a sandstone terrace overlooking the comings and go-

ings on Gandhi Chowk. Evening dinners are especially atmospheric.

our pick Little Italy (Map p325; ☎ 253397; mains Rs 80-120; ⏱ 9am-11pm) Set right next to the First Fort Gate, Little Italy is an atmospheric Italian restaurant, atop a lower section of the old fort wall. The interior is decorated with floor cushions, mirrorwork, terracotta lamps and a satin-tented ceiling, or you can sit outside on the rooftop, and look up to the floodlit fort ramparts – looking for all the world like a giant's sandcastle. It's romantic, and the bruschetta, pizza and pasta are excellent. And the beer is pretty good, too.

QUICK EATS

Dhanraj Bhatia Sweets (Map p325; Sadar Bazaar; sweets Rs 13/100g, samosas Rs 7) This place in Bhatia Market has been churning out traditional sweet treats for 10 generations. It's renowned in Jaisalmer and beyond for its local specialities, such as *ghotua ladoos* (sweetmeat balls made with gram flour) and *panchadhari ladoos* (made with wheat flour). Even if you don't grab a handful of sticky sweets or spicy samosas, this little shop is worth visiting just to watch the sweetmakers ply their trade. You will recognise it by the throng of locals waiting to buy sweets.

Mohan Juice Centre (Off Map p325; Bhatia Market; lassis Rs 7-16) Near the fort, this has a little sitting area – almost in the style of an ice-cream parlour – at the back. It sells assorted interesting lassis, such as honey and *makhania* (saffron-flavoured).

Bhang Shop (Map p325; Gopa Chowk; medium/strong lassi Rs 40/50, cookies Rs 50/70) Outside the First Fort Gate, below Little Italy (same owners), this 'shop' (not the most attractive establishment in town) offers lassis of different strengths as well as bhang cookies, cakes and chocolate (including special camel-safari packs). Note that bhang doesn't agree with everyone (see p360).

Shopping

Jaisalmer has a particularly stunning array of mirrorwork wall hangings – some of the best in Rajasthan – and is also famous for embroidery, rugs, blankets, bedspreads, oil lamps, old stonework and antiques. Watch out when buying silver items; the metal is sometimes adulterated with bronze.

Bellissima (Map p325; ☎ 254468; ⏱ 10am-9pm) This small shop near the Maharaja Mahal sells beautiful patchworks, embroidery, handmade paintings, bags, rugs, cushion covers and all types of Rajasthani art. It is the brainchild of Bobby (p328), of henna painting fame, and the proceeds assist women, in particular widows who unfortunately continue to endure social discrimination.

Hari Om (Map p325; ☎ 255122; ⏰ 10am-9pm) This family of silversmiths makes beautiful, delicate silver rings and bracelets featuring places and Hindu gods. Visitors have commissioned personalised wedding rings here and been delighted with the results.

Light of the East (Map p325; ⏰ 8am-9pm) On the laneway leading up to the Jain temples within the fort, this is an enthralling little shop selling crystals and rare mineral specimens, including zeolite, which fetches up to Rs 5000 depending on the quality. Ask the owner to show you the amazing apophyllite piece – unfortunately, it's not for sale.

There are several good *khadi* (homespun cloth) shops located around town that sell fixed-price carpets, shawls and woven garments. These include **Zila Khadi Gramodan Parishad** (Map p322), **Khadi Gramodyog Bhavan (Seemagram)** (Map p322; Dhibba; ⏰ 10am-6pm Mon-Sat) and **Gandhi Darshan Emporium** (Map p322; Gandhi Chowk; ⏰ 11am-7pm Fri-Wed). You can also pop into **Rajasthali** (Map p322; Gandhi Chowk; ⏰ 10am-8pm Mon-Sat) to check out prices – this is the government handicraft emporium, which sells all sorts of products ranging from cushion covers to wooden ornaments.

Getting There & Away
AIR
The airport, 2.5km south of town, has been intermittently closed and open for the last few years due to border tensions with Pakistan. It reopened in late 2007, when **Indian Airlines** (www.indianairlines.nic.in) and **Kingfisher Airlines** (www.flykingfisher.com) started services to Delhi (Rs 8000 one way) and Jodhpur. However these services stopped in early 2008. When/if services recommence it is quite likely other airlines will join or replace these two carriers. The Indian Airlines agent is **Crown Tours** (Map p322; ☎ /fax 251912), about 350m west of Amar Sagar Gate.

BUS
The main **RSRTC (Roadways) bus stand** (Map p322; ☎ 251541) is near the train station. Fortunately, all buses start at a more convenient bus stand southwest of the fort.

There are buses to Jodhpur (express/deluxe Rs 122/155, 5½ hours, hourly) and express buses to Bikaner (Rs 160, seven hours, four daily), Jaipur (deluxe Rs 341, 12 hours, one daily) and Barmer (express/deluxe Rs 66/77, three hours, hourly).

You can book private buses through most travel agencies and hotels. Private buses congregate near Hanuman Chowk and near Desert Boys Dhani south of the fort. Numerous buses go to Bikaner, Jaipur, Jodhpur (express/deluxe/sleeper Rs 70/90/110), Mt Abu (Rs 202), Ahmedabad (Rs 270) and elsewhere. Most private buses (except those going to Bikaner) require a change at Jodhpur. Buses also run to Ajmer (Rs 270, 12 hours) and Udaipur (Rs 250, 10 hours). Some travellers have found themselves in Jodhpur with a useless onward ticket, so make sure you clarify what you're getting.

TRAIN
There's a **reservation office** (⏰ 8am-8pm Mon-Sat, 8am-2pm Sun) at the train station.

There are numerous trains going to/from Jodhpur, including the *Jodhpur Express* (No 4809), which leaves Jaisalmer at 11.15pm, arriving in Jodhpur (sleeper/3AC Rs 157/411) at 5.35am. The *Jaisalmer Express* (4810) leaves Jodhpur at 11.15pm and arrives in Jaisalmer at 5.30am. The *Barmer-Jaisalmer-Delhi Express* (4060) leaves at 4pm, calls at Jodhpur (sleeper/3AC Rs 157/411) at 10pm, at Jaipur (sleeper/3AC Rs 256/690) at 5am and at Delhi (sleeper/3AC Rs 326/889) at 11.10am. Going the other way, the express (4059) leaves Delhi at 5.45pm and arrives in Jaisalmer at 1pm the following day.

From Jodhpur you can get train connections to other destinations (see p312).

Getting Around
AUTORICKSHAW
Bargain hard. An autorickshaw ride to Gadi Sagar costs about Rs 25 one way from the fort entrance. Autorickshaws from the train station into the city should be no more than Rs 30.

BICYCLE
A good way to get around is by bicycle. There are a number of places where you can hire, including one unsigned operator near Gandhi Chowk charging Rs 5 per hour or Rs 30 per day.

CAR & MOTORCYCLE

It's possible to hire jeeps from the **stand** (Map p322) near Hanuman Chowk. To Khuri or the Sam sand dunes expect to pay Rs 500 return with a one-hour wait. For Lodhruva, you'll pay Rs 700 return with a one-hour stop. A full day of sightseeing around Jaisalmer will cost around Rs 1000. To cut the cost, find other people to share with you.

Shiva Bikes (☎ 250531; scooter/motorbike per day Rs 300/400) is a licensed hirer with adequate motorbikes and scooters for exploring town and nearby sights.

AROUND JAISALMER

There are several fascinating places to visit in the desolate, wind-swept landscape around Jaisalmer. Beyond the major sights, the barren sand-dune desert stretches across the lonely border into Pakistan.

Due to the alleged arms smuggling across that border, most of Rajasthan west of National Hwy No 15 is a restricted area. Special permission is required from the **district magistrate** (☎ 02992-252201) in Jaisalmer to go there, and is usually only issued in exceptional circumstances. Places exempted are Amar Sagar, Bada Bagh, Lodhruva, Kuldhara, Akal, Sam, Ramkund, Khuri and Mool Sagar.

Bada Bagh

Located about 6km north of Jaisalmer, Bada Bagh is a fertile oasis with a huge old dam. It was built by Maharaja Jai Singh II in the 16th century and completed after his death by his son.

Above the gardens (closed to visitors) are picturesque royal **chhatris** (admission Rs 50, camera Rs 20; ☽ 6am-7pm), with beautifully carved ceilings and equestrian statues of former rulers. On the memorial of Maharaja Jeth Singh it is inscribed that on his death his queen and 10 concubines committed *sati*. Bada Bagh is now surrounded by wind turbines.

Amar Sagar

This once pleasant formal garden, 7km northwest of Jaisalmer, has fallen into ruin. The lake usually dries up several months into the dry season. According to locals, the step-wells here were built by prostitutes.

Nearby is a beautifully restored and finely carved 19th-century **Jain temple** (admission Rs 10, camera/video Rs 50/100; ☽ sunrise-sunset) that's well worth a look.

Lodhruva

About 15km northwest of Jaisalmer are the deserted ruins of Lodhruva, the ancient capital before the move to Jaisalmer. It was probably founded by the Lodra Rajputs, and passed to the ruler of Devagarh, Bhatti Devaraja, in the 10th century. In 1025 Mahmud of Ghazni laid siege to the town, and it was sacked various times over subsequent decades, prompting Jaisala to shift the capital to a new location – Jaisalmer.

The **Jain temples**, rebuilt in the late 1970s, are the sole reminders of the city's former magnificence. The **main temple** (admission Rs 20, camera/ video Rs 50/100; ☽ sunrise-sunset) enshrines a finely wrought silver image of Parasnath, the 23rd *tirthankar*, surrounded by fine sculptures.

The ornate rosette in the centre of the drum of the dome over the *mandapa* was carved from a single piece of stone, and before the temple is a beautiful *torana*. The small sculptures around the lower course of the inner sanctum are badly damaged, and still bear the scars of Muslim raids. Behind the inner sanctum is a 200-year-old carved Jaisalmer stone slab that bears carvings of the *tirthankars'* feet in miniature. The small temple to the right is dedicated to Adinath, the first *tirthankar*.

There is nowhere to stay in Lodhruva – the *dharamsala* beside the temple is for Jains only.

There are buses from Jaisalmer to Lodhruva (Rs 8, 20 minutes, four daily), though hiring a taxi (Rs 500-700 depending on time and other sites visited) is a far more comfortable option.

Mool Sagar

Situated 9km west of Jaisalmer, this is another pleasant, but rather neglected, small **garden and tank** (admission Rs 5; ☽ 8am-7pm). It belongs to the royal family of Jaisalmer and was originally built as a cool summer retreat. In the lemon grove there's a small Shiva temple carved from two pieces of sandstone.

Inside is the **Royal Camp Mool Sagar** (☎ 253801; www.jodhpurheritage.com; d Rs 6000), a luxury tented camp which mostly hosts tour groups with accommodation, excursion and entertainment packages.

Kuldhara

This small **village** (admission Rs 10, vehicle Rs 50; ☽ sunrise-sunset) is 25km west of Jaisalmer. Around 400 years ago, all the inhabitants of the 84 villages in the area left after a dispute with the prime minister, Salim Singh, whose *haveli* you can visit in Jaisalmer (see p327). The prime minister had taxed the Paliwals heavily, they had been looted and a daughter of one family had been kidnapped, but there was no response to their complaints, so the entire community upped and left. According to legend, they couldn't carry all their gold and silver, so they buried it. Several years ago some Westerners armed with metal detectors arrived at Kuldhara on motorcycles and found some valuable silver coins. Local villagers became suspicious and called the police, and the treasure hunters were apprehended and divested of their booty.

Some of the houses appear in remarkable condition, as they have been heavily restored for use as film sets – this is a popular Bollywood location. Kuldhara is also included on some of the extended camel treks.

Desert National Park & Sanctuary

This **national park** (Indian/foreigner Rs 5/10, guide Rs 200, vehicle Rs 100), 42km southwest of Jaisalmer, was established in 1980 to preserve the Thar Desert ecosystem, including the critically endangered Indian bustard *(Choriotis niergceps)*, known locally as *godawan*. It encompasses an area of 3162 sq km, an arid zone of sand dunes, thorn forest, scrub and sandy wastelands between Jaisalmer and Barmer, including the areas around Sam and Khuri. It is of interest to visitors with a curiosity in desert ecosystems, however there are no attractions for the layperson.

The park should be avoided during summer months, when temperatures soar to over 50°C. You need to bring a good supply of drinking water at any time. For more information, contact the Desert National Park's **deputy director** (☎ 02992-2522201) in Jaisalmer, from whom you need to obtain permission to visit the park.

Sam Sand Dunes

The silky **Sam sand dunes** (admission vehicle/camel Rs 50/80) lie on the edge of the Desert National Park, and are one of the most popular excursions from Jaisalmer. The dunes are 42km from the city, along a very good sealed road (which is maintained by the Indian army).

This is Jaisalmer's nearest real Sahara-like desert. It's best to be here at sunrise or sunset, and many camel safaris spend a night at the dunes. Just before sunset jeeploads of day-trippers arrive from Jaisalmer to be chased across the sands by tenacious camel owners offering short rides, dressed-up dancing children and young boys selling soft drinks. Yes, this place has become a massive tourist attraction, so don't set your heart on a solitary desert sunset experience. The hordes of people here at sunset lend the place something of a carnival atmosphere. If you want a slightly less touristy sand-dunes experience, try Khuri as an alternative (below).

Despite the tourist hype, it's still a magical place – and it's possible to frame pictures of solitary camels against lonely, wind-rippled dunes. A fascinating sight on a smaller scale is the desert dung beetle. Study a dune close up to spot these industrious little creatures rolling lumps of dung twice their size.

One tragic consequence of dune-hungry hordes is the debris and rubbish they leave behind. Visitors are now charged a fee to visit the dunes, money which could be put to good use to clean them up, but is more likely lining the pocket of some local official. If you feel strongly about the rubbish here, a letter to the **Chief Tourism Officer** (RTDC Tourism, Swagatam Campus, near train station, Jaipur 302006, Rajasthan) might have some effect. For further information, contact the Desert National Park's **deputy director** (☎ 02992-252201) in Jaisalmer.

SLEEPING & EATING

Most travellers prefer to visit the dunes on a day trip from Jaisalmer or as part of a camel safari. However, there are several places to stay – mostly upmarket tented camps catering to organised tours. There's also a straggling line of restaurants and tea shops at the dunes.

RTDC Hotel Sam Dhani (s/d Rs 875/1225) This hotel has good, though by no means luxurious, huts and tents and is in an appealing spot overlooking the dunes. It's a good idea to book ahead, through **RTDC Hotel Moomal** (☎ 02992-252392) in Jaisalmer, as the manager isn't always around.

GETTING THERE & AWAY

There are three daily buses to Sam (Rs 22, 1½ hours) from Jaisalmer.

Khuri

☎ 03014

Khuri is a small village 40km southeast of Jaisalmer, surrounded by desert sand dunes and wind turbines. Khuri is a relatively peaceful place with houses of mud and straw decorated with intricate patterns. And once the excitement of sunset is over, you have desert solitude under the brilliant star-studded sky. There are plenty of camps of mud huts and camel drivers eager to take you on the dunes, as well as throngs of holidaymakers. Be aware that the commission system is entrenched in the larger accommodation options here.

SLEEPING & EATING
Places to stay in Khuri are mostly basic, fanless thatched mud huts with wall paintings, set around a campfire area, though some have improved their facilities in recent years. All places listed here provide meals and can arrange camel safaris.

Badal House (☎ 274120; huts or r without bathroom incl meals Rs 125) Here you can stay in a family compound with a few charming small spotlessly clean huts and freshly painted rooms. Former camel driver Badal Singh is a lovely, gentle man who charges Rs 300 for a camel safari with a night on the dunes. Don't let touts warn you away. The phone number given here belongs to his brother Amal Singh, who can pass on a message. If you arrive by car ask your driver not to demand a commission as this is not included in the prices quoted here.

Khuri Guest House (☎ 274044; r Rs 150-2000; 🍽) This place has expanded into something of a complex, though it's still a friendly place, with cheap, basic rooms and huts with shared bathrooms, and more expensive AC rooms with private bathroom, as well as tents among the dunes. Room vacancy for independent travellers is dependent on group bookings from Delhi. Packages including a camel ride, cultural dance, dinner and accommodation, start at Rs 2000 per person per night.

Mama's Guest House (☎ 274042; gajendra_sodha 2003@yahoo.com; huts without bathroom incl dinner & breakfast per person Rs 500) This is a long-running place, with a circle of cosy whitewashed huts. A basic/luxurious overnight camel safari costs Rs 350/600.

Gangaur Guest House (☎ 274056; hameersingh@ yahoo.com; huts Rs 750, without bathroom Rs 500) This is a small place with yet another circle of snug huts. It offers packages, including one with a camel ride, dinner with traditional dance entertainment and breakfast, for Rs 750. It's closest to the dunes.

GETTING THERE & AWAY
There are at least four daily buses to Khuri from Jaisalmer (Rs 20, one hour).

Akal Wood Fossil Park
About 1km off the road to Barmer, 17km from Jaisalmer, are the amazing fossilised remnants of a 180-million-year-old **forest** (Indian/foreigner Rs 5/20, car Rs 10, bike Rs 2; 🕒 8am-5pm Apr-Oct, 8am-6pm Nov-Mar). They're a collection of fallen, broken logs protected by little corrugated-iron shelters. The largest fossil is 13.4m long and 0.4m wide. The climate here was once hot and humid – a stark contrast with today's dry desert. The fossil park is apparently 108 hectares, of which only 18 have been excavated. Near the entrance is a small display, where you get the chance to stroke an ancient red wood tree-trunk fossil.

A return taxi will cost around Rs 400.

BARMER
☎ 02982 / pop 83,517
Barmer is famed for its woodcarving, carpets, embroidery, block printing and other handicrafts, and it is also a great place to hunt for bargains. The small shops in the colourful Sadar Bazaar are a good place to start – exploring the narrow backstreets, you'll find artisans at work. Otherwise this desert town, 153km south of Jaisalmer, isn't very interesting, and few travellers make the trek out here. For details of Barmer's cultural festivals, see p301. The best part is the journey that takes you through peaceful, small villages, their mud-walled houses decorated with geometric designs. There is a particularly interesting village located south of Barmer (see p338).

Sleeping & Eating
Barmer's accommodation options are strictly at the budget end of the scale.

RTDC Hotel Khartal (☎ 222956; s/d Rs 300/400) Out of the town centre, this hotel is a very basic option. Rooms are adequate for weary travellers and basic meals are available.

Hotel Krishna (☎ 230826; r without/with AC Rs 300/700; 🍽) This is Barmer's best option. It is on the main street leading from the train station and staff are friendly and helpful. Rooms vary but all are acceptably clean.

Kailash Sarover Hotel (☎ 230030; Station Rd; s/d with AC Rs 770/870; 🍽) Further away from the station and on the opposite side of Station Rd (with

WESTERN RAJASTHAN

a spillover building nearby), this hotel offers OK but overpriced rooms.

Raj Restaurant (Station Rd; mains Rs 25-60; ☻ 7.30am-10.30pm) Between the train station and Hotel Krishna, Raj Restaurant is a jolly, typically grubby, little place that opens onto the street. It offers a range of veg dishes at reasonable prices.

Getting There & Away

From Barmer there are frequent buses to/from Jaisalmer (express/deluxe Rs 66/77, three hours) and Jodhpur (Rs 95, four hours). Buses leave from the main bus stand, which is about 1km north of the train station.

Trains to/from Barmer include the *Delhi-Jaisalmer–Barmer Express* (4059) which bifurcates and departs Jodhpur at 6.10am to arrive at Barmer (sleeper/3AC Rs 125/321) four hours later. The return train (4060A) departs Barmer at 6.30pm and arrives at Jodhpur at 10pm, where it joins up with 4060 from Jaisalmer and continues to Delhi. The rail link between Munabao in Barmer district, and Khokhraparkar in Pakistan, closed since 1965, reopened in 2006. The weekly *Thar Express* (see p376) runs from Jodhpur to Karachi via this line.

AROUND BARMER

About 35km from Barmer, the 10th- to 11th-century **Kiradu Temples** feature some very fine sculpture. These five temples conform to a style of architecture known as Solanki, and the most impressive is **Someshvara Temple**, which has a multiturreted spire. However, it's located in the sensitive border region near Pakistan, so you'll first need to contact the **district magistrate** (☎ 02982-220003), who will obtain the necessary permission from the superintendent of police for you to visit. You'll need to fill out an application form and submit a photocopy of your passport – usually if you ask for permission in the morning it will be granted by the afternoon.

South of Barmer the road leads 67km to **Dhorimmana**, a small, dusty market town with no specific attractions, but which is a busy meeting point for villagers living in the area. It's a chance to see wonderful tribal dress. The colourful villages along the route are also very traditional, consisting of huddles of mud huts among the desert scrub. This is a fascinating off-the-beaten-path excursion for those with their own transport.

BIKANER

☎ 0151 / pop 529,007

A dust-swirling desert city, Bikaner's finest sight is its fort, Junagarh, with its dazzlingly rich interiors. Close to the fort lies the old city, surrounded by a high crenellated wall. Within the walled city the streets feel medieval (despite the motorbike and rickshaw traffic) – narrow, dark and uneven, complete with open sewers, rubbish heaps, dark-red sandstone *havelis* and some exquisitely painted Jain temples.

Bikaner feels far less set up for tourism than other Rajasthan cities, though there are a lot of hotels here and a busy camel-safari scene. More and more visitors are opting to take desert camel safaris from Bikaner, thus avoiding the Jaisalmer hustle.

Many travellers come here to visit the notorious Karni Mata Temple, 30km south, where pilgrims worship thousands of holy rats. Less Brothers Grimm, but still fairy-tale, is the small temple town of Kolayat, with its holy lake and religious fair (p301), 54km to the south.

The city is also known for its traditional fire dances, performed by members of a Hindu religious sect called the Jas Naths. Today it's only possible to see this dance during the Bikaner Camel Festival (p301), in the village of Katriyasar, 40km from Bikaner on the Jaipur road.

History

The city was founded in 1488 by Rao Bika, a descendant of Jodha, Jodhpur's founder, and was another important staging post on the great caravan trade routes. Being closer to Delhi, Bikaner spent more time fighting the Mughals than other Rajasthan cities, but its harsh desert surroundings helped to defeat many of its enemies. Post Mughals, the city declined, though its geography excused it the attacks from the Marathas that plagued many other cities. By the 19th century the province was markedly backward, but managed to turn its fortunes around by trading camels with the British during the Afghan War. In 1886 it was the first desert princely state to install electricity.

Maharaja Ganga Singh (r 1898–1944) was one of Rajasthan's most notable and accomplished rulers. His clever diplomacy and canny economic sense helped develop Bikaner. He promoted the Ganga Canal, built between

1925 and 1927, which continues to irrigate a large area of arid land. He later led the Indian delegation to the League of Nations.

Orientation

The old city is encircled by a 7km-long wall with five entrance gates that was constructed in the 18th century. The fort and palace, built of similar reddish-pink sandstone as Jaipur's famous buildings, lie outside the city walls.

Information

For an online guide to Bikaner, check out www.realbikaner.com.

Bank of Baroda (☎ 2545453; ☯ 10am-2pm Mon-Fri, 10am-12.30pm Sat) Changes travellers cheques only.

Corporation Bank ATM Beside the fort, near the post office, accepts Cirrus cards.

Main post office (☯ 10am-1pm & 2-3pm Mon-Fri, 10am-1pm Sat) Near Junagarh.

New Horizons (Biscuit Gali; per hr Rs 20; ☯ 9am-9pm) Off Station Rd, this is one of the few internet places in Bikaner (other than the increasing number of hotels with convenient internet access). Be warned the equipment is old and the shoes-off policy has led at least one traveller to leave shoeless!

PBM Hospital (☎ 2525312; Hospital Rd)

State Bank of Bikaner & Jaipur Ambedkar Circle (☎ 2544361; ☯ noon-4pm Mon-Sat); public park, near Junagarh (☎ 2544034; ☯ 10am-2pm Mon-Fri, 10am-noon Sat) Changes cash and travellers cheques.

Tourist Reception Centre (☎ 2226701; ☯ 10am-5pm Mon-Sat) Near Pooran Singh Circle, in the RTDC Hotel Dhola Maru compound, about 1km from the city centre. It has various brochures (including a free map of Bikaner and a toilet that can be used by tourists). There is also a **counter** (☯ 3-6pm Mon-Sat) within the fort.

Sights

JUNAGARH

This most impressive **fort** (Indian/foreigner Rs 20/100, camera/video Rs 30/100, guide Rs 150; ☯ 10am-4.30pm) was constructed between 1588 and 1593 by Raja Rai Singh, a general in the army of the Mughal Emperor Akbar. Palaces and luxurious suites were added by subsequent maharajas. Unlike many Rajasthan forts, Junagarh doesn't command a hilltop position. However, it's no less imposing for that and – a credit to its planners and architects – it has never been conquered.

It's protected by a 986m-long wall with 37 bastions, and is surrounded by a (now dry) moat. The sandstone **Surajpol** (Sun Gate) is the main entrance and is where the guides line up to hussle trade. The palaces within the fort are on the southern side, and make a picturesque ensemble of courtyards, balconies, *chhatris*, towers and windows, with superb stone carving.

The handprints that can be seen close to the **Daulatpol** commemorate the wives of Rajput soldiers lost in battles, who committed *sati* on their husbands' funeral pyres.

You may be besieged by 'guides' offering tours before you arrive at the ticket counter. Unless you want an individual tour, this is unnecessary, as the ticket price includes a group tour with an official guide. The one-hour tours leave every 15 to 20 minutes. To visit at a leisurely pace, ask for your own guide, as larger groups rush around.

The gold-painted ceiling of the beautiful **Diwan-i-Khas** (Hall of Private Audience) was executed in 1631, and the silver *gaddi* of the maharajas can still be seen here. There's a courtyard paved with Italian tiles; through the fine lattice screens surrounding it, the women of the zenana could watch the activities below. Beside the **Phool Mahal** (Flower Palace), built during the reign of Maharaja Gaj Singh, is a marble statue of Surya, the sun god. Around the upper edges of the walls are paintings depicting Hindu gods.

The beautiful **Anup Mahal** was commissioned by Maharaja Karan Singh (r 1631–69). According to local lore, the maharaja was camping at Golkonda, in southern India, in his capacity as a general in the Mughal army, when an artist showed him fine works in gold. The artist told the maharaja that he was originally from Jaisalmer, but had migrated to southern India when a famine swept over his homeland. The maharaja was inspired by the proficiency and great beauty of the work he had been shown, and so he invited the artist to return to Bikaner, where the artist was given royal patronage.

The work of this artist and of his students features in the **Karan Mahal** and the **Anup Mahal**. Three types of work can be seen here: the *sonakin* style features white plaster decorated with delicate patterns and painted with gold leaf; the *jangali sunthari* style features plaster with a green backing that depicts floral motifs; and the *manovat* style features a pillar of clay that is embossed on plaster, the entire work painted with gold leaf.

In the **Badal Mahal** (Cloud Palace), the walls are painted with blue cloud motifs, and there's

BIKANER

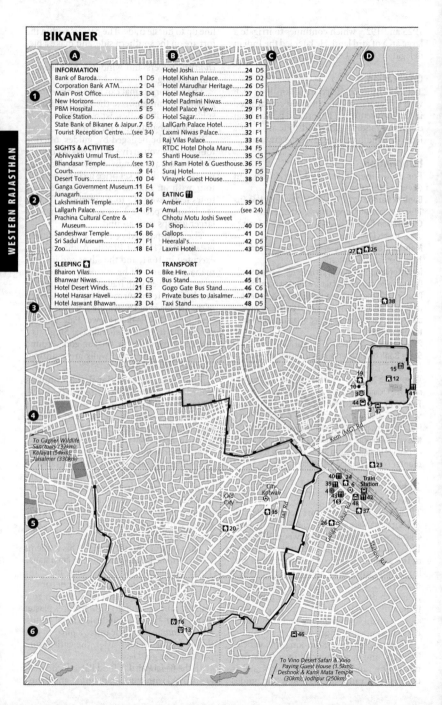

INFORMATION
Bank of Baroda	1	D5
Corporation Bank ATM	2	D4
Main Post Office	3	D4
New Horizons	4	D5
PBM Hospital	5	E5
Police Station	6	D5
State Bank of Bikaner & Jaipur	7	E5
Tourist Reception Centre	(see 34)	

SIGHTS & ACTIVITIES
Abhivyakti Urmul Trust	8	E2
Bhandasar Temple	(see 13)	
Courts	9	E4
Desert Tours	10	D4
Ganga Government Museum	11	E4
Junagarh	12	D4
Lakshminath Temple	13	B6
Lallgarh Palace	14	F1
Prachina Cultural Centre & Museum	15	D4
Sandeshwar Temple	16	B6
Sri Sadul Museum	17	F1
Zoo	18	E4

SLEEPING 🏠
Bhairon Vilas	19	D4
Bhanwar Niwas	20	C5
Hotel Desert Winds	21	E3
Hotel Harasar Haveli	22	E3
Hotel Jaswant Bhawan	23	D4
Hotel Joshi	24	D5
Hotel Kishan Palace	25	D2
Hotel Marudhar Heritage	26	D5
Hotel Meghsar	27	D2
Hotel Padmini Niwas	28	F4
Hotel Palace View	29	F1
Hotel Sagar	30	E1
LallGarh Palace Hotel	31	F1
Laxmi Niwas Palace	32	F1
Raj Vilas Palace	33	E4
RTDC Hotel Dhola Maru	34	F5
Shanti House	35	C5
Shri Ram Hotel & Guesthouse	36	F5
Suraj Hotel	37	D5
Vinayek Guest House	38	D3

EATING 🍽
Amber	39	D5
Amul	(see 24)	
Chhotu Motu Joshi Sweet Shop	40	D5
Gallops	41	D4
Heeralal's	42	D5
Laxmi Hotel	43	D5

TRANSPORT
Bike Hire	44	D4
Bus Stand	45	E1
Gogo Gate Bus Stand	46	C6
Private buses to Jaisalmer	47	D4
Taxi Stand	48	D5

To Gagner Wildlife Sanctuary (32km); Kolayat (54km); Jaisalmer (330km)

Kem (MG) Rd

Old City

City Kotwali

Castle Station Rd

Station Rd

Train Station

To Vino Desert Safari & Vino Paying Guest House (1.5km); Deshnok & Karni Mata Temple (30km); Jodhpur (250km)

WESTERN RAJASTHAN

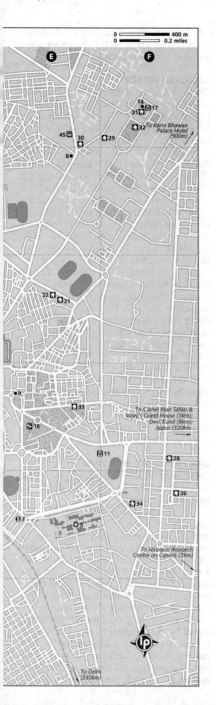

a statue here of Vishnu and Lakshmi. The large pillars beside the Karan Mahal were installed with the aid of elephants nearly 400 years ago.

The **Gaj Mandir** formed the private chambers of Maharaja Gaj Singh. The maharani's chamber is decorated with mirror tiles and gold painting, and there's wooden lac (resin) painting on the ceiling. The maharaja's chamber has a beautiful painted wood ceiling featuring florets and geometric motifs, and carved ivory doors.

In the **Hawa Mahal** (Palace of the Winds – used in the summer), there's an ingenious device said to have alerted the maharaja to potential enemies. A mirror positioned over the bed enabled Maharaja Dunga Singh to see the reflections of people walking across the courtyard below (this is the purpose of the mirror according to the official fort guides, but other motives might be suspected). The ceiling features floral arabesques and scenes of Krishna dancing. The decorative blue tiles were imported from both Europe and China.

There's an interesting museum exhibition (included in the ticket price), housed in several of the newer rooms of the palace. In the armoury are enormous bore guns that were used for shooting from the backs of camels, as well as the usual collection of sinister-looking pistols and swords.

In the **Diwan-i-Khas** of Ganga Singh are three massive, intricately carved arches and a throne of sandalwood. Here also can be seen a 56kg suit of armour, including chain mail, and sculptures of Krishna dancing and stealing the clothes of the *gopis*. Beautiful, if deadly, weapons, each an exquisite work of art – swords with carved ivory and crystal handles – can also be seen here. In a separate chamber are the royal vestments of Maharaja Ganga Singh, as well as items from his office. There's also an old biplane that was presented to Ganga Singh by the British government during WWI. This is one of only two models of this kind of plane in the world.

PRACHINA CULTURAL CENTRE & MUSEUM

The **museum** (Indian/foreigner Rs 10/50, camera Rs 10/25; 9am-6pm), across the main courtyard from Surajpol, is fascinating and well labelled. It focuses on the Western influence on the Bikaner royals before Independence, including crockery from England and France and menu cards from 1936, as well as some exquisite Rajasthani costumes, jewellery and textiles, and intriguing everyday ephemera.

There is a small shop and café at the museum, and a reference library containing a limited collection of books on Rajasthan, which is open to the public.

JAIN TEMPLES

Two Jain temples just inside the walled city are well worth seeking out. **Bhandasar Temple** (admission free; ⊕ 6am-7pm) is particularly beautiful, with yellow-stone carving and dizzyingly vibrant paintings. It's dedicated to the fifth *tirthankar*, Sumtinath, and the building was commissioned in 1468 by a wealthy Jain merchant, Bhandasa Oswal. It was completed after his death in 1514.

The interior of the temple is stunning. The pillars bear floral arabesques and depictions of the lives of the 24 Jain *tirthankars*. It's said that 40,000kg of ghee was used instead of water in the mortar, which locals insist seeps through the floor on hot days.

On the 1st floor of the three-storey temple are beautiful miniatures of the sentries of the gods. There are fine views over the city from the 3rd floor, with the desert stretching behind it to the west. The priest will undoubtedly ask for a donation in excess of Rs 100, of which half will go surreptitiously to your guide. In fact, a trust pays for the upkeep of the temples and this is how the priest earns pocket money.

The second Jain temple here is **Sandeshwar Temple** (admission free, camera/video Rs 20/30; ⊕ 6am-noon & 6-7pm). It's smaller than Bhandasar Temple, and has good carving around the door architraves and columns, and ornately carved, painted pillars. Inside the drum of the *sikhara* (spire) are almost ethereal paintings, and the sanctum itself has a marble image of Sandeshwar, flanked by smaller marble statues of other Jain *tirthankars*.

LAKSHMINATH TEMPLE

Behind Bhandasar Temple, to the right, is the splendid Hindu **Lakshminath Temple** (admission free, photography prohibited). It was built during the reign of Rao Lunkaran between 1505 and 1526. Lakshminath was the patron god of the rulers of Bikaner, and during major religious festivals a royal procession led by the maharaja paid homage at the temple. The elaborate edifice was maintained with tributes received from five villages and several shops, which were granted to the temple by Maharaja Ganga Singh (1880–1943). Around 9.30pm you may witness praying in Sanskrit.

LALLGARH PALACE

About 3km north of the city centre, this pink-golden sandstone **palace** was built by Maharaja Ganga Singh (1880–1943) in memory of his father, Lal Singh. It's out-and-out grandeur, with overhanging balconies and delicate latticework. The 1st floor contains the **Sri Sadul Museum** (Indian/foreigner Rs 10/20, camera/video Rs 20/50; ⊕ 10am-5pm Mon-Sat). It has fascinating old B&W photographs celebrating the slaughter of wildlife and some evocative maharaja accessories reflecting the former royals' privileged lifestyles. Artefacts include (empty) wine and sherry bottles, menu cards, European crockery and a brass vessel known as a *tokna* (used to collect revenue that was transported by camel to the Bikaner state treasury). There's even a funky old film projector made in New York in 1921. Other more pedestrian exhibits include Maharaja Karni Singh's golf tees, roller skates, typewriters and pink-shaded sunglasses. There's also a disturbing pictorial display of tiger carnage, including a picture of the five tigers shot in three minutes by Maharaja Ganga Singh in 1937.

At the time of writing there were plans to move the museum to new rooms in the palace and possibly increase the admission cost.

In front of the palace is a carriage from the maharaja's royal train (you can stay in the train; see p345).

GANGA GOVERNMENT MUSEUM

This **museum** (admission Rs 3, free Mon; ⊕ 9.30am-5pm), on the Jaipur Rd, houses a well-displayed, interesting collection.

Exhibits include terracotta ware from the Gupta period, a range of Rajasthani traditional musical instruments, rich gold paintings by local Usta artisans, miniature wooden models of the Gajner and Lallgarh palaces, and a miniature of the Royal Bikaner train with the roof folded back to reveal its comfortable amenities. There's a separate exhibition hall with exquisite carpets and royal vestments.

Other interesting exhibits include decrees issued by the Mughals to the maharajas of Bikaner, including one advising Rai Singh to proceed to Delhi 'without any delay and with utmost expedition and speed, travelling over as great a distance as possible during the day time as well as by night' as 'Emperor Akbar is dying'. It was issued by Crown Prince (who would shortly become Emperor) Jehangir.

There are also some fine oil paintings, including one entitled *Maharaja Padam Singhji avenging…the death of his brother, Maharaja Mohan Singhji by killing the Emperor's brother-in-law…He drew his sword, rushed upon his enemy and severed him in two with a blow which also left a mark upon the pillar.*

The sculptures include a beautiful, busty image of Devi, and a marble Jain sculpture of Saraswati dating from the 11th century.

Only still cameras (no videos) are permitted (no charge). The entrance to the museum is at the back of the building on the left-hand side.

Tours

The Tourist Reception Centre (p339) can arrange English-speaking guides (Rs 300 per day, with a maximum of four people).

Bhairon Vilas (p345) offers various tours, including a range of camel safaris, village tours, a jeep tour to Deshnok via a couple of the desert villages, and a tour to Kolayat (p348) and Gajner Wildlife Sanctuary (p347).

Most of the tour options cost from Rs 650 to 1500 per day, including transport, a guide and (sometimes) food. The trip to Gajner includes jeep transport into the sanctuary for wildlife spotting.

Sleeping

The **Tourist Reception Centre** (☎ 2544125) at the RTDC Hotel Dhola Maru has a list of families registered with Bikaner's Paying Guest House Scheme. Rates are Rs 200 to 600 per night.

BUDGET

Shri Ram Hotel & Guesthouse (☎ 2522651; www.yha india.org, www.hotelshriram.com; YHA dm Rs 60, s/d from Rs 200/300, s/d with AC from Rs 400/600; 🏠 🖳) In a quiet area east of town, 3km from the train and bus stations, this is an accommodation multiplex comprising a YHA affiliated youth hostel, guesthouse and hotel. Despite its diversity, it retains a family atmosphere. Rooms vary in size and comfort and are adequately clean. Free pickup from the train and bus stations is offered, and note the 9am checkout.

Vinayek Guest House (☎ 2202634; vinayakguest house@gmail.com; r Rs 80-300) This place offers five very different rooms in a quiet family house

BIKANER CAMEL SAFARIS

Bikaner is an excellent alternative to the Jaisalmer safari scene. The Bikaner version of the safari tends to involve more travel in a camel cart – less tiring but also less fun. There are also fewer sights than around Jaisalmer, but it's great if you want to ride in empty desert scrub (no wind turbines yet), sleep on dunes and see life in desert villages. There are fewer organisations running safaris here, so you're unlikely to encounter much hassle. In fact there are two main camel men and all the other operators contract camels and drivers from them. If your travel agent/hotel manager/rickshaw-wallah is talking down either of these gentlemen (a favourite sport in Bikaner), it is because they have tried to squeeze too much discount from one of the camel men and there has been a falling out. If you are quoted a discount price for an overnight trip you may well find yourself heading out to the camels in a rickshaw rather than a jeep.

The major (and recommended) operators include **Vino Desert Safari** (www.vinodesertsafari.com; see Vino Paying Guest House, p344), south of the city, opposite the Gopeshwar Temple, which has been operating since 1991. Vino offers two- to seven-day trips (Rs 500 to 1500 per day, depending on how much luxury you require and how much you use a jeep). The friendly, enthusiastic Vino speaks English, French and German.

Then there's Vijay Singh Rathore, the **Camel Man** (www.camelman.com; see Vijay's Guest House, p344), another friendly chap operating safaris since 1983, who runs basic half-day/full-day safaris for Rs 650/1000, and more upmarket excursions (beds with sheets are provided) for Rs 1300 to 1600 per day. Safaris range from half-day jaunts to 14-day trips all the way to Jaisalmer.

Also recommended is Kamal Saxena of **Desert Tours** (☎ 2521967; www.uniqueidea.org), a smaller operator who has a long experience organising safaris. He charges around Rs 800 per day and is located behind the main post office.

There are many different camel-trek routes, including trips to Khichan, home of the demoiselle cranes, and to the rat temple at Deshnok.

owned by the manager of the Urmul Trust. On offer is a free pick-up service, cooking lessons and camel safaris. There's no sign outside, but it's near Sher Singh's Flour Mill and Old Pugal House.

Vino Paying Guest House (☎ 2270445, 9414139245; www.vinodesertsafari.com; Ganga Shahar; s without bathroom Rs 100, d Rs 200-850) This guesthouse in a family home south of town is a cosy choice. Rooms vary widely and include standard hotel rooms as well as basic and cool adobe huts in the garden. All are excellent value, and the family is enthusiastic, helpful and welcoming and runs recommended safaris (see p343). Vino's family also gives free cooking lessons. It's opposite Gopeshwar Temple.

RTDC Hotel Dhola Maru (☎ 2529621, fax 2522109; dm Rs 100, s/d without AC Rs 500/600, with AC Rs 750/900; 🔀) This large hotel has spacious and tolerably clean rooms in a typically bland RTDC hotel complex including a featureless restaurant and a helpful tourist reception centre.

our pick Shanti House (☎ 2543306, 9461159796; inoldcity@yahoo.com; near Kotwali, Old City; s/d Rs 150/250) Run by the affable Gouri who is a fountain of information, this friendly, tidy and snug guesthouse is secreted in the old city. Take advantage of the free pickup from the train and bus stations otherwise you'll never find this place in the maze of laneways. There are just four rooms which boast real mattresses on the beds but have bucket hot water and squat toilets in the attached bathrooms. There is also a two-night minimum stay. The old city is quiet and atmospheric and once you get your bearings you'll enjoy wandering around.

Vijay's Guest House (☎ 2231244, 9829717331; www.camelman.com; Jaipur Rd; s/d from Rs 250/300-800) Camel safari organiser Vijay (see p343) runs this super-clean and friendly guesthouse. East of town, opposite Sophia School, it has a family atmosphere and vast rooms, some of which are air-cooled.

Hotel Marudhar Heritage (☎ 2522524; hmheritage2000@yahoo.co.in; Ganga Shahar Rd; s/d from Rs 250/350, with AC from Rs 550/650; 🔀 🖳) This is a friendly, well-kept and well-run option in a quiet location. There are rooms to suit most budgets that are plain and comfortable with TV and phone. You may wish to avoid the carpeted rooms which are a bit musty. There are nice views from the roof.

Hotel Joshi (☎ 2527700; Station Rd; s Rs 250-800, d Rs 350-900) Hotel Joshi bills itself as a 'Landmark in Vegetarian Hotels' and its clean, though

unexciting, rooms are the best of the cheapies available on Station Rd – the others hotels are quite depressing. It's conveniently near the train station, does a decent veg thali, and has 24-hour checkout.

Hotel Kishan Palace (☎ 2527762; www.hotelkishanpalaceheritage.com; 8B Gajner Rd; r Rs 300-750; 🔀) North of town, Kishan Palace is a reasonable option with spacious rooms that are showing their age and looking a little dusty. Meals are available, and there's free pick-up from the bus station.

Hotel Meghsar Castle (☎ 2527315; www.hotelmeghsarcastle.com; 9 Gajner Rd; r Rs 300-1050; 🔀 🖳) Next door to Kishan Palace, this hotel has old-fashioned rooms, some echoingly large, with cool, clean, tiled floors. It's a well-run, friendly place, with meals available in the garden. The front rooms can suffer a bit of traffic noise.

Hotel Harasar Haveli (☎ 2209891; www.harasar.com r Rs 300-2000) Most rickshaw-wallahs will want to bring you to this hotel next to Desert Winds – it's notorious for its commission-paying tactics. If you don't mind encouraging such behaviour, it's a great choice – big and efficient with clean, uncluttered rooms and even better deluxe rooms. Room prices can be bargained down if things are quiet or no commission is being paid. There's a pleasant rooftop restaurant with swing chairs. Camel safaris are available.

Suraj Hotel (☎ 2542740; surajhotel@yahoo.com; Rani Bazaar; s/d Rs 325/375, with AC Rs 625/675; 🔀) A good choice, off Station Rd near the train station, with 24-hour checkout. Check your bathroom for working plumbing but the rest of the room should be OK and there's a recommended restaurant in the basement (see opposite).

Hotel Palace View (☎ 2203463; hotelpalaceview@gmail.com; Lallgarh Palace Campus; s Rs 400-650, d Rs 600-700, s/d with AC Rs 900/1200; 🔀) This place is north of town, within the grounds of Lallgarh Palace, with – you've guessed it – palace views. The rooms are all different but all share the same care, cleanliness and attention to detail. The hotel is pleasant, small and efficient, in a very peaceful spot, with good-value, home-cooked meals.

Hotel Desert Winds (☎ 2542202; www.hoteldesertwinds.in; r Rs 400-1300; 🔀) This lovely hotel with squeaky-clean rooms is northeast of the fort and only about 1km from the train station, opposite Karni Singh Stadium. It's owned by a retired deputy director of Rajasthan Tourism, who can give you info about the city and organise camel safaris.

Hotel Padmini Niwas (☎ 2522794; padmi_hotel@ rediffmail.com; 148 Sadul Ganj; r without/with AC from Rs 450/750; ☒ ☲) Padmini Niwas has clean, carpeted rooms in a peaceful location. The owner is relaxed, and the small outdoor pool (Rs 100 for nonguests) is a bonus.

MIDRANGE
Hotel Jaswant Bhawan (☎ /fax 2548848; www.hotel jaswantbhawan.com; Alakh Sagar Rd; s/d Rs 600/800, with AC Rs 800/1000; ☒ ☲) This is a pleasant, quiet, welcoming place with a small garden, lounge bar and restaurant. The pricier rooms in this heritage house are spacious and airy. It's very handy for the train station without the noise of Station Rd, and you can use the excellent kitchen for self-catering.

ourpick Bhairon Vilas (☎ /fax 2544751; www.hotel bhaironvilas.tripod.com; r Rs 800-1800; ☒ ☲) Bikaner's prime minister once lived here (he had three wives, hence the 120-year-old building's four sections). The deep-red heritage hotel is now run by the prime minister's great-grandson, Harsh Singh, who's made it Bikaner's funkiest place to stay. Rooms are huge and eclectically decorated with antiques, bearskins and old family photographs. There's a snug bar crammed with old furnishings, a garden restaurant where traditional musicians sometimes play, and an interesting, if pricey, shop here called Vichitra Arts (see p346). Free pickup from the bus or train station is available and camel safaris and local tours (see p343) can be arranged.

Hotel Sagar (☎ 2520677; www.sagarhotelbikaner .com; Lallgarh Palace Campus; s/d from Rs 1000/1200; ☒) This hotel, north of town, is housed in a large pink building, the first place to the left of the driveway as you approach Lallgarh Palace. It offers a range of rooms, from thatched huts set in the garden to overfurnished grand rooms set in the main building, which surrounds a courtyard. All are a bit overpriced so don't forget to ask for a discount.

Raj Vilas Palace (☎ 2525901; www.rajvilaspalace.net; Public Park; s/d Rs 1950/3500; ☒ ☲) This newish cement palace boasts a brash and bright lobby, coffee shop, bar and restaurant. Unfortunately not as much money has been spent on the rather ordinary rooms and the swimming pool was already in a state of disrepair. Hopefully these are just teething problems for this business- and wedding-oriented hotel.

TOP END
Karni Bhawan Palace Hotel (☎ 2524701; www.hrhindia .com; Gandhi Colony; r from Rs 3000, ste Rs 5000) This hotel is about 500m east of the Lallgarh Palace Hotel and was briefly the residence of Maharaja Karni Singh. It's an ugly but grand red-and-white flourish of a building, cosy and well run. Huge suites are furnished in Art Deco style. A visit to stunning Gajner Palace Hotel outside Bikaner can be arranged (see p348).

Bhanwar Niwas (☎ 2529323; www.bhanwarniwas .com; Rampuri St, Old City; s/d from Rs 3500/4500; ☒ ☲) This place, in the beautiful and elaborate Rampuri Haveli, near the *kotwali* (police station) in the old city, has large, tastefully decorated rooms, featuring hand-painted wallpaper and antique furnishings. The atmospheric rooms are all very different, and are set around a peaceful, sun-dappled courtyard. The *haveli* was completed in 1927 for Seth Bhanwarlal Rampura, heir to a textile and real-estate fortune. In the entrance gate is a stunning blue 1927 Buick. Inside is pure uncluttered sumptuousness from the gilded sitting room to the grand dining hall. To get here turn left at the Kote Gate, and take the first right at Lady Elgin School. The hotel is close to a community of kitemakers, who can be seen practising their craft.

Lallgarh Palace Hotel (☎ 2540201; www.lallgarh palace.com; s/d from Rs 4000/4600; ☒ ☲) Some 3km north of the city centre, this pink-and-gold sandstone hotel is part of the maharaja's palace, dating from 1902, and has well-appointed, old-fashioned rooms around a courtyard. The pricier ones are huge, with lofty ceilings. There is an indoor pool (Rs 250 per hour for nonguests), as well as a billiard room, croquet facilities, and a resident masseur and astrologer.

Laxmi Niwas Palace (☎ 2202777; www.laxmi niwaspalace.com; s/d Rs 5500/5500; ☒) Beside Lallgarh Palace, north of town, this is a beautifully restored building with some lovely stone carving, opulent interiors and an oversupply of dead tiger photos. Rooms are enormous, elegant and evocative, with painted walls. The courtyard is overlooked by the old zenana, the bar is overlooked by stuffed heads, and there's a charming garden restaurant (see p346).

Eating
RESTAURANTS
Laxmi Hotel (Station Rd; mains Rs 30; ☷ 10am-10pm) This is one of four earthy veg joints which

crowd the entrance to a large *dharamsala* and tempt pilgrims with cheap tasty thalis.

Suraj Restaurant (☎ 2542740; Rani Bazaar; mains Rs 40-65; ☺ 6am-10.30pm) Situated beneath the Suraj Hotel (p344) off Station Rd, this is Bikaner's best-value thali joint. Choose between the 'mini', 'deluxe' and the highly recommended 'special' which can be shared between two people.

Amber (☎ 2220333; Station Rd; mains Rs 40-100; ☺ 6am-10pm) Amber is a cool, clean restaurant that is decorated in neutral tones with bench seating. It is well regarded and popular for veg fare, including Continental and South Indian dishes. On one side of the restaurant there's an Indian sweets counter, and on the other side is an ice-cream parlour and pizzeria.

Heeralal's (☎ 2204455; Station Rd; mains Rs 55-85; ☺ downstairs 7am-midnight, upstairs 12.30-11.30pm) Opposite the train station, this bright restaurant is a great place to wait for the train. Downstairs there are shiny booths, pizzas, burgers and South Indian snacks. Upstairs they deliver veg and nonveg dishes including tandoori, curries and Chinese in swish surrounds, but unfortunately no beer.

Gallops (☎ 3200833; mains Rs 90-175; ☺ 8am-10pm) This modern café/restaurant close to Surajpol is managed by the folks at Harisar Haveli, and the rickshaw-wallahs know it as 'Glops'. There are snacks such as pizzas, pakoras, and sandwiches, and a good range of Indian and Chinese veg and nonveg dishes. You can curl up on the outside leather lounge with a cold beer or a fuming hookah and be entertained by live music.

Hotel Laxmi Niwas Palace Garden Restaurant (☎ 2202777; mains Rs 80-150; ☺ noon-3pm & 7.30-10.30pm) Beside Laxmi Niwas Palace (p345), this excellent garden restaurant is a lovely place to eat – at least until the nights become too chilly. If it is obvious you are a tourist you will first be offered the menu from the hotel's plush, indoor **Swarn Mahal** (mains Rs 125-250). However, if you are looking for food less pricey and more spicy, then ask for the Garden Restaurant menu. Note that the beer is cheaper and that there is far less choice on this menu – veg and nonveg curries and some Chinese dishes. If you are lucky there's music in the evenings.

Bhanwar Niwas (☎ 2529323; set lunch/dinner Rs 350/375) A splendid place to eat, this hotel (p345) welcomes nonguests to its veg dining hall (notice is essential). You can have a drink before dinner in the courtyard.

QUICK EATS

Bikaner is noted for the *bhujiya*, which is a special kind of *namkin* (spicy nibbles), sold in the shops along Station Rd among other places.

Chhotu Motu Joshi Sweet Shop (Station Rd) This is Bikaner's best-loved sweet stop, with an assortment of Indian treats. Try milk-sweet *ras malai* (ricotta dessert with cardamom, nuts and sugar; Rs 16) and saffron *kesar cham cham* (Rs 6). The latter is a sausage-shaped sticky confection of milk, sugar and saffron; when bitten, it oozes a sweet sugar syrup. Fresh samosas (Rs 5) are available out the front in the mornings, and *bhujiya* costs Rs 9 per plate, *jalebis* (circular, deep-fried sweet) Rs 15 per plate.

Amul (Station Rd; ice cream Rs 10-15) On the ground floor of Hotel Joshi, there's a small ice-cream parlour selling popular Amul ice cream.

Shopping

Abhivyakti (Ganganagar Rd; ☺ 8.30am-6.30pm) Run by the Urmul Trust, a local NGO supported by Urmul Dairy (which has an outlet next door), Abhivyakti sells textiles produced by skilled artisans from local villages. The profits go directly to the producers, and to health and education projects in the surrounding villages, such as a girls' college. Take care, as rickshaw drivers and touts have taken visitors to other, commercial shops, claiming that they're run by the Urmul Trust.

The trust, founded in 1986, aims to provide primary health care and education to the people of the remote villages of Rajasthan, raise awareness of poor women's rights and promote the handicrafts of rural artisans, thus cutting out middlemen and commissions. You can pick up *pattus* (lovely handloom shawls), cushion covers, kurtas (shirts), *jootis* (traditional, pointy-toed Rajasthani shoes), puppets and more.

The Urmul Trust welcomes volunteers (see p371).

Vichitra Arts Based at Bhairon Vilas (see p345), this shop sells beautiful clothes including magnificent wedding skirts. It's pricey but interesting. There's an adjoining workshop with a resident artist painting miniatures.

Go to Usta St in the old city to see artisans making *usta* (gold-painted camel leather) products.

CAMEL-OLOGY

The camels reared at Bikaner's National Research Centre on Camels are of three breeds. The long-haired camels with hairy ears are the local Bikaner variety; they are renowned for their strength. The light-coloured camels are from Jaisalmer, and are renowned for their speed. The dark-coloured camels are from Gujarat, and the females are renowned for the quantity of milk they produce. The milk tastes a little salty and is reputedly good for the liver. If you have a cup of chai in a small desert village, you're quite possibly drinking camel milk. The stout of heart might even like to try fresh, warm camel milk at the farm. The camels on the farm are crossbred so, in theory, they should be the strongest, fastest and best milk-producing camels you'll find anywhere. Breeding season is from around December to March, and at this time the male camels froth disconcertingly at the mouth.

This is also a stud farm; locals bring their female camels here to be serviced free of charge. Female camels give birth every one and a half years, depending on their age and health, following a long (13-month) gestation period. A male camel can inseminate up to five cows per day.

Adult camels consume about 16kg of fodder in summer, and drink around 30L of water per day; in winter, they drink about 20L per day. In winter a healthy camel can work up to one month without food or water, and in summer up to one week.

Getting There & Away

BUS

The bus stand is 3km north of the city centre, almost opposite the road leading to Lallgarh Palace. If your bus is coming from the south, ask the driver to let you out closer to the city centre. Private buses to Jaisalmer congregate near the southern wall of the fort. There are numerous RSRTC and private buses to Agra (express/sleeper Rs 205/274, 12 hours), Ajmer (Rs 133, seven hours), Delhi (express/sleeper Rs 216/237, 11 hours), Jaipur (express/sleeper Rs 125/150, seven hours), Jaisalmer (Rs 146, eight hours), Jhunjhunu (Rs 87, five hours), Jodhpur (Rs 139, 5½ hours), Mandawa (Rs 50, four hours), and Udaipur (Rs 265, 12 hours).

TRAIN

To Jaipur, you can take the *Bikaner Howrah Superfast* (2308A), that leaves at 6.30pm (sleeper/3AC Rs 201/510, seven hours) or the *Jaipur-Bikaner Express* (4737/8), that departs at 9.20pm (sleeper/2AC Rs 178/654, 8½ hours). The *Ranakpur Express* (4707) leaves for Jodhpur at 9.45am (sleeper/3AC Rs 148/386, five hours). To Delhi, you can take the *Sampark Kranti Express* (2464A) that leaves at 5.20pm and arrives at Delhi Sarai Rohilla station at 5.40am (sleeper/3AC Rs 293/771).

Getting Around

An autorickshaw from the train station to the palace should cost Rs 20, but you'll certainly be asked for more. Bicycles can be hired near Bhairon Vilas for Rs 25 a day.

AROUND BIKANER

Devi Kund

The marble and red-sandstone royal **cenotaphs** of the Bika dynasty rulers, with some fine frescoes, are located 8km east of the centre of Bikaner. The white-marble *chhatri* of Maharaja Surat Singh is among the most imposing.

It costs Rs 150 return by rickshaw to get to this quiet spot.

National Research Centre on Camels

The **National Research Centre on Camels** (☎ /fax 0151-2230183; admission Rs 10, camera Rs 20, rides Rs 30, guides Rs 100; ☻ 2-6pm), 8km from central Bikaner, is possibly worth a look if camels take your fancy – you can visit the baby camels, go for a short ride and look around the small museum. There are about 230 camels, and three different breeds, reared here. The British Army had a camel corps drawn from Bikaner during WWI.

The on-site Camel Milk Parlour doesn't look much but can whip up a lassi for Rs 5. The round trip, including a half-hour wait at the camel farm, is around Rs 150 for an autorickshaw or Rs 300 for a taxi.

Gajner Wildlife Sanctuary

The lake and forested hills of this **reserve** (admission per jeep Rs 1000), 32km from Bikaner on the Jaisalmer road, are inhabited by wildfowl,

---

THE TEMPLE OF RATS

The Karni Mata Temple located at Deshnok is one of India's more challenging temples for Westerners – its resident mass of holy rodents is not for the squeamish. Karni Mata lived in the 14th century and performed many miracles during her lifetime. When her youngest son, Lakhan, drowned, Karni Mata ordered Yama, the god of death, to bring him back to life. Yama replied that he was unable to do this, but that Karni Mata, as an incarnation of Durga, could restore Lakhan's life. This she did, decreeing that members of her family would no longer die but would be reincarnated as *kabas* (rats), and that these *kabas* would return as members of her family. Around 600 families in Deshnok claim descent from Karni Mata and that they will be reincarnated as *kabas*.

The temple is an important place of pilgrimage; pilgrims are disgorged from buses every few minutes. Once at the village, they buy *prasad* (holy food offerings) in the form of sugar balls to feed to the rats. Eating *prasad* covered in holy rat saliva is also claimed by believers to bring good fortune, although most travellers are willing to take their word for it.

The pilgrims are anointed with a tikka made with ash from a holy fire in the inner sanctum, while the objects of their devotion run over their toes (sorry, no shoes permitted). Before the temple is a beautiful marble façade with solid silver doors, donated by Maharaja Ganga Singh. Across the doorway to the inner sanctum are repoussé silver doors – one panel shows the goddess with her charges at her feet. An image of the goddess is also enshrined in the inner sanctum. There are special holes around the side of the temple courtyard to facilitate the rats' movements, and a wire grille has been placed over the courtyard to prevent birds of prey and other predators consuming the holy rodents.

It's considered highly auspicious to have a *kaba* run across your feet – you'll probably find you'll be inadvertently graced in this manner whether you want it or not. White *kabas* are quite rare, although there are one or two at the temple, and sighting one augurs well for your spiritual progress.

What may seem unusual to Western eyes is devoutly believed by pilgrims – remember that this isn't a sideshow but a place of worship. And don't conveniently forget to remove your shoes!

---

wild boar, desert foxes, blackbucks and nilgai. It was once a royal hunting ground – many British luminaries have killed wildlife here. The reserve is only accessible by vehicle from Gajner Palace Hotel (below), which may be hired by nonguests.

SLEEPING & EATING

Gajner Palace Hotel (☎ 01534-275061; www.hrhindia .com; r from Rs 6000; 🛋) Right on the edge of a beautiful lake is the magnificent erstwhile royal winter palace and hunting lodge, in 2400 hectares. The sandstone palace is set in lush surroundings, and the rooms are lavishly furnished. Some of the rugs in the main palace were woven by prisoners of the Bikaner jail. There's a restaurant, and you can eat indoors or outdoors as you watch the birds bobbing on the lake.

GETTING THERE & AWAY

There are frequent daily buses (Rs 28) running to Gajner village, about 1km away from the hotel. A return taxi from Bikaner should

cost around Rs 600, including the two hours' waiting time.

Kolayat

Set around a temple-ringed lake, Kolayat is a beautiful, untouristed town, around 54km to the south of Bikaner. Kolayat is a holy place, with 52 ghats surrounding its lake. Visiting here is a worthy pilgrimage, and spending one day here can equal up to 10 years at another sacred place. Like Pushkar, it has a (rare) Brahma temple.

There are a number of very basic *dharamsalas*, but most won't accept tourists. **Bhaheti Dharamsala** (r with shared bathroom Rs 35), on the main ghat by the lakeside, is a reasonable place. Otherwise Kolayat is a good day trip from Bikaner.

The **Kapil Muni Mela** (fair) is held here in October or November, around the same time as the Pushkar Camel Fair (minus the camels and cattle, but with plenty of sadhus). The main temple at Kolayat is **Kapil Muni Temple** (🕑 closed 3-5pm).

There are regular buses from Bikaner (Rs 30, 1½ hours), or there's a train at 8.30am (1½ hours), returning at 4pm.

Deshnok

Most travellers coming to Bikaner make a beeline for the extraordinary **Karni Mata Temple** (www.karnimata.com; admission free, camera/video Rs 20/50; ☻ 4am-10pm) at this village 30km south of Bikaner (see opposite). The holy rodents of Karni Mata are considered to be incarnations of storytellers, and they run riot over the temple complex.

Two special festivals take place at the Karni Mata Temple around April/May and October/November. Ask at the **Tourist**

Reception Centre (☎ 0151-2544125) in Bikaner for the exact dates.

SIGHTS
Shri Karni Centenary Auditorium

The pictorial display in this **auditorium** (admission Rs 2; ☻ 7am-7pm), across the square from the temple, is worth a look. It tells the story of Karni Mata's life, with descriptions in English and Hindi.

GETTING THERE & AWAY

Buses from the main or Gogo Gate bus stands in Bikaner depart hourly for Deshnok (Rs 20, 30 minutes). A taxi (Rs 450 with a one-hour wait) is better and safer.

Directory

CONTENTS

ACCOMMODATION

Accommodation in Rajasthan ranges from simple whitewashed cells to glorious palaces and forts that have been converted into some of India's most luxurious, atmospheric and extraordinary hotels.

Accommodation listings are usually divided into budget, midrange and top-end categories. Recommendations within these listings are in ascending order of tariff. Roughly, the budget breakdown in this book is from around Rs 75 to Rs 800 (US$2 to

> **BOOK YOUR STAY ONLINE**
>
> For more accommodation reviews and recommendations by Lonely Planet authors, check out the online booking service at lonelyplanet.com/hotels. You'll find the true, insider lowdown on the best places to stay. Reviews are thorough and independent. Best of all, you can book online.

US$20) for a budget room, from around Rs 800 to Rs 4000 (US$20 to US$100) for midrange and from around Rs 4000 (US$100) upwards for the top end. However, this is a loose guide; many places have rooms covering a variety of categories – their upper-priced rooms are midrange, lower-priced ones are budget. Prices also vary depending on the season, the festival calendar, whether it's a tourist hot spot, and whether you are bedding down in the town or country. Standout options throughout this book are indicated by **our pick**.

Although most prices quoted here are for single and double rooms, many hotels will put an extra bed in a room to make a triple for about an extra 25%.

During the peak tourist season, which falls from mid-November to February, and some festivals, hotel rates can skyrocket and it can be tough even finding a bed – advance reservations are advisable.

Room quality can vary dramatically within properties, particularly budget properties, so try to inspect a few rooms first. For a bathroom low-down see Get to Know Your Bathroom, p352.

Some hotels operate on a 24-hour system (ie your time starts when you check in), while others have fixed checkout times – it pays to ask.

Credit cards are accepted at most top-end hotels and many midrange ones; however, few budget places will take them. Some hotels may request an upfront payment. If you're asked to sign a blank impression of your credit card, refuse to do so. If they insist, fill in an amount less than your estimated expenditure.

In some towns, notably Jodhpur, some hotels 'borrow' the name of a thriving competitor to confuse travellers. To avoid landing up at an inferior copycat, make sure that you know the *exact* name of your preferred hotel, and before paying the driver double-check that you're at the right place, as some cheeky chaps will try to off-load you at hotels where they receive fat commissions. Also see About Touts, p356.

Accommodation Options
BUDGET & MIDRANGE HOTELS

These options range from squalid dives to excellent-value and well-kept guesthouses. Most hotels in these categories come with ceiling fans. Shoestring travellers may like to consider bringing their own sheets and pillowcases, as some of the cheaper places have bed linen that even the most ferocious *dhobi-wallah* (washerman) couldn't whiten.

Midrange hotels offer you more comfort than their budget brothers, but they can be a mixed bag: some have dreary, boxlike rooms while others ooze character. Some of these hotels have 'air-cooled' rooms that are one step up from a ceiling fan and one step below air-conditioning. An air-cooler is a large (usually noisy) evaporative device built into a frame within a wall.

Some budget and midrange hotels lock their gates at night and remain unmanned on the outside, so let someone know if you intend coming back late.

CAMPING

There are few camping options in Rajasthan, though a couple of hotels allow you to camp in their grounds, as detailed in the Sleeping sections of regional chapters. Some budget hotels let travellers sleep on their rooftop (usually providing a mattress and some bedding) for a nominal charge.

PAYING GUEST HOUSE SCHEME (HOMESTAYS)

Rajasthan pioneered the Paying Guest House Scheme, so it's well developed in the state. Staying with a local family can be a stimulating change from dealing only with hoteliers. Prices range from budget to upper midrange – contact the local Rajasthan Tourism Development Corporation (RTDC) tourist offices for details (for contact information, see the individual regional chapters). Jaipur also has a reputable private scheme called Jaipur Pride (p164).

RAILWAY RETIRING ROOMS

These are found at train stations, and you can technically only stay here if you possess an ongoing train ticket. The rooms, which can range from substandard to adequate, are handy if you have an early morning train departure, although they can be noisy if it's a busy station. Most are let on a 24-hour basis, and usually offer dormitories (sometimes male only) and private rooms.

PRACTICALITIES

- Electricity is 230V to 240V, 50Hz AC and sockets are the three-round-pin variety. Blackouts are fairly common so bring a torch (flashlight) and the gear to protect delicate electronic equipment.

- Officially India uses the metric system for weights and measures. Terms you're likely to hear are lakhs (one lakh = 100,000) and crores (one crore = 10 million).

- Major English-language dailies include the *Hindustan Times, Times of India, Indian Express, Pioneer, Asian Age, Hindu, Statesman, Telegraph* and *Economic Times*. In Delhi there are several listings and general information guides: *Delhi City Guide, Delhi Diary, Explore Delhi, First City* and *Time Out Delhi*. Jaipur also has a couple of listings and tourist guides: *Jaipur Vision* and *Jaipur City Guide*. In Udaipur look out for *Out and About in Udaipur*.

- Read incisive current affairs in *Frontline, India Today*, the *Week, Sunday* and *Outlook*. For India-related travel articles get *Outlook Traveller*.

- The national (government) TV broadcaster is Doordarshan. More widely watched are satellite and cable TV; channels include BBC World, CNN, Discovery, Star Movies, HBO and MTV. TV (and radio) programme/frequency details appear in most English-language dailies.

- Government-controlled All India Radio (AIR) nationally transmits local and international news. There are also private channels broadcasting news, music, current affairs, talkback and more.

GET TO KNOW YOUR BATHROOM

All top-end and most midrange hotels in India have sit-down flush toilets with toilet paper. Some midrange and many budget hotels have a choice of squat and sit-down flush toilets. In the rock-bottom category squat toilets are the norm and toilet paper is rarely provided.

Some hoteliers refer to squat toilets as 'Indian-style' and sit-down flush toilets as 'Western-style'. In some places you may discover the curious hybrid toilet, which is a sit-down toilet with footpads on the edge of the bowl.

Throughout India, there's differing terminology for hotel bathrooms: 'common bath', 'without bath' or 'shared bath' means communal bathroom facilities. 'Attached bath', 'private bath' or 'with bath' indicates that the room has its own bathroom.

'Running', '24-hour' or 'constant' hot water indicates that there's hot water around the clock (not always the case in reality). At the cheapest level, some hotel bathrooms only have cold tap water so hot water is provided in buckets, sometimes only within certain hours and at a small charge.

Hotels that advertise 'room with shower' can be misleading. Even if a bathroom has a shower, check that it works before accepting the room. Some hotels surreptitiously disconnect showers to cut costs, while showers at other places render a mere trickle of water.

Some budget and midrange hotels have small hot-water tanks in the bathroom, which need to be switched on anywhere up to an hour before use.

In this book, hotel rooms have private bathroom unless otherwise stated.

RTDC ACCOMMODATION

RTDC hotels are government run and their facilities and service are not usually up to much. They may offer dorm beds (Rs 100 per person per night), and there are also usually two or three types of rooms available, all with private bathroom: ordinary, deluxe and superdeluxe. The local branch of the RTDC tourist office is often on the premises.

PALACES, FORTS & CASTLES

Rajasthan is famous for its wonderful palace, fort and castle hotels, most famous being the Lake Palace (p253) in Udaipur, Devi Garh (p253) near Udaipur, Rambagh Palace (p169) in Jaipur and Umaid Bhawan Palace (p310) in Jodhpur. But there are hundreds of others, and it often doesn't cost a fortune: some are the height of luxury and priced accordingly, but many are simpler, packed with character and in stunning locations.

As palaces and forts were not originally designed for tourism, the size and quality of rooms can vary, so look at a few rooms first.

Throughout Rajasthan you will discover many finely appointed historical buildings that have been converted into tourist accommodation. They are known as 'heritage hotels' and include *havelis* (traditional mansions), forts and former royal hunting lodges. Many of the RTDC tourist offices have a brochure that lists heritage

hotels, or you can check out the website http://heritagehotels.com.

TOP-END HOTELS

As major tourist centres, Rajasthan, Delhi and Agra have a bevy of top-end hotels, ranging from swanky five-star chains such as the Oberoi, Taj and Welcomgroup (affiliated to Sheraton), to less-glamorous four-starrers.

Note that US dollar rates often apply to foreigners, including to nonresident Indians (NRIs).

If you're interested in staying at a top-end hotel, it's often cheaper to book it through the internet. Nevertheless, unless the hotel is busy, you can nearly always score a discount from the rack rates.

Additional Costs
SEASONAL VARIATIONS

Most hoteliers in Delhi, Agra and Rajasthan crank up their high-season prices to around two to three times the low-season price – the process is gradual, so as the high season approaches, prices will creep up. The prices quoted in this book are high-season rates.

High season begins about a month before Christmas and includes the two months following. Some hotels charge higher rates for the brief Christmas and New Year period, or over major festivals such as Diwali (p360) and the

Pushkar Camel Fair (p209). Conversely, in the low season (from around April to September), prices at even normally expensive hotels can drop dramatically, creating some amazing bargains. Between low and high season there's a shoulder season with intermediate prices. It's *always* worth asking for a better rate if the hotel doesn't seem busy.

TAXES & SERVICE CHARGES

At most rock-bottom places you won't have to pay any taxes. Once you get into the top end of budget places, and certainly in midrange and top-end accommodation, you will usually have to pay a 8% to 10% 'luxury' tax on rooms over Rs 1000 plus 12.5% on food and beverages in hotels that attract the luxury tax on their rooms.

On top of taxes, many midrange and upmarket hotels have a 'service charge' (usually 8% to 10%). This may be restricted to room service and telephone use, or may be levied on the total bill. Rates quoted in this book exclude taxes unless otherwise indicated.

Many hotels raise their tariffs annually, some raise them when business is good, and some raise rates with an increase of popularity (often because they have had a good write-up in Lonely Planet!) – be prepared for increments on the rates quoted here.

ACTIVITIES

From exploring the desert on camelback, to being covered in Ayurvedic oils, Rajasthan has an exhilarating range of activities on offer.

Remember that travel agents often take a cut of what you pay and sell you on as clients to someone else. The end provider gets only part of what you paid and so you may get poor equipment, insufficient food or poor safety standards. If you are using an agent, try to deal with companies that are the end provider and ask if they're registered with the state government. Then ask if they're members of an accredited association such as the Travel Agents Association of India, Indian Association of Tour Operators or the Adventure Tour Operators Association of India – ask to see their accreditation. Ask official tourist offices for government-approved operators or, best of all, get recommendations from fellow travellers.

For information on camel, horse, jeep and wildlife safaris, see p368.

Ayurveda

Massages, treatments and assessments are available at various places, including Ashtaang, in Delhi (p107), and Kerala Ayurveda Kendra and Chakrapania Ayurveda in Jaipur (p161). There are also Ayurvedic hospitals in Udaipur (p248) and Bundi (p227) offering treatment.

Bird-watching

Rajasthan contains some renowned bird-watching sites, including World Heritage–listed Keoladeo Ghana National Park (p188); Ranthambhore National Park (p215); Khichan (see the boxed text, p318), near Phalodi; Sariska Tiger Reserve (p198); and Dungarpur (p263).

Boating

In southern Rajasthan, boats can be hired at Nakki Lake (p265) in Mt Abu, at Chambal Gardens (p230) in Kota, and on Pichola Lake (water-level permitting; p243) in Udaipur. At Jaisalmer, you can hire boats at Tilon-ki-Pol (p327).

Cycling

Ramesh Jangid, from Apani Dhani (p281) in Nawalgarh, Shekhawati, can organise cycling tours around the villages of Shekhawati, including informative commentaries on the region's remarkable paintings. Hotel Jamuna Resort (p287) in Jhunjhunu, Shekhawati, can also arrange cycling tours. Butterfield & Robinson offers more-upmarket organised bicycle tours (see p377 for more information).

Golf

It's possible to play golf in Jaipur (p161) and Jodhpur (p306); equipment is available for hire.

Swimming

Quite a few of the upmarket hotels allow non-guests to use their swimming pools. Expect to pay anywhere from Rs 100 to 500 for this privilege, which should include a towel.

Trekking

Various operators can organise treks in the Aravalli Range. Ramesh Jangid (see p280) organises treks that include a guide, all meals, transport and accommodation in village homes, tents and *dharamsalas* (pilgrims guesthouses).

DIRECTORY

You can also make short treks in the marvellous Aravalli hills around Mt Abu (p268). Other places worth exploring are around Udaipur (p249), Ranakpur (p261) and Kumbalgarh (p260), which have stunning scenery.

BUSINESS HOURS

Official business hours are from 9.30am to 5.30pm Monday to Friday. Unofficially they tend to be from 10am to 5pm.

Most banks are open from 10am to 2pm (some from 9am to 1pm and 1.30pm to 4pm) on weekdays, and from 10am to noon on Saturday – there are often variations, so it pays to check. In the bigger cities and tourist centres there are invariably foreign-exchange offices that stay open for longer.

In most cities, the main post office is open from 10am until 5pm on weekdays (some close for lunch any time between 1pm and 2pm) and on Saturday until noon (and occasionally on Sunday).

Shop hours vary regionally, but most tend to open from around 10am to 6pm and close once a week (often on Sunday).

In the more popular tourist areas, such as Udaipur, Jaisalmer and Pushkar, many shops open at around 9am and don't close until about 7pm, and half close on Sunday.

In this book we note opening hours of major sights and activities. Restaurants are generally open from 8am to 11pm daily; specific hours are provided in listings.

CHILDREN

Being a family-oriented society, India is a child-friendly destination. But travelling with kids in India can be hard work, requiring constant vigilance – be especially cautious of road traffic. Any long-distance road travel should include adequate stops, as rough roads can make travel more tiring than usual, especially for little ones. Train is usually the most comfortable mode of travel, especially for long trips. Always carry sufficient clean drinking water, snacks and amusements (books, toys, portable DVD players etc).

Health risks, such as diarrhoea (p391), can be much more of a threat to children than adults. If your child takes special medication, bring along an adequate stock in case it's not easily found locally.

For helpful hints, see Lonely Planet's *Travel with Children*, and the travelling with

Children section of Lonely Planet's Thorn Tree forum (http://thorntree.lonelyplanet. com) for more advice.

Practicalities

Many hotels have 'family rooms' or will happily provide an extra bed, and the more upmarket hotels may offer baby-sitting facilities and kid's activity programmes. Upmarket hotels have cable TV featuring children's channels such as Cartoon Network.

Regarding restaurants, it's usually the upmarket ones that supply high chairs. Restaurants rarely have dedicated nappy-changing rooms. For more information on eating, see p71.

Standard baby products such as nappies (diapers) and powdered milk are available in larger towns.

Sights & Activities

Allow several days for children to acclimatise to India's explosion of sights, smells, tastes and sounds. Start with short outings and include child-friendly attractions (generally more prevalent in bigger cities), such as the sound-and-light show of Delhi (p98), and fun museums such as Delhi's doll museum (p108). For other ideas in Delhi see Delhi for Children (p108). Chokhi Dhani (p172), near Jaipur, is a great place for children, and they'll love the elephants at Amber Fort (p178).

Wildlife, camel and horse safaris are also worth considering (see p368).

Travelling is usually much better out of the larger towns – without the hectic traffic and hassle, children will be safer and will find it much easier to adapt. Mt Abu and Bundi make great places to relax with the kids. Bear in mind, however, that you won't find the facilities and comforts of the cities unless you pop into plush hotels.

CLIMATE CHARTS

The climate of Rajasthan can be neatly divided into four seasons: premonsoon, monsoon, postmonsoon and winter. *Kharif* (monsoon) and *rabi* (winter) are the two main crop-growing seasons. For comprehensive details, see p17.

COURSES

To find out about new courses that may now be on offer, inquire at tourist offices, ask fellow travellers and check local newspapers

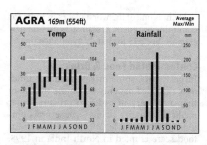

AGRA 169m (554ft)

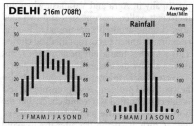

DELHI 216m (708ft)

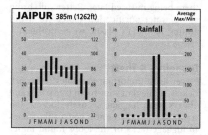

JAIPUR 385m (1262ft)

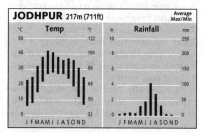

JODHPUR 217m (711ft)

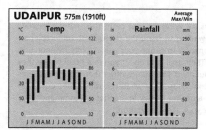

UDAIPUR 575m (1910ft)

and magazines. For information on arts and crafts see p53, and for cooking courses, see p73.

Arts & Crafts

There are myriad arts and crafts courses available in Rajasthan.

Jaipur Blue pottery can be tried at Kripal Kumbh (p163). For block printing and blue pottery head to Sakshi (p163), about 16km south of Jaipur in Sanganer Village.

Jhunjhunu Tuition in local Shekhawati painting is offered at Hotel Jamuna Resort (p287).

Nawalgarh *Bandhani* (tie-dye) and other crafts are offered at Apani Dhani (p280).

Udaipur Painting lessons are offered at Ashoka Arts (p250).

Astrology

Those fascinated by the future can take lessons in astrology at the Rajasthan Astrological Council & Research Institute (p163) in Jaipur.

Ayurveda, Meditation & Yoga

There are many places in Rajasthan, Agra and Delhi offering meditation and yoga courses – ask around for recommendations. For places that don't levy a charge, donations are much appreciated. Try the following:

Delhi (p108) Hatha yoga at Ashtaang. Meditation and yoga at Dhyan Foundation. Various forms of yoga at Morarji Desai National Institute of Yoga. Meditation and various forms of yoga, including asanas and pranayama (traditional breath control) at Studio Abhyas. Buddhist meditation at Tushita Meditation Centre.

Jaipur Vipassana meditation at Dhammathali Vipassana Meditation Centre (p163) and yoga (p164) at Yoga Sadhana Ashram and Madhavanand Girls College.

Mt Abu Raja Yoga meditation at Brahma Kumaris Spiritual University (p267).

Udaipur Hatha yoga at Ashtang Yoga Ashram (p250).

Languages

Apani Dhani and Ramesh Jangid's Tourist Pension (p280) in Nawalgarh can arrange Hindi lessons.

Music & Performing Arts

Places to hone your musical and dance skills include Maharaja Sawai Mansingh Sangeet Mahavidyalaya (p163), Jaipur, where you can learn sitar, tabla, flute and classical Indian dance; various places in Udaipur (p250) where teachers offer sitar, tabla and flute lessons; and Saraswati

DIRECTORY

Music School (p210) and Pushkar Music School (p210) in Pushkar for tabla, flute, singing and *kathak* (classical Indian dance) lessons.

CUSTOMS REGULATIONS

The usual duty-free regulations apply for India, that is, 1L of alcohol and 200 cigarettes or 50 cigars or 250g of tobacco.

You are permitted to bring in expensive items, such as video cameras and laptop computers; they may have to be entered on a 'Tourist Baggage Re-export' form to ensure you take them out with you when you go (although this isn't always policed).

Technically, you're supposed to declare any amount of cash or travellers cheques over US$10,000 on arrival. Officially, you're not supposed to take Indian currency into or out of India.

If entering India from Nepal, you are not entitled to import anything free of duty.

There are certain restrictions about what you can take out of India – see p365.

DANGERS & ANNOYANCES

Indian cities have occasionally been targeted by bombers, typically associated with the situation in Kashmir. In May 2008 Jaipur suffered such an attack. However rare such attacks may be, it makes sense to check the security situation with embassy travel advisories and local newspapers.

Like anywhere else in the world, common sense and caution are your best weapons against theft or worse. Chat with other travellers and tourism officials in order to stay abreast of the latest potential hazards. Also check the India branch of Lonely Planet's **Thorn Tree forum** (http://thorntree.lonelyplanet.com) where travellers often post warnings about problems they've encountered. Women travellers should see p371.

Delhi is one of the worst places in India for scamming travellers, as scamsters prey on new arrivals. See p95 for handy avoidance tips.

Contaminated Food & Drink

In past years, some private medical clinics have provided patients with more treatment than necessary in order to procure larger medical insurance claims – get several opinions where possible. Worse still, a serious food scare erupted in North India in 1998, principally in Agra and Varanasi, when numerous travellers became sick and two died after eating purposely contaminated food at restaurants linked to corrupt medical clinics. This scam has thankfully been quashed, but there's always the chance it could reappear.

Water (see Drinking Water, p391) can also be a potential problem. Always ensure the seal is intact on bottled water and check that the bottom of the bottle hasn't been tampered with. Crush plastic bottles after use to avoid them being misused later. Better still, bring along water-purification tablets to avoid adding to India's plastic waste problem – see p83.

Druggings & Theft

Never leave important valuables (passport, tickets, money) in your room (see p363) and always keep luggage securely locked. On trains, keep your gear near you; padlock bags to luggage racks or the loops found under some train seats. Thieves tend to target popular tourist train routes, such as Delhi to Agra. Be extra alert during train departure times, when the confusion and crowds are at their worst. Airports are another place to exercise caution, as after a long flight you're unlikely to be at your most alert.

Occasionally tourists (especially those travelling solo) are drugged and robbed on train or bus journeys. Unwary travellers are

---

ABOUT TOUTS

Rajasthan, Delhi and Agra are magnets for touts, all vying for your cash. Their natural habitats are airport terminals and bus or train stations, waiting to snare the fresh (most vulnerable) arrivals. Often they're rickshaw- or taxi-wallahs. Some try to gauge your vulnerability by enquiring whether it's your first trip to India – say it isn't. Their goal is to divert you to a hotel where they earn commission. Some hotels refuse to pay touts and you'll more often than not hear stories about those places being 'full', 'under renovation', 'closed' or whatever. Nine times out of 10 they'll be just that – stories. Think twice before agreeing to stay in any hotel recommended by a tout, as you'll be paying through the nose for your accommodation.

befriended, offered a spiked drink (to send them to sleep) and their valuables are then stolen. It's wise to politely decline drinks or food offered by relative strangers (use your instincts), particularly if you're alone.

Unfortunately, some travellers make their money go further by helping themselves to other people's – take care. For stolen or lost travellers cheques, contact the Amex or Thomas Cook office in the closest capital city – to locate nationwide branches contact their Delhi offices (p91).

Holi Festival

Although the Holi festival (p360) is mostly good fun, there have been incidences of people being doused with toxic substances mixed in water, sometimes leaving them with scars. During Holi, there's also a tradition of guzzling alcohol and consuming cannabis-derived bhang in the form of lassis, pakoras and cookies. Female travellers have been groped by spaced-out blokes – particularly in touristy areas. Officials advise women to avoid venturing onto the streets alone during Holi.

Other Important Warnings

Gem scams are a major problem in Rajasthan, especially in Jaipur (see p154) and Agra (p133), and many people have been conned by dealers who convince them to part with large sums of money for gems to resell at home. The gems are usually overpriced and often valueless.

Be careful using credit cards when shopping. If you're told that the merchant won't forward the credit slip for payment until you've received the goods, don't believe a word of it. No trader will send you as much as a postcard until they have received the full amount for the goods. Don't let your credit card be taken out the back to be processed – make sure transactions take place in front of you to avoid multiple imprints of your card by unscrupulous traders.

Precautions

A good travel-insurance policy is essential. If you have something stolen, report it immediately to the police. Ensure you get a statement proving you have done so – essential if you want to make an insurance claim. Note that some policies require you to report a theft to the police within a certain amount of time after you realise you've been robbed.

It's a good idea to keep photocopies of your important documents (passport, insurance documents etc) in a separate place, in case they do get pinched.

Always keep a stash of emergency cash in case you lose your travellers cheques, and in that same place (ie separate from your travellers cheques) keep a record of the cheques' serial numbers, proof-of-purchase slips, encashment vouchers and your photocopied passport details (data and visa pages).

To rapidly replace lost travellers cheques you need the proof-of-purchase slip and the numbers of the missing cheques (some places require a photocopy of the police report and a passport photo). If you don't have the cheque numbers, Amex (or whichever company has issued them) will contact the place where you bought them.

DISCOUNT CARDS
Senior Cards

For those aged over 65, Indian Airlines offers 50% discount on domestic air travel and Jet Airways offers 25% discount. Discounts on other air carriers may emerge as competition among airlines increases (ask travel agents). However, cut-price fares on budget airlines may well be cheaper than discounted full fares. If you're over 60 you're entitled to a 30% discount on train travel.

Student & Youth Cards

Student cards are of limited use nowadays – many student concessions have either been eliminated or replaced by 'youth fares' or other age concessions. Hostels run by the Indian Youth Hostels Association are part of the Hostelling International (HI) network; an HI card entitles you to standard discount rates. Members of YMCA/YWCA are also entitled to standard discounts on accommodation.

Foreigners aged below 30 receive a 25% discount on full-price domestic air tickets. Again, standard fares on budget airlines may be cheaper still.

EMBASSIES & HIGH COMMISSIONS
Indian Embassies & High Commissions

The following represent just some of India's missions around the world. For comprehensive contact details see www.meaindia .nic.in (click on the 'Missions and Posts Abroad' link).

Apart from the main mission, there are Indian consulates in many countries – inquire locally for these.

Australia (☎ 02-6273 3999; www.hcindia-au.org; 3-5 Moonah Place, Yarralumla, ACT 2600)

Bangladesh (☎ 02-9889339; http://199.236.117.161; House 2, Rd 142, Gulshan I, Dhaka)

Bhutan (☎ 02-322162; www.eoithimphu.org; India House Estate, Thimphu)

Canada (☎ 613-744 3751; www.hciottawa.ca; 10 Springfield Rd, Ottawa, Ontario K1M 1C9)

France (☎ 01 40 50 70 70; www.amb-inde.fr; 15 Rue Alfred Dehodencq, 75016 Paris)

Germany (☎ 030-257950; www.indianembassy.de; Tiergartenstrasse 17, 10785, Berlin)

Ireland (☎ 01-497 0843; www.indianembassy.ie; 6 Leeson Park, Dublin 6)

Israel (☎ 03-5291999; www.indembassy.co.il; 140 Hayarkon St, Tel Aviv – 61033)

Italy (☎ 064 88 46 42; www.indianembassy.it; Via XX Settembre 5, 00187 Rome)

Japan (☎ 0332 622 391; www.embassyofindiajapan.org; 2-2-11 Kudan Minami, Chiyoda-ku, Tokyo 1020074)

Myanmar (Burma; ☎ 01-240633; www.indiaembassy .net.mm; 545-547 Merchant St, Yangon)

Nepal (☎ 014 410900; www.south-asia.com/embassy -india; 336 Kapurdhara Marg, Kathmandu)

The Netherlands (☎ 0703 46 97 71; www.indian embassy.nl; Buitenrustweg 2, 2517 KD, The Hague)

New Zealand (☎ 04-473 6390; www.hicomind.org.nz; 180 Molesworth St, Wellington)

Pakistan (☎ 0512 206950; G5, Diplomatic Enclave, Islamabad)

Sri Lanka (☎ 012 421605; www.hcicolombo.org; 36-38 Galle Rd, Colombo 3)

Thailand (☎ 0 2258 0300; www.indianembassy.gov .in/bangkok; 46 Soi Prasarnmitr, Soi 23, Sukhumvit Rd, Bangkok 10110)

UK (☎ 020-7836 8484; www.hcilondon.net; India House, Aldwych, London WC2B 4NA)

USA (☎ 202-939 9806; www.indianembassy.org; 2536 Massachusetts Ave NW, Washington DC 20008)

Embassies & High Commissions in India

Most missions operate from 9am to 5pm Monday to Friday (some close between 1pm and 2pm).

If your country's mission is not listed below, that doesn't necessarily mean it's not represented in India – see the local phone directory, *Delhi Diary* magazine, or call one of the missions listed here for relevant contact details.

The following are located in Delhi:

Australia (Map pp102-3; ☎ 011-41399900; www .ausgovindia.com; 1/50G Shantipath, Chanakyapuri)

Bangladesh (Map pp92-3; ☎ 011-24121389; www .bhcdelhi.org; EP39 Dr Radakrishnan Marg, Chanakyapuri)

Bhutan (Map pp102-3; ☎ 011-26889230; Chandragupta Marg, Chanakyapuri)

Canada (Map pp102-3; ☎ 011-41782000; www.dfait -maeci.gc.ca/new-delhi; 7/8 Shantipath, Chanakyapuri)

France (Map pp102-3; ☎ 011-24196100; www.france -in-india.org; 2/50E Shantipath, Chanakyapuri)

Germany (Map pp102-3; ☎ 011-26871831; www .new-delhi.diplo.de; 6/50G Shantipath, Chanakyapuri)

Ireland (Map pp102-3; ☎ 011-24626741; www.ireland inindia.com; 230 Jor Bagh)

Israel (Map pp102-3; ☎ 011-30414500; www.delhi .mfa.gov.il; 3 Aurangzeb Rd)

Italy (Map pp102-3; ☎ 011-26114355; www.amb newdelhi.esteri.it; 50E Chandragupta Marg, Chanakyapuri)

Japan (Map pp102-3; ☎ 011-26876564; www.in.emb -japan.go.jp; 50G Shantipath, Chanakyapuri)

Malaysia (Map pp102-3; ☎ 011-26111291; www .kln.gov.my/perwakilan/newdelhi; 50M Satya Marg, Chanakyapuri)

Myanmar (Burma; Map pp102-3; ☎ 011-24678822; 3/50F Nyaya Marg, Chanakyapuri)

Nepal (Map pp102-3; ☎ 011-23327361; Barakhamba Rd)

The Netherlands (Map pp102-3; ☎ 011-24197600; www.holland-in-india.org; 6/50F Shantipath, Chanakyapuri)

New Zealand (Map pp92-3; ☎ 011-26883170; www .nzembassy.com; 50N Nyaya Marg, Chanakyapuri)

Pakistan (Map pp102-3; ☎ 011-24676004; 2/50G Shantipath, Chanakyapuri)

Singapore (Map pp92-3; ☎ 011-46000915; www .mfa.gov.sg/newdelhi; E6 Chandragupta Marg, Chanakyapuri)

South Africa (Map pp92-3; ☎ 011-26149411; www .sahc-india.com; B18 Vasant Marg, Vasant Vihar)

Sri Lanka (Map pp102-3; ☎ 011-23010201; www .slmfa.gov.lk; 27 Kautilya Marg, Chanakyapuri)

Switzerland (Map pp102-3; ☎ 011-26878372; www .eda.admin.ch; Nyaya Marg, Chanakyapuri)

Thailand (Map pp102-3; ☎ 011-26118104; www .thaiemb.org.in; 56N Nyaya Marg, Chanakyapuri)

UK (Map pp102-3; ☎ 011-24192100; www.ukindia .com; Shantipath, Chanakyapuri)

USA (Map pp102-3; ☎ 011-24198000; http://newdelhi .usembassy.gov; Shantipath, Chanakyapuri)

FESTIVALS & EVENTS

Rich in religion and tradition, Rajasthan has scores of vibrant festivals. Most holidays and festivals follow either the Indian lunar calendar (a complex system determined by astrologers) or the Islamic calendar (which falls about 11 days earlier each year; 12 days earlier in leap years), and therefore change annually relative to the Gregorian calendar. The India-wide holidays and festivals listed here are arranged according to the Indian lunar (and Gregorian) calendar which starts in Chaitra (March or April) – contact local tourist offices for exact festival dates, as many are variable.

Many festivals in India occur during Purnima (full moon), which is traditionally auspicious.

The 'wedding season' generally falls between the cooler months of November and March (the dates revolve around auspicious timings set by astrologers). During this period you're likely to see at least one wedding procession on the street, which will be a merry mix of singing, dancing and a loud brass band.

The following represent major national festivals – for more details about regional ones see the Festivals in… boxed texts at the beginning of individual chapters.

Chaitra (March/April)

Mahavir Jayanti Jain festival commemorating the birth of Mahavira, the founder of Jainism.

Ramanavami Hindus celebrate the birth of Rama. In the week leading up to Ramanavami, the Ramayana is read and performed.

Easter This Christian holiday marks the Crucifixion and Resurrection of Christ.

Eid-Milad-un-Nabi An Islamic festival celebrating the birth of the Prophet Mohammed.

Vaisakha (April/May)

Muharram This 10-day Muslim festival commemorates the martyrdom of Imam Hussain, the Prophet Mohammed's grandson.

Baisakhi A Sikh festival commemorating the day that Guru Gobind Singh founded the Khalsa, the Sikh brotherhood. The Guru Granth Sahib, the Sikh holy book, is read at gurdwaras (Sikh temples). Feasts and dancing follow.

Buddha Jayanti This 'triple-blessed festival' falls on the full moon (usually in May, sometimes in late April or early June) and celebrates Buddha's birth, enlightenment and attainment of nirvana.

Jyaistha (May/June)

No major festivals currently fall during this period.

Asadha (June/July)

No major festivals currently fall during this period.

Sravana (July/August)

Naag Panchami This Hindu festival is dedicated to Ananta, the serpent upon whose coils Vishnu rested between universes. Snake charmers do a roaring trade.

Raksha Bandhan (Narial Purnima) On the full-moon day girls fix amulets known as *rakhis* to the wrists of their (not necessarily blood-related) brothers to protect them in the coming year. The brothers reciprocate with gifts.

Bhadra (August/September)

Independence Day This public holiday on 15 August marks the anniversary of India's Independence in 1947.

Drukpa Teshi The first teaching given by Buddha is celebrated during this festival.

Ganesh Chaturthi This joyful festival marks the birth of the popular elephant-headed god, Ganesh. On the last day of the festival clay idols of Ganesh are paraded through the streets before being ceremoniously immersed in a river, sea or tank.

Janmastami The anniversary of Krishna's birth is celebrated with happy abandon – in tune with Krishna's own mischievous moods. Devotees fast all day until midnight.

Shravan Purnima On this day of fasting, high-caste Hindus replace the sacred thread that they wear looped over their left shoulder.

Pateti Parsis celebrate their new year at this time.

Ramadan (Ramazan) This 30-day dawn-to-dusk fast marks the ninth month of the Islamic calendar, the month during which the Prophet Mohammed had the Quran revealed to him in Mecca. This festival moves forward 11 days each year and is due to begin in late September in 2008, 22 August 2009 and 11 August in 2010.

Asvina (September/October)

Navratri (Festival of Nine Nights) For nine happy nights, this Hindu festival leading up to Dussehra is dedicated to the goddess Durga, who valiantly beheaded a menacing demon. Goddesses Lakshmi and Saraswati, of wealth and learning respectively, also get special praise. During the day Hindus take part in rituals, fasting and prayer. Then after sundown there's often tabla-accompanied *dandiya raas* (folk dancing with sticks). Some regions also have nightly *garbas* (folk dances without the sticks).

Dussehra (Durga Puja) This festival celebrates Durga's victory over the buffalo-headed demon Mahishasura. In many places it culminates with the burning of huge images of the demon king Ravana and his accomplices, symbolic of the triumph of good over evil. In Delhi (and elsewhere) it's also known as Ram Lila (Life Story of Rama), with fireworks and re-enactments of the Ramayana. It's particularly spectacular in Kota.

Gandhi Jayanti This public holiday is a solemn celebration of Mohandas (Mahatma) Gandhi's birthday on 2 October with prayer meetings at the Raj Ghat in Delhi, where he was cremated.

DIRECTORY

Eid al-Fitr This feast celebrates the end of Ramadan; festivities continue for three days.

Kartika (October/November)

Diwali This is the happiest festival of the Hindu calendar, celebrated on the 15th day of Kartika. At night decorative oil lamps are lit to show Rama the way home from his period of exile. The festival is also dedicated to the goddesses Lakshmi and Kali. In all, it lasts five days. On the first day, houses are thoroughly cleaned and doorsteps are decorated with intricate *rangolis* (chalk/powder designs). Day two is dedicated to Krishna's victory over Narakasura, a legendary tyrant. Day three is spent worshipping Lakshmi. Traditionally, this is the beginning of the new financial year for companies. Day four commemorates the visit of the friendly demon Bali whom Vishnu put in his place. On the fifth day men visit their sisters to have an auspicious tikka put on their forehead. Giving sweets has become as much a part of Diwali as the lighting of oil lamps and firecrackers.

Govardhana Puja A Hindu festival dedicated to the holy cow.

Aghan (November/December)

Nanak Jayanti The birthday of Guru Nanak, the founder of Sikhism, is celebrated with prayer readings and processions.

Eid al-Adha This Islamic occasion commemorates the Prophet Ibrahim's readiness to obey god even to the point of sacrificing his son.

Pausa (December/January)

Christmas Day Christians celebrate the anniversary of the birth of Christ on 25 December.

Magha (January/February)

Republic Day This public holiday on 26 January celebrates the anniversary of India's establishment as a republic in 1950. Celebrations are held in Jaipur, but it's most spectacular in Delhi, where there's a military parade along Rajpath. As part of the same celebration, three days later a Beating of the Retreat ceremony takes place in Delhi.

Vasant Panchami Heralds the onset of spring. People worship Saraswati, goddess of wisdom and knowledge, on this day, and make floral offerings, dress in yellow, cook yellow rice and exchange yellow sweets — yellow represents the ripening of the spring crops. It's held on the 5th day of Magha.

Phalguna (February/March)

Holi This is one of the most exuberant Hindu festivals, when people celebrate the beginning of spring by throwing coloured water and *gulal* (powder) at one another. Don't wear good clothes, be ready to duck, and expect to look like a *gulab jamun* (a red, sticky sweet) at the end of the day (women see also p357). Udaipur and Jaisalmer are both excellent venues to celebrate Holi. On the night before Holi, bonfires are built to symbolise the destruction of the evil demon Holika.

Muharram An Islamic festival commemorating the martyrdom of the Prophet Mohammed's grandson, Imam.

Shivaratri This day of Hindu fasting is dedicated to Shiva, who danced the *tandava* (cosmic dance) on this day. Temple processions are followed by the chanting of mantras and anointing of lingams (phallic symbols).

FOOD

Sampling India's amazing cuisine is an adventure in itself. For comprehensive coverage of Rajasthan's culinary scene see p64.

GAY & LESBIAN TRAVELLERS

As with relations between heterosexual Western couples travelling in Rajasthan – both married and unmarried – gay and lesbian travellers should exercise discretion and refrain from displaying overt affection towards each other in public. For more information see p41.

The Mumbai publication *Bombay Dost* is a gay and lesbian magazine available at a limited number of bookshops and newsstands in Delhi.

For further information about India's gay scene, there are some excellent websites, including **Gay Bombay** (www.gaybombay.org), **Humsafar** (www.humsafar.org) and the Delhi-based **Humrahi** (www.geocities.com/WestHollywood/Heights/7258).

HOLIDAYS

In India there are three national public holidays: Republic Day (26 January), Independence Day (15 August) and Gandhi Jayanti (2 October). There are usually also holidays during major festivals (sometimes only followed by certain religious denominations), which include Diwali, Dussehra and Holi (all

---

BEWARE OF THOSE BHANG LASSIS!

Although it's rarely printed in menus, some restaurants in Rajasthan clandestinely whip up bhang lassi, a yogurt and iced-water beverage laced with bhang, a derivative of marijuana. Commonly dubbed 'special lassi', this often potent concoction doesn't agree with everyone. Some travellers have been stuck in bed for several miserable days after drinking it; others have become delirious.

REGIONAL FESTIVAL CALENDAR

Look at the Festivals in... boxed texts at the beginning of each regional chapter for detailed coverage. Following is a quick reference for dates of the major regional fairs and festivals up to the year 2010:

Festival & location	2008	2009	2010
Nagaur Fair (p301), Nagaur	13-16 Feb	2-5 Feb	22-25 Feb
Baneshwar Fair (p224), Baneshwar	17-21 Feb	5-9 Feb	26-30 Jan
Jaisalmer Desert Festival (p301), Jaisalmer	19-21 Feb	7-9 Feb	28-30 Jan
Brij Festival (p185), Bharatpur	2-4 Feb	2-4 Feb	2-4 Feb
Elephant Festival (p148), Jaipur	21 Mar	10 Mar	28-30 Feb
Kaila Devi (p185), Karauli	8-9 Apr	29-30 Mar	18-19 Mar
Shri Mahavirji Fair (p185), Chandangaon	14-20 Apr	3-9 Apr	24-30 Apr
Gangaur (p148), Jaipur	8-10 Apr	29-31 Mar	18-20 Mar
Mewar Festival (p224), Udaipur	3 Apr	23 Mar	12 Mar
Summer Festival (p224), Mt Abu	18-20 May	7-9 May	26-28 Mar
Teej (p148), Jaipur	4-5 Aug	24-25 Jul	12-13 Aug
Kajli Teej (p224), Bundi	18-19 Aug	8-9 Aug	26-27 Aug
Ramdevra Fair (p301), Ramdevra	9-10 Sep	29-30 Aug	17-18 Sep
Dussehra (p224), Kota	7-9 Oct	26-28 Sep	15-17 Oct
Marwar Festival (p301), Jodhpur	13-14 Oct	3-4 Oct	21-22 Oct
Pushkar Camel Fair (p209), Pushkar	5-13 Nov	25 Oct-2 Nov	13-21 Nov
Chandrabhaga Fair (p224), Jhalrapatan	12-14 Nov	1-3 Nov	20-22 Nov
Kolayat Fair (p301), Kolayat	9-18 Nov	29 Oct-7 Nov	17-26 Nov

three are Hindu), Nanak Jayanti (Sikh), Eid al-Fitr (Islamic), Mahavir Jayanti (Jain), Buddha Jayanti (Buddhist) and Easter and Christmas (Christian). For dates see above.

Most businesses (offices, shops etc) and tourist sites close on public holidays. Apart from more crowding, public transport tends to remain unaffected during festivals. Remember that accommodation at festival destinations can be difficult to get and room rates increase dramatically. It's wise to make reservations well in advance if you intend visiting during major festivals. You'll also need to book train tickets well in advance.

INSURANCE

A travel insurance policy to cover theft, loss and medical problems is wise – health insurance is vital (see p386). Be aware that some policies specifically exclude dangerous activities, which can include trekking. There is a wide variety of policies available, so check the small print.

If you have to make a claim later, ensure you keep all documentation. Check that the policy covers an emergency flight home. Note that it is crucial to get a police report if you've had anything stolen, as insurance companies may refuse to reimburse you without one.

INTERNET ACCESS

Most travellers make constant use of internet cafés and free web-based email such as Yahoo (www.yahoo.com) or Hotmail (www.hotmail.com).

If you're travelling with a notebook or hand-held computer, be aware that your modem may not work once you leave your home country. The safest option is to buy a reputable 'global' modem before you leave home, or buy a local PC-card modem if you're spending an extended time in any one country. For more information on travelling with a portable computer, see www.teleadapt.com.

Internet outlets in Rajasthan are spreading fast – most towns have email facilities and so do most midrange hotels. In bigger towns there are usually several broadband cafés. It usually costs around Rs 10 to 60 per hour. Some places enforce a minimum time of 15 minutes.

See also p21 for internet resources.

LAUNDRY

Unless a hotel has its own in-house laundry, your clothes will be washed by a dhobi-wallah. You hand over your dirty clothes in the morning and you'll usually get them back washed and pressed that same evening for a minimal cost. If you don't think your gear will stand up to being thrashed clean, then hand wash them yourself or give them to a drycleaner. Washing powder can be bought cheaply in small sachets all over the place.

LEGAL MATTERS

If you find yourself in a sticky legal predicament, contact your embassy (see p357). Travellers are subject to Indian laws and in the Indian justice system it can often seem that the burden of proof is on the accused.

You should carry your passport at all times, and the less you have to do with local police the better. If you are asked for a bribe the prevailing wisdom is to pay it, as the alternative can be a trumped up prosecution. Again it's better to avoid any situation where you might be asked for a bribe.

Drugs

India has long been known for its smorgasbord of illegal drugs, but would-be users should be aware of the severe risks. Apart from opening yourself up to being taken advantage of by dealers and/or police, if convicted on a drugs-related charge, sentences are for a *minimum* of 10 years and there is no remission or parole. Cases can take several years to appear before a court while the accused waits, locked up. In addition, there's usually a hefty monetary fine. The police have been getting particularly tough on drugs-related issues involving foreigners so you should take the risk seriously.

Smoking

The Indian government has banned smoking in public places in Delhi. Transgressors face a mere Rs 100 fine, which probably accounts for the ban's limited success.

MAPS

There is a dearth of high-quality maps in India. Some of the better possibilities include TTK's Discover India series, which has a number of state, regional and city maps. Eicher produces an excellent *Delhi* street atlas, as well as useful foldaway city maps. The Survey of India publishes decent city, state and country maps, while the Indian Map Service has a *Rajasthan* road atlas (based on Survey of India maps). There's also the *Rajasthan Road Atlas,* published by Anada Sahitya Prakashan and Gyan Vigyan Prakashan, which has 1:600,000 maps of each district. Nelles Maps

publishes a *Western India* map, which has pretty good coverage of Rajasthan, but it can be hard to find in India. All these maps are stocked at good bookshops and some modern petrol stations.

Throughout Rajasthan, tourist offices stock local maps, which are often dated and lacking in essential detail, but they're still reasonably useful for general orientation.

MONEY

The rupee (Rs) is divided into 100 paise (p). There are coins of five, 10, 20, 25 and 50 paise and Rs 1, 2 and 5, and notes of Rs 10, 20, 50, 100, 500 and 1000.

Whenever you change money, take your time and check each note even if the wad appears to have been stapled together. Some bills look quite similar, so check them carefully. Don't accept any filthy, ripped or disintegrating notes, as you'll have difficulty in getting people to accept these (you can change them at the Reserve Bank of India as a last resort). Remember, you must present your passport whenever changing currency and travellers cheques.

It can be difficult to use large denomination notes because of a seemingly perpetual lack of change in shops, taxis etc, so it's a good idea to maintain a constant stock of smaller currency.

For information about costs, read p19. See inside the front cover for exchange rates.

Outside Rajasthan's main cities, the State Bank of Bikaner & Jaipur (SBBJ) or the State Bank of India (SBI) are usually the places to change money. In the more remote regions, few banks offer exchange facilities, so use banks in the main tourist centres before heading out into the desert – although you'll have no trouble changing money at Bikaner or Jaisalmer.

ATMs

Twenty-four hour ATMs linked to international networks are common in many places in Rajasthan. This means that travellers can now rely on debit cards as a primary cash source. A cash or travellers cheque back-up is recommended in case you lose or break your card, or if ATMs are temporarily out of order – a fairly regular annoyance, especially in smaller towns. You shouldn't rely on ATMs as your sole source of cash if you're planning to travel beyond the larger towns or away from tourist centres, as they either won't be available, or may not accept foreign cards. Alternatively, ensure you withdraw adequate cash from ATMs in big cities before striking out into the outback.

ATMs usually accept Cirrus, Maestro, MasterCard, Plus and Visa (but not always all cards). Banks in India that currently accept foreign cards include Citibank, HDFC, ICICI, UTI, HSBC, SBI, Standard Chartered, IDBI, SBBJ and Corporation Bank.

Your bank is likely to impose higher charges on international transactions, so once in India it's generally more economical to withdraw big amounts of money at once rather than make lots of small transactions. *Always* check in advance with your home bank whether your card can indeed access banking networks in India and, if so, what the charge per transaction is and whether they have schemes to minimise these.

Several travellers have reported ATMs snatching back money if you don't remove it within around 30 seconds. Conversely, some people have said that machines can take more than 30 seconds to release cash, so don't hastily abandon the ATM assuming something has gone wrong.

The ATMs listed in this book's regional chapters all accept foreign cards (but not necessarily all types of cards). Keep the emergency lost and stolen numbers for credit cards in a safe place and report any loss or theft immediately.

Cash
It's no problem changing money in bigger towns. However, it's advisable to have some US dollars or pounds sterling (the most widely accepted currencies) in cash in case you're unable to change travellers cheques or use a credit card, especially in smaller places.

Credit Cards
Most major cities and tourist centres accept credit cards, with MasterCard and Visa being the most widely accepted. Cash advances on major credit cards can be made at various banks (although rarely in smaller towns). For details about whether you can access home accounts in India, inquire at your bank before leaving.

Credit cards are accepted at almost all top-end hotels and at some midrange ones, but it's rare that budget hotels and restaurants accept them. Regularly check your banking online for errant transactions which should be reported to your credit-card company as soon as possible.

Encashment Certificates
By law, foreign currency must be changed at official moneychangers or banks, which give you an encashment certificate (a money-exchange receipt that is valid for three months). They are required to re-exchange rupees exceeding Rs 10,000 into foreign currency when departing India. Encashment certificates are also needed for tax clearance certificates (below). Some shipping agents may request them as well.

International Transfers
Naturally it's preferable not to run out of money but, if you do, you can have money transferred in no time at all (at a charge of course) via Thomas Cook's Moneygram service or at Western Union, both of which have branches throughout India. To collect cash, you need to bring along your passport and the name and reference number of the person who sent the funds.

Moneychangers
Usually open for longer hours than the banks, private moneychangers are a convenient option and are virtually everywhere. However, it pays to check the bank rates first, and as with anywhere, check you are given the correct amount.

Security
The safest place for your money and your passport is next to your skin, in a moneybelt or pouch. Never, ever carry these things in your luggage or a shoulder bag. Bum bags are not recommended either, as they advertise that you have a stash of goodies. Never leave your valuable documents and travellers cheques in your hotel room (including under your mattress). If the hotel is a reputable one, you should be able to use the hotel safe.

It's wise to peel off at least US$100 and keep it stashed away separately from your main horde, just in case.

Finally, separate your big notes from your small ones so you don't display large wads of cash when paying for things.

Tax Clearance Certificates
If you have a visa enabling you to stay in India for more than six months, you must

technically get a tax clearance certificate to leave the country. This is to prove that you financed your stay in India with your own money rather than through working in the country. For details, contact a local Foreigners' Regional Registration Office (in Delhi or Jaipur). You'll need to show your passport, visa extension form, any other appropriate paperwork and a bunch of bank encashment certificates.

Tipping, Baksheesh & Bargaining

In tourist restaurants or hotels, where a service fee (amounts vary regionally) is usually already added on to your bill, tipping is optional. In smaller places, where there is no service fee, a tip is appreciated. Hotel and train porters expect around Rs 20 to carry bags, and hotel staff also expect around the same to provide services above and beyond the call of duty. It's not mandatory to tip taxi or autorickshaw drivers.

Baksheesh can be defined as a 'tip'. Baksheesh also refers to giving alms to beggars. Many Indians implore tourists not to hand out sweets, pens or money to children, as it's positive reinforcement to beg. Instead you may prefer to donate to a school or charitable organisation (see Volunteer Work, p369).

Apart from at fixed-price shops, bargaining is the norm in India – see The Art of Haggling, below.

Travellers Cheques

All major brands are accepted in India, with Amex and Thomas Cook being the most widely traded. Pounds sterling and US dollars are the safest bet, especially beyond the major cities. Charges for changing travellers cheques vary from place to place and bank to bank.

If you lose your cheques, contact the Amex or Thomas Cook office in the closest capital city – to find details of branches nationwide contact their offices in Delhi (p91).

PHOTOGRAPHY

For useful tips and techniques on travel photography, read Lonely Planet's *Guide to Travel Photography; Travel Photography: Landscapes;* and *Travel Photography: People & Portraits.*

Digital processing and memory cards are available from photographic shops in the larger cities and most tourist destinations. Internet cafés will generally download images onto DVD and CD (for around Rs 100).

Colour print film-processing facilities are still readily available in most Indian cities. You'll only find colour slide film available in

---

THE ART OF HAGGLING

Haggling is a must in most parts of India. Shopkeepers in tourist hubs are accustomed to travellers who have lots of money and little time to spend it. It's not unusual to be charged at least double, or even triple the 'real' price.

So how do you know if you're being overcharged and need to strike back with some serious haggling? Well, you're safe in government emporiums, cooperatives and modern shopping complexes, where the prices are usually fixed. But in most other shops that cater primarily to tourists, be prepared to don your haggling hat. The kind of places that usually fall into this category include handicraft, carpet, painting, souvenir and clothing shops.

The first 'rule' to haggling is never to show too much interest in the item you want to buy. Secondly, don't buy the first item that takes your fancy. Wander around and price things, but don't make it obvious. Otherwise if you return to the first shop the vendor will know it's because they are the cheapest.

Decide how much you would be happy paying and then express a casual interest in buying. If you have absolutely no idea of what something should really cost, start by slashing the price by half (even more in touristy spots). This is usually completely unacceptable to the vendor but it works as a good starting point to haggle for a happy compromise. You'll find that many shopkeepers lower their so-called 'final price' if you proceed to head out of the shop saying you'll 'think about it'.

Haggling is a way of life in India, but it should never turn ugly. Keep in mind exactly how much a rupee is worth in your home currency so you don't lose perspective, and if a vendor seems to be charging an unreasonably high price and is unwilling to negotiate, simply look elsewhere.

the major cities. Always check the use-by date on all film stock.

Restrictions

India is touchy about photographs being taken of places of military importance – this can include train stations, bridges, airports, military installations and sensitive border regions.

Places of worship (temples and mosques) may prohibit photography. If in doubt, ask.

PHOTOGRAPHING PEOPLE

Some people are more than happy to be photographed, but care should be taken in pointing cameras at people, especially women. Again, if in doubt, ask. A zoom is a less intrusive means of taking portraits – even when you've obtained permission to take a portrait, shoving a lens in your subject's face can be disconcerting. A reasonable distance between you and your subject will help reduce your subject's discomfort, and will result in more natural shots.

POST

Indian postal and poste restante services are generally good. Expected letters almost always arrive and letters you send do invariably reach their destination, though they may take up to three weeks. Even though the Indian postal system is fairly reliable, don't count on a letter or package getting through if there's anything of market value inside it. Amex in major city locations offers an alternative to the poste restante system for holders of Amex cards.

Some cities have courier services (such as DHL) that can reliably arrange speedy air freight around the world; from Delhi DHL charges around Rs 2700 for 1kg to Australia, Europe or the USA.

Receiving Mail

Ask senders to address letters to you with your surname in capital letters and underlined, followed by poste restante, main post office and the city or town in question. Many 'lost' letters are simply misfiled under given (first) names, so always check under both your names. Also ask senders to provide a return address, just in case you don't collect your mail. Letters sent via poste restante are generally held for one month before being returned. To claim mail, you'll need to show your passport. It's best to have any parcels sent to you by registered post.

Sending Mail

Posting aerogrammes/postcards overseas costs Rs 8.50/8 and for airmail letters the cost is Rs 15. For postcards, it's not a bad idea to stick on the stamps *before* writing on them. This is because post offices can give you as many as four stamps per card, which can cover up your carefully composed missive.

Posting parcels is quite straightforward, and prices vary depending on the weight. The parcel counter usually closes in the early afternoon, so if you want to send something, it's best to go to the post office in the morning. In the main cities, there's usually a person at the post office who sews parcels up in cheap linen. The post office will have the necessary customs declaration forms. To avoid paying duty at the delivery end, specify that the contents are a 'gift' under the value of Rs 1000.

Parcel post has a maximum of 20kg to 30kg depending on the destination, and charges vary depending on whether it goes by air or sea. A 1kg parcel by air/sea costs Rs 570/450 to Australia, Rs 645/500 to Europe, and Rs 645/480 to the USA.

It is often cheaper to send packages under 2kg as registered letters. You also have the option of EMS (Express Mail Service; delivery within three days) for around 30% more than the airmail price.

Books or printed matter can go by book post (maximum 5kg), which is considerably cheaper than parcel post, but the package must be wrapped a certain way: make sure that it can be opened for inspection along the way, or that it's wrapped with the two ends exposed so that the contents are visible. A customs declaration form is usually not necessary. The overseas bookpost rates start at Rs 260 for 1kg to any international destination.

Be cautious with places that offer to mail things to your home address after you have bought them. Government emporiums are usually fine but in many other places it pays to do the posting yourself.

SHOPPING

Rajasthan (and Delhi) really is one of the easiest places to spend money, with its busy bazaars, colourful arts and crafts, gorgeous fabrics, miniature paintings, and much more. The cardinal rule is to bargain and bargain hard.

Be careful when purchasing items that include delivery to your home country. You may well be given assurances that the price includes all charges, but this is not always the case.

Be aware that sellers often claim that miniature paintings are antiques; this is rarely the case. For other important warnings also read p154.

Avoid buying products that further endanger threatened species and habitats. It's illegal to export ivory products or any artefact made from wild animals. Articles over 100 years old are not allowed to be exported from India without an export clearance certificate. If you have doubts about any item and think it could be defined as an antique, you can check with branches of the Archaeological Survey of India. In Delhi, contact the Director of Antiquities, **Archaeological Survey of India** (Map pp102-3; ☎ 011-23017443; Janpath; ☒ 9.30am-1.30pm & 2-6pm Mon-Fri), located next to the National Museum.

Detailed information on what is best to buy in each region is given in the regional chapters. For information on buying Rajasthani arts and crafts, see the Rajasthani Arts & Crafts chapter, p53.

SOLO TRAVELLERS

Perhaps the most significant issue facing solo travellers is cost. Single-room rates at guesthouses and hotels are sometimes not much lower than rates for a double; some midrange and top-end places don't even offer a single tariff, though you can try to bargain down the double rate.

If you tire of your own company, never fear: Rajasthan, Delhi and Agra are tourist hubs, so it's easy to meet other travellers – head for popular hotels and restaurants.

Although most solo travellers experience no major problems in India, remember that some (locals and travellers alike) may view lone tourists as an easy target for theft. Don't be paranoid, but, like anywhere in the world, it's wise to stay on your toes in unfamiliar surroundings.

For important information specific to women, see p371.

TELEPHONE

Even in the tiniest of towns you will find private call booths with direct local, interstate and international dialling (PCO/STD /ISD); these are invariably cheaper than calls made from hotels. A digital meter means you can keep an eye on what the call costs, and you receive a print-out when the call is finished.

Throughout most of India, interstate calls from booths (not hotels) charge the full rate from around 9am to 8pm. After 8pm the cost slides, with the cheapest time to call being between 11pm and 6am. Interstate calls are half rate on Sunday.

India's White Pages are found at www.india whitepages.com, and the Yellow Pages at www .indiayellowpages.com.

Domestic Calls

Telephone numbers in Rajasthan have an annoying tendency to change. Call ☎ 197 for local telephone-number inquiries. Reverse-charge (collect) operators can be reached on ☎ 186.

International Calls

Direct international calls from call booths (not hotels) cost an average of Rs 22 to 40 per minute depending on the destination. The cheapest international calls can be made through internet cafés using Net2phone, Skype or a similar service. Calls cost from as little as Rs 5 per minute.

In some centres PCO/STD/ISD booths may offer a 'call-back' service – you ring your folks or friends, give them the phone number of the booth and wait for them to call you back. The booth operator charges about Rs 5 to 10 per minute for this service, plus the cost of the preliminary call.

Mobile Phones

If you bring your mobile phone to India, you'll find local mobile networks are cheap to use and getting hooked up to the mobile phone network is straightforward. Calls (even international) are delightfully cheap by world standards.

In most towns you simply buy a prepaid mobile phone kit (SIM card and phone number) from any phone shop or other outlet, such as PCO/STD/ISD booths, internet cafés and grocery stores. The most popular (and reliable) companies are Airtel, Hutch, and BSNL.

The SIM card itself costs about Rs 150 but you usually pay for an additional amount of credit to get started. You then buy recharge cards (top-ups) from any phone shop for between Rs 100 and Rs 3400. Credit must usually be used (or topped up) within a fixed period (ie 15 to 60 days) and remember that the amount you pay for a credit top-up is not the amount you get on your phone – state taxes and service charges come off first, so for a top-up of Rs 500 you'll get around Rs 375 worth of calls. Note that with some networks, recharge cards are being replaced by direct credit, where you pay the vendor and the credit's deposited straight to your phone – ask which system is in use before you buy.

Calls made within the state/city where you bought the SIM card are cheap – less than Rs 1 per minute – and you can call internationally for less than Rs 25 per minute. SMS messaging is even cheaper. The more credit you have on your phone, the cheaper the call rate.

The downside to the whole thing is that the prepaid system is not truly national – major cities and all states have their own network, which means that your SIM card will work fine in the city/state you bought it, and you only pay for calls you make. If you move outside that network area you will have to ensure that it has roaming capabilities. Call rates are a little higher and you will be charged for incoming as well as outgoing calls.

Some travellers have reported difficulties in using their mobile even within states (either no coverage at all or frequent cut-offs). In addition, international texting is reliable on some days and not others.

As the mobile phone industry is an evolving one, mobile rates, suppliers and coverage are all likely to develop over the life of this book.

Phone Codes

To make a call *to* India from overseas, dial the international access code of the country you're in, then ☎ 91 (international country code for India), the area code (drop the initial 0; this zero only applies for calls made within India) and the local number. See this book's regional chapters for area codes.

To make an international call *from* India, dial ☎ 00 (international access code from India), then the country code (of the country you are calling), the area code and the local number.

Also available is the Home Country Direct service, which gives you access to the international operator in your home country. For the price of a local call, you can then make reverse-charge (collect) or phonecard calls. Some countries and their numbers:

Country	Number
Australia	☎ 0006117
Canada	☎ 00016788
Germany	☎ 0004917
Japan	☎ 0008117
The Netherlands	☎ 0003117
Singapore	☎ 0006517
Spain	☎ 0003417
UK	☎ 0004417
USA	☎ 000117

TIME

India is 5½ hours ahead of GMT/UTC, 4½ hours behind Australian Eastern Standard Time (EST) and 10½ hours ahead of American EST. The local standard time is known as IST (Indian Standard Time), although many affectionately dub it 'Indian Stretchable Time'.

TOILETS

Public toilets are generally confined to tourist sites (eg museums), upmarket shopping complexes and cinemas, but they can be scarce, and cleanliness is variable.

When it comes to effluent etiquette, it's customary to use your left hand and water, not toilet paper. A strategically placed tap, usually with a little plastic jug nearby, is available in most bathrooms. If you can't get used to the Indian method, bring your own toilet paper (widely available in towns). However, paper, sanitary napkins and tampons are going to further clog an already overloaded sewerage system. Often a bin is provided so that you can dispose of such items.

TOURIST INFORMATION
Local Tourist Offices

There are RTDC tourist offices (often called Tourist Reception Centres) in most places of interest in Rajasthan. Staff range from being extraordinarily helpful to useless and grumpy, but can almost always supply glossy brochures and local maps.

There is a **RTDC Tourist Reception Centre** (Map pp92-3; ☎ 011-3381 884; Tourist Reception Centre, Bikaner House, Pandara Rd, Delhi) in Delhi, and **Government of India tourist offices** (Delhi India Tourism Delhi; Map p100; ☎ 011-23320005; 88 Janpath, Delhi; Jaipur Map pp152-3; ☎ 0141-2372200; Hotel Khasa Kothi; ☟ 9am-6pm Mon-Fri) in Delhi and Jaipur.

Tourist Offices Abroad

The **Government of India** (Ministry of Tourism; www.in credibleindia.org) maintains tourist offices in other

DIRECTORY

countries where you can obtain brochures and leaflets. India tourist offices abroad:

Australia Sydney (☎ 02-9264 4855; info@indiatourism .com.au; Level 2, Piccadilly, 210 Pitt St, Sydney, NSW 2000)

Canada Toronto (☎ 416-962 3787; indiatourism@bellnet .ca; 60 Bloor St, West Suite 1003, Toronto, Ontario, M4W 3B8)

France Paris (☎ 01 45 23 30 45; intourparis@aol.com; 11-13 Blvd Haussmann, F-75009, Paris)

Germany Frankfurt am-Main (☎ 069-2429490; info@ india-tourism.com; Basolar Strasse 48, D-60329, Frankfurt am-Main 1)

Italy Milan (☎ 028 053 506; info@indiatourismmilan .com; Via Albricci 9, Milan 20122)

The Netherlands Amsterdam (☎ 0206 208 991; info .nl@india-tourism.com; Rokin 9/15, 1012 KK Amsterdam)

UK London (☎ 020-7437 3677; info@indiatouristoffice .org; 7 Cork St, London W1S 3LH)

USA Los Angeles (☎ 213-380 8855; indiatourismla@ aol.com; Room 204, 3550 Wiltshire Blvd, Los Angeles, CA 900102485); New York (☎ 212-586 4901; ad@itonyc.com; Suite 1808, 1270 Ave of the Americas, NY 100201700)

TOURS

The RTDC offers a range of package tours covering various destinations in Rajasthan, and including transport, accommodation (usually at RTDC hotels), sightseeing and guide; entry charges are extra. For more information, contact the **RTDC Tourist Reception Centre** (Map pp92-3; ☎ 011-3381884, 3383837; www.rajasthantourismindia .com; Bikaner House, Pandara Rd, Delhi, 110011).

Many travel agencies offer excursions in Rajasthan. One of the few outfits in Rajasthan that promotes sustainable tourism is **Alternative Travels** (☎ 01594-222239; Apani Dhani, Nawalgarh, Shekhawati). Ramesh Jangid of Alternative Travels can organise camel and cycling trips around the painted towns of Shekhawati, treks in the Aravalli Range and homestays with villagers, as well as tours elsewhere in India. For more details on his Rajasthan tours, see p280.

Other agencies:

Indo Vacations (Map pp152-3; ☎ 0141-9414312872; www.indien-reise.com in German; 312-6 Valmiki Rd, Raja Park, Jaipur)

Rajasthan Travel Service (Map pp152-3; ☎ 0141-2365408; www.rajasthantravelservice.com; ground fl, Ganpati Plaza, MI Rd, Jaipur)

Crown Tours (Map pp152-3; ☎ 2363310; Palace Rd, Jaipur)

Safaris

CAMEL SAFARIS

It's possible to take a camel safari lasting from an hour up to several weeks. Camel-safari central is Jaisalmer (see Jaisalmer Camel Safaris, p330), in western Rajasthan, and prices vary according to what is provided. Basic safaris start at about Rs 600 per person per day, which includes meals, but you pay more for greater comfort. You can also take safaris from Khuri (p336), near Jaisalmer. Bikaner (see Bikaner Camel Safaris, p343) is another centre, and many travellers head here to avoid the Jaisalmer hype (note you're more likely to travel by camel cart here, rather than on camelback). A less-visited area for camel trekking is that around Osiyan (p317), 65km from Jodhpur.

The Pushkar area (p210) is also popular, and a couple of operators in Shekhawati (p275) offer camel treks into the countryside, around towns full of interesting painted *havelis*.

HORSE & JEEP SAFARIS

Some hotels can arrange horse safaris – the best options are in Udaipur at the Kumbha Palace and Pratap Country Inn (see p248). The Dundlod Fort (p284), in Shekhawati, can arrange horse safaris for experienced riders – on spectacular Marwari horses – around the Shekhawati region and further afield.

For most horse safaris, you are required to bring your own riding hat and boots – call ahead to check. The best time to ride is during the cooler months (between mid-October and mid-March).

Quite a few hotels, particularly in western Rajasthan, offer jeep safaris, which are also usually available at palace hotels in remote regions. One-day jeep safaris to the Bishnoi villages (p314) around Jodhpur are another popular option.

WILDLIFE SAFARIS

The state's major wildlife sanctuaries are in eastern Rajasthan. Wildlife safaris are available by jeep at Sariska Tiger Reserve (p198) and at Ranthambhore National Park (p215). Another option at Ranthambhore is a trip in a canter (open-topped truck). At Keoladeo Ghana National Park (p188), motorised vehicles are prohibited, but you can see the park by cycle-rickshaw or bicycle.

TRAVEL PERMITS

Due to the hostilities between India and Pakistan, foreigners are prohibited from going within 50km of the India–Pakistan border (with the exception of those travelling to Pakistan on the *Thar Express* (p376). Special permission is required from the **District Magistrate** (☎ 02992-252201) in Jaisalmer to travel to most of Rajasthan west of National Highway No 15, and is only issued in exceptional circumstances. Places exempted are Amar Sagar, Bada Bagh, Lodhruva, Kuldhara, Akal, Sam, Ramkund, Khuri and Mool Sagar.

Permission is required from the **District Magistrate** (☎ 02982-220003) in Barmer to travel to Kiradu, which is about 35km from Barmer near the border with Pakistan.

TRAVELLERS WITH DISABILITIES

India's crowded public transport, crush of people in urban areas and variable infrastructure can test the hardiest traveller. If you have a physical disability or are vision impaired, these pose a greater challenge. However, seeing the way the mobility-impaired locals whiz through traffic in modified bicycles proves that nothing is impossible.

India has limited wheelchair-friendly hotels (mostly top end), restaurants and offices. Staircases are often steep. Footpaths, where they exist, are often riddled with holes, littered with debris and packed with pedestrians, severely hindering movement.

Try to prebook ground-floor hotel rooms and, if you use crutches, bring along spare rubber caps for the tips as they can wear down quickly in India.

If your mobility is considerably restricted you may like to consider travelling with an able-bodied companion. Additionally, hiring a car with a driver will make moving around a whole lot easier (see p379).

Organisations that may offer further advice include the **Royal Association for Disability and Rehabilitation** (RADAR; ☎ 020-7250 3222; www .radar.org.uk; 12 City Forum, 250 City Rd, London EC1V 8AF, UK) and **Mobility International USA** (MIUSA; ☎ 541-3431284; www.miusa.org; PO Box 10767, Eugene, OR 97440, USA).

VISAS

You must get a visa *before* arriving in India. Six-month multiple-entry tourist visas (valid from the date of issue) are issued to nationals of most countries (check visa options with the Indian embassy in your country) regardless of whether you intend staying that long or re-entering the country. Visas cost A$75 (an extra A$15 service fee applies at consulates)

for Australians, US$60 for US citizens and UK£30 for Britons.

You won't be issued a visa to enter India unless you hold an onward ticket, which is taken as sufficient evidence that you intend to leave the country.

Extended visas (up to five years) are possible for people of Indian descent (excluding those in Pakistan and Bangladesh) who hold a non-Indian passport and live abroad. A special People of Indian Origin (PIO) card is also possible (valid for 15 years). Contact your embassy (see p357) for more details.

Visa Extensions

Fourteen-day extensions are possible under exceptional circumstances from Foreigners' Regional Registration Offices (FRROs) in Jaipur and Delhi, but it's rare that you'll get an extension on a tourist via.

In Delhi, the **FRRO** (Map pp92-3; ☎ 011-26195530; Level 2, East Block 8, Sector 1, Rama Krishna Puram; ☯ 9.30am-1.30pm & 2-3pm Mon-Fri) is behind the Hyatt Regency hotel. Come here for visa extensions or replacement visas (if you've had your lost/stolen passport replaced).

For those with a good reason, the FRRO issues 14-day visa extensions, free for nationals of all countries except Japan (Rs 390), Sri Lanka (from Rs 135), Russia (Rs 1860) and Romania (Rs 500). Bring your confirmed air ticket, one passport photo and a photocopy of your passport (the information and visa pages).

VOLUNTEERING

Numerous charities and aid agencies have branches in India and, although they're mostly staffed by locals, there are some opportunities for foreigners. It's advisable to write in advance and, if you're needed, you'll be of far more use if you can commit enough time to be of help. A week on a hospital ward may salve your conscience, but you may do little more than get in the way of the people who work there long term.

Flexibility in the work you are prepared to do is also really vital. Some charities are inundated with requests from foreign volunteers who want to help babies in an orphanage, for instance, but few are willing to work with adults who have physical or mental disabilities. Know the level of work involved before you sign up and consider whether you are a good match for the organisation and its philosophy.

Overseas Volunteer Placement Agencies

For long-term posts, the following organisations may be able to advise:

Action Without Borders (☎ 212-8433973; www .idealist.org; Suite 1510, 360 West 31st St, New York, NY 10001, USA)

AidCamps International (☎ 020-8291 6181; www .aidcamps.org; 5 Simone Ct, Dartmouth Rd, London SE26 4RP, UK)

Australian Volunteers International (☎ 03-9279 1788; www.ozvol.org.au; PO Box 350, Fitzroy VIC 3065, Australia)

Co-ordinating Committee for International Voluntary Service (☎ 01 45 68 49 36; www.unesco .org/ccivs; Unesco House, 31 Rue François Bonvin, 75732 Paris Cedex 15, France)

Global Volunteers (☎ 651-407 6100; www.global volunteers.org; 375 East Little Canada Rd, St Paul, MN 55117-1628, USA)

Voluntary Service Overseas (VSO; ☎ 020-8780 7200; www.vso.org.uk; 317 Putney Bridge Rd, London SW15 2PN, UK)

Working Abroad (France office ☎ /fax 04-68 26 41 79; www.workingabroad.com; PO Box 454, Flat 1, Brighton, BN1 3ZS, East Sussex, UK)

Other useful sites:
- www.volunteerabroad.com
- www.ethicalvolunteering.org
- www.studyabroad.com
- www.responsibletravel.com

Programmes in Delhi & Rajasthan

Following are details of some of the programmes operating in Delhi and Rajasthan that may have volunteering opportunities available; contact them in advance rather than just turning up. Donations of money or clothing from travellers will also receive a warm welcome. Some nongovernmental organisations (NGOs) may also offer you volunteer work – for details visit www.india nngos.com.

Note that unless otherwise indicated, volunteers are always expected to cover their own costs, including accommodation, food and transport.

DELHI

There are two branches of Mother Teresa's Kolkata-based Missionaries of Charity in the Civil Lines area that welcome volunteers: **Shishu Bhavan** (Map pp92-3; ☎ 011-23950181; 12 Commissioners Lane) looks after infants (female volunteers only) while **Nirmal Hriday** (Map pp92-3;

☎ 011-23952180; 1 Magazine Rd) cares for the sick, destitute and dying.

Concern India Foundation (Map pp92-3; ☎ 011-26210997, delhi@concernindia.org; A-52 1st fl, Amar Colony, Lajpat Nagar 4) may be able to link volunteers with current projects – contact it in advance to ascertain possibilities.

SOS Children's Village (Map pp102-3; ☎ 011-24359450; www.soscvindia.org; A7 Nizammudin West) assists orphaned, abandoned and destitute children. Volunteers may be needed to teach English. You must apply in advance and a minimum three-month commitment is requested. See below for more information about SOS.

RAJASTHAN

Animal Aid Society (Map p242; ☎ 0294-3111435; www .animalaidunlimited.com; Chota Hawala Village, Udaipur) is an animal hospital that rescues and treats injured and destitute animals and sterilises street dogs. For more details see Animal Aid Society, p79.

The first organisation in Rajasthan to provide services under one roof for people living with cerebral palsy and other neural conditions, **Disha – Centre for Special Education, Vocational Training and Rehabilitation** (Map pp152-3; ☎ 0141-2393319, 2391690; disha_jaipur@hotmail.com; 450 AB Nirman Nagau, Kings Rd, Jaipur) provides special education, home management, staff training, counselling and advocacy. Volunteers from the fields of physiotherapy, speech therapy, special education, sports, arts and crafts and vocational counselling are welcomed.

The animal hospital **Help in Suffering** (HIS; Map pp152-3; ☎ 0141-2760803; www.his-india .org.au; Jaipur) welcomes qualified voluntary vets (three-/six-/12-month commitments). Write to: Help in Suffering, Maharani Farm, Durgapura, Jaipur 302018, Rajasthan. Visitors are welcome at the shelter in Jaipur, and donations are also gratefully accepted. For more information see Help in Suffering, p179.

The Jaipur branch of the **Indian National Trust for Art and Cultural Heritage** (Intach; Map pp152-3; ☎ 0141-2228275; www.intach.org; B14/A Bhawani Singh Rd, Jaipur) and Jaipur Virasat, a local heritage organisation linked to it, are working to preserve the vast cultural and physical heritage of Rajasthan's capital, and to increase awareness of heritage issues. You can volunteer to work in various capacities. The focus is on restoration and conservation work, but you can also help if you have skills in promotion, art or administration. You need to stay for a minimum of one month.

Les Amis du Shekhawati (Friends of Shekhawati; ☎ 01594-222239; www.apanidhani.com; Nawalgarh) aims to preserve Shekhawati's rich artistic heritage. The society's work includes educating villagers about the importance of the paintings, as well as promoting the region. You can be involved in painting restoration, promotion or teaching English or French to trainee guides. Architects who can help with creating a record of the *havelis* in Shekhawati will also be welcomed. Contact the society through Apani Dhani ecofarm.

The NGO **Marwar Medical & Relief Society** (☎ 0291-2545210, 2571620; Mandore Guest House; www .mandore.com; Mandore, Jodhpur) works to address drug-addiction problems and provide medical services in the Jodhpur district. It welcomes short-term volunteers for its Village Project.

Missionaries of Charity (Map pp152-3; ☎ 0141-2365804; Vardhman Path, C-Scheme, Jaipur), a branch of Mother Teresa's Kolkata-based order, provides a refuge for the destitute, many of whom are mentally ill or disabled.

Seva Mandir (☎ 0294-2450960; Old Fatehpura, Udaipur) develops natural resources, health promotion and literacy programmes. Volunteers can observe or participate in development work for a minimum of two weeks at this NGO.

SOS Worldwide runs more than 30 programmes across India. In Jaipur **SOS Children's Village** (Map pp152-3; ☎ 0141-2280262; Jhotwara Rd, Jaipur) looks after orphaned, destitute and abandoned children, who are cared for by unmarried women, abandoned wives and widows. Volunteers teach English and help the children with their homework. SOS also educates children (particularly girls) who come in for the day. The organisation only accepts volunteers prepared to commit for one year. You can also sponsor a child's education. SOS Children's Village is opposite the Petal Factory.

Urmul Trust (☎ 0151-2523093; Ganganagar Rd, Bikaner) provides primary health care and education to the people of around 500 villages in Rajasthan; raises awareness among the women of the desert of their rights and privileges in society; and promotes the handicrafts of rural artisans, with its profits going directly back to them. There is volunteer work (minimum one month) available in social welfare, teaching English, health care or possibly helping with implementation and overseeing of projects.

WOMEN TRAVELLERS
Attitudes Towards Women

India is a largely conservative country, and the clothing and culturally inappropriate behaviour of some travellers (not to mention Western TV programmes) seems to have had a ripple effect on the perception of foreign women in general. An increasing number of female travellers have reported some form of sexual harassment (predominantly lewd comments and groping) despite making a concerted effort to act and dress conservatively. While there's no need to be concerned to the point of paranoia, you should be aware that your behaviour and dress code is under scrutiny.

Rajasthan is usually a perfectly safe place for women travellers, even those travelling alone, but you will have to put up with some aggravation. Getting constantly stared at is, unfortunately, something you'll have to get used to. Just be thick-skinned and don't allow it to get the better of you. It's best to refrain from returning stares, as this may be considered a come-on; dark glasses can help. A good way to block out stares in restaurants is to take along a book or postcards to write home. Other harassment women have encountered include provocative gestures, jeering, groping and being followed. Exuberant special events (such as the Holi festival, p357) can be notorious for this.

Women travelling with a male partner are less likely to be harassed. However, a foreign woman of Indian descent travelling with a non-Indian male may cop disapproving stares; having a non-Indian partner is still not condoned in parts of India.

Ultimately, there are no sure-fire ways of shielding yourself from harassment, even for those who do everything 'right'. You're essentially going to have to use your judgment and instincts, as there isn't a blanket rule. If the warnings here make travel in India seem a little daunting, remember that most men are not out to bother you, and the problems mentioned here are just things to be aware of.

Clothing

Warding off sexual harassment is often a matter of common sense and culturally appropriate behaviour. What you wear helps enormously. Baggy clothing that hides the contours of your body is the way to go.

Wearing Indian dress makes a positive impression and, although we've had a few reports of women still being groped, most find it curtails harassment. The *salwar kameez* (the long tunic and baggy trouser combination), widely worn by Indian women, is practical, comfortable, cool in hot weather and shows respect for the Indian dress code. The dupatta (long scarf) worn with this outfit is handy if you visit a shrine that requires your head to be covered.

Going into public wearing a choli (small blouse worn under a sari) or a sari petticoat (which many foreign women mistake for a skirt) is like strutting around half-dressed, so it's best avoided.

You can read other women travellers' experiences at www.journeywoman.com, which has a section devoted to dress.

Staying Safe

To keep discussions short, get to the point as quickly and politely as possible. Getting involved in inane conversations with men can be misinterpreted as a come-on. Statements such as 'do you have a boyfriend?' or 'you are looking beautiful' should start alarm bells ringing. Some women wear a pseudo wedding ring, or announce early on in the conversation that they are married or engaged (whether they are or not). This often proves effective in putting men off, though it may provoke questions on how you're coping during this sexual hiatus.

If, despite your efforts, you still get the feeling that a man's encroaching on your space, he probably is. A firm request to keep away is usually enough to take control of the situation, especially if it's loud enough to draw the attention of passers-by. Alternatively, the silent treatment can be a remarkably good way of getting rid of unwanted male company.

When interacting with men on a day-to-day basis, adhere to the local practice of not shaking hands – instead, relay respect by saying the traditional *namaste*.

Female film-goers will probably feel more comfortable (and decrease the chances of harassment) by going to the cinema with a companion.

Lastly, it's wise to arrive in towns before dark and always avoid walking alone at night, especially in isolated areas.

Taxis & Public Transport

Officials recommend that solo women prearrange an airport pick-up from their hotel if their flight is scheduled to arrive late at night. If that's not possible, catch a prepaid taxi and make a point of (in front of the driver) writing down the car registration and driver's name and giving it to one of the airport police. In 2004 a prepaid-taxi driver (from Delhi's international airport) was charged with the murder of an Australian woman and although authorities have assured travellers that the prepaid system is now safer, most solo women (especially to Delhi) still prefer to prearrange an airport pick-up or wait until daybreak before leaving the airport.

Whenever you catch a taxi, avoid doing so late at night (when many roads are deserted) and never agree to more than one man (the driver) in the car. The driver will invariably try to convince you that it's 'just his brother' or 'for more protection' etc, but authorities warn against it, so heed their advice. Women are also advised against wearing expensive-looking jewellery as it can make them a target for assault.

On extended train and bus travel, being a woman has some advantages. You go to the front of the ticket queue, and on trains there are special women-only carriages. Solo women have reported less hassle in the more expensive classes on trains, especially on overnight trips. When travelling overnight, try to get the uppermost berth, which will give you more privacy (and distance from potential gropers).

On public transport, sit next to a woman; if you can't, don't hesitate to return any errant limbs, put some item of luggage in between you and, if all else fails, move. You're also within your rights to tell him to shove off – loudly enough to shame the guy into leaving you alone.

Transport

CONTENTS

GETTING THERE & AWAY

ENTERING THE COUNTRY

Entering India by air or land is relatively straightforward, with standard immigration and customs procedures. For customs information see p356.

Passport

To enter India you must have a valid passport, visa (see p369) and onward/return ticket. Once in India, if your passport is lost or stolen, immediately contact your country's representative (see p358). It's wise to keep photocopies of your passport and airline ticket.

AIR

Airports & Airlines

Most travellers fly into Delhi or Mumbai for Rajasthan. A small number of international flights serve Jaipur – for details, inquire at travel agencies and see www.indianairports.com.

Delhi (DEL; Indira Gandhi International Airport; www .delhiairport.com; ☎ 011-25652011)

Mumbai (BOM; Chhatrapati Shivaji International Airport; www.mumbaiairport.com; ☎ 022-26829000)

India's national carrier is **Air India** (www.air india.in), which also carries passengers on some domestic sectors of international routes. **Indian Airlines** (www.indianairlines.in), **Jet Airways** (www.jetair ways.com), and **Kingfisher Airlines** (www.flykingfisher .com), India's major domestic carriers, also fly

THINGS CHANGE...

The information in this chapter is particularly vulnerable to change. Check directly with the airline or a travel agent to make sure you understand how a fare (and ticket you may buy) works and be aware of the security requirements for international travel. Shop carefully. The details given in this chapter should be regarded as pointers and are not a substitute for your own careful, up-to-date research.

internationally. The safety records of airlines can be viewed on www.airsafe.com/index .html. For details about India's domestic airlines see p376.

The major airlines servicing India are listed below (see their websites for contact details):

Aeroflot (code SU; www.aeroflot.org) Hub: Sheremetyevo International Airport, Moscow.

Air Canada (AC; www.aircanda.com) Hub: Vancouver Airport.

Air France (AF; www.airfrance.com) Hub: Charles de Gaulle, Paris.

Air India (AI; www.airindia.com) Hub: Indira Gandhi International Airport, Delhi.

Alitalia (AZ; www.alitalia.com) Hub: Fiumicino International Airport, Rome.

American Airlines (AA; www.aa.com) Hub: Dallas Airport.

Austrian Airlines (OS; www.aua.com) Hub: Vienna International Airport.

Biman Bangladesh Airlines (BG; www.bangladeshon line.com/biman) Hub: Zia International Airport, Dhaka.

British Airways (BA; www.british-airways.com) Hub: Heathrow Airport, London.

Cathay Pacific Airways (CX; www.cathaypacific.com) Hub: Hong Kong International Airport.

Druk Air (KB; www.drukair.com.bt) Hub: Paro Airport.

El Al Israel Airlines (LY; www.elal.co.il) Hub: Ben Gurion, Tel Aviv.

Emirates (EK; www.emirates.com) Hub: Dubai International Airport.

Gulf Air (GF; www.gulfairco.com) Hub: Bahrain International Airport.

Iran Air (IR; www.iranair.nl) Hub: Tehran International Airport.

Japan Airlines (JL; www.jal.com) Hub: Narita Airport.

TRANSPORT

CLIMATE CHANGE & TRAVEL

Climate change is a serious threat to the ecosystems that humans rely upon, and air travel is the fastest-growing contributor to the problem. Lonely Planet regards travel, overall, as a global benefit, but believes we all have a responsibility to limit our personal impact on global warming.

Flying & Climate Change

Pretty much every form of motor travel generates CO_2 (the main cause of human-induced climate change) but planes are far and away the worst offenders, not just because of the sheer distances they allow us to travel, but because they release greenhouse gases high into the atmosphere. The statistics are frightening: two people taking a return flight between Europe and the US will contribute as much to climate change as an average household's gas and electricity consumption over a whole year.

Carbon Offset Schemes

Climatecare.org and other websites use 'carbon calculators' that allow jetsetters to offset the greenhouse gases they are responsible for with contributions to energy-saving projects and other climate-friendly initiatives in the developing world – including projects in India, Honduras, Kazakhstan and Uganda.

Lonely Planet, together with Rough Guides and other concerned partners in the travel industry, supports the carbon offset scheme run by climatecare.org. Lonely Planet offsets all of its staff and author travel.

For more information check out our website: lonelyplanet.com.

Kenya Airways (KQ; www.kenya-airways.com) Hub: Jomo Kenyatta International Airport, Nairobi.
KLM – Royal Dutch Airlines (KL; www.klm.com) Hub: Schiphol Airport, Amsterdam.
Kuwait Airways (KU; www.kuwait-airways.com) Hub: Kuwait International Airport.
Lufthansa Airlines (LH; www.lufthansa.com) Hub: Frankfurt International Airport.
Malaysia Airlines (MH; www.malaysiaairlines.com) Hub: Kuala Lumpur International Airport.
Pakistan International Airlines (PK; www.piac.com .pk) Hub: Jinnah International Airport, Karachi.
Qantas Airways (QF; www.qantas.com.au) Hub: Kingsford Smith Airport, Sydney.
Qatar Airways (QR; www.qatarairways.com) Hub: Doha International Airport.
Royal Nepal Airlines Corporation (RA; www.royal nepal.com) Hub: Kathmandu Airport.
Singapore Airlines (SQ; www.singaporeair.com) Hub: Changi Airport, Singapore.
Sri Lankan Airlines (UL; www.srilankan.aero) Hub: Bandaranaike International Airport, Colombo.
Swiss International Airlines (LX; www.swiss.com) Hub: Zurich International Airport.
Thai Airways International (TG; www.thaiair.com) Hub: Bangkok International Airport.

Many international airlines are represented by the following agencies, which are located in Jaipur Towers in Jaipur:

Interglobe Air Transport (Map pp152-3; ☎ 0141-2360532; Jaipur Towers, MI Rd; ☺ 9.30am-6pm Mon-Sat) Represents United Airlines, SAS, Syrian Arab Airlines and Virgin.
Jetair Ltd (Map pp152-3; ☎ 0141-2368640; Jaipur Towers, MI Rd; ☺ 9.30am-1pm & 1.30-6pm Mon-Sat) Represents American Airlines, Royal Jordanian Airlines, Austrian Airlines, Gulf Air, Biman Bangladesh and Kenya Airways.

Tickets

As travellers aren't generally issued a tourist visa to India unless they have an onward/return ticket, few visitors buy international tickets in India itself. For those who do require a ticket, international schedules and fares are available from travel agents in India.

International fares to India fluctuate according to the low, shoulder and high seasons. The fares we've given in this section represent the average fares of various carriers servicing India. Individual carriers have not been specifically mentioned as their routes and fares are subject to change over the life of this book. Contact your travel agent or check out the internet to get up-to-the-minute ticket prices and schedules.

Online ticket sales are handy for straightforward trips with few or no connecting flights. However, travel agencies are recommended for special deals, sorting out tricky connections and organising insurance and Indian visas. Here are a few reputable international online ticket sites:

Ebookers (www.ebookers.com)
Expedia (www.expedia.com)
Flight Centre International (www.flightcentre.com)
Flights.com (www.tiss.com)
STA Travel (www.statravel.com)
Travelocity (www.travelocity.com)

AFRICA

Rennies Travel (www.renniestravel.com) and **STA Travel** (www.statravel.co.za) have offices throughout southern Africa. Check their websites for branch details.

Return fares to Mumbai are around US$600 from Nairobi and around US$500 from Johannesburg.

ASIA

STA Travel Hong Kong (☎ 22360262; www.statravel.com.hk); Japan (☎ 0353-912 922; www.statravel.co.jp); Singapore (☎ 6737 7188; www.statravel.com.sg); Thailand (☎ 2236 0262; www.statravel.co.th) has branches all around Asia. Another resource in Japan is **No 1 Travel** (☎ 0332-056 073; www.no1-travel.com); in Hong Kong try **Four Seas Tours** (☎ 2200 7760; www.fourseastravel.com/fs/en).

Nepal

A return flight from Kathmandu is about US$300 to Delhi and US$450 to Mumbai.

Pakistan

Be aware that flights between Pakistan and India are often suspended when relations between the two countries turn sour. At the time of writing, flights were operating. It costs around US$180 for a return flight from Lahore to Delhi, US$300 between Karachi and Delhi and US$200 between Karachi and Mumbai.

Thailand

Bangkok is the most popular departure point from Southeast Asia into India. Various flights go from Bangkok, including to Delhi and Mumbai (from around US$500 return).

AUSTRALIA

STA Travel (☎ 1300 733 035; www.statravel.com.au) and **Flight Centre** (☎ 133133; www.flightcentre.com.au) have offices throughout Australia. For online bookings, try www.travel.com.au.

There is usually at least one stop in a Southeast Asian city en route to India,

though Qantas has direct flights to Mumbai. The return fares to Delhi and Mumbai from Australian cities are all fairly similarly priced – you can expect to pay anywhere between A$1200 and A$1700, depending on the season.

CANADA

Travel Cuts (☎ 800-667 2887; www.travelcuts.com) is Canada's national student travel agency. For an online booking try www.expedia.ca and www.travelocity.ca.

From Canada, most flights to India are via Europe but a number of reasonably priced fares are also available from Vancouver via one of the major Asian cities.

The return fare from Vancouver to Delhi or Mumbai is from around C$1500.

CONTINENTAL EUROPE

Flight options from Europe are similar to those from the UK, with many of the cheaper flights from major European cities via the Middle East. There is a plethora of deals so shop around.

For fares from European destinations to the various Indian hubs, try the agencies below or peruse the internet.

France
Some recommended agencies:
Anyway (☎ 08 92 89 38 92; www.anyway.fr, in French)
Nouvelles Frontières (☎ 08 25 00 07 47; www.nouvelles-frontieres.fr, in French)
OTU Voyages (www.otu.fr, in French) Specialises in student and youth travellers.
Voyageurs du Monde (☎ 01 40 15 11 15; www.vdm.com, in French)

Germany
Some recommended agencies:
Expedia (www.expedia.de, in German)
Just Travel (☎ 089-747 33 30; www.justtravel.de)
STA Travel (☎ 01805 456 422; www.statravel.de, in German)

Italy
CTS Viaggi (☎ 064 62 04 31; www.cts.it, in Italian)

The Netherlands
Airfair (☎ 0206 20 51 21; www.airfair.nl, in Dutch)

Spain
Barcelo Viajes (☎ 902 11 62 26; www.barceloviajes.com, in Spanish)

TRANSPORT

NEW ZEALAND

Both **Flight Centre** (☎ 0800 243 544; www.flightcentre .co.nz) and **STA Travel** (☎ 0508 782 872; www.statravel .co.nz) have countrywide branches. For online bookings try www.travel.co.nz.

Flights between India and New Zealand all go via southeast Asia. Return fares from Auckland to Delhi start at about NZ$1600.

UK & IRELAND

Discount air travel is big business in London so always check the latest deals on offer. Advertisements for many travel agencies appear in the travel pages of the weekend broadsheet newspapers.

Good places to start hunting for competitive quotes:

Ebookers (☎ 0871-2335000; www.ebookers.com)
Flight Centre (☎ 0870-0890 8099; www.flightcentre .co.uk)
STA Travel (☎ 0870-0160 0599; www.statravel.co.uk)
Trailfinders (☎ 08450585858; www.trailfinders.co.uk)
Travel Bag (☎ 0800-8048911; www.travelbag.co.uk)

USA

Discount travel agencies in the USA are known as consolidators (although you won't see a sign on the door saying 'Consolidator'). San Francisco is the ticket consolidator capital of America, although some good deals can be found in Los Angeles, New York and other big cities. As fares are so variable, consult travel agents and scan the internet to nail the best deal.

For online bookings try the following websites:

■ www.cheaptickets.com
■ www.expedia.com
■ www.itn.net
■ www.lowestfare.com
■ www.orbitz.com
■ www.sta.com
■ www.travelocity.com

LAND
Rajasthan to Pakistan

The weekly *Thar Express* (aka *JU MBF Link Express*, 4889) runs from Jodhpur to Karachi. In Jodhpur it leaves from Bhagat ki Kothi station on Saturday at 1.00am and reaches Munabao on the border at 7.00am. From Munabao you take a Pakistan Railways train. The Pakistan side of the border is Khokhraparker.

You must have a valid visa to Pakistan from India to travel on this train. The train is an ordinary (uncomfortable) mail train. The cost is Rs 98/163 in second-class seating/sleeper. Tickets can only be booked at Jodhpur (ie not online), and have to be booked not more than 15 days before departure.

GETTING AROUND

AIR

Within Rajasthan, there are airports in Jaipur, Jaisalmer, Jodhpur and Udaipur. However, Jaisalmer is closed throughout the year when tensions are high along the Pakistan border.

A nifty booklet containing updated domestic air schedules and fares is *Excel's Timetable of Air Services Within India* (Rs 50; published monthly). It's available at various city newsstands and bookshops.

At the time of writing, the airlines listed below offered domestic services to various Indian destinations (see their websites for the latest). These airlines have offices in major Indian cities (for contact details see the websites and the Getting There & Away sections of some regional chapters):

Air India (www.airindia.in) The national carrier flies between Delhi and Mumbai. Note that most of these flights leave from international terminals (check in advance).

Air India Express (www.airindiaexpress.in) Air India's budget subsidiary with numerous domestic and several short-range international destinations.

Indian Airlines (www.indianairlines.in) India's major domestic carrier offers flights to numerous destinations within India and to neighbouring countries. It is the major player in Rajasthan, serving Agra, Delhi, Jodhpur, Jaisalmer (when the airport is open), Udaipur and Mumbai (see Getting There & Away in the relevant city for prices). The service gets mixed reports and their safety record is not as good as other domestic carriers.

IndiGo (www.goindigo.in) An emerging budget carrier flying between Mumbai, Delhi and Jaipur.

Jet Airways (www.jetairways.com) Rated by many as India's best airline, with efficient staff and a modern fleet, serving Delhi, Jaipur, Jodhpur, Mumbai and Udaipur.

Kingfisher Airlines (www.flykingfisher.com) Giving Jet Airways a good run for its money, Kingfisher flies between Delhi, Mumbai, Jaipur, Jodhpur and Udaipur.

Spicejet (www.spicejet.com) Another low-cost airline that includes Jaipur, Mumbai and Delhi in its network.

BICYCLE

Rajasthan offers an immense array of experiences for a long-distance cyclist. Nevertheless, long-distance cycling is not for the faint of heart or weak of knee. You'll need physical endurance to cope with the roads, traffic and climate.

Try to read some books on bicycle touring, such as Bicycling Magazine's *Guide to Bike Touring: Everything You Need to Know to Travel Anywhere on a Bike.* Cycling magazines provide useful information and their classifieds sections are good places to look for a riding companion. Also have a look at the websites for **Cyclists Touring Club** (www.ctc.org.uk) and the **International Bicycle Fund** (www.ibike.org).

If you're a serious cyclist or amateur racer and wish to get in touch with counterparts while in India, there's the **Cycle Federation of India** (☎ /fax 011-23392578; Yamuna Velodrome, IGI Sports Complex, Delhi). For anything bicycle-related in Delhi, head for Jhandewalan Cycle Market (Map pp92–3), which has imported and domestic new and secondhand bikes and spare parts.

Bicycle Tours

If you want to splash out, try **Butterfield & Robinson** (☎ 416-864 1354; www.butterfield.com; 70 Bond St, Toronto M5B 1X3, Canada) who offer biking expeditions through Rajasthan starting and ending in Delhi, returning via Agra. The all-inclusive tours last for 11 days, which are divided into walking and riding days.

Bring Your Own Bike

Most travellers prefer to buy a bike in India, but by all means consider bringing your own. Mountain bikes are especially suited to India – their sturdier construction makes them more manoeuvrable and less prone to damage, and allows you to tackle rocky, muddy roads unsuitable for lighter machines. Inquire in your home country about air transport and customs formalities. When transporting your bike, remove pedals, all luggage and accessories, turn the handlebars, cover the chain and let the tyres down a bit.

It may be hard to find parts, especially wheels, for touring bikes with 700C wheels. Parts for bicycles with 66cm wheels (of variable standards) are available.

Carry a good lock and use it. Consider wrapping your bicycle frame in used inner tubes – this not only hides fancy paint jobs, but protects them from knocks.

Hire & Purchase

Even in the smallest towns there is usually at least one outlet that hires out bikes but they tend to be rickety bone-rattlers that are only good for short distances. Charges tend to be around Rs 5 per hour, or around Rs 35 per day.

You may like to buy a bike in India and your best bet is to shop around to get a feel for brands and prices. There are many brands of Indian clunkers, including Hero, Atlas, BSA and Raleigh. Raleigh is considered the finest quality, followed by BSA, which has many models including some sporty jobs. Consider bringing your own saddle, rack and good-quality panniers. Get a machine fitted with a stand and bell.

Reselling is usually a breeze. Count on getting about 60% to 70% of what you paid, if it was a new bike. A local bicycle-hire shop will probably be interested.

Repairs & Maintenance

For Indian bikes, there are plenty of repair 'shops' (some are no more than a puncture-wallah with his box of tools under a tree), which makes maintenance delightfully straightforward. The puncture-wallahs will patch tubes for a nominal cost.

If you bring your own bicycle to India, you will need to be prepared for the contingencies of part replacement or repair. Several travellers have warned that it is not at all easy locating foreign parts. Ensure you have a working knowledge of your machine. Bring all necessary tools with you as well as a compact bike manual with diagrams – Indian mechanics can work wonders, and illustrations help overcome the language barrier. Roads don't often have paved shoulders and are very dusty, so keep your chain lubricated, and bring a spare.

Roads & Distances

It's obviously more pleasurable to ride on quieter roads – avoid big cities where the chaotic traffic can be a real hazard for cyclists. National highways can also be a nightmare with speeding trucks and buses. Always make inquiries before venturing off-road.

Avoid leaving anything on your bike that can easily be removed when it's unattended.

TRANSPORT

ROAD DISTANCES (KM)

	Agra	Ahmedabad	Ajmer	Alwar	Bharatpur	Bikaner	Bundi	Chittorgarh	Delhi	Jaipur	Jaisalmer	Jodhpur	Kota	Mt Abu	Mumbai	Udaipur
Agra	---															
Ahmedabad	889	---														
Ajmer	388	526	---													
Alwar	172	798	272	---												
Bharatpur	56	658	332	116	---											
Bikaner	665	754	233	462	497	---										
Bundi	438	485	163	347	382	396	---									
Chittorgarh	579	364	191	463	523	424	121	---								
Delhi	195	916	392	163	251	470	465	583	---							
Jaipur	232	657	138	143	174	354	205	345	259	---						
Jaisalmer	853	296	490	762	822	333	653	657	882	543	---					
Jodhpur	568	511	205	477	537	243	368	372	597	317	285	---				
Kota	453	522	200	383	418	432	36	158	504	242	690	405	---			
Mt Abu	737	221	375	647	707	569	418	297	767	465	572	326	455	---		
Mumbai	1204	554	1071	1343	945	1299	1041	928	1461	1202	1341	1056	1005	766	---	
Udaipur	637	252	274	551	581	506	233	112	664	347	545	260	270	185	797	---

You may like to bring along a padlock and chain. However, don't be paranoid – your bike is probably safer in India than in many Western cities.

If you've never cycled long distances, start with 20km to 40km a day and increase this as you gain stamina and confidence. Be warned that asking directions can send you on a wild-goose chase.

For an eight-hour pedal an experienced cycle tourist will average 70km to 100km a day on undulating plains, or 50km to 70km in mountainous areas on sealed roads; cut this by at least one-third for unsealed roads. The distance you cycle may be dictated by available accommodation; not all villages have a place to stay. If you're cycling in a hot climate, try to get your cycling done by noon as the sun may be too strong in the afternoon. Hotels also fill up in the afternoon and it's usually dark by 6pm, so these are additional reasons to get an early start.

BUS

The state government bus service is **Rajasthan State Road Transport Corporation** (RSRTC; www.rsrtc.gov

.in), otherwise known as Rajasthan Roadways. Often there are privately owned local bus services as well as luxury private coaches running between major cities. These can be booked through travel agencies.

Although the bus network is comprehensive and reliable, many travellers prefer to travel by train, as it's a smoother ride and doesn't involve the nerve-wracking zigzagging of road travel. Buses are best suited to short journeys; if you've got a long trip, particularly overnight, opt for a train if there's a choice. The big advantage of buses over trains is that they travel more frequently and getting one usually involves less predeparture hassle. It's best to avoid night travel when driving conditions can be more hazardous.

The condition of buses largely affects the comfort of the journey – private buses are often the most comfortable option, though the deluxe RSRTC buses (Volvo and Gold Line) are now very good. Choose a seat between the axles, as this generally minimises the bumpiness of a trip.

Your luggage is usually stored in an enclosed compartment at the back of the bus –

the company may charge a few rupees for this. Alternatively, baggage is carried for free on the roof and if this is the case, it's worth taking some precautions. Firstly, ensure your bag is adequately padlocked. Make sure it's tied on securely and that nobody dumps a heavy tin trunk on top of your gear. Theft can be a problem so keep an eye on your bags during any stops en route (which are ideal times to stretch your legs anyway).

On long-distance bus trips, chai stops seem to be either far too frequent or agonisingly infrequent. Toilet facilities for women are often inadequate. It's worth taking earplugs (or headphones), as some bus drivers love to crank up bus stereos or videos.

Local city buses, particularly in the larger cities, are fume-belching, human-stuffed, mechanical rattletraps that travel at breakneck speed, except when they are stuck in traffic. Within cities it's more convenient and comfortable to opt for an autorickshaw or taxi.

Bus Types

On the main routes in Rajasthan you have a basic choice of ordinary, express and deluxe. Express and deluxe buses make fewer stops than ordinary buses – they're still usually crowded though. The fare is marginally higher than ordinary buses, but worth every rupee.

The RSRTC also operates some divisions in the deluxe category: on selected routes there are Gray Line (sleeper) buses – these have beds and make overnight trips more comfortable. Beds have a bunk-bed arrangement, with rows of single beds, each with a curtain for privacy, so they are usually fine even for women travelling alone.

Silver Line is a so-called superdeluxe service and the buses have a reasonable level of comfort. Air-conditioned (air-con) Volvo and Gold Line buses are the best and serve the routes between Jaipur and Delhi, Agra and Udaipur.

Private buses also operate on most Rajasthan routes; apart from often being quicker and usually more comfortable, the booking procedure is much simpler than for state-run buses. However, private companies can often change schedules at the last minute to get as many bums on seats as possible. They can be cheaper than the RSRTC buses.

Costs

Fares and journey times differ according to the transport provider, class and distance. The fares with private operators can be influenced by the time of year, the condition of the bus and sometimes by your bargaining skills. On state buses, a deluxe bus from Delhi to Jaipur costs around Rs 270 (Rs 370 to Rs 460 in air-con), an express from Udaipur to Mt Abu costs Rs 105, and a deluxe from Jodhpur to Jaisalmer costs Rs 168.

Reservations

Advance reservations are often not possible on 'ordinary' buses, so it pays to arrive a bit early to bag a seat. Other bus services do usually take advance reservations and it's wise to book ahead as seats can fill up fast, especially on popular routes.

Many bus stations have a separate women's queue, although this isn't always obvious because the relevant sign (where it exists) is rarely in English and there may not be women queuing. More often than not, the same ticket window will handle the male and the female queue so women travellers should sharpen their elbows and make their way to the front, where they will get almost immediate service.

CAR
Hire
CAR & DRIVER

Long-distance car hire that includes a driver is an excellent way to get around Rajasthan. Spread among, say, four people it's not expensive and you have the flexibility to go where you want when you want.

Most local taxis will quite happily set off on a long-distance trip in Rajasthan. Inquiring at a taxi rank is the cheapest and easiest way to organise this. Alternatively, you can ask a travel agency or your hotel to book one for you. Although they may well be taking a cut for their service, you have the security of having someone to go to should the driver and car and your belongings disappear in the night.

Rates with the Rajasthan Tourism Development Corporation (RTDC) are from Rs 4.75/6 per kilometre for a non air-con/air-con Ambassador, with a 250km minimum per day and an overnight charge of Rs 125 to Rs 300.

Expect to pay around Rs 4 per kilometre if you arrange a non air-con car directly with

TRANSPORT

TIPS FOR HIRING A CAR & DRIVER

Try to get a driver who speaks at least some English and who is knowledgeable about the region(s) you intend visiting. Night travel is best avoided.

More than a few travellers have shelled out much more money than is reasonable, paying for the driver's accommodation and meals (even booze!), completely unaware that his lodging and meal cost has already been factored into the fee. Make sure you understand the accommodation and meal arrangements for the driver *before* paying the car-hire company and ensure this is made clear to the driver *before* you set off. The charge that's quoted should include an allowance for the driver's daily living expenses (ie food and lodging) as well as petrol (hire rates may fluctuate in tune with petrol prices). Note that there's often a vehicle entry fee into other states, which costs extra. You also have to pay extra for any car-parking or car-entry fees you may incur.

For longer trips, when it comes to where the driver stays overnight, this is for him to decide and should never be your headache (many choose to sleep in the back seat of the car thus pocketing their accommodation allowance).

Be aware that many hotels in Rajasthan don't permit drivers onto their premises (to sleep or eat, even if you're paying). That's because the commission racket has created all sorts of headaches for hotels and, while your intentions may be warm-hearted, the hotel owners are the ones who may face problems with demanding drivers long after you've departed India. Although some places don't mind drivers joining guests at hotel restaurants, respect those that refuse entry – if in doubt, ask. If you want to shout your driver a meal, there are good independent restaurants not attached to hotels that welcome one and all.

Finally, and very importantly, it's imperative to set the ground rules from day one. Many travellers have complained of having their holiday completely dictated by their driver. Politely, but firmly, let the driver know at the onset that you're the boss – it can make the difference between a carefree journey and a strained one.

Shop around to find the best deal and before paying anything, get in writing what you've been promised to avoid 'misunderstandings' later. Before setting off it's wise to inspect the car and meet the driver.

A tip is in order at the conclusion of your journey; anything from Rs 75 per day is reasonable (more if you're happy with the service).

---

a taxi driver, or if you haggle hard with an agency – with a Rs 100 overnight charge and a minimum charge of 250km per day. If you're hiring for several days, try to negotiate a better deal.

If you're only going one way, remember that you have to pay for the driver to return to your starting point. Your driver may ask you for an advance of a few hundred rupees at the start of the trip to pay for petrol. To hire a car with driver for use only within one city (eg Delhi) expect to pay Rs 600 per day for a nonair-con vehicle, around Rs 800 for an air-con vehicle. There's usually an eight hour, 80km limit per day (additional charges apply if you exceed these).

SELF-DRIVE

Currently there are no agencies in Rajasthan offering self-drive vehicles. Self-drive hire is possible in Delhi, but given the hair-raising driving conditions most travellers opt for a car with driver. Major car-hire companies in India include Budget and Hertz.

In some cities, such as Delhi, it's possible to hire or buy motorcycles, and you'll often need to produce a driving licence of some sort (see p382). An International Driving Licence can also come in handy for other identification purposes, such as bicycle hire.

HITCHING

Hitching in India isn't a realistic option, as you're likely to only be offered rides by truck drivers (not private cars). You're then stuck with the quandaries of: 'will the driver expect to be paid?' and 'will they be unhappy if I don't offer to pay or will they want too much?' Women are strongly advised against hitching.

LOCAL TRANSPORT

Although there are comprehensive local bus networks in most major towns, unless you have time to familiarise yourself with the routes, you're better off sticking to taxis, autorickshaws or cycle-rickshaws, or hiring bicycles.

A basic rule applies to any form of transport where the fare is not ticketed, fixed or metered: agree on the fare beforehand. If you fail to do that you can expect enormous arguments and hassles when you get to your destination. And agree on the fare clearly – if there is more than one of you make sure it covers all of you (the price quoted should be per vehicle, not per person). If you have baggage make sure there are no extra charges, or you may be asked for more at the end of the trip. If a driver refuses to use the meter, or insists on an extortionate rate, simply walk away – if he really wants the job the price will drop. If you can't agree on a reasonable fare, find another driver.

Other useful tips when catching taxis and rickshaws:

- Always have enough small change, as drivers rarely do, which can be a real hassle, especially at night.
- If you are staying or dining at a top-end venue and you need to catch a rickshaw, try walking a few hundred metres down the road to avoid the drivers who hang outside assuming you're a cash cow.
- Finally, it's a good idea to carry around a business card of the hotel in which you are staying, as your pronunciation of streets, hotel names etc may be incomprehensible to drivers. Some hotel cards even have a nifty little sketch map clearly indicating their location.

Fares are often steeper (as much as double the day fare) at night and some drivers charge a few rupees extra for luggage. Many autorickshaw drivers are right into the commission racket – see p356.

Autorickshaw & Tempo

An autorickshaw is a noisy three-wheel device powered by a two-stroke motorcycle engine with a driver up front and seats for two (or sometimes more) passengers behind. They don't have doors and have just a canvas top. They are also known as scooters or autos.

They're generally about half the price of a taxi, though the meters are rarely used, and follow the same ground rules as taxis. Because of their size, autorickshaws are often faster than taxis for short trips and their drivers are decidedly nuttier. Hair-raising near-misses are

guaranteed and glancing-blow collisions are not infrequent; thrill seekers will love them!

Tempos are somewhat like large autorickshaws. These ungainly looking three-wheel devices operate like minibuses or share taxis along fixed routes (at fixed fares). Unless you're spending a lot of time in one city, they're impractical.

Cycle-rickshaw

Cycle-rickshaws are effectively three-wheeler bicycles with a seat for two passengers behind the driver. You'll find them in parts of Delhi, in Jaipur and in many smaller towns.

As with taxis and autorickshaws, fares must be agreed upon in advance. A typical ride in a cycle-rickshaw is between 1km and 3km and costs roughly between Rs 20 and Rs 40. Remember this is extremely strenuous work and the wallahs are among India's poorest, so a tip is appreciated and haggling over a few rupees unnecessary.

Share Jeep

Share jeeps supplement the bus service in many parts of Rajasthan, especially in areas off the main road routes, such as many of the towns in Shekhawati.

Jeeps leave when (very) full, from well-established 'passenger stations' on the outskirts of towns and villages; locals should be able to point you in the right direction. They are usually dirt cheap and jam-packed and tend to be more dangerous than buses (drivers are even crazier). Most travellers find them too crowded and claustrophobic for long journeys.

Taxi

Most towns have taxis, and most of them (certainly in the major cities) are metered. Getting a metered fare, however, is rather a different situation. First of all the meter may be 'broken'. Threatening to get another taxi will often miraculously 'fix' it. Opt for prepaid taxis where available.

Another problem with taxis is that their meters may be outdated. Fares are adjusted upwards so much faster and more frequently than meters are recalibrated that drivers often have 'fare adjustment cards' indicating what you should pay for your trip compared to what the meter indicates. This is, of course, open to abuse. You have no idea if you're being shown the right card or if the taxi's meter has actually been recalibrated and you're being shown the card anyway.

The only answer to all this is to get an idea of what the fare should be before departure (ask at information desks, hotel receptions etc) and possibly agree on a fare with the driver beforehand. You'll soon develop a feel for what the meter says, what the cards say and what the two together should indicate.

MOTORCYCLE

Cruising solo around India by motorcycle offers the freedom to go when and where you desire. There are also some excellent motorcycle tours available (see right), which take the hassle out of doing it alone.

Helmets, leathers, gloves, goggles, boots, waterproofs and other protective gear are best brought from your home country, as they're either unavailable in India or are of variable quality. You'll also need a valid International Driving Licence.

Hire

Organised tours provide motorcycles, but if you're planning an independent trip, bikes can be hired at negotiable prices. You'll probably have to leave a cash deposit (refundable) and/or your air ticket.

In Delhi, Lalli Motorbike Exports (right) rents out Enfields (minimum three weeks; a 500cc machine for three/eight weeks costs Rs 13,000/23,000). There are places to hire (or purchase) motorbikes and scooters in Pushkar and Jaisalmer.

On the Road

Given the overall road conditions in India, motorcycling is not without hazards and ideally should only be undertaken by experienced riders. Hazards range from goats crossing the road to defunct abandoned trucks and of course the perpetual potholes and unmarked speed humps. Rural roads sometimes have grain crops strewn across them to be threshed by passing vehicles – it can be a real hazard for bikers.

Avoid covering too much territory in one day. A lot of energy is spent simply concentrating on the road, making long days exhausting and potentially dangerous. On the busy national highways expect to average 50km/h without stops; on smaller roads, where conditions are worse, as little as 10km/h is not an unrealistic average. On the whole, on good roads, you can easily expect to cover a minimum of 100km a day (up to or over 300km with minimal stops). Night riding should be avoided.

For long hauls, putting the bike on a train can be a convenient option. You'll pay about as much as a 2nd-class passenger fare for the bike. The petrol tank must be empty, and there should be a tag in an obvious place with name, destination, passport number and train details. When you pack the bike, remove the mirrors and loosen the handlebars to avoid damage.

Organised Motorcycle Tours

Motorcycle tours usually operate with a minimum number of people and some can be tailor-made. Below are some reputable options (see websites for contact details, itineraries and prices):

Ferris Wheels (www.ferriswheels.com.au)

H-C Travel (www.hctravel.com)

Indian Motorcycle Adventures (http://homepages .ihug.co.nz/~gumby)

Indian Shepherds (www.asiasafari.com)

Lalli Singh Tours (www.lallisingh.com)

Moto Discovery (www.motodiscovery.com)

Saffron Road Motorcycle Tours (www.saffronroad .com)

Purchase

Buying a secondhand machine is a matter of asking around and a good place to start is with mechanics. Do your homework thoroughly and shop around to get an idea of the latest models on the market and their costs. Also try to speak to other bikers.

In Delhi the area around Hari Singh Nalwa St in Karol Bagh is full of places buying, selling and hiring out motorcycles. The reputation of many places is variable, but Lonely Planet consistently receives good reports about **Lalli Motorbike Exports** (Map pp92-3; ☎ 011-25728579; www .lallisingh.com; 1740-A/55 Basement, Hari Singh Nalwa St, Karol Bagh Market). Run by the knowledgeable Lalli Singh, this place deals in sales (secondhand and new bikes), hiring, spares and servicing of Enfields only. It also offers other services such as arranging motorbike transport in India and collecting your bike from your final destination if it's not Delhi.

Prices for new Enfield models are listed at www.royalenfield.com. For a new bike, you'll also have to pay Rs 4500 for comprehensive one-year insurance and lifetime road tax and registration. You may like to invest a little more to get extras such as a luggage rack, protection bar, backrest, rear-view mirrors, lockable fuel tap, petrol filter, complete tool kit and loud horn (you're looking at an extra Rs 4000 to Rs 4500 for all of these). An Enfield 500cc gives about 25km/L. Their tanks hold 14L, though you can get a customised 18L to 20L tank for an extra cost.

A secondhand Enfield 500cc (two to three years old, without servicing) costs Rs 35,000 to Rs 65,000, depending on the condition. It's advisable to get it serviced before you set off (around Rs 10,000 to Rs 15,000).

When the time comes to sell your bike, expect to get around Rs 30,000 for a secondhand Enfield 500cc (in reasonable condition) and about Rs 35,000 to Rs 45,000 if you purchased it as a new machine.

An obvious tip perhaps, but don't part with your money until you have the ownership papers, receipt and affidavit signed by a magistrate authorising the owner (as recorded in the ownership papers) to sell the machine.

Ownership papers are much more straightforward for a new bike than for a secondhand one. Each state has a different set of ownership-transfer formalities – inquire locally about current requirements.

It takes about a week (up to two weeks for secondhand machines) to get the paperwork done. If you wish to buy a new Enfield, you can contact the dealer in advance so that the paperwork will be ready by the time you arrive in India.

Repairs & Maintenance

Original spare parts from an 'authorised dealer' can be expensive compared to copies available from your spare-parts-wallah. Delhi's Karol Bagh Market (p119) is a good place for parts for all Indian and imported bikes. If you plan on going to remote regions, take basic spares with you (valves, piston rings etc) as they may not be readily available.

For all machines (particularly older ones), make sure you regularly check and tighten all nuts and bolts, as Indian roads and engine vibration tend to work things loose quickly. Check the engine and gearbox oil level regularly – with the quality of oil it's advisable to change it and clean the oil filter every couple of thousand kilometres.

PUNCTURES

Given the road conditions, the chances are you'll make at least a couple of visits to a puncture-wallah. These phenomenal fix-it men are found almost everywhere, but it's good to have the tools to at least remove your own wheel. It's worth buying new tyres if you purchase a secondhand bike with worn tyres.

TRAIN

To take a train is to ride in India's bloodstream. **Indian Railways** (www.indianrail.gov.in) runs over 14,000 trains a day, and moves 14 million passengers daily to any of 6856 stations. At first the system can seem impenetrable. However, it becomes easier (if never straightforward) once you get used to it, and train travel is generally more comfortable than bus travel, especially for long trips. Delhi has a suburban train network and metro, which is usually fine during the day, but can become unbearably crowded during peak hours.

There are tourist quotas for many express trains, and special offices or counters for foreigners in major cities and tourist centres (you are supposed to bring money-exchange receipts or ATM slips if paying for tickets with rupees, but these are rarely asked for). Many stations have left-luggage rooms with nominal daily charges.

Train services to certain destinations are often increased during major festivals or other peak travel periods. Be especially careful during these times as there have sometimes been reports of passengers being crushed to death on overcrowded platforms. Other things to beware of (at all times) are passenger drugging and theft of your belongings – see p356.

We've listed major trains throughout this book but there are many more. If you intend on doing a lot of train travel, it's worth getting the national *Trains at a Glance* booklet (Rs 50; available at various train stations or at city bookshops and newsstands). It contains extensive details and there are timetables covering each regional zone. It takes a bit more than a glance to work these out, but once you've mastered it you will be hooked.

For comprehensive online information about the Indian railway system, a valuable resource is www.seat61.com/India.htm.

Classes

Shatabdi express trains are same-day services between major and regional cities. These are

TRANSPORT

PALACES ON WHEELS

To travel maharaja-style, try the RTDC *Palace on Wheels* and *Heritage on Wheels* services.

Palace on Wheels (www.palaceonwheelsindia.com) operates weekly tours of Rajasthan, departing from Delhi every Wednesday (September to April). The itinerary covers Jaipur, Jaisalmer, Jodhpur, Ranthambhore National Park, Chittorgarh (Chittor), Udaipur, Keoladeo Ghana National Park and Agra. It's a mammoth stretch in seven days, but most of the travelling is done at night. This train once used the maharajas' original carriages, but these became so ancient that new carriages were refurbished to look like the originals. The train has two dining cars and a bar, and each coach, containing four doubles with private bathroom, is attended by a splendidly costumed captain and attendant.

If you can't afford to do the trip for real, go for a virtual chug on the website. From October to March tariffs per person are US$3920/2905/2380 for single/double/triple occupancy. From September to April it costs US$2905/2205/1820. The price includes tours, admission fees, accommodation and all meals.

The *Heritage on Wheels* (www.heritageonwheels.com) is a similarly luxurious train which departs Jaipur and explores the Bikaner and Shekhawati regions before returning to Jaipur on the fourth day. The tariff per person per day for single/double/triple occupancy is US$300/200/150.

Bookings can be made online or at the **RTDC Tourist Reception Centre** (Map pp102-3; ☎ 011-23381884; Bikaner House, Pandara Rd, Delhi 110011) or at the **RTDC Central Reservations Office** (Map pp152-3; ☎ 0141-2202586; MI Rd; ⏰ 10am-5pm Mon-Sat) in Jaipur.

---

the fastest and most expensive trains, with only two classes: air-con executive chair and air-con chair. Shatabdis are comfortable, but the glass windows cut the views considerably compared to nonair-con classes on slower trains, which have barred windows and fresh air.

Rajdhani express trains are long-distance express services running between Delhi and the state capitals, and offer air-con 1st class (1 air-con), 2-tier air-con (2 air-con), 3-tier air-con (3 air-con) and 2nd class. Two-tier means there are two levels of bunks in each compartment, which are a little wider and longer than their counterparts in 3-tier. Costing respectively a half and a third as much as 1 air-con, 2 air-con and 3 air-con are perfectly adequate for an overnight trip.

Other express and mail trains have 2 air-con coaches, chair car, nonair-con sleeper (bring your own bedding), nonair-con 2nd class, and finally there are unreserved tickets. A sleeper costs around a quarter as much as 2-tier air-con. For more details see *Trains at a Glance,* or big stations often have English-speaking staff at inquiry counters who can help with picking the best train. At smaller stations midlevel officials, such as the deputy station master, usually speak English.

For an excellent description of the various train classes (including pictures) see www.seat61.com/India.htm; scroll down to the 'What are Indian trains like?' heading.

Costs

Fares are calculated by distance. For a full rundown on fares see www.indianrail.gov.in or *Trains at a Glance*. On most trains, if your journey is longer than 500km, you can take one break (for two days maximum) but you must have your ticket endorsed by the station master or ticket collector at the station you stop at.

Bedding is free in 1 air-con, 2 air-con and 3 air-con sleepers, but you'll need your own for ordinary sleepers. Meals are free on Rajdhani and Shatabdi trains, and cheap meals are available on other trains.

The major stations have accommodation called 'retiring rooms', which are a basic option if you have a valid ticket.

Tickets are refundable (opposite) but a fee applies; there are no refunds on lost tickets.

Seniors over 60 years of age are entitled to a 30% discount on train tickets.

Reservations

To make a reservation you must fill out a form stating which class you want and the train's name and number. For overnight journeys it's best to reserve your place a couple of days in advance. If there's no special counter or office for foreigners at the station (New Delhi's International Tourist Bureau is recommended), you'll have to adopt local queuing practices, which range from reasonably orderly lines to mosh pits. There are sometimes separate ladies' queues, but usually the same window handles men and women. Women should simply proceed to the front of the queue, next to the first male.

If you don't want the hassle of buying a ticket yourself, many travel agencies and hotels are in the business of purchasing train tickets for a small commission. But watch out for small-fry travel agents who promise express-train tickets and deliver tickets for obscure mail or passenger trains, *or* get you a waiting list reservation rather than a seat or bunk. Only leave a small deposit, if any, and check the ticket carefully before paying.

Reserved tickets show your berth and carriage number. Efficient railway staff will also stick lists of names and berths on each reserved carriage, as well as writing the carriage number in chalk.

If you can't buy a reserved seat, ask if there's a waiting list. If you are on the waiting list, it will say 'wl' on your ticket followed by a number, which gives the number of your position in the queue. You can ask when you buy what the likelihood is that you will get a seat.

Alternatively, you could buy unreserved tickets – which go on sale about an hour before departure – and try to upgrade it. Find a reserved-class carriage and a spare seat, and seek out the conductor (officially the Travelling Ticket Examiner – TTE). Explain you could only buy an unreserved ticket and ask about vacancies. With luck, the conductor will be happy to oblige. You pay the difference between the ordinary fare and the fare of whichever class you're in, plus a small excess charge of around Rs 30.

ONLINE RESERVATIONS

It's possible to book train tickets online at www.irctc.co.in though many travellers have found it a fruitless exercise in trying. Helpful tips on making online bookings are available at the website www.seat61.com/India.htm; scroll down to the 'How to book – from outside India' heading.

REFUNDS

Tickets are refundable but fees apply. If you present more than one day in advance, a fee of Rs 20 to Rs 70 applies. Steeper charges apply if you seek a refund less than four hours prior to departure, but you can get some sort of refund as late as 12 hours afterwards.

When refunding your ticket you officially have a magic pass to go to the front of the queue, as the next person may require the spot you're surrendering. We've never seen if this works in practice.

Health Dr Trish Batchelor

CONTENTS

While the potential dangers of travelling in India can seem quite ominous, in reality few travellers experience anything more than an upset stomach. Hygiene is generally poor throughout the country, so food- and water-borne illnesses are common. Travellers tend to worry about contracting infectious diseases, but infections are a rare cause of *serious* illness or death in travellers. Pre-existing medical conditions such as heart disease, and accidental injury (especially traffic accidents), account for most life-threatening problems.

Fortunately, most travellers' illnesses can either be prevented with some common-sense behaviour or be treated easily with a well-stocked traveller's medical kit. The following advice is a general guide only and does not replace the advice of a doctor trained in travel medicine.

BEFORE YOU GO

Pack medications in their original, clearly labelled containers. A signed and dated letter from your physician describing your medical conditions and medications, including generic names, is very useful. If carrying syringes or needles, be sure to have a physician's letter documenting their medical necessity. If you have a heart condition, bring a copy of your ECG taken just prior to travelling.

If you take any regular medication, bring double the amount you need in case of loss or theft. You'll be able to buy many medications over the counter in India without a doctor's prescription, but it can be difficult to find some of the newer drugs, particularly the latest antidepressant drugs, blood-pressure medications and contraceptive pills.

INSURANCE

Even if you're fit and healthy, don't travel without health insurance – accidents do happen. Declare any existing medical conditions you have, as the insurance company WILL check if your problem is pre-existing and will not cover you if it is undeclared. You may require extra cover for adventure activities, such as rock climbing. If you have health insurance at home that doesn't cover you for medical expenses abroad, consider getting extra insurance. If you're uninsured, emergency evacuation is: bills of over US$100,000 are not uncommon.

Ask in advance if your insurance plan will make payments directly to providers or reimburse you later for overseas health expenditures. (In many countries doctors expect payment in cash.) Some policies offer lower and higher medical-expense options; the higher ones are chiefly for countries that have extremely high medical costs, such as the USA. You may prefer to take out a policy that pays doctors or hospitals directly to avoid having to pay on the spot and claim later. If you have to claim later, make sure you keep all documentation. Some policies ask you to call (reverse charges) a centre in your home country, where an immediate assessment of your problem is made.

MEDICAL CHECKLIST

Recommended items for a personal medical kit:

- antibacterial cream, eg Muciprocin
- antibiotic for skin infections, eg Amoxicillin/Clavulanate or Cephalexin
- antifungal cream, eg Clotrimazole
- antihistamine – there are many options, eg Cetrizine for daytime and Promethazine for night
- antiseptic, eg Betadine

- antispasmodic for stomach cramps, eg Buscopan
- contraceptive(s)
- decongestant, eg Pseudoephedrine
- DEET-based insect repellent
- diarrhoea medication – consider an oral rehydration solution (eg Gastrolyte), diarrhoea 'stopper' (eg Loperamide) and anti-nausea medication (eg Prochlorperazine); antibiotics for diarrhoea include Norfloxacin and Ciprofloxacin, for bacterial diarrhoea Azithromycin, and for giardia or amoebic dysentery Tinidazole
- first-aid items such as scissors, Elastoplasts, bandages, gauze, thermometer (but not mercury), sterile needles and syringes, safety pins and tweezers
- Ibuprofen or another anti-inflammatory
- indigestion tablets, eg Quick Eze or Mylanta
- iodine tablets (unless you are pregnant or have a thyroid problem) to purify water
- laxative, eg Coloxyl
- migraine medication if you suffer from them
- paracetamol
- permethrin to impregnate clothing and mosquito nets
- steroid cream for allergic or itchy rashes, eg 1% to 2% hydrocortisone
- sunscreen and hat
- throat lozenges
- treatment for thrush (vaginal yeast infection), eg Clotrimazole pessaries or Diflucan tablet
- Ural or equivalent if you are prone to urine infections

VACCINATIONS

Specialised travel-medicine clinics are your best source of information; they stock all available vaccines and will be able to give specific recommendations for you and your trip. The doctors will take into account factors such as past vaccination history, the length of your trip, activities you may be undertaking, and underlying medical conditions, such as pregnancy.

Most vaccines don't give immunity until at least two weeks after they're given, so visit a doctor four to eight weeks before departure. Ask your doctor for an International Certificate of Vaccination (otherwise known as the yellow booklet), which will list all the vaccinations you've received.

Recommended Vaccinations

The World Health Organization (WHO) recommends that travellers to India be up to date with measles, mumps and rubella vaccinations. Other vaccinations it recommends:

Adult diphtheria and tetanus Single booster recommended if none given in the previous 10 years. Side effects include sore arm and fever.

Hepatitis A Provides almost 100% protection for up to a year; a booster after 12 months provides at least another 20 years' protection. Mild side effects such as headache and sore arm occur in 5% to 10% of people.

Hepatitis B Now considered routine for most travellers. Given as three shots over six months. A rapid schedule is also available, as is a combined vaccination with Hepatitis A. Side effects – usually headache and sore arm – are mild and uncommon. In 95% of people lifetime protection results.

Polio In 2004 polio was still present in India. Only one booster is required as an adult for lifetime protection. Inactivated polio vaccine is safe during pregnancy.

Typhoid Recommended for all travellers to India, even if you only visit urban areas. The vaccine offers around 70% protection, lasts for two to three years and comes as a single shot. Tablets are also available; however, the injection is usually recommended as it has fewer side effects. Sore arm and fever may occur.

Varicella If you haven't had chickenpox, discuss this vaccination with your doctor.

Immunisations recommended for long-term travellers (those going away for more than one month) or those at special risk:

Japanese B Encephalitis Three injections in all. Booster recommended after two years. Sore arm and headache are the most common side effects. Though rare, an allergic reaction comprising hives and swelling can occur up to 10 days after any of the three doses.

Meningitis Single injection. There are two types of vaccination. The quadrivalent vaccine gives two to three years' protection, and the meningitis group C vaccine gives around 10 years' protection. Recommended for long-term backpackers aged under 25.

Rabies Three injections in all. A booster after one year will then provide 10 years' protection. Side effects are rare – occasionally headache and sore arm.

Tuberculosis (TB) A complex issue. Adult long-term travellers are usually advised to have a TB skin-test before and after travel, rather than vaccination. Only one vaccine needs to be given in a lifetime.

Required Vaccinations

Yellow fever is the only vaccine required by international regulations. Proof of vaccination will only be required if you have visited a country in the yellow-fever zone within the six

HEALTH

days prior to entering India. If you are travelling to India from Africa or South America you should check to see if you require proof of vaccination.

INTERNET RESOURCES

There's a wealth of travel-health advice on the internet. **LonelyPlanet.com** (www.lonely planet.com) is a good place to start. Some other suggestions:

Centers for Disease Control and Prevention (CDC; www.cdc.gov) Good general information.

MD Travel Health (www.mdtravelhealth.com) Provides complete travel-health recommendations for every country; updated daily.

World Health Organization (WHO; www.who.int/ith/) Its superb book *International Travel & Health* is revised annually and is available online.

FURTHER READING

Lonely Planet's *Healthy Travel – Asia & India* is pocket sized and packed with useful information about pre-trip planning, emergency first aid, immunisation and disease information, and what to do if you get sick on the road. Other recommended references include *Traveller's Health*, by Dr Richard Dawood, and *Travelling Well*, by Dr Deborah Mills – check out the website of **Travelling Well** (www.travellingwell.com.au).

IN TRANSIT

DEEP VEIN THROMBOSIS

Deep vein thrombosis (DVT) occurs when blood clots form in the legs during flights, chiefly because of prolonged immobility. The longer the flight, the greater the risk. Though most blood clots are reabsorbed uneventfully, some may break off and travel via the blood vessels to the lungs, where they may cause life-threatening complications.

The chief symptom of DVT is swelling or pain of the foot, ankle, or calf, usually but not always on just one side. When a blood clot travels to the lungs, it may cause chest pain and difficulty in breathing. Travellers with any of these symptoms should immediately seek medical attention.

To prevent the development of DVT on long flights you should walk about the cabin, perform isometric compressions of the leg muscles (ie contract the leg muscles while sitting), drink plenty of fluids, and avoid alcohol and tobacco.

JET LAG & MOTION SICKNESS

Jet lag is common when crossing more than five time zones; it results in insomnia, fatigue, malaise or nausea. To avoid jet lag drink plenty of (nonalcoholic) fluids and eat light meals. Upon arrival, seek exposure to natural sunlight and readjust your schedule (for meals, sleep etc) as soon as possible.

Antihistamines such as dimenhydrinate (Dramamine), promethazine (Phenergan) and meclizine (Antivert, Bonine) are usually the first choice for treating motion sickness. Their main side effect is drowsiness. A herbal alternative is ginger, which works like a charm for some people.

IN INDIA

AVAILABILITY OF HEALTH CARE

There are plenty of English-speaking doctors in urban centres. Most hotels have a doctor on call – if you're staying at a budget hotel and they can't help, try contacting an upmarket hotel to find out which doctor they use. Some cities now have clinics catering specifically to travellers and expats. These are usually more costly than local facilities but are worth it, as they will offer a superior standard of care. Additionally, staff at these clinics understand the local system, and are aware of the safest local hospitals and best specialists. They can also liaise with insurance companies should you require evacuation. It is difficult to find reliable medical care in rural areas.

If you're seriously ill, contact your country's embassy (see p358), which usually has a list of recommended doctors and dentists.

Treatment at public hospitals is generally reliable, though private clinics offer the advantage of shorter queues. However, there have been reports that some private clinics have bumped up the level of treatment to more than is necessary in order to procure larger medical-insurance claims.

In even the smallest Rajasthani town you will find at least one well-stocked pharmacy (selling everything from malaria medication to nail-polish remover). Many are open until late. Many pharmaceuticals sold in India are manufactured under licence from multinational companies, so you'll probably be familiar with many brand names. Before buying medication over the counter, always check the expiry date and ensure the packet is sealed. Don't accept items that have been poorly stored (eg lying in a glass cabinet that's exposed to the sunshine).

INFECTIOUS DISEASES
Coughs, Colds & Chest Infections
Around 25% of travellers to India will develop a respiratory infection. This usually starts as a virus and is exacerbated by environmental conditions such as pollution in the cities or cold and altitude in the mountains. A secondary bacterial infection, marked by fever, chest pain and coughing up discoloured or blood-tinged sputum, will commonly intervene. If you have the symptoms of an infection, seek medical advice or commence a general antibiotic.

Dengue
This mosquito-borne disease is becoming increasingly problematic in the tropical world, especially in the cities. As there is no vaccine available it can only be prevented by avoiding mosquito bites. The mosquito that carries dengue bites day and night, so use insect avoidance measures at all times. Symptoms include high fever, severe headache and body ache (dengue was previously known as 'breakbone fever'). Some people develop a rash and experience diarrhoea. There is no specific treatment – just rest and paracetamol. Do not take aspirin as it increases the chance of haemorrhaging. See a doctor to be diagnosed and monitored.

Hepatitis A
A problem throughout the region, this food- and water-borne virus infects the liver and causes jaundice (yellow skin and eyes), nausea and lethargy. There is no specific treatment for hepatitis A; you need to allow time for the liver to heal. All travellers to India should be vaccinated against hepatitis A.

Hepatitis B
The only sexually transmitted disease that can be prevented by vaccination, hepatitis B is spread by body fluids (eg by sexual contact). The long-term consequences can include liver cancer and cirrhosis.

Hepatitis E
Hepatitis E is transmitted through contaminated food and water. It has similar symptoms to hepatitis A but is far less common. It is a severe problem in pregnant women and can result in the death of both mother and baby. There is currently no vaccine, and prevention is by following safe eating and drinking guidelines.

HIV
HIV is spread via contaminated body fluids. Avoid unsafe sex, unsterile needles (including in medical facilities) and procedures such as tattoos. The growth rate of HIV in India is one of the highest in the world.

Japanese B Encephalitis
This viral disease is transmitted by mosquitoes and is rare in travellers. Like most mosquito-borne diseases, it's becoming a more common problem in affected countries. Most cases occur in rural areas, and vaccination is recommended for travellers spending more than one month outside cities. There is no treatment, and a third of infected people will die, while another third will suffer permanent brain damage.

Malaria
Considering it's such a serious and potentially deadly disease, there is an enormous amount of misinformation about malaria. You must get expert advice as to whether your trip will put you at risk. For most rural areas, the risk of contracting malaria far outweighs the risk of any tablet side effects. Before you travel, seek medical advice on the right medication and dosage for you.

Malaria is caused by a parasite transmitted by the bite of an infected mosquito. The most important symptom of malaria is fever,

HEALTH

but general symptoms such as headache, diarrhoea, cough or chills may also occur. Diagnosis can only be made by taking a blood sample.

Two strategies should be combined to prevent malaria – mosquito avoidance and antimalarial medications. Most people who catch malaria are taking inadequate or no antimalarial medication.

Travellers are advised to take to the following steps to prevent mosquito bites:

- Use an insect repellent that contains DEET on exposed skin. Wash this off at night, as long as you're sleeping under a mosquito net. Natural repellents such as citronella can be effective but must be applied more frequently than products containing DEET.
- Sleep under a mosquito net impregnated with permethrin.
- Choose accommodation with screens and fans (if not air-conditioned).
- Impregnate clothing with permethrin in high-risk areas.
- Wear long sleeves and trousers in light colours.
- Use mosquito coils.
- Spray your room with insect repellent before going out for your evening meal.

A variety of medications are available. The effectiveness of the Chloroquine and Paludrine combination is now limited in many parts of south Asia. Common side effects include nausea (in 40% of people) and mouth ulcers.

The daily tablet Doxycycline is a broad-spectrum antibiotic with the added benefit of helping to prevent a variety of tropical diseases such as leptospirosis, tick-borne disease and typhus. The potential side effects include photosensitivity (a tendency to sunburn), thrush in women, indigestion, heartburn, nausea and interference with the contraceptive pill. More serious side effects include ulceration of the oesophagus – you can help prevent this by taking your tablet with a meal and a large glass of water, and never lying down within half an hour of taking it. It must be taken for four weeks after leaving the risk area.

Lariam (Mefloquine) has received much bad press, some of it justified, some not. This weekly tablet suits many people. Serious side effects are rare but include depression, anxiety, psychosis and fits. Anyone with a history of depression, anxiety, any other psychological disorder or epilepsy should not take Lariam. It is considered safe in the second and third trimesters of pregnancy. Tablets must be taken for four weeks after leaving the risk area.

The new drug Malarone is a combination of Atovaquone and Proguanil. Side effects are uncommon and mild, most commonly nausea and headache. It is the best tablet for beachgoers and for those on short trips to high-risk areas. It must be taken for one week after leaving the risk area.

Rabies

Around 30,000 people die from rabies in India each year. This uniformly fatal disease is spread by the bite or lick of an infected animal – most commonly a dog or monkey. You should seek medical advice immediately after any animal bite and commence post-exposure treatment. Having a pre-travel vaccination means the post-bite treatment is greatly simplified. If an animal bites you, gently wash the wound with soap and water, and apply an iodine-based antiseptic. If you are not prevaccinated, you will need to receive rabies immunoglobulin as soon as possible, and this is almost impossible to obtain in much of India.

STDs

Sexually transmitted diseases most common in India include herpes, warts, syphilis, gonorrhoea and chlamydia. People carrying these diseases often have no signs of infection. Condoms will prevent gonorrhoea and chlamydia but not warts or herpes. If after a sexual encounter you develop any rash, lumps, discharge or pain when passing urine, seek immediate medical attention. If you have been sexually active on your travels, have an STD check when you return home.

Tuberculosis

While TB is rare in travellers and in western countries, it is not rare in India and long-term travellers should take precautions. Vaccination is usually only given to children under the age of five, but adults at risk are advised to undergo pre- and post-travel TB testing. The main symptoms are fever, cough, weight loss, night sweats and tiredness.

Typhoid

This serious bacterial infection is also spread via food and water. It gives a high and slowly progressive fever and a headache, and may be accompanied by a dry cough and stomach pain. It is diagnosed by blood tests and treated with antibiotics. Vaccination is recommended for all travellers spending more than a week in India. Be aware that vaccination is not 100% effective, so you must still be careful with what you eat and drink.

TRAVELLER'S DIARRHOEA

Traveller's diarrhoea is the most common problem that affects travellers – between 30% and 70% of people will suffer from it within two weeks of starting their trip. In over 80% of cases, traveller's diarrhoea is caused by a bacteria (there are numerous potential culprits), and therefore responds promptly to antibiotics. Treatment with antibiotics will depend on your situation – how sick you are, how quickly you need to get better, where you are etc.

Traveller's diarrhoea is defined as the passage of more than three watery bowel actions within 24 hours, plus at least one other symptom such as fever, cramps, nausea, vomiting or feeling generally unwell.

Treatment consists of staying well hydrated; rehydration solutions like Gastrolyte are best for this. Antibiotics such as Norfloxacin, Ciprofloxacin or Azithromycin will kill the bacteria quickly.

Loperamide is just a 'stopper' and doesn't get to the cause of the problem. It can be helpful, though, for example if you have to go on a long bus ride. Don't take Loperamide if you have a fever, or blood in your stools. Seek medical attention quickly if you do not respond to an appropriate antibiotic.

Amoebic Dysentery

Amoebic dysentery is rare in travellers but often misdiagnosed by poor-quality labs. Symptoms are similar to bacterial diarrhoea: fever, bloody diarrhoea and generally feeling unwell. You should always seek reliable medical care if you have blood in your diarrhoea. Treatment involves two drugs: Tinidazole or Metronidazole to kill the parasite in your gut and then a second drug to kill the cysts. If left untreated, complications such as liver or intestinal abscesses can occur.

> **DRINKING WATER**
>
> ■ Never drink tap water.
>
> ■ Bottled water is generally safe – check the seal is intact at purchase.
>
> ■ Avoid ice.
>
> ■ Avoid fresh juices – they may have been watered down.
>
> ■ Boiling water is the most efficient method of purifying it.
>
> ■ The best chemical purifier is iodine. It should not be used by pregnant women or those with thyroid problems.
>
> ■ Water filters should also filter out viruses. Ensure your filter has a chemical barrier such as iodine and a small pore size, eg less than four microns.

Giardiasis

Giardia is a parasite that is relatively common in travellers. Symptoms include nausea, bloating, excess gas, fatigue and intermittent diarrhoea. The parasite will eventually go away if left untreated, but this can take months. The treatment of choice is Tinidazole, with Metronidazole being a second-line option.

ENVIRONMENTAL HAZARDS
Air Pollution

Air pollution, particularly vehicle pollution, is an increasing problem in most of India's major cities. If you have severe respiratory problems, speak with your doctor before travelling to any heavily polluted urban centres. This pollution also causes minor respiratory problems such as sinusitis, dry throat and irritated eyes. If troubled by the pollution leave the city for a few days and get some fresh air.

Food

Eating in restaurants is the biggest risk factor for contracting traveller's diarrhoea. Ways to avoid it include eating only freshly cooked food, and avoiding shellfish and food that has been sitting around on buffets. Peel all fruit, cook vegetables and soak salads in iodine water for at least 20 minutes (avoid iodine if you are pregnant or have thyroid problems). Eat in busy restaurants with a high turnover of customers. For more on safe eating, see Street Food Dos & Don'ts, p72.

Heat

With temperatures hitting 45°C and over in the summer months, heatstroke and heat exhaustion are serious dangers for travellers used to cooler climes; for most people it takes at least two weeks to adapt. Swelling of the feet and ankles is common, as are muscle cramps caused by excessive sweating. Prevent these by avoiding dehydration and excessive activity in the heat. Take it easy when you first arrive. While it's best to avoid salt tablets (they aggravate the gut), it does help to drink rehydration solution or eat salty food. Treat cramps by stopping activity, resting, rehydrating with double-strength rehydration solution and gently stretching.

Dehydration is the main contributor to heat exhaustion. Symptoms include a feeling of weakness, headache, irritability, nausea or vomiting, sweaty skin, a normal or slightly elevated body temperature, and a fast, weak pulse. Treatment involves getting the sufferer out of the heat and/or sun, fanning them and applying cool wet cloths to the skin. Lay the sufferer flat with their legs raised, and rehydrate them with water containing a quarter of a teaspoon of salt per litre. Recovery is usually rapid, but it's common to feel weak for some days afterwards.

Heatstroke is a serious medical emergency. Symptoms come on suddenly and include weakness, nausea, a hot, dry body with a body temperature of over 41°C, dizziness, confusion, loss of coordination, fits and eventually collapse and loss of consciousness. Seek medical help, and cool the person by getting them out of the heat, removing their clothes, fanning them and applying cool wet cloths or ice to their body, especially to the groin and armpits.

Prickly heat is a common skin rash caused by excessive perspiration getting trapped under the skin. The result is an itchy rash of tiny lumps. Treat it by moving out of the heat and into an air-conditioned area for a few hours and by having cool showers. Creams and ointments clog the skin, so they should be avoided. Locally bought prickly-heat powder can be helpful.

Insect Bites & Stings

Bedbugs don't carry disease, but their bites are very itchy. They live in the cracks of furniture and walls, and then migrate to the bed at night to feed on you. You can treat the itch with antihistamines. Lice inhabit various parts of your body but most commonly your head and pubic area. Transmission is via close contact with an infected person. Lice can be difficult to treat, and you may need numerous applications of an anti-lice shampoo such as permethrin. Pubic lice are usually contracted from sexual contact.

Ticks are contracted after walking in rural areas. They're commonly found behind the ears, on the belly and in the armpits. If you have had a tick bite and experience symptoms such as a rash at the site of the bite or elsewhere, fever or muscle aches you should see a doctor. Doxycycline prevents tick-borne diseases.

Bee and wasp stings mainly cause problems for people who are allergic to them. Anyone with a serious bee or wasp allergy should carry an injection of adrenaline (eg an Epipen) for emergency treatment. For others, pain is the main problem – apply ice to the sting and take painkillers.

Skin Problems

Fungal rashes are common in humid climates. Two common rashes affect travellers. The first occurs in the moist areas that get less air, such as the groin, the armpits and between the toes. It starts as a red patch that slowly spreads and is usually itchy. Treatment involves keeping skin dry, avoiding chafing and using an antifungal cream such as Clotrimazole or Lamisil. *Tinea versicolor* is also common – this fungus causes small, light-coloured patches, most commonly on the back, chest and shoulders. See a doctor.

Cuts and scratches become easily infected in humid climates. Take meticulous care of any cuts and scratches to prevent complications such as abscesses. Immediately wash all wounds in clean water and apply antiseptic. If you develop signs of infection (increasing pain and redness), see a doctor. Divers and surfers should be particularly careful with coral cuts, as they easily become infected.

Sunburn

Even on a cloudy day sunburn can occur rapidly. Always use a strong sunscreen (at least factor 30), making sure to reapply it after a swim, and always wear a wide-brimmed hat and sunglasses outdoors. Avoid spending too much time in the sun during the hottest part of the day (10am to 2pm). If you become sunburnt, stay out of the sun until you have recovered, apply cool compresses and take painkillers for the discomfort. A 1% hydrocortisone cream applied twice daily is also helpful.

WOMEN'S HEALTH

Pregnant women should receive specialised advice before travelling. The ideal time to travel is in the second trimester (between 16 and 28 weeks), when the risk of pregnancy-related problems is at its lowest and when pregnant women generally feel at their best. Always carry a list of quality medical facilities available at your destination and ensure you continue your standard antenatal care at these facilities. Avoid travel in rural areas with poor transportation and medical facilities. Most of all, ensure travel insurance covers all pregnancy-related possibilities, including premature labour.

Malaria is a high-risk disease in pregnancy. The WHO recommends that pregnant women

do NOT travel to areas with Chloroquine-resistant malaria. None of the more effective antimalarial drugs is completely safe in pregnancy.

Traveller's diarrhoea can quickly lead to dehydration and result in inadequate blood flow to the placenta. Many of the drugs used to treat various diarrhoea bugs are not recommended in pregnancy. Azithromycin is considered safe.

In a lot of places, supplies of sanitary products (pads, rarely tampons) are readily available. Birth-control options may be limited, so bring adequate supplies of your own form of contraception. Heat, humidity and antibiotics can all contribute to thrush. Treatment is with antifungal creams and pessaries such as Clotrimazole. A practical alternative is a single tablet of Fluconazole (Diflucan). Urinary tract infections can be precipitated by dehydration or long bus journeys without toilet stops; bring suitable antibiotics.

HEALTH

Language

CONTENTS

The huge number of languages spoken in India helps explain why English is still widely spoken more than 50 years after the British left, and why it's still the official language of the judiciary. There are 22 languages recognised in the constitution, and over 1600 minor languages spoken according to the last census. While the locals in Rajasthan, Agra and Delhi may be speaking Punjabi, Urdu, Marwari, Jaipuri, Malvi or Mewati to each other, for you Hindi will be the local language of choice. If you do have the urge to delve into the indigenous languages of the region, Lonely Planet's *India Phrasebook* is the tool for you.

Despite major efforts to promote Hindi as the national language of India, phasing out English, many educated Indians speak English as virtually their first language. For the large number of Indians who speak more than one language, it's often their second tongue. Although you'll find it very easy to get around India with English, it's always good to know at least a little of the local language.

HINDI

Hindi is written from left to right in Devanagari script. While the script may be unfamiliar, English speakers will recognise many of Hindi's grammatical features.

Hindi is also marked depending on the gender of the speaker or the gender of a noun (and its adjective). In this language guide we give the options for male and female speaker, marked 'm' and 'f' respectively.

For a far more comprehensive guide to Hindi, get a copy of Lonely Planet's *Hindi, Urdu & Bengali Phrasebook*. For a guide to the main regional languages of the country (including Rajasthani), look for Lonely Planet's *India Phrasebook*.

PRONUNCIATION

Most Hindi sounds are similar to their English counterparts, but there are a few tricky ones. There's a difference between 'aspirated' and 'unaspirated' consonants – the aspirated ones are pronounced with a strong puff of air, like saying 'h' after the sound. There are also 'retroflex' consonants, where the tongue is curled up and back to 'colour' the sound. The simplified transliterations we've used in this language guide, however, don't include these distinctions.

Pronunciation of vowels is important, especially length (eg **a** compared to **aa**). The combination **ng** after a vowel indicates 'nasalisation' (pronounced through the nose).

Pay attention to the consonant sounds listed below. All others are the same as in English.

Vowels

a	as the 'u' in 'sun'
aa	as in 'father'
ai	as in 'hair' before a consonant; as in 'aisle' at the end of a word
au	as in 'haul' before a consonant; as the 'ou' in 'ouch' at a word's end
e	as in 'they'
ee	as in 'feet'
i	as in 'sit'
o	as in 'shot'
oo	as in 'fool'
u	as in 'put'

Consonants

ch	as in 'cheese'
g	always as in 'gun', never as in 'age'
r	slightly trilled
y	as in 'yak'

EMERGENCIES

Help!	*mada keejiye!*
Stop!	*ruko!*
Thief!	*chor!*
Call a doctor!	*daaktar ko bulaao!*
Call an ambulance!	*embulains le aanaa!*
Call the police!	*pulis ko bulaao!*
I'm lost.	*maing raastaa bhool gayaa/gayee hoong* (m/f)

Where is the ...?	*... kahaang hai?*
police station	*taanaa*
toilet	*gusalkaanaa*

I wish to contact my embassy.
maing apne dootaavaas ko fon karnaa chaahtaa/ chaahtee hoong (m/f)

ACCOMMODATION

Where is the (best/cheapest) hotel?
sab se (achaa/sastaa) hotal kahaang hai?
Please write the address.
zaraa us kaa pataa lik deejiye
Do you have any rooms available?
kyaa koee kamraa kaalee hai?
I'd like to share a dorm.
maing dorm me teharnaa chaahtaa/chaahtee hoong (m/f)

I'd like a ...	*mujhe ... chaahiye*
double room	*dabal kamraa*
room with a bathroom	*gusalkaanevaalaa kamraa*
single room	*singal kamraa*

How much for one night/week?
ek din/hafte kaa kiraayaa kitnaa hai?
May I see it?
kyaa maing kamraa dek saktaa/saktee hoong? (m/f)
Is there any other room?
koee aur kamraa hai?
Where's the bathroom?
gusalkaanaa kahaang hai?

bed	*palang*
blanket	*kambaal*
key	*chaabee*
shower	*shaavar*
toilet paper	*taailet pepar*
water (cold/hot)	*paanee (tandaa/garam)*
with a window	*kirkeevaalaa*

CONVERSATION & ESSENTIALS

The word 'please' is usually conveyed through the polite form of the imperative, or through other expressions. This book uses polite expressions and the polite forms of words.

Hello.	*namaste/namskaar*
Goodbye.	*namaste/namskaar*
Yes.	*jee haang*
No.	*jee naheeng*
Thank you.	*shukriyaa/danyavaad*
You're welcome.	*koee baat naheeng*
Excuse me/Sorry.	*kshamaa keejiye*
How are you?	*aap kaise/kaisee haing? (m/f)*
Fine, and you?	*maing teek hoong aap sunaaiye?*
What's your name?	*aap kaa shubh naam kyaa hai?*

DIRECTIONS

Where's a/the ...	*... kahaang hai?*
bank	*baink*
consulate	*kaungnsal*
embassy	*dootaavaas*
Hindu temple	*mandir*
mosque	*masjid*
post office	*daakkaanaa*
public phone	*saarvajanik fon*
public toilet	*shauchaalay*
town square	*chauk*

Is it far from/near here?
kyaa voh yahaang se door/nazdeek hai?

HEALTH

Where is a/the ...?	*... kahaang hai?*
clinic	*davaakaanaa*
doctor	*daaktar*
hospital	*aspataal*

I'm sick. *maing beemaar hoong*

antiseptic	*ainteeseptik*
antibiotics	*ainteebayotik*
aspirin	*(esprin) sirdard kee davaa*
condoms	*nirodak*
contraceptives	*garbnirodak*
diarrhoea	*dast*
medicine	*davaa*
nausea	*gin*
syringe	*sooee*
tampons	*taimpon*

LANGUAGE DIFFICULTIES

Do you speak English?
kyaa aap ko angrezee aatee hai?
Does anyone here speak English?
kyaa kisee ko angrezee aatee hai?
I understand.
maing samjhaa/samjhee (m/f)

SIGNS	
प्रवेश/अन्दर	Entrance
निकार/बाहर	Exit
खुला	Open
बन्द	Closed
अन्दर आना [निषि/मना] है	No Entry
धूम्रपान करना [निषि/मना] है	No Smoking
निषि	Prohibited
गर्म	Hot
ठंडा	Cold
शोचालय	Toilets

I don't understand.

maing naheeng samjhaa/samjhee (m/f)

Please write it down.

zaraa lik deejiye

NUMBERS

Where English numbers are counted in tens, hundreds, thousands, millions and billions, the Hindi numbering system uses tens, hundreds, thousands, hundred thousands and ten millions. A hundred thousand is one lakh *(laak)*, and 10 million is one crore *(kror)*. These words are almost always used over their English equivalents.

Once into the thousands, written numbers have commas every two places, not three.

1	ek
2	do
3	teen
4	chaar
5	paangch
6	chai
7	saat
8	aat
9	nau
10	das
11	gyaarah
12	bara
13	terah
14	chaudah
15	pandrah
16	solah
17	satrah
18	attaarah
19	unnees
20	bees
21	ikkees
22	baaees

30	tees
40	chaalees
50	pachaas
60	saat
70	sattar
80	assee
90	nabbe/navve
100	sau
1,000	hazaar
100,000	ek laak (written 1,00,000)
10,000,000	ek kror (written 1,00,00,000)

SHOPPING & SERVICES

Where's the nearest ...?

sab se karib ... kah hai?

bookshop	kitaab kee dukaan
chemist/pharmacy	davaaee kee dukaan
general store	dukaan
market	baazaar
washerman	dobee

Where can I buy (a/an) ...?

maing ... kah kareed sakta hoong?

I'd like to buy (a/an) ...

mujhe ... karidnaa hai

clothes	kapre
colour film	rangin film
envelope	lifaafaa
handicrafts	haat kee banee cheeze
magazines	patrikaae
map	nakshaa
newspaper (in English)	(angrezee kaa) akbaar
paper	kaagaz
razor	ustaraa
soap	saabun
stamp	tikat
toothpaste	manjan
washing powder	kapre done kaa saabun

a little	toraa
big	baraa
enough	kaafee
more	aur
small	chotaa
too much/many	bahut/adik

How much is this?

is kaa daam kyaa hai?

I think it's too expensive.

yeh bahut mahegaa/mahegee hai (m/f)

Can you lower the price?

is kaa daam kam keejiye?

Do you accept credit cards?

kyaa aap kredit kaard lete/letee haing? (m/f)

TIME & DATES

What time is it?	*kitne baje haing?*
It's (ten) o'clock.	*(das) baje haing*
Half past (ten).	*saare (das)*
Five past (ten).	*(das) baj kar paangch minat hain*
When?	*kab?*
now	*ab*
today	*aaj*
tomorrow/yesterday	*kal (kal is used for both, but the meaning is clear from context)*
day	*din*
evening	*shaam*
month	*maheenaa*
morning	*saveraa/subhaa*
night	*raat*
week	*haftaa*
year	*saal/baras*
Monday	*somvaar*
Tuesday	*mangalvaar*
Wednesday	*budvaar*
Thursday	*guruvaar/brihaspativaar*
Friday	*shukravaar*

Saturday	*shanivaar*
Sunday	*itvaar/ravivaar*

TRANSPORT

When's the ... bus?	*... bas kab jaaegee?*
first	*pehlaa/pehlee (m/f)*
next	*aglaa/aglee (m/f)*
last	*aakiree*

What time does the ... leave?
... kitne baje jaayegaa/jaayegee? (m/f)
What time does the ... arrive?
... kitne baje pahungchegaa/pahungchegee? (m/f)

boat	*naav (f)*
bus	*bas (f)*
plane	*havaaee jahaaz (m)*
train	*relgaaree (f)*

How do we get to ...?
... kaise jaate haing?
I'd like a one-way/return ticket.
mujhe ek ektarafaa/dotarafaa tikat chaahiye

1st class	*pratam shreni*
2nd class	*dviteey shreni*

LANGUAGE

Glossary

This glossary is a sample of words and terms you may encounter on your travels through Rajasthan, Delhi and Agra. For definitions of food and drink, see p74.

agarbathi – incense

Agnikula – Fire Born; name of the mythological race of four *Rajput* clans who were manifested from a sacred fire on Mt Abu; one of the three principal races from which *Rajputs* claim descent

ahimsa – nonviolence and reverence for all life

angrezi – foreigner

apsara – celestial maiden

Aryan – Sanskrit word for 'noble'; people who migrated from Persia and settled in northern India

ashram – spiritual community or retreat

autorickshaw – a noisy three-wheeled device with a motorbike engine and seats for two passengers behind the driver

Ayurveda – the ancient and complex science of Indian herbal medicine and healing

azan – Muslim call to prayer

bagh – garden

baithak – salon in a *haveli* where merchants received guests

baksheesh – tip, donation (alms) or bribe

bandh – general strike

bandhani – tie-dye

Banjaras – nomadic tribe, believed to be the ancestors of Europe's Gypsies

baori – well, particularly a step-well with landings and galleries

betel – nut of the betel tree; chewed as a stimulant and digestive in a concoction know as *paan*

bhang – dried leaves and flowering shoots of the marijuana plant

Bhil – tribal people of southern Rajasthan

bhojanalya – basic restaurant or snack bar; known elsewhere in India as a *dhaba*

bidi – small, hand-rolled cigarette, really just a rolled-up leaf; also spelt as *beedi*

bindi – forehead mark

Bishnoi – tribe known for their reverence for the environment

Bodhi Tree – *Ficus religiosa*, under which Buddha attained enlightenment

bor – forehead ornament; also known as a *tikka* or *rakhadi*

Brahmin – member of the priest caste, the highest Hindu caste

Buddha – Awakened One; the originator of Buddhism; also regarded by Hindus as the ninth incarnation of Vishnu

bund – embankment, dyke

bunti – wooden block used in block-printing fabric; also known as a *chhapa*

cantonment – administrative and military area of a Raj-era town

chajera – mason employed by Marwari businessmen of Shekhawati to build *havelis*

chakki – handmill used to grind grain

chappals – sandals

charpoy – simple bed made of ropes knotted together on a wooden frame

chaupar – town square formed by the intersection of major roads

chhan – see *dogla*

chhapa – wooden block used in block-printing fabric; also known as a *bunti*

chhatri – cenotaph (literally 'umbrella')

chitera – painters of *havelis* in Shekhawati

choli – sari blouse

chowk – town square, intersection or marketplace

chowkidar – caretaker; night watchman

chudas – bangles worn by Rajasthani women

chureil – evil spirit; also known as a *dakin*

crore – 10 million

cycle-rickshaw – three-wheeled bicycle with seats for two passengers behind the rider

dacoit – bandit

dakin – evil spirit

Dalit – preferred term for India's *Untouchable* caste

dalwar – sword

dargah – shrine or place of burial of a Muslim saint

darshan – offering or audience with someone; viewing of a deity

darwaza – gateway or door

dhaba – hole-in-the-wall restaurant or snack bar; boxed lunches delivered to office workers

dharamsala – pilgrims guest house

dhobi ghat – place where clothes are washed

dhobi-wallah – person who washes clothes

dhoti – length of fabric worn by men, which is drawn up between the legs

dhurrie – cotton rug

Digambara – Sky Clad; a Jain sect whose monks show disdain for worldly goods by going naked

Diwan-i-Am – hall of public audience

Diwan-i-Khas – hall of private audience

dogla – building adjacent to a village dwelling in which livestock and grain are kept; also known as a *chhan*

dupatta – long scarf for women often worn with the *salwar kameez*

durbar – royal court; also a government

gaddi – throne of a Hindu prince

ganja – dried flowering tips of marijuana plant

gaon – village

garh – fort

ghat – steps or landing on a river; range of hills or road up hills

ghazal – Urdu song derived from poetry; sad love theme

ghoomer – dance performed by women during festivals and weddings

gopis – milkmaids; Krishna was very fond of them

gram panchayat – government at the village level

Gujjars – people traditionally engaged in animal husbandry

gurdwara – Sikh temple

guru – teacher or holy person

Harijan – name (no longer considered acceptable) given by Gandhi to India's *Untouchables*, meaning 'children of god'

hathi – elephant

hathphool – ornament worn on the back of the hand by Rajasthani women

haveli – traditional, ornately decorated rseidence

hijra – eunuch

hookah – water pipe

howdah – seat for carrying people on an elephant's back

IMFL – Indian Made Foreign Liquor; beer or spirits produced in India

Induvansa – Race of the Moon (Lunar Race); one of the three principal races from which *Rajputs* claim descent

jagirdari – feudal system of serfdom imposed on the peasants of Rajasthan

Jagirdars – feudal lords of Rajasthan

jali – carved marble lattice screen; also refers to the holes or spaces produced through carving timber

Jats – traditionally people who were engaged in agriculture; today Jats play a strong role in administration and politics

jauhar – ritual mass suicide by immolation, traditionally performed by *Rajput* women after military defeat to avoid dishonour

jhonpa – village hut with mud walls and thatched roof

jogi – priest

jootis – traditional leather shoes of Rajasthan; men's *jootis* often have curled-up toes; also known as *mojaris*

Julaha – weaver caste

kabas – the holy rats believed to be the incarnations of local families at Karni Mata Temple at Deshnok

Kalbelias – nomadic tribal group associated with snake charming

karma – Hindu, Buddhist and Sikh principle of retributive justice for past deeds

kashida – embroidery on *jootis*

kathputli – puppeteer; also known as a *putli-wallah*

khadi – homespun cloth; Mahatma Gandhi encouraged people to spin *khadi* rather than buy English cloth

khadim – Muslim holy servant or mosque attendant

kharfi – monsoon

kheis – shawl; also known as a *pattu*

kot – fort

kotwali – police station

Kshatriya – cwarrior or administrator caste, second in the caste hierarchy; Rajputs claim lineage from the Kshatriyas

kuldevi – clan goddess; every Hindu family pays homage to one

kund – lake or tank

kundan – type of jewellery featuring *meenakari* on one side and precious stones on the other

kurta – long cotton shirt with either a short collar or no collar

lakh – 100,000

lingam – phallic symbol; symbol of Shiva

loharia – form of *bandhani* that gives a ripple effect

lungi – worn by men, this loose, coloured garment (similar to a sarong) is pleated by the wearer at the waist to fit snugly

madrasa – Islamic college

Mahabharata – Vedic epic poem of the Bharata dynasty; describes the battle between the Pandavas and the Kauravas

mahal – house, palace

maharaj kumar – son of a maharaja; prince

maharaja – literally 'great king'; princely ruler; also known as maharana, maharao and maharawal

maharani – wife of a princely ruler or a ruler in her own right

Mahavir – the 24th and last *tirthankar*

mahout – elephant driver/keeper

mandana – folk paintings in red chalk on village dwellings

mandapa – chamber before the inner sanctum of a temple

mandir – temple

mantra – sacred word or syllable used by Buddhists and Hindus to aid concentration; metric psalms of praise found in the *Vedas*

Marathas – warlike central Indians who controlled much of India at times and fought against the *Mughals* and *Rajputs*

marg – major road
masjid – mosque
Marwar – kingdom of the Rathore dynasty that ruled from Mandore, and later from Jodhpur
mataji – female priest; also a respectful form of address to a mother or older woman
meenakari – type of enamelwork used on ornaments and jewellery
mehfilkhana – Islamic building in which religious songs are sung
mehndi – henna; intricate henna designs applied by women to their hands and feet
mela – fair, festival
Mewar – kingdom of the Sisodia dynasty; ruled Udaipur and Chittorgarh
Moghul – see Mughal
mojaris – see *jootis*
moksha – release from the cycle of birth and death
monsoon – rainy season; June to October
moosal – pestle
mosar – death feast
Mughal – Muslim dynasty of Indian emperors from Babur to Aurangzeb (16th to 18th centuries)

namaz – Muslim prayers
nawab – Muslim ruling prince or powerful landowner
nilgai – antelope
niwas – house, building
NRI – Non-Resident Indian

odhni – headscarf
okhli – mortar; bowl for grinding grain with a *moosal*
Om – sacred invocation that represents the essence of the divine principle

paag – turban; also called *pagri* and *safa*
paan – chewable preparation made from betel leaves, nuts and lime
pagri – see *paag*
pahar – hill
panchayat sammiti – local government representing several villages
panghat poojan – ceremony performed at a village well following the birth of a child
pattu – shawl; also known as *kheis*
payal – anklet worn by Rajasthani women
PCO – public call office
pida – low folding chair featuring decorative woodcarving, traditionally made in Shekhawati and Bikaner
pitar – soul of a dead man
pitari – soul of a woman who has died before her husband
pol – gate
prasad – sacred food offered to the gods
puja – literally 'respect'; offering or prayer

purdah – custom among some conservative Muslims (also adopted by some Hindus, especially the Rajputs) of keeping women in seclusion; veiled
putli-wallah – puppeteer; also known as a *kathputli*
Rabari – nomadic tribe from Jodhpur area
raga – any conventional pattern of melody and rhythm that forms the basis for free composition
raj – rule or sovereignty; British Raj (sometimes just Raj) refers to British rule before 1947
raja – king; also *rana*
Rajputs – Sons of Princes; Hindu warrior caste, former rulers of western India
rakhadi – forehead ornament; also known as a *bor* or *tikka*
rana – see *raja*
rani – female ruler; wife of a king
rawal – nobleman
reet – bride price; opposite of dowry
Road – railway town that serves as a communication point to a larger town off the line, eg Mt Abu and Abu Road
RSRTC – Rajasthan State Road Transport Corporation
RTDC – Rajasthan Tourism Development Corporation

sadar – main
sadhu – ascetic, holy person, one who is trying to achieve enlightenment; usually addressed as 'swamiji' or 'babaji'
safa – see *paag*
sagar – lake, reservoir
sahib – respectful title applied to a gentleman
sal – gallery in a palace
salwar kameez – traditional dresslike tunic and trouser combination for women
sambar – deer
sapera – snake charmer; traditionally associated with the Kalbelias tribe
sati – suicide by immolation; banned more than a century ago, it is still occasionally performed
Scheduled Tribes – government classification for tribal groups of Rajasthan; the tribes are grouped with the lowest casteless class, the Dalits
shikar – hunting expedition
Sikh – member of the monotheistic religion Sikhism, which separated from Hinduism in the 16th century and has a military tradition; Sikh men can be recognised by their beards and turbans
sikhara – temple-spire or temple
silavat – stone carvers
Singh – literally 'lion'; a surname adopted by Rajputs and Sikhs
Sufi – Muslim mystic
Suryavansa – Race of the Sun (Solar Race); one of the three principal races from which Rajputs claim descent

tabla – pair of drums
tempo – noisy three-wheeled public transport; bigger than an autorickshaw

thakur – Hindu caste; nobleman
tikka – a mark devout Hindus put on their foreheads with *tikka* powder; also known as a *bor* or *rakhadi*
tirthankars – the 24 great Jain teachers
tonga – two-wheeled passenger vehicle drawn by horse or pony
toran – shield-shaped device above a lintel, which a bridegroom pierces with his sword before claiming his bride
torana – elaborately sculpted gateway before temples
tripolia – triple gateway

Untouchable – lowest caste or 'casteless', for whom the most menial tasks are reserved; the name derives from the belief that higher castes risk defilement if they touch one; formerly known as Harijan, now Dalit

Vaishya – merchant caste; the third caste in the hierarchy
Vedas – Hindu sacred books; collection of hymns composed during the 2nd millennium BC and divided into four books: Rig-Veda, Yajur-Veda, Sama-Veda and Atharva-Veda

wallah – man; added onto almost anything, eg *dhobi-wallah, chai-wallah, taxi-wallah*

yagna – self-mortification

zenana – women's quarters
zila parishad – government at district level

The Authors

LINDSAY BROWN
Coordinating Author, Jaipur, Eastern Rajasthan, Western Rajasthan

After completing a PhD on evolutionary genetics and following a stint as a science editor and a sojourn on the subcontinent, Lindsay started working for Lonely Planet. Lindsay is a former Publishing Manager of the Outdoor Activity Guides at Lonely Planet, and he returns to the subcontinent to trek, write and photograph whenever possible. He has also contributed to Lonely Planet's *South India, Nepal, Bhutan,* and *Pakistan & the Karakoram Highway* guides, among others.

AMELIA THOMAS
Delhi, Agra, Northern Rajasthan (Shekhawati), Southern Rajasthan, Rajasthani Arts & Crafts

Amelia Thomas is a writer and journalist working throughout the Middle East, India and beyond. She has worked on numerous Lonely Planet titles and takes special delight in Delhi and its culinary treasures. Amelia has three toddlers – with a fourth baby on the way as this book was researched – who love tagging along on far-flung train journeys, and especially enjoy pointing out strange contraptions in Shekhawati *haveli* (traditional, ornately decorated residence) murals. Her recent book *The Zoo on the Road to Nablus*, tells the true story of the last Palestinian zoo.

CONTRIBUTING AUTHORS

Anirban Mahapatra wrote the History and Culture chapters of this guide. He is a journalist, writer and photographer based in Delhi, and travelled extensively through Rajasthan and northern India during his three-year stay in the Indian capital. His primary interests include exploring the multifaceted culture and living tradition of India and its people.

Dr Trish Batchelor wrote the Health chapter of this guide. She is a general practitioner and travel medicine specialist who works at the CIWEC Clinic in Kathmandu, Nepal, as well as being a Medical Advisor to the Travel Doctor New Zealand clinics. Trish teaches travel medicine through the University of Otago, and is interested in underwater and high-altitude medicine, and in the impact of tourism on host countries. She has travelled extensively through Southeast and East Asia and particularly loves high-altitude trekking in the Himalayas.

LONELY PLANET AUTHORS

Why is our travel information the best in the world? It's simple: our authors are passionate, dedicated travellers. They don't take freebies in exchange for positive coverage so you can be sure the advice you're given is impartial. They travel widely to all the popular spots, and off the beaten track. They don't research using just the internet or phone. They discover new places not included in any other guidebook. They personally visit thousands of hotels, restaurants, palaces, trails, galleries, temples and more. They speak with dozens of locals every day to make sure you get the kind of insider knowledge only a local could tell you. They take pride in getting all the details right, and in telling it how it is. Think you can do it? Find out how at **lonelyplanet.com**.

Behind the Scenes

THIS BOOK

This edition of *Rajasthan, Delhi & Agra* was written by Lindsay Brown and Amelia Thomas, with contributions by Anirban Mahapatra. Dr Trish Batchelor wrote the Health chapter. The 1st edition was written by Abigail Hole, Sarina Singh and Martin Robinson.

This guidebook was commissioned in Lonely Planet's Melbourne office, and produced by the following:

Commissioning Editor Sam Trafford
Coordinating Editor Alison Ridgway
Coordinating Cartographer Jolyon Philcox
Coordinating Layout Designer Jacqueline McLeod
Managing Editor Brigitte Ellemor
Managing Cartographers Shahara Ahmed, Adrian Persoglia
Managing Layout Designer Adam McCrow
Assisting Editors Adrienne Costanzo, Laura Crawford, Robyn Loughnane, Alan Murphy
Assisting Cartographer Joanne Luke
Assisting Layout Designers Paul Iacono, Jacqui Saunders, Cara Smith
Cover Designer Pepi Bluck
Project Manager Craig Kilburn
Language Content Coordinator Quentin Frayne

Thanks to Holly Alexander, Helen Christinis, David Connolly, Diana Duggan, George Dunford, Owen Eszeki, Jennifer Garrett, Lisa Knights, Erin McManus, Mandy Sierp, Marg Toohey, Celia Wood

THANKS
LINDSAY BROWN

Thanks to fellow authors Amelia Thomas and Anirban Mahapatra, and to Sarina Singh and Sam Trafford in Melbourne. It was great to receive enthusiastic help from so many people in Rajasthan, and I particularly thank the following for their invaluable assistance: Dicky Singh and Satinder Singh in Jaipur, Joshi in Jodhpur, and Loise and Chanesar in Jaisalmer. For their prowess on the road, a huge thanks to drivers Sher Singh and Shankar. And finally thanks to Jenny, Pat and Sinead at home.

AMELIA THOMAS

Many thanks to Sam Trafford, Lindsay Brown, Alison Ridgway, Jolyon Philcox and the rest of the Lonely Planet team, for making this book a pleasure to work on. Thanks to Dan Smolar and Nich Hastings for their Delhi-based baby-sitting services, to the patient staff at the Manor and Palace Heights who provided piles of pancakes for

THE LONELY PLANET STORY

Fresh from an epic journey across Europe, Asia and Australia in 1972, Tony and Maureen Wheeler sat at their kitchen table stapling together notes. The first Lonely Planet guidebook, *Across Asia on the Cheap*, was born.

Travellers snapped up the guides. Inspired by their success, the Wheelers began publishing books to Southeast Asia, India and beyond. Demand was prodigious, and the Wheelers expanded the business rapidly to keep up. Over the years, Lonely Planet extended its coverage to every country and into the virtual world via lonelyplanet.com and the Thorn Tree message board.

As Lonely Planet became a globally loved brand, Tony and Maureen received several offers for the company. But it wasn't until 2007 that they found a partner whom they trusted to remain true to the company's principles of travelling widely, treading lightly and giving sustainably. In October of that year, BBC Worldwide acquired a 75% share in the company, pledging to uphold Lonely Planet's commitment to independent travel, trustworthy advice and editorial independence.

Today, Lonely Planet has offices in Melbourne, London and Oakland, with over 500 staff members and 300 authors. Tony and Maureen are still actively involved with Lonely Planet. They're travelling more often than ever, and they're devoting their spare time to charitable projects. And the company is still driven by the philosophy of *Across Asia on the Cheap*: 'All you've got to do is decide to go and the hardest part is over. So go!'

hungry toddlers to fling about, and to the dozens of Delhi, Agra and Udaipurites who offered help, advice, and tips throughout.

OUR READERS

Many thanks to the travellers who used the last edition and wrote to us with helpful hints, useful advice and interesting anecdotes:

Louise Acreman, Robert Agasucci, Karin Amnå, Kristaps Andersons, Rosi Aryal, Paul De Barros, Chris Beall, Ollie Blake, Martin Bockshammer, Christoph Bratzler, Kathrin Buegl, Brian Cargille, Carmen Carmen, Lin Castang, Philip Cole, Sarah Cotton, JK Diepeveen, Rakhi Doshi, Tony Ellery, Chris Emerson, Anthony Finlay, Daniel Fox, Ritesh Gadhia, Paul Gardner, Robert Gay, Eve Goldie, Ann-Maree Grant, Per Gulden, Kate Hawthorn, Richard Hayes, Willy Houthtoofd, Charles Hugh-Jones, Jakobien Huisman, Lisa Hunter, Catherine Iannello, Simon Ives, Graham James, Paolo De Jong,

Wayne Kennedy, John Lucas, Hugh Major, Rohan Malhotra, Jozef Malocha, Laura Manetti, Thomas Mangnall, CJ Manley, Bertrand Marotte, Elise Massip, William Mcconnachie, Eddy De Mol, Monique Muller, Mairead O'Dwyer, Mahesh Parameswaran, Chitra Parpia, Jeremy Parsons, Werner Racky, Jan Reynders, Klaas Ruitinga, Anita Rye, Maximilian Schoen, Upendra Shrimali, David Simmons, Andy Sobel, Alexandra & Depy Spyratos, Mark Stainforth, Paul Starkey, Matthew Steer, Lisa Strychar, Ramsey Su, Sandra Talanti, Lauren Taylor, André Tempelaar, Annalisa Tozzo, Anna Vazquez, Danny Vendramini, Ron Versleijen, Estelle Wechsler, Dennis Wiesenborn, Pamela Winter, Daniel Wurm, Paolo Zevi

ACKNOWLEDGMENTS

Many thanks to the following for the use of their content:

Globe on title page ©Mountain High Maps 1993 Digital Wisdom, Inc.

SEND US YOUR FEEDBACK

We love to hear from travellers – your comments keep us on our toes and help make our books better. Our well-travelled team reads every word on what you loved or loathed about this book. Although we cannot reply individually to postal submissions, we always guarantee that your feedback goes straight to the appropriate authors, in time for the next edition. Each person who sends us information is thanked in the next edition – and the most useful submissions are rewarded with a free book.

To send us your updates – and find out about Lonely Planet events, newsletters and travel news – visit our award-winning website: **www.lonelyplanet.com/contact**.

Note: we may edit, reproduce and incorporate your comments in Lonely Planet products such as guidebooks, websites and digital products, so let us know if you don't want your comments reproduced or your name acknowledged. For a copy of our privacy policy visit www.lonelyplanet.com/privacy.

Index

INDEX

INDEX

INDEX

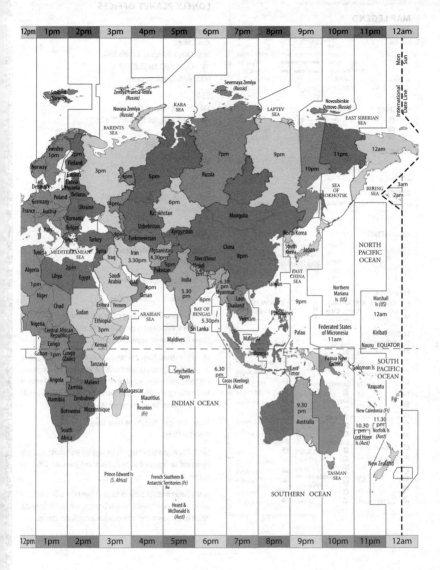

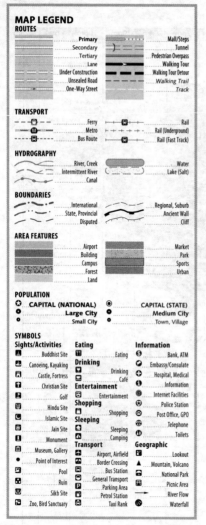

MAP LEGEND

ROUTES

Primary	Mall/Steps
Secondary	Tunnel
Tertiary	Pedestrian Overpass
Lane	Walking Tour
Under Construction	Walking Tour Detour
Unsealed Road	Walking Trail
One-Way Street	Track

TRANSPORT

Ferry	Rail
Metro	Rail (Underground)
Bus Route	Rail (Fast Track)

HYDROGRAPHY

River, Creek	Water
Intermittent River	Lake (Salt)
Canal	

BOUNDARIES

International	Regional, Suburb
State, Provincial	Ancient Wall
Disputed	Cliff

AREA FEATURES

Airport	Market
Building	Park
Campus	Sports
Forest	Urban
Land	

POPULATION

○ CAPITAL (NATIONAL)	⦿ CAPITAL (STATE)
● Large City	● Medium City
○ Small City	○ Town, Village

SYMBOLS

Sights/Activities	Eating	Information
Buddhist Site	Eating	Bank, ATM
Canoeing, Kayaking	**Drinking**	Embassy/Consulate
Castle, Fortress	Drinking	Hospital, Medical
Christian Site	Café	Information
Golf	**Entertainment**	Internet Facilities
Hindu Site	Entertainment	Police Station
Islamic Site	**Shopping**	Post Office, GPO
Jain Site	Shopping	Telephone
Monument	**Sleeping**	Toilets
Museum, Gallery	Sleeping	**Geographic**
Point of Interest	Camping	Lookout
Pool	**Transport**	Mountain, Volcano
Ruin	Airport, Airfield	National Park
Sikh Site	Border Crossing	Picnic Area
Zoo, Bird Sanctuary	Bus Station	River Flow
	General Transport	Waterfall
	Parking Area	
	Petrol Station	
	Taxi Rank	

LONELY PLANET OFFICES

Australia
Head Office
Locked Bag 1, Footscray, Victoria 3011
☎ 03 8379 8000, fax 03 8379 8111
talk2us@lonelyplanet.com.au

USA
150 Linden St, Oakland, CA 94607
☎ 510 250 6400, toll free 800 275 8555
fax 510 893 8572
info@lonelyplanet.com

UK
2nd fl, 186 City Rd,
London EC1V 2NT
☎ 020 7106 2100, fax 020 7106 2101
go@lonelyplanet.co.uk

Published by Lonely Planet Publications Pty Ltd
ABN 36 005 607 983

© Lonely Planet Publications Pty Ltd 2008

© photographers as indicated 2008

Cover photograph: Boy dancing on decorated floor, Hugh Sitton/Corbis. Many of the images in this guide are available for licensing from Lonely Planet Images: www.lonelyplanetimages.com.

Printed through Colorcraft Ltd, Hong Kong.
Printed in China.